Marketing for Tourism and Hospitality

A Canadian Perspective

Simon Hudson

University of Calgary

Australia   Canada   Mexico   Singapore   Spain   United Kingdom   United States

THOMSON

NELSON

**Marketing for Tourism and Hospitality:
A Canadian Perspective**

Simon Hudson

Editorial Director and Publisher:
Evelyn Veitch

Executive Editor:
Veronica Visentin

Senior Marketing Manager:
Chantal Lanning

Publisher's Representative:
Cher Bond

Senior Developmental Editor:
Elke Price

Photo Researcher:
Karen Becker

Permissions Coordinator:
Karen Becker

Production Editor:
Tammy Scherer

Copy Editor:
Tara Tovell

Proofreader:
Eliza Marciniak

Indexer:
Maura Brown

Senior Production Coordinator:
Hedy Sellers

Creative Director:
Angela Cluer

Interior Design:
Peter Papayanakis

Cover Design:
Peter Papayanakis

Cover Images:
Main: Steve Mason/Photodisc
     Green/Getty Images
Inset, top: © Ariel
     Skelley/Corbis/Magma
Inset, centre: © Charles O'Rear/
     Corbis/Magma
Inset, bottom: © Paul A. Souders/
     Corbis/Magma

Compositor:
Courtney Hellam

Printer:
Transcontinental

**National Library of Canada
Cataloguing in Publication**

Hudson, Simon
     Marketing for tourism and hospitality: a Canadian perspective / Simon Hudson.

Includes index.
ISBN-13: 978-0-17-622468-4
ISBN-10: 0-17-622468-8

     1. Tourism—Canada—Marketing. 2. Hospitality industry—Canada—Marketing.
I. Title.

G155.C2H82 2004
338.4'7917104'0688
C2004-900466-2

Brief Contents

Contents

Special Interest Boxes

MARKETING IN ACTION

PROFILES

SNAPSHOTS

Preface

Tourism is an increasingly important sector of the Canadian economy. In 2002, Canada attracted 20 million international overnight visitors who spent nearly $14 billion, making tourism one of Canada's top foreign-exchange earners. Almost 10 percent of Canada's labour force works in tourism, accounting for 1.4 million jobs. By 2005, it is expected that more than 1.7 million tourism positions will exist in Canada's work force. The World Tourism Organization ranks Canada as the ninth most popular destination in the world.

Alongside the growth of the tourism industry, tourism education has expanded rapidly over the last few decades, reflecting the growing recognition of tourism (and the travel and hospitality industries that serve it) as one of the world's most significant economic, social, and environmental forces. Tourism education and training has been developed at various levels, ranging from highly vocational courses to higher research degrees. The growth reflects the widely held belief that one of the major challenges the industry faces is to recruit, develop, and retain employees and managers who have appropriate educational backgrounds.

Yet despite this obvious interest in the subject of tourism, until now there has been no text that specifically deals with tourism and hospitality marketing in Canada. There are many tourism marketing books, the majority of which are aimed at the American or European markets, but none of them are relevant to Canadian students in particular. There is also very little material available for the marketing practitioner in relation to marketing tourism and hospitality products in Canada. *Marketing for Tourism and Hospitality: A Canadian Perspective* is therefore long overdue. Marketing is a subject of vital concern in tourism because it is the principal management influence that can be brought to bear on the size and behaviour of this major global market. The main sectors of the tourism industry—travel organizers, destination organizations, transportation, and various product suppliers—combine to manage visitors' demands through a range of marketing influences.

This very readable text's unique focus on Canada makes it suitable for use in both educational and professional contexts. Over 70 up-to-date examples and case studies from all over Canada are included, covering all sectors of tourism and hospitality. The case studies at the end of each chapter examine the marketing of diverse tourism products, such as sport and adventure tourism, nostalgia tourism, space tourism, wine tourism, urban ecotourism, and native tourism. Some readers will be fascinated to learn why Roots Air failed while WestJet Airlines succeeded; why Four Seasons Hotels and Resorts has such a successful positioning strategy; how Canadian Mountain Holidays sells heliskiing trips with no advertising; and how the Sheraton Suites Calgary Eau Claire consistently wins awards for service excellence. Others will be interested to know how Catch became Canada's Best New Restaurant; how bed and breakfasts in Canada market themselves on the Internet; why the backpacker is getting older and richer; and why the fast-food market is targeting a healthier consumer.

As well as offering numerous Canadian examples, the book provides comprehensive coverage of essential marketing principles, such as developing a marketing plan, understanding consumer behaviour, doing marketing research, and implementing the marketing mix. The text also includes sections on contemporary marketing issues such as integrated marketing communications, Internet marketing, responsible marketing, and internal marketing.

Marketing for Tourism and Hospitality: A Canadian Perspective begins with a chapter dedicated to the tourism and hospitality environment in Canada. **Chapter 1** starts by providing an introduction to tourism and hospitality marketing in general by discussing the definition and role of marketing and its importance in tourism. A synopsis of services marketing theory highlights the unique characteristics of services and introduces important service marketing models, such as the services marketing triangle and the services marketing mix. The chapter then focuses on tourism in Canada and analyzes the key players in Canada's tourism industry. The remainder of the chapter examines the marketing environment's microenvironmental and macroenvironmental forces, and the ways in which they affect an organization's ability to serve its customers.

Successful marketing in tourism and hospitality requires careful planning and execution. **Chapter 2**, which focuses on the development of a marketing plan in the tourism and hospitality industry, discusses the eight key steps in the marketing planning process. Practical examples from various sectors of the tourism industry are also provided.

Chapter 3 considers behavioural trends in tourism by reviewing tourism motivational studies, examining typologies of tourists, and discussing the external factors that influence consumer behaviour. The chapter includes a section devoted to organizational buying behaviour, as well as an analysis of current trends in consumer behaviour that are affecting tourism marketing today.

Chapter 4, on marketing research in tourism and hospitality, begins with a description of the type of applied research conducted in tourism, which is followed by a discussion of the various stages in the research process. The chapter then describes the various methodologies available to researchers and discusses the relative merits of primary and secondary research. The next part of the chapter looks at sampling and highlights five common research problems. The effective use of research in decision making is then considered, and a final section discusses trends in tourism marketing research.

Chapter 5 begins by introducing the peculiarities of the tourism product and the idea that tourism and hospitality products are a group of selected components or elements brought together in a "bundle" to satisfy needs and wants. The chapter includes sections on the different product levels, product planning, the product life cycle model, and the positioning strategies available to organizations in the tourism and hospitality fields. An in-depth analysis of branding in tourism is supported by two case studies—one about the growth of chefs as brands and the other about the re-branding of The Manitoba Museum. The final section of the chapter discusses the concept of packaging.

Chapter 6, on pricing, begins by looking at the impact that various corporate objectives have on pricing. The key factors determining a company's pricing decisions are discussed, along with the contribution of economics to pricing. The basic approaches to pricing are then examined, and an important discussion on yield management follows. The difference between strategic pricing and tactical pricing is then explained, and the final section of the chapter looks at the specific characteristics of the tourism and hospitality industry that affect pricing policy.

Chapter 7 examines the various ways of distributing a tourism and hospitality product. It begins by looking at the nature and types of distribution channels and the different functions of a distribution system. The key intermediaries involved in the tourism distribution system are then discussed, and a consideration of channel conflict and organization follows. Finally, the process of designing a company's distribution system and ensuring the effective execution of the distribution strategy is examined.

The next three chapters explore the various marketing communications methods used by tourism and hospitality providers. **Chapter 8** begins with an introduction that explains the role and types of promotion tools used in tourism and hospitality, and a section on the communications process follows. The chapter then discusses the rise of integrated marketing communications—the recognition that advertising can no longer be crafted and executed in isolation from other promotional mix elements. The communication techniques of advertising and sales promotion are then considered.

Chapter 9 begins by focusing on public relations. It examines the roles and functions of public relations and the main public relations techniques used in tourism and hospitality. Personal selling is the subject of the next section, which discusses the roles and objectives of personal selling, the sales process, and the roles of a sales manager. The chapter concludes with a section on word-of-mouth communication, an important but often misunderstood form of promotion in tourism.

Chapter 10 examines two important and growing areas of tourism and hospitality marketing: direct marketing and Internet marketing. The key advantages of direct marketing are discussed in the first section of this chapter, as are the major direct marketing tools. The remainder of the chapter discusses the six ways in which the Internet is being used by the tourism and hospitality industry: direct e-marketing, advertising, distribution and sales, providing information, customer service and relationship marketing, and marketing research.

Chapter 11 begins by defining internal marketing and describing the four key steps in the internal marketing process. The next section, on service quality, includes segments on the "gaps model" of service quality, methods of measuring service quality, and behavioural consequences of service quality. The third section discusses loyalty and relationship marketing. Various customer retention strategies are introduced, as are the benefits of relationship marketing to both company and customer. The final part of the chapter discusses service recovery and offers guidelines for tracking and handling complaints.

Chapter 12 considers both the opportunities and challenges inherent in the marketing of destinations and begins by discussing the principles of destination marketing. In the opening section destinations are defined, characterized, and classified. A summary of the objectives and benefits of destination marketing is followed by a more in-depth look at the role of destination marketing organizations (DMOs). A short section on identifying target markets is followed by a section on tourism development that stresses the growing importance of responsible marketing. The two strategies used in marketing destinations— promotion and facilitation—are then considered, after which a review of the theories on destination branding follows. Finally, the chapter looks at the marketing of two sectors of the tourism market that are particularly important for destinations: events and conferences, and sport and adventure tourism.

PEDAGOGICAL FEATURES

The objective of all chapters in this text is to cover the basic tourism and hospitality theories well while omitting unnecessary detail. Careful selection of topics, appropriate depth of coverage, and concise writing help to achieve this objective. Current examples from all types and sizes of tourism and hospitality businesses are used in the text discussion.

Each chapter contains the following pedagogical features:

Opening Vignette

These stories have been designed to draw students into the chapter by presenting a real-life example that is carefully linked to the material covered in the chapter.

Objectives

Objectives are provided at the beginning of each chapter to identify the major areas and points covered in the chapter and to guide the learning process.

Chapter Overview

A brief introductory section at the beginning of each chapter summarizes the material that is to be presented.

Chapter Summary

Each chapter ends with a summary that distills the main points of the chapter. This synopsis serves as a quick review of important topics covered and as a helpful study guide.

Key Terms

Throughout each chapter, key terms appear in **boldface** in the text and have corresponding definitions in the margins. A list of these terms, including page numbers, appears at the end of each chapter, making it easy for students to check their understanding of important terms in the chapter.

Discussion Questions and Exercises

Each chapter ends with discussion questions that provide students with an opportunity to review how well they have learned the material in the chapter.

Case Study

Each chapter contains an up-to-date and relevant case study. As a collection, these studies cover a variety of tourism and hospitality sectors and regions. Designed to foster critical thinking, the case studies illustrate actual business scenarios that stress several concepts found in the chapter. End-of-case questions encourage students to spot issues, analyze facts, and solve problems.

Web Sites

Web addresses of companies discussed in the chapter are provided for students who wish to further explore topics presented in the text.

Endnotes

Bibliographical references for sources cited within each chapter are provided in a numbered end-of-chapter list.

Special Interest Boxes

Boxed features in each chapter help students to connect principles to practice more easily. Three types of feature boxes are interspersed throughout the text.

Marketing in Action

Marketing in Action boxes (one per chapter) provide in-depth examples of the practical application of the tourism and hospitality marketing theory discussed in each chapter.

MARKETING IN ACTION

GLOBAL STUDY FINDS TRAVELLERS' NEEDS NOT BEING MET BY THE TRAVEL INDUSTRY

In 2002, a team of anthropologists in Tokyo, London, Israel, New York, Los Angeles, Chicago, Orlando, and Las Vegas gathered data from a global sample of travellers and identified basic needs that are not being met by the travel industry. These findings were used to locate and understand points within the travel experience where industries such as hotels, rental car companies, attractions, and cruises can better meet the needs of their customers.

Profiles

Profiles (one per chapter) highlight achievements of successful individuals or organizations in the tourism and hospitality industry. Those profiled in these boxes were chosen for their expertise in specific areas related to the chapter material.

PROFILE

JEANNIE HENKE, MILLENIUM SUN TRAVEL

I began my home-based travel agency approximately nine years ago. I was in the unique position of working for an airline, and I was bridging relationships with retail travel agencies in the community. For the next two to three years, I worked as a sales rep making referrals to A-list travel agencies and making a small commission. At that time, most suppliers (wholesalers and tour operators) did not recognize agents working on their own through their home.

Snapshots

Snapshots (two per chapter) provide examples of real-life cases. These are used to illustrate a particular concept or theoretical principle presented in the chapter.

SNAPSHOT

FAST-FOOD INDUSTRY TARGETS HEALTHIER CONSUMER

We have become a nation of fatties. According to Statistics Canada, almost half of Canadian adults are overweight, and the incidence of obesity among children is rising. While lack of exercise and overeating certainly contribute to widening waistlines, health activists say that fast food, with its obscene portion sizes and lack of nutrition, is the real culprit in our super-sized population. Just as the tobacco industry was slapped with lawsuits, sin taxes, and marketing restrictions, the fast-food industry's role in the health of Canadians is now being closely scrutinized.

SUPPLEMENTS

Instructor's Manual/Test Bank

The Instructor's Manual includes answers to discussion questions and exercises, case study questions, and a test bank.

www.hudson.nelson.com

This rich Web resource to accompany the first edition of *Marketing for Tourism and Hospitality: A Canadian Perspective* provides resources for both the instructor and the student. The Student site includes true/false and multiple-choice questions, Internet exercises, PowerPoint® slides, career information, and more. The Instructor site includes the Instructor's Manual/Test Bank and PowerPoint® slides.

ACKNOWLEDGMENTS

I am grateful to the many individuals who helped to make *Marketing for Tourism and Hospitality: A Canadian Perspective* a reality. In particular, I would like to thank the team at Nelson Thomson Learning, especially Elke Price and Veronica Visentin.

This book has benefited tremendously from the people in the tourism industry who took the time to talk to me and to provide me with valuable material for the book. Those people are too numerous to list, but I thank them all. I would also like to thank my wife, Louise, whose patience—while I (from her perspective) "tapped away incessantly" during my sabbatical in the South Pacific—was commendable (and unbelievable!). Finally, I am indebted to the reviewers who took the time to review the manuscript so professionally. I would like to extend my gratitude to the reviewers listed below:

Julie Aumais, Mohawk College

Candace Blayney, Mount Saint Vincent University

Marc Bussieres, St. Lawrence College

Mark Elliott, Douglas College

Marion Joppe, University of Guelph

Brenda Hodgins, Red Deer College

Georgina King, Seneca College

Ian McVitty, Algonquin College

Iain Murray, University of Guelph

Sue Nickason, Georgina College

Steve Renton, Assiniboine Community College

Margaret Shaw, University of Guelph

Arlene Shieven, British Columbia Institute of Technology

Marc Simard, Nova Scotia Community College

Michael Tittel, Vancouver Community College

David Wright, Seneca College

I would also like to thank Joyce Twizell for all her help with the tables and diagrams.

About the Author

Simon Hudson, Ph.D., M.B.A., B.A., Dip.M.

Simon Hudson is an associate professor in tourism management at the University of Calgary in Canada. He has held previous academic positions at universities in England, and has also worked as a visiting professor in Austria, Switzerland, Fiji, New Zealand, and Australia. Prior to working in academia, Dr. Hudson spent several years working in the tourism industry in Europe, and now consults for the industry in Alberta and British Columbia. Dr. Hudson has written two books in addition to *Marketing for Tourism and Hospitality: A Canadian Perspective. Snow Business* was the first book to be written about the international ski industry, and *Sports and Adventure Tourism* was published in 2003. The marketing of tourism is the focus of his research, and his work has resulted in numerous published journal articles and book chapters. He has made many tourism conference presentations, and has been invited to several international locations as a keynote speaker, including China, New Zealand, and the United States.

The Tourism Marketing Environment

1

AN ADVENTURE WITH BRUCE POON TIP

In 1991, Bruce Poon Tip withdrew every last penny in his bank account to open his own travel company that would take tourists to emerging countries in Central and South America. Due to the risky nature of the travel industry at that time, caused by the persistent Gulf War, the banks were unwilling to lend him any money. Poon Tip would not be discouraged and, as a result, he stretched the limit of his credit card to follow his vision. Today, G.A.P Adventures

is one of the 10 largest adventure companies in the world. At 21, Poon Tip found his G.A.P concept when he travelled in Thailand for $10 a day and stayed with the hill tribes. "It wasn't my first visit, but it was my most genuine," says Poon Tip, who recently consulted on *Survivor*. "That was when I knew others would want authentic travel experiences." Born in Trinidad, Poon Tip runs his company based on his commitment to developing mutually beneficial international relationships, incorporating values and respect for local cultures, and promoting ecotourism. His $35 million business, which sells trips to 100 destinations through its 21 offices worldwide, does more to promote sustainable tourism than any other company in the business.

G.A.P Adventures and Bruce Poon Tip have been recognized by many organizations as leaders in business practices and leadership. In 2003, Poon Tip won Entrepreneur of the Year in Canada, as well as the National Citation for Entrepreneurship. In addition to receiving an award as one of Canada's top 40 Canadians Under 40, Poon Tip has also been honoured as one of Canada's top five entrepreneurs by *Canadian Business* and as one of Canada's 100 leaders of tomorrow. Poon Tip also received the Global Traders Leadership award from the government for his groundbreaking ideas in exporting services. He has also spearheaded a postgraduate diploma program for Humber College on Ecotourism and Adventure Travel. Recently, he was asked by the World Bank and UNESCO to be on a team visiting the People's Republic of China to lecture on sustainable development. In January 2002, Poon Tip was the only Canadian operator invited to attend the United Nations' launch of the Year of Ecotourism in New York.

Poon Tip believes that ecotourism does not have to be small-scale. "Most people say ecotourism means 'leave only footprints,' " he says. "I disagree with that. I think that we've got to get those 10 000 people off the cruise ships and into 200 small groups. I think that tourists can leave behind a huge impact." To that end, Poon Tip has worked with the World Bank to help impoverished villages finance tourist lodges and teach communities to profit through tourism. Six communities in Bolivia, for example, now sustain themselves through such initiatives, which helps reduce their dependence on logging and the drug trade. He is also making efforts to reel in less eco-minded tourists with his new company, Real Traveller. It offers essentially the same products, but without G.A.P's rather loud emphasis on sustainability. It is designed, he explains, to appeal to customers who do not want to travel with "a bunch of tree huggers." Poon Tip says the spinoff is also a strategy to block competitors. "Instead of waiting for big business to come in and start a competing company, we thought we'd start it ourselves." At the same time, he also launched a software company to sell other small tour operators the booking software G.A.P spent two years developing.

G.A.P Adventures doubled in size in October 2002 with the purchase of Vancouver's Global Connections (GC). While the latter's substantial Latin American free independent traveller (FIT) product line adds a new dimension to the Toronto-based adventure specialist, it is GC's flight consolidation operation that has those at G.A.P excited. For Poon Tip, adding airline seats to his expanding roster of products rectifies one of his "biggest mistakes" in 10 years of operations—"ignoring flights!" Unimpressed by the airline sector's low margins, Poon Tip says he has diligently tried to stay away from selling airline seats, but admits his failure to do so has been holding G.A.P back, adding, "It's really become quite ridiculous." Into the bargain, G.A.P also gained a ready-made FIT program that, combined with G.A.P's groups, will make G.A.P the largest independent Canadian tour operator for Latin America, according to Poon Tip, who projected $35 million in sales for the merged operation in 2002.

Sources: Baginski, M. (2002). GC acquisition fills large G.A.P. Retrieved October 10, 2002, from http://www.canadatourism.com/en/ctc/ctx/ctxnews/search/newsbydateform.cfm; G.A.P Adventures Web site: http://www.gapadventures.com; B. Poon Tip, personal communication, February 28, 2003.

Objectives

On completion of this chapter, readers should understand

- what is meant by tourism and hospitality marketing;
- the unique characteristics of services;

- who the key players are in Canada's tourism industry; and
- the various macroenvironmental forces shaping the tourism industry in Canada.

Chapter Overview

The opening vignette is an example of a Canadian success story in the tourism industry. By understanding and adapting to a changing environment, G.A.P Adventures has become one of the largest adventure companies in the world. This book begins with a chapter dedicated to the tourism and hospitality environment in Canada. The chapter begins by providing an introduction to tourism and hospitality marketing in general by discussing the definition and role of marketing and its importance in tourism. A synopsis of services marketing theory highlights the unique characteristics of services and introduces important service marketing models, such as the services marketing triangle and the services marketing mix. The chapter then focuses on tourism in Canada and analyzes the key players in Canada's tourism industry. The marketing environment is made up of microenvironmental and macroenvironmental forces, and the remainder of the chapter examines the major environmental forces that affect an organization's ability to serve its customers.

INTRODUCTION TO TOURISM AND HOSPITALITY MARKETING

tourism market

a market that reflects the demands of consumers for a very wide range of travel and hospitality products

Tourism is a powerful economic force providing employment, foreign exchange, income, and tax revenue. The **tourism market** reflects the demands of consumers for a very wide range of travel and hospitality products, and it is widely claimed that this total market is now being serviced by the world's largest industry. The World Tourism Organization (WTO) estimated that in 2002 international arrivals of 715 million people (19.7 million in Canada) generated receipts of US$463 billion. The WTO also estimated that in 2001 employment in the travel and tourism economy comprised over 200 million jobs or 8.2 percent of total employment. WTO's Tourism 2020 Vision forecasts that international arrivals are expected to reach over 1.56 billion by the year 2020. Of these worldwide arrivals in 2020, 1.18 billion will be intra-regional and 377 million will be long-haul travellers.[1]

The Influence of Marketing on Tourism

Marketing is a subject of vital concern in tourism because it is the principal management influence that can be brought to bear on the size and behaviour of this major global market. Figure 1.1 shows the vital linkages between demand and supply in tourism, which are fundamental to an understanding of the role of marketing. The figure shows the relationship between market demand, generated in areas of origin, and product supply, mainly at visitor destinations. In particular, the model shows how the main sectors of the tourism industry—travel organizers, destination organizations, transportation, various product suppliers—combine to manage visitors' demand through a range of marketing influences.

The marketing mix is in the centre of the diagram, and it is discussed in more detail later in the chapter. However, it is important to note that the influence of this marketing activity is likely to vary according to visitors' interests and circumstances. For example, domestic visitors travelling by car to stay with friends or relatives may not be influenced by destination marketing in any way, whereas first-time buyers of package tours to exotic destinations may find that almost every aspect of their trip is influenced by the marketing decisions of the tour operator they choose. In between these two examples, a business traveller will select his or her own destination according to business requirements, but may be influenced as to which airline or hotel he or she selects.

Knowledge of the customer, and all that it implies for management decisions, is generally referred to as consumer or marketing orientation. A detailed understanding of consumer characteristics and buying behaviour is central to the activities of marketing managers, and therefore consumer behaviour is the topic of Chapter 3.

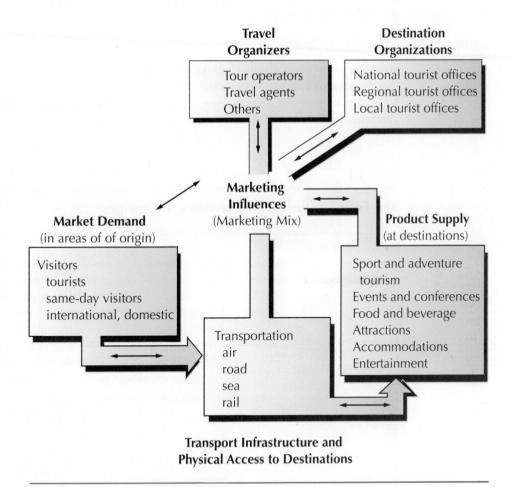

Figure 1.1 The Systematic Linkages between Demand and Supply: The Influence of Marketing

Source: Middleton, V. T. C., & Clarke, J. (2001.) *Marketing in travel and tourism.* Oxford: Butterworth-Heinemann.

marketing

the process of planning and executing the conception, pricing, promotion, and distribution of ideas, goods, and services to create exchanges that satisfy individual (customer) and organizational objectives

Marketing has been defined as "the process of planning and executing the conception, pricing, promotion, and distribution of ideas, goods, and services to create exchanges that satisfy individual (customer) and organizational objectives."[2] The marketing concept is a business philosophy that defines marketing as a process intended to find, satisfy, and retain customers while the business makes a profit. Central to both these definitions is the role of the customer and the customer's relationship to the product, whether that product is a good, a service, or an idea. The tourism and hospitality sector, like other service sectors, involves a combination of tangible and intangible products. A hotel is a mixture of goods (beds, food, telephone, and communication systems) that are linked with a range of services (front desk, housekeeping, room service, finance, and accounting). A tourist attraction such as a Canadian national park is a combination of facilities (hotels, shops, visitor centres) situated within a physical attraction (the mountains and rivers), offering a range of services (guided tours, interpretation, education, etc.). This whole package of tangible and intangible products is perceived by the tourist as an experience, and represents the core of the tourism product.

Unique Characteristics of Services

As can be seen from the above, tourism and hospitality incorporate both goods and services. Goods are easier to measure, test, and evaluate, while services provide a greater challenge. Service products are commonly distinguished from goods products by four unique characteristics listed in Table 1.1.

Table 1.1

The Four Unique Characteristics of Services

CHARACTERISTIC	DESCRIPTION
1. Intangibility	Service products cannot be tasted, felt, seen, heard, or smelled. Prior to boarding a plane, airline passengers have nothing but an airline ticket and a promise of safe delivery to their destination. To reduce uncertainty caused by service intangibility, buyers look for tangible evidence that will provide information and confidence about the service.
2. Inseparability	For many services, the product cannot be created or delivered without the customer's presence. The food in a restaurant may be outstanding, but if the server has a poor attitude or provides inattentive service, customers will not enjoy the overall restaurant experience. In the same way, other customers can affect the experience in service settings.

CHARACTERISTIC	DESCRIPTION
3. Heterogeneity	Service delivery quality depends on who provides the services. The same person can deliver differing levels of service, displaying a marked difference in tolerance and friendliness as the day wears on. Lack of consistency is a major factor in customer dissatisfaction.
4. Perishability	Services cannot be stored. Empty airline seats, hotel rooms, daily ski passes, restaurant covers—all these services cannot be sold the next day. If services are to maximize revenue, they must manage capacity and demand since they cannot carry forward unsold inventory.

Services Marketing Models

Several models and frameworks have been developed over the years to assist in making services marketing and management decisions at both the strategic and implementation levels. Two of these will now be discussed: the services marketing triangle and the services marketing mix. Both of these frameworks address the challenges inherent in services, and each of them can be used to assess and guide strategies, as well as provide a roadmap for implementation planning.

The Services Marketing Triangle

The **services marketing triangle** (see Figure 1.2 on page 8) shows the three interlinked groups that work together to develop, promote, and deliver services. These key players—the company, the customers, and the providers—are labelled on the points of the triangle. Between these three points there are three types of marketing that must be successfully carried out for a service to succeed: external, interactive, and internal marketing. For all services, especially for tourism and hospitality services, all three types of marketing activities are essential for building and maintaining relationships. Through its external marketing efforts, a company makes promises to its customers regarding what they can expect and how it can be delivered. Traditional marketing activities (such as those discussed in Chapters 8, 9, and 10) facilitate this type of marketing, but for services, other factors such as the servicescape and the process itself help to set customer expectations.

Keeping promises, or interactive marketing, is the second kind of marketing activity captured by the triangle. Interactive marketing occurs in the "moment of truth" when the customer interacts with the organization and the service is produced and consumed. From the customer's point of view, the most vivid impression of service occurs in the service encounter or the moment of truth. It is in these encounters that customers receive a snapshot of the organization's service quality, and each encounter contributes to the customer's overall satisfaction and willingness to do business with the organization again.

Finally, internal marketing takes place through the enabling of promises. Promises are easy to make, but unless providers are recruited, trained, provided with tools and appropriate internal systems, and rewarded for good service, the promises may not be kept. Internal marketing is discussed in more depth in Chapter 11.

services marketing triangle

a model that illustrates the three interlinking groups that work together to develop, promote, and deliver services: the company, the customer, and the provider

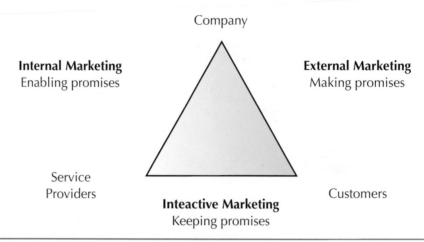

Figure 1.2   The Services Marketing Triangle

Source: Zeithaml, V. A., & Bitner, M. J. (2000.) *Services marketing: integrating customer focus across the firm*. New York: McGraw-Hill, 16.

The Marketing Mix for Services

services marketing mix

the original four P's of the marketing mix—product, place, promotion, and price—plus the people, the physical evidence, and the process

Another way to begin addressing the challenges of services marketing is to think creatively about the **services marketing mix**—through an expanded marketing mix for services. The marketing mix may be defined as "the mixture of controllable marketing variables that the firm uses to pursue the sought level of sales in the target market."[3] The original four P's of the marketing mix, introduced in 1961,[4] are product, place, promotion, and price. Because services are usually produced and consumed simultaneously, customers are often part of the service production process. Also, because services are intangible, customers will often be looking for any tangible cue to help them understand the nature of the service experience. These facts have led service marketers to conclude that they can use additional variables to communicate with and satisfy their customers. Acknowledgement of the importance of these additional variables has led service marketers to adopt the concept of an expanded marketing mix for services, shown in Table 1.2. In addition to the traditional four P's, the services marketing mix includes people, physical evidence, and process.

The people element includes all human actors who play a part in service delivery and thus influence the buyer's perceptions—namely the firm's personnel, the customer, and other customers in the service environment. The physical evidence is the environment in which the service is delivered and where the firm and customer interact, and any tangible components that facilitate performance or communication of the service. Table 1.2 gives some examples of tangible evidence or cues used by service organizations. Finally, the process is the actual procedures, mechanisms, and flow of activities by which the service is delivered. The three new marketing mix elements are included in the marketing mix as separate elements because they are within the control of the firm and any or all of them may influence the customer's initial decision to purchase a service and the customer's level of satisfaction and repurchase decisions. The traditional elements as well as the new marketing mix elements are explored in depth in later chapters.

Table 1.2

Expanded Marketing Mix for Services

	PRODUCT	PLACE	PROMOTION	PRICE

Traditional 4 P's of Marketing	Physical good features
	
	Quality level
	Accessories
	Packaging
	Warranties
	Product lines
	Branding
		Channel type
		
		Exposure
		Intermediaries
		Outlet locations
		Transportation
		Storage
		Managing channels
			Promotion blend
			
			Salespeople
			  number
			  selection
			  training
			  incentives
			
			Advertising
			  targets
			  media types
			  types of ads
			  copy thrust
			
			Sales promotion
			Publicity
				Flexibility
				
				Price level
				Terms
				Differentiation
				Discounts
				Allowances

	PEOPLE	PHYSICAL EVIDENCE	PROCESS

Additional 3 P's of Services Marketing	Employees
	  recruiting
	  training
	  motivation
	  rewards
	  teamwork
	
	Customers
	  education
	  training
		Facility design
		Equipment
		Signage
		Employee dress
		
		Other tangibles
		  reports
		  business cards
		  statements
		  guarantees
			Flow of activities
			  standardized
			  customized
			Number of steps
			  simple
			  complex
			
			Customer involvement

Source: Booms, B. H., & Bitner, M. J. (1981). Marketing strategies and organizational structures for service firms. In J. H. Donnelly & W. R. George (Eds.), *Marketing services* (pp. 47–51). Chicago: American Marketing Association.

TOURISM IN CANADA

Tourism is an increasingly important sector of the Canadian economy. In 2001, the World Tourism Organization ranked Canada as the ninth most popular destination in the world. Canada's share of the international tourism travel market that same year was 2.8 percent. The tourism Gross Domestic Product reached $22.4 billion, and total government revenues from

Table 1.3

Travel to and within Canada by Province Visited in 2001

PROVINCE	CANADIAN RESIDENTS (000s)	U.S. RESIDENTS (000s)	OVERSEAS RESIDENTS (000s)
Atlantic Region	7 901	1 213	274
Quebec	15 924	2 336	1 016
Ontario	26 200	7 900	1 838
Manitoba/Saskatchewan	7 071	559	131
Alberta	9 195	1 020	875
British Columbia	9 547	3 783	1 524
Total	**75 838**	**16 811**	**5 658**

Source: Canadian Tourism Commission. (2003). *Canadian tourism facts and figures 2001*. Retrieved August 15, 2003, from http://www.canadatourism.com/en/ctc/ctx/ctx-news/search/newsbydateform.cfm.

tourism were $16.7 billion. In 2002, Canada attracted 20 million international overnight visitors, who spent $17.8 billion, making tourism one of Canada's top foreign exchange earners. Tourism in Canada provides jobs in many sectors—transportation, accommodation, food and beverage services, recreation and entertainment, and travel agencies. Estimates indicate that in 2002 employment directly related to tourism totalled 585 900, an increase of 0.5 percent over 2001. As for outbound tourism, Canadians made 17.6 million overnight trips outside Canada in 2002, down 3.8 percent from 2001. Domestically, Canadians spent almost $34 billion on tourism in Canada, an increase of 1.8 percent over 2001 domestic travel spending. Table 1.3 shows travel to and within Canada by province visited in 2001.

KEY PLAYERS IN CANADA'S TOURISM INDUSTRY

The key players in Canada's tourism industry are outlined in Figure 1.3. They include private and nonprofit sector services, public sector services, suppliers (transportation, accommodation, food and beverage services, attractions, events and conferences, and sport and adventure tourism), intermediaries, and the customers (tourists/travellers) themselves. Each will be discussed in turn below.

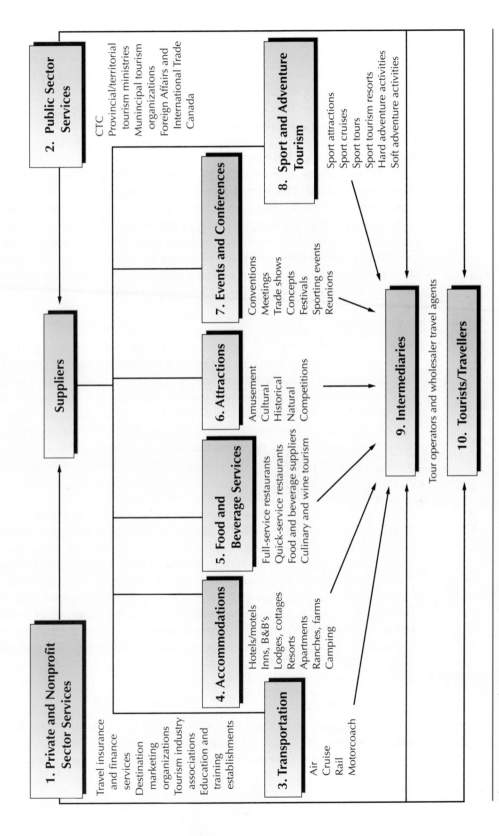

Figure 1.3 Key Players in Canada's Tourism Industry

1. Private and Nonprofit Sector Services

The private and nonprofit sector includes tourism industry associations such as the Association of Canadian Travel Agents (ACTA); Canadian Standard Travel Agency Registry (CSTAR); financial and banking services; educational institutions; the media, such as the Canadian Travel Press; and insurance services. Although many companies have found it more difficult to obtain insurance since September 11, 2001, inbound Canadian tour or receptive operators and tourism product and service suppliers received some good news at the 2001 Rendezvous Canada show in Halifax, Nova Scotia. Operators and suppliers can now take advantage of a new insurance program provided by Export Development Canada (EDC), which protects them against foreign tour operator default or bankruptcy. The accounts receivable insurance covers up to 90 percent of losses suffered if the U.S. or foreign tour operator cannot or will not pay; the insured tourism contracts and payment vouchers also become a "bankable asset" and can be used as security for a new line of credit. Beyond these practical aspects, the insurance program will allow operators and suppliers to grow their business with foreign tour companies with which they might not have done business without the insurance protection.

2. Public Sector Services

Public sector involvement is led by the Canadian Tourism Commission (CTC), a Crown corporation representing provincial and regional tourism associations, government agencies, hoteliers, tour operators, airline companies, and attractions owners. The key role of the CTC is to design, deliver, and fund marketing and research initiatives in partnership with the above groups. The government of Canada contributes about $65 million annually to the CTC. Public sector involvement also comes from provincial tourism ministries, regional organizations, and municipal tourism organizations. Other important tourism groups in the public sector include those responsible for national parks and for national heritage.

Under the umbrella of each provincial tourism organization, there are a number of public, quasi-public, and independent organizations, which work independently and in cooperation to create more attractive tourism products. For example, Ontario has the Southern Ontario Tourism Organization (SOTO), the Niagara Economic Tourism Development Corporation (NECTOR), the Niagara Parks Commission (park-based) and Niagara Falls Tourism (city-based). At a state or provincial level, marketing agencies spend millions of dollars promoting tourism. Their marketing programs target both individual travellers and travel trade intermediaries. Often they enter into cooperative marketing with suppliers, carriers, intermediaries, and other destination marketing organizations. Chapter 12, on destination marketing, explores these issues in more detail.

3. Transportation

a) The Airline Industry

Canada is a signatory to the Open Skies Policy, which has opened the borders and allowed foreign carriers greater access to Canadian customers, allowing customers greater choice. The Open Skies Policy agreement took effect in 1995, with the result that airlines and not governments now decide which transborder routes they can fly. Over 90 new scheduled routes have been added by Canadian and American carriers since the signing of the agreement and 40 percent have been added in Toronto alone.

Airline deregulation around the world has led to the development of no-frills, low-cost airlines, operating mainly out of secondary airports. Calgary-based WestJet is a Canadian example (see Case Study in Chapter 11), and more recently Jetsgo and Air Canada's Tango and Zip have entered the discount market to compete with WestJet. In Canada, there has been much debate about the structure of the airline industry and the role of "open skies." Some commentators have stated that Canada's tourism markets are being undermined by an air transport policy suitable for the 1930s but totally unfit for the competitive world we live in today. "Our current airline policy is based on the single premise of protecting air carriers. This is absolutely contrary to the role of government, which is to protect consumers," says Dr. Tretheway, vice-president and Senior Economist of InterVISTAS Consulting Inc.[5]

b) The Cruise Industry

In 2000, the direct economic impact of cruise spending in Canada amounted to about $500 million. British Columbia cities Victoria and Vancouver receive more cruise ship business each year, Victoria being the largest receiver. Victoria posted a big jump in cruise ship arrivals, from 70 in 2001 to 110 in 2002. The port of Vancouver has also had a good run of growth, based on the steady expansion of the Alaska-bound cruise industry over the past two decades. The number of departures from Vancouver was about 280 in 2002, with 25 visiting ships recorded the same year. Cruising has also grown in Eastern Canada. Passenger counts increased by more then 340 percent, from just over 47 000 in 1998 to about 160 000 in 2002. The largest cruise line companies in the world are regular customers of ports in Nova Scotia such as Halifax and Sydney and include such industry leaders as Carnival Corporation, Royal Caribbean International, and P&O. On average, each passenger spends about $95 on shore. In 2002, that equated to more than $16 million to the local economies.

c) Railways

A single carrier, VIA Rail Canada, dominates the passenger rail industry. VIA serves over 3.8 million passengers annually, and of those, 3.2 million ride the train between Toronto and Quebec City. The flagship of the industry is *The Canadian*, which runs from Toronto to Vancouver, attracting over 150 000 passengers a year, most of them tourists. VIA claims to have been the world's first railway to provide interactive online access to timetables and fares, followed by ticket reservation and payment capability. The Rocky Mountaineer is another Canadian success story (see Case Study in Chapter 9).

However, there are many more railway operators in Canada. In British Columbia, for example, the Pacific Wilderness Railway takes people to the top of Malahat Mountain, on Vancouver Island. There is also the Okanagan Valley Wine Train, which provides excursions into the province's wine-growing regions. In Winnipeg, tourists can take the Prairie Dog Central, a steam train that runs into the prairies, and in Ontario they can choose between the Polar Bear Express, which runs through the wilderness from Cochrane to Moosonee, and the Agawa Canyon Train out of Sault Ste. Marie. In Hull, Quebec, the

Hull-Chelsea-Wakefield Steam Train takes visitors for a five-hour journey into the past, and in the Yukon, the historic White Pass & Yukon Route Railway will take tourists between White Pass, Yukon, and Skagway, Alaska.

d) Motorcoach Operators

A strong and viable motorcoach industry has a significant impact on the tourism industry. As a rule of thumb, one overnight motorcoach tour operator generates approximately $7000 per day for the economy. On a yearly basis, the CN Tower reports more than 6000 coach visits and Niagara Falls reports over 40 000 visits. Even less populated areas receive significant coach business: in 2002, 958 coaches entered Prince Edward Island, bringing 35 948 people to that province. In terms of annual ridership densities, scheduled bus passenger traffic makes up about 3 billion passenger kilometres (20 percent), while charter and other passenger traffic makes up about 11 billion passenger kilometres (80 percent). Motorcoach tour passengers have traditionally been seniors or those over 50 years of age, but ridership has diversified recently with the increase of specialized tours based on pursuits such as theatre and soft adventure. Indeed, charter passengers are of all ages, usually brought together by a specific event or a common interest (e.g., country and western tours or casino trips).

4. Accommodations

The accommodation sector in Canada is dynamic and characterized by fast-paced change. In 2000, almost 17 000 traveller accommodation establishments generated $11.8 billion in revenue, up 4.1 percent from 1999. Hotels and motels accounted for 88 percent of all traveller accommodation revenue, with other accommodations, like bed and breakfasts, contributing the remaining 12 percent. Hotel ownership has shifted dramatically, resulting in the concentration of hotel assets in the hands of a few portfolio investors. Three real estate investment trusts, including Legacy Hotels, Canadian Income Hotel Properties, and Royal Hosts, own more than 80 hotels with over 17 000 rooms. Similar to global trends, acquisitions are expected to continue across North America, and branding has become increasingly important.

In Canada, 76 percent of hotels with 100 rooms or more are attached to a brand. The larger hotel brands operating in Canada include Best Western (see *Snapshot* in Chapter 7, pp. 229–232), Choice, Fairmont (see Case Study in this chapter), Four Seasons (see the opening vignette in Chapter 2), Hilton, Holiday Inn, Howard Johnson, Hyatt, Marriott, Radisson, Ramada, Sheraton, and Westin. Canadian hotel transaction volume reached an estimated $540 million in 2002, approximately 18 percent below the $656 million reported in 2001 and some 59 percent below the $1.3 billion achieved in 1998.

However, second-home ownership has been growing. Canada is still a cottager's paradise, with 10 percent of Canadians owning recreational properties, and demand is soaring. On Nova Scotia's South Shore, for example, prices for vacation properties have doubled in the past decade.[6] Land around Kingsburg, Ontario, was selling for $247 000 per hectare in 2001, and 16 percent of the province's coast was owned by nonresidents. In other parts of Canada, companies like Intrawest, which are developing four-season resorts, are investing heavily in real estate development and profiting from vacation ownership. For example, in Whistler, British Columbia, building investment has exceeded

$2 billion since the establishment of this municipality in 1975. Now, with more than 55 000 beds, and 18 000 of those within 500 metres of the lifts, Whistler boasts the most ski-in/ski-out beds of any mountain recreation resort in North America.

5. Food and Beverage Services

Another important supplier to the tourism industry is the food and beverage sector. In 2001, the Canadian restaurant business was worth $32.2 billion and grew 6.6 percent in the same year, despite the economic downturn. Full-service restaurants strongly outpaced the quick-service sector, and consumer demand was so resilient that restaurateurs managed to pass along an average 3.2 percent price increase, largely the result of buying produce with a weak Canadian currency and high labour and energy costs. One reason for the resilience is that dining out is now an integral element in the lives of Canadians, who are more educated about food and wine than ever before. Consumers' time is more valuable because of lifestyle changes such as longer working weeks and more dual-career families, making dining out or eating food prepared outside the home more common than in previous generations.

Although culinary experiences are rarely paramount when one thinks of tourism in Canada, there are a number of interesting developments in the field. Canadians are taking part in the international movement toward the use of indigenous, locally cultivated products and the development of regional cuisine. Atlantic seafood and Alberta beef have long been culinary draws, but there is increasing use of more specialized products such as Saskatoon berries, Quebec cheeses, and wild Arctic musk ox. Such regional cuisine has the potential to be an increasingly important tourism resource, and Canadian tour operators are beginning to package cuisine in unique and innovative ways. For example, First Island Tours, in British Columbia, features a "Gourmet Trail" and an "Ale Trail." Baillarge Cultural Tours offers a "Cuisines of Quebec" tour that includes visits to local producers of maple sugar, cider, vinegar, and liqueurs, as well as to a traditional flourmill.

6. Attractions

As with other sectors of the tourism industry, attractions are increasingly polarized between a few large attractions and thousands of small and micro-sized enterprises. Within the range of visitor management techniques available to attractions, marketing is increasingly seen as fundamental to success. It is recognized as the best way of generating revenue to contribute to the cost of operation and maintenance of the resource base, to develop and sustain satisfying products, to create value for money, and to influence the volume and seasonality patterns of site visits.

Attractions can be classified as natural or human-made. Canadians are extremely proud of their 39 national parks, 3 marine conservation areas, and over 850 natural historic sites. In a recent survey, Canadians stated that after "O Canada" and the flag, they consider these natural and cultural attractions to be their premier source of identity and pride.[7] Experiencing these special places is a top motivator of both domestic and international travel, and a vital component of Canada's multi-billion dollar tourism industry. Canadian attractions profiled in this book include Pier 21 in Nova Scotia and West Edmonton Mall in Alberta.

7. Events and Conferences

Events and conferences often play a key role in bringing business and leisure travellers to destinations. These events can vary from conventions and exhibitions for the business market to huge sporting events like the Olympics or the soccer World Cup, which attract millions of sport tourists. From the destination's perspective, event tourism is the development and marketing of events to obtain economic and community benefits. To the consumer, it is travel for the purpose of participating in or viewing an event. The marketing of events and conferences is discussed more fully in Chapter 12.

8. Sport and Adventure Tourism

The marketing of sport and adventure tourism, also covered in more detail in Chapter 12, is a fast-growing segment of the Canadian tourism industry. Sport travel in Canada is valued at approximately $1.3 billion annually or 4 percent of the tourism market.[8] There are currently about 200 000 sport events that occur annually in this country, and nearly 40 percent of travellers participate in, or are spectators at, a sport event every year. Adventure tourism is also on the increase. This type of travel brings together travel, sport, and outdoor recreation, and three key factors have facilitated its growth: a deferring of control to experts; a proliferation of promotional media, including brochures; and the application of technology in adventurous settings.[9] Adventure tourism is often classified according to activity, where "hard" adventure tourism activities include mountaineering, white-water rafting, scuba diving, and mountain biking, and "soft" adventure activities include camping, hiking, biking, animal watching, horseback riding, canoeing, and water skiing.

9. Intermediaries

The key intermediary players in the tourism industry are tour operators and wholesalers, destination marketing companies, travel agents, travel specialists, and Web-based intermediaries. (A detailed analysis of intermediaries can be found in Chapter 7). Both tour operators and wholesalers are organizations that offer packaged vacation tours to the general public. These packages can include everything from transportation, accommodation, and activities, to entertainment, meals, and drinks. Destination Marketing Companies (DMCs) are private sector companies that also act as inbound tour operators. Travel agents are the most widely used marketing intermediaries in the tourism industry, but the emergence of new and cheaper distribution tools such as the Internet has placed the future role of travel agents in doubt.

10. Tourists/Travellers

As mentioned earlier, Canada attracted 19.6 million international overnight visitors in 2001. Nearly 70 percent of these visitors came to Canada during the second and third quarters of the year. The origins of these visitors are discussed in detail in Chapter 3, but the United States is clearly Canada's most important international market, accounting for over 78 percent of trips.[10] As for domestic tourists, 14.5 million overnight trips were recorded in Canada in 2001. Tourists can be classified as leisure and business travellers, both of which are discussed in Chapter 3. Business travel has been hardest hit by events in 2001, as new airline restructuring, security clampdowns, and people's widespread reluctance to leave home has driven the cost and hassle of corporate travel sky high.

In addition, Canadians frequently travel abroad. In 2002, Canadians took nearly 13 million trips outside the country. Seventy-seven percent of the Canadian population over the age of 15 travelled abroad at least once that year, spending $15.5 billion on international travel. The United States is the most popular destination, accounting for 4.6 million or 76 percent of the total international outbound trips.

PROFILE

THE CANADIAN TOURISM COMMISSION: RESPONDING TO SEPTEMBER 11, 2001

According to Jim Watson, former president and CEO of the Canadian Tourism Commission, "One cannot reflect on 2001 without envisioning the horrible and tragic images of September 11, and what those acts of terrorism did not only to our industry, but to the world as we knew it." While tourism revenues and travel to and from Canada have grown in recent years, 2001 saw an economic slowdown. This downturn in the economy was further affected by the terrorist attacks in the United States on September 11. The impact on tourism was devastating, and immediately following the events, the Canadian Tourism Commission (CTC) and its partners came together to try to mitigate the impact and put in place several initiatives to help restore consumer confidence and stimulate travel. Industry-led, market-driven, and research-based, the Canadian Tourism Commission is a Crown corporation that works in partnership with the tourism industry and provincial and territorial governments to market Canada as a four-season destination.

The CTC was quick to respond in the aftermath of the tragic events of September 2001 by promptly providing useful and timely information to the industry and by launching successful marketing campaigns in Canada and the United States to promote tourism to and within Canada. They received a one-time federal contribution of $15 million for a

domestic and U.S. marketing campaign and, internally, they redirected $5 million for the campaign.

The domestic marketing campaign, launched in November 2001 and aimed at encouraging Canadians to keep travelling domestically, used television, cinema, print, and e-marketing. The campaign portrayed Canada as an exciting and unique travel experience in a familiar setting. As a result, 60 percent of Canadians said they were very likely to consider a trip within Canada in the next year, and CTC's consumer Web site (www.travelcanada.ca) posted a 200 percent increase in the number of visitors over the same period a year earlier. Wave II of the "Travel Canada" campaign, with its "There's no place like home" theme line, appeared in print media, on national television, and in movie theatres across Canada. "Altogether, it's apparent that Canadians, as well as foreign tourists, are interested in travelling to Canada and experiencing our country," says Jim Watson.

In order to attract the U.S. market, the CTC put forward an unprecedented effort in communication, dialogue, coordination, and marketing. In addition to the historic long-haul concentration, marketing efforts were immediately focused on northern tier/border states and the driver market. Coupled with a favourable exchange rate, and the fact that

PROFILE *continued*

Americans travelled closer to home, the 2001 overnight trips and corresponding spending targets were exceeded. "Travel in Canada is definitely on the rise and the recovery seems to be quicker than we initially forecasted," says Watson. "The CTC's marketing initiatives appear to be effective in encouraging Canadians and Americans to visit Canada following the tragic events of September 2001. Moreover, overall results for 2001 are more positive than we expected."

Month-to-month results published by Statistics Canada indicate that total international overnight travel to Canada in December 2001 increased significantly, by 5.1 percent, the second consecutive monthly increase since August 2001. The number of overseas trips showed the largest rebound, at 11.3 percent; in fact, 7 of Canada's top 12 overseas markets returned to pre-September levels. For its part, travel from the United States to Canada increased by 3.8 percent. On the

other hand, further results from Statistics Canada point to a very modest decrease of 0.1 percent in international overnight travel to Canada for 2001, compared to the previous year, with a total of 19.6 million overnight tourists. The slowing economies and the tragedies in the United States were largely responsible for this result, with overseas travel from the United States being more affected than travel to Canada from that country. Overall, in light of research results posted earlier by the CTC, predicting an improvement in the travel sector later in 2002, the international travel flows to Canada in December 2001 confirmed that the recovery of the Canadian tourism industry was on track.

Sources: Canadian Tourism Commission. (2002). President's message. *CTC Annual Report 2001.* Ottawa: Author, 2; Desaulniers, G. (2002). Recovery of Canadian tourism industry on fast pace. Retrieved February 18, 2002, from http://www.canadatourism.com/en/ctc/ctx/ctx-news/search/newsbydateform.cfm.

MICRO- AND MACROENVIRONMENTS

Microenvironment

microenvironment

forces close to the organization that can affect its ability to serve its customers: the organization itself, marketing channel firms, customer markets, and a broad range of stakeholders or publics

The marketing environment is made up of a microenvironment and a macroenvironment. The **microenvironment** consists of forces close to the organization that can affect its ability to serve its customers: the organization itself, marketing channel firms, customer markets, and a broad range of stakeholders or publics (see Figure 1.4). For a tourism marketer, these factors will affect the degree of success in attracting target markets, so it is important to understand their importance. This book discusses most of these components in detail: competitors in Chapter 2, customers in Chapter 3, intermediaries in Chapter 7, and the various publics in Chapter 9. However, it is important to acknowledge the influence that the company and its suppliers will have on achieving marketing objectives.

Marketing managers need to work closely with other departments in the company, as all of these departments will have some impact on the success of marketing plans. Every tourism organization will differ as to how many departments it has and what they are called. However, finance is normally responsible for finding and using the funds required to carry out marketing plans, accounting has to measure revenues and costs in order to

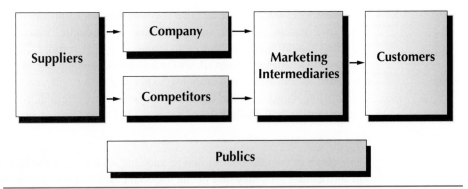

Figure 1.4   Major Components in a Company's Microenvironment

evaluate marketing objectives, and human resources will be crucial in supporting a service marketing culture (see Chapter 11). Suppliers also have an important role to play in supporting marketing objectives. Suppliers are firms and individuals that provide the resources needed by the company to produce its goods and services. Marketing management must pay close attention to trends and developments affecting suppliers, and to changes in supply availability and supply costs. At a micro level, hotels and exhibition centres contract with restaurant companies to supply food and beverage services. In turn, these restaurants will have their own favoured suppliers of produce. On a macro basis, tourist destinations will need suppliers in the form of airlines, hotels, restaurants, ground operations, meeting facilities, and entertainment.

Macroenvironment

macroenvironment

the larger societal forces that affect the microenvironment: competitive, demographic, economic, environmental and natural, technological, political, cultural and social, and legal forces

The **macroenvironment** comprises the larger societal forces that affect the entire microenvironment, and this will shape opportunities and pose threats. The macroenvironment consists of the eight major forces shown in Figure 1.5, and tourism businesses need

Figure 1.5   Major Forces in a Company's Macroenvironment

to take into consideration the fact that they operate in a competitive national and international environment. Although an organization cannot control many of these external factors, they should never be allowed to come as a total surprise. A planned response to potential environmental issues allows for a balanced, thoughtful reaction—a process often referred to as "environmental scanning." This chapter's *Profile*, on the Canadian Tourism Commission, shows how the Canadian tourism industry responded to an external influence on tourism in Canada that was not predicted—the terrorist attacks of 2001.

Competitive Forces

Being aware of who the competition is, knowing what their strengths and weaknesses are, and anticipating what they may do are important aspects for understanding the macroenvironment. The marketing concept states that to be successful a company must satisfy the needs and wants of consumers better than its competitors. Furthermore, competitive advantage is now widely accepted as being of central importance to the success of organizations, regions, and countries. As we enter the third millennium, the world of tourism is becoming increasingly competitive. Although competition occurs between hotels, airlines, tour operators, travel agents, and other tourism services, this inter-enterprise competition is dependent upon and derived from the choices tourists make between alternative destinations. Competition therefore centres on the destination. Countries, states, regions, and cities now take their role as tourist destinations very seriously, committing considerable effort and funds toward enhancing their touristic image and attractiveness. As a consequence, destination competitiveness has become a significant part of tourism literature, and evaluation of the competitiveness of tourism destinations is increasingly being recognized as an important tool in the strategic positioning and marketing analysis of destinations.

As a result of globalization, additional countries are now aware of the importance of tourism to their economies. These countries have therefore increasingly targeted international tourism markets, augmenting their investment in marketing to attract international visitors and increase foreign earnings. Canada's major competitors in overseas markets are the United States, Australia, New Zealand, and South Africa. While revenues related to overnight international travel to Canada have grown in recent years, Canada's competitive position in this sector has eroded. There has been a decline in the number of tourists coming from Japan, France, and Germany over the last decade, representing a measurable opportunity cost of $2.3 billion in international receipts from Canada's largest markets.[11]

Competition is intensifying to grab a larger share of the expected growth in outbound travel from China. The World Tourism Organization expects that by the year 2020, China will become one of the world's major outbound tourism markets, generating globally 100 million tourists, or 6.2 percent of the world total. Competitive product, price, and quality, as well as access to and delivery of tourism goods and services will be the major success factors in attracting new Chinese outbound tourists and encouraging repeat travellers in the next decade and beyond.

Demographic Forces

demographics

statistics that describe the observable characteristics of individuals

Demographics are statistics that describe the observable characteristics of individuals, including our physical traits, such as gender, race, age, and height; our economic traits, such as income, savings, and net worth; our occupation-related traits, including education; our location-related traits; and our family-related traits, such as marital status and number and age of children. According to David Foot, author of *Boom, Bust & Echo*, demographics explain about two-thirds of everything.[12] For example, the dramatic increase in popularity of golf over the last 25 years is explained by golf's popularity among aging baby boomers who are entering a stage of life that enables them to spend more time on the golf course.

In fact, the single most notable demographic trend in Canada is the aging population. The over-50 segment, sometimes referred to as the maturing or greying market, is nearly 30 percent of the population, and this market has a keen interest in travel and leisure services. Other demographic trends affecting the marketing of tourism in Canada include the relatively slow population growth, the continued increase in education and service sector employment, increasing ethnic diversity, the demise of the traditional family, and the geographic mobility of the population. In addition to understanding general demographic trends, marketers must also recognize demographic groupings that may turn out to be market segments because of their enormous size, similar socioeconomic characteristics, or shared values. Such segments in Canada are discussed in Chapter 2.

MARKETING IN ACTION

INDUSTRY TARGETS FAMILY TRAVEL

Over the last few decades, more and more Canadians have started taking their families on business trips, extending the annual meeting or conference week to include a weekend of fun and exploration in the destination city. The trend has spurred hotels, resorts, and other meeting locations to offer more children's programs for the days when parents have to go to work. Companies specializing in entertaining and catering for children during business meetings have also sprung up. More Convention and Visitors' Bureaus are including "Families Welcome" sections in their mail-out packets, mentioning historic sites, child-friendly museums and restaurants, and ecotours.

The lodging industry, encouraged by the growing number of children and teens in North America, has responded by developing family-friendly programs and incentives across the country. Many hotels offer "kids stay/eat free" programs, and most resort properties offer some type of children's program that incorporates entertainment and education.

The North American hotel industry leader in attracting children is perhaps Hyatt, with its Camp Hyatt for children ages 3 to 12. Introduced in 1989, the program offers low-cost activities for children at 16 Hyatt Resorts in the continental United States, Hawaii, and the Caribbean. Each resort offers its own supervised activities and rates for morning, afternoon, and evening sessions. Activities can include (depending on the location) canoeing, horseback riding, square dance lessons, movies, games, karaoke, swimming and waterslides, crafts, hiking on nature trails, photography and dance lessons, and deep-sea fishing. Hyatt Resort surveys say that while Camp Hyatt may be a plus in attracting meetings, their primary users are vacationers or attendees at family gatherings such as weddings and reunions.

In Canada, the Delawana Inn Resort on Georgian Bay, north of Toronto, recently received the 5 Star award from the Hotel Fun 4 Kids rating program. The Web-based company, now in its third year, rates hotels and

MARKETING IN ACTION *continued*

resorts according to the level of services offered for children. The 5 Star award is given only to hotels and resort properties that have demonstrated outstanding children's programs, activities, and facilities. Delawana has exhibited continuous improvement, with its expansion of supervised children's programs, natural history family activities, and a new children's play area. Family evening entertainment continues seven days a week through the summer. Hotels and resorts that receive a 5 Star rating are thoroughly evaluated by Maureen Hall, president of Hotel Fun 4 Kids, who makes personal visits and evaluates the level of services and facilities offered.

Hall says, "It requires a real commitment to kids on the part of a hotel or resort to receive a 5 Star rating, the top rating under the Hotel Fun 4 Kids program. Not only has Delawana Inn met all of the criteria, but in many cases has surpassed the traditional rating requirements with its facilities, including the resort's proximity to so many outdoor nature activities and an enthusiastic recreation director that has put together a great schedule of activities for children and families at Delawana." Delawana has partnered with several of the nearby natural attractions in the Southern Georgian Bay Area, including the Georgian Bay Islands National Park, Wye Marsh Wildlife Area, and Sainte-Marie among the Hurons, to enhance the experiences of every guest at the resort.

Cruise lines are also working to increase the age range of their clientele by making a vacation in the open seas appealing not only to adults but to their children as well. Family cruising has increased every year for the past six years as a result of these efforts. Norwegian Cruise Lines (Kid's Crew) and Carnival (Camp Carnival) have programs specially designed for the younger traveller. "Families are a huge part of our marketing

mix," says Bob Dickinson, Carnival president. "Oftentimes, children's input can make or break the final vacation decision, and with the Carnival Pride, we've gone to great lengths to create a stimulating environment with a variety of activities and amenities that appeal to parents and kids alike." Disney Cruise Line is also attractive to families, boasting nearly an entire deck designed just for kids. In 2002, Disney added more than 30 new programs and activities for kids and teens, specifically designed with five different age groups in mind.

However, the prospects for the family travel industry worldwide are not good. IPK International is predicting that the industry will change dramatically in the next few years because of evolving demographics. According to IPK, family travel actually decreased more than any other type of travel between 2000 and 2002. Europeans took nearly 79 million family holidays abroad in 2001, 4 percent less than the record level in 2000, marking the first decline in this sector since the Gulf War in 1991. Terrorism fears have dampened all forms of tourism, but the downward shift in family travel owes more to a decline in disposable income and to unemployment fears among the middle classes. Families are reacting more strongly to this economic psychology than other markets, family sizes are shrinking, and the overall population is aging in Europe and North America.

Sources: Alexander, A. (2002, November 20). Shakeup expected in family travel. *The Globe and Mail,* p. T4; Hall, M. (2002). Delawana inn resort earns 5 Star Rating. Retrieved June 18, 2002, from http://www.canadatourism.com/en/ctc/ctx/ctx-news/search/newsbydateform.cfm; Sharpe, K. (2002). Cruise lines target a much younger market. *Tourism, 30*(19), 17–22; Tindell, K. (2001). Family travel: A market close to home. *HSMAI Marketing Review,* Fall/Winter, 43–45.

Economic Forces

economic forces

those forces that affect
consumer purchasing
power and spending
patterns

Economic forces in the environment are those that affect consumer purchasing power and spending patterns. Total purchasing power depends on current income, prices, savings, and credit, so marketers must be aware of major economic trends in income and of changing consumer spending patterns. In Canada, for example, average total income per family rose from $61 133 in 1996 to $68 318 in 2000. Average expenditure per household reached $57 742 in 2001 and $3453 of that was on leisure and recreation. Total expenditure on holiday trips (80 km or more) also rose from just over $18 million to $24.5 million in 2001, $8 million of that being spent in Ontario.

Price changes and exchange rates can also have a significant impact on tourism. The upward pressure on the prices of travel packages has eroded Canada's competitiveness in major overseas markets. Since 1995, the travel price index in Canada has increased by 21.4 percent, much more than the consumer price index, which increased by 8.9 percent in the same period. The situation has been aggravated in several markets as a result of a drop in the rate of currency exchange. Between 1995 and 2000, currencies in Germany, France, and Japan lost an average of 25 percent against the Canadian dollar. As a direct result, travel packages to Canada from these countries became more expensive. On the other hand, favourable exchange rates with countries like the United Kingdom have worked to Canada's advantage.

Budget cutbacks can have severe impacts on smaller tourism businesses. For example, spending cuts recently forced the closure of the Wascana, Saskatchewan, heritage site that was the boyhood home of the man known as Canada's populist prime minister, John Diefenbaker. The tiny wooden shack, with its sloping shingle roof and rusting black stovepipe, has seen tens of thousands of visitors since it opened in 1967. But since the beginning of 2002, it has remained surrounded by a chainlink fence topped with barbed wire. At its peak in the 1970s, the homestead attracted more than 30 000 people during the tourist season. However, only 6000 visited in 2001, and in light of the $18 000 needed for repairs and other costs, the Wascana authority responsible for operations at the site decided there were other areas in which it could better spend its money.

Environmental and Natural Forces

The last four decades have witnessed a dramatic increase in environmental consciousness worldwide. Media attention given to the greenhouse effect, acid rain, oil spills, ocean pollution, tropical deforestation, and other topics has raised public awareness about environmental issues. This environmental awareness has had an impact on the tourism industry. International leisure travellers are increasingly motivated by the quality of destination landscapes, in terms of environmental health and the diversity and integrity of natural and cultural resources. Studies of German and U.S. travel markets indicate that environmental considerations are now a significant element of travellers' destination-choosing process, down to—in the case of the Germans—the environmental programs operated by individual hotels.[13] It has been suggested that 40 percent of Canadians consider the environmental track record of both holiday company and destination when booking a holiday.[14]

The growing concern amongst consumers for the protection of the environment has clearly attracted the attention of companies seeking to profit from environmentally sound marketing practices. Surveys have shown that consumers are more likely to choose one brand over another if they believe the brand will help the environment, and environmental quality is a prevailing issue in making travel-related decisions. This has led to the "greening" of attractions, hotels, and even resorts, and to an increase in the number of environmentally friendly tourism products. An increasing emphasis is also being placed upon evaluating the likely environmental impacts of any tourism development, with environmental audits, environmental impact analysis, and carrying capacity issues being taken more seriously.

The natural environment will also have an impact on tourism marketing. Geography is a major factor in international marketing, and Canadian operators have exploited Canada's amazing variety of scenery and landforms. Banff National Park in the Canadian Rocky Mountains, for example, is an internationally acclaimed tourist destination receiving over five million visitors a year (see *Snapshot*, pp. 25–26). For more than 115 years, tourism has played a central role in the economy of Banff and the region, and, in 1998, visitor spending on goods and services in Banff National Park reached $954 million.[15] International and domestic visitors are attracted by the spectacular Rocky Mountain scenery, abundant wildlife, and outstanding recreational opportunities. However, the problem of travel time and distance from major overseas markets presents a challenge for Canadian marketers, and as a tourism destination, Canada has been losing market share to the competition over the past decade.

Finally, uncontrollable natural forces can have a negative impact on the tourism industry. For example, in 2003, fears of sudden acute respiratory syndrome (SARS) resulted in a huge number of cancelled trips to Toronto and millions of dollars in lost tourism revenue. Toronto brings in $7.2 billion in tourism revenue and plays host to more than 16 million visitors. But during March, April, and May of 2003, the aggregate decline in tourism expenditures in the Toronto area was estimated at almost $190 million. In April, for example, the city lost between $15 million and $20 million after an international conference was cancelled. Thousands of cancer researchers decided against attending their annual convention in Toronto, and a trip by Wisconsin students to the Toronto International Music Festival was also called off at the same time because of concerns about SARS.

Technological Forces

The most dramatic force shaping the future of tourism and hospitality is technology. The accelerated rate of technological advancement has forced tourism organizations to adapt their products accordingly, particularly in terms of how they develop, price, distribute, and promote their products. Technology facilitates the continual development of new systems and features that improve the tourism product. Technology has allowed for extra security in hotels and resorts, thanks to security systems and safety designs. It has also created new entertainment options for travellers, such as in-room movies and video games. Some hotels, and even airplanes, are now outfitted with the Internet, to cater to the technological needs of today's consumer.

The Internet fits the theoretical marketing principle in the travel industry because it allows suppliers to set up direct links of communication with their customers. Canadians are turning in increasing numbers to the Internet to help them plan and book their travel. The dollar value of travel that Canadians book over the Internet is expected to increase to $4.2 billion by 2004, from $662 million in 1999, a six-fold increase in five years. Internet use overall grew by 45 percent between 1998 and 2001, and Canadians looking for travel packages are keen users of the Internet; 77 percent of travellers are browsing the Internet for information, and more than two in three package travellers used the Internet to help plan summer trips.[16] The travel industry has been quick to realize the potential of the Internet, but research in this area is still at an early stage. As Internet technology is relatively new, there is still little knowledge of the consumer buying process online, and the impact of the Internet on travel intermediaries is still uncertain.

Technology is also beginning to have an impact on consumer research, as tourism organizations realize the potential of database management and the value of relationship marketing. Databases of customer profiles and customer behaviour are the basis for effective direct marketing. In tourism, the collection and analysis of data streams that now flow continuously through distribution channels and booking systems provide the modern information base for strategic and operational decisions of large organizations. The rate of technological change as databases connect and interact indicates that the speed and quality of information flows will be further enhanced in the coming decade.

Political Forces

Marketing decisions are strongly affected by developments in the political environment. This environment is made up of government agencies and pressure groups that influence and limit the activities of various organizations and individuals in society. Government policies can have far-reaching implications for the tourism industry. For example, the nation of Myanmar (formerly called Burma) receives very few tourists because of the turbulent political situation in the country. While Thailand welcomes 10 million visitors annually, Myanmar barely mustered up 200 000 in 2001, the vast majority of which were Asian bu~~siness~~
contemplating a visit to any country with a history of human-rights a~~buses~~
good example—are faced with an ethical dilemma: keep yourself ~~and~~
away, or go and bear witness, facilitate the exchange of ideas, and su~~pport~~

Two cases discussed in this chapter illustrate the influence ~~of politics on~~
tourism: the effect of parliamentary legislation on development in ~~Banff national~~
parks (see *Snapshot* below), and the effect of the terrorist attacks ~~of 9/11 on the~~
tourism industry in Canada (see *Profile*). The latter incident illust~~rates how, com-~~
bined with social issues, can have a powerful impact on tourism. A~~lthough~~
the target was not tourism, terrorist attacks on tourists are also see~~n as an~~
effective way to gain maximum international attention and to put ~~pressure on~~
government at all levels.

SNAPSHOT

POLITICAL INFLUENCES IN BANFF NATIONAL PARK

An example of how government policies have affected tourism in Canada comes from Banff National Park, in Alberta. In 1885, John A. Macdonald's government established

the initial federal land reserve in the Bow River Valley, creating Canada's first national park. Banff Park was then established as a tourist zone catering to a largely British elite.

SNAPSHOT *continued*

In 1909, the park boundaries were expanded, a Banff warden service was established, and hunting was banned. The park superintendent had to approve all building plans, and the preservation and repopulation of wildlife began with a buffalo paddock and the importation of moose from Ontario. As a reaction to the growing number of day visitors who had come along with the first road in 1911, conservation and preservation became a popular cause. It was taken up by two early conservation groups, the Alpine Club of Canada and the National Parks Association of Canada, and became enshrined in the National Parks Act of 1930. This original Parks Act placed the use and enjoyment of the park by the human population first and foremost, and this encouraged the first alpine ski resort at Sunshine in 1932. By the late 1960s, Sunshine had been joined by the ski resorts of Lake Louise and Mount Norquay, as Banff became a playground for the masses.

However, the environmental movement worldwide was gathering speed, and in 1996, the Minister of Canadian Heritage appointed the Banff–Bow Valley (BBV) Task Force to assess the cumulative environmental effects of development in the park. The task force for the Banff–Bow Valley Study made over 400 recommendations, including stricter limits to growth; creative visitor management programs; the refocusing and upgrading of the role of tourism; and improvements in education, awareness, and interpretation programs

for tourists and residents. For ski resorts in particular, it recommended capping skier numbers and prohibiting night use of ski hills. In response to the BBV report, Ottawa took a much more active role in the park's future. In 1998, the government imposed controversial limits on commercial development in the Banff town site. Then, in the spring of 2000, Sheila Copps, the heritage minister, introduced legislation in Parliament outlining new rules for restrictive development in Banff and other national parks. These new policies would cut back ski area operations, cap daily skier capacity, and restrict future expansions in Banff and Jasper National Parks.

The new Act moves ecological integrity to the top of the park's management agenda. However, owners of the ski areas in the park are far from happy with this new legislation, and they are pursuing legal action against Parks Canada and Sheila Copps over these new policies, saying that the government measures were taken without consulting them and without obtaining the environmental assessment required under the Canadian Environmental Assessment Act. They say that their 30-year leases allow them to build lifts, clear trees, and cut glades, but the government is now prohibiting them from doing so. The conflict is still going on.

Source: Hudson, S. (2002). Environmental management in the Rockies: The dilemma of balancing National Park values while making provision for their enjoyment. *Journal of Case Research, 22*(2), 1–14.

Cultural and Social Forces

cultural environment

institutions and other forces that affect society's basic values, perceptions, preferences, and behaviours

Marketing's consumer focus relies on an understanding of who the markets are, what motivates them, and how to appeal to them. Understanding the cultural environment is thus crucial for marketing decision making. This **cultural environment** includes institutions and other forces that affect society's basic values, perceptions, preferences, and behaviours. Cultural values influence consumer behaviour, and marketers tend to concentrate on dominant cultural values or core values. A grouping technique that is used to track trends in cultural values is psychographics, which determines how people spend their time and resources (activities), what they consider important (interests and values), and what they think of themselves and the world around them (opinions). Psychographics is discussed more fully in Chapter 3. Core values are slow and difficult to change, but secondary values are less permanent values that can sometimes be influenced by marketers. These values serve as the basis for subcultures, and again, distinct subcultures in Canada are given more attention in Chapter 3.

Major cultural trends in Canada that affect the tourism industry include

1. calls for increased responsibility on the part of those who drink as well as those who sell and serve alcoholic beverages;
2. the desire to develop individuality in order to be seen and treated as different from others (egonomics);
3. the tendency to act and feel younger than one's age (down-aging);
4. the urge to change one's life to a slower but more rewarding pace (cashing out);
5. the refusal to tolerate shoddy products and poor service (the vigilant consumer);
6. acceptance of the gay and lesbian community;
7. concerns for the environment;
8. an increasing desire for smoke-free restaurants and hotels; and
9. the desire to regularly eat out.

According to author Charles Leadbeater, Canada is also in the middle of a nostalgia boom.[18] The more rapidly people are propelled into an uncertain future, the more they yearn for the imagined security of the past. Not only have Canadians become more interested in history, but the scale, richness, and diversity of the history they are interested in has also expanded enormously in the past 30 years. This subject is given more attention in Chapter 3, but the following *Snapshot* provides a good example of an attraction in Nova Scotia that has capitalized on this nostalgia boom.

SNAPSHOT

PIER 21 RESPONDS TO GROWTH IN NOSTALGIA TOURISM

A National Historic Site, Pier 21 is a unique tourism facility that offers the visitor the opportunity to understand the difficult early immigration process that many people had to withstand. Winner of a national award for being the Best New Attraction in 2001, Pier 21 operates as a learning facility and an informational and experiential tourism destination. Located in Halifax, Nova Scotia, Pier 21 presents an experience that no other destination in Canada can provide: an in-depth look at what over one million people went through to make a new life in a new country. It also provides a place to honour the members of Canada's armed forces who served in World War II.

First operational in 1928, Pier 21 was the gateway to Canada for more than one million immigrants until its closure in 1971. Ships would arrive, and immigrants would begin the

final process leading to their new lives in Canada. No more that 250 people at once would disembark and be led to the Assembly Room. From there, they filed into the Examination Room for a medical exam and an immigration interview. If successful, the immigrants could take trains to their final destination. During World War II, Pier 21 also operated as the departure point for the troops who sailed to Europe to engage in battle. Today, the Wall of Service, located on the World War II Deck, stands as a tribute to the sacrifices made by members of the Canadian military to ensure the freedoms enjoyed by many nations.

In 1999, Pier 21 re-opened to honour the contributions of immigrants to building Canada and to acknowledge the sacrifice of Canadian troops. Today, it operates as a non-profit society and offers a variety of services to special interest groups, visitors, and the local community. Pier 21 also has a comprehensive

educational program that it offers to schools to give children the opportunity to gain first-hand knowledge of what it may have been like to be an early immigrant coming to Canada.

In March 2003, on the day of Pier 21's 75th anniversary, the Pier 21 Society announced a five-year strategic vision for a transformed Pier 21. The objective of the vision was to expand Pier 21's existing immigration span of 1928–1971 to an all-inclusive heritage program. The future model of Pier 21 will connect with most of Canadian society, instead of relating only to the 20 percent of Canadians who have a personal connection to the present Pier 21. The new plan was announced in Montreal at a Pier 21 fundraising gala dinner, "Footprints on the Pier." "The future Pier 21 will speak to contemporary Canadians, reaching further than the immigrants during the Pier 21 era," says Pier 21 CEO Robert Moody. "There is a wonderful opportunity for Pier 21 to become Canada's national immigration heritage centre. Over the next five years, Pier 21 will evolve to tell the story of all immigrants to Canada; from the time of first contact with our First Nations people to present-day immigration, Pier 21 will celebrate how all our people have contributed to the building of our country. It will celebrate Canada's cultural diversity," says Sherry Porter, chair of the Pier 21 Society.

Sources: Pier 21 promotional printed material; Pier 21 Education Kit; Pier 21 Web site: http://www.pier21.ca.

Legal Forces

The tourism industry has witnessed an increase in legislation and regulation that affects business, normally enacted to protect companies and consumers from unfair business practices. Government regulation also aims to protect society's interests against unrestricted business behaviour, as profitable business activity does not always improve the quality of life within a society. Hence the regulations in many parts of Canada that restrict smoking in restaurants and hotels. In fact, government agencies have become involved in the regulation of everything from food-handling practices in restaurants to fire codes for hotels. Travellers are seen as good sources of revenue by politicians, as witnessed by the increasing number of provinces in Canada that are implementing hotel taxes.

Most countries have laws that permit governments to restrict foreign trade when such trade could adversely affect the economy of the country or when such trade is in conflict with foreign policy. There are laws about the level of foreign investment permitted and the amount of money that can be transferred out of the country, and immigration laws affect the transfer of staff internationally from one multinational property to another. All laws have an impact on investment and development in the tourism industry. More specifically, laws regarding landing taxes for aircraft, health regulations, gaming licences, and visa and entry permits all affect the tourism industry in one way or another.

An example of how recent legislation in Canada has affected the tourism industry comes from the marine sector. New legislation intended to establish uniform liability insur-ations for all passenger-carrying boats came into effect in August 2001. The ability Act, passed by the federal government, has not been well received by the dustry, particularly by adventure tourism operators across Canada. The new law eet of canoes, kayaks, or river rafts in the same insurance category as a Great enger cruise ship. Small operators have already gone out of business because they ord the new insurance. One component of the Act that has adventure operators ncerned prevents the use of liability waivers. Operators have successfully used or many years to prevent or defend against lawsuits in case of accident. The fear is ance companies, which have in the past supported or even demanded these small s' use of waivers, will simply refuse to insure water-based adventure businesses or insurance prohibitively expensive.

[handwritten note: The airline industry is heavily regulated by the gov't of Canada. The new no fly list.]

CHAPTER SUMMARY

Tourism and hospitality incorporate both goods and services. Goods are easier to measure, test, and evaluate, but services provide a greater challenge. Service products are com-monly distinguished from goods products by four unique characteristics: intangibility, inseparability, heterogeneity, and perishability. The services marketing triangle shows the three interlinked groups that work together to develop, promote, and deliver services. These key players are the company, the customers, and the providers. The triangle also suggests that three types of marketing must be successfully carried out for a service to suc-ceed: external, interactive, and internal marketing. The expanded marketing mix for serv-ices includes the traditional four P's—product, price, place, and promotion—as well as the more recently added people, physical evidence, and process.

Tourism is an increasingly important sector of the Canadian economy. The World Tourism Organization (WTO) ranks Canada as the ninth most popular destination in the world. Canada's share of the international tourism travel market in 2001 was 2.8 percent. The key players in Canada's tourism industry are private and nonprofit sector services, public sector services, suppliers (transportation, accommodation, food and beverage serv-ices, attractions, events and conferences, and sport and adventure tourism), intermediaries, and the customers (tourist/travellers) themselves.

The marketing environment is made up of a microenvironment and a macroenvironment. The microenvironment consists of actors and forces close to the organization that can affect its ability to serve its customers: the organization itself, marketing channel firms, customer markets, and a broad range of stakeholders or publics. The macroenvironment comprises the larger societal forces that affect the entire microenvironment and shape opportunities and pose threats. The macroenvironment consists of eight major forces: competitive, demographic, economic, environmental and natural, technological, political, cultural and social, and legal.

KEY TERMS

cultural environment, p. 26	marketing, p. 6	services marketing triangle,
demographics, p. 20	microenvironment, p. 18	p. 7
economic forces, p. 23	services marketing mix, p. 8	tourism market, p. 4
macroenvironment, p. 19		

DISCUSSION QUESTIONS AND EXERCISES

1. Why do managers in tourism and hospitality need to understand the services marketing triangle and the services marketing mix?

2. Choose one key player in the tourism industry and suggest how it should deal with the unique characteristics of services outlined in Table 1.1. For example, how do airlines overcome the perishability of their product?

3. Which of the key players in Canada's tourism industry outlined in Figure 1.3 are more vulnerable to external influences such as the September 11 terrorist attacks?

4. Choose one of the transport sectors discussed in the chapter (airlines, cruises, railways, or motorcoach operators) and update the material presented in the text. How is this sector performing in today's environment?

5. As a tourist destination, Canada has been losing market share to the competition for the last decade. What factors are contributing to this, and what do you suggest the CTC do to make Canada more competitive?

6. What are the key challenges facing the Canadian tourism and hospitality industry today? Which of these are controllable and which are uncontrollable?

CASE STUDY

FAIRMONT HOTELS: WEATHERING THE STORM

Fairmont has come a long way in a short time. The historic Canadian Pacific (CP) Hotels & Resorts chain's rapid-fire series of acquisitions beginning in 1998 included a merger with Fairmont Hotels. The merged company has since become a huge player in the North American hotel industry. CP now operates 77 hotels with about 30 000 rooms, employs 28 000 people, and in 2001 reported revenues of US$1.6 billion. After merging with Fairmont, which had seven properties in the United States, many of them historic hotels in major cities, Canadian Pacific (CP) adopted the Fairmont name for all its hotels, apart from the Delta properties, after consumer surveys showed that the CP name was virtually unknown in the United States.

Besides owning hotel properties in places such as Lake Louise and Banff, Fairmont owns the management firm Delta Hotels and has a 34 percent stake in Legacy Real Estate Investment Trust. In the United States, where the hospitality sector took a harder financial hit than Canada did after September 11, 2001, Fairmont has ownership interests in Copley Plaza Boston, Kea Lani Maui, and Scottsdale Princess. Fairmont also manages landmark properties, such as the Plaza in New York and the Fairmont San Francisco. In the weeks after September 11 attacks on the United States, Fairmont struggled as many guests cancelled their reservations not only at the two stately hotels in Banff National Park, but across the chain's hotels in Canada, the United States, and abroad. However, Fairmont, spun off from the Canadian Pacific Empire in October 2001, has weathered the economic storm well.

Fairmont was severely tested in its early days as a publicly traded entity whose beginnings coincided with September 11. Share prices fell as a reaction to the widespread cancellations of room reservations and predictions that business and leisure travel faced a prolonged slump. William Fatt, the company's CEO, was forced to withdraw Fairmont's previously stated projections, which anticipated a 5 percent increase in pre-tax profits for 2001. "In these circumstances, it is uncertain how the travel and lodging industry will be affected…. reduced travel will impact the earnings performance of the industry as a whole," Fatt says.

However, as travel dollars started trickling back in, Fairmont stock recovered well—much faster than some observers had anticipated. The sharp run-up in Fairmont shares from mid-November 2001 through to early January 2002 reflected optimism toward how its operations would fare in 2003, as well as excitement over its expansion plans—such as the planned seven-storey convention centre at Lake Louise, which will enhance Fairmont's position in the Rockies. The company is perhaps also seeing the payoff from developing what is known as the most comprehensive environmental program in the North American hotel industry.

The long-term industry trends and Fairmont's unique assets point to a strong performance. But its ambitious growth strategy could be jeopardized by reduced cash flow, due to the curtailment of business and leisure travel in 2001 and to a shortage of risk capital for Fairmont's planned rapid expansion in the United States and outside of North America. That expansion is important in establishing the Fairmont brand outside of Canada, where it still derives about half its profit. Despite an impressive acquisition campaign over the last five years, which has seen the addition of properties in the United States, Mexico, Bermuda, and Barbados, Fairmont still depends on just 9 of its 77 hotels for about two-thirds of its total earnings. These include 3 resort hotels at Whistler and at Banff National Park, which alone account for 35 percent of earnings and make the chain vulnerable to seasonal factors such as poor conditions for skiing.

In Canada, Fairmont is synonymous with grand hotels, owing to its historic railway properties, but it is not nearly so well established outside Canada. In contrast to Four Seasons Hotels Inc., a chief rival in the luxury market, Fairmont lacks a presence in several major U.S. business centres. And it has no properties outside North America, apart from a project underway in Dubai. Assembling a truly global collection of hotels will require patience—Four Seasons spent more than 20 years scouting locations and securing the financing for properties in Tokyo and Paris that opened during the last decade. Despite its similar vulnerability to downturns in business travel, Four Seasons has a consistency of product and profit that makes it the industry favourite amongst investors. The company sticks with its formula of small-scale premium-priced hotels, regardless of location.

Delta, on the other hand, would seem to be a distraction to Fairmont. A large operator of mid-market hotels in Canada, Delta does not feed customers to the larger Fairmont hotels and is of limited use as a vehicle for U.S. expansion, given Delta's lack of brand recognition south of the border. It has been suggested that Delta, which accounts for only 4 percent of the parent company's profit, is reminiscent of CP's failed experiments with business hotels in Germany and Israel, its Red Oak and Le Baron small-city hotels in Canada, and the mid-market Doubletree chain in the U.S., all since abandoned.

However, today, Fairmont has US$1 billion worth of borrowing power for building and buying new hotels, and Fatt relishes the buying opportunities that arise in tough times. "There will people out there with properties not performing as they'd like," says Fatt, "or creditors pressuring them to sell, and they're eager to dispose of those properties." Lately, Fairmont has been very successful in turning around distressed properties that have been acquired at modest prices, then selling them to Legacy Hotels, a real estate investment trust.

Source: Olive, D. (2001, September 19). Beyond Banff Springs. *Financial Post*, p. B8.

QUESTIONS

1. Apply the eight major forces of the macroenvironment to the Canadian hotel industry today. What are the major forces shaping the future for Fairmont?
2. How has Fairmont coped with changes in the macroenvironment in Canada?
3. How does Fairmont compare to its competitors in Canada?
4. This case was written in 2002. How is Fairmont doing now?

WEB SITES

www.aircanada.ca
Air Canada

www.banffnationalpark.com
Banff National Park (BNP)

www.canadabyrail.ca
Canada by Rail

www.canadatourism.com
Canadian Tourism Commission (CTC)

www.travelcanada.ca
Canadian Tourism Commission's travel Web site

www.cruising.org
Cruise Lines International Association

www.delawana.com
Delawana Inn Resort

www.fairmont.ca
Fairmont Hotels & Resorts

www.gapadventures.com
G.A.P Adventures

www.greenhotels.com
Green Hotels Association

www.greentourism.ca
Green Tourism Association of Toronto

www.pier21.ca
Pier 21

www.westjet.com
WestJet Airlines

www.world-tourism.org
World Tourism Organization

ENDNOTES

1. World Tourism Organization. (2003). *Tourism highlights*. Retrieved April 14, 2003, from http://www.world-tourism.org.
2. AMA board approves new marketing definition. (1985, March 1). *Marketing News,* 1.
3. Kotler, P. (1984). *Marketing management: Analysis, planning, implementation and control* (8th ed.). Upper Saddle River, NJ: Prentice Hall, 92.
4. McCarthy, E. J. (1981). *Basic marketing, a managerial approach* (7th ed.). Georgetown, ON: Irwin.
5. Tretheway, M. (2002). Air access: Canada's achilles heel? In M. Joppe (Ed.), *Accessing destinations—Getting there from here*. Proceedings of TTRA Conference, September 29–October 1, Edmonton, AB. Available on CD-ROM.
6. Demont, J. (2002, May 28). Paradise lost. *Maclean's, 114*(22), 22–25.
7. Parks Canada and TIAC sign historic accord. (2002). *Tourism,* 6(3), 12.
8. Sport Tourism Impact. (2002). *Tourism,* 6(6), 6.
9. Beedie, P., & Hudson, S. (2003). The commodification of mountaineering through tourism. *Annals of Tourism Research, 30*(3), 625–643.
10. Canadian Tourism Commission. (2002). Major markets overview. *CTC Annual Report 2001,* 7.
11. Canadian Tourism Commission. (2002). *Strategic plan 2002–2004*. Ottawa: CTC, 4.
12. Foot, D. (2000). *Boom, bust & echo: Profiting from the demographic shift in the 21st century*. Toronto: MacFarlane Walter & Ross, 313.
13. Ayala, H. (1996). Resort ecotourism: A paradigm for the 21st century. *Cornell Hotel and Restaurant Administration Quarterly, 37*(5), 1–9.
14. Kiernan, P. (1992, August 21). Earth bound. *Marketing Week,* 26–30.
15. Hudson, S. (2002). Environmental management in the Rockies: The dilemma of balancing National Park values while making provision for their enjoyment. *Journal of Case Research, 22*(2), 1–14.
16. Canadians logging on to destination web sites. (2001). Retrieved September 26, 2001, from http://tourismtogether.com/tourismweb/news/buzz/sep.
17. Hopfner, J. (2002, May 11). The Myanmar paradox. *The Globe and Mail,* p. T1.
18. Leadbeater, C. (2002, July 6–7). Longing for the way we were. *Financial Times Weekend,* p. IV.

2

Developing a Marketing Plan

POSITIONING "FOUR" SUCCESS

Toronto-based Four Seasons Hotels and Resorts is an excellent example of distinctive positioning leading to global competitive success. Four Seasons operates 58 luxury hotels and resorts in 27 countries around the world, turning over more than $300 million a year. It wins awards at an unprecedented level in industry publications as the leading player in the luxury hotel and resort business worldwide. Ten or more of its hotels routinely make lists of the top 100 hotels in the world, and the company often appears on the *Fortune* list of best places to work. Its revenue per available room (RevPAR) in the highly competitive U.S. market is more than 30 percent higher than that of its closest chain competitor, Ritz-Carlton. Countries and cities around the world encourage Four Seasons to build hotels in their jurisdiction because the presence of a Four Seasons signals a high-quality location.

The success of the company has been derived from making an integrated set of choices that are highly distinctive from competitors'. Its goal was to develop a brand name synonymous with an unparalleled customer experience, and to meet these aspirations it chose to focus exclusively on serving high-end travellers. This is in direct contrast to large competitors such as Hyatt, Marriott, Hilton, and Westin, all of which compete across the spectrum of hotel classes, thereby struggling to establish consistent high-end service and branding.

Using high prices as a means of positioning, Four Seasons hotels raise their prices when competitors come near them. Even when September 11, 2001, and the SARS outbreak of 2003 led to increased costs and lower occupancy levels, Four Seasons decided to maintain its room rates despite moves by competitors to slash prices. CEO Isadore Sharp believes the room rates are easily justified. "It isn't what you might call a discretionary expense, as most luxury items are," he says. "We provide a service. When travellers can rely on prompt room service, their suit being properly pressed, and their messages actually reaching them," says Sharp, "they realize this is a great value."

Another key early strategic choice for Four Seasons was to pursue a truly global strategy by developing an ever-growing portfolio of hotels and resorts in key destinations around the world. This distinguished Four Seasons from the bulk of smaller high-end competitors. The final key strategy was to specialize as a hotel manager, not a developer and owner. This was a distinct choice in the industry until Marriott divided its business into hotel ownership and hotel management companies. Because its business model means Four Seasons doesn't own most of its hotels, the capital risk is low, and the company boasts a sound balance sheet. Indeed, even in punishing economic cycles, the brand remains highly valued by investors—unusual for a place that often charges three or four times the price of a typical Sheraton.

An interesting development in the company's history is its movement into new territory with the launch of a luxury catamaran cruise in the Maldives. Called the Island Explorer, the cruise offers a level of luxury not seen in this part of the world before. According to visitors, the boat lives up to its Four Seasons billing in terms of both service and activities. In fact, the Island Explorer is equal parts catamaran and luxury hotel; the staff of 25 includes not only a captain and several diving instructors, but three chefs, a massage therapist, and an on-board marine biologist. Four Seasons' plan is to sustain equilibrium between private charters and general cruises.

Because the Four Seasons strategy is unique and is ensconced in an activity system that would force competitors to make unacceptable trade-offs, its competitors have been disinclined to imitate Four Seasons, despite its obvious success. The result is a Canadian global leader with attractive growth prospects for the future.

Sources: Four Seasons Hotels reports hit to profit in first quarter. (2002, May 11). *The Globe and Mail*, p. B2; Libin, K. (2003). Four Seasons Hotels. *Canadian Business*, *76*(12), 48; Marr, G. (2003, February 27). Four Seasons posts 18% earnings decline. *Financial Post*, p. FP3; Martin, R. (2002, May 13). Conquer the world and triumph in Canada. *Financial Post*, p. FP11; Sharp, I. (2000). The unseen precondition of long-term success. Presentation at the World Tourism Education & Research Centre's Air Canada Distinguished Lecture Series, University of Calgary, Calgary, AB. Thursday, April 27, 2000.

Objectives

On completion of this chapter, readers should understand

- the eight key steps in the marketing planning process;
- the importance of the corporate connection;
- analysis and forecasting;

- setting goals and objectives;
- targeting and positioning;
- tactics and action plans; and
- how marketing planning is conducted in various sectors of the tourism industry in Canada.

Chapter Overview

The opening vignette highlights the importance of successful positioning in today's marketing environment. Positioning is an important part of marketing planning, which is the subject of this chapter. Successful marketing in tourism and hospitality requires careful planning and execution. In its principles, marketing planning is no more than a logical thought process in which all businesses should engage. It is an application of common sense, as relevant to a small bed and breakfast as it is to an international airline. The chapter proposes that there are eight key steps in the marketing planning process. Each of these steps is discussed in turn, and practical examples are given from various sectors of the tourism industry.

INTRODUCTION TO MARKETING PLANNING

marketing plan

a written, short-term plan that details how an organization will use its marketing mix to achieve its marketing objectives

strategic marketing plan

a written plan for an organization covering a period of three or more years into the future

The term **marketing plan** is widely used to mean a short-term plan for two years or less. This chapter is devoted to the development of such plans. A **strategic marketing plan** on the other hand is different, as it covers three or more years. A marketing plan serves a number of purposes within any tourism organization: it provides a road map for all future marketing activities of the firm; it ensures that marketing activities are aligned with the corporate strategic plan; it forces marketing managers to review and think through objectively all steps in the marketing process; it assists in the budgeting process to match resources with marketing objectives; and it creates a process to monitor actual against expected results.

A systematic marketing planning process consists of eight logical steps, as outlined in Figure 2.1. For the strategic marketing plan, the first four stages may be more detailed, but any short-term marketing plan should also include an assessment of these steps. Each step feeds into the next one. A marketing plan is not a stand-alone tool, so the first stage is examining the goals and objectives of the organization as a whole and then developing a marketing plan that will support the company's mission statement, corporate philosophy, and corporate goals. Once the corporate connection has been clarified, the next stage is defining the current situation, reviewing the effectiveness of current activities, and identifying opportunities. This is the "analysis and forecasting" stage. The third stage is concerned with defining marketing goals and objectives derived logically from the previous stages of the planning process.

At the fourth stage, target markets should be selected from the previously developed list of available segments, and once the market has been segmented and a target market identified, the next step in the marketing plan is positioning. Market positioning is ultimately how the consumer perceives the good or service in a given market, and is used to achieve a sustainable competitive advantage over competitors. The fifth stage of the marketing plan involves selecting and developing a series of strategies that effectively bring about the required results. This part of the plan shows how the organization intends to use the 7 P's. The marketing plan needs to address the resources required to support the strategies and meet the objectives, and resource requirements are the focus of the plan's sixth stage. The seventh stage of the marketing plan is concerned with marketing control and how objectives will be achieved in the required time, using the funds and resources requested. Finally, at the eighth stage, the marketing plan should be communicated both internally and externally to achieve maximum impact. Most marketing plans will contain an **executive summary** of the whole plan, and this should be no more than a few pages in length. A good approach is to sum up each of the sections and present them in the order in which they appear.

The role played by each section of the marketing plan will now be discussed in more detail.

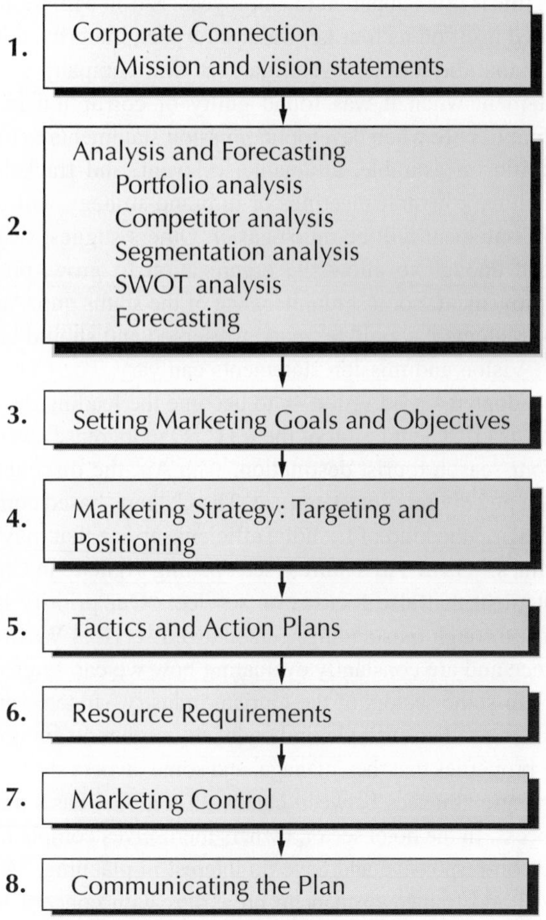

executive summary

a few pages, usually positioned at the beginning of the marketing plan, that sum up the plan's main sections

1. Corporate Connection
   Mission and vision statements

2. Analysis and Forecasting
   Portfolio analysis
   Competitor analysis
   Segmentation analysis
   SWOT analysis
   Forecasting

3. Setting Marketing Goals and Objectives

4. Marketing Strategy: Targeting and Positioning

5. Tactics and Action Plans

6. Resource Requirements

7. Marketing Control

8. Communicating the Plan

Figure 2.1   Marketing Planning: An Eight-Step Process

1. THE CORPORATE CONNECTION

goals

the primary aims of the organization

objectives

the specific aims that managers accomplish to attain organizational goals

mission statement

a brief simple phrase or sentence that summarizes the organization's direction and communicates its ethos to internal and external audiences. It also answers the question, "What business are we in?"

"smart" rule

rule used in the development of the mission statement in order to ensure that the statement is **s**pecific, **m**easurable, **a**ttainable, **r**elevant, and **t**rackable

A good marketing plan begins with the fact that the only purpose of marketing is to support the enterprise. Marketing planning should therefore reflect the goals and objectives of the organization as a whole. The mission or vision statement reflects the organization's philosophy, and the goals and objectives as set out in the business plan become the basis of planning for all departments. Marketing's responsibilities in relation to the corporate vision are usually outlined in one or more separate marketing-specific documents. Goals can be defined in terms such as sales growth, increased profitability, and market leadership, whereas objectives are the activities that will accomplish the goals. A vision statement usually answers the question, "What do we want to be?", whereas the mission statement will answer the question, "What business are we in?" Whereas the vision describes where the organization wants to be in some future time, the mission is a broader statement about an organization's business and scope, goods or services, markets served, and overall philosophy.

A mission statement should be more than a page in the employee handbook; it is the company's best tool for holding itself accountable to employees, customers, and investors. Unfortunately, the majority of mission statements don't reflect an organization's reality, and this is often apparent to employees. Enron's mission statement noted that the company prided itself on its four key values: respect, integrity, communication, and excellence. It is clear that the former seventh-largest U.S. company was not living up to its own mission statement when it was found guilty of corruption in 2002. Companies could use the "smart" rule when developing mission statements to ensure that the mission statement is **s**pecific, **m**easurable, **a**ttainable, **r**elevant, and **t**rackable. That way, its usefulness as a benchmark in staff meetings or in brand strategy will increase, and living up to the mission statement will be much easier. Others suggest that the mission statement should be broad enough to allow the organization to grow, providing scope for innovation and improvement, not just maintenance of the status quo. And finally, it is argued that the mission statement should be market-oriented and should be inspirational and motivating.[1]

Vision and mission statements can vary. The Canadian Tourism Commission (CTC) has adopted a bold vision—"to become the leading destination marketing organization in the world." The mission of the CTC is "to increase awareness of and interest in Canada as a four-season tourist destination." Zip Air, the discount carrier launched by Air Canada, has a punchy mission statement. The Calgary-based company says it is "committed to providing … the kind of friendly, efficient service that maybe you've been missing with other airlines." G.A.P Adventures (see opening vignette in Chapter 1) has the following mission statement that also focuses on service: "Our priority is to satisfy every customer, every time, through outstanding, personalized service! We are dedicated to the customer experience and are constantly evaluating how we can improve this experience."

In some sectors of the tourism industry, strategic and marketing planning faces many challenges. For example, in hotels and restaurants, major chains commonly do not own all the properties that they manage, and some owners show little interest in long-term planning. Strategic alliances between chains on a global basis may further complicate the planning process. In the hotel sector, owners themselves complain that hotel management companies are non-responsive and have no interest in planning. Managers have commonly been educated and trained to manage properties with concern for areas such as maintenance and front-desk operations but have received little or no training in strategic planning.

These unique management and ownership structures can complicate the process of strategic planning. Planning at the destination level also presents some fundamental differences and challenges, which are addressed in Chapter 12.

2. ANALYSIS AND FORECASTING

The next stage of the marketing plan is defining the current situation. It is essential that each component of the business be reviewed in order to ensure that resources can be allocated efficiently. Several models exist for reviewing effectiveness and identifying opportunities, but those proven by time and practical application across a range of industries include portfolio analysis, competitor analysis, segmentation analysis, SWOT (strengths, weaknesses, opportunities, and threats) analysis, and forecasting.

Portfolio Analysis

portfolio analysis

an approach to evaluating a very diverse group of goods and services, based on long-term planning and economic forecasts

Boston Consulting Group (BCG) model

a technique designed to show the performance of an individual product in relation to its major competitors and the rate of growth in its market

Portfolio analysis first became popular in the 1960s, when many organizations sought to improve their profitability by diversifying their activities so as not to keep all their eggs in one basket. The **Boston Consulting Group (BCG) model** was one of the most popular approaches to evaluating a very diverse group of goods and services, based on long-term planning and economic forecasts. The model adopts the view that every product of an organization can be plotted on a two-by-two matrix to identify those offering high potential and those that are drains on the organization's resources.

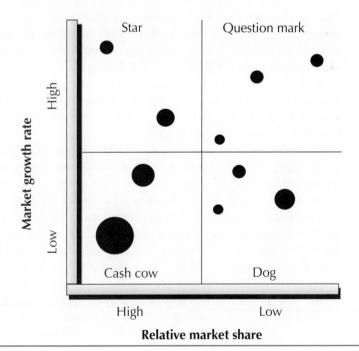

Figure 2.2   The Boston Consulting Group (BCG) Model

market share

the percentage relationship of an organization's sales to total industry sales

cash cow

a product that generates a high volume of income in relation to the cost of maintaining its market share

dog

a product that provides neither cash flow nor long-term opportunities and does not hold great promise for improved performance

stars

products that have a dominant share of a fast-growing market

question marks

fairly speculative products that have high-risk potential. They may be profitable, but because they hold a small market share, they may be vulnerable to competition

In Figure 2.2, the horizontal axis represents market share, and the vertical axis represents anticipated market growth. High market share means that a business is a leader in that good or service; low market share indicates that either the marketplace is heavily competitive or a good or service has not had widespread market acceptance. A good or service can then take up one of four theoretical positions on the model. A cash cow is a product that generates cash and turnover, but the long-term prospects are limited. The company in Figure 2.2 operates two cash-cow businesses. A dog provides neither cash flow nor long-term opportunities and does not hold great promise for improved performance. In the illustration, the company has three dogs.

Stars are products that have a dominant share of a fast-growing market. Although they may not generate a large amount of cash at present, they have potential for high returns in the future. Question marks are fairly speculative products that have high-risk potential. They may be profitable, but because they hold a small market share, they may be vulnerable to competition. Goods or services go through the product life cycle, which can affect where they are positioned on the BCG model. A new product may be in the "question mark" cell; as it becomes successful it moves into the "star" category, and then moves on to become a "cash cow" before it starts into decline and becomes a "dog."

A good example of a tourism product that has taken up all four positions in the BCG model is the Concorde jet airplane. Beginning as a "question mark," the delta-winged marvel, a product of 1960s technology and optimism, quickly became a "star" as business executives and stars asserted their status by happily spending thousands of dollars to save a few hours of travelling time. The plane created a "jet set" that could leave London at 10:30 a.m. and be in New York at 1:30 p.m. The product soon became a "cash cow," and more than 2.5 million passengers flew on British Airways' Concordes after they entered service in 1976. Twenty Concordes were built over a 25-year period, but filling the 100 seats on a Concorde became increasingly difficult for three reasons: first, a horrific crash on July 25, 2000, which tarnished Concorde's safety record; second, the impact of the September 11 attacks on transatlantic travel; and finally, an economic downturn in 2002, which proved to be the final straw. For three years, Concorde could be classified as a "dog." In April 2003, it was announced that the supersonic airline run by British Airways and Air France would be retired that year because of slumping ticket sales. Customers were no longer willing to pay the high prices: an unrestricted one-way ticket on the Concorde cost about $20,000 in 2003.

Portfolio analysis is useful because it allows managers to compare a range of diverse products and look at their current contribution (in terms of cash flow) and future potential (in terms of market share). The disadvantages are that it focuses on the company's existing range of products and services, but does not allow for the development of new ideas and does not assess the activities of competitors. Finally, although the BCG model and other portfolio management models are a good way to analyze the basic position and contribution of products and services, they have received some criticism in terms of their ability to withstand economic instability, especially during high-inflation periods.

In 2001, the CTC developed a Market Portfolio Analysis (MPA) model to help evaluate the potential and performance of markets and then establish priorities based on the results.[2] Canada's international tourism market is concentrated largely in the United States, which provides almost 60 percent of Canada's international tourism receipts (see Figure 2.3).

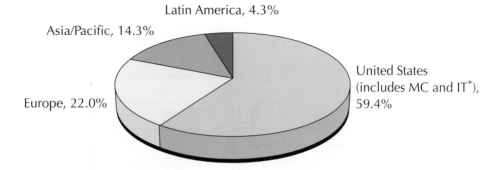

*Meetings, conventions, and incentive travel

Figure 2.3   Canada's International Tourism Receipts, 2002

Source: Canadian Tourism Commission. (2002). *Strategic plan 2002–2004*. Ottawa: CTC, 6.

While this level of concentration offers a relatively secure source of international receipts for Canada, it increases Canada's vulnerability to a major economic downturn in this market. Accordingly, Canada must address a twin challenge: to secure existing business from its current market base and to expand promotional efforts to develop alternative sources of tourism earnings in markets other than Canada's major international markets.

As part of a portfolio analysis, an organization should assess each good and service in terms of its position on the product life cycle. This concept is discussed in Chapter 5 (see pp. 144–145).

Competitor Analysis

Information on the number and type of competitors, their relative market shares, the things they do well, and things they do badly will assist in the planning process. **Competitor analysis** will also highlight market trends and the level of loyalty of consumers. Competitors can be divided into four broad categories: **direct competitors** offer similar goods and services to the same consumer at a similar price; **product category competitors** make the same product or class of products; **general competitors** provide the same service; and **budget competitors** compete for the same consumer dollars. In addition to the existing competition, there is also the threat of potential competition in the form of new entrants—for example, an American hotel chain expanding into Canada. Figure 2.4 on page 42 shows the forces that determine the competitive environment in an industry, as summarized by Michael Porter.[3]

Porter also suggests that there are only three generic strategies for dealing with competition: low-cost leadership, differentiation, and focus. **Low-cost leadership** is the simplest and most effective strategy, but it requires large resources and strong management to sustain. A low-cost leadership strategy is used when a firm sets out to become the low-cost producer in its industry. Low-cost producers typically sell a standard, or no-frills, product and place considerable emphasis on reaping scale or absolute cost advantages from all sources. It may be short-lived, as it is easy for competitors to match a low price

competitor analysis

a review of competitors that allows the organization to identify and highlight the market trends and the level of loyalty of consumers

direct competitors

companies that offer similar goods and services to the same consumer at a similar price

product category competitors

companies that produce the same product or class of products

general competitors

companies that provide the same service

budget competitors

companies that compete for the same consumer dollars

low-cost leadership

the simplest and most effective strategy for dealing with competition, but one requiring large resources and strong management to sustain. It may be short-lived, as it is easy for competitors to match a low price in an attempt to drive off the challenge

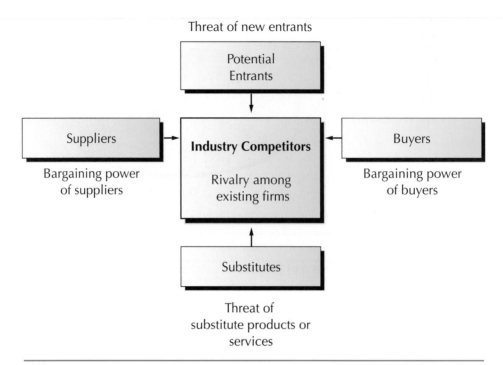

Figure 2.4   Forces Driving Industry Competition

Source: Porter, M.E. (1980). *Competitive strategy: Techniques for analyzing industry and competitors.* New York: Free Press, 4.

differentiation

a strategy that consists of an innovative technological breakthrough, which can take competitors a long time to imitate. A competitive advantage can be gained by a product that is newer, better, and/or faster

focus

a strategy that concentrates on designing a good or service to meet the needs of one segment of the market better than the competition does

in an attempt to drive off the challenge. **Differentiation** is a strategy that consists of an innovative technological breakthrough, which can take competitors a long time to imitate. A competitive advantage can be gained by a product that is newer, better, and/or faster. The improvement can be in performance, durability, reliability, or service features. A **focus** strategy concentrates on designing a good or service to meet the needs of one segment of the market better than the competition does. All three of these generic strategies are based on the organization's creation of a unique position for itself, which distinguishes its offerings from those of its competitors by price, product features, or the way in which it serves the needs of a particular segment. This process, known as "positioning," is discussed later in the chapter (see pp. 54–55).

Segmentation Analysis

segmentation analysis

the practice of dividing total markets up into groups on the basis of similar characteristics

Segmentation analysis refers to the way in which organizations identify and categorize customers into groups defined by similar characteristics and similar needs or desires. The concept of segmentation is widely adopted in tourism marketing, as few companies in the industry attempt to appeal to an entire market. The principles of segmentation are based on the premise that a market can be readily divided into segments for the commercial purpose of targeting offerings. The core advantage of segmentation is that customers will be more satisfied with the product because it has been designed with their needs in mind. Their social needs are also satisfied because they will be mixing with people like themselves and avoiding incompatible types. If an organization knows exactly which segments it wishes to reach, it can select the media most likely to be read, heard, or seen by those consumers, and so spend less on general mass-market advertising. If it knows the lifestyles and attitudes of that segment and the benefits they are seeking from the product, the advertising message can be made more persuasive.

There are effectively two broad approaches to analysis of customer segments: segmentation by trip descriptors, such as short haul, long haul, visiting friends and relatives, etc., and segmentation by tourist descriptors, such as "grey panthers" (early retired and interested in travel) or "adventure explorers" (those seeking unusual and new destinations). Recently, researchers have started focusing on the growing visiting friends and relatives (VFR) market.[4] Seaton and Palmer suggest that this interest in VFR tourism has grown because of the recognition that: (a) it is a category that is growing worldwide for a whole range of social and political reasons; (b) in some destinations it is the principal source of tourists; and (c) it may be more significant in financial terms than had formerly been thought.[5]

The criteria used most often by tourism and hospitality suppliers to segment the market are as follows.

- *Demographic segmentation* uses the primary variables of age, gender, family life cycle, and ethnicity to segment the markets. Bust Loose Holidays, for example, uses age and lifestyle stage variables to segment the holiday market by attracting singles who attend universities or colleges.
- *Psychographic segmentation* divides buyers into different groups based on social class, lifestyle, and personality characteristics. Pyschographics and lifestyle segmentation is based on personality traits, attitudes, motivations, and activities, and is discussed in more detail in Chapter 3 (see pp. 79–80). People in the same demographic group can have very different psychographic profiles.
- *Geographic segmentation* is the division of markets according to geographical boundaries, such as countries, provinces/states, regions, cities, or neighbourhoods. In Canada, market segmentation is often limited to understanding the more lucrative international tourist market, but destination organizers are beginning to recognize the significance of local and provincial residents and the impact that they have on tourism receipts, particularly since September 11, 2001.[6]
- *Benefit segmentation* segments customers based on the benefits they desire, such as education, entertainment, luxury, or low cost. Customers weigh different features of a service, and these are evaluated to form the basis of benefit segmentation. Holidaymakers staying at the Fairmont Chateau Laurier in Ottawa, for example, would value benefits such as a spa, room service, and valet parking, whereas speed skaters staying at the Village Park Inn in Calgary would value its proximity to public transit and attractions such as the Olympic Oval.
- *Behaviour segmentation* divides the market into groups based on the various types of buying behaviour. Common bases include usage rate (light, medium, and heavy), user status (former users, nonusers, potential users, first-time users, and regular users of a product), loyalty status (many people stay in five-star hotels as much for the status it confers on them as for the additional comfort), buyer-readiness stage, and occasions. On special occasions, people are prepared to pay more for special treatment, so many restaurants now have deals for children's birthday parties, while hotels and cruise lines have special honeymoon suites.

In sum, the heart of any marketing plan is careful analysis of available market segments and the selection of the appropriate target markets. A common mistake within tourism and hospitality is the selection of inappropriate segments (see the Case Study in this chapter). Marketing managers commonly make errors by allowing or encouraging the acquisition of low-yield segments in an effort to maintain occupancy. At the opposite end of the spectrum, managers often feel they are attracting low-spend segments, and attempt to attract a more affluent segment. The problem is that this is often done without significant changes to the product or service. When developing a marketing plan, marketers can gather information concerning market segments from two sources. Internal data can be analyzed by looking at business cards, guest registrations, credit card receipts, customer surveys, direct observations, and staff perceptions. External data can be gathered from published industry information, from marketing research, or by making guesstimates after talking with competitors, vendors, and others in the industry.

Segmentation assists strategic planning in a number of areas. In general terms segmentation is undertaken in order to develop marketing programs appropriate to identified groups. This involves matching media to known targets; choosing retail outlet locations that conform to customer traffic patterns (e.g., for travel agents); suggesting creative marketing approaches (e.g., for the cover of a brochure designed for a specific market); estimating and forecasting the likely volume and value of a market; estimating the catchment area for an attraction; and above all, designing or improving the product to the known needs and preferences of particular customer groups.

Market segmentation is a dynamic process because customer trends are not static. It is thus important to carry out regular—preferably continuous—tracking studies to monitor changes happening in the market. One of the most recent trends in tourism and hospitality has been a "demassification" of the market, in which a greater number of niche markets are replacing the mass ones of the past.[7] (For example, Table 2.1 profiles the growing soft outdoor adventure tourist market). As a result, **niche marketing** is increasing, whereby products are tailored to meet the needs and wants of narrowly defined geographic, demographic, or psychographic segments. Technology has reduced the costs of creating a special product for each customer, making a degree of customization possible in several areas of tourism and hospitality. For example, travel agents have access to databases of accommodations, car rental companies, and airlines, so that from their computer terminal they can quickly put together an itinerary and make bookings to create a customized package for a client. With requests for customized and personalized vacations rising sharply, both agents and traditional tour operators are changing their businesses to meet that demand. Instead of booking only air and hotel, agents are arranging customized wine tastings, visits to artisan workshops, and private after-hours tours of the British crown jewels and the Vatican.[8] All this makes market segmentation an even more essential requirement of effective tourism marketing than it has been in the past.

Among activity-based market segments identified in the Canadian Tourism Commission's new series of TAMS (Travel Activities and Motivation Survey) analysis, soft outdoor adventure enthusiasts are the largest market, in both the United States and Canada. Travellers were classified as soft outdoor adventure enthusiasts based on their participation levels in various outdoor activities. Table 2.1 highlights some of the key findings from the soft outdoor adventure report.

The *Snapshot* on page 46, profiling Knight Inlet Lodge, is a good example of a company capitalizing on this growing market for soft outdoor adventure tourism.

niche marketing

the tailoring of products to meet the needs and wants of narrowly defined geographic, demographic, or psychographic segments

Table 2.1

Highlights of the TAMS Soft Outdoor Adventure Report

On both sides of the border, a substantial market exists for soft outdoor adventure—5.3 million adult Canadians and 35.5 million adult Americans. These are the largest segments of those analyzed by the CTC.

Among travellers with recent leisure travel experience in Canada, 4.4 million were Canadian (representing the largest segment having travelled recently in Canada) and 7.1 million were Americans (representing the second largest segment, behind heritage enthusiasts).

Canadian travellers appear to have a stronger outdoors and winter orientation than do their American counterparts, but top activities of choice for both groups of enthusiasts were typically "warm weather" activities.

The three most popular activities chosen by these travellers were wildlife viewing, hiking/backpacking in wilderness settings, and fishing.

Soft outdoor adventure enthusiasts are concentrated at the younger end of the adult age spectrum. Close to three quarters of American and one half of Canadian outdoor enthusiasts are between 18 and 44 years and are underrepresented at the older end of the age spectrum.

Canadian soft outdoor adventure enthusiasts have relatively narrow tourism interests compared to the more wide-ranging interests of the corresponding American group; 40 percent were also heritage enthusiasts. Different packaging and marketing strategies may be required on each side of the border to reach outdoor-oriented tourists, based on differences in interests and on overlap with other activity segments.

Compared with other activity-based market segments, less foreign competition exists for both Canadian and American soft outdoor adventure enthusiasts, although the United States offers strong competition for a sizeable minority of Canadians in this segment and for virtually all American soft outdoor adventurers.

The majority of soft outdoor adventure enthusiasts live in adult-only households. However, they are more likely than the "typical" tourist to have children living in their households.

The Canadian soft outdoor adventure group was the most homogeneous of all segments, with more than 9 in 10 members being Canadian-born. This will have a significant influence on future market potential, since Canada's population growth is being fuelled by immigration.

While the actual rate of growth of this segment is expected to be positive over the next 25 years, it is going to grow at a substantially slower rate than it would have if the population structure were to remain the same. Changes in amenities and services offered by tourism businesses may be required to better accommodate the needs and interests of an aging population. Efforts will also have to be made to entice new Canadians to experience Canada's natural settings.

Source: Soft outdoor adventure. (2003). *Tourism*, 7(4), 16.

SNAPSHOT

GRIZZLY BEAR VIEWING AT THE KNIGHT INLET LODGE

One might not want to encounter a grizzly bear face to face, but in a remote area of the Pacific Northwest on Vancouver Island, B.C., the Knight Inlet Lodge welcomes visitors to view them from a safe distance on a Knight Inlet Grizzly Bear Adventure tour. Knight Inlet is one of the top grizzly bear viewing spots in the world, according to Dean Wyatt, owner and operator of the Knight Inlet Lodge.

Knight Inlet Lodge is a floating lodge, and displays an assortment of construction styles dating from the early 1940s, when the original float housed a logging camp. Recent construction has provided modern accommodation, and the lodge now hosts a maximum of 30 guests in its 12 rooms and offers a variety of packages and activities. "Our feature product is grizzly bears, but our claim to fame is the variety of wildlife that we can offer people," says Wyatt. "Our target market is anyone interested in wildlife and we are a great family destination. Seventeen percent of our guests are from the U.S., so this market is important to us. It has the largest ecotourism market in the world, and this is the fastest-growing segment of the tourism market today." Equipment is supplied with every package, including boots, suits, rain gear, and cooler boxes.

The lodge is situated near one of the largest concentrations of grizzly (brown) bears in B.C. It is not uncommon for up to 40 bears to be within a few miles of the lodge during the peak fall season when the salmon are running up the Glendale River. And while the bears are abundant in the fall, it is not the only season that grizzlies frequent the area around the lodge. Starting in April, both black and grizzly bears begin emerging from hibernation and head to the cove and the estuary to feed on the succulent new spring growth. Even in mid-summer, when many of the bears have moved into the surrounding timber clearings to feast on berries, several bears can be seen each day as they move in and around the estuary and along the logging roads.

But grizzly bear viewing is not the only activity offered to tourists. As part of the 2003 wildlife and photography adventure packages, the company offered daily killer whale and marine wildlife watching tours at world-renowned Johnstone Strait. Groups are often rewarded with close encounters with killer whales, as well as with porpoises, playful white-sided dolphins, sea lions, seals, and occasionally humpback or minke whales. Other activities offered include bird-viewing excursions, scenic inlet cruises, rain forest hiking trips, salmon fishing, hiking tours, tracking tours, kayaking itineraries, and a jet-boat tour to the head of Knight Inlet. A best-selling package is the Safari trip, which consists of a round-trip float plane from Campbell River on Vancouver Island, three nights' accommodation, all meals, including Dungeness crab, plus two full and one partial day with the grizzlies and orcas in the wilderness.

Sources: Rosa, T. (2001, July 2). Grizzly bear viewing tops roster of activities. *Travel Weekly* 60(53), 16; Knight Inlet Grizzly Bear Adventure Tours Web site: http://grizzlytours.com.

SWOT Analysis

SWOT analysis

a technique that provides scope for an organization to list all its strengths, weaknesses, opportunities, and threats

SWOT is an acronym for **s**trengths, **w**eaknesses, **o**pportunities, and **t**hreats. A SWOT analysis provides scope for an organization to list all its *strengths* (those things it does best and its positive product features) and its *weaknesses* (problems that affect its success). These factors are always internally focused. For hotels and visitor attractions, location may be a major strength, or the strength may lie in the skills of certain staff members. Strength may also lie in historical artifacts or architectural style, or it may reflect having a particularly favourable consumer image. Once identified, strengths are the basis of corporate positions and can be promoted to potential customers, enhanced through product augmentation, or developed within a strategic framework. In the opening vignette of this chapter, several strengths of the Four Seasons Hotels and Resorts can be identified, including its reputation, brand equity, and global positioning.

Weaknesses, ranging from aging products and declining markets to surly customer contact staff, must also be identified. Once identified, they may be subject to management action designed to minimize their impact or to remove them where possible. Weaknesses and strengths are often matters of perception rather than "fact," and may be recognized only through consumer research. Again, using Four Seasons as an example, weaknesses could include not being diversified enough and therefore being vulnerable to negative external environmental impacts.

Opportunities are events that can affect a business, either through its reaction to external forces or through its addressing of its own weaknesses. An opportunity identified recently by Four Seasons Hotels and Resorts is in private charters and general cruises, a move that may improve the group's weakness of not being diversified enough.

Threats are those elements, both internal and external, that could have a serious detrimental effect on a business. Despite the efforts of the CTC after September 11, the subsequent downturn in the economy had a devastating impact on tourism in Canada. By the end of 2002, Four Seasons had not recovered from the aftereffects of September 11, and it sharply underperformed Fairmont Hotels & Resorts on the Toronto Stock Exchange. The subsequent Iraq war and concerns about sudden acute respiratory syndrome (SARS) led to a huge number of cancelled trips to North America and to thousands of dollars in lost tourism revenue for all hotels in Canada, including Four Seasons.

A SWOT analysis is usually best undertaken early in the planning process, and in large organizations a SWOT is often carried out for each division. For example, a convention hotel would conduct a SWOT on the property as a whole, but might also undertake a separate exercise for the functions area, restaurants, retail outlets, and recreation facilities. To enhance their own foresight and bring to bear an independent, fresh vision, it is common practice in large market-oriented businesses for managers to commission consultants to carry out regular audits of all aspects of their business, including a SWOT analysis. The *Snapshot* on page 48 presents the SWOT analysis carried out by Travel Alberta in order to assess the competitive position of Alberta in the global marketplace in 2003.

SNAPSHOT

TRAVEL ALBERTA SWOT ANALYSIS

Strengths

- Alberta is one of the greatest outdoor and adventure destinations in the world.
- Alberta has unique, world-class heritage, historical, and cultural products.
- Albertans are friendly and welcoming.
- Alberta landscapes and products are varied and accessible.
- Alberta has available capacity in shoulder seasons at value prices.
- Alberta has strong winter products, including world-class resorts.
- Alberta has no provincial sales tax, making it a more affordable destination.

Weaknesses

- Alberta's great outdoors and adventure products are taken for granted by Albertans.
- Albertans have too little awareness of the wide range of travel experiences available in Alberta.
- Albertans have no sense of urgency to travel in Alberta, and they often lack specific knowledge of Alberta's tourism product.
- Albertans tend not to think of themselves as tourists or as being on vacation when travelling within Alberta.
- Albertans have a perception that travel opportunities are better and more exotic elsewhere.
- Albertans have a perception that little or no product is available during peak seasons and on weekends.

Opportunities

- To promote the broad and diverse range of unique products available across the province, in order to increase awareness and visitation—especially in rural areas.
- To develop mini-vacation experiences and packages within Alberta, based on customer needs and demands.
- To improve industry marketing knowledge and ability to package products, based on consumer demand and needs, in order to produce an international, export-ready product.
- To package more winter products, in addition to alpine skiing.
- To use the competitive advantage the weak Canadian dollar provides against other travel destinations abroad.
- To enhance "Visiting Friends and Relatives (VFR)" offerings and packages.
- To target new Alberta residents and their respective friends and relatives.

Threats

- Pent-up demand for travel outside Canada, particularly to the United States, is growing.
- Advertising aimed at Albertans from the United States, British Columbia, and other destinations is increasing.
- A greater variety of products and promotion is entering the market from the United States and other destinations.

Source: Travel Alberta. (2003). *Strategic tourism marketing plan 2003–2006*. Edmonton: Author, 12.

Forecasting

forecasting

a market-research–
based but future-
oriented process that
relies on expectations,
vision, judgment, and
projections for factors
such as sales volume
and revenue trends,
consumer profiles,
product profiles,
price trends, and
trends in the external
environment

Because information is never perfect and the future is always unknown, no one right conclusion can ever be drawn from the evidence gathered in the SWOT process. As a result, forecasting becomes an important stage in the planning process to support a SWOT. **Forecasting** is market-research–based but future-oriented, and it relies on expectations, vision, judgment, and projections for factors such as sales volume and revenue trends, consumer profiles, product profiles, price trends, and trends in the external environment. Because the future for tourism and hospitality products is subject to volatile, unpredictable factors and competitors' decisions, the goal of forecasting is not accuracy but careful and continuous assessment of probabilities and options, with a focus on future choices. Forecasting recognizes that most marketing mix expenditure is invested months ahead of targeted revenue flows. Since marketing planning is focused on future revenue achievement, it is necessarily dependent upon skill, judgment, foresight, and realism in the forecasting process.

There are two main sets of forecasting techniques: qualitative and quantitative. *Qualitative* techniques are those that seek to estimate future levels of demand, based on detailed subjective analysis. They include sales staff estimates, senior management opinions, and buyers' intention surveys. Two more sophisticated qualitative techniques are the Delphi technique and scenario planning. The Delphi technique involves obtaining expert opinions about the future prospects for a particular market without the experts actually meeting or necessarily knowing at any stage the composition of the panel. Long-term scenario planning is undertaken by larger organizations such as hotel or airline companies. This is a systematic attempt to predict the composition of the future market environment in 10–25 years' time and the likely impacts on the company.

Quantitative techniques rely on analysis of past and current data. In some instances this implies the simple projecting of future demand in terms of past trends, and in other instances unravelling casual determinants need to be considered. A number of well-tested methods are used; however, most require a degree of statistical ability. Time-series, non-causal techniques involve the forecasting of future demand on the basis of past trends. Causal methods attempt to show, by using regression analysis, how some measure of tourism demand is influenced by selected variables other than time. Finally, computer simulations are becoming more popular—trend-curve analysis and multiple regressions are combined mathematically to generate a computer model that simulates tourism demand.

Scott Meis of the CTC has the following to say about forecasting:

> It bears saying that forecasting is an imperfect science. We use a set of parameters, such as exchange rates, gross domestic product, established travel trends, and so forth. After drawing on the expertise of our researchers and factoring in assumptions from what we know of the past, we run the variables through analytical models to produce statistics for the future—the number of overnight trips, the purpose of travel, expected revenues (the total number of dollars coming from a particular market), and expected yields (the average expenditure per visitor). Once we have these preliminary estimates, we consult with our sales force and directors in the various markets, who keep us informed of other factors we have not considered. And then, if appropriate, we adjust our forecasts to make our estimates as accurate and useful as possible.

Like weather forecasting, tourism forecasting becomes more useful the more often it is done. And, like weather forecasting, people are beginning to realize that while we cannot be precisely right all the time, we are close enough to the mark, often enough, so that our forecasts are useful. Indeed, this may be the real benefit of forecasting. Just as important as the numbers you get is the exercise of asking and finding out what they are most likely to be. This process of reaching out to the future is important for any forward-looking organization. It's the discipline that counts, the discipline to face the future and plan for it. None of us, at the CTC or anywhere, can be content any more with only understanding the past. To paraphrase Ontario-born economist John Kenneth Galbraith, "Economists don't produce forecasts because they know any better than anyone else what will happen; they do so because they are asked."[9]

3. SETTING MARKETING GOALS AND OBJECTIVES

Goals are the primary aims of the organization, and *objectives* the specific aims that managers accomplish to achieve organizational goals. Although most writers tend to link the terms and define them as desired results, some make distinctions. Baird, for example, defines goals as "the organization's primary intended accomplishments," whereas objectives are "the specific aims that managers accomplish to achieve organizational goals."[10] Goals can be defined in terms of sales growth, increased profitability, and market leadership. Objectives are the activities that will accomplish the goals. For example, the goal of sales growth for a hotel could become an objective of a 20 percent increase in accommodation sales and a 30 percent increase in food and beverage sales. The goal of increased profitability could be translated into objectives of a 15 percent increase in profits across the board, and a goal of market leadership could be translated into objectives for each city in which a hotel chain operates.

Marketing objectives at the tactical level derive logically from the previous stages of the planning process. To be effective and actionable in practice, tactical marketing objectives must be

- integrated with long-term corporate goals and strategy;
- precise and quantified in terms of sales volume, sales revenue, or market share;
- specific in terms of which products and which segments they apply to;
- specific in terms of the time period in which they are to be achieved;
- realistic and aggressive in terms of market trends (revealed in the situation analysis) and in relation to budgets available;
- agreed and endorsed by the managers responsible for the programs of activity designed to achieve results; and
- measurable directly or indirectly.[11]

If these criteria are not fully reflected, the objectives will be less than adequate for achieving the success of the business, and the marketing programs will be harder to specify and evaluate. The more thorough the previous stages of the marketing plan, the easier the task of specifying precise objectives. To ensure profitability and to remain competitive in today's marketplace, it has become necessary to establish several sub-objectives. For instance, a thousand-room hotel will undoubtedly have two broad objectives: average occupancy and average room rate. By themselves, these objectives do not serve as sufficient guides for developing marketing strategies. A set of sub-objectives might therefore include occupancy per period of time, the average room rate by type of room, and annual sales by each salesperson. Each marketing support area needs to be guided by a set of sub-objectives. This includes areas such as advertising, promotion, public relations, market research, and sales.

4. MARKETING STRATEGY: TARGETING AND POSITIONING

Targeting

target market
a clearly defined group of customers whose needs the company plans to satisfy

No area of the marketing plan surpasses the selection of **target markets** in importance. If inappropriate markets are selected, marketing resources will be wasted. High-level expenditures on advertising or sales will not compensate for misdirected marketing effort. Target markets should be selected from a previously developed list of available segments. These include segments currently served by the organization and newly recognized markets. A target market is simply the segment at which the organization aims its marketing message. It is a group of customers who have been identified, for whom the offering should be tailor-made, and to whom the organization will direct the majority of its marketing time, resources, and attention. Implicitly, the nonprofitable customers should be given less attention. A target market generally has four characteristics. It should be groups of people or businesses that are well-defined, identifiable, and accessible; members should have common characteristics; they should have a networking system so that they can readily refer the organization to one another; and they should have common needs and similar reasons to purchase the product or service.

Target marketing offers many advantages. Sales in the target market are higher than lost sales in the non-target segments. The company is therefore better off financially. The company also develops a competitive advantage after tailoring its products and campaigns to the needs and wants of the target customers. Organizations that use target marketing are more profitable because their customers are usually willing to pay a higher price for a product that is made just for them. Also, targeted customers are the most loyal customers an organization will have if the product or service is above average and successfully meets customer expectations. However, far too many marketing managers in tourism and hospitality simply select last year's target markets. Although it is normally true that the majority of target markets will remain the same, new ones appear, and the order of importance of segments can change between years. *Marketing in Action* on pages 52–53 highlights how A&W has targeted baby boomers. This sector, born between 1947 and 1966, represents about a third of the Canadian population, and is a very attractive market for the tourism and hospitality industry. Two other target markets growing in attractiveness for the tourism industry are the gay market and the senior market.

The gay tourism market offers enormous growth for the Canadian tourism industry. The market is estimated at $40 billion, compared to a U.S. market potential of $400 billion.[12] Montreal will continue to play a major role in this market as it prepares to host the 2006 Gay Games. The city is expected to welcome 19 000 athletes, 5000 artists, and over 250 000 visitors from Canada alone, as it stages 22 sporting events and cultural activities during the seven-day international event. Tourism Montreal anticipates that the 2006 Gay Games will have $150 million in economic impact. Canada is not the only country targeting this niche market. The British Tourist Authority's (BTA) campaign to attract gay and lesbian travellers from the United States is evidenced by the launch of the 2002 edition of its gay travel guide, as well as by new strategies for building a market niche that it says has already produced "gratifying" results. The decision to begin targeting gay and lesbian travellers from the United States was made in 1997. The BTA has subsequently expanded the campaign with the introduction of a larger travel guide and a dedicated gay and lesbian Web site.[13]

The senior market is another growing market increasingly targeted by the hospitality industry. This market is both lucrative and unique because it is less tied to seasonal travel, involves longer trips, and is not wedded to midweek or weekend travel, so it can boost occupancy rates for business and leisure travel properties. Choice Hotels identified the potential of this market in 2000 and in all its hotel brands offered a space-available 30 percent discount to seniors. Available to travellers aged 50 or over, the discount encouraged impulse travel and a change of travel plans to take advantage of that discount. The success of the campaign can be seen in the rise of senior occupancy to 38 percent of Choice's business.

Evaluation of potential target markets involves examining the segment's size and growth, the segment's structural attractiveness, and the firm's own objectives and resources. In terms of size, the American travel market is an important market segment for many Canadian tourism companies, as stressed earlier in the chapter. The transformation of Canadian Pacific (CP) Hotels & Resorts into Fairmont Hotels & Resorts demonstrated this importance (see Case Study in Chapter 1, pp. 30–32). The merger of these two companies, and the subsequent name change, was part of Canadian Pacific's targeting and positioning strategy. While the CP brand was relatively unfamiliar to many Americans, the Fairmont brand was very well known in the United States, and was associated with luxury, prestige, and high levels of service quality. Thus, in order to target the Americans, and to differentiate itself from other luxury accommodation providers in Canada, the company adopted the better-known brand name.

MARKETING IN ACTION

A&W TARGETS THE BABY BOOMER

A&W isn't the only fast-food chain trying to appeal to the ubiquitous baby boomers. But with a history that dates back to 1956, no other burger chain can claim to have raised boomers on fast food. Today, nearly empty-nesters, the boomers no longer have to eat where the kids want. And after all these years, it appears A&W still tops their list. "Some of our competitors might say they're going after the baby-boomer market because it is such a big market, but they can't do what we do because we have a tremendous linkage to the boomer genera-tion," says Jeff Mooney, chair and CEO of Vancouver-based A&W Food Services of Canada Inc.

For Mooney, the brand's strong heritage comes down to simple demographics. "We raised the boomers on fast food. They got older, got married, and got kids. Then McDonald's came along in the 1970s and bet that a four-year old screaming for a toy would win over an adult wanting a good hamburger. So as the boomers had children, that part of the market flourished. Now, the boomers' kids are grown and the adults are free to make their own choices about fast food." Some believe that despite being in a very competitive field, the fact that A&W are going after the older demographics as opposed to the younger adults or kids bodes well for their future because the boomer demographic is expanding. A&W President Paul Hollands adds, "Regardless of generations, A&W has a huge appeal and bridges right back to the incoming generations. The brand has broad appeal because we are true to what we are. We're really about good food."

A&W, which bills itself as Canada's first hamburger quick-service restaurant, has come a long way since first arriving in Canada nearly 50 years ago. The company was born in 1919 in Lodi, California, when Roy Allen and Frank Wright opened a sidewalk stand and later a drive-in, serving a creamy drink called root beer. A&W came to Canada in 1956 when two operators, Dick Bolte and Orval Helwege, opened their first drive-in on Portage Avenue in Winnipeg. The concept's popularity quickly grew, and by 1966, A&W operated more than 200 drive-in locations across Canada. Today, the company operates 609 restaurants across Canada, and it posted

sales of $433 million in 2001. A&W is the country's third largest burger chain by sales volume, behind McDonald's ($2.24 billion) and Wendy's ($476 million), and it employs 17 000 people.

According to Mooney, A&W is a strategy-driven company. "That means everything that happens in our business—from major deci-sions about how the organization works to what goes on the placemats in our restau-rants—is driven by this strategy," he says. A&W's current strategy involves a continued focus on the baby boomers; an expansion into the Ontario, Quebec, and Atlantic mar-kets; and developing a well-branded street presence. In 2002, the company began revi-talizing its 300 free-standing restaurants with "retro" design and new exterior and interior signs.

Looking ahead, Mooney is confident that demographics will play a key role in the com-pany's future success. "The two largest groups in the Canadian population right now are 35 to 44 and 45 to 54, and that's right where our customers are," he says. "And so the next 10 to 15 years are just a spectacular opportu-nity for growth for our company. We think we can have 1500 locations in this country, so we're excited about the future."

Interestingly, he doesn't seem worried about the trend toward baby boomers choosing healthy options. The company's view is people taking a "cumulative approach" to diet. This means, as Mooney explains, if someone eats bran flakes with skim milk for breakfast, salmon for dinner, then what is wrong with eating an A&W burger with onion rings for lunch?

Source: Harris, R. (2002). Adult appeal. *Foodservice and Hospitality, 35*(10), 26–29.

Positioning

Once the market has been segmented and a target market identified, the next step in the marketing plan is positioning. **Positioning** is a communications strategy that is a natural follow-through from market segmentation and target marketing. Market positioning is ultimately how the consumer perceives the product or service in a given market, and is used to achieve a sustainable competitive advantage over competitors. Three steps are necessary to develop an effective position in the target market segment: product differentiation, prioritizing and selecting the competitive advantage, and communicating and delivering the position.

Step One: Product Differentiation

Product differentiation, a term coined by Michael Porter, describes a technique that enables organizations to seek to gain competitive advantage by offering a product that has features not available in the offerings of competitors. Product differentiation has the potential to assist companies in gaining a competitive edge and can distinguish them from competitors by offering competitive advantages. A competitive advantage offers greater value to the consumer by providing benefits that justify a higher price. These advantages can be established through product attributes, features, services, level of quality, style and image, and price range. The key elements will shape how the consumer perceives the product. Physical attribute differentiation is achieved by enhancing or creating an image in the consumer's mind through tangible evidence. For example, Quality Inn offers a very simple physical appearance, communicating a clean, safe, cheap place to sleep. Fairmont Hotels & Resorts, on the other hand, combine elaborate an exterior with a luxurious interior to inspire feelings of comfort, relaxation, and prestige.

Service differentiation is an increasingly important way of gaining competitive advantage. Service quality has been increasingly identified as a key factor in differentiating service products and building a competitive advantage in tourism. The process by which customers evaluate a purchase, thereby determining satisfaction and likelihood of repurchase, is important to all marketers, but especially to services marketers because, unlike their manufacturing counterparts, they have fewer objective measures of quality by which to judge their production.[14] Several studies have examined the association between service quality and more specific behavioural intentions, and there is a positive and significant relationship between customers' perceptions of service quality and their willingness to recommend the company or destination.[15] Likewise, research on service quality and retaining customers suggests that willingness to purchase again falls considerably once services are rated below good.[16]

Step Two: Prioritizing and Selecting the Competitive Advantage

Positioning is much like a ranking system, and an organization must decide where it wants to be on the hierarchy. Some companies have an image of high quality, service, and price—others, of being low-budget. Neither image is better or worse. However, once the position is established, it is very difficult to change it in the consumer's mind. Therefore, companies must be very cautious in selecting the most effective combination of competitive advantages to promote and to contribute to building their positioning strategy.

It is important to promote not only one benefit to the target market, but to develop a **unique selling proposition (USP)**, a feature of a product that is so unique that it distinguishes the product from all other products. The goal of a USP is for a company to establish itself as the number one provider of a specific attribute in the mind of the target market. The attribute chosen should be desired and highly valued by target consumers. If the marketing mix elements build the brand and help it to connect with the customer year after year, the total personality of the brand, rather than the trivial product differences, will decide its ultimate position in the market. Although it is difficult in the tourism industry to find an effective USP, in such a competitive and free market, it is essential to offer something new. Package holidays tend to offer similar deals, with only minor differences. Therefore, it is important for a company to create a new good, service, or benefit that can be offered to consumers by it alone. Travel Cuts is an excellent example of a Canadian company that utilizes USP effectively. It offers student-discounted fares through its International Student Identity Card program—something that no other travel company offers.

Step Three: Communicating and Delivering the Position

The final goal of an organization in the positioning process is to build and maintain a consistent positioning strategy. The overall aim of tourism providers is to attract attention from potential customers and to delight them with product offerings that cannot be beaten by competitors. Programs and slogans that support the organization's position must be continuously developed and promoted in order to establish and maintain the organization's desired position in the consumer's mind. Quality, frequency, and exposure in the media will determine how successful the positioning strategy will be.

branding

a method of establishing a distinctive identity for a product based on competitive differentiation from other products

Tourism and hospitality providers try to differentiate their products by using branding, a method of establishing a distinctive identity for a product based on competitive differentiation from other products. Branded products are those whose name conjures up certain images—preferably positive ones—in consumers' minds. These images may relate to fashion, value, prestige, quality, or reliability. Image is an important element of customer perception. If a hotel chain has an image of quality, staying at the hotel will provide benefits to business customers who want to project a successful image to their clients or colleagues. Some brands are recognized for their reliability. It is comforting, for example, to know that a Best Western property will meet certain standards, and that selecting one will be a reliable choice, even if the traveller is unfamiliar with the specific property or region. Hotels in particular brand specific properties within their group to identify different categories of product. (See Chapter 5 for a more detailed discussion of branding.)

5. TACTICS AND ACTION PLANS

Although no single strategy will be suitable for all organizations, marketing planning provides the opportunity to understand the operating environment and to choose options that will meet the organization's goals and objectives. Planning involves selecting and developing a series of strategies that effectively bring about the required results. Among the types of strategies that can be considered are

- *making good investment decisions.* Selecting the best, most effective use of financial resources is crucial. This will include reviewing the product's life cycle and doing a portfolio analysis.
- *diversifying.* While it is important to ensure that resources are allocated to those markets showing the best potential yields, the possibility of disruptions to markets must also be taken into account. Diversification can provide an important cushion.

- *planning for the long term.* Tourism marketing campaigns can have long lead times. The cumulative effect of promotions may take a while to produce measurable results. Building effectiveness over time is just as important as generating instant results.
- *seizing new opportunities.* Being aware of consumer trends, fads, fashions, and attitudinal shifts will also help an organization to identify opportunities. Being flexible enough to respond to market developments will give an organization a strong competitive edge.
- *developing strategic partnerships.* It is important to identify customers, suppliers, and competitors with whom it is possible to develop an enhanced working relationship. Strategic alliances offer the opportunity to increase profits for all participants.

Marketing strategies are designed as the vehicle to achieve marketing objectives. In turn, marketing tactics are tools to support strategies. Far too often, strategies and tactics have little relationship to objectives. This is always an error, and is commonly the result of one or more of the following:

- the desire to maintain the status quo. Strategies and tactics do not change because they are perceived to be working, even though solid proof of their effectiveness seldom exists.
- incompetent managers who do not want to risk their positions by implementing new strategies
- failure to engage in marketing planning or to view the processes as being serious and meaningful to decision making
- undue heavy influence of outside vendors, such as advertising agencies, which do not wish to change direction or try new vehicles
- failure to understand the relationship between objectives, strategies, and tactics.

Applying the Marketing Mix

Action programs comprise a mix of marketing activities that are undertaken to influence and motivate buyers to choose targeted volumes of particular products. This part of the marketing plan shows how the organization intends to use the 7 P's introduced in Chapter 1 (see pp. 8–9). Table 2.2 shows the activities that should be included in this section of the marketing plan. The third column lists the chapters in this book where these topics are covered in detail. A marketing mix program or marketing campaign expresses exactly what activities will take place in support of each identified product/market subgroup on a week-by-week basis.

Table 2.2

Specific Strategies Included in the Action Plan

STRATEGIES	MARKETING MIX ELEMENTS (P'S)	CHAPTER
Product strategies	Product Physical evidence Process	5
Pricing strategies	Price	6
Distribution strategies	Place	7
Advertising strategies	Promotion	8
Sales promotion and merchandising strategies	Promotion	9
Public relations strategies	Promotion	9
Sales strategies	Promotion	9
Direct marketing strategies	Promotion	10
Internet marketing strategies	Place Promotion	10
Internal marketing strategies (personnel, managing service quality, etc.)	People Process	11

PROFILE

THE MARKETING PLAN FOR SUPERIOR NORTH: A PYRAMID APPROACH

The Superior North region of Northwestern Ontario is located on the rugged and scenic north shore of Lake Superior and stretches roughly 350 kilometres from east to west. Commonly referred to as the "Top of Superior" because of its geographic location relative to Lake Superior, the Superior North region encompasses the communities of Dorion, Hurkett, Red Rock, Nipigon, Lake Helen First

PROFILE *continued*

Nation, Pays Plat First Nation, Rossport, Schreiber, Terrace Bay, Marathon, Pic River First Nation, and Manitouwadge.

The tourism industry has always existed in Superior North, but has never reached a level at which it could be considered a prime economic generator. There are two key reasons for this situation. First, the mining and forestry industries have been paramount economic engines and employers for decades. Second, communities and individual businesses/operators have traditionally marketed tourism individually on a very small scale, with limited financial and human resources, which left them unable to compete against larger, established tourist attractions.

However, in recent years, the Marathon and District Chamber of Commerce has entered into a synergistic partnership with the Superior North Community Futures Development Corporation (hereafter referred to as "the partnership"). The partnership has endeavoured to serve as a project champion in undertaking a new approach to marketing and

developing tourism in the Superior North region. The fundamental concept is to dynamically market and promote all communities and businesses/operators in the region under a single, four-season destination umbrella. This approach is not unique in its concept, but it is completely nontraditional for Superior North. Tourism marketing and development in the region hold the potential to aid in diversifying and strengthening local and regional economies that have traditionally been dependent on the natural resource-based industries of mining and forestry.

The partnership has formulated a strategic tourism marketing plan for Superior North, using a formal vision and a practical planning approach. The marketing plan is built around the model of a pyramid— "a bottom up" approach to development (see Figure 2.5). The first level of the pyramid focuses on developing the concept of "regionalization" to capitalize on the theory of "economies of scale." It has been extensively proven that there is

Figure 2.5   The Pyramid Approach to Development

PROFILE *continued*

strength in numbers, and for Superior North tourism to cultivate new revenues and expand local infrastructure, all communities of the region must realize the value in marketing as a single, uniquely northern destination.

With the concept of regionalization established as a building block, the second level of the pyramid is formed on the concept of a tourism resource audit. This audit develops an inventory of all direct and related tourism products in the region. Having a critical knowledge of all market-ready tourism products supports developing the marketing plan based on the concept of assets-based planning. The resource audit provides a clear view of the region's tourism strengths, weaknesses, opportunities, and threats (SWOT) within all economic sectors. From the SWOT analysis, demand generators can be identified and developed, and a differentiation strategy can be developed for the Superior North region to gain a competitive advantage.

Using assets-based planning, the third level of the pyramid consists of the actual marketing strategies and their tactical thrusts designed to increase and drive tourism traffic to the Superior North region. The key to the productivity of the developed marketing strategies and thrusts is to design practical, innovative initiatives that build on the region's strengths and capitalize on burgeoning opportunities. The carrying out of the marketing strategies and thrusts is appropriately detailed and methodical, and it employs a step-by-step approach to implementation and responsibilities. Some of the developed strategies and thrusts are

- creative branding strategy/thrust;
- partnership development strategy/thrust;
- integrated communications strategy/thrust;

- stakeholder outreach strategy/thrust;
- tourism package development strategy/thrust;
- regional/community team building (belief building) strategy/thrust;
- destination management system strategy/thrust;
- ecotourism development strategy/thrust;
- festival/theme events strategy/thrust; and
- Aboriginal tourism development strategy/thrust.

With all marketing strategies designed and thrusts implemented, the peak of the pyramid and its reciprocation is the measuring and evaluation of the marketing strategies and thrusts based on their effectiveness and productivity. It is crucial that the overall marketing effort be tracked because this will serve as the foundation to establish performance indicators and benchmarks. In turn, the identified indicators and benchmarks will form the basis for a marketing plan expansion and future plan development. The measurement and evaluation phase is pivotal in developing the sustainability of tourism as a strong economic engine in Superior North, and this will ensure its futurity. But the partnership recognizes that for tourism to develop and serve as a sustainable revenue generator in the future, new tourism infrastructure must be planned, funded, and developed. The creation of new assets will increase the region's critical mass and this in turn will create new demand generators and core attractions to draw tourists and revenues to Superior North.

Source: D. Skworchinski, Regional Communications and Strategic Development Coordinator, Superior North Community Futures Development Corporation, personal communication, May 26, 2003.

6. RESOURCE REQUIREMENTS

The marketing plan needs to address the resources required to support the marketing strategies and meet the objectives. Such resources include personnel, equipment and space, budgets, intra-organizational support, research, consulting, and training. A common error in writing a marketing plan is developing strategies that are probably highly workable but for which there is insufficient support. Generally, the most costly and difficult resource needed to ensure the success of marketing/sales strategies in tourism and hospitality businesses is personnel. Management commonly views the addition of personnel as unnecessary, impractical, or unwise, given budgetary restrictions.

Of prime importance in analyzing resource requirements is the budget. Setting a budget that provides the marketing department with sufficient resources to deliver its plan is essential. However, in most organizations, various departments compete for funds, and it is not always easy to convince management that the marketing budget should have a priority claim in limited funds. Although this is less of an issue in commercially oriented organizations, it can be a major problem in arts and entertainment organizations and non-profit groups. The idea of spending money on marketing (which is frequently not viewed as a core activity) at the expense of collections, maintenance, acquisitions, or expanding performance programs is often a very contentious issue.

The marketing budget determines the amount of money that has to be spent in advance of bookings, reservations, and purchases in order to secure targeted sales volumes and revenue. The budget represents the sum of the costs of individual marketing mix elements judged necessary by marketing managers to achieve specified objectives and targets. There will normally be a range of options as to how each marketing objective will be achieved—more or less advertising, more or less price discounting, and so on. Marketing managers are required to consider these options and the associated costs, using judgment, experience, and analysis of previous results. If an evaluation of objectives and the cost of marketing tasks demonstrate that planned resources are inadequate, then additional budgets will be needed or the objectives must be amended.

7. MARKETING CONTROL

The penultimate step in the planning process is to ensure that objectives will be achieved in the required time, using the funds and resources requested. In order to measure effectiveness, evaluation programs have to be put in place, and regular monitoring needs to occur. There is little value in preparing a one-year marketing plan and including an evaluation methodology that commences toward the end of the operating year. This will not allow enough time to identify potential problems or initiate remedial action.

Because objectives have been set in quantifiable terms, regular reviews of sales forecasts and quotas, assessments of expenditure against budget, and data collection and analysis will provide guidance on how well objectives are being met. If a problem arises, contingency plans can be activated. Effective contingency plans are considered well before emergencies or problems arise. Reacting under pressure is rarely as effective as preplanning. If, as part of the original process, alternatives are considered, it is more likely that they will be successful. The most important reason for insisting on precision in setting objectives is to make it possible to measure results. Such results for a tourism business might be flow of bookings against planned capacity, enquiry and sales response related to any advertising, customer awareness of advertising messages measured by research surveys, sales response to any price discounts and sales promotions, sales response to any merchandising efforts by travel agents, consumer use of Web sites and flow of bookings achieved, and customer satisfaction measurements.

Most marketing plans are written to cover a one-year action plan in detail, with references made to the longer term—traditionally three years and five years. While the corporate goals may be longer-term (often as long as 10 or 20 years), the actual objectives are usually defined in terms of a much shorter time frame. Some organizations base their marketing plans on their funding cycles. Some art organizations or government departments on three-year funding cycles prepare business and marketing plans that cover the full funding period. Even these, however, stress the importance of regular review and re-evaluate their action plan sections on a 12-month basis.

8. COMMUNICATING THE PLAN

Involving as many staff members as possible in the process of setting objectives and drawing up plans that communicate well is an important aspect of motivating staff at all levels and securing enthusiastic participation in the implementation process. This involvement is a subject of increasing attention in many tourism and hospitality organizations;[17] it is especially important for service businesses, in which so many staff members have direct contact with customers on the premises. It is a good idea to time the stages in marketing planning so that managers and as many staff as possible in all departments can take some part in initiating or commenting on draft objectives and plans. Where target setting and evaluation are linked with some form of performance incentives, the motivation of staff is likely to be easier to secure. Motivation can be damaged if objectives are continuously changed or if there is no opportunity to debate their practicality in operation. While marketing planning is conducted primarily to achieve more efficient business decisions, its secondary benefit is to provide a means of internal participation and communication, vital in creating and sustaining a high level of organizational morale.

Marketing plans must be sold to many people. Internally, these include members of the marketing and sales department, vendors and advertising agencies, and top management. Marketing plans are also important in communicating to stakeholders outside the company. Approaching banks or other investors—for example, in tourism projects funded by government sources—invariably requires a business plan in which marketing is a primary component. Where money is granted, evidence of results will be required through a formal evaluation process. In terms of presenting the report, many readers, both inside and outside the organization, will be impatient and will want the conclusions immediately. The executive summary is therefore a key section of the report. Indeed, it can be assumed that some staff—and perhaps senior executives and board members—will read only the executive summary. In general, an executive summary should be between two and six pages. It should avoid the use of jargon, and it should highlight the key objectives and action aspects of the plan and budget, leaving the analysis of current situations and detailed market analyses for the main document.

CHAPTER SUMMARY

A marketing plan serves a number of purposes within any tourism organization: it provides a road map for all marketing activities of the firm for the future; it ensures that marketing activities are in agreement with the corporate strategic plan; it forces marketing managers to review and objectively think through all steps in the marketing process; it assists in the budgeting process to match resources with marketing objectives; and it creates a process to monitor actual against expected results. There are eight logical steps in a systematic marketing planning process:

1. *Corporate connection.* Marketing planning should reflect the goals and objectives of the organization as a whole.
2. *Analysis and forecasting.* This includes portfolio analysis, competitor analysis, segmentation analysis, and SWOT analysis. Forecasting becomes an important stage in the planning process to support a SWOT.
3. *Setting marketing goals and objectives.* Goals are the primary aims of the organization, and objectives are the specific aims that managers accomplish to achieve organizational goals.
4. *Marketing strategy: Targeting and positioning.* Target markets should be selected from the previously developed list of available segments. Positioning is a natural follow-through from market segmentation and target marketing.
5. *Tactics and action plans.* This part of the marketing plan shows how the organization intends to use the 7 P's.
6. *Resource requirements.* The marketing plan needs to address the resources required to support the strategies and meet the objectives.
7. *Marketing control.* This step in the planning process is to ensure that objectives will be achieved in the required time, using the funds and resources requested.
8. *Communicating the plan.* This is an important aspect of motivating staff at all levels and securing participation in the implementation process.

KEY TERMS

Boston Consulting Group (BCG) model p. 39	general competitors, p. 41	product differentiation, p. 54
branding p. 55	goals, p. 38	question marks, p. 40
budget competitors p. 41	low-cost leadership, p. 41	segmentation analysis, p. 42
cash cow p. 40	marketing plan, p. 36	"smart" rule, p. 38
competitor analysis p. 41	market share, p. 40	stars, p. 40
differentiation, p. 42	mission statement, p. 38	strategic marketing plan, p. 36
direct competitors, p. 41	niche marketing. p. 44	SWOT analysis, p. 47
dog, p. 40	objectives, p. 38	target market, p. 51
executive summary, p. 37	portfolio analysis, p. 39	unique selling proposition (USP), p. 54
focus, p. 42	positioning, p. 54	
forecasting, p. 49	product category competitors, p. 41	

DISCUSSION QUESTIONS AND EXERCISES

1. Examine the mission statement for a local tourism or hospitality organization. Does it reflect the "smart" rule described in this chapter? If not, try to redefine the statement.
2. Choose a large tourism or hospitality enterprise in Canada and apply the BCG matrix to the various products and services on offer. Does the organization have a balanced portfolio?
3. Four Seasons has achieved success through distinctive positioning. Think of another three examples of tourism organizations that have clearly understood the significance of positioning. Describe their target markets.
4. It is suggested in the chapter that competitors can be divided into four broad categories. Take an example from the Canadian tourism industry (a hotel chain perhaps) and list its competitors under the four categories.
5. The chapter highlights three target markets growing in attractiveness for the tourism industry. Segment the tourists that your region attracts. Are there any segments of the travel market that are not being targeted? Why not?
6. Go out and find a marketing plan from a tourism organization in your area. Does it follow the eight steps of the planning process outlined in this chapter? How is it different?

CASE STUDY

ROOTS AIR: A SHORT HISTORY

The story of Roots Air began early in 2000, with a cryptic voice mail message from Ted Shetzen, the man behind Roots Air, to Leo Desrochers, the chief operating officer of Skyservice Airlines Inc., a Toronto-based charter carrier that mostly ferried travellers south in the winter. Mr. Desrochers's acquaintance with Mr. Shetzen went way back, to the days when both worked at Air Canada. Shetzen's message was brief and to the point, saying only: "It's time."

From those two words emerged a plan to steal away a small portion of Air Canada's most profitable customers—business flyers—by enticing them with celebrity pitchmen and promises of great food, plush lounges, and excellent service, all at lower prices. A main attraction of the new venture was its branding agreement with Roots, the clothing empire founded by Michael Budman and Don Green. Roots invested $5 million for the right to put its name on the carrier and design the uniforms, lounges, and other promotional items. Trading on the trendy image of the apparel retailer, the timing of the new airline seemed encouraging. The merger of

Air Canada and Canadian Airlines was not going well, and there was reason to believe there were a lot of disgruntled travellers looking for an alternative.

A key element of the Roots Air strategy was to use brand new A320 and A330 aircraft but exploit Skyservice's existing infrastructure to operate at low cost. "We basically saw an opportunity to carve a place out for ourselves in the business market, not with high expectations of market share, not competing with Air Canada everywhere, but enough to allow us an adequate return on capital," recalled Desrochers. Roots had two service tiers: gold and silver. Gold included luxury items such as leather-covered seats, whereas silver service was tailored for the more price-sensitive business traveller. In March 2001, a Roots silver-class fare was about $800 one-way from Vancouver to Toronto. Air Canada's fare was almost $2,000 for the same journey.

As well as targeting the business traveller, Roots Air was looking to attract consumers who wanted to associate themselves with the cachet of the retailer, Roots Canada. But apart from outfitting its cabin staff and baggage personnel in the hip designs that have made Roots famous from Hollywood to the Olympics, Roots Air did not forge a clear marketing message. A major advertising campaign by Grey Worldwide of Toronto touted the Roots Air image, with a jazzy Web site, large banners inside and outside major airports, and print ads in major daily newspapers. The agency tried to entice customers and executives and travel agents with moody, black-and-white photos unconventional for the airline industry. This led to further criticisms that the Roots message was unclear.

As far as public relations were concerned, Michael Budman and Don Green, co-founders of the Roots apparel phenomenon, were conspicuously absent in the airline's development phase, choosing not to play the Richard Branson role of playful, ubiquitous promoters—probably the only chance Roots Air had of making an impression on jaded air travellers. If they deferred to Russell Payson, CEO of Skyservice, it was perhaps with the knowledge that the Roots owners' previous non-retail fling with a Roots hotel in Colorado in the early 1990s was a flop.

But in general, the goals of the new airline were too ambitious. An offering circular was sent out in June 2000, by Research Capital Corp., to raise $35 million to fund the venture. It included a pro forma statement showing that Skyservice's revenue would increase to $548.3 million from $228.9 million in the first year of Roots Air's operation, starting with four planes and adding two more by the end of the year. By comparison, WestJet, arguably Canada's most successful airline ever, took five years to attain those numbers, reaching them only in 2000 after it had grown to 22 aircraft. "The expectations were not realistic, particularly for a start-up airline in its first year of operations," says Kobus Dietzsch, who worked in marketing planning and analysis in Roots Air. A more realistic expectation would have been for $175 million in revenue the first year, says Dietzsch.

Other assumptions made at the outset were also dubious. For example, the plan was based on a 50/50 mix of business and leisure customers, whereas 20 percent business class is considered good by most industry standards. In estimating

traffic, the original plan was premised on having 71 percent of its silver and 78 percent of its gold business seats filled during August, a time when such traffic tapers off. "The real problem was that we had too many business-class seats on airplanes," says Russel Payson, president of Skyservice.

Confusion was rampant within Skyservice leading up to and beyond its first Roots Air flight on March 26, 2001. "Despite the excitement of launching a new airline, there is a feeling of being overwhelmed by the enormity of the task and compressed timeline," said a consultant's study done by Marketing Matters for Skyservice in mid-January. Even basic scheduling decisions raised intractable problems. The airline did not know 11 days before March 26 whether or not it would be flying Calgary–Toronto on the first day. The flight was ultimately cancelled. Only one interline agreement (despite plans for many more) with other carriers to receive and hand off passengers was signed by the launch date. Even that deal with Air Tahiti fell apart after Roots Air announced on the first day that it would not fly to Los Angeles, where it was to connect with the Pacific Island carrier. This further hurt earnings projections, since initial expectations were that a significant portion of revenue would come from arrangements with other airlines. Desrochers states that it was difficult to negotiate such agreements because potential partners wanted to see Roots Air up and running before signing.

Perhaps the biggest fiasco came on launch day, when the carrier was forced to cancel two of its inaugural flights because one of its planes had not arrived on time. Compounding the problem was a mistaken entry in the travel agent computer reservation system, showing Roots Air operating a 316-seat Airbus A330 when in fact the plane was a 120-seat A320. As a result, the aircraft was oversold and Roots' Mr. Budman and his guests found themselves bumped.

Other problems ran deeper, and included internal disorganization and in-fighting between the low-end charter side of Skyservice, which operated the Roots Air scheduled flights, and the Roots Air people who aimed to be high-end. Skyservice operational people began referring derogatorily to those in the Roots Air marketing arm as the "hangar people" because they were holed up in a different building. Cultural differences also had a negative effect on the advertising, which was crucial to attracting customers and of prime importance to the Roots clothing partners, for whom marketing has always been fundamental. Mark Stoiber, creative director of the Roots Air account at Grey Advertising says, "With two very different cultures coming together, understandably there was tension and the stakes were very high. Is it a price-driven thing or a style-driven thing?"

One month after launching, it was clear that a host of assumptions on which Roots Air had been based were incorrect. It was now clear that Air Canada did in fact have a hammerlock on corporate Canada, and business traffic was not materializing. Calgary passengers in particular were not as disaffected with Air Canada as had been believed, and the Roots Air brand was not resonating with the public as expected. Finally, the Roots Air's service aspirations were being thwarted by the charter mentality of Skyservice. Promising more legroom, shorter line-ups, better food, and real china in the promotional material, the airline found that it just could not deliver on promises.

There were simply too few passengers to sustain the business. During its short life, on average Roots Air flew less than 60 percent full. While some flights had 80 percent loads, others were much worse, such as the Calgary–Toronto run on May 3, 2001, the day the airline announced it would shut, when the 120-seat plane had only five people on board. The low loads overturned the economics of the operation, with the result that Roots Air lost money on virtually every flight. Payson says the carrier was losing $1 million a week, a significant expense for a company the size of Skyservice, which had revenue of about $110 million in the fiscal year ending April 30, 2000. In the end, having lost about $7.5. million, Skyservice opted for a deal with Air Canada that called for shutting down Roots Air on May 4, 2001, and for the two to collaborate on running a new low-cost carrier. The low-cost plan fell apart, but the deal allowed for an orderly closure with no passengers left stranded and no creditors left unpaid.

Sources: Bramham, D. (2001, March 27). Roots air: Not quite flight of fancy. *Vancouver Sun*, p. F1; Fitzpatrick, P. (2002, January 31). Up, up … and down: Roots, a short history. *Financial Post*, pp. 1, 14; Laucius, J. (2001, May 5). Roots air couldn't compete with frequent fights. *Ottawa Citizen*, p. D1.

QUESTIONS

1. What went wrong with the Roots Air? Were there elements of the marketing plan outlined in this chapter that did not receive sufficient attention?
2. Since the writing of this case, several groups in Canada have started up new carriers. What can they learn from the experiences of Roots Air?
3. The text lists the criteria used most often by tourism and hospitality suppliers to segment the market. What particular segments was Roots Air trying to attract and what methods did it use to segment the market? Was it successful?
4. The Roots brand has never travelled very far beyond its established position in leisure apparel. Why do you think that is?

WEB SITES

www.awrestaurants.com
   A&W Restaurants

www.bustloose.com
   Bust Loose Holidays

www.carnival.com
   Carnival Cruise Line

www.choicehotels.com
   Choice Hotels

www.disney-cruise-vacations.com
Disney Cruise Vacations

www.fourseasons.com
Four Seasons Hotels and Resorts

www.knightinletlodge.com
Knight Inlet Lodge

www.ncl.com
Norwegian Cruise Line

www.ritzcarlton.com
Ritz-Carlton Hotels and Resorts

www.tourismvancouver.com
Tourism Vancouver

www.travelcuts.com
Travel Cuts Travel Agency

www.visitbritain.com
Visit Britain

www.4321zip.com
Zip Airline

ENDNOTES

1. Dickman, S. (1999). *Tourism & hospitality marketing*. Oxford: Oxford University Press, 33.
2. Canadian Tourism Commission. (2002). *Canadian Tourism Commission strategic plan, 2002–2004*. Ottawa: Author, 14.
3. Porter, M. E. (1980). *Competitive strategy: Techniques for analyzing industry and competitors*. New York: Free Press, 4.
4. Jackson, R. T. (1990). VFR tourism: Is it underestimated? *Journal of Tourism Studies, 1*(2), 10–17.
5. Seaton, A. V., & Palmer, C. (1997). Understanding VFR tourism behaviour: The first five years of the United Kingdom Tourism Survey. *Tourism Management, 18*(6), 345–355.
6. Hudson, S., & Ritchie, J. R. B. (2002). Understanding the domestic market using cluster analysis: A case study of the marketing efforts of Travel Alberta. *Journal of Vacation Marketing, 8*(3), 263–276.
7. Crawford-Welch, S. (1991). Marketing hospitality in the 21st Century. *International Journal of Contemporary Hospitality Management, 3*(3), 21–27.
8. Whitlock, S. (2001, September). The world on a platter. *Travel + Leisure,* 176–179.
9. Meis, S. (2002). Forecasting for the tourism industry. *Tourism, 6*(5), 15.
10. Baird, L., & Post, J. (1990). *Management, functions and responsibilities.* New York: Harper & Row, 104–105.
11. Middleton, V. T. C., & Clarke, J. (2001). *Marketing in travel and tourism.* Oxford: Butterworth-Heinemann, 209.
12. Gay tourism sector growing in Canada. (2002). *Tourism, 6*(3), 10.
13. BTA launches 2002 edition of gay and lesbian campaign (2002). Canadian Tourism Commission press release. Retrieved February 5, 2002, from http://www.canadatourism.com/en/ctc/ctx/ctxnews/search/newsbydateform.cfm.
14. Zeithaml, V. A., Berry, L. L., & Parasuraman, A. (1988). Communication and control processes in the delivery of service quality. *Journal of Marketing, 52,* 35–48.
15. Zeithaml, V. A., Berry, L. L., & Parasuraman, A. (1996). The behavioural consequences of service quality. *Journal of Marketing, 60,* 31–46.
16. Gale, B. (1992). Monitoring customer satisfaction and market-perceived quality. *American Marketing Association Worth Repeating Series*, No. 922CSO 1. Chicago: American Marketing Association.
17. Middleton, V. T. C., & Clarke, J. (2001). *Marketing in travel and tourism.* Oxford: Butterworth-Heinemann, 213.

CHAPTER

Consumer Behaviour

3

BACKPACKERS WITH GOLD CARDS

Few modern social developments are more significant and less appreciated than the rise of backpacker travel. The tens of thousands of young Australians, Germans, Britons, Americans, and others who wander the globe, flitting from Goa to Costa Rica, from Thailand to Tasmania, are building what may be the only example of a truly global community. Nobody has an accurate way of guessing the size of the backpacker market, but the growth of the Lonely Planet brand offers an approximation. The first Lonely Planet guidebook was stapled together on an Australian kitchen table in the early 1970s; 30 years later, the company publishes more than 600 titles.

The backpacking market is a tourism market that doesn't get a lot of attention or coverage in Canada, and one that is not well understood by the industry. However, it appears that young Canadians are catching up to their counterparts from other cultures, such as the British, for whom a "gap year" spent travelling abroad is a rite of passage. Travel agents have noticed a huge increase in new customers willing to ditch the matching luggage and take on the challenges of living out of a backpack. In Canada, the average visiting backpacker spends $3366 during the course of a trip, and travellers who are 33 years old and younger generate about one third of overnight stays in Canadian accommodation properties.

Here are some important facts about typical international backpackers:

- They tend to be between the ages of 18 and 35, with a major subsegment in the 18 to 25 range.
- Backpackers use inexpensive, communally oriented accommodations like hostels, which offer shared rooms and guest facilities.
- Although backpackers tend to represent a lower "daily spend" than other tourism segments, their length of stay is usually much greater, making their overall financial impact greater.
- These travellers also provide regional benefits by visiting more of the country than a standard tourist, tending to spend their travel dollars in the country on independent itineraries, injecting money into local economies.

But there is evidence that the traditional backpacker profile is changing. John Hughes, a British expatriate who runs a Web site for backpackers in Asia, says that young people taking breaks in schooling, and those seeking temporary employment and learning opportunities abroad have largely replaced the travellers of old who wandered footloose and fancy-free as far and long as their money would take them. And there are some older ones who come back drawn by fond memories of their younger backpacking days. "It seems to me that a lot of backpackers have plastic in their back pockets whereas they didn't before," says Hughes. "They're better organized and getting more packaged." Backpackers are also not necessarily western these days.

Backpacker destinations are attracting growing numbers of Koreans, Taiwanese, and Hong Kong citizens, and a vast potential market is seen in China and India.

Backpackers are also getting older. Hostel owners say they are seeing a marked increase in the number of North Americans, Australians, and Europeans in their thirties and forties backpacking through Asia and Africa. As people marry later, make more money earlier, and switch careers more often, many are tapping into savings to have an extended adventure before going back to the grind. Moreover, companies that value their employees are bowing to their workers' wanderlust by granting travel sabbaticals. Those travel patterns are being catered to by on-the-cheap guidebooks that increasingly are giving more expensive options to the more grown-up market.

These moves have brought new tensions to the adventure of the backpacker trail. Younger, more traditional backpackers say the sense of community they cherish in hostels is being lost as the richer backpackers use the accommodations only to sleep. "These new backpackers can take away from the communal aspect of what these backpacker hostels started out as," complains Lauren Robers, manager of Whale House Backpackers in Hout Bay, near Cape Town. Traditional backpackers, she says, use hostels as one-stop social outlets—inexpensive places to sleep and meet travellers from around the world to share adventures and travelling tips with. But older backpackers often rent cars and flash credit cards to ditch the hostel and fellow tourists for (in this case) camel safaris or white-linen wine-tasting evenings in Cape Town's excellent wine regions. "The double rooms people are building defeat the object of the backpackers: The dorm rooms get people talking to each other," she said. "It's sort of a fight in the industry now. You can lose the whole concept of the hostel."

Sources: Backpackers lift an economy. (2002, September 25). *The Vancouver Sun*, p. A15; Cousineau, A. (2002, November 2). Backpackers really do have more fun. *Calgary Herald*, p. TS04; Daley, B. (1999, September 29). Slumming it, with a gold card. *National Post*, p. B9; Gray, D. (2002, July 27). The new backpacker: Less scruffy and stinky, more moneyed and packaged. *Times–Colonist*, Victoria, B.C., p. D2.

Objectives

On completion of this chapter, the readers should understand

- the importance of consumer behaviour within tourism marketing;

- the major factors influencing consumer behaviour;

- some of the typologies of tourist roles;

- the underlying principles of organizational buying behaviour; and

- some of the trends in consumer behaviour influencing tourism marketing today.

Chapter Overview

The opening vignette is an excellent example of changing behavioural patterns among tourists—in this case, the backpacker. This chapter looks at behavioural trends in tourism, but begins by reviewing tourism motivational studies, which examine why people travel and—to a lesser extent—why they choose not to. Such studies seek to explain psychological and sociopsychological factors such as attitudes, beliefs, perceptions, culture, and lifestyles, and their effect on purchasing behaviour. These variables that make up internal motivation have been analyzed with a view to developing typologies of tourists who carry out tourist roles. The second part of the chapter focuses on such typologies of tourists. The link between internal and external driving forces provides an insight into how visitors learn about, and—more importantly—perceive, tourism offerings in the marketplace. The third section in the chapter, therefore, examines the external factors that influence consumer behaviour. The fourth section looks at the stages of the buying process, and this is followed by a section devoted to organizational buying behaviour, as tourism marketers need to understand both the decision-making criteria used and the process of decision making that groups and organizations go through in buying tourism services. The final section looks in-depth at some of the trends in consumer behaviour affecting tourism marketing today.

CONSUMER BEHAVIOUR AND TOURISM MARKETING

consumer behaviour analysis

the study of why people buy the products they do and how they make decisions

The cornerstone of marketing theory is the satisfaction of the consumer. Therefore, the marketer needs to understand three related aspects of **consumer behaviour analysis**: consumer motivations, consumer typologies, and the consumer purchasing process. Most tourism and hospitality organizations have an imperfect picture of their customer, and few monitor patterns of consumer behaviour at a level of detail necessary to remain competitive. Many organizations consider that they are sufficiently close to their visitors and therefore do not commit resources to more formal consumer studies. Others are constrained by limited marketing budgets and by the fact that researching consumer motivation and the buying process can be a time-consuming and difficult process. In fact, most organizations rely almost entirely on the scanning of secondary consumer data, combined with management observation and judgment. However, in a rapidly changing environment, conclusions drawn from secondary data can be out of date in no time. Consumer patterns recorded in 2000, for example, will most likely have changed by the year 2005, but many companies might still be using this type of information as a benchmark.

FACTORS INFLUENCING CONSUMER BEHAVIOUR

Figure 3.1 shows the various factors that influence a consumer's behaviour. Motivation is often seen as a major determinant of consumer behaviour, but cultural, personal, and social influences will also have an important effect on consumer purchases. Each of the influences in Figure 3.1 will be discussed here in turn.

Motivations

motivations

inner drives that people have that cause them to take action to satisfy their needs

needs

the gaps between what customers have and what they would like to have, seen as the force that arouses motivated behaviour

Motivations are inner drives that cause people to take action to satisfy their needs. The case for an improved understanding of consumer motivation is convincing. It is one of the most effective ways of gaining competitive differential advantage, as discussed in Chapter 2 (p. 54–55). Understanding the key triggers that lead to the purchase of a tourism or hospitality product, such as a visit to an attraction or a hotel booking, is recognized as one of the main factors in the success of competitive organizations. Many industry critics consequently see motivation as a major determinant of the tourist's behaviour. Central to most content theories of motivation is the concept of need. **Needs** are seen as the force that arouses motivated behaviour, and it is assumed that, to understand human motivation, it is necessary to discover what needs people have and how they can be fulfilled. Maslow, in 1943, was the first to attempt to do this with his needs hierarchy theory, now the best-known of all motivation theories (see Figure 3.2 on page 72).

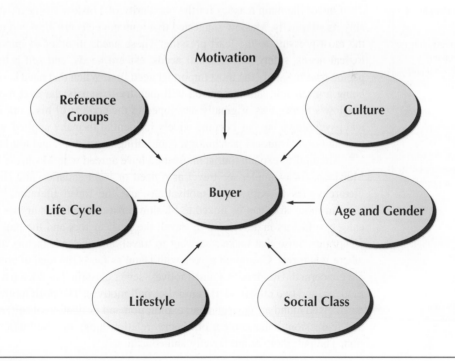

Figure 3.1   Factors Influencing Consumer Behaviour

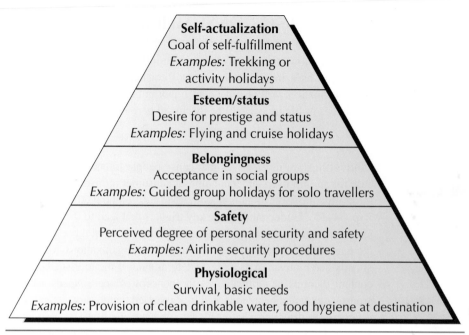

Figure 3.2   Maslow's Hierarchy of Needs

Source: Maslow, A. H. (1943). A theory of human motivation. *Psychological Review, 50*, 370–396.

Maslow's hierarchy of needs

Maslow's theory that human needs are arranged in a hierarchy, from the most pressing to the least pressing; these needs in order of importance are physiological needs, safety needs, social needs, esteem needs, and self-actualization needs

One of the main reasons for the popularity of Maslow's hierarchy of needs is probably its simplicity. Maslow suggested that human needs are arranged in a hierarchy, from the most pressing to the least pressing. These needs in order of importance are physiological needs, safety needs, social needs, esteem needs, and self-actualization needs. A person tries to satisfy the most important need first. When that need is satisfied, it will stop being a motivator, and the person will then try to satisfy the next most important need. Maslow's theory was originally developed in the context of his work in the field of clinical psychology, but has become widely influential in many applied areas such as industrial and organizational psychology, counselling, marketing, and tourism.

Attempts to explain tourist motivation have agreed with Maslow's hierarchy. Mill and Morrison, for example, see travel as a need or want satisfier, and show how Maslow's hierarchy ties in with travel motivations and the travel literature.[1] Similarly, Dann's tourism motivators can be linked to Maslow's list of needs. He argues that there are basically two factors in a decision to travel: the push factors and the pull factors.[2] The push factors are those that make you want to travel, and the pull factors are those that affect where you travel. Crompton agrees with Dann as far as the idea of push and pull motives are concerned. He identifies nine motives, seven classified as sociopsychological or push motives, and two classified as cultural or pull motives. The push motives are escape from a perceived mundane environment; exploration and evaluation of self; relaxation, prestige, and regression; enhancement of kinship relationships; and facilitation of social interaction. The pull motives are novelty and education.[3]

Krippendorf, in an enlightening book on tourism, sees a thread running through all these theories of tourism motivation. First, travel is motivated by "going away from" rather than "going toward" something; second, travellers' motives and behaviour are markedly self-oriented. The author classifies these theories into eight explanations of travel: recuperation and regeneration, compensation and social integration, escape, communication, freedom and self-determination, self-realization, happiness, and broadening the mind.[4]

Other factors influencing motivation and purchase include learning, beliefs and attitudes, and perception. **Learning** refers to the way in which visitors receive and interpret a variety of stimuli. People gain experience through taking holidays, by listening to others, and through a variety of other sources. From these experiences a consumer will develop a mental inventory of expectations about places—a catalogue of good and bad holiday experiences. These form the basis of learned criteria that will be recalled when selecting future holidays and destinations. **Beliefs** refer to the thoughts that people have about most aspects of their life. As far as tourism is concerned, consumers will have beliefs about companies, products, and services, including tourism offerings and destinations. Such thoughts can be positive, such as trust or confidence in a certain hotel or tour guide, or negative, such as a feeling about lack of security on airlines, or fear of injury on the ski slopes. **Attitudes** are more difficult to change, as they are ingrained feelings about various factors of an experience. For many Americans, for example, it may be difficult to accept, after the events of September 11, 2001, that flying by plane is a safe method of travelling.

Finally, **perception** is an overall mind-picture of the world, shaped by information that people filter and then retrieve. Thus, perception is inextricably bound to the concepts of bias and distortion. People choose to interpret different stimuli in different ways, ignoring some factors while enhancing others. This is known as selective perception. People often perceive tourism offerings in a way that compliments their self-image. In this way tourism products are viewed as bundles of benefits that are personal to the consumer. It is, however, through the technical factors (which are called "significative stimuli") that the marketer can seek to change perceptions.

Marketers sometimes use a technique known as **perceptual mapping** to identify the relationship between the level of perceived importance of certain aspects of a product on the part of the tourist and the actual performance on the part of the supplier. Figure 3.3, from a 2001 research report by the Canadian Tourism Commission, shows German market perceptions of price versus value for seven long-haul destinations (see page 74). An average value score was calculated for each destination, based on respondents' perceptual ratings of all value-related attributes of the destination, weighted by their overall importance to this market. An average price score was calculated in the same way, based on price perceptions. The graph in Figure 3.3 shows that Canada rates extremely well on perceived value, placing ahead of all destinations other than Australia/New Zealand. In terms of price, Canada is in the middle, being bested by the Caribbean, Asia, and Australia/New Zealand.

Consumer attitudes are a consumer's enduring favourable or unfavourable cognitive evaluations, emotional feelings, and action tendencies toward some object or idea. As these attitudes and perceptions evolve, travel industry organizations must try to stay ahead without venturing too far off course. Some changes are evident years in advance—for example, few failed to anticipate the impact the aging baby boomers would have on the

learning

the way in which visitors receive and interpret a variety of stimuli

beliefs

the thoughts that people have about most aspects of their life

attitudes

ingrained feelings about various factors of an experience

perception

an overall mind-picture of the world, shaped by information that people filter and then retrieve

perceptual mapping

technique used to identify the relationship between the level of perceived importance of certain aspects of a product on the part of the tourist and the actual performance on the part of the supplier

consumer attitudes

a consumer's enduring favourable or unfavourable cognitive evaluations, emotional feelings, and action tendencies toward some object or idea

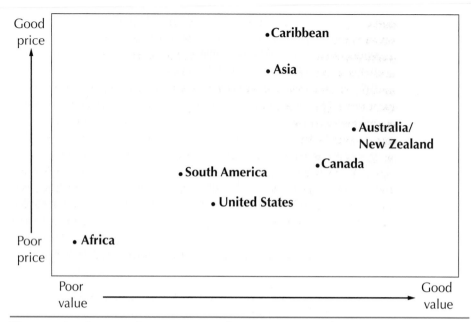

Figure 3.3 German Consumers' Market Perceptions of Price versus Value for Different Long-Haul Destinations

Source: Canadian Tourism Commission. (2002). *Germany consumer research: Research report 2002–2005.* Retrieved September 17, 2003, from http://www.canadatourism.com/en/ctc/ctx-news/search/newsbydateform.cfm.

industry. Others changes, however, are unforeseeable. After September 11, 2001, many in the hospitality industry had to quickly adapt strategies to suit customers whose perceptions and needs changed literally overnight. Destinations began to focus on the geographic demographic of the driver market. Restaurants, too, had to adapt to changing needs. Ed Michalski, president of Management Insight, a hospitality consulting firm, says that "For some, comfort food had a new appeal, while for others, suddenly it seemed the time to try something new and be more adventurous."[5] Michalski also says that people are increasingly demanding high-quality ingredients, service, and presentation, whether they are eating pork chops or prime rib. "There's so much access to information about fine foods, with the popularity of food magazines, the food channel and cooking shows on television, that people are much more knowledgeable than they used to be, and restaurants have to upgrade their products and services."

Culture

culture

the norms, beliefs, and rituals that are unique to each person

Culture can be defined as the norms, beliefs, and rituals that are unique to each person. These different factors influence how we live, communicate, and think about certain things; culture can also often dictate how a person will act in a certain situation. In terms of self-image and the satisfaction of underlying tensions, most people seek to satisfy their desires in a way that fits into societal norms. For example, it is acceptable to be a green consumer in tourism, but sex tourism is viewed disparagingly. Awareness of cultural shifts

MARKETING IN ACTION

GLOBAL STUDY FINDS TRAVELLERS' NEEDS NOT BEING MET BY THE TRAVEL INDUSTRY

In 2002, a team of anthropologists in Tokyo, London, Israel, New York, Los Angeles, Chicago, Orlando, and Las Vegas gathered data from a global sample of travellers and identified basic needs that are not being met by the travel industry. These findings were used to locate and understand points within the travel experience where industries such as hotels, rental car companies, attractions, and cruises can better meet the needs of their customers.

The report, published by Carlton Donofrio Partners Inc., views "travel" as a brand. The collaborative nature of the travel industry makes it unique in that consumers come into contact with numerous products, services, and people each time they travel. The study examines the sum of all these interactions, which is one "travel" brand experience.

More specifically, the researchers found that consumers see travel as a process; they plan their trip, travel via some mode (air, train, ship, car), stay at their destination for a time,

then pass back through the same mode to get home. They found that if one part of the process is in distress, the whole process suffers. The study concludes that this travel process is powered by three variables—the three needs that travellers seek to fulfill. The most basic is that of *control* over their travel experience. People also demand a consistent level of *service* throughout the whole process. And ultimately, people want an experience that brings them the *joy* of travel. The needs of control, service, and joy must be satisfied throughout the planning, mode, and destination stages.

Figure 3.4 illustrates the differences between the ideal travel brand experience and that of today. The ideal model begins with a high level of control during the planning stage. Travellers, especially leisure travellers, slowly relinquish control as they move through their travel brand process. By the time they reach the destination, they want to turn a good deal of control over to someone else,

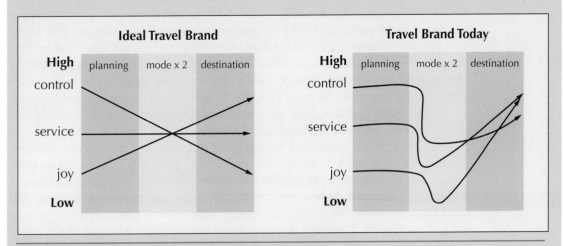

Figure 3.4 The Ideal Travel Brand and the Travel Brand Today

MARKETING IN ACTION *continued*

whether it's to the leisure resort or the business lodging chain. They want things taken care of *for* them, not *by* them. Ideally, the service level remains consistent through every step of the travel brand experience. Travellers expect at least a satisfactory level of service at each stage of their trip. The joy level rises from planning to a peak at the destination part of the travel experience. In today's experience, however, these fundamental travel needs are not being satisfied. The major source of this distress is the mode, or means of transportation, and people cannot easily plan their trip or truly enjoy their destination because of that disruption. Thus, needs are met minimally in the mode and this in turn lowers the level of satisfaction throughout the whole process.

The Carlton Donofrio study suggests that the travel industry re-focus on needs—on satisfying control, service, and joy—to balance today's travel brand experience. More specifically, the research group offers some strategies and tactics that will satisfy these customer needs. It suggests that the industry answer three strategic questions in order to balance today's travel experience:

1. How can you spread your influence across the entire travel process (from planning to mode to destination to home)?
2. How do you currently satisfy the three basic customer travel needs: control, service, and joy?
3. How can you improve on that for tomorrow?

In sum, the study found that travel is no longer a fluid process, but is now broken up by anxieties that leave many consumers re-evaluating their reasons for travel. Companies who, by the nature of their business, are able to touch a traveller only at one point in his or her experience should look to expand their influence to span many segments of the travel experience. By doing so, they will be recognized for increasing the level of customer service in unique ways that go beyond traditional measures and outside their usual boundaries.

Source: Carlton Donofrio Partners Inc. (2002, May 13). Global study on travel examines consumer behaviours. Retrieved May 13, 2002, from http://carltondonofrio.com/study.cfm.

is equally important. For example, smokers are increasingly being prohibited from smoking in social places, especially on transport carriers and in restaurants. One of the most accepted theories in cross-cultural and marketing research was developed by Gert Hofstede.[6,7] He defined culture as "the collective mental programming of the people in an environment," and stated that "culture is not a characteristic of individuals; it encompasses a number of people who were conditioned by the same education and life experience."

Other aspects of culture that are appropriate to motivational studies include languages, societal practices, institutions, and subcultures. The transmission of culture is primarily through the spoken and written word, but also through symbolic gestures, including the ways in which people are expected to be greeted by others. Cultural practices include how we divide the day and our attitudes toward opening hours for shops or restaurants. Institutions, such as the church, the media, and educational systems, will affect cultural patterns. The church, for example, seeks to retain a special day for worship and hence is reluctant to sanction secularization of this day, often in opposition to the promoters of tourism. Finally, most societies comprise a number of subcultures that exhibit variations of behaviour as a result of ethnicity or regional differentiation.

Age and Gender

As mentioned in Chapter 2 (p. 43), a traditional way of segmenting markets has been by age. For example, a recent survey of travellers over 50 found that seniors are seeking out adventure and hands-on experiences.[8] According to the survey, the older generation are looking for the following on a trip: experience and learning about new cultures first-hand, especially meeting the locals (43 percent); expert tour guides who can share their culture (17 percent); plenty of time to explore each travel site (15 percent); worry-free experiences (8 percent); and meeting and socializing with fellow travellers (8 percent).

The senior market today is both lucrative and unique because it is less tied to seasonal travel, involves longer trips, and is not wedded to midweek or weekend travel, so it can boost occupancy rates for business and leisure travel opportunities. For the senior market, too, perceived value is much more important than price.[9] After people retire, they may stay loyal to brand names they know best, but the price points will have to be suitable to a retirement income as well.[10] Disney's recent push to attract visitors in their fifties and sixties to its theme parks is a good indicator that the baby boomer bandwagon is picking up momentum as the majority of the population in North America starts sliding down the backside of middle age. Some believe that this will result in a decline in the number of family restaurants and quick-food service, as these were products demanded by the baby boomers, who are now aging.

In some societies gender can influence consumer behaviour, in terms of societal expectations of the roles men and women should play. Gender segmentation has long been used in marketing clothing, hairdressing, cosmetics, and magazines. But more recently it has been applied to tourism and hospitality products and services. For example, the number of women travelling for work purposes has been growing steadily for two decades, and vocal women travellers have influenced the introduction of better-lit parking garages, higher-quality soaps and lotions in hotel bathrooms, and improved room-service fare. Travel industry experts say that women travellers are more demanding and discerning than their male counterparts. Their main concerns are safety and security, followed by comfort and convenience.

SNAPSHOT

LONGING FOR THE WAY WE WERE

There was once a place where neighbours greeted neighbours in the quiet of summer twilight. Where children chased fireflies. And porch swings provided easy refuge from the cares of the day. The movie house showed cartoons on Saturday. The grocery stores delivered. There is a place that takes you back to that time of innocence. A place of caramel apples and cotton candy, secret forests and hopscotch on the street. That place is here again.

This is how Disney sold the idea behind its model Florida town, Celebration. Model towns such as Celebration and attractions like

SNAPSHOT *continued*

Pier 21 in Canada (see *Snapshot* in Chapter 1, p. 27–28) are prime examples of utopian nostalgia—places where everything is freshly minted to look old. From films to music, from cars to architecture, we are using new technology to return us to the past, to deliver better versions of old experiences. According to author Charles Leadbeater, Internet-linked, digital-television-watching, brand conscious, globally connected societies such as Canada are in the middle of a nostalgia boom. The more rapidly we are propelled into an uncertain future, the more we yearn for the imagined security of the past. "Globalization promotes a yearning for local roots and identities. Our immersion in the digital and virtual world creates a demand for tactile and tangible skills at home: cooking, gardening, and decorating. The growth of individualism makes us yearn for a time when we imagined that we lived in real communities, with a sense of shared memory and moral commitment," says Leadbeater.

Not only have we become more interested in history, but the scale, richness, and diversity of the history we are interested in has also expanded enormously in the past 30 years. History used to be about stately homes, battles, and kings and queens. Now it can be about everything from pencils to maple syrup,

from toys to matches, from kitchens to bricks. The participative culture of nostalgia has been driven by the rise of do-it-yourself history, often as a direct response to social dislocation. Compiling family history began as a mass activity in the 1970s, precisely at a time when social mobility was felt to be rising markedly. The Internet has also opened up a huge new arena for populist nostalgia. The Web site Friends Reunited, which has more than four million members who are searching for friends from their younger days, is a vast expression of participatory nostalgia.

The extension of the healthy lifespan, by about two years per decade since 1945, has allowed an entirely new demographic to emerge: the "young old," who are over 50 but want to behave as if they are still 30. This expanding and affluent group has no intention of fading away, and it is one of main markets for nostalgia products. The nostalgia boom perhaps explains why, in the 21st century, societies that make their living mainly from services, finance, media, and creative industries are so obsessed by the fate of old industries like farming and railways, which exert a powerful nostalgic pull on people's emotions.

Source: Leadbeater, C. (2002, July 6–7). Longing for the way we were. *Financial Times Weekend*, p. IV.

Social Class

social class

the position one occupies within society, determined by such factors as income, wealth, education, occupation, family prestige, value of home, and neighbourhood

Social class is still considered to be one of the most important external factors influencing consumer behaviour. Social class is the position one occupies within society, and it is determined by such factors as income, wealth, education, occupation, family prestige, value of home, and neighbourhood. As a rule, the higher the level of disposable income people have, the more likely they are to travel, and premium income earners tend to be those people who have studied at a higher educational level. Table 3.1 shows wealth and income by age group in Canada. It is clear that the 35 to 54 age group—today's baby boomers—have the largest income, whereas the 55 to 64 age group has the biggest family net worth. The advertising industry in Canada has been criticized for an emphasis on youth to the exclusion of wealthy, somewhat older consumers.[11] Established customers should be regarded as the most valuable asset a company has. There is no need to try to convince them to change; they already

Table 3.1

Wealth and Income by Age Group in Canada

AGE	% OF TOTAL POPULATION (AS OF JULY 2001)	AVERAGE FAMILY INCOME, 1998 (000s)	AVERAGE FAMILY NET WORTH, 1999 (000s)
<24	32.3	$26	$40.6
25–34	14.1	$40.5	$88.3
35–44	17.1	$45.9	$194.6
45–54	14.5	$53.2	$338.7
55–64	9.4	$46.4	$455.1
65+	12.7	$32.0	$332.0

Source: Statistics Canada. (2003). *Wealth and income by age group in Canada.* Retrieved February 17, 2003, from http://www.statcan.ca.

believe in the company and its products. The primary aim of marketing to these customers should be to solidify and expand the relationship. The message should reassure them of the wisdom of their choice and encourage them to expand that relationship with related products. Better still, it should inspire them to make this relationship a family tradition. The return a company receives for dollars spent on such marketing is enormous.

Lifestyle

lifestyle analysis

examines at the way people allocate time, energy, and money

psychographic analysis

attempts to measure people's activities, interests, and opinions

VALS™

a typology framework that divides the population into eight lifestyle groups, defined according to factors such as self-image, aspirations, values, and products used.

Marketers are increasingly segmenting their markets by consumer lifestyles. **Lifestyle analysis** examines the way people allocate time, energy, and money. Lifestyle analysis tends to exclude demographic traits, so researchers in marketing have combined demographic and psychological variables into a concept called "psychographics." **Psychographic analysis** attempts to measure people's activities, interests, and opinions. By profiling the way groups of people live, it is possible to predict their travel motivations and purchases. One of the best-known categorizations in this area is the **VALS™** typology framework, which divides the population into eight lifestyle groups, defined according to factors such as self-image, aspirations, values, and products used. The original VALS conceptual model categorized people according to their values and then identified various consumer behaviours that go with these values. However, SRI International, a leading consultant in the area of consumer research, discovered that the relationship between values and purchase was not very strong, so they developed the current VALS system, which groups values and other psychological traits.

As can be seen in Figure 3.5 on page 80, distinguishes between seven psychographic groups: thinkers, achievers, experiencers, believers, strivers, makers, and survivors. Members of each group hold different values and maintain different lifestyles. The position of a person in the VALS framework depends on the person's primary motivations (ideas, achievement, or self-expression) include income, education, self-confidence, health, eagerness to buy, and energy level.

Life Cycle

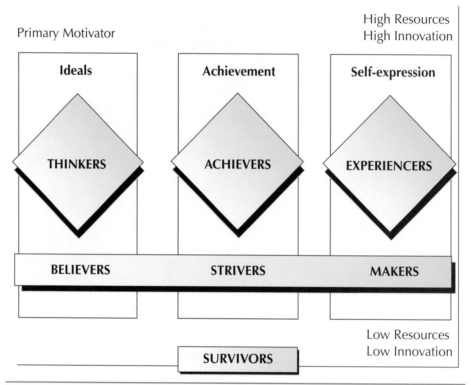

Figure 3.5   The VALS™ Typology Framework

Source: SRI Consulting Business Intelligence.

family life cycle

the stages through which families might pass as they mature

life cycle model

suggests that travel patterns and destinations vary as people move through their life cycle

The concept of the **family life cycle**—the stages through which families might pass as they mature—is based on the premise that when people live together, their way of life changes. Single people are likely to behave differently than couples, and if couples subsequently have children, their lifestyle changes more radically, as does their level of financial and other commitments. Many authors have applied the **life cycle model** to tourism, suggesting that travel patterns and destinations vary as people move through their life cycle.[12,13] The model works well when investigating the traditional nuclear family composed of two parents and one or more children. It does not, however, purport to represent the increasing proportion of households that do not fall into this pattern, such as single-parent families, extended family networks, and those who remain single throughout their life.

Reference Groups

reference groups

groups that have a direct (face-to-face) or indirect influence on a person's attitude or behaviour

Learning also takes place through sharing values and expectations with others in a variety of social **reference groups**, including the family, college, workplace, or church. This brings exposure to a normative set of values, i.e., those that set a tone as to how we should behave morally in society. For example, experienced travellers who have been exposed to other cultures and to people who are less fortunate than they are influencing a new trend of volunteer tourism. The World Tourism Organization (WTO) has noticed that there is "an increasing tendency among contemporary travel consumers to view travel as a means for enhancing the quality of their own lives by building on a philosophy of doing well while doing something good for society."[14] The WTO and other tourism organizations that monitor trends in the travel industry say it is precisely the growing number of well-heeled, well-educated older travellers—people who are indeed concerned with "doing something good for society"—who have been driving the demand for such developing niche markets as educational tourism, ecotours, agritourism, and cultural tourism. Travellers can take a "volunteer vacation" and give their time and expertise to help in projects in developing countries. These trips aren't free, but they're often cheaper than conventional tours.

TYPOLOGIES OF TOURISTS

allocentrics

travellers who prefer exotic destinations, unstructured vacations rather than packaged tours, and more involvement with local cultures

psychocentrics

travellers who prefer familiar destinations, packaged tours, and "touristy" areas

The discussion so far has been about the variables that influence tourist behaviour. But many tourism researchers have tried to explain tourist behaviour by developing typologies of tourists who carry out various tourism roles. The tourist motivation model proposed by Stanley Plog is one of the most widely cited typologies of tourists.[15] According to Plog, travellers may be classified along two dimensions: allocentrism/psychocentrism and energy. Travellers who are more **allocentric** are thought to prefer exotic destinations, unstructured vacations rather than packaged tours, and more involvement with local cultures. **Psychocentrics**, on the other hand, are thought to prefer familiar destinations, packaged tours, and "touristy" areas. Later, Plog added the concept of energy, which describes the level of activity desired by the tourist: high-energy travellers prefer high levels of activity, while low-energy travellers prefer less activity.

Plog found that the majority of the population was neither allocentric nor psychocentric, but "midcentric"—somewhere in the middle (see Figure 3.6 on page 82). It has been argued, however, that Plog's theory is difficult to apply, as tourists will travel with different motivations on different occasions.[16] There are many holidaymakers who will take a winter skiing break in an allocentric destination, but will then take their main holiday in a psychocentric destination.

Smith has also criticized Plog's model.[17] Using data from seven nations, he tested the model's basic hypothesis as well as its applicability to other countries. He concluded that his test of the allocentric/psychocentric model failed to support the hypothesized association between personality types and destination preferences. He even criticized tourism researchers for relying on untested hypotheses for explanations about how the tourist system works.

In addition to Plog, other tourism researchers have tried to explain tourist recreational behaviour by developing typologies of tourist roles. Most are based on empirical data obtained from questionnaires and/or personal interviews. Cohen's typology—one of the first—proposed four classifications of tourists: (1) the organized mass tourist, highly dependent on the "environmental bubble," purchasing all-inclusive tours or package holidays; (2) the individual mass tourist, who is more autonomous and free than those in the previous group; (3) the explorer, who seeks new areas but would sometimes opt to step back into comfortable accommodation, etc.; and (4) the drifter, who avoids any kind of "tourist establishment." Cohen also introduced a differentiation between the "institutionalized" and "noninstitutionalized" forms of tourism. The first two tourist roles can be regarded as institutionalized types, as they deal with the institutionalized tourist system. The latter two roles are categorized as noninstitutionalized types, since they do not depend on services offered by the tourist establishment.[18]

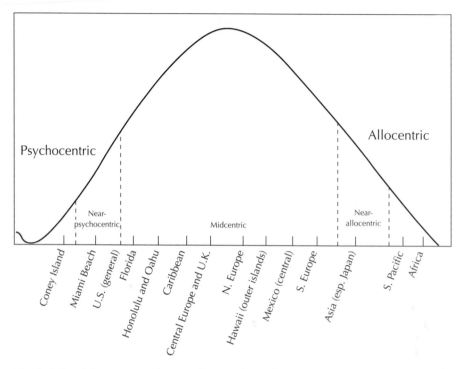

Psychocentric

Allocentric

Near-
psychocentric

Midcentric

Near-
allocentric

Coney Island

Miami Beach

U.S. (general)

Florida

Honolulu and Oahu

Caribbean

Central Europe and U.K.

N. Europe

Hawaii (outer islands)

Mexico (central)

S. Europe

Asia (esp. Japan)

S. Pacific

Africa

The height of the curve indicates the number of travellers in each category.

Figure 3.6   Plog's Classification of Tourists

Source: Plog, S.C. (1974). Why destination areas rise and fall in popularity. *Cornell Hotel and Restaurant Quarterly*, 14(4), 58.

Following Cohen, other researchers have developed different typologies of tourist roles, and although the array of typologies present different numbers of types of tourist (from four to seven), the same characteristics appear in each of the types described: looking for adventure; discovering new cultures versus following accustomed daily habits; attaching importance to nature and authenticity; and seeking relaxation, sun, sand, and sea.

PROFILE

TYPOLOGIES OF ALBERTA'S DOMESTIC TOURISTS

In 2001, Travel Alberta undertook a consumer behaviour study and used cluster analysis to segment domestic tourists based on their deci-sion-making behaviour. Results indicated that there were five distinct types—or markets—among domestic tourists in Alberta. (See

PROFILE *continued*

Chapters 4 and 8 for more on this study.) These five types/markets are discussed below.

1. The Young Urban Outdoor Market

The youngest of all clusters (average age 38 years), the Young Urban Outdoor market is made up equally of males and females, and over 20 percent are single. An important niche within the cluster is the young student population that has time and dollar constraints. School schedules, visits to family and friends, and budgets are all factors that influence their decision to take a trip. These sporty life-lovers are very active outdoor enthusiasts. Whether it is recreation, winter sports, summer sports, or leisure activities, the members of the Young Urban Outdoor market do it outside. Word of mouth is not only a key source of travel information, but it is also the most effective way to communicate with this cluster. Of all clusters, this market segment shows the highest use of the Internet for getting travel information.

2. The Indoor Leisure Traveller Market

The second youngest of all clusters (average age 41 years), the Indoor Leisure Traveller market is very much a female cluster; almost 70 percent are female. Married, with children and lower household incomes, people in this cluster live more in the nonurban regions of Alberta's North, Heartland, and South. Budget and visiting family and friends are key factors affecting their decision to travel. The Indoor Leisure Traveller market is very much leisure-oriented. Indoor museums and resorts are key destinations these travellers like to visit when on an overnight trip in Alberta. Willing to travel further in distance and time than other clusters, the Indoor Leisure Traveller likes shopping, fine hotels, horseback riding, sightseeing, and campfires. Word of mouth, television, and magazines are key sources of travel information for the Indoor Leisure Traveller market.

3. The Children First Market

The Children First market is the only cluster whose members say that children's sports and competition schedules have a high influence on them taking trips in Alberta. Either male or female, with an average age of 43 years, they married and have more children than those in any other cluster. Spread around all tourism regions, the Children First market has the highest income of all clusters. Consequently, budget is not a factor that influences travel decisions, and these travellers are not apt to use discount coupons. While travel activities range across the outdoor spectrum, activities for the Children First market tend to revolve around children and family. Word of mouth and television are the most effective ways to convey information about accommodations, prices, and leisure activities to the Children First market.

4. The Fair Weather Friends Market

The second oldest cluster (average age 44 years), the Fair Weather Friends market is influenced to travel only by family or friends and weather conditions. With a low marriage rate, few children, and slightly more males in the cluster, visiting family and friends is a key factor in making a travel decision. This market has moderate level incomes and few budget concerns, so members of this cluster have the time and resources to travel. While people in this cluster do participate in a full range of activities when on a trip, their incident rate of activities is lower compared to those in the previous clusters. The best informed of all clusters, the Fair Weather Friends know a lot about the province and places to visit. Word of mouth, newspapers, Internet, and tourist information centres are key sources of travel information for this cluster; however, word of mouth and television are considered the most effective communication methods.

PROFILE *continued*

5. The Older Cost-Conscious Traveller Market

The oldest cluster (average age 45 years), the Older Cost-Conscious Traveller market is influenced by cost/value for money spent and the sense of a safe and secure environment. Members of this slightly female-oriented cluster tend to be married, but this cluster also has a high divorced, widowed, and/or single contingent. Its members' middle to lower incomes are reflected in their budget and travel expense concerns, along with a high coupon use. The Older Cost-Conscious Traveller market is outdoors-oriented and is likely to take part in summer sports and leisure activities when travelling in Alberta.

With more information and awareness of travel opportunities, this market would take more trips. Word of mouth, newspapers, AMA, Tourist Information, and television are the most effective means for getting travel information to this cluster group.

Marketing in Action in Chapter 8 shows how this behavioural research was used to develop a successful promotional campaign called the "Travel Alberta Made to Order" campaign.

Source: Hudson, S., & Ritchie, J. R. B. (2002). Understanding the domestic market using cluster analysis: A case study of the marketing efforts of Travel Alberta. *Journal of Vacation Marketing, 8*(3), 263–276.

THE BUYING PROCESS

Before discussing the buying process, it is important to recognize that various buying situations will have an influence on this process. First of all, consumers are likely to display various levels of commitment, depending on the nature of the purchase. It has been suggested that there are three such levels:[19]

1. *Extended problem solving*. In this situation, such as the decision to take a long-haul holiday, the consumer is likely to be have deep level of commitment, to make a detailed search for information, and to make an extensive comparison of the alternatives.
2. *Limited problem solving*. In this situation, the consumer will have some degree of knowledge or experience already, but many factors will be taken for granted and the information search will be far more limited. A second holiday at a favourite skiing destination may be purchased in this way.
3. *Habitual problem solving*. This is a repeat purchase of a tried and tested short break or day excursion, which requires little or no evaluation. The purchase is made primarily on the basis of a previous satisfactory experience and a good understanding of the destination or brand name of the tourism or hospitality offering.

Role adoption will also influence the buying process, and it is proposed that there are five roles:[20]

1. *Initiator*: the person who starts the purchasing process and who gathers information;
2. *Influencer*: a person or persons who express preferences in choice or selection of information—this can be a group of friends, relatives, or a partner;

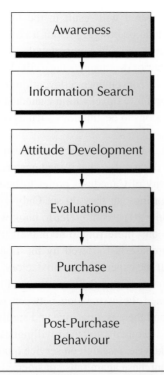

Figure 3.7 The Consumer Buying Process

3. *decider*: the person who has the financial control and possibly the authority within a group of people to make the purchase;
4. *buyer*: the person who actually makes the purchase, visits the travel agent, and obtains the tickets, etc.; and
5. *user*: the person or persons who consume the purchase and actually go on the trip.

The consumer buying process for tourism is often regarded as being similar to that involved in the purchase of other products and services. The assumption is that a consumer moves through a number of stages leading up to a purchase. Figure 3.7 outlines these stages.

The process begins with *awareness*, but according to CanadaTravel.ca, most Canadians are unaware of the broad range of products and services offered in Canadian communities. This Internet company helps solve this problem by providing domestic and global consumers with a complete range of information and booking services for participating Canadian communities and local tourism businesses. CanadaTravel.ca sends regular newsletters, providing a variety of information on festivals, events, and getaways to over 60 000 consumers.

The next stage in the buying process involves the buyer *obtaining more information*, and as suggested previously, there are likely to be various levels of commitment depending on the nature of the purchase. Recent surveys show that the Internet plays a major role when Canadians research and book travel: nearly 8 out of 10 Canadians who are connected to the Internet use it as a source of travel information and planning.[21] This information search will result in the *formation of an attitude*, perhaps reinforcing an existing attitude or bringing about a change on the part of the buyer. At the *evaluation* stage, the buyer will make more detailed comparisons. For example, a consumer may consider a number of destinations and will choose based on choice criteria such as price, recommendation, convenience, convention, etc. A 2002 survey showed that 33 percent of Canadians prefer to travel within Canada's borders, but a close 27 percent are taking more exotic excursions to destinations such as the Caribbean, Mexico, Europe, South America, and Asia.[22]

Subject to time and financial constraints, the consumer will then make the *purchase*. Contrary to the mindset that Canadians are last-minute bookers, the same survey showed that a majority of Canadians prefer to book their vacations months in advance, with 55 percent reporting that they do so. Only 4 percent of Canadians book vacations days in advance, while 20 percent prefer to book weeks in advance. And 15 percent of Canadians are spontaneous, preferring to book their trip on the spur of the moment.

The purchase is followed by the final stage of the buying process, *post-purchase behaviour*. If the experience is satisfactory, the visitor may purchase the same type of holiday in the future. Often the importance of this stage is underestimated, but several studies have examined the association between service quality and more specific behavioural intentions, and there is a positive and significant relationship between customers' perceptions of service quality and their willingness to recommend the company or destination to others.[23] Likewise, research on service quality and retaining customers suggests that willingness to purchase again falls considerably once services are rated below good.[24]

ORGANIZATIONAL BUYER BEHAVIOUR

Decision Making for Organizations

Tourism marketers need to understand both the decision criteria used and the decision-making process undergone by groups and organizations in buying tourism services. The process is likely to be quite different for group buyers, and there can be many individuals or groups involved in making decisions for the conference market. These include the users, influencers, deciders, and buyers. It has been argued that in order to close a sale within a business-to-business market, the supplier has to identify and satisfy all stakeholders in the decision-making unit and treat each accordingly.

A marketer will also need to understand the buying phases for organizations. The conference market, for example, follows a pattern of group decision making, and the "buy phase" has been described as follows: problem recognition, general need description, product specification, supplier search, proposal solution, supplier selection, order routine specification, and performance review.[25] These buy phases sometimes take a long period of time, depending on the size of the conference or the complexity of arrangements, with lead times of two or three years in some instances and longer ones for mega events such as the World Cup soccer tournament.

The process is also affected by the nature of the purchase, as it can be a new purchase, a modified re-buy, or a straight re-buy.[26] A new purchase involves a high degree of risk, as the client is buying a facility or service for the first time. A modified re-buy is less risky, as the client has bought a service offering before, perhaps at another hotel or conference centre within the group, but now seeks to modify the purchase. This might mean a new venue or new specifications for service levels. The straight re-buy is the least risky purchase situation, as it involves, for example, re-ordering a service at the same venue.

Having identified the key decision makers and phases in the purchase process, the marketer must then establish which criteria the decision makers use to differentiate between suppliers. Webster and Wind suggest that four main factors influence the decision-making criteria of organizational buyers: environmental, organizational, interpersonal, and individual.[27] These factors are constantly changing, so it is essential to frequently re-evaluate market trends.

For example, since the terrorist attacks in the United States on September 11, 2001, cost cutting and cost control have become major elements in new corporate travel policies. A survey of businesses one year after the attacks revealed that 40 percent had either cut back or eliminated luxury travel for their employees; 39 percent had redefined nonessential travel; 29 percent were using more economy hotels in place of high-end properties; 26 percent said they were processing more car rentals; and 22 percent indicated they had increased their use of low-cost carriers.[28] The same survey said that company travel was down by as much as 20 percent compared to the same period a year before, and business travel to Canada was expected to be weak in 2002. After September 11, videoconferencing companies reportedly doubled their business; Web conferencing—in which participants can share and manipulate data simultaneously on screen—is also attracting customers.[29]

The events of September 11, 2001, have also had a major impact on the behaviour of business travellers. Immediately after the attacks, some business travellers did not consider the big cities to be safe, and most executives demonstrated a preference for confining travel to national borders or nearby countries.[30] London, like New York and other large urban centres, suffered a decline in business travel. This led to the emergence of destinations with less of a glamour factor. There was a noticeable move away from the traditionally favoured city destinations such as New York, Los Angeles, and Washington, toward

destinations perceived as safer, such as those in Asia and Canada. The U.S. hotel industry was the worst affected by September 11, 2001, as US$1 billion of conference business was cancelled in the immediate aftermath.

The Behaviour of Business Travellers

The behaviour of business travellers is significantly different than that of leisure travellers. In fact, according to experts, executives do not see travel as a perk but rather as another source of stress.[31] Executives feel that they have no proper balance between home life and work life, and that it causes problems in their relationships with partners and children. And it is not just the business traveller who suffers. A recent study found that people whose spouses travel frequently on business suffer more mental health problems than those whose partners remain at home.[32] Short, frequent trips away from home have a worse effect on people than longer, less frequent trips. The study recommended that workers travel no more than 90 days a year and that companies allow employees to decline making too many trips; it also suggested videoconferencing and flexible work arrangements as substitutes for travel. Unfortunately, few businesses pay attention to the damaging effect travel can have on their employees. The paradox is that travel costs the company money, and much business travel has been made redundant by modern communication technologies such as telephone conferencing and videoconferencing.

Airlines spend a lot of time and money trying to understand the needs of their business travellers. As the demographic gets wider for this group (as it has been doing for the last decade), zeroing in on what services and programs would most appeal to this group is becoming more difficult.[33] The group is not necessarily unified in terms of age, dress, or tastes, or in terms of what its members want to do or have in business class. Whether a flight is inbound for business or outbound for home makes a difference in what a customer expects from an airline, and the key for airlines is to offer their customers the ability to work or play. Work-related technology—laptop power plugs and in-air phones—are obligatory for any airline interested in attracting the business traveller. For passengers' downtime, not much has changed: movies, food, and drink remain required staples. The selection in the last category has become much broader, due in part to the fact that 30 to 40 percent of frequent business passengers are women, and women don't always want a beer or a soft drink. One factor that is consistent among all passengers, however, is the need for space, and airlines are always looking for ways to increase personal space for passengers. Air Canada redesigned its international business class service in 2003 to provide customers with more legroom and more seat recline space.[34] Executive First cabins were reconfigured to provide 150 cm standard pitch of legroom, and seats were changed to recline to a 151-degree position. Space is an equally important service consideration on the ground. It is standard to isolate first or business class passengers from those flying economy with special lounges and facilities devoted to their needs. Computer hook-ups, boardrooms, and entertainment centres are now standard requirements. Air Canada's Vancouver lounge even offers its frequent flyers a small 18-hole putting green. The spacious 9 x 18 m arrivals lounge is fitted out in Canadian maple wood and decorated in warm, muted colours. The lounge seats 20 people and has a spa area with six private shower bathrooms, one for the disabled; shower users' clothes can also be left for steaming or pressing for valet staff. Nearly 400 people use the spas each month.[35] The two work areas in the business centre have telephone, fax, copier, printer, and Internet hook-up facilities, and the buffet offers beverages, freshly baked croissants, Danish pastries, and bagels.

TRENDS IN CONSUMER BEHAVIOUR

As mentioned in Chapter 1 (pp. 26–27), many major cultural trends in Canada affect the tourism industry, such as the desire to develop individuality in order to be seen and treated as different from others and the tendency to act and feel younger than one's age. This final section of the chapter focuses on a range of trends or demands in consumer behaviour that are influencing tourism and hospitality marketing today.

Learning and Enrichment

Today's travellers are seeking experiences that provide them with a greater insight, increased understanding, and a personal connection to the people and places they visit. Rather than choose their vacation by the destination, many are first determining the experiences they want, and then choosing the destination where these experiences are located. **Learning and enrichment travel** refers to vacations that provide opportunities for authentic, hands-on, or interactive learning experiences, featuring themes such as adventure, agriculture, anthropology, archaeology, arts, culture, cuisine, education, forestry, gardening, language, maritime culture, mining, nature, science, spirituality, sports, wine, and wildlife—to name only a few!

learning and enrichment travel

refers to vacations that provide opportunities for authentic, hands-on, or interactive learning experiences

Canada is a stage for some of the best learning and enrichment travel experiences in the world. Authentic, hands-on, and interactive themed experiences—including cuisine and wine, gardens, arts and culture, natural phenomena, wildlife viewing, heritage, and history—can be found throughout Canada. An example of an attraction in Canada that is capitalizing on new consumer demand for enrichment and learning is "Dynamic Earth," in Sudbury, Ontario. The $14.35 million interpretive facility opened in 2003 on the former Big Nickel Mine site. The attraction offers an authentic northern experience, providing visitors with the opportunity to experience the unique geology and rich mining heritage of this northern Ontario city. Interactive exhibits, multimedia theatre shows, and a unique site interpretation enable visitors to discover the geology of the Sudbury Basin and the strong connection between the mines and the community over the past 100 years. In addition to the high-tech displays, visitors hear real-life stories, told by real miners, about the difficulties early miners were forced to face and overcome. Through the tales of various other characters, visitors also learn how historical events have shaped the Sudbury community and have brought about some of the activities happening in the region today.

The Learning & Enrichment Travel Alliance, a newly launched national Canadian travel alliance representing members from a variety of tourism businesses in Canada from coast to coast, has created a business-to-business Web site (www.letacanada.com) that allows the user to easily find these segmented experiences as well as vacations incorporating multiple experiences in Canada. This Web site can be used to match vacation experiences with the interests of the user. Members of the travel trade and the media can research experiences in Canada by theme, season, supplier name, and destination. The site offers a free service to members of these two sectors who are interested in using the site for researching, generating story ideas, developing products, locating experiences by theme, finding a company name or destination, accessing helpful information, sourcing prepackaged learning vacations, and accessing resources to assist in planning vacations for their clients.

Concern for the Environment

International leisure travellers are increasingly motivated to select a destination for the quality of its environmental health and the diversity and integrity of its natural and cultural resources. Studies of German and U.S. travel markets indicate that environmental considerations are now a significant aspect of travellers' destination-choosing process, down to—in the case of the Germans—the environmental programs operated by individual hotels. It has also been suggested that 40 percent of Canadians consider the environmental track record of both holiday company and destination when booking a holiday.

Certainly in the United States, the growth in special-interest, nature-oriented travel reflects an increasing concern for the environment. A recent study also showed that approximately 80 percent of American travellers believe it is important that hotels take steps to preserve and protect the environment. According to the study, 70 percent are willing to pay as much as $150 more for a two-week stay in a hotel that has a "responsible environmental attitude," and 55 percent are more likely to book a hotel that purports to be environmentally friendly.[36] This is good news for Fairmont Hotels & Resorts, which has the most comprehensive environmental program in the North American hotel industry.

Even restaurants are taking the green route. Chanterelle Country Inn, on the Cabot Trail in Cape Breton, Nova Scotia, offers a "green environment" and "Cape Breton fresh" cuisine. Besides recycling and precycling, the inn uses only organic and fragrance-free facial, bath, and laundry soaps, as well as cleaning products; linens and bedding of natural fibres; and solar power for water and space heating. Its water comes from a deep well fed by a spring. All dishes are prepared in its own kitchens, using organic and locally produced ingredients. Its dining room also stocks organically grown wines.

Health-Consciousness

A more health-conscious society, and the desire on the part of tourists to be active on holiday has resulted in a dramatic increase in sport and adventure tourism[37] (see Chapter 12, pp. 414–421, for more on this sector of tourism). Patterson has examined the demographic characteristics of baby boomers and their growing interest in adventure tourism as they age.[38] Baby boomers are generally healthier, financially better off, better educated, and more interested in novelty, escape, and authentic experiences than were previous cohorts of older people. Many baby boomers and senior adult groups are consequently opting for more physically challenging and "adrenalin-driven" activities.

The demographics of the baby-boom bulge are also having an impact on the health and wellness industry. U.S. statistics show that from 1997 to 1999 Americans made 250 million visits to traditional medical practitioners, and another 280 million to nontraditional medical practitioners. Health and wellness centres are springing up in many tourism destinations. A Canadian example is in Canmore, situated in the Rockies near Banff National Park, where TGS Properties is developing a resort offering a myriad of traditional and nontraditional services. The design of the resort will be similar to Whistler, built around a central core of facilities. Canmore tourism officials believe that the health and wellness concept, which is not weather- or snow-dependent, provides a real opportunity to eliminate the slow shoulder season. It is also a form of tourism that offers better wages than the traditional service industry jobs. Canmore has already become something of a magnet for alternative health therapists, who offer everything from acupuncture to reflexology to herbology.

SNAPSHOT

FAST-FOOD INDUSTRY TARGETS HEALTHIER CONSUMERS

We have become a nation of fatties. According to Statistics Canada, almost half of Canadian adults are overweight, and the incidence of obesity among children is rising. While lack of exercise and overeating certainly contribute to widening waistlines, health activists say that fast food, with its obscene portion sizes and lack of nutrition, is the real culprit in our super-sized population. Just as the tobacco industry was slapped with lawsuits, sin taxes, and marketing restrictions, the fast-food industry's role in the health of Canadians is now being closely scrutinized.

But the quick-service industry is responding. Burger giants that built their empires selling high-fat, high-calorie food, are heeding the call for healthier options. In March 2001, Toronto-based Burger King Restaurants of Canada launched the BK Veggie, later adding greens to the menu, including a Chicken Caesar Salad and a dinner-sized salad. Wendy's followed suit in February 2002 with a new line of salads introduced in Canada and the United States. The chain said sales were brisk, and in the second quarter of 2002 the company attributed its 7.3 percent increase in same-store sales in part to the new salads.

McDonald's jumped on the "better-for-you" bandwagon in June 2002 by launching its "Lighter Choices" menu. Research conducted by the Toronto-based chain suggested that consumers want menu options from morning to evening that fit the balanced lifestyle they are looking for. Sales are going well, contrary to the chain's earlier foray into healthier food. Poor sales of its salads and the McLean Deluxe burger, introduced in the early 1990s, forced the chain to abandon its lower-fat choices. As of January 2003, sales of the Lighter Choices menu had already met the company's expectations, accounting for about 5 percent of the total annual $2.24 billion sales.

But perhaps the most successful venture into healthier fast food has come from Subway, which has turned its low fat and calorie content into a marketing coup. Subway's "7 under 6 menu" (seven sandwiches that each contain less than six grams of fat) was introduced in 1997, but the company ramped up promotions when it learned that Jared Fogel, a once 425-pound (193 kg) college student, lost 245 pounds (111 kg) on a diet consisting of Subway turkey and veggie subs. Positioning itself as a healthy fast-food alternative has certainly paid off for Subway. In Canada, the company is number 10 on the list of top 100 foodservice companies, generating sales of $632 million in 2001. Les Winograd, public relations manager for Subway says, "Customers are recognizing Subway as a healthier alternative, but we also have items on the menu for people who are not as concerned with that subject."

So while the fast-food industry's role in our growing national girth is up for debate, both health groups and the industry agree that the trend toward healthy eating will continue. But just as fast-food restaurants are marketing soy patties and salads, they are continuing to fill menus with double burgers, bacon

SNAPSHOT *continued*

toppings, and old-fashioned milk shakes. French fries are still the number one item at these restaurants, followed by hamburgers, according to CREST/NPD Foodservice Information Group. Will it be the fast-food industry or the consumer that has the final choice of what to eat in the quick-service sector?

Source: Harris, R. (2003). Fast food, fat nation. *Foodservice and Hospitality, 25*(11), 39–45.

Customization

Requests for customized and personalized vacations are also rising sharply, and both agents and traditional tour operators are changing their businesses to meet that demand. In addition to booking air and hotel reservations, agents and outfitters today are arranging customized wine tastings, visits to artisan workshops, and private after-hour tours of the British crown jewels and the Vatican. Even at companies like Butterfield & Robinson and Abercrombie & Kent—both of which have been primarily associated with pre-arranged tours—requests for customized trips, known in industry-speak as FITs (foreign independent travel) are increasing. Kristina Rundquist, spokesperson for the American Society of Travel Agents, says that there are two parallel trends now: people who want personalized service and those who want highly specialized trips: "Many tourists have precious little time for vacations, so they like to make sure they get exactly what they want, whether it's a boutique hotel or a special kind of restaurant. They need someone who will listen and cater to their needs."[39]

One Canadian travel company that has always been customer-driven, with its "personal touch philosophy," is Nahanni Wilderness Adventures (NWA). Owned and managed by outfitters David and Wendy Hubbard, NWA has been operating river tours on the Nahanni River for over 40 years. NWA has a wide range of quality trip packages and dates available for customers to choose from. The company has over 15 different packages available and fashions each trip according to customer experience, type of activity, and time and price constraints. Despite the high level of variety in the packages on offer, NWA also advertises private trips to "customize your dream adventure." Such trips could include a family vacation or a do-it-yourself package for which the company will rent out equipment and help arrange charter flights. "From the start, customizing trips has been our specialty," says David Hubbard.

Convenience and Speed

The increasing desire for convenience and speed is having its greatest impact on the restaurant sector in Canada. According to NPD Group Canada, drive-through sales are on the rise across the service restaurant category.[40] Since NPD began tracking drive-through sales in 1994, sales have risen by a remarkable 250 percent. At Tim Hortons, bagel sales have risen to the extent that the company now accounts for half the bagels sold through food services in Canada. Tim Hortons has more than 2000 outlets in Canada, and another 140 in the United States. "Consistency and quality"—the price of entry in the food business—are the main elements Tim Hortons seeks to provide its customers, with "speed of service" following close behind. The need to emphasize speed is borne out by the company's sales data, which reveals that, like McDonald's, Tim Hortons outlets with drive-through windows conduct 50 percent of their business with passing motorists. But convenience includes more than just speed. For drivers, it also means food they can eat without worrying about making a mess. For people who take public transit, convenience takes the form of restaurant outlets in malls, hospitals, and entertainment complexes. And for groups of people with varied tastes, convenience can be found in combo locations—locations with two or three different restaurants offering a wide range of food types. For example, when Tim Hortons and Wendy's Restaurants of Canada—both owned by U.S.-based Wendy's International—put two outlets in the same location, the sales of the individual units go up.

Experiences

experience

occurs when a company intentionally uses services as the stage, and goods as props, to engage individual customers in a way that creates a memorable event

According to Pine and Gilmore, today's consumer desires what the industry is calling "**experiences**," which occur when a company intentionally uses services as the stage, and goods as props, to engage individual customers in a way that creates a memorable event. More and more travel organizations are responding by explicitly designing and promoting such events. As services, like goods before them, increasingly become commodified, experiences have emerged as the next step in the "progression of economic value." From now on, leading-edge companies—whether they sell to consumers or businesses—will find that the next competitive battleground lies in staging experiences.[41]

An experience is not an amorphous construct; it is as real an offering as any service, good, or commodity. In today's service economy, many companies simply wrap experiences around their traditional offerings to sell them better. To realize the full benefit of staging experiences, however, businesses must deliberately design engaging experiences that command a fee. Commodities are fungible, goods tangible, services intangible, and experiences memorable. Buyers of experiences value what the company reveals over a period of time. While prior economic offerings—commodities, goods, and services—are external to the buyer, experiences are inherently personal, existing only in the mind of an individual who has been engaged on an emotional, physical, intellectual, or even spiritual level. Thus, no two people can have the same experience, because each experience derives from the interaction between the staged event (like a theatrical play) and the individual's state of mind.

Experiences have always been at the heart of the entertainment business—a fact that Walt Disney and the company he founded have creatively exploited. But today the concept of selling an entertainment experience is taking root in businesses far removed from theatres and amusement parks. At theme restaurants such as the Hard Rock Cafe, Planet Hollywood, and the House of Blues, the food is just a prop for what's known as "eatertainment." And stores such as Niketown, Cabella's, and Recreational Equipment Incorporated draw consumers in by offering fun activities, fascinating displays, and promotional events (sometimes labelled "shoppertainment" or "entertailing"). But experiences are not exclusively about entertainment; companies stage an experience whenever they engage customers in a personal, memorable way. For example, WestJet airline goes beyond the function of transporting people from point A to point B, and competes on the basis of providing an experience. The company uses its base service (the travel itself) as the stage for a distinctive en route experience—one that attempts to transform air travel into a respite from the traveller's normally frenetic life.

CHAPTER SUMMARY

Understanding the consumer's needs and buying process is the foundation of successful marketing. By understanding the buyer's decision-making process, the various participants in the buying procedure, and the major influences on buying behaviour, marketers can acquire many clues about how to meet buyer needs. The key factors that influence consumer behaviour are motivation, culture, age and gender, social class, lifestyle, life cycle, and reference groups.

It has been suggested that there are three levels of buying of commitment, which are dependent on the nature of the purchase: extended problem solving, limited problem solving, and habitual problem solving. It is also proposed that there are five buying roles: initiator, influencer, decider, buyer, and user. A consumer moves through a number of stages leading up to purchase: awareness, information gathering, formation of an attitude, evaluation, purchase, and post-purchase.

A marketer will also need to understand the buying phases for organizations. The conference market, for example, follows a pattern of group decision making, and the "buy phase" has been described as follows: problem recognition, general need description, product specification, supplier search, proposal solution, supplier selection, order routine specification, and performance review.

The behaviour of business travellers is significantly different than that of leisure travellers. For example, business travellers do not see travel as a perk but rather as another source of stress. Hence some sectors of the tourism industry, such as airlines, are spending considerable effort trying to understand the needs of their business travellers in order to satisfy them.

There are a range of trends or demands in consumer behaviour that are influencing tourism and hospitality marketing today. These include the desire for learning and enrichment travel, concern for the environment, a more health-conscious society, the desire on the part of tourists to be active on holiday, requests for customized and personalized vacations, the increasing desire for convenience and speed, and the desire for experiences.

KEY TERMS

allocentrics, p. 81	learning, p. 73	needs, p. 71
attitudes, p. 73	learning and enrichment travel,	perception, p. 73
beliefs, p. 73	p. 89	perceptual mapping, p. 73
consumer attitudes, p. 73	life cycle model, p. 80	psychocentrics, p. 81
consumer behaviour analysis,	lifestyle analysis, p. 79	psychographic analysis, p. 79
p. 70	Maslow's hierarchy of needs,	reference groups, p. 80
culture, p. 74	p. 72	social class, p. 78
experience, p. 93	motivations, p. 71	VALS™, p. 79
family life cycle, p. 80		

DISCUSSION QUESTIONS AND EXERCISES

1. Using the opening vignette and all the material on consumer behaviour in this chapter, create a profile of a typical backpacker. How is he or she different in behaviour from other types of travellers, such as the packaged or the business traveller?

2. Where would you place the backpacker on Plog's continuum? What are likely to be the popular backpacker destinations of the future? Are there some destinations that are not capitalizing on this market?

3. Why is the post-purchase behaviour stage included in most models of the buying process?

4. Consider the trends in consumer behaviour discussed at the end of the chapter. Can you think of any other trends that have emerged since this book was published?

5. Discuss the roles that each member of the family plays in the decision-making process when choosing a holiday. Is there any evidence that children have an influential role?

6. *Marketing in Action* in the chapter alludes to tactics that will satisfy the customer's need for control, service, and joy. If you were managing a tour-operating business, what tactics could you employ to satisfy these needs?

CASE STUDY

"ROUTES TO LEARNING"

One of the major trends in tourism today is the desire of the tourist to have a learning experience as a part of the vacation. Educational travel has boomed over the past few decades. A recent survey found that half of North American travellers want to visit art, architectural, or historic sites on vacations, while one-third would like to learn a new skill or activity. Of course, the idea for self-improvement is nothing new. Young gentlemen of the 18th and 19th centuries who set out on the Grand Tour were looking for a dose of classical culture spiced with some pleasant debauchery as part of the package. But putting the label "educational" on vacation trips is becoming increasingly popular these days.

Thirty years ago almost no travel companies catered specifically to these self-improvement desires. It seems that 1975 was when everything started to change. That summer, a few hundred people gathered on five New Hampshire college campuses for the first Elderhostel program—the brainchild of activist Marty Knowlton and university administrator David Bianco, who wanted to create new opportunities for travellers in their sixties, seventies, and beyond. That same year, a few hundred other travellers boarded chartered 707s bound for England, France, and U.S.S.R., where they took part in the first large-scale study tours sponsored by the Smithsonian Institution. This program was the granddaddy of all the museum, alumni, and association tours that have since fanned out to the unlikeliest parts of the globe. Table 3.2 on page 96 gives some examples of educational trips from around the world.

Elderhostel International Inc. now claims to offer the "world's most diverse and affordable selection of learning adventures" for those 55 and older. Routes to Learning Canada (formerly Elderhostel Canada) is the provider of all Canadian

Table 3.2

Trips to Learn By

The Road to Compostela. Brush up on medieval history in Spain, retracing the route of St. James the Great. ACE Study Tours, *877/465-9050; www.study-tours.org; June 9–21, 2002*

India: Birding and Wildlife Safari. Bird-watching in the Ranthambore Tiger Reserve, Keoladeo Ghana National Park, and the Yamuna River grasslands. Massachusetts Audubon Society, *800/289-9504; www.massaudubon.org; February 7–23, 2002; $2650 per adult, $1745 per child.*

Family Dinosaur Discovery: In the Grand Valley of the Colorado River. Dig for bones and learn how to prepare fossils for preservation. American Museum of Natural History's Discovery Tours, *800/462-8687; www.discovery.org; July 20–26, 2002; $2650 per adult, $1745 per child.*

Focus on Deserts of Southern Africa. Chris Rainier, former assistant to Ansel Adams, leads this photography workshop. Mountain Travel–Sobek, *888/687-6235; www.mtsobek.com; August 25–September 12, 2002; prices not yet available.*

Opera Lover's France: Paris. See three operas, attend a lecture on each, and sit in on a rehearsal. Smithsonian Study Tours, *877/338-8687; www.smithsonianstudytours.org; November 13–22, 2001; $6195 per person.*

L.L. Bean Outdoor Discovery Introductory Fly-Fishing Camp. Learn the basics at this workshop on Maine's Kennebago Lake. L.L. Bean's Outdoor Discovery Schools, *888/552-3261; www.llbean.com; September 9–13, 2001; $1195 per person.*

Berlin: Building the New City. Visit the city's most important buildings, including Foster's Reichstag and Eisenman's Jewish Museum. Archetours, *800/770-3051; www.archetours.com; August 24–31, 2002; $4595 per person.*

Cuba: Language and Culture. Study Spanish in Havana. Global Exchange, *800/497-1994, ext. 234; December 1–15, 2001; $1300 per person.*

The Human Odyssey: A Search for Our Beginnings. Travel on a 50-seat private jet to see Lascaux, the remains of Lucy in Ethiopia, Persepolis in Iran, and more. Archaeological Institute of America, *800/748-6262; www.archaeological.org; November 3–20, 2001; $32 950 per person.*

learning programs for Elderhostel International Inc. and is a good example of a Canadian operator that provides and coordinates educational travel programs for Canadians and visitors to Canada.

Routes to Learning Canada (RLC) works with tourism providers across Canada and abroad to create learning opportunities for discriminating travellers. The company states its purpose as follows:

"Routes to Learning Canada collaborates with learning providers to create, nurture, enable and ensure quality learning opportunities for Canadians or visitors to Canada." RLC's mission and guiding principles centre on environmental and cultural sensitivity. In addition, the company focuses on benefitting the host communities as well as the "learners" that participate in its programs.

Most RLC programs include accommodation with a private bath, all meals, transportation, applicable entrance fees, resource specialists, information packages, and modest gratuities. This all-inclusive aspect is very appealing, especially for older, and perhaps retired, travellers or for those who are not interested in working out the individual travel details themselves. With the baby boomer population aging, one can imagine that this sort of travel will become increasingly popular.

The name change of Elderhostel Canada to Routes to Learning Canada may be significant for a few reasons—most importantly, to promote the company to the baby boomer generation, as they tend to retire younger than retirees of the past and may not identify with the word "elder." Several of the programs RLC provides for Elderhostel are designed to be "intergenerational," to allow grandparents, adult parents, and grandchildren to travel and learn together. Another service offered by RLC is the creation and provision of programs for corporations. It is also able to provide a number of support services for these programs, including evaluation, quality control, and promotional and accounting assistance.

RLC provides programs in each region of Canada, as well as in overseas destinations ranging from Cuba to the United Kingdom to Australia and New Zealand. The company provides a wide variety of learning possibilities by offering the following programs: "train trek"; festival and event; fine arts/performing arts; heritage and multicultural; First Nations' and native peoples'; shipboard and study cruise; cultural immersion; horticultural; food and wine; and active and outdoors programs, which include bicycling, birding, and walking/trekking/hiking.

The following is a sample program description for "Jewels of the St. Lawrence: A Discovery Cruise":

Discover the staggering variety of one of the world's great rivers as you explore the jewel of the St. Lawrence from Kingston to Québec City. You will encounter Québec City. You will encounter the Québecois joie de vivre, found nowhere else in North America, and the legacy of North America's only walled city. Lectures on board ship and on land centre on the magic of the Thousand Islands, the deep historical root of the United Empire Loyalists territory in Brockville and the living history of Upper Canada Village. Field trips include Notre Dame du Cap Shrine at Trois Rivieres, the International Seaway and its lock system; Upper Canada Village; Fort Wellington; and Boldt Castle. Enjoy a two hour guided lecture of Montréal with free time before and after dinner on your own.

Each program description also includes information on the activity level, be it relaxed, moderate, or active, as well as a list of the types of study leaders for the program, be they historians, expert guides, internationally trained chefs, wine experts, or even whale research biologists. The wealth of information provided about each program allows consumers to be enticed and drawn to the programs that will suit them best.

Because of the intensity of work and the limited time for travel and relaxation in the 21st century, travellers find it critical to get the most out of each travel opportunity. When these travellers retire from the workforce, they may perceive this stage in their life as a chance to make up for lost time. It is clear that the programs designed and offered by RLC are intended to provide an "experience" for the traveller rather than a mere vacation. As noted earlier in the chapter (see p. 93), trends in tourism suggest that experience-seekers are going to become an ever-increasing part of the tourism and travel market.

Sources: *Elderhostel: For first-time visitors.* (2003). Retrieved May 1, 2003, from http://elderhostel.org; Goodheart, A. (2001, September). The educational quest. *Travel + Leisure,* 98–101. *Routes to Learning Canada.* (2003). Retrieved May 1, 2003, from http://www.routestolearning.ca

QUESTIONS

1. Why is it that demand for educational tourism has mushroomed in the last few decades?
2. Can Maslow's hierarchy of needs explain the motivation behind these trips?
3. Explain why a company such as Routes to Learning Canada will increasingly draw the attention of the baby-boomer generation.
4. Do some research yourself to find some examples of educational holidays offered around the world.

WEB SITES

www.astanet.com
American Society of Travel Agents

www.elderhostel.org
Elderhostel International Inc.

www.letacanada.com
The Learning & Enrichment Travel Alliance

www.nahanniwild.com
Nahanni Wilderness Adventures

www.ntaonline.com
National Tour Association

www.pier21.ns.ca
Pier 21 (Nova Scotia)

www.routestolearning.ca
Routes to Learning Canada

www.travelalberta.com
Travel Alberta

www.disney.go.com
Walt Disney World

ENDNOTES

1. Mills, A. S., & Morrison, A. M. (1985). *The tourism system: An introductory text.* Englewood Cliffs, NJ: Prentice-Hall.
2. Dann, G. (1977). Anomie, ego-enhancement and tourism. *Annals of Tourism Research, 4,* 184–194.
3. Crompton, J. L. (1979). Why people go on pleasure vacation. *Annals of Tourism Research, 6*(4), 408–424.
4. Krippendorf, J. (1987). *The holidaymakers.* London: Heinemann.
5. Sutherland, S. (2002, May). Hospitality trends. *Alberta Venture*, 49–53.
6. Hofstede, G. (1980). Motivation, leadership, and organization: Do American theories apply abroad? *Organizational Dynamics*, 9, 42–63.
7. Hofstede, G. (1983). National cultures in four dimensions: A research-based theory of cultural differences among nations. *International Studies of Management & Organization, 13*, 46–75.
8. Lanning, T. G. (2002, June 13). Seniors choose a variety of travel destinations. *South Bend Tribune.*
9. Colbert, J. (2000, January). Older, wiser, and richer. *Lodging*, 59–62.
10. Sutherland, S. (2002, May). Hospitality trends. *Alberta Venture*, 49–53.
11. Bond, D. E. (2002, March 18). Advertisers shun affluent boomers at their peril. *The Globe and Mail*, p. B8.
12. Pearce, P. L. (1993). Fundamentals of tourist motivation. In D. Pearce & W. Butler (Eds.), *Tourism and research: Critiques and challenges* (pp. 113–134). London: Routledge.
13. Oppermann, M. (1995). Travel life cycle. *Annals of Tourism Research, 22*(3), 535–552.
14. Mature travellers and volunteer holidays. (2002, February 2). *The Edmonton Journal*, p. K2.

15. Plog, S. C. (1974). Why destination areas rise and fall in popularity. *Cornell Hotel and Restaurant Quarterly, 14*(4), 55–58.

16. Gilbert, D. C. (1991). An examination of the consumer behavior process related to tourism. In Cooper, C. (Ed.), *Progress in tourism* (Vol. 3, pp. 113–134). London: Belhaven.

17. Smith, S. L. J. (1990). A test of Plog's allocentric/psychocentric model: Evidence from seven nations. *Journal of Travel Research, 28*(4), 40–43.

18. Cohen, E. (1972). Toward a sociology of international tourism. *Social Research, 39*(1), 164–182.

19. Howard, J. A., & Sheth, J. N. (1969). *The theory of buying behaviour,* New York: Wiley.

20. Engel, J. F., Blackwell, R. D., & Miniard, P. W. (1990). *Consumer behaviour.* Orlando, FL: Dryden.

21. Hardenne, J. (2003, January 8). Surfing for travel. *The Globe and Mail*, p. T1.

22. Baginski, M. (2002). *Poll predicts positive outlook for industry.* Retrieved November 20, 2002, from http://www.canadatourism.com/en/ctc/ctx/ctx-news/search/newsbydateform.cfm.

23. Zeithaml, V. A., Berry, L. L., & Parasuraman, A. (1996). The behavioral consequences of service quality. *Journal of Marketing, 60*, 31–46.

24. Gale, B. (1992). Monitoring customer satisfaction and market-perceived quality. *American Marketing Association Worth Repeating Series*, No. 922CSO 1. Chicago: American Marketing Association.

25. Radburn, D. (1997). Organizational buyer behaviour. In L. Lumsdon (Ed.), *Tourism Marketing*, (pp. 52–63). London: Thomson Business Press.

26. Robinson, P., Faris, C., & Wind, Y. (1967). *Industrial buying and creative marketing.* Boston: Allyn and Bacon.

27. Webster, F., & Wind, Y. (1972). *Organizational buying behaviour.* Englewood Cliffs, NJ: Prentice Hall.

28. *NBTA survey sees biz travel still down.* (2002). Retrieved September 16, 2002, from http://www.canadatourism.com/en/ctc/ctx/ctx-news/search/newsbydateform.cfm.

29. Cohen, A. (2001, October 2). Frequent flyers forced to think twice. *Financial Times*.

30. Safety first for business travellers. (2002, February 15). *Financial Times*.

31. Cohen, A. (2000, January 31). Business takes all the fun out of travel. *National Post*, p. C17.

32. Tong, T. (2002, March 8). Business travellers' spouses pay psychological price. *National Post*, p. A1.

33. Cuthbert, W. (2000, January 31). The changing face of first class. *National Post*, p. C17.

34. Air Canada launching new Executive First. (2002). *Canadian Travel Press*. Retrieved September 19, 2002, from http://www.canadatourism.com/en/ctc/ctx/ctxnews/search/newsbydateform.cfm.

35. Air Canada popular with business travellers. (2000, January 15). *Lloyds List*, 11.

36. Americans going green? (2002). *Tourism, 6*(8), p. 12.

37. Hudson, S. (Ed.). (2003). *Sport and adventure tourism.* Binghampton, NY: Haworth.

38. Patterson, I. (2002). Baby boomers and adventure tourism: The importance of marketing the leisure experience. *World Leisure, 2*, 4–10.

39. Whitlock, S. (2001, September). The world on a platter. *Travel + Leisure*, 176–178.

40. Allossery, P. (2002, March 4). Fast food in high gear. *Financial Post*, p. FP6.

41. Pine, B. J. II, & Gilmore, J. H. (1998). Welcome to the experience economy. *Harvard Business Review, 76*(4), 97–108.

CHAPTER

Marketing Research

4

RESIDENT ATTITUDES SURVEY IN ONTARIO

In May 2002, a Resident Attitudes Survey was undertaken by Superior North in Ontario (now the North of Superior Tourism Association), using the Marathon & District Chamber of Commerce's annual trade show as the survey venue. The purpose of this survey was twofold:

1. To gain insight into the perspectives and perceptions Superior North residents have toward regional tourism development; and

2. To serve as a tool in fostering positive community attitudes toward tourism and economic development—i.e., community belief-building.

A questionnaire was developed, and 113 respondents completed it. A nonprobability convenience sample was used as the survey method. This method is based on the selection of readily available respondents. It does not provide definitive statistical findings, but it does provide informational exploratory research.

Interpretation and analysis of the surveys identified the following principal attitudes:

- 99 percent of respondents supported community or regional tourism development;
- 40 percent of respondents had concerns regarding community or regional tourism development;
- 89 percent of respondents believed they benefitted personally from community or regional tourism development;
- 32 percent of respondents believed that certain places or attractions should not be developed for tourism;
- 46 percent of respondents felt tourism contributed a medium amount of revenue to local and regional economies; and
- 24 percent of respondents felt that the following theme statement best described the Superior North region: "Superior North. An exciting adventure, a relaxing escape."

Respondents identified the following as prime tourism opportunities for community or regional development:

- marina and waterfront development;
- Lake Superior development;
- fishing and hunting;
- snowmobiling;
- national and provincial parks;
- nature and wilderness settings;
- outdoor activities (hiking, walking, biking, skiing, golfing, canoeing, etc.); and
- ecotourism.

Upon completion and analysis of the Resident Attitudes Survey, the results were used to develop a framework for a Superior North Strategic Tourism Marketing Plan. The plan is a logistical document available to all regional stakeholders and acts as a "common game plan" in capitalizing on the economic impacts of tourism. More intrinsically, the research was used to form the foundation of "product teams" inside the tourism plan. These teams were developed on the basis of consumer trends and patterns identified in the research. (It is believed that what residents of the region view as tourism opportunities would generally be viewed the same way by those visiting the region.) The following are the defined product teams:

Touring and Attractions

Scenic viewing, provincial and national parks, camping, motorcycles, visiting interpretive centres, visiting museums, visiting parks, golfing, shopping, boating, the Great Lakes Heritage Coast, and the National Marine Conservation Area.

Adventure and Experience (Summer/Winter)

Hiking, biking, skiing (downhill and cross-country), snowboarding, snowmobiling, canoeing, and kayaking.

Fishing and Hunting

Offshore, inland, and ice fishing (includes fishing festivals and derbies), and big and small game hunting.

Cultural Festivals and Themed Events

Music festivals, drag-racing festivals, Aboriginal powwows, and community events and celebrations, etc.

Source: D. Skworchinski, regional communications and strategic development coordinator, Superior North Community Futures Development Corporation, personal communication, May 26, 2003.

Objectives

On completion of this chapter, readers should understand

- what is meant by marketing research;
- the types of applied marketing research employed in the tourism industry;
- the key stages in the marketing research process;

- the relative merits of the various methodologies available to researchers;
- how marketing research can be used for effective decision making; and
- the current trends in tourism marketing research.

Chapter Overview

The opening vignette is a real-life example of a research project undertaken by a tourism organization that was used to develop a framework for a marketing plan (see *Profile* in Chapter 2 for more details of this marketing plan). The project raises many questions that will this chapter will address. For example, were the objectives realistic? Was the sample selection appropriate? Were the results used for effective decision making?

This chapter focuses on marketing research in tourism and hospitality and begins with an introduction to marketing research, its definition, and its role in the tourism and hospitality industry. A description of the type of applied research conducted in tourism is followed by a focus on the various stages in the research process. A section then describes the various methodologies available to researchers and discusses the relative merits of primary versus secondary research. The next part of the chapter looks at sampling, and five common research problems are then highlighted. The effective use of research in decision making is discussed, followed by the final section on trends in tourism marketing research.

INTRODUCTION TO MARKETING RESEARCH

marketing information system (MIS)

the way in which an organization gathers, uses, and disseminates its research in the marketing context

Research should form the basis of an ongoing system for gathering data about the company, its products, and its markets. Often, managers, in the course of their everyday duties, gather intelligence informally and subconsciously by observing, listening to discussions, talking to colleagues in the industry, and reading trade journals and papers. Valuable as this process is, it should be supported by more formal procedures carried out in a systematic and scientific manner. The way in which an organization gathers, uses, and disseminates its research in the marketing context is generally referred to as the **marketing information system (MIS)**. The success of an MIS depends on the quality of the information, its accuracy and relevance, and the way it is collected, interpreted, and applied. A key component of the MIS is the marketing research process.

Researchers and managers seldom address the definition of what constitutes marketing research. To further complicate the issue, the terms "market research" and "marketing research" are often used interchangeably, sometimes within the same document. Gerhold[1] asserts that there is no difference between the two terms and that they can both be defined as "any scientific effort to understand and measure markets or improve marketing performance". Kinnear et al.[2] distinguish between the two terms, arguing that the focus of market research is on the analysis of markets, whereas marketing research extends the role and character of research and emphasizes the contact between researchers and the marketing management process. This chapter adopts the term **marketing research** exclusively, defining it as the systematic and objective search for and analysis of information relevant to the identification and solution of any problem in the field of marketing.[3]

The marketing research process is one of the key distinctions between a management organization that has a sales orientation and one that has a true marketing orientation.[4] A sales-oriented manager's primary goal is to maximize the sales of or revenues from whatever product or service the organization is offering. This orientation developed out of the older production or technology management orientation as the supply for the goods and services produced eventually caught up with demand. The management orientation then changed from producing the goods and services to selling them. As the number and type of selling functions increased, the costs of selling also increased until managers started looking for more efficient selling processes. The marketing orientation that developed was subtle in its evolution but dramatic in its results. The focus shifted from selling what was produced to producing what would sell. The key to this process was learning what the customer wanted through accurate and effective marketing research.

marketing research

the systematic and objective search for and analysis of information relevant to the identification and solution of any problem in the field of marketing

MARKETING RESEARCH IN TOURISM AND HOSPITALITY

In a critique of marketing research theory and methodology in the tourism industry, Baker et al. suggest that the travel and tourism industry is progressing through the stages of the management development process to a true marketing orientation.[5] Various public and private sector tourism service providers can be found at each stage of the development process, depending upon the nature of the services provided and the extent of the competition. The most important point of this evolution of management orientation is that the true marketing orientation is the most efficient, and the marketing research process is the key to that efficiency. Marketing research is only a resource for management decision making, not a substitute for it. Tourism managers who understand this point will better meet their customers' demands for goods and services and simultaneously use fewer resources to provide those goods and services. Good research is the key to good customer service. If the research is not effective, efficient, or accountable, then the tourism management decision process is at best not supported and at worst erroneously influenced.

Just as Baker et al. have provided a critique of tourism research, Morrison recently reflected on hospitality research.[6] Despite acknowledging that during recent decades hospitality research has made considerable advancements, he highlights a significant degree of debate concerning the definitional, philosophical, and conceptual dimensions of hospitality. Morrison's conclusions call for definitional precision in hospitality; a clearly articulated research philosophy locating hospitality as a specialist field of study within the social science landscape; an enhanced degree of research philosophy awareness by researchers; and the benefits of formulating and agreeing on an internally valid conceptual framework.

According to McIntosh et al., there are six reasons for conducting tourism and hospitality research:

1. to identify, describe, and solve problems in order to increase the efficiencies of day-to-day tourism operations;

2. to keep tourism and hospitality firms in touch with trends, changes, predictions, etc. related to their markets;
3. to reduce the waste produced by tourists and tourist organizations;
4. to develop new areas of profit by finding new products, services, markets, etc.;
5. to help promote sales in situations where research findings are of interest to the public; and
6. to develop goodwill, as the public thinks well of firms that are doing research in order to better meet consumers' needs.[7]

Unfortunately, in tourism and hospitality many smaller organizations feel that "real" marketing research is a costly and time-consuming luxury only available to large companies that have professional research staffs, sophisticated computers, and almost unlimited budgets. Other organizations see marketing research as something to be undertaken when a major event is about to occur—the introduction of a new product, the acquisition of a new property, or a change in target markets. Its value at these junctures is recognized, but its ability to contribute to an organization's success on a day-to-day basis is often overlooked. Another common problem in the tourism industry is that organizations are not making full use of the information that already exists and is easily accessed. Sometimes information is available and studies are done, but the results are either ignored or not fully considered in the final decision-making process. This lack of attention happens when the information is not in accord with the prevailing view of management or when the information has not been properly analyzed and clearly presented.

APPLIED RESEARCH IN TOURISM AND HOSPITALITY

Most marketing research is classified as applied research, which is undertaken to answer specific questions. It differs from pure research (done by scientists at universities or by government authorities), which is aimed at the discovery of new information. Applied research in tourism and hospitality can be grouped into eight categories: research on consumers; research on products and services; research on pricing; research on place and distribution; research on promotion; research on competition; research on the operating environment; and research on a destination. Table 4.1 lists some of the typical research programs undertaken within these categories.

Table 4.1

Applied Research in Tourism and Hospitality

1. RESEARCH ON CONSUMERS	
Identifying existing markets	Identifying general trends in demographics and psychographics
Identifying potential markets	
Identifying lapsed consumers	Identifying changes in attitudes and behaviour patterns (generally)
Testing customer loyalty	
Developing detailed consumer profiles	Identifying changes in attitudes and behaviour patterns (product-specific)

TABLE 4.1 *continued*

2. RESEARCH ON PRODUCTS AND SERVICES

Measuring attitudes toward existing products or services	Evaluating competitors' products
	Evaluating consumer attitudes toward décor, presentation, and packaging
Identifying potential new products that may be at the end of their product life cycle	Evaluating consumer attitudes about combinations of products and services (bundles of product attributes)
Identifying products that are considered acceptable substitutes/alternatives	

3. RESEARCH ON PRICING

Identifying attitudes toward prices	Identifying costing policies of competitors
Testing attitudes toward packages and individual pricing	Testing alternative pricing strategies
	Testing payment processes (credit cards, electronic funds, transfers, etc.)
Identifying costs	

4. RESEARCH ON PLACE AND DISTRIBUTION

Identifying attitudes toward location	Identifying potential demand for product or services at other locations
Identifying attitudes toward buildings/premises	Identifying cooperative opportunities for distribution of information or services
Identifying attitudes on virtual sites	

5. RESEARCH ON PROMOTION

Testing and comparing media options	Testing new communications options (Internet, e-mail, Web pages)
Testing alternative messages	Identifying cooperative opportunities
Testing competitors' messages and their effectiveness	Measuring advertising and promotion effectiveness

6. RESEARCH ON COMPETITION

Measuring awareness	Identifying specific competitive advantages (locations, suppliers, etc.)
Measuring usage	Identifying cooperative opportunities
Identifying levels of customer loyalty	
Identifying competitors' strengths and weaknesses	

7. RESEARCH ON THE OPERATING ENVIRONMENT

Economic trends	Political climate and trends
Social trends	Technological developments and their impact
Environmental issues	

TABLE 4.1 *continued*

8. RESEARCH ON A DESTINATION

Measuring residents' attitudes	Identifying tourism activities
Benchmarking	Identifying spending patterns
Measuring customer loyalty	Branding research

A veritable explosion of new journals has been introduced as an outlet for academic publication of research in hospitality and tourism. A recent inventory, while neither exhaustive nor exclusive, yielded a count of 69, as listed in Table 4.2.

Table 4.2

An Inventory of Tourism and Hospitality Publications

GENERAL INTEREST	TOURISM	FOOD SERVICES
The Cornell Hotel & Restaurant Administration Quarterly	Annals of Tourism Research	Journal of Restaurant & Foodservice Marketing
International Journal of Hospitality Management	ACTA Turistica	Journal of Nutrition, Recipe, and Menu Development
Journal of Hospitality and Tourism Research	Asia Pacific Journal of Tourism Research	Journal of College and University Foodservice
FIU Hospitality Review	Current Issues in Tourism	Journal of Foodservice Systems
International Journal of Contemporary Hospitality Management	Event Tourism	Journal of Agricultural & Food Information
	Information Technology & Tourism	
Journal of Quality Assurance in Hospitality & Tourism	International Journal of Tourism Research	Journal of Nutrition for the Elderly
The Journal of Applied Hospitality Management	Journal of Convention & Exhibition Management	Journal of the American Dietetic Association
Australian Journal of Hospitality Management	Journal of Ecotourism	NACUFS Journal (National Association of College & University Foodservices)
	Journal of Sports Tourism	
The Consortium Journal: Journal of HBCU	Journal of Sustainable Tourism	School Foodservice Research Review
	Journal of Travel Research	
	Journal of Travel & Tourism Research	

TABLE 4.2 *continued*

International Journal of Hospitality and Tourism Administration	Journal of Vacation Marketing	Journal of Food Production Management
Praxis: The Journal of Applied Hospitality Management	Pacific Tourism Review	Journal of Food Products Marketing
ANATOLIA	Teoros International	Journal of Foodservice Business Research
Scandinavian Journal of Hospitality and Tourism	Tourism Analysis	Journal of Culinary Science
Tourism and Hospitality Research	TOURISM: An International Interdisciplinary Journal	
Journal of Hospitality & Leisure for the Elderly	The Tourist Review	
Journal of Convention & Exhibition Management	Tourism, Culture & Communication	
Journal of Hospitality & Leisure Marketing	Tourism Economics	
Journal of Tourism and Hospitality Education	Tourism Geographies	
Hotel & Motel Management	Tourism Management	
International Journal of Hospitality Information Technology	Tourism Recreation Research	
Journal of Gambling Studies	Tourism Today	
Journal of Hospitality Financial Management	Tourismus Journal	
	Tourist Studies	
	Travel & Tourism Analyst	
	Journal of Teaching in Travel & Tourism	
	Journal of Human Resources in Hospitality & Tourism	
	Journal of Travel & Tourism Marketing	
	Journal of Tourism Studies	
	Tourism Intelligence Quarterly	
	Papers de Turisme	

Source: Rutherford, D. G., & Samenfink, W. H. (2002). Out for the count: A response. *International Journal of Hospitality Management, 21*(2), 111–117.

consumer research

one type of applied research that focuses on the consumer

competitor intelligence

keeping track of competition by having a clear understanding of who the competition is and knowing how the company is doing in comparison to the competitors

Consumer research is one type of applied research, and cases in this chapter look at consumer studies in food services (see *Profile*, pp. 112–113), consumer research conducted by Seaflight Hydrofoil and the Canadian Tourism Commission (see *Marketing in Action* below), and a consumer behavioural study by Travel Alberta (see *Snapshot*, pp. 118–120). Another important type of applied research is **competitor intelligence**. If a company wants to keep track of competition, it requires a clear understanding of who the competition is, as well as knowledge of how the company is doing in comparison to the competitors. Competitor intelligence is available through a variety of sources, including competitors' annual reports, local tourism authorities and state tourism departments, magazine articles, speeches, media releases, brochures, and advertisements. It is important, too, to recognize what is meant by "the competition"—see Chapter 2 for a discussion of four broad categories of competition (p. 41). As previously noted, information about the number and type of competitors, their relative market shares, the things they do well, and the things they do badly will assist in the planning process. A review of the competition will also highlight market trends and the level of loyalty of consumers.

While some information is willingly shared, to get a true picture of how the competition is doing, a firm often needs to undertake research. The form of this research varies from business to business. For a tourist attraction or food operation, it could be as simple as counting the number of cars in the parking lot at various times, or actually going into the facility to see how busy it is. For a hotel, it might mean checking room availability at particular times or watching for advertisements of special offers and discounts. For tour operators, it may involve counting the number of competing coaches at major destinations and collecting tour brochures and schedules. Participant observation is also often used to gather competitor intelligence. For example, executives of airlines might travel with competitors, or hotel managers might check in to competitor hotels. These are effective ways of gathering valuable knowledge for research purposes.

MARKETING IN ACTION

SEAFLIGHT HYDROFOIL LISTENS TO CUSTOMERS

Seaflight Hydrofoil is a ferry-style transport service that operates a fleet of hydrofoils from May to early November, carting passengers across Lake Ontario. The ships can carry more than 130 passengers in just over one hour. The most popular routes, between Toronto and Niagara Falls, feature full-day and overnight packages that include wine tours and other attraction tickets.

In 2002, the company decided to elicit customer feedback using its Web site (www.seaflights.com). Customers could log on to the site and offer opinions and suggestions. Seaflight listened closely to customers, and responded by incorporating many of their suggestions as new features for the following season. "We are taking people's opinions on how they would use our service," said operations manager Janos Radics. "I would like to hear what people think and alter and add routes to our service during the season."

The research identified many tourists with time restrictions, so in response the company introduced some new products. The company

MARKETING IN ACTION *continued*

decided to operate three daily one-hour tours around Toronto for tourists who don't have time for a Niagara Falls excursion but still want to see the city. The runs visit Toronto Harbour as well as making a tour from Scarborough Bluffs in the east to Etobicoke in the west. A combination package was made available that included the one-hour run and a city tour of Toronto aboard a double-decker bus operated by Grey Line. Additional customer demand also resulted in new charter service to Oshawa and a direct route between Cobourg and Rochester. Furthermore, the success of packages to Niagara Falls and Niagara on the Lake prompted the 28 wineries in Jordan Harbour, Grimsby, and Beamsville to contact Seaflight about summer service to their ports. As a result, packages featuring wine tours and lunch were made available to all three destinations.

Along with more packages, passengers saw an improvement in the onboard entertainment and services. The research program identified a desire for more of the onboard wine tastings that had been such a big hit the previous year, so Seaflight offered the special occasions more frequently in 2002, a move also requested by many local wineries. A new 32-seat first-class section was also offered, which included a separate, private coach for wine tour packages in Niagara. Seaflight also responded to demand from families and single parents by offering a new variety of family packages.

Source: Seaflight not resting on laurels. (2002). Retrieved March 19, 2002, from http://www. canadatourism.com/en/ctc/ctx/ctxnews/search/ newsbydateform.cfm.

STAGES IN THE RESEARCH PROCESS

In undertaking research, there are a number of steps that should be followed, as outlined in Figure 4.1.

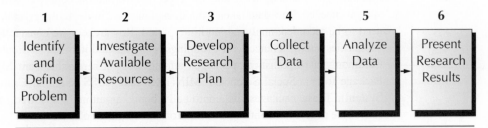

Figure 4.1 Stages in the Research Process

1. Identify and Define the Problem

Before beginning the task of gathering information, it is first necessary to identify the problem for which research is required. This step is crucial to ensure that any information collected is relevant. As well as formulating an aim, specific research questions (objectives) should be stipulated at the outset. These objectives will determine the type of information required. There are three types of objectives for a marketing research project:

1. *exploratory*, to gather information that will help define the problem and suggest hypotheses;
2. *descriptive*, to describe the size and composition of the market; and
3. *causal*, to test hypotheses about cause-and-effect relationships.

2. Investigate Available Sources

There is little point embarking upon a research program involving the collection of primary data if information is already available. Seeking out available information will involve a search of internal data generated and recorded by the organization as well as an examination of available secondary sources of data. Such information should then be assessed to establish the extent to which the research questions can be tackled using this information alone.

3. Develop the Research Plan

secondary data

information that already exists somewhere, having been collected for another purpose

primary data

information collected for the specific purpose at hand

Specific information needs need to be determined from the research objectives. Research objectives must be translated into specific information needs. Two types of data may be used to meet the manager's information needs: **secondary data**, consisting of information that already exists somewhere, having been collected for another purpose, and **primary data**, consisting of information collected for the specific purpose at hand. A full discussion of both types of data collection follows this section.

4. Collect Data

Upon development of a research plan, data should be collected using the method(s) selected. The data collection phase of the marketing research process is generally the most expensive and the one most frequently subject to error. Great care should be taken to avoid bias, which, if introduced, could render results meaningless. This is a particular problem associated with the interview and observation methods.

5. Analyze Data

The collected data must be processed and analyzed to pull out important information and findings. The methods used and the type of information collected will determine the analysis needed. Raw data taken from questionnaires, in-depth interviews, checklists, etc. need to be recorded, analyzed, and interpreted. Researchers are constantly searching for similarities and differences, for groupings, patterns, and items of particular significance. Commonly used statistical packages among tourism researchers are SPSS (Statistical Package for the Social Sciences), MINITAB, and NCSS (Number Cruncher Statistical System). These packages are continually being monitored, reviewed, and updated to reflect the process of continuous evolution in computer software.

6. Present Research Results

Information needs to be tabulated and interpreted, so that recommendations can be made regarding an appropriate course of action to take. This will almost certainly involve the presentation of a report that summarizes the results of the research. This report enables the management of the organization to make decisions based on the newly acquired information.

RESEARCH METHODOLOGY

The increased importance of tourism management decision making has caused more attention to be focused on the theories and methodologies of the tourism research process. A recurrent theme has emerged in the travel research literature concerning the appropriateness of specific types of tourism research and certain methodological applications. There are several approaches to collecting data, but two key decisions that have to be made are as follows:

- *Primary versus secondary data.* In planning a research project, it is sensible to consider whether it is worth going to the expense of collecting new information (primary data, where the researcher is the primary user) or whether existing data (secondary data, where the researcher is the secondary user) will be sufficient. In practice, it may be necessary to collect both types of information. The various types of primary and secondary research are explored later in this chapter (see pp. 113–121).
- *Qualitative versus quantitative research.* Qualitative research methods and techniques give rise to qualitative (subjective) information, whereas quantitative research is research to which numerical (empirical) estimates can be attached. There has been much debate recently about appropriate methods for leisure research, with some authors arguing for extended use of qualitative research over quantitative research. In tourism research, quantitative and qualitative research approaches seem to coexist without the sort of apparent rivalry seen in leisure studies. It is possible for research to be conducted entirely quantitatively, entirely qualitatively, or using a mixture of both. In fact, it is common for large-scale quantitative research to be planned on the basis of prior exploratory qualitative studies.

The distinction between the two methods is indicated in Table 4.3. Both research methods possess distinct limitations and weaknesses, but both also have redeeming characteristics. The choice between the two must be determined by the situation in which research takes place, not by some misguided search for rigour simply for its own sake.

qualitative research
research methods and techniques that use and give rise to qualitative (subjective) information

quantitative research
research to which numerical (empirical) estimates can be attached

Table 4.3

Qualitative versus Quantitative Research

COMPARISON DIMENSION	QUALITATIVE RESEARCH	QUANTITATIVE RESEARCH
Types of questions	Probing	Limited probing
Sample size	Small	Large
Information per respondent	Much	Varies
Administration	Interviewer with special skills required	Fewer special skills required
Types of analysis	Subjective, interpretive	Statistical, summarizing

TABLE 4.3 *continued*

COMPARISON DIMENSION	QUALITATIVE RESEARCH	QUANTITATIVE RESEARCH
Hardware	Tape recorders, projection devices, video equipment, pictures	Questionnaires, computers, printouts
Ability to replicate	Low	High
Training of the researcher	Psychology, sociology, social psychology, consumer behaviour marketing, marketing research	Statistics, decision models, decision support systems, computer programming, marketing research
Types of research	Exploratory	Descriptive or causal

Source: McDaniel, C. D., Jr., & Gates, R. (1993). *Contemporary marketing research* (2nd ed.). Minneapolis–St. Paul, MN: West, 126.

PROFILE

RESEARCH IN THE FOODSERVICE INDUSTRY

Research in the foodservice industry is a subject that has received minimal attention in the literature on tourism. In a recent article, Johns and Pine reviewed the literature related to consumer studies in food service, organizing it into four sections representing different schools of research (see Table 4.4). "Survey research" includes studies of consumers as groups, while the work reviewed under "experimental research" involves test situations in which different factors have been manipulated. Studies under "economics and geography" represent alternative quantitative approaches to consumer research. Under "sociology and anthropology" is included a range of qualitative research that provides complimentary insights into the restaurant experience.

Most quantitative studies in foodservice consumer research are concerned with some aspect of segmentation, i.e., characterizing segments, identifying needs, or positioning specific offerings relative to specific segments. A large amount of work in this field has established a coherent structure linking restaurant attributes to repeat business. Many studies use expectancy-disconfirmation theory (how well actual performance confirms or disconfirms expectations) and the relationship between the quality of the offering and likelihood of repeat business has been demonstrated using sophisticated multivariate techniques. Examples come from Nayga and Capps, who relate demand for different types of restaurants to different socioeconomic segments,[8] and from Binkley, who showed that demographic and income differences have less of an effect upon demand for fast food than does the population density of metropolitan areas.[9]

The experimental research tradition regards eating out as a function of the food itself and the situation in which it is eaten. Surprisingly, the physical surroundings in

PROFILE *continued*

Table 4.4

Summary of the Four Areas of Foodservice Consumer Research

AREA	PRACTICAL FOCUS	METHODS USED	THEORETICAL FOCUS	EXAMPLES OF AUTHORS
Survey research	Segmentation Targeting Positioning	Geodemographic, attitude, and behavioural-based surveys Modelling	Attribute theory Expectancy-disconfirmation Repeat business	Nayga & Capps (1994) Binkley (1998)
Experimental research	Customer preferences	Control of specific variables	Factors affecting food preference	Bruner (1990) Love (1995) Birch et al. (1984)
Economics and geography	Spatial and socioeconomic location	Analysis of secondary data	Population flow and behaviour	Holm et al. (1995) Smith (1985)
Sociology and anthropology	Individual experience Wider social context	In-depth interview Observation Literature review	Power relations Social impacts Semiotics	Jamal (1996) Finkelstein (1989)

which food is eaten have been given comparatively little attention, despite offering very attractive targets for experiment. The effects of image, colour, and music were extensively investigated in retail settings in the 1960s and 1970s.[10] More recently, it has been claimed that McDonald's uses colour and image to manage the behaviour of patrons.[11] Taste experiments have shown that the time of day, and also the speed of a meal,[12] affect taste perceptions, and social context experiments reveal that the amount people eat increases with the number of people in a group.

Economic reports of the restaurant business appear frequently in the trade periodicals, but are generally limited in scope, are descriptive rather than analytical, and quickly become outdated. National statistics are offered by government publications in many countries, and deeper analyses of national data occasionally find their way into more permanent literature.[13] No serious attention seems to have been paid to forecasting or to assessing the contribution of the restaurant business to local or national economies. Similarly, the geography of eating out seems to be a neglected area of research, apart from some work by Smith.[14]

Social and anthropological studies have the potential to enrich consumer research in the foodservice industry by casting light on the individual experience that underlies consumer responses. Most studies have been more concerned with the societal effects of the foodservice industry (Jamal, for example, presents an interesting study of acculturation of the British public through increased availability of Indian foods),[15] but a few researchers have used semiotics and discourse analysis to access consumers' deeper meanings.[16] This approach may represent a way to understand perceptions of restaurant experiences.

In general, Johns and Pine see a need for studies to seek new techniques and to exchange ideas and perspectives between disciplines—particularly as many of the articles

reviewed have been published outside the usual hospitality management journals. The eclectic approach of the review contributes in some measure to this process.

Source: Johns, N., & Pine, R. (2002). Consumer behaviour in the food service industry: A review. *International Journal of Hospitality Management, 21*(2), 119–134.

SECONDARY RESEARCH

Secondary data is data that already exists for an established purpose, and secondary research is also referred to as documents and desk research. It includes information collected from internal sources such as occupancy rates, sales figures, attendance figures, types of services sold, etc. In-house surveys can also be valuable sources of data. As well, data can be collected from external sources. Government agencies such as the Canadian Tourism Commission (CTC) compile statistics on visitor arrivals, how much they spend, where they are coming from, etc. As well as generating a considerable amount of statistical data at the macro level, government is also responsible for a number of tourism-related publications (*Tourism*, a journal published monthly by the CTC, is one example). Hotels, travel agents, tour operators, and airlines all have associated trade bodies that compile information on their members and the market. The trade press can provide a regular supply of information. In Canada, *Travel Week* claims to be the best-read travel trade publication. Journals (see Table 4.2), periodicals, and reports can be useful sources of information, as can conference papers, speeches, and annual reports. Searching the Internet, while sometimes a time-consuming process, can also reveal other potential sources of information, as can chat groups and online newsletters. It is worth noting, however, that the accuracy of such information is not guaranteed, so checking the reliability of the source is important.

Collecting secondary data is more cost-effective than starting from scratch to acquire the information. It may still be necessary to identify major gaps and fill them in by undertaking the required research, but using and incorporating information that already exists in the market research program can save significant amounts of time and money. However, the major disadvantage of secondary data is that it does not always meet the specific requirements or objectives of a research project. Because it hasn't been collected specifically to address the problem being studied, it may not include everything that would be useful. Research from the CTC may not break regional tourism statistics into precisely the units that are required, or it may have categories different from those that are really desired.

PRIMARY RESEARCH

Qualitative Research Techniques

The term "qualitative" is used to describe research methods and techniques that use and give rise to subjective rather than empirical information. In general, the approach is to collect a great amount of "rich" information from relatively few people. Potential purposes of qualitative research include developing hypotheses concerning relevant behaviour and attitudes; identifying the full range of issues, views, and attitudes that should be pursued in large-scale research; and understanding how a buying decision is made. Qualitative research can be used in unstructured and structured situations.

Unstructured Situations

Participative observation falls into this category, in which a tourism field researcher may adopt one of four different roles. The first is the "complete participant," where the researcher becomes a genuine participant, and the second is the "participant as observer," where researchers reveal their intentions. Third, "observers as participants" also reveal themselves as researchers, and will participate in the normal social process, but make no pretence of being participants. The fourth type, "the complete observer," simply observes without being involved. There are five issues that affect the researcher as an understanding participant/observer: problems arising from familiarity; the nature of the relationship between researcher and informant; to what extent local knowledge provides access to data; ethical and political questions; and subsequent responsibilities to respondents. Other issues the researcher must consider in participant observation studies are sampling (discussed later in this chapter) and recording and classifying responses.

Other unstructured qualitative research methods include using conversation as a source of data, as well as using letters and postcards. Case studies have also been used for tourism research. Tourism case studies require informed observation, and it is possible to discern the developments of thought within the literature based on case studies.

Mystery shopping, the name given to participant observation in the commercial sector, has become a common market research technique in tourism and hospitality. In the services context, mystery shopping provides information about the service experience as it unfolds, and helps to develop a richer knowledge of the experiential nature of services. One example of such a study is that by Boote and Mathews, who were employed by Whitbread PLC to develop guidelines for the siting of middle-market restaurant outlets.[17] Part of their research involved participant observation of customers at lunchtime and in the evenings, so as to identify whether the actual clientele matched the intended market segment. This author also used mystery shoppers to test travel agent recommendations in the United Kingdom.[18] Results from investigating 156 travel agents indicated that the majority of travel agents owned by large tour operators will attempt to push the holidays of their parent company rather than give impartial advice to consumers.

Structured Situations

Qualitative research also permits more structured situations in which the researcher can play a more proactive role, although that role is more facilitative than directive. At the initial stages of tourism research, it may be necessary to follow up a conversation, and if the research is intended to generate quantitative data, to develop items for scales to be used on a questionnaire. Hence, there is a need to clearly identify the constructs that inform the attitudes toward specific destinations, behaviours, or experiences that are being surveyed. One effective method of identifying these constructs is the **repertory grid technique**, which requires respondents to select from a group of three items. In this research process, the question posed to respondents is along the lines of "looking at three destinations, which one do you think is different and why?" The object is to elicit the basis of comparison.

The constructs underlying an attitude can be revealed in other ways, one of which is the use of **projection techniques**. These may be called "what if?" techniques, as they involve measures to get subjects to respond to hypothetical, or projected, situations. For example, subjects might be asked to indicate how they would spend a particular sum of money if given a free choice, or would spend additional leisure time if it were made available. Another projection technique is to show respondents a picture or cartoon representing a particular situation, and to ask them to state what they think is actually happening or what one cartoon character is saying to another. The concept behind many of these projection techniques is that respondents tend to give socially acceptable answers in normal interviews, whereas if they answer for another character, they are able to project on that character those unacceptable feelings that they may be actually be feeling. The techniques are based on Freudian psychoanalysis, which posits that anxiety is easily dealt with by the ego if it is projected and attributed to some external part of the respondent's world.[19]

The idea of interviewing groups of people together rather than individually is becoming increasingly popular in market research. In a **focus group**, the interviewer becomes the facilitator of a discussion rather than an interviewer as such, in order to obtain representative views of a wider population. A focus group is usually fairly homogeneous in nature and comprises 8 to 10 people. It is important that those selected have little experience of working in a focus group, as the researcher wishes to obtain views representative of a wider population, not from expert "opinion givers" who are used to the dynamics of a focus group.

Ryan believes that the advantages of using focus groups for obtaining views arise from the social dynamics of the group, which he categorizes as being

- *synergism*: a wider range of ideas can result from a cumulative group effect, as opposed to individual interviews;
- *snowballing*: one comment can elicit a whole range of additional confirmatory or modifying statements;
- *security*: focus groups can generate a social ease, reducing the insecurity or defensiveness that often arise in an interview situation;
- *spontaneity*: it is likely that focus groups will elicit more spontaneous views; and
- *stimulation*: the members of the group can stimulate each other to participate in group discussion.[20]

Focus groups are commonly used in commercial research, especially in the development and monitoring of advertising campaigns. They are beginning to be widely used in the world of tourism, and are often used for obtaining feedback on holiday brochures. Groups are asked to respond to the layout, pictures, text, and typeface of brochures, to help companies find those that appeal most to various market niches. The Westin Hotel Group brings in meeting planners for focus groups to find out more about their needs and wants. Mark Nisbett, director of sales and marketing at The Westin Edmonton, says that

repertory grid technique

structured research technique that requires respondents to select from a group of three items

projection techniques

called "what if?" techniques, as they involve measures to get subjects to respond to hypothetical, or projected, situations

focus group

type of research in which the researcher acts as a facilitator to obtain views representative of a wider population; usually comprises 8 to 10 people the feeling he perceives in these buyers is, "'Finally someone is asking for our opinion.'" Nisbett continues, "Buyers were very excited to be involved, and we learned so much about what is going on in their industry today."

virtual focus groups

online "chat" sessions, in which one to dozens of pre-recruited respondents type in responses to a guided online discussion

Virtual focus groups are also becoming more common. Online "chat" sessions, in which one to dozens of pre-recruited respondents type in responses to a guided online discussion, can be used effectively to bring together participants from virtually anywhere to discuss a client issue, activities, and experiences, or provide feedback on products. While virtual focus groups will not always be able to replace in-person interviews, the time- and cost-saving benefits of such groups make them a very useful tool for researchers—especially for gathering Web site feedback with participants when they are using the Internet.

in-depth interview

a qualitative research technique in which an interviewer will meet an interviewee for about 45 minutes to one hour

In-depth interviews tend to be used for three main reasons. First, they are used in situations where the limited number of subjects renders quantitative methods inappropriate. Second, they are used when information obtained from each subject is expected to vary considerably, i.e., when the question of "what percentage of respondents said what" is not relevant. Third, in-depth interviews can be used to explore a topic as a preliminary stage in planning a more formal questionnaire-based survey.

Interviews can be structured, unstructured, or a combination of the two. The unstructured interview differs from a conversation in the sense that both parties are aware of an agenda of question and answer. The structured interview involves a number of skills on the part of the researcher. For example, questionnaire-drafting skills, such as determining the sequence of questions and their precise content, are key. Other required skills are the interpersonal skills involved in conversation and being able to "lead" the interviewee. Also, the researcher must develop the skills of recording responses accurately; very often interviews are taped and a word-for-word transcription is prepared.

There are various ways of going about the analysis of interview transcripts, but it is imperative that the researcher returns to the terms of reference and statement of objectives and begins to evaluate the information gathered in relation to the questions posed. Recently, a variety of computer packages have become available to analyze interview transcripts.

Quantitative Research Techniques

Traditionally, most consumer research studies have been based on questions identified in market decision making, to be posed to random samples of existing or potential customers. The Travel Alberta study at the end of this chapter (see Case Study) is typical of such research. This study found that the top activities on leisure trips for Albertans are visiting family and friends (75 percent), taking trips that involve outdoor recreation (67 percent), and visiting resort towns and attractions (39.5 percent). All these trends are quantifiable dimensions that can be used for future decision making. This is quantitative research, meaning a study to which numerical estimates can be attached. Quantitative research is usually based on "structured" questionnaires, in which every respondent is asked the same questions. Because the range of possible answers is printed on questionnaires, variations to suit individual respondents are not possible.

However, quantitative data can also be collected via observations. Some researchers believe that this is one of the most effective ways to actually gain knowledge about consumers. Tracking studies, for example, are used in museums, galleries, and tourist attractions to monitor people's activities. Tracking studies provide information on what people do, the amount of time they spend on various activities, and the order in which they do things. Other types of observation include counting the number of people in a dining room at various times of the day, counting the number of cars in the parking lot, counting the number of people entering a casino, and even seeing which way people move through a museum or an art gallery.

The Questionnaire or Survey Method

A review of the methods used in collecting tourism and hospitality research data shows that the questionnaire technique or survey method is the most frequently used. The survey method includes factual surveys, opinion surveys, or interpretive surveys, all of which can be conducted by personal interview, telephone, mail, or by electronic means.

Factual surveys are by far the most beneficial. "When you are on holiday, what activities do you engage in?" was a question used by Travel Alberta in the survey discussed in the Case Study in this chapter. Respondents should be able to give accurate information in response to such a question. In an **opinion survey**, the respondent is asked to express an opinion or make an evaluation or appraisal. For example, in the same survey by Travel Alberta, Albertans were asked about their opinions toward package holidays. In **interpretive surveys**, the respondent acts as an interpreter as well as a reporter. Subjects are asked why they chose a certain course of action—why they chose a particular package, for example. While respondents can reply accurately to "what" questions, they often have difficulty replying to "why" questions. Therefore, while interpretive research may give a researcher a feel for consumer behaviour, the usefulness of the results tends to be limited.

Personal interviews tend to be much more flexible than either mail or telephone surveys because the interviewer can adapt to the situation and the respondent. Typically, one can obtain much more information by personal interview than by other means, as personal interviewers can observe the situation as well as ask questions. A major limitation of the personal interview method, however, is its relatively high cost. An interview takes a considerable amount of time to conduct, and there is always the possibility of personal interviewer bias. *Telephone surveys* are conducted much more rapidly and at less cost than are personal interviews. Telephone was Travel Alberta's chosen method for collecting data. Speed and low cost are the primary advantages of telephone interviews; however, these interviews tend to be less flexible than personal interviews, and they also have to be brief. Computer-assisted telephone interviewing using random dialling is very popular in North America. *Mail surveys* involve mailing the questionnaire to carefully selected sample respondents and requesting them to return the completed questionnaires. Advantages are that a large geographical area can be covered, respondents can fill out the survey at their own convenience, and personal interview bias is absent. The greatest problems with mail surveys are the lack of a good list and lack of adequate response.

Finally, a relatively new way of conducting research is the use of *electronic surveys* that ask consumers questions and immediately record and tabulate the results. Computer-type electronic equipment might be placed in a hotel lobby, mall, or other high-traffic location (for example, Whistler Resort collects data from its skiers using electronic devices placed up and down the main street). Alternatively, respondents may be asked to complete a survey online. Internet-based survey methodology is gaining increasing popularity, and it is predicted that as much as 60 to 80 percent of research will be conducted via the Web in the near future.[21] The *Snapshot* on pages 119–120 shows how Travel Alberta used the Web to gather valuable customer information. (See also Chapter 10 for information related to online research.)

factual survey
the respondent is asked to state certain facts, such as age or number of children

opinion survey
the respondent is asked to express an opinion or make an evaluation or appraisal

interpretive survey
the respondent acts as an interpreter as well as a reporter

SNAPSHOT

USING THE WEB TO GATHER CONSUMER DATA

In November 2002, Travel Alberta began its first e-marketing campaign, which had an impressive response. The campaign was a pilot project intended to gauge the interest of Web consumers visiting the Travel Alberta Web site in submitting valuable information about their interests and travel plans. Several ski packages with a variety of industry partners formed the incentive, which was integral to encouraging Web consumers to sign up. A pop-up message on both the U.S. and Canadian home pages presented the offer in an attractive format to all "Americas Web" visitors and encouraged them to participate by featuring a contest to win a ski vacation.

"The objectives met our expectations and exceeded our targets in terms of the quality of data we have available with which to make future marketing decisions," says Klaus Roth, Travel Alberta Portfolio Manager. Approximately 2600 entries were received during the campaign period from November 1, 2002, to February 15, 2003, the majority of entries being submitted in late January and early February. "This finding has certainly made us think differently about consumer travel timelines," says Roth. "Though we would have expected more sign-ups in the latter months of 2002, it points to the fact that consumers are making travel plans much closer to their date of travel."

The significant increase in Web traffic during the months of January and February (an 87 percent increase compared with 2002) strongly reinforced the growing popularity of the Web as a key travel planning tool. In addition, the data collected offered a rich summary of the activities Web visitors are seeking, their anticipated travel dates, and

basic demographics of the users. "The results validate all of the research we have about online consumer travel preferences," says Roth. "In fact, the spread of data reinforces the messages, demographics, and markets we focus on in our "Americas" program. These are highly qualified travel consumers that want to talk with us and visit Alberta."

Seventy-five percent of contest entrants were from the United States, and the remainder were from Canada. Top locations of entrants from all primary "Americas" markets were Ontario, California, British Columbia, Texas, Florida, Saskatchewan, New York, Illinois, Pennsylvania, and Georgia. Nearly 50 percent of entrants asked to receive information in the future from Travel Alberta and its preferred partners. Twenty-five percent of respondents indicated that they plan to travel to Alberta in the summer of 2003, the majority intending to do so later in the year and in the spring/summer of 2004. Preferred activities included sightseeing (20 percent), skiing (15 percent), hiking (15 percent),

SNAPSHOT *continued*

culture (12 percent), urban pursuits (11 percent), trail riding (9 percent), fishing (7 percent), cycling (6 percent), and golf (6 percent).

Based on the success of the pilot project, the "Americas" marketing team was planning a more aggressive campaign for the spring/summer 2003 season. "We are aligning our efforts with those of the Canadian Tourism Commission (CTC) to leverage opportunities to reach more qualified consumers," said Roth. "In addition, strategic partnerships with leading Internet providers and Web portals, including the acquisition of highly qualified e-mail distribution lists will ensure that we drive the maximum traffic possible from our primary markets to the Web site," added Roth. The new campaign would feature a similar incentive, offering a chance to win an Alberta summer vacation, with support from a variety of industry partners.

Source: Lundy, H. (2003). *Travel Alberta's first e-marketing campaign a success!* Retrieved March 3, 2003, from www.tourismtogether.com.

Questionnaire Design

The value of a survey questionnaire rests with its design. As there are so many ways in which a questionnaire can be formulated to perform its task, it is difficult to develop a set of rules. Each questionnaire is unique. Consequently, the design of questionnaires has been referred to as an art that is influenced by the researcher's knowledge of the population, the subject matter, common sense, experience, and pilot work.

According to Crouch, questionnaires have four main purposes:[22]

1. *To collect relevant data.* When drafting each question, the researcher should always ask, "What use will the answers be?" This relates back to the definition and purpose of the research, but also tests whether the question is phrased so as to produce the desired information.

2. *To make data comparable.* The wording of the questions and alternative answers should be clear and not open to more than one interpretation. The language employed should be simple so that it can be understood by all respondents. Sentences should be kept short and to the point. Carrying out a pilot survey on a small sample is useful for detecting any ambiguities.

3. *To minimize bias.* The phrasing of questions can bias the response given. For example, if a question begins with "you don't think, do you …," a negative response is likely to be given, and if a question begins with "shouldn't something be done about …," a positive response is the likely outcome. Care should be taken to avoid wording questions that lead respondents to feel that one answer will be regarded as more acceptable than others.

4. *To motivate the respondent.* The respondent must be made to feel that answering the question will be interesting, useful, and not time-consuming. If the questionnaire is too long, this can be demoralizing for the interviewer and respondent, thus affecting both refusal rates and the quality of the data. The survey should begin with interesting questions, not with requests for personal details like "how much do you earn?" These questions can be placed at the end of the questionnaire.

In the past, quantitative research has frequently been more acceptable to tourism practitioners than qualitative research has. Traditionally, travel research has been conducted in-house, which is a reflection of both narrow profit margins and an ignorance of the benefits that skilled independent researchers can offer. The result has been a proliferation of amateurishly designed questionnaires, many of which can be found in hotel rooms or which are given to tourists on charter planes on the return journey home. There is also a tendency to distribute customer satisfaction questionnaires to as many clients as possible, without worrying too much about what percentage will respond and whether there will be any built-in response bias among respondents. Further, there has been very little research on the validity or accuracy of questionnaire data used in leisure and tourism studies. One study found that in a survey of tennis participation, respondents exaggerated their level of participation by as much as 100 percent. This suggests that the researcher and the user of research results should always bear in mind the nature and source of the data. Questionnaire surveys rely on information from respondents, and what respondents say depends on their own powers of recall, on their honesty, and, fundamentally, on the questions asked of them.

benchmarking

a management technique that allows companies to compare how well they are performing relative to their competitors

More recently, the practice of benchmarking has received attention from tourism market researchers. **Benchmarking** is essentially a management technique that allows companies to compare how well they are performing relative to their competitors. To date, the limited application of benchmarking within tourism and hospitality industries has been confined mainly to hotels.[23] Benchmarking initiatives might include collecting guest satisfaction scores. For Sheraton Hotels and Resorts, measuring guest satisfaction is a crucial part of marketing research, and plays an important role in internal marketing. Guest satisfaction scores (GSS) are closely monitored by the research group, and results are shared with all hotels and all employees. To measure satisfaction, Sheraton Hotels has commissioned NFO Worldwide Group to send out a questionnaire to every customer that stays in a Sheraton property in North America. Chapter 11's opening vignette profiles the Sheraton Suites Calgary Eau Claire, which was awarded the Starwood Select Best in Brand in North America for both 2001 and 2002, with the highest guest satisfaction score among 240 Sheraton properties.

SAMPLING

Because of the expenses associated with research, marketing managers often find themselves grappling with the question of how many people must be surveyed in order to obtain accurate responses. It is almost impossible—and not very cost effective—to interview every product user or potential product user. Therefore, a company's decisions are based on the opinions and reactions of a sample of the population. The sample selection process is as follows:

1. *Define the population.* The first stage in the sampling process is specification of the target population.

2. *Specify the sample frame.* This is a specification of the listing, directory, or roster from which the sample will be chosen.

3. *Select the sampling method.* The researcher has to decide whether a probability or nonprobability approach will be applied to draw the sample and exactly how the sample members will be selected. There is a wide range of both probability and nonprobability sampling methods. The key difference between the two is that in probability sampling, a statistical evaluation of sampling error can be undertaken; such an assessment is not possible for samples drawn by nonprobabilistic methods. Therefore the more accurate form of sampling is the probability method, in which each unit of the population has a known, but not necessarily an equal, chance of selection. Techniques subsumed within this method are simple, random, systematic, stratified, cluster, multi-phase, and area sampling.

4. *Determine sample size.* The selection of sample size has received considerable attention from critics of tourism research. It is not difficult to find examples of tourism research projects in which the sample size has been determined by no known or accepted theoretical practice. Baker et al. suggest that there are two basic approaches for the tourism researcher interested in accountability and efficiency: required size per cell and the traditional statistical model.[24] The required size per cell approach requires approximately 30 responses for each demographic cell of data. For example, two genders, four ethnic groups, and four age groups would require a sample size of 960 (2 x 4 x 4 x 30). The traditional statistical model is based on a management specification of allowable error (*e*), the level of confidence in the sampling process (*z*), and the variance in the population (@). The sampling size is thus expressed as: $n = z@ / e$

    One important aspect of the traditional statistical method of sample size determination is that the sample must be randomly selected; every member of the population of interest must have a known chance of being selected. This is a key to eliminating systematic bias. Another important point is that if questionnaire respondents are all basically alike, a small sample size is required, no matter how large the population. This is often a fundamentally difficult concept for researchers and managers alike to accept. Sample size is not a function of population size: it is a function of population variance. Large-scale data collection is very costly, and quite often not needed.

5. *Draw the sample and collect the data.* The final stage in the sampling process is the implementation stage, in which the sample is chosen and surveyed.

The sampling procedure adopted will have a direct impact on the validity of the results, so if the survey is to be the principal tool for data collection, careful consideration must be given to the technique employed and the sample size chosen.

COMMON RESEARCH ERRORS

There are many potential pitfalls in conducting research; the most common four errors are discussed here.

1. Not Including Enough Qualitative Information

Most surveys reported in trade magazines provide descriptive information. For example, an American Express survey of business people in 2002 reported that business travellers were using more online booking tools to make travel arrangements. However, to use this information, tourism suppliers and intermediaries need to know specifically what online tools these business travellers are using, what they believe is an effective Web site, how long they stay online per transaction, etc. All these questions could be asked in face-to-face interviews or in focus groups with business travellers.

2. An Improper Use of Sophisticated Statistical Analysis

It is possible for a multitude of errors to creep into the research process if collection, tabulation, and analysis are not done properly. In today's environment, tabulation is likely to take place on the computer; a number of excellent packages are available for this purpose. However, statistical conclusions must be interpreted in terms of the best action or policy for the organization to follow. This reduction of the interpretation to recommendations is one of the most difficult tasks in the research process.

3. Failure to Have a Sample That Is Representative of the Population

A sample is a segment of the population selected to represent the population as a whole. Ideally, the sample should be representative, so that the researcher can make accurate estimates of the thoughts and behaviours of the larger population. It is doubtful that the samples used by both Superior North (see the opening vignette) and Seaflight Hydrofoil (see *Marketing in Action*) were representative of the population as a whole. Care must therefore be taken in interpreting, and acting on, the results of these studies. And in the *Snapshot* below, the Canadian Tourism Commission acknowledges that their International Travel Survey had begun to yield data whose quality was eroding—partly because a smaller and smaller percentage of travellers' questionnaires were returned.

4. Problems with Interpretation

In many cases, results from research can be interpreted the wrong way. In the opening vignette, the assumption was made by Superior North researchers that what residents of the region view as tourism opportunities would generally be viewed the same way by those visiting the region. However, this is not always the case. Too often, local residents do not appreciate the assets they have in their region that might appeal to tourists.

SNAPSHOT

THE INTERNATIONAL TRAVEL SURVEY (ITS)

The Research Program at the Canadian Tourism Commission (CTC) is fundamental to the success of the CTC. It establishes the importance of the tourism industry to the Canadian economy in terms of employment size and growth, foreign exchange earnings,

SNAPSHOT *continued*

tax revenues for all levels of government, and gross domestic product (GDP). The information the CTC provides has proved invaluable in gaining visibility for the tourism industry and drawing attention to some of the obstacles to the growth of the industry that are of a regulatory or financial nature (air transportation policy, taxation policies, customs practices, etc.).

While the CTC carries out regular market surveys regarding consumer perceptions, behaviours, and travel patterns in every major international market, it acknowledges that there is still a need for tourism organizations to get to know their customers better. One area that has seen significant improvements in recent years is in the collection of data from traffic flows across Canada's borders. The International Travel Survey (ITS) measures these flows and creates a profile of visitors' characteristics, travel habits, and spending while they are in this country. In this way, trends can be spotted for international tourism traffic, predictions can be made for forecasting, and information can be produced for decision making. Conducted by Statistics Canada in partnership with the CTC, the ITS produces numbers that are released on a monthly, quarterly, and annual basis.

The ITS is an ongoing study and has been in process since the 1920s. It initially consisted of a simple form, requiring very little time to complete. As travel and tourism grew over the decades, so did the form length—and the number of forms—required to keep track of visitors to Canada. But for many reasons, the survey had begun to yield data whose quality was eroding—partly because a smaller and

smaller percentage of travellers' questionnaires were returned. So beginning in the late 1990s, the CTC research committee began to address the whole logic and design of the ITS, and to develop a new vision more suitable to the needs of the tourism industry, notably rationalizing it to focus on Canada's major ports of entry and key international markets.

Among the changes made is the supplementation of paper questionnaires (handed out by custom officers to overseas residents as they enter Canada) with personnel interviews with some of these visitors as they leave. Also, the number of languages in which surveys are conducted has increased from 2 to 10, and sampling has been concentrated on the major and medium-sized Canadian airports. In addition to changing the way data is collected, the methods used to derive the estimates have been improved to better reflect the different characteristics of business and leisure travellers from some key overseas markets.

Rebuilding the ITS has not been an easy task. Traditional surveys use a stable population, but the ITS involves millions of moving targets. The field work for the ITS also requires an enormous amount of effort and more than 3700 people to complete it each month. But the CTC is on the right track. Users of the new ITS numbers include the federal governments, the CTC, most large Canadian cities, and the U.S. government.

Sources: Canadian Tourism Commission. (2002). *Canadian Tourism Commission strategic plan, 2002–2004.* Ottawa: Author, 13; Meis, S. (2002). New era in research. *Tourism, 6*(8), 15.

EFFECTIVE USE OF MARKETING RESEARCH IN DECISION MAKING

There is little doubt that in an industry as dynamic and expansive as tourism, research must play a critical role in its development. Not only should research be undertaken by every organization, whether large or small, to assist in the task of practical decision making at a strategic level, but it should also be acknowledged as important at the academic level for its shedding of valuable light on the development of tourism on a global basis. For research to be worthwhile, it has to be acted upon. In this chapter, examples have been given of tourism organizations like Superior North, Seaflight Hydrofoil, and Sheraton Hotels and Resorts, which have used research results to make important strategic decisions.

Research is never an exact science, but it can reduce the margins of error to which hunches on their own are subject. The feasibility study, for example, is an essential prerequisite to any new project, whether it is the launch of a new company, the introduction of a new logo, or the development of a new product. Above all, the success of research will be contingent on three conditions:

1. Sufficient resources must be allocated to do the job properly, both in terms of time and money.
2. Managers must be willing to believe the results of the research when they become available, even if they conflict with the management's own preconceived views.
3. The results should be used. All too frequently, research is commissioned in order to avoid making an immediate decision. Expensively commissioned research is then left to gather dust in a drawer instead of being used to enable managers to make better decisions on the future direction of the company's strategy.

TRENDS IN TOURISM MARKETING RESEARCH

Research in tourism marketing has matured over the last few decades, fuelled by a proliferation of texts and journals specifically related to the subject. Given the importance of tourism marketing in the management of tourism and hospitality, it is important that students as well as practitioners understand the forces that are shaping the future of marketing in the tourism industry and how these forces direct tourism research. Increased competition, increasingly expectant consumers, consolidation in many sectors of the industry, rapid technological improvements—all these factors have opened up new avenues of research. Three key areas that are underresearched, and therefore underrepresented in academic literature, are the impact of the Internet on tourism marketing, consumer research in an increasingly fragmented marketplace, and integrated marketing communications.

In recent years, tourism marketing has gone through fundamental changes, caused by the pursuit of global strategies based on strategic alliances and by the breakdown of commercial borders and advances in new technologies—particularly communication and distribution technologies. These factors have greatly facilitated the commercialization of tourism products. Today, the *Internet* is a key tool in tourism marketing for both industrialized and developing countries. The Internet fits the theoretical marketing principle in the travel industry because it allows suppliers to set up direct links of communication with their customers. The travel industry has been quick to recognize the potential of the Internet, but research in this area is still at an early stage. As Internet technology is relatively new, there is still little knowledge of the consumer buying process online, and the impact of the Internet on travel intermediaries is still uncertain.

Technology is also beginning to have an impact on consumer research, as tourism organizations recognize the potential of database management and the value of relationship marketing. The importance of researching tourist satisfaction and dissatisfaction, service quality gaps, and consumer travel patterns is now evident, and the segmentation or classification of tourism consumers in an increasingly *fragmented market* is becoming more and more critical. As tourists become more sophisticated in their behaviour, so too must research become more sophisticated in order to understand and explain this behaviour. Understanding the consumer's needs and buying process is the foundation of successful marketing. The "grand models" of consumer behaviour have been transformed by tourism academics interested in the tourism choice process. However, this "borrowing" of theories from those who have concentrated on more tangible products has hampered the development of realistic models.

Finally, one of the most important advances in marketing in recent decades has been the rise of *integrated marketing communication*—the recognition that advertising can no longer be crafted and executed in isolation from other promotional mix elements. As tourism markets and the media have grown more complex and fragmented, consumers find themselves in an increasingly confusing marketing environment. Tourism marketers must respond to this consumer confusion by conveying a consistent, unified message in all their promotional activities. Destinations are therefore beginning to understand the importance of branding and resort positioning, but to date, research in this area has been mainly exploratory.

CHAPTER SUMMARY

The way in which an organization gathers, uses, and disseminates its research in the marketing context is generally referred to as the Marketing Information System (MIS). A key component of the MIS is the marketing research process: the systematic and objective search for and analysis of information relevant to the identification and solution of any problem in the field of marketing.

In undertaking research, these steps should be followed: identify and define the problem; investigate available sources; develop the research plan; collect data; analyze data; and present research results. There are several approaches to collecting data, but two key decisions that have to be made are whether to use primary or secondary data and whether to use qualitative or quantitative research. Secondary data is data that already exists for an established purpose, and this type of research is also referred to as documents and desk research. Primary research involves collecting new information and can be divided into unstructured and structured situations. Unstructured research includes participative observation, and structured research includes techniques such as the repertory grid technique, projection techniques, and focus groups. These techniques are forms of qualitative—or subjective—research.

Quantitative research is research to which numerical estimates can be attached. It is usually based on "structured" questionnaires, in which every respondent is asked the same questions. The questionnaire technique or survey method is the most frequently used method of collecting tourism and hospitality research data. The survey method includes factual surveys, opinion surveys, and interpretive surveys, all of which can be conducted by personal interview, mail, telephone, or by electronic means. Questionnaires have four main purposes: to collect relevant data, to make data comparable, to minimize bias, and to motivate the respondent.

The sample selection process is as follows: define the population; specify the sample frame; select the sampling method; determine sample size; and draw the sample and collect the data.

There are many potential pitfalls in conducting research; the most common four errors are not including enough qualitative information; an improper use of sophisticated statistical analysis; failure to have a sample that is representative of the population; and problems with interpretation. In addition, the success of research will be contingent on three conditions: sufficient resources must be allocated to do the job properly, both in terms of time and money; managers must be willing to believe the results of the research when they become available; and the results should be used.

Certain factors such as increased competition, increasingly expectant consumers, consolidation in many sectors of the industry, and rapid technological improvements have all opened up new avenues of research. Three key areas that are underresearched, and therefore underrepresented in academic literature, are the impact of the Internet on tourism marketing, consumer research in an increasingly fragmented marketplace, and integrated marketing communications.

KEY TERMS

benchmarking, p. 121	interpretive survey, p. 118	projection techniques, p. 116
competitor intelligence, p. 107	marketing information system	qualitative research, p. 111
consumer research, p. 107	(MIS), p. 102	quantitative research, p. 111
factual survey, p. 118	marketing research, p. 103	repertory grid technique, p. 116
focus group, p. 116	opinion survey, p. 118	secondary data, p. 110
in-depth interview, p. 117	primary data, p. 110	virtual focus groups, p. 117

DISCUSSION QUESTIONS AND EXERCISES

1. Do some research and find an example of a local tourism or hospitality organization that has recently published research results. How have they used the results for decision making?

2. If you owned a high-class restaurant and wanted to improve the level of service offered by your staff, how could observational research help you accomplish your goal?

3. How does secondary data differ from primary data, and what are the main tourism sources of secondary data in Canada?

4. Differentiate between qualitative and quantitative research and give specific examples of how each could be used by a hotel.

5. How would a tour operator go about collecting competitor intelligence on the success of tours through Canada?

6. As marketing research manager for a large destination-marketing organization, how might you use focus groups to collect information?

CASE STUDY

ALBERTA RESIDENT TRAVEL BEHAVIOUR RESEARCH STUDY, 1999–2000

Alberta is the fourth largest province in Canada, with a population of just under three million, and is divided by Travel Alberta into six tourism destination regions (TDRs): Alberta North, Edmonton and area, Alberta Central, Calgary and area, Canadian Rockies, and Alberta South. Each TDR receives equal funding for both marketing coordination and regional tourism marketing services. In 1999, Alberta's total tourism revenues totalled $4.2 billion, and the region received 13 million overnight stays. Of these, 7.5 million were Albertans travelling within Alberta, and along with the 9.2 million same-day visitors from Alberta they spent more than $2.1 billion within the province. An important component of Travel Alberta's marketing plan is the effective marketing of the province to Albertans as a world-class destination close to home, in the face of increasing incentives to travel elsewhere. The plan intends to encourage residents to travel more frequently in Alberta and into new areas of the province. However, there has always been a poor understanding of the consumer in Alberta, so part of the 1999 marketing plan included embarking on an in-province travel behaviour study, so that future marketing activities could be segmented by demography, sociography, geography, travel interests, and preferences of Albertans.

The overall aim of the research study was to establish a better understanding of the domestic travel market in Alberta, as a basis for the development of a marketing campaign. More specifically, the research had three main objectives:

1. To measure the factors important in choosing Alberta destinations.
2. To assess the current image and perceptions of the Alberta vacation product among identified market segments.
3. To understand how travel decisions are made and how travel information is acquired.

To accomplish the research objectives, both qualitative and quantitative methods were used, to allow for accurate understanding upon which to base decisions. This approach combined two different but complimentary methodologies.

Phase 1: Qualitative Research

Twelve focus groups were conducted in the six tourist destination regions. These exploratory groups were conducted with residents across Alberta to look at their leisure travel preferences and habits within the province. The results of these focus groups helped frame and validate questions regarding tourism behaviours for the quantitative survey conducted in Phase 2.

Phase 2: Quantitative Research

Survey research was conducted with a sample of 13 445 Albertans. Telephone surveys were conducted between October and December 1999, and they took an average of 35 minutes to complete. Screening criteria required the respondent to be over 18, and to have travelled within Alberta on at least one overnight leisure trip in the previous 12 months, for a distance of no less than 80 km from home. A randomly generated sample list of Albertans was purchased, and 15 computer assisted telephone interviewing (CATI) stations were used to allow interviewers to key answers directly into SPSS (a statistical software program). The survey was divided into six main sections: travel decisions for making trips in Alberta; travel product perceptions; travel factors that influence people to take trips in Alberta; perceptions of activity packages; media and information needs; and demographics.

Basic frequency tables were generated for each question, and data was compared across regions to identify patterns of similarity and difference among the tourists regions. Cluster analysis was then used to search for relatively homogenous groups of shared characteristics within given populations.

Results

Overall, 22 percent of telephone calls resulted in a completed interview (3017 respondents). Of the 78 percent that were not completed, 58 percent refused participation, another 22 percent were ineligible, 10 percent of numbers were not in service, and the remaining 10 percent were unreachable. A sample size of 3017 provides an overall margin of error at $+/-1.78$ percent, 19 times out of 20. At a 95 percent confidence level, these statistical parameters mean that there is a 5 percent probability that the sample population data would not reflect the larger population, plus or minus the margin of error.

Province-Wide Findings

When it comes to taking a short leisure trip (one to three nights away from home), on average Albertans are prepared to travel for 342 km, or for a period of four hours. Just over half of Albertans (57 percent) plan for a trip such as this for one to four weeks in advance. The top activities on leisure trips are visiting family and friends (75 percent), taking trips that involve outdoor recreation (67 percent), and visiting resort towns and attractions (39.5 percent). People who visit family and friends tend to make an average of 5.8 trips per year, while outdoor recreation accounts for an average of 4.5 trips per year, and those that visit resorts and attractions make an average of 2.6 trips a year.

The top three factors that influence people when they make decisions about where to take a trip in Alberta include cost and value for money spent, having a sense of being in a safe and secure environment, and making a visit to family and friends. When asked to rate statements about travelling within the province, most respondents said that the mountains, forests, and parks make a trip in Alberta special. Next to that, they like to take trips in Alberta where they can explore and do new things.

Overall, most Albertans prefer to choose their activities when they get to their destination. If activity packages were available, 77 percent said they would be more likely to consider discount packages that offer a variety of choices of activities and/or events, and 74 percent would be attracted to packages that offer tickets to a special event and include transportation, hotel accommodations, and some meals. Another 70 percent would consider a package that offers self-guided sightseeing tours to outlying attractions or events and includes nightlife and hotel accommodations.

The majority of Albertans (57 percent) feel they are "somewhat well informed" about travel opportunities that exist within the province, and less than one-third (27 percent) feel "well informed." The remaining 16 percent feel they are "not very well informed at all" about travel opportunities within Alberta. Word of mouth (47 percent) is the primary source of information people rely on for knowing about places to go and things to see in Alberta. While one-third (34 percent) relies on the newspapers, 24 percent go to the Alberta Motor Association (AMA), and almost as many (23 percent) go to tourist information centres. The information they look for in order to plan their leisure trips is accommodations, leisure activities that are near their destination, costs, and campgrounds and hiking trails in the area.

Cluster Profiles

In this study, discriminant analysis showed that the five-cluster solution correctly classified 93.1 percent of respondents into the right cluster, and that a statistically significant difference existed between the clusters. To put a face to the clusters, names were assigned that are indicative of the key characteristics that make them uniquely different as a group. Table 4.5 presents a summary and comparison of all of the characteristics of each cluster. (See Chapter 3, pp. 82–84, for a more detailed discussion of each of the five clusters.)

The table shows some striking similarities between the clusters. These include the fact that, in all clusters, a limited view of travel opportunities is evident, as reflected in an overall preference for "mountains, forests, and parks," even though Albertans say they want to "explore and do new things." For all the clusters, visiting friends and relatives and

Table 4.5

Summary Table Showing Characteristics of Each Cluster

	CLUSTER ONE Young Urban Active Outdoor N=520 730	CLUSTER TWO Indoor Leisure Traveller N=586 285	CLUSTER THREE Children First Traveller N=446 516	CLUSTER FOUR Fair Weather Friends N=445 280	CLUSTER FIVE Older Cost-Conscious Traveller N=754 501
	18.9%	21.3%	16.2%	16.2%	27.4%
Demographics					
	M=49% F=51%	M=31% F=69%	M=50% F=50%	M=59% F=41%	M=44% F=56%
	Average Age: 37.5	Average Age: 40.2	Average Age: 42.5	Average Age: 44.2	Average Age: 44.8
	12% under $25 000	12% under $25 000	7% under $25 000	10% under $25 000	11% under $25 000
	16% $100 000+	9% $100 000+	19% $100 000+	13% $100 000+	11% $100 000+
	66% Married	70% Married	75% Married	62% Married	62% Married
	23% Not Married	13.5% Not Married	9% Not Married	21% Not Married	18% Not Married
	Children: 54%	Children: 63%	Children: 66%	Children: 33%	Children: 30%
	Edmonton: 38.5%	Edmonton: 25%	Edmonton: 30%	Edmonton: 34%	Edmonton: 33%
	Calgary: 32%	Calgary: 23%	Calgary: 27%	Calgary: 27%	Calgary: 28%
	North: 14%	North: 18%	North: 15%	North: 16%	North: 14%
	South: 8%	South: 17%	South: 13%	South: 12.5%	South: 13%
	Heartland: 8%	Heartland: 17%	Heartland: 13%	Heartland: 11%	Heartland: 12%
Decision Factors (in descending order of influence)					
	School holidays	Sense of safe and secure environment	Children's sports/ competitions	Visit family and friends	Sense of safe and secure environment
	Cost/value for money spent	Cost/value for money spent	Sense of safe and secure environment	Weather conditions	Cost/value for money spent
	Sense of safe and secure environment	Weather conditions			Weather conditions

TABLE 4.5 *continued*

Decision Factors (in descending order of influence) continued

Visit family and friends	Packages or discounts	Cost/value for money spent	Quality of accommodations
Weather conditions	Visit family and friends	Children/family-oriented activities	Visit family and friends
Variety of activities offered	Quality of accommodations	Visit family and friends	
	Children/family-oriented activities	Variety of activities	
	School holidays	Weather conditions	
	Large city attractions	School holidays	
	Small town events and attractions		

Travel Statements

Mountains, forests, and parks	Mountains, forests, and parks	Mountains, forests, and parks	Mountains, forests and parks
Explore and do new things	Explore and do new things	Explore and do new things	Explore and do new things

Most Popular Travel Activities (top four)

Visiting friends and relatives	Visiting friends and relatives	Visiting friends and relatives	Visiting friends and relatives
Outdoor recreation	Outdoor recreation	Outdoor recreation	Outdoor recreation
Indoor leisure activities	Resort towns and attractions	Outdoor summer sports	Resort towns and attractions
Resort towns and attractions	Indoor leisure activities	Outdoor leisure activities	Indoor leisure activities

Note: The N at the top of each column refers to the provincial population that falls into these clusters. The % represents the percentage of the population that is likely to fall into the individual clusters.

TABLE 4.5 *continued*

CLUSTER ONE Young Urban Active Outdoor N=520 730	CLUSTER TWO Indoor Leisure Traveller N=586 285	CLUSTER THREE Children First Traveller N=446 516	CLUSTER FOUR Fair Weather Friends N=445 280	CLUSTER FIVE Older Cost-Conscious Traveller N=754 501
18.9%	21.3%	16.2%	16.2%	27.4%
Activity Packages People Would Consider				
Discount packages with variety	Discount packages with variety	Discount packages with variety	Tickets to special events with extras	Discount packages
Tickets to special events with extras	Tickets to special events with extras	Tickets to special events with extras	Discount packages	Tickets to special events with extras
Self-guided tours	Self-guided tours	Self-guided tours	Tickets to special events with extras	Self-guided tours
Hiking, lodging, catering, campfires and cabins	Hiking, lodging, catering, campfires and cabins	Hiking, lodging, catering, campfires and cabins	Self-guided tours	Hiking, lodging, catering, campfires and cabins
	Shopping, theatre, fine dining, and hotels		Hiking, lodging, catering, campfires and cabins	Shopping, theatre, fine dining, and hotels
	Separate activities			Separate activities
Self-Designed Packages (in order of preference)				
Outdoor recreation	Outdoor recreation	Outdoor recreation	Outdoor recreation	Outdoor recreation
Accommodation	Accommodation	Accommodation	Outdoor summer sports	Accommodation
Outdoor summer sports	Outdoor leisure activities	Outdoor summer sports	Outdoor leisure activities	Outdoor summer sports
Outdoor leisure activities	Outdoor summer sports	Outdoor leisure activities	Accommodation	Outdoor leisure activities
Meals	Meals	Meals	Meals	Meals

TABLE 4.5 *continued*

Sources of Information Used (in order of preference)

Word of mouth	Word of mouth	Word of mouth	Word of mouth
Newspapers	Newspapers	Newspapers	Newspapers
Tourist information centres	Alberta Motor Association	Alberta Motor Association	Alberta Motor Association
Internet	Other (prior experience and radio)	Other (radio and prior experience)	Other (radio and prior experience)
Other (radio and Travel Alberta)	Internet	Internet	Television
Alberta Motor Association		Tourist information centres	Internet
		Alberta Motor Association	

Perceived Effectiveness of Communication Methods

Word of mouth	Word of mouth	Word of mouth	Word of mouth
Television	Television		Television
Campground guides			
Tourist information centres			
Newspapers			
Alberta Motor Association			
Glossy brochures			
Magazines			

Note: The N at the top of each column refers to the provincial population that falls into these clusters. The % represents the percentage of the population that is likely to fall into the individual clusters.

participating in outdoor recreation were given as the two main reasons for travelling in Alberta. In addition, the most effective way for providing Albertans with information regarding destinations, activities, and special events within the province, and the one they rely on the most, is word of mouth. Albertans were also intrigued by the idea of packages that offer value. This was a significant finding, in that few tourism operators in Alberta were offering packages to Albertans at this time, and their experiences of packaging tourism products and services was quite limited. But although Albertans do have these commonalities, the results show that the domestic market in Alberta can be divided into distinct segments that display key characteristics that make them uniquely different as a group. Cluster Three, the "Children First" market, for example, was a group that had not previously been identified in any research study, and yet it represents nearly half a million potential travellers. The "Fair Weather Friends" cluster was also unique in that it was influenced to travel only by family or friends and weather conditions.

The study has a number of theoretical implications. First, it has shown the power of cluster analysis to reveal relatively homogenous groups of shared characteristics within given populations. The results also support previous research that suggests that the visiting friends and relatives (VFR) market is a significant part of domestic tourism and deserves more recognition. This segment in Alberta takes nearly six trips a year, while outdoor recreation accounts for an average of 4.5 trips per year, indicating that the short-break market is also a distinct and valuable tourism segment.

Of course, an effective market segmentation study should result in the more efficient and effective use of marketing and promotional dollars, especially in advertising. The resulting Travel Alberta promotional campaign sought to use the data generated from the research for such marketing and promotional purposes. (*Marketing in Action* in Chapter 8, on pages 255–257, provides details of this process.)

Source: Hudson, S., & Ritchie, J. R. B. (2002). Understanding the domestic market using cluster analysis: A case study of the marketing efforts of Travel Alberta. *Journal of Vacation Marketing*, *8*(3), 263–276.

QUESTIONS

1. What were the key differences between Phase I and Phase II of the research program?
2. Do you think the methodologies employed were sufficient to achieve the research objectives? What other methods could have been used?
3. Take a closer look at Table 4.5. Apart from the similarities highlighted above, what else do the results signify?
4. Before looking at Chapter 8 (*Marketing in Action*), how would you use this segmentation research to make more efficient and effective use of marketing and promotional dollars?

WEB SITES

www.seaflights.com
Seaflight Hydrofoil

www.sheraton.com
Sheraton Hotels and Resorts

www.sheratonsuites.com
Sheraton Suites Calgary Eau Claire

www.nosta.on.ca
Superior North in Ontario

www.travelalberta.com
Travel Alberta consumer Web site

www.tourismtogether.com
Travel Alberta industry Web site

ENDNOTES

1. Gerhold, P. (1993). Defining marketing (or is it market?) research. *Marketing Research,* *5*(Fall), 6–7.

2. Kinnear, T., Taylor, J., Johnson, L., & Armstrong, R. (1993). *Australian marketing research.* Sydney, Australia: McGraw-Hill.

3. Green, P., Tull, D., & Albaum, A. (1988). *Research for marketing decisions* (5th ed.). Englewood Cliffs, NJ: Prentice-Hall.

4. Baker, K., Hozier, G.C., Jr., & Rogers, R. D. (1994). Marketing research theory and methodology and the tourism industry: A nontechnical discussion. *Journal of Travel Research, 32*(3), 3–11.

5. Ibid.

6. Morrison, A. (2002). Hospitality research: A pause for reflection. *International Journal of Tourism Research, 4,* 161–169.

7. McIntosh, R. W., Goeldner, C. R., & Ritchie, J. R. B. (1995). *Tourism: Principles, practices, philosophies* (7th ed.). New York: Wiley.

8. Nayga, R. M., & Capps, O. (1994). Impact of socio-economic and demographic factors on food away from home consumption: Number of meals and type of facility. *Journal of Restaurant and Foodservice Marketing, 1*(2), 45–69.

9. Binkley, J. K. (1998). Demand for fast food across metropolitan areas. *Journal of Restaurant and Foodservice Marketing 3*(1), 37–50.

10. Bruner, G. C. (1990). Music, mood and marketing. *Journal of Marketing, 54,* 94–104.

11. Love, J. F. (1995). *McDonald's behind the arches.* New York: Bantam Books.

12. Birch, L. L., Billman, J., & Richards, S. S. (1984). Time of day influences food acceptability. *Appetite, 5*(3), 109–116.

13. Holm, F., Falkebo, M., Salmiovirta, T., Ramstad, A. H., & van Roy, H. (1995). Analysis of retailing in the Nordic countries. *International Trends in Retailing, 12*(2), 3–31.

14. Smith, S. L. J. (1985). Location patterns of urban restaurants. *Annals of Tourism Research, 12*(4), 581–602.

15. Jamal, A. (1996). Acculturation: The symbolism of ethnic eating among contemporary British consumers. *British Food Journal, 98*(10), 12–26.

16. Finkelstein, J. (1989). *Dining out: A sociology of modern manners.* Cambridge, UK: Polity.

17. Boote, J., & Mathews, A. (1999). Saying is one thing; doing is another: The role of observation in marketing research. *Qualitative Market Research: An International Journal, 2*(1), 15–21.

18. Hudson, S., Snaith, T., Miller, G. A., & Hudson, P. (2001). Distribution channels in the travel industry: Using mystery shoppers to understand the influence of travel agency recommendations. *Journal of Travel Research, 40*(2), 148–154.

19. Ryan, C. (1995). *Researching tourist satisfaction: Issues, concepts, problems.* London: Routledge.

20. Ibid.

21. Lipke, D. J. (2000). You've got surveys. *American Demographics, 22*(11), 42–45.

22. Crouch, S. (1986). *Marketing research for managers.* London: Heinemann.

23. Kozak, M., & Rimmington, M. (1999). Measuring tourist destination competitiveness: conceptual considerations and empirical findings. *Hospitality Management, 18,* 273–283.

24. Baker, K. J., Hozier, G.C., Jr., & Rogers, R. D. (1994). Marketing research theory and methodology and the tourism industry: A nontechnical discussion. *Journal of Travel Research, 32*(3), 3–7.

The Tourism and Hospitality Product

THE COOLEST PLACE IN TOWN: QUEBEC'S ICE HOTEL

Using 12 000 tonnes of snow and 400 tonnes of ice, a Canadian entrepreneur has created a fully functional luxury hotel that is attracting international attention as the hottest winter experience in North America. For Jacques Desbois, the man behind Quebec's coolest overnight lodging, sleeping in a snow shelter in winter is "a beautiful experience, a purification." As founder of the Ice Hotel, a concept he imported from Sweden, Desbois gave North Americans a chance to purify in 2001. About 40 000 people visited the hotel's Montmorency Falls site, including 1500 who spent the night. Media coverage was worldwide, and the following year the hotel received 60 000 visitors, 3500 staying overnight. The soft-spoken Desbois was named Quebec's Tourism Personality of the Year for 2001.

Building on the runaway fascination, the promoters expanded the Ice Hotel in 2002, from 6 to 31 rooms. Ten of these are "suites" that have more than one bed and are decorated with ice sculptures. Ordinary rooms are furnished with just a bed and candleholder. To give guests something to do, the hotel site was moved to the Duchesnay "station écotouristique" northeast of Quebec City. Run by Sépaq, the organization that operates Quebec's parks and wildlife reserves, Duchesnay is an 89 km^2 forested area on a lake, offering opportunities for cross-country skiing, ice fishing, snowshoeing, dogsledding, or just walks in the woods.

Duchesnay is also a mini-village that Sépaq converted from structures belonging to a former forestry school. Guests eat their breakfast and dinner in the reception and restaurant building. Three log pavilions contain 40 rooms, and the 14 fully equipped lakeside chalets can accommodate from 4 to 12 guests. For people wanting it both ways, a package is available including one night at the ice hotel and one night in a warm room at the "station" for $388 per person, double occupancy, including breakfast and dinner for the two days and use of Duchesnay's outdoor facilities, except for dogsledding.

The ice hotel itself, including meals and a welcome cocktail, costs $229 per person, double occupancy, in an ordinary room and $279 in a suite. If you can't find an adventurous partner, an ordinary room is a steep $345 and a suite $558. A tour of the hotel provides both enchantment and shivers. On the enchanting side, two art galleries display ice sculptures of fish, swans, human figures, and more. One gallery honours nature and the municipality of Sainte-Catherine-de-la-Jacques-Cartier, in which Duchesnay is located, and the other, which includes a long house, celebrates Iroquois native culture. A wedding chapel has an ice altar with a shining star in the background. Less encouraging are rooms with snow floors, no windows, and beds made of ice blocks. However, sleepers are separated from the ice by a wood frame, 8 cm of dense foam, and deerskins. The hotel supplies sleeping bags rated for arctic conditions, which is more than enough protection as interior temperatures are unlikely to fall below −10°C. Humidity makes the indoor air seem chillier, however, and a tomb-like silence pervades the hotel, even the bar, which is named after sponsor Absolut Vodka. In the morning, a hotel employee comes by with a wake-up coffee or hot chocolate.

Peppered with questions about cold, Desbois replies that only 1 percent of guests leave the hotel without sleeping through the night. "Just follow the advice to change to dry clothes and don't drink much alcohol. Make sure to breathe outside your sleeping bag to avoid building up humidity." Guests are given a half-hour information session on how to keep warm before going to their rooms. As for why anyone would sleep in an ice hotel, Desbois answers, "We're an adventure service, not a lodging service. There's a kind of pride you feel after surviving a night in the Ice Hotel. This is how we present the product." About 30 percent of the guests are American, said Desbois, who is known as Mr. Igloo around Quebec City, for the igloo villages he builds at carnival time. Canadians, who are used to snow, account for 63 percent of guests. To see the hotel without sleeping over, tours of 30 to 45 minutes cost only $14, after which you can have access to the hotel for the whole day. The visitor ticket then becomes a season pass.

For more information on the Ice Hotel, go to www.icehotel-canada.com and the Duchesnay station écotouristique site, at www.sepaq.com/Duchesnay.

Source: Leney, P. (2002, January 19). Ice Hotel's aim is adventure not comfort. *Montreal Gazette*, p. G5.

Objectives

On completion of this chapter, readers should understand

- the components of the tourism and hospitality product;

- the various levels of products or services;

- the tools used in product planning;

- the concepts of packaging and branding; and

- new product development in the tourism and hospitality sector.

Chapter Overview

tourism and hospitality products

a group of selected components or elements brought together in a "bundle" to satisfy needs and wants

The opening vignette provides a classic example of how unusual and varied the tourism product can be. This chapter begins by introducing the peculiarities of the tourism product and the idea that **tourism and hospitality products** are a selected group of components or elements brought together in a "bundle" to satisfy needs and wants. The next section looks at the three levels of tourism products—the core product, the tangible product, and the augmented product—and these product levels are then applied to theme parks. Product planning is the focus of the next section, which begins by describing the five basic market/product options, and then discusses the usefulness of a features/benefits analysis. A critique of the product life cycle model is then followed by a discussion of various positioning strategies available to organizations in the tourism and hospitality fields. An in-depth analysis of branding in tourism is supported by two cases. One discusses the growth of chefs as brands, and the other looks at the re-branding of the Manitoba Museum. The next section of the chapter gives attention to the concept of packaging, and the final part of the chapter looks at new product development and the various theoretical stages a company can follow in developing a new product or service.

INTRODUCTION TO THE TOURISM AND HOSPITALITY PRODUCT

Product decisions, with all their implications for the management of tourism and hospitality operations, influence not only the marketing mix, but also a firm's long-term growth strategy and its policies for investment and human resources. Product specifications largely determine the corporate image and branding an organization is able to create in the minds of its existing and prospective customers.[1] Tourism constitutes such a wide span of products that it has to be considered in terms of sectors rather than as a single industry, as discussed in Chapter 1 (see pp. 9–17). These sectors include accommodations, attractions, transportation, travel organizers, and destination organizations, among others (see Figure 1.3). This diversity is matched by an even greater diversity of component features specific to each tourism product sector, which need to be considered and managed in providing individual products for particular markets. The conceptualization of tourism and hospitality products as a group of selected components or elements brought together in a "bundle" to satisfy needs and wants is a vital image for marketing managers.

From the standpoint of a potential customer considering any form of tourist visit, the product may be defined as a bundle or package of tangible and intangible components, based on activity at a destination. The package is perceived by the tourist as an experience that is available for a price. There are five main components in the overall product: destination attractions and environment; destination facilities and services; accessibility of the destination; images of the destination; and price.[2] Although these components are combined and integrated in the visitor's overall experience, they are capable of extensive and more or less independent variation over time. Intrawest, for example, has transformed the natural environment in Canada and created popular purpose-built tourist winter destinations. But it is in the promotional field of images and perceptions that some of the most interesting planned changes occur, and these are marketing decisions (see Chapter 12 for examples).

PRODUCT LEVELS

For many years, marketing theory has differentiated between three levels of product offering. The three levels can be seen as a continuum, with the product's most basic benefit at one end, and a range of add-on benefits, not directly related to the product's essential purpose, at the opposite end. These three levels are:

core product

the basic need function served by the generic product

tangible product

the specific features and benefits residing in the product itself—styling, quality, brand name, design, etc.

augmented product

the add-ons that are extrinsic to the product itself but may influence the decision to purchase

- **Core product:** the basic need function served by the generic product. For an airline or train, the core product is transportation; for a hotel, the core benefits offered are shelter and rest.
- **Tangible product:** these are the specific features and benefits residing in the product itself—styling, quality, brand name, design, etc.
- **Augmented product:** the add-ons that are extrinsic to the product itself but may influence the decision to purchase. Augmented features may include credit terms, after-sales guarantees, car parking, etc.

Although these levels were defined with manufactured products in mind, they do apply, with modifications, to tourism and hospitality goods and services. For example, Swarbrooke has applied the three levels to theme parks (see Figure 5.1).

Conceptualizing the product in these three areas allows the tourism marketer to appraise the comparative advantages and consumer appeal of his or her product versus those of others. In a highly competitive market, it is unlikely that any supplier will have an advantage in the core benefits, and differentiation is instead likely to reside in the second and third levels. For example, most theme parks offer excitement and thrills for consumers, but will compete with each other on the variety and quality of rides, or the quality of the surrounding environment.

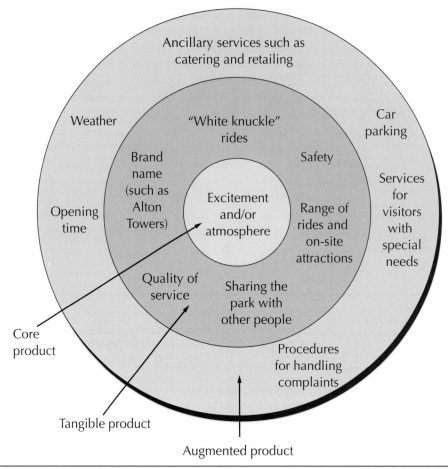

Figure 5.1   The Three Levels of Product—Example of a Theme Park

Source: Swarbrooke, J. (1995). *The development and management of visitor attractions.* Oxford: Butterworth-Heinemann.

PHYSICAL EVIDENCE AND THE SERVICESCAPE

servicescape

the environment in which the service is delivered and in which the firm and customer interact, and any tangible components that facilitate performance or communication of the service

An important part of the augmented product is the physical environment. Because many tourism and hospitality services are intangible, customers often rely on tangible cues, or physical evidence, to evaluate the service before its purchase and to assess their satisfaction with the service during and after consumption. As explained in Chapter 1 (see p. 7), the physical evidence is the environment in which the service is delivered and in which the firm and customer interact, and any tangible components that facilitate performance or communication of the service. The physical facility is often referred to as the "**servicescape**," and is very important for tourism and hospitality products such as hotels, restaurants, and theme parks, which are dominated by experience attributes. Disney, for example, effectively uses the servicescape to excite its customers. The brightly coloured displays, the music, the rides, and the costumed characters all reinforce the feelings of fun and excitement that Disney seeks to generate in its customers.

General elements of physical evidence are shown in Table 5.1. They include all aspects of the organization's servicescape that affect customers, including both exterior attributes (such as signage, parking, and landscape) and interior attributes (such as design, layout, equipment, and décor).

Table 5.1

Elements of Physical Evidence

SERVICESCAPE FACILITY EXTERIOR	SERVICESCAPE FACILITY INTERIOR	OTHER TANGIBLES
Parking	Layout	Uniforms
Landscape	Equipment	Business cards
Signage	Signage	Stationery
Exterior design	Air temperature	Invoices
	Interior design	Brochures
	Lighting	Web pages
		Employee dress

Consumer researchers know that the design of the servicescape can influence customer choices, expectations, satisfaction, and other behaviours. Retailers know that customers are influenced by smell, décor, music, and layout. Arby's, the fast-food chain, uses the servicescape to position its restaurants as a step above other quick-service outlets. With carpeted floors, cushioned seating, and a décor "superior" to other fast-food chains, the company asserts that the interior ambience of Arby's outlets contributes to attracting diners. Design of work environments can also affect employees' productivity, motivation, and satisfaction. The challenge in many tourism and hospitality settings is to design the physical space and evidence so that it can support the needs and preferences of customers and employees simultaneously.

Employees and customers in service firms respond to dimensions of their physical surroundings in three ways—cognitively, emotionally, and physiologically—and these responses influence their behaviours in the environment. First, the perceived servicescape may elicit *cognitive* responses, including people's beliefs about a place and their beliefs about the people and products found in that place. For example, a consumer study found that a travel agent's office décor affected customer attributions of the travel agent's behaviour.[3]

In addition to influencing cognitions, the perceived servicescape may elicit *emotional* responses that in turn influence behaviours. The colours, décor, music, and other elements of the atmosphere can have an unexplained and sometime subconscious affect on the moods of people in the place. Servicescapes that are both pleasant and arousing have been termed "exciting," while those that are pleasant and non-arousing, or sleepy, are called "relaxing." Unpleasant servicescapes that are arousing are "distressing," while unpleasant, sleepy servicescapes are "gloomy."[4] Finally, the servicescape may affect people in purely *physiological* ways. Noise that is too loud may cause physical discomfort, the temperature of a room may cause people to shiver or perspire, the air quality may make it difficult to breathe, and the glare of lighting may decrease ability to see and may cause physical pain. All of these physical responses will influence whether people remain in and enjoy a particular environment. For example, it is well known that the comfort of seating in a restaurant influences how long customers stay, and Arby's is clearly attempting to differentiate itself from other fast-food chains that seek quick customer turnover and therefore provide minimum comfort.

In Chapter 3, the discussion of consumer trends pointed out that today's consumer desires experiences (see p. 93), and more and more businesses are responding by explicitly designing experiences with themed servicescapes. At themed restaurants such as the Hard Rock Cafe, Planet Hollywood, or the Rainforest Cafe, the food is just a prop for what's known as "eatertainment." Retailers are also creating themes that tie merchandising presentations together in a staged experience. A popular tourist attraction in Las Vegas is the Forum, a mall that displays its distinctive theme—an ancient Roman marketplace—in every detail. The Simon DeBartolo Group, which developed the mall, fulfills this motif through a panoply of architectural effects. These include marble floors, stark white pillars, "outdoor" cafes, living trees, flowing fountains—and even a painted blue sky with fluffy white clouds that yield regularly to simulated storm, complete with lighting and thunder. Every mall entrance and every storefront is an elaborate Roman recreation. Every hour inside the main entrance, statues of Julius Caesar and other Roman luminaries come to life and speak. "Hail, Caesar!" is a frequent cry, and Roman centurions periodically march through on their way to the adjacent Caesars Palace casino.

Despite the increased emphasis on the servicescape in designing experiences, companies that fail to provide consistently engaging experiences, overprice their experiences relative to the value perceived, or overbuild their capacity to stage them will see pressure on demand, pricing, or both. The Rainforest Cafe and Planet Hollywood have both encountered trouble because they have failed to refresh their experiences. Guests find nothing different from one visit to the next. Disney, on the other hand, avoids staleness by frequently adding new attractions and even whole parks such as the Animal Kingdom, in 1998, and California Adventure, in 2001. This last US$1.4 billion project, which also included construction of a first-class hotel, was designed to accommodate 30 000 people a day, to add to the 70 000 visitors that come to Disneyland across the street. Many of those visitors originate from the Western Canadian cities of Calgary, Edmonton, and Vancouver. Covering 55 acres, California Adventure is a high-energy park, celebrating the dreams of the many Americans who came to California and reflecting the highlights and the pop culture of the state today. It features attractions a little wilder and a lot more grown up than the original Disneyland; these attractions are situated in three themed areas: Paradise Pier, Golden State, and Hollywood Pictures Backlot.

PRODUCT PLANNING

Product Mix

product mix

the portfolio of products that an organization offers to one market or several

The most basic decisions a tourism organization has to make are what business it is in and what product mix is appropriate to it. The **product mix** is the portfolio of products that an organization offers to one market or several. Five basic market/product options exist: [5]

1. several markets/multi-product mixes for each (e.g., mass tour operators that offer a wide range of multi-destination packages to a variety of market segments);
2. several markets/single product for each (e.g., airlines with a product for business and economy class travellers);
3. several markets/single product for all (e.g., a national tourist organization promoting a country);
4. single market/multi-product mix (e.g., a specialist tour operator with a range of cultural tours aimed at a wealthy, educated market); and
5. single market/single product (e.g., a heliskiing operator targeting the very rich).

features

the objective attributes of a tourism product

benefits

the rewards the product gives the consumer

The decision on which product mix option to adopt depends upon many factors, including the strength and value of consumer demand in the different markets, the level of competition in each market, and the distinctive competence of the organization to service the markets adequately. The starting point in product analysis and planning is thus an analysis of the consumer and competitive offerings in relation to the goals and product capacity of the tourism organization. The most successful products emerge when the marketing planning steps outlined in Chapter 2 are followed. Portfolio and SWOT analysis are discussed there (see pp. 39–41 and p. 47); another useful method of analyzing the tourism product is by considering its features and benefits. **Features** consist of the objective attributes of a tourism product; **benefits** are the rewards the product gives the consumer. The difference between the two is shown in Table 5.2.

Table 5.2

Features and Benefits Analysis for Tourism and Hospitality Products

TOURISM PRODUCT ITEM	PRODUCT FEATURE	CONSUMER BENEFIT
Pier 21	Archived information	Connect to origins
WestJet flights	Low service	Low-cost travel
Whistler Resort	All lifts near hotel rooms	Ski in, ski out facility
Manitoba Museum	Interactive facilities	An entertaining place to learn
Nahanni adventure tour	Quality kayaks and rafts	Reconnecting with nature

Product Life Cycle

**product life cycle
(PLC) analysis**

a way of plotting prod-
ucts or services to
identify what stage they
are at in their life
cycle; a valuable way
of reviewing a
product's past and cur-
rent position and
making predictions
about its future

One of the most basic product analysis tools is the **product life cycle (PLC) analysis** (see Figure 5.2). Plotting products or services to identify what stage they are at in their PLC is a valuable way of reviewing a product's past and current position and making predictions about its future. As part of a portfolio analysis (see Chapter 2, pp. 39–41), an organization should access each good and service in terms of its position in the product life cycle. *Product development* begins when the company finds and develops a new product idea. The *introduction* phase is a period of slow sales and low profits because of the investment required for product introduction. The *growth* phase is characterized by increasing market acceptance and substantial improvement in profits. The *maturity* phase is a period of slow sales but high profits as the product is well entrenched in the marketplace and has an acceptable market share. However, when sales begin to drop because competitors are moving into the marketplace, the product enters the *decline* stage. Profits and market share decline, and major costs may be involved in redeveloping, refurbishing, or maintaining the product.

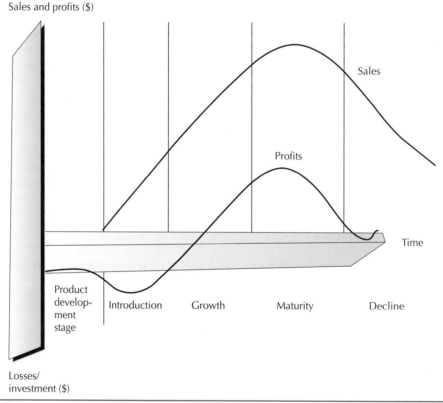

Figure 5.2   The Product Life Cycle

Using the PLC concept to develop marketing strategy can be difficult. Strategy is both a cause and a result of the PLC. At the introduction stage, promotion spending is likely to be high in order to inform consumers about the new product and encourage them to buy it. A company will focus on selling to buyers who are ready to buy, usually higher-income groups. Prices tend to be on the high side because of low output, production problems, and high promotion costs and other expenses. *Marketing in Action* in this chapter shows the experiences of Catch restaurant in Calgary during the restaurant's introduction stage. At the growth stage, the early adopters will continue to buy, and later buyers will start following their lead, encouraged by favourable word of mouth. Competitors will enter the market, attracted by the opportunity for profit, and they will introduce more product features that will expand the market. In the growth stage, the organization faces a trade-off between high market share and high current profit. By investing heavily in product improvement, promotion, and distribution, it can capture a dominant position. But it sacrifices maximum current profit in the hope of making this up in the next stage.

When sales start to slow down, the product will enter the maturity stage, and this lasts longer than the previous two stages and poses stronger challenges to marketing management. Most products or services are in this stage, and it is a phase that is characterized by heavy competition. The only way to increase sales is to lure customers away from competition, and so price wars and heavy advertising are common. At this stage, an aggressive product manager will seek to increase consumption by modifying markets and/or products. The product manager may also try to improve sales by changing one or more of the marketing mix elements. In the decline stage, some firms will withdraw from the market. Those that remain may reduce the number of their product offerings or the number of market segments they are targeting. They may also reduce the promotion budget as well as prices. For each declining product, management must decide whether to maintain, harvest, or drop it.

However, the PLC is not as simple as it sounds in theory, and according to one writer "its supposed universal applicability is largely a myth."[6] The study of the PLC pattern for a particular product has to take into account the market the product is in. For example, if a product is showing no growth or decline, it may still be very successful if the market as a whole is in decline. Another complication of the PLC is that a product that is in overall decline may be losing its customers from one market segment but increasing appeal or holding steady with another. Ski areas, for example, have been very successful in attracting an increasing number of snowboarders over the past decade, despite a drop in the number of downhill skiers. In addition, although the PLC concept is neat on paper, it is often difficult to determine what particular stage a product is at. Finally, even assuming that a product's life cycle position can be determined, it may not be obvious what action should be taken.

However, despite these problems, the PLC is a valuable concept to operationalize, since it forces the organization to analyze trends for its product in relation to the overall market and the segments within it, in order to assess future marketing requirements. Ski areas, for example, have adapted to the growth in snowboarders referred to above by changing the products they offer; most successful ski areas these days have designated areas for snowboarders. A related concept for analyzing destinations is that of the tourism area life cycle, which is discussed in Chapter 12 (see pp. 398–399).

Positioning

positioning

establishing an image for a product or service in relation to others in the marketplace

Positioning is the bedrock of product management. Chapter 2 introduces the concept as the natural follow-through of market segmentation and market targeting, and highlights the three steps necessary to develop an effective position in the target market segment (see pp. 54–55). The objective of positioning is to create a distinctive place in the minds of potential customers. Positioning in tourism should evoke images of a destination or product in the customer's mind—images that differentiate the product from the competition and also convey that it can satisfy their needs and wants. Effective positioning should direct all of the marketing functions of a business. Advertising and promotions, as well as decisions on price, product, and distribution channels must all be consistent with positioning goals. Often, these marketing functions will be driven by a **positioning statement**, which is a phrase that reflects the image the organization wants to create. The positioning statement for the Manitoba Museum, for example (see *Profile*), is "Encouraging Discovery." This statement encapsulates what the Manitoba Museum stands for, the essence of what the museum does, and how it does it.

There are an endless number of positioning strategies, and selection of the appropriate approach is vital to the success of a tourism organization. Burke and Resnick have identified four key positioning strategies that are not mutually exclusive and may therefore be used individually or in combination:

- positioning relative to target market (e.g., business travellers, families with children under 10, etc.);
- positioning by price and quality (e.g., a premium product such as a room at the Four Seasons Hotel);
- positioning relative to a product class (e.g., a tour operator positioning its products within a winter sports tourism category); and
- positioning relative to competitors (e.g., the Hertz Rental Car campaign "We try harder," which drew attention to the fact that Hertz was not market leader but would work harder to catch up with its competitors).[7]

Arby's uses a combination of the above positioning strategies. The company's restaurants and menus are generally targeted at attracting an adult population with more sophisticated, grown-up tastes. This is a brand positioning that not only distinguishes Arby's from certain other quick-service chains but also caters directly to the fastest-growing demographic sector in North America. Aiming to create the same kind of passion demonstrated by football or hockey fans, the company's vision is focused on developing customers who are fanatics about eating at Arby's restaurants—people who will often go out of their way to get an Arby's roast beef or market fresh sandwich. The company's driving principle is to be a "cut above" in all areas of the brand's operations. The unwavering objective is to make Arby's the best fast-food option in the industry: the brand consumers prefer because of its cut-above employees, cut-above food, cut-above service, and cut-above facilities. Whether or not Arby's succeeds with this positioning strategy remains to be seen.

Another example of a new restaurant positioning itself in the Canadian market is highlighted in *Marketing in Action* on pages 147–148. The owners of the restaurant Catch, in Calgary, identified a gap in the Calgary market for a unique, upscale dining experience with atmosphere, and so offered high-quality food at high prices, placing great emphasis on the servicescape.

positioning statement

a phrase that reflects the image an organization wants to create

MARKETING IN ACTION

CANADA'S "BEST NEW RESTAURANT"—CATCH

The realities of opening a new business—especially a new restaurant—can be far removed from the theories presented in marketing textbooks. Catch, voted "Canada's Best New Restaurant" by *enRoute* magazine in 2002, was due to open in time for the Calgary Stampede. The owners were just hoping that would be Stampede 2001 and not Stampede 2002. After two arduous years in development, one of the most eagerly anticipated restaurants in Canada did finally open in the summer of 2002, in downtown Calgary.

Why did the development take so long? One of the owners, Stephan Reid, explains that partway through the project, the owners decided the restaurant should be of a grander scale than they had originally envisioned. "We decided to provide something that didn't exist in Calgary—a unique fine dining experience. We decided to offer very high quality food at high prices but with a unique, fun atmosphere." They were keen for the restaurant to be a showpiece for their company, Creative Restaurants Inc., and to be "the finest restaurant in the city." So they reviewed the plans and began to make significant changes. The owners spent months travelling throughout North America, looking at restaurant design, focusing specifically on researching fish restaurants on the West Coast. Working to retain the historic nature of the old Bank of Canada building—the site of the new restaurant—also took time, as approval from both the civic and provincial historic committees took longer than anticipated.

As the concept of the restaurant grew, so did the development budget. This was eventually pegged at $5.6 million—a vast amount for a new restaurant. Reid says it would have been half as expensive and would have taken far less time to build the same property from scratch. But he and his partners, Darren Gurr and Clay Riddell, are pleased with the results. Catch is a three-storey, three-concept facility, with room for about 300 diners, that starts on the ground floor with what the owners call a "reasonably rowdy" oyster bar. The look is exposed sandstone, wood booths, a pounded tin ceiling, and a shiny new kitchen. With its front doors opening up directly on to Stephen Avenue, the Catch Oyster Bar attracts both Calgary executives and visiting hotel and conference goers. The ground floor features not only an oyster bar, but its very own private "white wine" dining room, which hosts up to 26 guests surrounded by a showcase white wine cellaring system. The menu features a broad range of fresh oysters, clams, and mussels, as well as shellfish risotto and Dungeness crab. Tables are turned around faster in the oyster bar, where the average amount spent is approximately $42.

MARKETING IN ACTION *continued*

On the second floor, patrons spend an average of $65 on their meal, and tend to stay longer. Here, the atmosphere is more contemporary, and includes a light wood floor, large windows, nouveau chandeliers, and another clean, open kitchen. The menu shares the fresh features of the ground floor, but expands into Nova Scotia lobster, roasted monkfish, and braised Queen Charlotte halibut. This is the place for serious dining, and it has a calmer, more relaxed atmosphere than downstairs. Unique to Calgary is the Creative Events facility on the third level of this historic building. The Events Centre is completely encased in glass, providing a view of the Calgary Tower as well as the rest of the Calgary skyline. The Events Centre is booked for conferences, creative corporate functions, weddings, and special occasions, or just for a large group to enjoy a special culinary experience.

Before the restaurant opened, the owners brought in star chef Michael Noble from Vancouver. He ran a test kitchen at Bonterra, one of Catch's sister restaurants, where he tried out some of his recipes. Response was highly favourable. Now the former Canadian Federation of Chefs & Cooks Chef of the Year (1999–2000) and Iron Chef competitor has his own kitchen and staff to work with, and has become an attraction in his own right.

"It is a show—a production—and people come in just to see our celebrity chef. He is a huge draw," says Stephan McQueen, the restaurant's general manager. Noble, a two-time Bocuse D'Or competitor, has earned the respect of his peers the hard way, via a long and successful career. Fiercely competitive, Noble's motto, "Don't fail!," has rubbed off on the staff. He is often in-house to speak with guests in the dining room, and his visibility puts additional pressure on the kitchen team, Noble says. No one wants to embarrass the chef by causing complaints of poorly prepared or plated food.

When they first opened the restaurant's doors, the owners encountered a challenge in the fact that the Calgary consumer did not know what to expect from Catch, and it took some time before the bookings came rolling in. "Catch is a place you need to come to first in order to understand why to come there the next time," said McQueen, "and therefore it was both trial and positive word of mouth that eventually persuaded people to come and see what we were all about." Initially there were complaints about the size of food portions offered in the restaurant: "It took people from Calgary time to realize that fine dining is not all about getting large portions of food," said McQueen. Now the restaurant takes in $10 000 to $15 000 on an average day, with about 180 sittings on the first floor and 120 on the second. In fact, in December, Catch was taking in $26 000 to $28 000 per day. However, the perception still exists among Calgarians that Catch is an expensive dining spot. "You get what you pay for," Noble says, somewhat impatiently.

How long will it be before the $5.6 million investment is paid off? "Of course, our shareholders would like payback real soon," says McQueen. "But it is a huge hill to climb, and with that kind of investment we have to be successful for a long time." Fortunately for Catch, the media attention generated from being voted "Canada's Best New Restaurant" has been exceptional. "It was a complete surprise," said McQueen, "but it has been a huge free promotion for us." In fact, Catch spends only one percent of total sales on marketing, as the owners believe that free publicity, along with word of mouth, will bring the customers in. Only time will tell.

Sources: Gilchrist, J. (2002, June 9). Catch it if you can. *Calgary Herald*, p. C6; Hobsbawn-Smith, D. (2003). Shooting for the stars. *Calgary*, 5(1), 36; S. McQueen, general manager, Catch restaurant, personal communication, January 31, 2003.

BRANDING

branding

a method of establishing a distinctive identity for a product based on competitive differentiation from other products

The practice of **branding** developed in the field of packaged goods as a method of establishing a distinctive identity for a product based on competitive differentiation from other products. Branding was commonly achieved through naming, trademarking, packaging, product design, and promotion. Successful branding gave a unique identity to what might otherwise have been a generic product. This identity produced a consistent image in the consumer's mind, which facilitated recognition and quality assurance. In the 19th century, products such as Beecham's Pills, Cadbury's Chocolate, and Eno's Salts were early users of branding. These days, the market in packaged goods is dominated by brands, and in the last few decades branding has also been widely recognized in services marketing. A "brand," in the modern marketing sense, offers the consumer relevant added value—a superior proposition that is distinctive from competitors' and that imparts meaning above and beyond the product's functional aspects.

Branding in services offers a solution to some of the problems in services marketing discussed in Chapter 1 (see pp. 6–7)—in particular those of consistency and product standardization. Branding can be a way of unifying services, which is why it has been particularly developed in hotel marketing. Research shows that nearly 90 percent of bookings are made with branded hotel chains, and 9 out of 10 consumers can distinguish between chains, franchise operators, and independents.[8] For large hotel companies that have a wide variety of properties, grouping them into brands can

- unify them into more easily recognizable smaller groups;
- enable each branded group to be targeted at defined market segments; and
- enable product delivery, including human resource management, to be focused on creating a specific set of benefits for a specific market.

SNAPSHOT

CHEFS AS BRANDS

Some of the most successful and fastest-growing consumer brands today are chefs. Chefs used to be limited to working in the back of restaurants and creating great meals that consumers loved to eat. But now they are moving to the forefront and becoming their own brands. Many chefs today have their names attached to multiple product lines and have their hands in a wealth of restaurants and business. They are a new breed of chef—one that understands how powerful a brand name can be in the marketplace. And they are following popular marketing theory, which states that if you find a product that works, you should create brand extensions from it. Chefs like Wolfgang Puck, Emeril Lagasse, Rob Feenie, Michael Smith, and a host of other celebrity chefs are the main draw, and brand extension of their names to a variety of products—from restaurants, cookbooks, and cookware to marinades, spices, and prepackaged meals—is making them very rich.

SNAPSHOT *continued*

With so many outlets through which they can now reach the public, these chefs have truly become celebrities. The explosion of television cooking shows, which has led to the creation of entire cable television stations devoted to the subjects of food and cooking, allows these chefs to market themselves nearly every day to millions of viewers. For example, Ming Tsai, owner of one restaurant in the United States, is the host of two shows on the Food Network that reach almost 70 million homes. Canadian-made "Cook Like a Chef" is just one of a number of shows that have made Food Network Canada into one of the country's most successful specialty channels. The network's audience drawn from its target demographic—adults aged 25 to 54—grew by at least 25 percent and as much as 50 percent in every quarter of 2002.

The Internet is also increasing in value for these brand names. The medium brings chefs a wide-reaching sales channel that they couldn't find elsewhere. While you can find most of Emeril Lagasse's spices, marinades, salad dressings, and pasta sauces in practically every supermarket, he also has a Web site that sells products from pans and cookbooks to chef's clothing and gift certificates. Because of this exposure, celebrity chefs routinely sell more than 100 000 copies of their cookbooks,

and they are making millions of dollars in annual revenues on products that have nothing to do with restaurants.

How far can you extend a chef's name as a brand? Tsai currently has a highly successful restaurant and cookbook, but he is now looking to extend his brand even further. Tsai recently started his own company, Ming East West, which he says he founded "to leverage my TV personality to slowly build a brand and go into other business." He is launching products such as oils, marinades, rubs, and a full pantry series, and also coming out with a lower-end line of products that brings basic kitchen items—pots, knives, tongs, steamers—into as many consumers' homes as possible.

For celebrity chefs—as for many consumer products—marketing is all about connecting with an audience. "These celebrity chefs are so hot because they are so touchable," says industry publicist Lisa Ekus. "Consumers can see them, taste their food, feel like they are really getting something from them. That intimacy is invaluable when it comes to marketing. It allows them to turn themselves into successful brands."

Sources: Cohen, A. (2001, December). Look who's cooking now. *Sales & Marketing Management, 152*(12), 30–36; Turner, C. (2003, March 31). Edible peep show. *The Globe and Mail*, p. R3.

In the past, branding was often seen mainly as a matter of promotion and of creating the right image through advertising and publicity. But marketing managers now recognize that successful branding involves the integrated deployment of product design, pricing policies, distribution selection, and promotion. The case for branding is stronger for tourism products that offer the possibility for differentiation in several areas of the marketing mix. This is why branding has been particularly successful in hotel and restaurant marketing (see *Snapshot*, pp. 149–150). Branding of restaurants, hotels, and airlines developed extensively in the United States in the 1980s and 1990s, and companies in the rest of the world are following suit. The momentum is driven mainly by large organizations that recognize that, to remain competitive, they need to offer several products to different markets instead of relying upon a monolithic presence in one main one.

Apart from the advantages already mentioned, Middleton and Clarke suggest that branding in tourism offers other specific advantages:[9]

- Branding helps reduce medium- and long-term vulnerability to the unforeseen external events that so beset the tourism industry. Recovery time after an event such as the terrorist attacks of September 11, 2001, is likely to be shorter for a well-established brand.
- Branding reduces risk for the consumer at the point of purchase by signalling the expected quality and performance of an intangible product. It offers either an implicit or explicit guarantee to the consumer.
- Branding facilitates accurate marketing segmentation by attracting some consumer segments and repelling others. For an inseparable product, onsite segment compatibility is an important marketing issue.
- Branding provides the focus for the integration of stakeholder effort, especially for the employees of an organization or the individual tourism providers of a destination brand.
- Finally, branding is a strategic weapon for long-range planning in tourism, as can be seen in the case of the Manitoba Museum (see *Profile*).

It should be recognized that a competitive brand is a live asset and not a fixture, and therefore its value may depreciate over time if starved of investment and marketing and management skill. Brand decay may begin if a brand is over-stretched into new products that damage its essence, or following a merger or takeover. The Case Study in Chapter 1 shows how Canadian Pacific adopted the Fairmont name for all its hotels, apart from the Delta properties, after consumer surveys showed that the CP name was virtually unknown in the U.S. market.

The airline industry in Canada has seen numerous brand extensions over the last few years. In 2002, Air Canada launched three regional brands: Tango, Zip, and Jazz. The new Jazz brand was launched after a two-year consolidation process of Air Canada's regional carriers: AirBC, Air Nova, Air Ontario, and Canadian Regional. "Our objective in creating our new brand was to build on the strengths of the four existing brands," says Joseph Randell, president of Air Canada Jazz. "Each of these carriers had strong brand awareness within their regions, and the new name reflects these qualities and acts as a metaphor for being youthful, vibrant, innovative, flexible and part of the local community." The Air Canada family can be seen in Table 5.3 on page 152; it was extended in 2003 with the addition of Destina.ca and a full-service travel Web site (see *Snapshot* in Chapter 7, pp. 220–221). However, Air Canada's brand extensions have been criticized by one commentator, who suggests that Air Canada will continue to create sub-brands and companion services "in its never-ending quest to provide the travelling public with the illusion that they have a choice."[10]

Table 5.3

The Air Canada Family

AIRLINE	SERVICE	EXPRESS CHECK-IN	E-TICKETING	AEROPLAN
Air Canada	Full service	★	★	★
Tango	Low fares	★[2]	★[3]	★[4]
Air Canada Jazz	Full service (regional)	★	★	★
Zip	Low fare/high value	★	★	★
Air Canada Jetz	Specialty charter		★	
Other Businesses (Air Canada Vacations)	Vacation packages	★		★
Destina.ca	Full service travel Web site	★	★	★
Air Canada Cargo	Cargo service			
Air Canada Technical Services	Transport Canada–approved maintenance organization			

[1] Interline: Travellers can use a single itinerary to transfer between carriers.
[2] Except for Terminal 3 at Pearson International Airport (Toronto).
[3] Mandatory.
[4] All Aeroplan® miles accumulated on Tango do not count toward Aeroplan® top-tier status. Consult www.aeroplan.com for further details.
[5] Eligible Maple Leaf ™ Lounge customers only.
[6] Through Air Canada code share.

brandicide

the process of taking a well-known brand and extending it into a new area that will "kill" the brand

Extending or stretching a brand can be dangerous. Marketers sometimes use the term "**brandicide**" to describe the process of taking a well-known brand and extending it into a new area that will "kill" the brand. Companies are increasingly attempting to stretch their proven expertise into new areas. A combination of factors has made companies more eager than ever to stretch their brands further and more boldly. Advances in technology have reduced barriers to entry in new sectors. Companies have developed stronger and more knowledgeable relationships with customers, and the cost and difficulty of developing new brands is encouraging companies to exploit the brands they already have. But there can be a cost to leveraging brand equity. If a brand loses credibility in one sector—as Roots did after failing in the airline industry (see Case Study in Chapter 2)—this tainted sector can contaminate everything else that bears the brand's name. So "brandicide" should be avoided.

STAR ALLIANCE BENEFITS	RAPIDAIR	EXECUTIVE FIRST/ EXECUTIVE CLASS	MAPLE LEAF LOUNGE	CONCIERGE	INTERLINE[1]
★	★	★	★	★	★
			★[5]		
★		★	★	★	★
★[6]			★		★[6]
			★	★	
		★	★		

PROFILE

THE MANITOBA MUSEUM

In 2002, The Manitoba Museum announced a change in corporate identity that would integrate the Manitoba Museum of Man and Nature, the Manitoba Planetarium, and the Manitoba Science Centre under the umbrella of The Manitoba Museum.

The designers tasked with creating the new logo were asked that the three main facilities and areas of program and activity, the Museum, Planetarium, and Science Gallery, be represented. The logo's three triangles symbolize the three facilities. They come together to form a whole: a reverse "M" reflecting the "M" in museum and Manitoba.

PROFILE *continued*

All three triangles are necessary to create the "M," as all three facilities are necessary to the formation of the Manitoba Museum. Each triangle is also different from the others, which represents the uniqueness of each of the three facilities (see logo on page 153).

The graphic is bold and contemporary, yet has an established, timeless feel appropriate for the Manitoba Museum. Gold was chosen as the logo's colour because of its many positive connotations and its integrative qualities. Gold is the symbol of ultimate achievement, value, and quality. Gold is also a colour seen widely in nature: Manitoba's prairie glows gold with wheat, sunflowers, canola, and mustard. Gold is also a colour that is common in astronomical bodies: our own golden sun is the source of life on Earth and the centre of our solar system. And gold is among the most important and precious of the metals found on Earth.

The photograph above shows a three-dimensional exhibition in the museum's Orientation Gallery. The display is integral to the museum as it introduces the museum to visitors, whose journey begins with a life-size scene of one of the last great 19th-century Red River buffalo hunts. A Métis hunter on horseback closes in on a herd of wide-eyed bison, thus dramatically introducing the

philosophical theme of the museum: the interrelationship of human beings and the natural environment.

The positioning statement and service promise, "Encouraging Discovery," encapsulates what the Manitoba Museum stands for, the essence of what the museum does, and how it does it. It was necessary that the positioning statement reflect and integrate all of the museum's products and services across all three areas of activity. The Museum Galleries, the Planetarium, and the Science Gallery all encourage visitors to discover the wonders of the world and universe. All three facilities employ disciplines and sciences focused on inquiry and discovery in establishing, caring for, and interpreting the heritage collections and in the presentation of the principles of physical science, astronomy, and space science.

"Encouraging Discovery" was the phrase in the Manitoba Museum's mission statement considered to be the most appropriate descriptor of what the museum does. This goal is the common element in all areas of the museum's endeavour and the element that most closely reflects the opinions and descriptions provided by the membership and the community in survey responses.

The process of developing the museum's new corporate identity occurred over a number of years, in concert with the physical changes brought about by the Capital Building Renewal Program and the development of The Futures Project—A Strategic Plan, 2000–2005. Thousands of museum members, donors, supporters, stakeholders, and members of the community at large from across the province were asked to participate in the development process by providing opinions and suggestions concerning the museum's important attributes, character, and messages, and by providing feedback on a variety of logo and positioning statement designs. This consultative approach provided invaluable information from a broad

PROFILE *continued*

constituency about what the Manitoba Museum means to people and how it should be presented. The museum learned what people want, expect, and receive from the museum. Respondents stated that the museum was an engaging and social environment and that "the museum is an established reliable resource offering unique options for discovery."

They also said that "the museum is an entertaining place to learn and enjoy the process of discovery." The resulting corporate identity package is a reflection of this research process.

Source: Liette, R. (2002). We have changed! Retrieved July 4, 2002, from http://www.canadatourism. com/en/ctc/ctx/ctx-news/search/newsbydateform.cfm.

PACKAGING

packaging

the process of combining two or more related and complementary offerings into a single-price offering

In the tourism and hospitality industry, **packaging** is the process of combining two or more related and complementary offerings into a single-price offering. A package may include a wide variety of services, such as lodging, meals, entrance fees for attractions, entertainment, transportation costs, guide services, or other similar activities. Travel packages have become increasingly popular over the years. They are attractive because they benefit both the consumer and participating businesses by providing convenience and value to the consumer and added revenue for businesses.

More specifically, packaging provides several customer benefits, including

- easier budgeting for trips: the customer pays at one time and has a good idea of the trip's total cost;
- increased convenience, which saves time and prevents aggravation;
- greater economy, as the cost to the customer is usually more economical than purchasing the package components individually;
- the opportunity to experience previously unfamiliar activities and attractions; and
- the opportunity to design components of a package for specialized interests.

For tourism operations, packages are attractive for the following reasons:

- They can improve profitability by allowing businesses to price at a premium by adding special good and services.
- They can smooth business patterns. Packaging during low demand periods may add attractive features to the service or product, thus generating additional business.
- They allow joint marketing opportunities, which can in turn reduce promotional costs.
- They can be an effective tool for tailoring tourism products for specific target markets.

In Canada, the tourism industry is becoming increasingly sophisticated and innovative with its packaging. The Case Study in this chapter gives numerous examples of day and weekend packages offered via the Internet. Two more packaging examples come from Quebec: On the Magdalen Islands, Tour Trends offers three- and four-night packages that enable people to see some of the hundreds of thousands of harp seals that gather in the area to give birth. A helicopter ride to ice floes with a guide is provided. Packages start at $1419 per person, based on a double booking, and include accommodation, transfers, some meals, the helicopter trip, a visit to the Seal Interpretation Centre, tours, cross-country skiing, and a cocktail.[11]

On the St. Lawrence, Groupe Dufour has successfully packaged cruising with hotels.[12] With four hotels strategically located near the St. Lawrence from Quebec City to Tadoussac, and with four day-cruise ships plying the river, Groupe Dufour has one of the most singular tourist offerings in the region. "We are the only company offering hotels and cruises at the same time," boasts company official Michelle Blais. "We are the only company bringing guests to each property by boat. That's the power we have." According to Blais, groups account for about 50 percent of the company's business. "That's why travel agents and operators are so important to us," Blais says. "We want to heighten the relationship and we want them to know that our Web site—www.familledufour.com—is transactional."

NEW PRODUCT DEVELOPMENT

Product Options in New and Existing Markets

Developing new products is different from maintaining existing ones, and planning for both kinds of product will differ according to whether the products are targeted at existing markets or new ones. Holloway and Plant have provided a useful matrix to illustrate the permutations of market/product interaction that are possible and the product moves that might be suitable for each (see Figure 5.3). According to the model, a company has four alternatives.

1. Market Penetration

market penetration
modifying an existing product for the current market

First, it can follow a **market penetration** strategy by modifying an existing product for the current market. Improvements to an existing product can render that product so new as to make it seen by prospective purchasers as a genuinely new product. Starbucks, for example, has recently adapted its menu to local tastes around the country in an attempt to increase patronage by current customers.

2. Market Development

market development
identifying and developing new markets for current products

The second strategy, **market development**, calls for identifying and developing new markets for current products. If an existing product is launched to a new market that is unfamiliar with it, that product is also, for all intents and purposes, a new product. Arby's, the American restaurant chain, for example, has expansion in Canada as a primary objective. Adding to the 130 units already operating in Canada, company projections call for substantial new growth across the country. But perhaps the best example of a fast-food company developing new markets for current products is Subway (see *Snapshot* in Chapter 3, pp. 91–92). Positioning itself as a healthy fast-food alternative, the company turned its low fat and calorie content into a marketing coup.

3. Product Development

product development
developing a genuinely new product to be sold to existing customers

The third strategy, **product development**, involves developing a genuinely new product to be sold to existing customers. In 2002, the Royal Botanical Gardens in Ontario (RBG) received a combined $18 million from the government of Ontario and the federal government to begin an ambitious expansion that will transform RBG into a year-round tourist attraction and cultural institution. "An expanded RBG Centre will allow us to offer more special events, changing exhibits, and innovative programs that are designed for all ages," says Mark Rizzo, chair of the Board of Directors for Royal Botanical Gardens.[13] Royal Botanical Gardens is the largest tourist attraction between Toronto and Niagara Falls, hosting 500 000 visitors a year.

4. Diversification

diversification

seeking opportunities outside the present business

Diversification growth makes sense when good opportunities can be found outside the present business. Three types of diversification can be considered. First, the company could seek new products that have technological or marketing synergies with existing product lines, even though the product may appeal to a new class of customers (concentric diversification). Second, the company might search for new products that could appeal to its current target market (horizontal diversification). Finally, the company might seek new businesses that have no relationship with the company's current technology, products, or markets (conglomerate diversification). The Case Study in Chapter 2, on Roots Air, provides an example of a failed diversification attempt.

Market

	Existing	New
New **Product**	**Product Development** Introduce new product to present market	**Diversification (example)** Launch new product to new market
Existing	**Market Penetration** Modify existing product for present market	**Market Development** Reposition present product to attract new market

Figure 5.3 Product Options in New and Existing Markets

Source: Holloway, J. C., & Plant, R.V. (1992). *Marketing for Tourism.* London: Pitman, 73.

Approaches to New Product Development

A company must develop new products to survive. New products can be obtained through acquisition or through new product development (NPD). There is a reasonably established approach to NPD, but Scheuing and Johnson have proposed a model for new service development (NSD), based on a review of other models and research into 66 U.S.-based service firms.[14] The model has 15 steps and 4 main stages (see Figure 5.4 on page 158).

The first stage (steps 1–3) of NSD focuses on how new ideas are generated and developed. The development process must begin with a precise formulation of *objectives and strategy*. A well-designed strategy drives and directs the entire innovation effort and imbues it with effectiveness and efficiency. The second step is for companies to ensure that they have organized or *structured* their plan in such a way as to enable innovation to take place. In large companies, this may involve setting up a research and development

	Stage	Step	
New idea generation and development	1.	(1) (2) (3)	Objectives and strategy Structure Idea generation and screening
Go/no go	2.	(4) (5) (6) (7)	Concept development Concept testing Business analysis Project authorization
Test design	3.	(8) (9) (10) (11)	Service design and testing Process design and testing Marketing design and testing Personnel training
Evaluation	4.	(12) (13) (14) (15)	Service testing Test marketing Launch Post-launch review

Figure 5.4   New Service Development (NSD) Model

Source: Scheuing, E. E., & Johnson, E. M. (1989). A proposed model for new service development. *The Journal of Services Marketing, 3*(2), 30.

(R & D) department. The third step consists of *idea generation and screening*. New ideas can be drawn from external sources, or be generated internally through consultation and brainstorming. Often the most powerful idea source is customer feedback.

The idea generation and development stage of NSD is followed by the second stage—the "go/no go" stage—comprising four steps (steps 4–7) that enable the company to decide whether or not it will proceed with the new development. *Concept development* requires that the surviving ideas be expanded into fully fledged concepts, especially if there is a significant service element. *Concept testing* is a research technique designed to evaluate whether a prospective user understands the idea of the proposed good or service, reacts favourably to it, and feels it provides benefits that answers unmet needs. The sixth step, *business analysis*, should represent a comprehensive investigation into the business implications of each concept. The *project authorization* step occurs when top management commits corporate resources to the implementation of a new idea. In an industry such as tourism, which consists of many small organizations, it is likely that 90 percent of companies have just one person or department in the company to authorize all innovative projects.[15]

Once the go-ahead has been given, the third stage of NSD—test design—is reached, in which detailed design and implementation of the innovation is carried out (steps 8–11). At this point, the new concept is converted into an operational entity. This requires *design and testing*. For a service, this activity should involve both the input of prospective users and the active cooperation of the operations personnel who will ultimately be delivering the service. It may also be necessary to design new production *processes* or develop new equipment.

This stage also includes *marketing design and testing*. To complete the test design phase, all employees should be familiarized with the nature and operational details of the new service. For instance, research into flight catering showed that 91 percent of airlines engaged in *personnel training*, whereas only 68 percent of food manufacturers did so.[16]

The final stage of NSD is the evaluation of the new innovation, comprising four steps (steps 12–15). *Service testing* should be used to determine potential customer acceptance of the new service, while a pilot run ensures its smooth functioning. An example comes from Prince Edward Island, where a pilot project was undertaken to determine whether package tours for farm and rural attractions were destined to become a growing industry. The pilot tour ran for five days, for eight participants, and the entire package cost $50, including food, accommodation, and any admissions. The project was carried out to determine if there was any potential in developing an innovative agritourism product for future growth.[17]

The next step, *test marketing*, examines the saleability of the new service, and a field test should be carried out with a limited sample of customers. With the delivery system and marketing in place and with the service thoroughly tested, the company should next initiate the full-scale *launch*, introducing the service product to the entire market area. Different sectors tend to evaluate their new services/products in slightly different ways. For instance, fast-food operators use market surveys, whereas foodservice contractors rely more on after-sales for customer feedback. The final step, *post-launch review*, should be aimed at determining whether the strategic objectives were achieved or whether further adjustments are needed.

Sheuing and Johnson suggest that firms should not rigidly follow this model but instead consider it as a framework from which to select those activities they deem necessary for the specific development they are undertaking. In fact, research studies have shown that tourism organizations do not follow a systematic NSD process.[18,19] It has been suggested that the systematic and formal approach to innovation is likely to be adopted only when one of the following is true: new products with major process impact are developed; a number of interrelated innovations are being developed simultaneously; product life cycles are long; competitors are unlikely to enter the market with a similar product or service; the new product is protected by licence or patent; or the innovation is original or "new to the world."[20]

The tourism and hospitality market clearly has few of these characteristics. Innovation is likely to follow a shorter, simplified development process when minor modifications are made to existing products or services; there is no licence protection; the "new" product is largely a copy of a competitor's product; innovation is not part of a major change program; and competitors are actively innovating. In 2003, a Canadian charter airline and package tour company went from introductory announcement to actually rolling down the runway in eight months. HMY Airways and its partner Companion Holidays were launched just 245 days after the company's chair, David Ho, announced his intention to launch a Vancouver-based charter airline and vacation company. "To go from the drawing board to launch that quickly is amazing," says B.C. minister of state Kevin Falcon. Clearly, the company did not follow as systematic and formal an approach to NSD as that suggested in Figure 5.4.

An organization also creates internal conditions that either foster or hinder innovation. Often, these are strongly influenced by the external environment. Conditions that may encourage a systematic but rigid approach to innovation are a bureaucratic culture, mature marketplace, the involvement of external consultants, and formal research and development departments. Conditions that encourage a dynamic and flexible approach to innovation are the following: growing supply chain integration; an organizational culture founded on innovation; industry association sponsorship; creative and entrepreneurial leadership; and deregulated markets. These conditions are likely to be more typical of organizations in tourism and hospitality, as there are many small, highly entrepreneurial firms, such as weekendtrips.com (see Case Study), operating in a largely deregulated marketplace.

SNAPSHOT

EXAMPLES OF NEW PRODUCTS

Gourmet Holidays

Cooking getaways are all the rage these days. Celebrity chefs such as Nigella Lawson, Emeril Lagasse, Bobby Flay, and Ken Kostick have made cooking cool. Torontonians are flocking to weekend gourmet cooking classes with seasoned chefs in gorgeous settings outside the city. Via Rail ran a "gourmet train" in 2003, from Toronto to Montreal, and gastronomic adventure packages are proving so popular that many places, like the pretty Butternut Inn in Port Hope, Ontario, are booked up as much as two months in advance.

Mobile Check-in

Ticket agents from Air Canada recently sported wireless IBM computers and clipped mobile printers to their belts to help deal with long line-ups during peak periods. The tech gear also helps them assist with big groups and special-needs fliers. Agents swipe a passenger's credit card or frequent flier card and pull up the reservation. They can also enter information on the mini touch-screen pad, check in the passenger, and print the boarding pass. The whole process can take less than 60 seconds.

Smart Glasses

For a customer wishing for a quick refill after finishing a drink, a new glassware system developed by Mitsubishi Electric Research Laboratories will alert bar staff to his or her needs. A small microprocessor, which costs about the same as a can of pop, is installed in the base of the glass, along with a transponder coil. The glass itself is coated with conductive material and powered by another coil embedded in the drink. Drink-level data is continuously sent to an automated system, such as a kitchen display. Waiters can also receive the fill-up information on a wireless device. Each glass has its own identification number, so staff can keep track of thirsty patrons even if they move around a bar or restaurant.

Flying Casinos

The Israeli government has given the go-ahead for "flying casinos"—specially fitted planes that will give gamblers a four-hour spin in the air. By leaving Israeli airspace, the planes will get around the country's gambling ban. Three flights a day will be run by an Icelandic airline, starting in 2003. The project, a private initiative of Israeli investors and financiers from abroad, is expected to generate about US$50 million a year in revenue for Israel.

Branded Hotel Floors

American Express and the Sheraton Vancouver Wall Centre Hotel have partnered to open a floor of the hotel dedicated to business accommodations for American Express credit card holders. Located on the 27th floor, the "American Express Club Floor" features a private lounge with business service centre, direct access to boardrooms and fitness facilities, dedicated front-desk check-in and a late 4:00 p.m. check out. According to officials, guests using the club floor pay the same price for their room as Amex's negotiated standard room rate and benefit from a host of value-added services and amenities. These include complimentary continental breakfast, all-day coffee and tea, evening hors d'oeuvres, international and local newspapers, and 24-hour room service.

Partner-Swapping for Skiers in Switzerland

A French travel company is offering chalet holidays for partner-swappers. Papillon des Alpes is selling breaks for "swingers" in Verbier, Switzerland, which cost about $1200 a week and are aimed at "broadminded, adventurous couples." Although the company's brochure includes explicit pictures, it says: "It is not necessary to actually have sex with other people to have a good time."

Canada's First Resort-Based Astronomical Observatory

The Delta Grandview Resort in the heart of the Muskokas opened the Echo Valley Astronomical Observatory in the fall of 2000, primarily for public viewing of celestial objects. The tree-storey, domed observatory houses a state-of-the-art 40 cm Schmidt-Cassegrain telescope, identical to those used for public viewing at the largest mountain-top research observatories in North America. The telescope is powerful enough to reveal celestial objects 10 000 times fainter than the faintest objects visible to the naked eye. Renowned for dark skies free from light pollution, Muskoka provides optimum conditions for astronomical viewing, and astronomer Robin Tapley leads guests on guided tours of the sky to see a multitude of cosmic sights.

The First Nude Airline!

What was billed as the first nude airline flight took off from Miami International Airport on May 3, 2003, destined for Cancun, Mexico. Once the plane reached cruising altitude, passengers enjoyed their flight clothes-free. Castaways Travel, based in Houston, which specializes in nude travel, put together the package. The cost for the round trip was US$499, which included a towel to sit on. Once in Cancun, the package group headed an hour south to the Eldorado Resort and Spa for a clothing-free week for an additional $770 to $1050 per person.

Iceberg Tourism

Every spring, icebergs make their way south from Greenland to the Newfoundland coast—"blue gems within white gems," as Annie Proulx called them in her bestseller *The Shipping News*. These icebergs have become an important part of Newfoundland's $620 million dollar tourism industry, as tourists flock to see the 10 000- to 15 000-year-old pieces of ice. Tour operators like Northland Discovery Tours have seen their businesses grow steadily for the last five years, although they now face competition from drink manufacturers that are harvesting the icebergs to make iceberg vodka and other bottled drinks. However, the harvesting has become an attraction in itself, attracting media attention and TV crews from all over the world. So whichever way you look at it, icebergs have becomes good business for Newfoundland tourism.

Anti-Terror Tour Packages

American and Canadian tourists in Israel are being offered a five-day package of counter-terrorism training, complete with a mock terror attack. The Shiloh tour package, costing about $8000, includes a stay at an Israeli army bunker, military-style food, hand-to-hand combat in the desert, and training on how to understand the mentality of terrorists. Tour participants are taught how to handle attackers, such as a knife-wielding intruder in a synagogue or a bomber on a bus.

Participants are given their own army fatigues and a chance to sit in an Israeli F-15 fighter jet. On the last day, they have the opportunnity to use their new training when they are divided into "Arabs" and "Jews" for a paintball fight.

Sources: *Amex, Sheraton team up in Vancouver* (2002). Retrieved January 24, 2002, from http://www.canadatourism.com/en/ctc/ctx/ctx-news/search/newsbydateform.cfm; Buhasz, L. (2002, June 5). Israel approves flying casinos. *The Globe and Mail*, p. T3; Copans, L. (2003, March 6). Firm offers anti-terror tour package. *Calgary Herald*, p. A5; Gourmet holidays. (2002, May 18). *National Post*, p. T04; Hughes, M. (2002, Spring). Delta Grandview Resort: Magical setting on Fairy Lake. *North American Inns*, 36–38; Ready for takeoff. (2003, January 23). *Calgary Sun*, p. 37; Tech travel. (2002, July). *Backbone Magazine*, 8; Womack, S. (2003, December 31). Firm offers wife-swapping for the off-piste husband. *Daily Telegraph*, p. 3.

CHAPTER SUMMARY

Tourism and hospitality products are a group of selected components or elements brought together in a "bundle" to satisfy needs and wants. There are three levels of tourism products: the core product, the tangible product, and the augmented product. An important part of the augmented product is the physical environment—often referred to as the "servicescape." This is very important for tourism and hospitality products such as hotels, restaurants, and theme parks, which are dominated by experience attributes.

The most basic decisions a tourism organization has to make are what business it is in and what product mix is appropriate to it. The product mix is the portfolio of products that an organization offers to one market or several. Five basic market/product options exist: several markets/multi-product mixes for each; several markets/single product for each; several markets/single product for all; single market/multi-product mix; and single market/single product.

One of the most basic product analysis tools is product life cycle (PLC) analysis; an organization should assess each product and service in terms of its position on the product life cycle. The five stages of the PLC are product development, introduction, growth, maturity, and decline.

Positioning is the bedrock of product management, and its purpose is to create a distinctive place in the minds of potential customers. Four key positioning strategies that are not mutually exclusive and may be used in combination are positioning relative to target market; positioning by price and quality; positioning relative to a product class; and positioning relative to competitors.

Branding developed in the field of packaged goods as a method of establishing a distinctive identity for a product based on competitive differentiation from other products. The case for branding is stronger for tourism products that offer the possibility for differentiation in several areas of the marketing mix. This is why branding has been particularly successful in hotel and restaurant marketing.

In the tourism and hospitality industry, packaging is the process of combining two or more related and complementary offerings into a single-price offering. Packaging provides several customer benefits, including easier budgeting for trips; increased convenience; greater economy; the opportunity to experience previously unfamiliar activities and attractions; and the opportunity to design components of a package for specialized interests. For tourism operations, packages are attractive because they can improve profitability; they can smooth business patterns; they allow joint marketing opportunities; and they can be an effective tool for tailoring tourism products for specific target markets.

Developing new products is different from maintaining existing ones, and planning for both kinds of product will differ according to whether the products are targeted at existing markets or new ones. Holloway and Plant suggest that a company has four alternatives in developing new products: market penetration, market development, product development, and diversification.

New products can be obtained through acquisition or through new product development (NPD). There is a reasonably established approach to NPD, but Scheuing and Johnson have proposed a model for new service development (NSD). It has four main stages. The first stage focuses on how new ideas are generated and developed. This stage is followed by the "go/no go" stage, in which the company decides if it will proceed with the new development. Once the go-ahead has been given, the test design stage is reached, in which detailed design and implementation of the innovation is carried out. The final stage of NSD is service evaluation.

KEY TERMS

augmented product, p. 139	market development, p. 156	product life cycle (PLC)
benefits, p. 143	market penetration, p. 156	analysis, p. 144
brandicide, p. 152	packaging, p. 155	product mix, p. 143
branding, p. 149	positioning, p. 145	servicescape, p. 140
core product, p. 139	positioning statement, p. 146	tangible product, p. 139
diversification, p. 157	product development, p. 156	tourism and hospitality
features, p. 143		products, p. 138

DISCUSSION QUESTIONS AND EXERCISES

1. Apart from the illustrations provided in the chapter, give some examples of businesses that are responding to consumer desires for experiences. How are they using the servicescape to deliver these experiences?

2. Think of a particular tourism or hospitality organization in which you believe physical evidence is particularly important in communicating with and satisfying customers. What information would you give to the manager of that organization to convince him or her of the importance of physical evidence in the organization's marketing strategy?

3. Reread the *Marketing in Action* feature on Catch restaurant. Apply the three levels of product to the restaurant. Where would you place the restaurant on the product life cycle (PLC), and how are the owners trying to position the restaurant? How important is the servicescape for Catch?

4. It has been suggested that companies can commit "brandicide" by stretching a well-known brand too far. Think of a brand that has done this. What was it that killed it off? Take a tourism brand you are familiar with and keep stretching it. How far can you go?

5. Review Figure 5.3, "Product Options in New and Existing Markets," and think of an example (not already given in the text) of each strategy from the tourism industry.

6. Why is it that many research studies have found that services rarely follow the new service development (NSD) steps outlined in Figure 5.4?

CASE STUDY

WEEKENDTRIPS.COM

Canadians are turning in increasing numbers to the Internet to help them plan and book their travel. The dollar value of travel that Canadians book over the Internet is expected to increase to $4.2 billion by 2004, from $662 million in 1999—a six-fold increase in just five years. Internet use overall has grown by 45 percent in the last three years, and Canadians looking for travel packages are keen users of the Internet. In 2003, 77 percent of travellers are browsed the Internet for information, up 10 percent from 2002, and more than two in three package travellers used the Internet in 2003 to help plan summer trips.

A parallel trend is seeing Canadians lacking the time for frequent, extensive holidays. The amount of time they spend working has been increasing steadily since 1992, and fast-paced work environments that place intense demands on individuals are the norm today. For many, time is at a

premium, and people are often too busy to dedicate the time, energy, and imagination necessary to arrange all the elements of a comprehensive weekend getaway.

Responding to these trends is weekendtrips.com, a Toronto-based travel and leisure company that focuses on designing short-term getaways and sells them via the Internet. Building on its network of partners in the travel, hospitality, and recreation industries, the company uses its resources to package and market weekend experiences. In Canada, the development and marketing of weekend getaways is led primarily by hotels and inns, small leisure activity operators, and tourist trade associations. For the most part, these operators act independently, often with limited marketing resources. While a number of informative resource guides were available to consumers, until weekendtrips.com came along, there was no company that offered a comprehensive selection of pre-arranged weekend experiences. The company was founded by two friends, Francesco Contini and Marawan El-Asfahani, who were sitting in a Toronto café a few years ago, commenting on how uneventful their weekend had been and, for that matter, how routine every weekend had become. Both agreed that their lives were so hectic that it was hard to find the time to plan something eventful for the weekend. So they created weekendtrips.com, and now El-Asfahani, who has an extensive background in the hospitality industry and is a co-founder of Oxygen Design + Communications, lends his vision, entrepreneurship, and marketing savvy to the company. "There are fifty-two weekends every year—that's fifty-two opportunities to see new places and have new experiences" says El-Asfahani. Contini, who has spent most of his career in the travel industry, oversees the operation of the company.

Weekendtrips.com offers a diverse range of weekend programs: multi-day cultural getaways in vibrant urban centres; adventurous canoeing excursions along remote northern rivers; and guided nature appreciation day trips for children at conservation areas and more. The variety of travel packages suits singles, couples, and families—people of all ages, interests, and budgets. The trips are as diverse as gliding over Southern Ontario or taking a four-day culinary spree in Bologna, Italy's gastronomic capital. Other ideas include sailing in Ontario's Prince Edward County, cycling tours in Mennonite country, photography workshops, cave exploration, gardening seminars, and off-road motorcycling, to name just a few. "We recognize that our clients are busy, so we want to make it as simple as possible for them to take off for the weekend. For instance, when we develop a trip, not only do we provide accommodation and travel arrangements, but we also take care of any necessary gear and equipment," says Contini.

The company offers both day trips and weekend trips (see Table 5.4 on page 166). For example, a day trip on offer at the end of 2001 was the Santa Claus Express, designed to make last minute holiday shopping stress-free. As other frustrated shoppers battled street traffic and crowded parking lots, Santa Claus Express participants travelled by bus between four downtown Toronto shopping neighbourhoods. Purchases could be stored on the bus, leaving participants free to continue their shopping expedition unencumbered. The trip cost was $19.95 per person plus GST. An example of a weekend trip offered in the same year was a three-day trip to the U.S. Grand Prix, held September 30, 2001, at the new track on the infield of the Indianapolis oval—one of racing's holiest sites. For $499 per person, weekendtrips.com provided charter bus transportation from Southern Ontario, two nights' accommodation, and a ticket to the race.

The advent of the Internet has brought many new opportunities, and by allowing weekendtrips.com to deliver frequently changing product information to a mass market in a cost-effective way, the Internet has increased dramatically the economic viability of the weekendtrips.com business model. Each week, consumers can browse the weekendtrips.com Web site and select from a variety of offers. By centralizing the fragmented resources and expertise of its partners, the Web site becomes a point of reference, a reliable source of ideas for the weekend. By simplifying the decision-making process, the company encourages weekend travel and leisure, thereby creating new market opportunities for weekendtrips.com and all it partners.

Table 5.4

Packages on Offer by Weekendtrips.com

DAY TRIPS	SATURDAY AND SUNDAY	LONG WEEKENDS
Fall cycling tours	Wine country getaway	Affordable New York
Fall adventure sailing	Country Inn getaway	Barefoot in the Bahamas
Good-earth cooking	Escape the world	San Francisco's edgy side
Mile-high rendezvous	Quintessential golf	Southern California escape
ATV train ride	Hiking at Blue Mountain	Bologna gastronomy delight
Explore underground	Old Quebec by private plane	Taliesin West desert weekend
Introduction to rock climbing	Sailing in Prince Edward County	
Introduction to photography	Get thee to a spa	
Skydiving course	Montreal by rail	
Kayaking on the Bay	Delicious diversions	
Waterfall photography workshop	Sheik Yerbouti	
Aerial discovery	Sex in the city	
Spiderman's Elora Gorge	Love me tender	
Charley's Angels	One starry night in Elora	

Sources: *Canadians logging on to destination Web sites*. (2000). Retrieved September 26, 2000, from http://tourismtogether.com/tourismweb/news/buzz/sep; F. Contini, general manager, weekendtrips.com, personal communication, April 14, 2003; Hudson, S., & Lang, N. (2002). A destination case study of marketing tourism online: Banff, Canada. *Journal of Vacation Marketing*, 8(2), 155–165; weekendtrips.com Web site: www.weekendtrips.com.

QUESTIONS

1. How do you explain the growth in the short-break tourism market?
2. Take a look at the products that weeendtrips.com are promoting today. Can you think of any new ideas for short breaks?
3. How do you see the future for weekendtrips.com? Which of the four strategies in Figure 5.3 would you recommend for the company?
4. Where would you place weekendtrips.com on the product life cycle (PLC), and what marketing strategies should the company be following because of this position?

WEB SITES

www.arbys.com
Arby's

www.creativeri.com
Catch restaurant, in Calgary

www.disney.com
Disney

www.vegas.com/shopping/forumshops
The Forum, Las Vegas

www.familledufour.com
Groupe Dufour

www.eberg.ca
Iceberg tourism

www.manitobamuseum.mb.ca
The Manitoba Museum

www.tourtrends.com/customtours
Tour Trends

www.weekendtrips.com
Weekendtrips.com

ENDNOTES

1. Middleton, V. T. C., & Clarke, J. (2001). *Marketing in travel and tourism.* Oxford: Butterworth-Heinemann.
2. Ibid.
3. Bitner, M. J. (1990). Evaluating service encounters. *Journal of Marketing, 54*(April), 69–82.
4. Russell, J. A., Ward, L. M., & Pratt, G. (1981). An affective quality attributed to environments. *Environment and Behaviour, 13*(3), 259–288.
5. Seaton, A. V., & Bennett, M. M. (1996). *Marketing tourism products: Concepts, issues, cases.* Thomson Business Press.
6. Mercer, D. (1992). *Marketing.* Oxford: Blackwell, 295.
7. Burke, J. F., & Resnick, B. P. (1991). *Marketing and selling the travel product.* Cincinnati, OH: South-Western.
8. Gilpin, S. (1994). Branding in the hotel industry. Where are we now? Paper presented at the CHME Conference, Napier University, Edinburgh, April 5–7.
9. Middleton, V. T. C., & Clarke, J. (2001). *Marketing in travel and tourism.* Oxford: Butterworth-Heinemann.
10. *Flying the crowded skies.* (2002, April 27). *National Post,* p. B5.
11. *Tour trends highlight Quebec's Magdalen Islands.* (2002, January 31). Retrieved January 31, 2002, from http://www.canadatourism.com/en/ctc/ctx/ctxnews/search/newsbydateform.cfm.
12. *Groupe Dufour has the power.* (2002, May 9). Retrieved May 9, 2002, from http://www.canadatourism.com/en/ctc/ctx/ctx-news/search/newsbydateform.cfm.
13. Butler, D. (2002). Royal Botanical Gardens receives $18 million to begin expansion project. Retrieved October 9, 2002, from http://www.canadatourism.com/en/ctc/ctx/ctx-news/search/newsbydateform.cfm.
14. Scheuing, E. E., & Johnson, E. M. (1989). A proposed model for new service development. *The Journal of Services Marketing, 3*(2), 25–34.
15. Jones, P., Hudson, S., & Costis, P. (1997). New product development in the UK tour-operating industry. *Progress in Tourism and Hospitality Research, 3*(4), 283–294.
16. Jones, P. (1995). Innovation in flight catering. In P. Jones and M. Kipps (Eds.), *Flight Catering* (pp. 163–175). London: Longman.
17. Sharratt, S. (2002, September 28). Pilot project tests farm-gate tourism. *The Guardian* (Charlottetown), p. A5.
18. Jones, P., Hudson, S., & Costis, P. (1997). New product development in the UK tour-operating industry. *Progress in Tourism and Hospitality Research, 3*(4), 283–294.
19. Easingwood, C. J. (1986). New product development for service companies. *Journal of Product Innovation Management, 3*(3), 296–312.
20. Jones, P., Hudson, S., & Costis, P. (1997). New product development in the UK tour-operating industry. *Progress in Tourism and Hospitality Research, 3*(4), 283–294.

CHAPTER

Pricing

6

"SAVE TIME, SAVE MONEY"—SKI BY THE HOUR AT BANFF MOUNT NORQUAY

"Save time, save money." This is the slogan used by Alberta ski area Banff Mount Norquay to promote its skiing-by-the-hour concept. In 1995, the resort introduced to market the concept of hourly skiing, which has ultimately proved to be an extremely successful long-term pricing strategy. The resort decided to test the waters in 1995 by introducing a mid-week-only two-hour ticket called a "flex-time" ticket, targeted at the local market.

Reaction to the flex-time ticket was extremely positive—skiers who had never been to Norquay were turning up for a couple of hours of skiing and then going back to work. Hourly skiing opened up a new market, so after two seasons Norquay decided to expand the idea by introducing two-, three-, four-, and five-hour tickets, seven days a week. "We found it was not abused, and it did not cannibalize existing business," says Robert Cote, Norquay's

director of marketing. "People bought a two-hour ticket because they only wanted to ski for two hours—they wouldn't normally have bought a day ticket, and they wouldn't have bought a season's pass because they didn't ski enough to make it worthwhile."

According to Cote, hourly skiing takes down all the barriers to skiing that would normally prevent people from coming. "We knew everyone liked Norquay, but it wasn't accessible from a customer's point of view. If someone wanted to ski for the morning they had to buy a whole day's lift ticket, and if they wanted a half day, they had to wait until mid-day. This meant Norquay was imposing its timetable on customers. Now we have put customers in control of their own day."

Competitors have not followed Norquay's lead on hourly tickets, mainly because the competitors are not as close to Banff or Calgary, and also because the layout of their resorts is not conducive to hourly skiing. For hourly skiing to succeed, a close proximity to the client base is necessary. Norquay's proximity to Banff allows visitors to the city to snatch a few hours of skiing on arrival or departure day, or to put in a half-day of skiing before an afternoon at the hot springs or shopping. Locals can also come up just for a short period. "The way the lifts are laid out here, you can do a lot of skiing in two hours. At other resorts it may not work because they are bigger and more spread out."

For Cote, the most significant advantage to skiing by the hour is that skiers now feel they are getting value for money. "There is a general perception that the sport of skiing is expensive. I don't think it is the actual money spent—I think it is a whole-value equation. Normally, if you don't make it by 9 a.m. for the first lift, you are not going to get full value for your lift ticket. You are going to leave with an unused portion and leave with the feeling of being ripped off. Our slogan is 'save time, save money.'" Cote adds, "The biggest thing here is saving time. In today's society with all the time demands placed on people, time is the most valuable commodity out there. People want to ski, but they don't necessarily want to commit so much time to it. Unfortunately, the full-day/half-day scenario of purchasing lift tickets just doesn't allow that. It all of a sudden puts a high demand on people's time."

In 2002–2003, in response to customer demand for even more flexibility, Norquay decided to increase from hourly increments to half-hourly increments. The resort's ski-by-the-hour ticket options are shown in Table 6.2 (see p. 188). The 2001–2002 season was the first winter in which gross sales from the different hourly tickets exceeded sales from full-day tickets—the three-hour ticket being the most popular, followed by two-hour and four-hour tickets. But full-day sales have remained steady, so hourly tickets have not adversely affected sales of full-day tickets. And skiing by the hour has become so popular at Norquay that Cote tags the skiing-by-the-hour concept onto all resort promotions. "After six years of it, people are really catching on to it, and it is becoming associated with us," he says.

Source: R. Cote, director of marketing, Mount Norquay, personal communication, February 15, 2003.

Objectives

On completion of this chapter, readers should understand

- the key factors determining pricing decisions;
- the contribution of economics to pricing;
- the specific characteristics of the tourism and hospitality industry that affect pricing policy;

- the key approaches that companies take toward pricing in tourism;
- how prices are calculated for new products;
- yield management as it applies to tourism; and
- the difference between strategic pricing and tactical pricing in tourism.

Chapter Overview

The opening vignette highlights an unusual pricing approach for a ski operator, but one that has proven to be extremely successful. This chapter begins by looking at the impact of various corporate objectives on pricing. These objectives may be profit maximization, target rate of return, market share, survival, or growth. Even if these objectives are not explicit, they can have a significant impact on pricing. The second section highlights the key factors determining pricing decisions. As well as marketing objectives, these include costs, other mix variables, channel member expectations, buyer perceptions, competition, and legal and regulatory restrictions.

The third part of the chapter focuses on the contribution of economics to pricing. This includes a discussion of the interaction between supply and demand, and the importance of elasticity of demand. Generally, companies use pricing as part of their positioning of a product, employing one of three basic approaches: premium pricing, value-for-money pricing, and undercut pricing. These approaches are examined here, using three hotel groups in Canada as examples. The next main section discusses the basic approaches to pricing, which fall into three general categories: cost-based methods, demand-based methods, and competition-oriented pricing. Pricing strategies for new products are the subject of the next part of the chapter, which discusses prestige pricing, market skimming, and penetration pricing. Other pricing techniques are then examined, followed by a discussion of yield management. The difference between strategic pricing and tactical pricing is then explained, and the final section of the chapter looks at the specific characteristics of the tourism and hospitality industry that affect pricing policy.

INTRODUCTION TO PRICING

Pricing is crucial to the successful marketing of any product or service, but it is often the least understood of the marketing mix elements. The prices that an organization charges for its products must strike a balance between gaining acceptance with the target market and making profit for the organizations. Even in not-for-profit organizations, the pricing of products and services is the key to encouraging consumption. The pricing element of the marketing mix is unique in that it is the only one that directly affects an organization's revenues, and hence its profits. The fields of finance and economics have much to contribute in setting prices, but on their own perhaps do not lead to the best pricing decisions.

Other marketing mix decisions will often interact with pricing decisions. Product quality (both real and perceived) needs to be considered in light of price. Knowledge of the "**price–quality trade-off**" compels decision makers to recognize that consumers might accept a higher cost for a better quality of product. Similarly, with regard to brand image—often the consequence of marketing communications decisions—lesser-known brands might command lower prices. Finally, pricing decisions must take into account the needs of the distributor. Distributors will sell a product only if they will obtain a certain profit margin.

As with other elements in the marketing mix, pricing should be treated as a tool to achieve corporate and marketing objectives. If the target market has been clearly identified, and a decision has been made about where a product is to be positioned, then pricing will become easier to determine. Companies choosing to position their products in the mass market and to enter a field with many competitors will need to adopt a very careful pricing policy. Those seeking to appeal to niche markets may have slightly more price flexibility, since they have fewer competitors and perhaps more points of difference between their products and others in the niche.

price–quality trade-off
acceptance of the higher cost of a better quality of product

FACTORS DETERMINING PRICING DECISIONS

Whatever the strategy of the organization is, clear pricing objectives should be established before price levels are set. The key factors determining pricing decisions are shown in Figure 6.1 on page 172. They are as follows.

1. Organizational and Marketing Objectives

The most common objectives are **profit maximization, target rate of return, market share**, and survival. For some organizations, such as Parks Canada, objectives are not only commercial in their nature, and pricing decisions are made for societal reasons—such as raising entry fees to reduce the social and environmental impacts of increasing numbers of visitors. Other objectives may include being perceived as offering outstanding value for money, or being the brand leader in the marketplace. The first may be reflected in lower prices, whereas the second goal could lead to high prices in the long term.

profit maximization
corporate objective that causes managers in organizations to make decisions in such a way as to maximize profits

target rate of return
corporate objective that aims to achieve a particular return on the assets employed in an organization

2. Costs

The setting of prices should incorporate a calculation of how much it costs the organization to produce the product or service. If the company is profit-oriented, a margin will be added to the cost price to derive the selling price. An organization could also decide to sell below cost for a period of time, which is often referred to as a tactical price reduction, discussed later in the chapter (see p. 197).

market share
the percentage relationship of an organization's sales to total industry sales

3. Other Marketing Mix Variables

Pricing decisions always have an interaction with the other elements of the marketing mix. Consider the example of Canadian Mountain Holidays, which sells expensive heliskiing holidays. The high price of this product must be reflected in other elements of the marketing mix. A high level of personal service is included as part of the promotional package, and the quality of the lodges must meet expectations that the high price has generated in the minds of the customers. Price usually gives the consumer the first indication

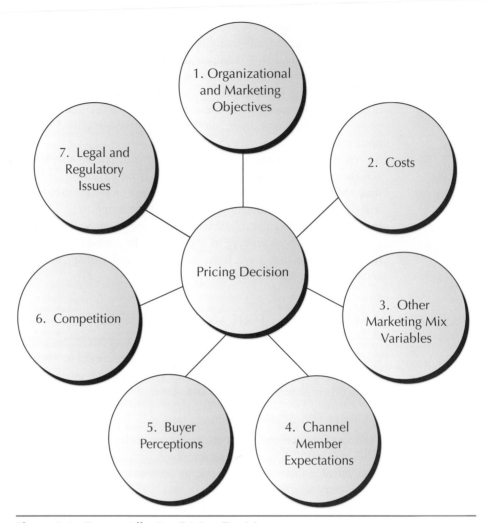

Figure 6.1   Factors Affecting Pricing Decisions

Source: Dibb, S., Simkin, L., Pride, W. M., & Ferrell, O. C. (1994). *Marketing: Concepts & strategies* (2nd ed). London: Houghton-Mifflin.

of perceived product quality. Distribution of the holidays takes place via an exclusive channel system of overseas agents, reflecting the high-quality image and resulting high price.

4. Channel Member Expectations

A marketer must consider the intermediaries in the distribution channel when pricing a product or service. Travel agents, for example, will expect to earn commissions for their efforts. However, some stakeholders in the travel industry, such as airlines, car rental companies, and international hotel chains, have been quick to grasp the potential of marketing and selling their services online. They have recognized an opportunity to bypass agents and sell their basic products and services directly to the customer. Increasingly, package holiday tour operators are including direct sales via the Internet in their sales strategy, thus bypassing the travel agent.

5. Buyer Perceptions

The prices set for travel products and services must reflect customers' perceptions in the target market. The key is whether customers perceive that the price they have paid represents good value for money and matches their quality expectations. In tourism and hospitality, consumers expect a high level of service and special features if a high price is being charged. For example, after paying $7000, a CMH heliskier can expect lodges to contain a fully stocked bar, a sauna and Jacuzzi, and even a resident qualified massage therapist.

6. Competition

In competitive markets, organizations will be trying to win customers from competitors in two ways. Price competition involves offering the product or service at a lower price than the price charged by the competition. In a very competitive marketplace, organizations are likely to resort to intense price competition to sell goods and services. Non-price competition, on the other hand, is concerned with trying to increase market share or sales by leaving the price unchanged but persuading target customers that their offering is superior to that offered by the competition. Such a strategy is more typical in oligopolistic markets, in which there are few competitors.

7. Legal and Regulatory Issues

There may be legal and regulatory restrictions that control the ways in which an organization fixes prices. For example, an organization such as The Manitoba Museum (see *Profile* in Chapter 5), which is subsidized by the government, may be put under pressure to keep prices low to encourage people to visit. Legal restrictions are often placed on the practice of price fixing and collusion. Additionally, there are a number of organizations, quasi-governmental and industrial, that exercise some influence on pricing policies and strategies, a fact that marketing managers must bear in mind.

SNAPSHOT

PRICING FOR FRACTIONAL OWNERSHIP

Fractional ownership is real estate's hot new growth segment, accounting for US$520 million in sales in the United States in 2002. At its most basic, fractional ownership occurs when two or more owners or families buy and share title to a single recreational property. The advantages for consumers is that they get more house for their buck than if they bought it alone, all maintenance and upkeep are shared, and the buyer has title to a piece of real estate that can be freely sold through a realtor. Some fractional ownerships offer the benefits of being able to exchange the properties for worldwide destinations, similar to the traditional time share model, and this can provide added appeal for consumers. Fractional properties have been booming in the United States, but Canada represents a relatively untapped market for this type of business. The market penetration rate is only about one-third of the U.S. rate for households with comparable incomes.

SNAPSHOT *continued*

Canadian Mountain Cabins is a new company capitalizing on this growing demand for fractional properties. In 2002, the company created a log cabin resort in the Purcell Mountains near Kimberley, B.C. The "cabins in the woods" product was specifically designed for whole or fractional ownership. "The fractional ownership of log cabins came from extensive market research indicating two types of demand," says Andy Harris, director of Canadian Mountain Cabins. "One, the demand from owners with restricted time to use a recreational property, and these owners typically use no more than 22 days a year; and secondly the demand from visitors for an authentically Canadian type of accommodation."

The fractional buyers typically live within a four-hour drive or a two-hour flight of their second home. "Owners are buying multiple fractional interest in properties to suit their lifestyle, with the real estate investment taking a secondary priority. Baby boomers are test driving their retirement with fractional ownership, picking property in destinations that match their plans when they ease off work," says Harris. A professional property manager was hired by the company so that the cabins could be rented to visitors when the owners were unable to use them.

Fractional ownership is not just limited to bricks and mortar. "We are seeing people buying a log cabin for skiing and golf, but they also may purchase fractional ownership of a yacht on the West Coast," Harris says. One4 Yacht Fractions, based on Granville Island in Vancouver, has pioneered this market with extensive service so that owners can turn up, stock the fridge, and sail off. "We make it easy for busy owners to enjoy the pride of ownership and their yacht without all the hassle usually associated with boat maintenance," says Colin Jackson, director of One4 Yacht Fractions.

As for the price, whole ownership of the log cabins is about $330 000, and fractional interests cost between $90 000 and $199 000. Monthly condo fees vary depending on the level of service chosen, and can be anywhere from $120 to $280 per month. For the yachts, a fully equipped Bavaria 44 sailing yacht costs about $550 000, whereas quarter shares are $130 000 and include the first year's moorage and insurance. Monthly payments for these services start in year two at $250 per month.

Source: A. Harris, director of Canadian Mountain Cabins, personal communication, May 23, 2003.

CONTRIBUTIONS OF ECONOMICS TO PRICING

Economists contend that producers of a commodity are more likely to provide that commodity if the price for it in the marketplace is high. This is coupled with the suggestion that buyers are more likely to purchase more of the commodity if prices are low. From this comes the idea that the quantity produced and consumed and the price acceptable to each party will be in equilibrium at some point. This is shown in Figure 6.2.

Unfortunately, this simplistic model is unlikely to be useful as a mathematical way of determining prices because it assumes that certain conditions need to be present for the process to occur. One of these is the assumption that consumers have perfect knowledge, and know all the prices from all the producers. Although the use of the Internet is

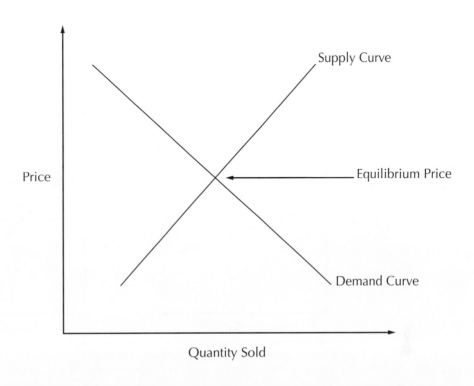

Figure 6.2   The Interaction of Supply and Demand

increasing, the likelihood of such wide consumer knowledge occurring is small in the travel industry. Another assumption of the model is that there are many small producers, whereas consolidation in many sectors of tourism and hospitality has reduced competition, meaning that prices are less free to move than the model suggests. Although the model may not help pricing decisions in a mathematical or graphical way, it does not mean that the concept is completely redundant. For instance, if a service producer has a feeling that the market is undersupplied—such as was the situation of Air Canada after September 11, 2001—he or she may tend to increase prices. Similarly, if a buyer senses that the market is oversupplied, he or she may try to negotiate lower prices—as happened in the hotel market after the terrorist attacks, the war in Iraq, and the outbreak of severe acute respiratory syndrome (SARS).

Elasticity of Demand

elasticity of demand

the sensitivity of customer demand to changes in the prices of services

The raising and lowering of prices generally has an effect on the level of sales. The analysis of buyers' reactions to price change employs the concept of the **elasticity of demand**. This is represented by the formula:

$$\text{Price elasticity of demand} = \frac{\%\ \text{change in quantity demanded}}{\%\ \text{change in price}}$$

If demand increases in line with price cuts then the product or service is said to be elastic. But if demand remains relatively unaltered by price changes, the product or service is said to be inelastic. In the tourism and hospitality industry, many products are elastic—as prices fall, demand increases. However, there are many occasions when this is not true. Business travel is often inelastic, and popularity or fashion may render a destination or restaurant inelastic. Figure 6.3 shows two demand curves—for an elastic and an inelastic product. As with knowledge of the state of supply and demand, managers are not often in a position to know mathematically the value of elasticity for a product. They may not have access to all price and quantity data, or the service may be new and there may therefore be no historical data from which to derive the slope of the demand curve.

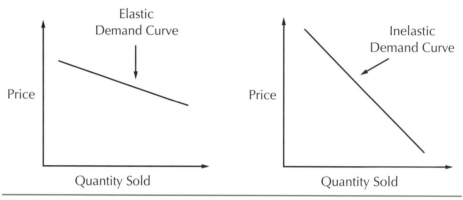

Figure 6.3   Elastic and Inelastic Demand Curves

Price elasticity can be affected by a number of factors, including the customer's perception of the uniqueness of the product, the availability and awareness of substitutes, and how the consumer budgets. For example, a leisure traveller buying a holiday for personal use will have one perspective on price value; if the same person uses a company charge account, he or she may have another set of values. If consumers are purchasing something for someone else to use, they may be prepared to spend more—or less—than they would spend on themselves. Price elasticity of demand gives management a statistical method to measure whether or not the organization's prices are too high or low. In setting prices, a company will want to know what levels of demand it is likely to experience at different prices. For a new product this is hard to gauge. The two most common methods of assessing demand are

1. asking potential customers what they would be willing to pay for the product; and
2. test marketing the product at different prices in different regions.

willingness to pay (WTP) assessment

asking potential customers what they would be willing to pay for the product

The first method is often called **willingness to pay (WTP) assessment**. The Case Study in this chapter reports on a research study engaged to measure the willingness to pay for "greener" products in Banff National Park. The difficulty with this method is that what people say they will do does not always translate into actual behaviour when the product is launched. In test marketing, the second method, it is difficult to control all the factors apart from price that will influence consumer decisions in different areas.

PRICING AND POSITIONING

Generally, companies use pricing as part of their positioning of a product, employing one of three strategic approaches: premium pricing, value-for-money pricing, and undercut pricing.[1]

1. Premium Pricing

premium pricing

setting prices above market price, to reflect either the image of quality or the unique status of the product

In **premium pricing**, a decision is made to set prices above market price, to reflect either the image of quality or the unique status of the product. The product may be new, or it may have unique features not shared by competitors, such as a tour that offers access to areas not normally open to the public. Finally, the company itself may have such a strong reputation that the brand image alone is sufficient to merit a premium price. The Four Seasons Hotel chain follows this strategy in setting prices. Promoted as upscale, full-service hotels, Four Seasons will, on occasion, raise prices to the highest level in the area. This strategy has been extremely successful in the past, with Four Seasons boasting an impressive 72.6 percent average occupancy and an average daily room rate of US$417 across its 12 728 rooms in 42 properties located in 25 countries worldwide.[2]

2. Value-for-Money Pricing

value-for-money pricing

charging medium prices and emphasizing that the product represents excellent value for money at this price

In **value-for-money pricing**, the intention is to charge medium prices and emphasize that the product represents excellent value for money at this price. Organizations with well-established reputations for service generally do well with such a pricing strategy. According to the readers' poll in the March 2002 issue of *Travel & Leisure* magazine, guests staying at properties in the Fairmont Hotels & Resorts collection are consistently maximizing the value of their dollar by receiving exceptional service, unique offerings, and renowned hospitality at an affordable price.

3. Undercut Pricing

undercut pricing

setting prices lower than the competition and using the price as a trigger to purchase immediately

Sometimes called "cheap value" pricing, the objective in **undercut pricing** is to undercut the competition by setting lower prices, and the lower price is used as a trigger to purchase immediately. Unit profits are low, but satisfactory overall profits are achieved through high turnover. This strategy is often used by organizations seeking a foot in or rapid expansion into a new market. The Super 8 hotel chain is an example of a company that has engaged in undercut pricing to foster rapid growth and expansion in each new market it enters. The company prices competitively to attract new customers and take business away from competitors. Super 8 has developed a very different price–demand relationship than the Four Seasons, mentioned above. However, it must be noted that the average occupancy at Super 8 is lower than Four Seasons', at 64 percent, even though the average daily room rate is considerably less (US$44.55). This may be an indication that Super 8's incredible growth rate (a new property opened every 2.3 days between 1996 and 2000) is causing a squeeze in the marketplace as Super 8 locations become too close to one another.[3]

Any of these policies can be seen as "fair-pricing" policies. A fair price can be defined as one that the customer is happy to pay while the company achieves a satisfactory level of profit. Thus a premium-pricing policy is acceptable, provided that the customer receives the benefits appropriate to the price. Only when companies are able to force up prices against the consumers' will, such as in the case of monopolies, can it be said that fair pricing is inoperative. A **monopoly** is a supply situation in which there is only one seller.

monopoly

a supply situation in which there is only one seller

BASIC APPROACHES TO PRICING

Organizations involved in the marketing of tourism, leisure, and hospitality products use different methods of calculation to set prices. Pricing methods fall into three main categories:

1. Cost-Based Methods

cost-based pricing

adding a certain dollar amount or percentage to the actual or estimated costs of a service to arrive at a final price

fixed costs

costs that not vary with the amount of the service provided

variable costs

costs that increase as more of a service is provided

break-even analysis

a pricing technique that considers fixed and variable costs, customer volumes, and profit margins

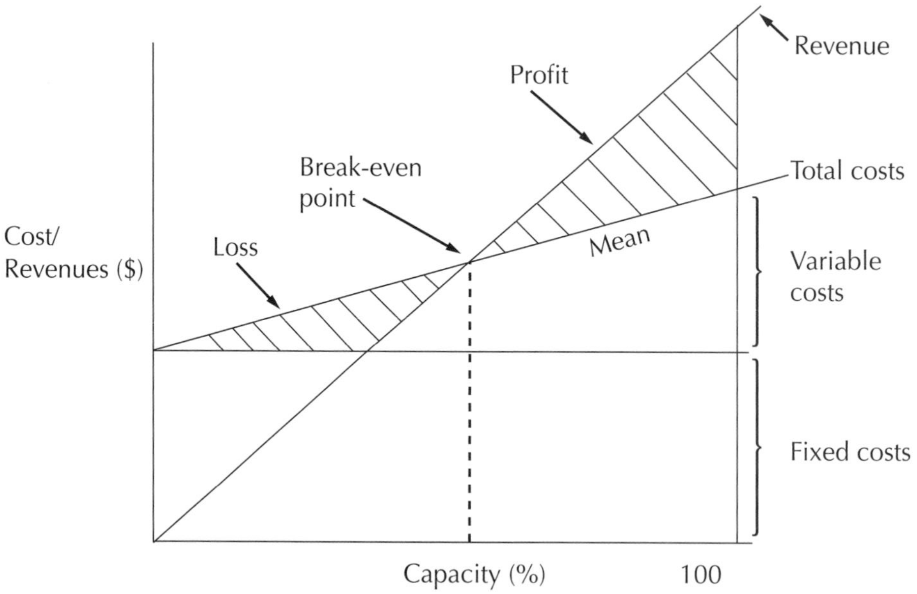

Cost-based pricing—the addition of a certain dollar amount or percentage to the actual or estimated costs of a service to arrive at a final price—draws heavily on the accounting discipline of costing. To use this method, it is necessary to understand the differences in the nature of costs. At the simplest level, costs can be split into two types. **Fixed costs** are costs that do not vary with the amount of the service provided. Hence, a hotelier has the fixed cost of owning the hotel to bear, whether or not rooms are occupied. **Variable costs**, on the other hand, are those that do increase as more of a service is provided. For example, the energy and cleaning costs of a hotel will increase as more guests occupy the rooms. These two cost elements can be combined with revenue—which should increase as more of the service is sold—to give a picture of when an operation becomes profitable. Known as **break-even analysis** or cost/profit/volume (CPV) analysis, the interaction of these elements can be shown graphically. Figure 6.4 shows the break-even point for a hypothetical hotel that has high fixed costs.

Figure 6.4 The Break-Even Point for a Hypothetical Hotel

cost-plus pricing

adding a standard mark-up to the cost of the product to reach the price charged

Having established the cost of doing business, the simplest approach to pricing is to then add a standard mark-up to the cost of the product, known as **cost-plus pricing**. A restaurant manager might decide that all wines will be marked up by 100 percent and all food dishes will be marked up by 60 percent. For example, a bottle of wine purchased at $12 will be sold for $24, and a steak dinner that costs $10 (including both fixed and variable costs) will be sold for $16. Clearly, this approach to pricing takes little account of market forces, and while costs do have to be covered in the long run, policies have to respond more to changing market conditions and what the market will bear. However, the concept of marginal costing, which attempts to identify the cost of one or more unit of a product, is an important one in cost-plus pricing, since it offers the marketing manager a flexible tool for pricing. For example, in the case the of an airline ticket for a flight across Canada, the additional cost of carrying one more passenger is extremely small: an added meal, a minute addition to fuel, etc. Therefore, once break-even is achieved, it becomes very attractive to price the "marginal seat" (any remaining seats over the number that have to be sold to break even) at a price that will attract market demand from those unwilling to pay regular fares.

For conventional manufactured products, there are strong arguments against this policy, one being the unfairness of some customers paying one price and others paying less. This can lead to complaints and to prospective buyers delaying purchase and waiting for discounts. However, in the tourism and hospitality industry, where the timing of consumption of the product is critical, the market seems to accept the principle of paying less for a service consumed at short notice; hence the common practice of agents selling discounted holidays or airline seats at the last minute. Pricing to give a contribution to cost is also acceptable to many organizations in tourism, as the product offered may support the sale of other products such as travel insurance. Similarly, this type of pricing may allow for the use of spare capacity, as in the transportation business. In the short term, **promotional pricing** (a temporary reduction in price) may be the springboard for other complementary products or may be used to destroy rival products.

promotional pricing

a temporary reduction in price

buyer-based pricing (sensitivity pricing)

allows for high prices when the demand is high and for lower prices when the demand is low, regardless of the cost of the product

2. Demand-Based Methods

Sometimes called "**buyer-based pricing**" (or "**sensitivity pricing**"), techniques in the demand-based category share the feature of giving major consideration to the consumer. These methods allow for high prices when the demand is high and for lower prices when the demand is low, regardless of the cost of the product. An example is accommodation in Banff, Alberta, which tends to be more expensive in summer than in winter due to higher demand during the summer months. Demand-based pricing allows an organization to charge higher prices and to therefore make higher profits as long as the buyers value the products above the cost price. Segmentation is often used to price travel and tourism products, using time (prices tend to be more expensive during school holidays) and age (children usually pay less for attractions), for example, as the basis for segmenting the market.

psychological pricing

using slightly lower prices to give consumers the perception of added value

Deeper understanding of the way consumers perceive prices can lead to **psychological pricing**. This usually manifests itself as prices that avoid barriers. For example, a $1000 holiday may seem psychologically cheaper if offered at $999. Similarly, in order to present a simplified choice of product to the consumer, **price lining**—pre-establishing price lines (levels) that the company feels confident will attract customers—may be employed. For example, a whale-watching trip may be priced at $75 but may not include lunch. The same trip including lunch would be priced at $100—even though lunch can be

price lining

pre-establishing price lines (levels) that the company feels confident will attract customers provided at a low cost, the $25 is added to make the offer clearly distinct. As long as consumers perceive the gap as representing a clear difference of price and quality, they should accept the distinction. The mistake not to make is to price many products with marginal differences and prices, as this may lead to consumer confusion.

Another important type of demand-based pricing, particularly in organizational buying, is **negotiating**, a technique used to establish prices when at least two parties are involved and they have a conflict of interest with respect to one or more issues about the product. Hotel space, exhibition services, and transport seats are all examples of tourism and hospitality products that are often block-booked by buyers, be they tour operators or specialist buyers. And the negotiation of the pricing of holidays does not always have to involve hard currency. A 62-year-old Saskatchewan man who has waited more than two and a half years for surgery struck a novel deal with a U.S. surgeon who agreed to operate on his hernia in exchange for a free duck-hunting trip. Nevada-based Dr. Murray performed the surgery in April 2003, in exchange for a duck-hunting excursion worth about US$2000.[4]

3. Competition-Oriented Pricing

In **competition-oriented pricing**, an organization fixes the prices of products in relation to competitors' prices; this is often also called **going-rate pricing**. This method offers the advantage of giving the organization the opportunity to increase sales or market share, but it is a dangerous approach to pricing, as it does not focus on either costs or the consumer. The arguments for this approach are that the industry will have developed prices that are acceptable to the marketplace and there is little to be gained by offering different prices (so-called "industry wisdom"). The counter-argument is that there may be the opportunity to offer different prices (and therefore to possibly achieve better profits) that the majority of the industry has ignored.

Some companies use competitors' prices as a target to be undercut. Those adopting this approach will need to be sure of their cost structures compared to others'. The danger is that competitors may have supply links that give them some type of cost advantage, or have some kind of "hold" on customers, such as a strong loyalty scheme. In this case, prices charged may not be a true indication of either costs or price sensitivity. If, for example, the owner of a seafood restaurant has a half share in a fishing trawler with a relative, the price of fish may be much lower than for someone shopping at the fish market. Generally, undercutting will be a difficult position to sustain if the price cutter does not have lower costs in the long term. It may also lead to price wars.

Some organizations, like airlines, may be competition-oriented to the extent that they use prices to try to drive out competition, perhaps to give themselves a long-term monopoly. There is a view in the travel industry that "destroyer" pricing leads to a decline in safety standards and quality. In the current climate, airlines should be reluctant to pursue pricing policies that may affect their credibility with regard to safety. However, third parties like tour operators are less reluctant to use undercutting when the responsibility for the provision of standards and safety is largely left to their suppliers—for example, to hotels and attractions. The trade tends to be moderated by third parties such as travel agents, who must give companies feedback on consumer responses to falling standards or concerns on safety.

negotiating

a technique used to establish prices when at least two parties are involved and they have a conflict of interest with respect to one or more issues about the product

competition-oriented pricing (going-rate pricing)

technique in which an organization fixes the prices of products in relation to competitors' prices

PROFILE

ZIP AIMS FOR LOW COST/ LOW PRICE LEADERSHIP

In 2002, Air Canada's CEO Robert Milton concluded that the only way to cut domestic losses and return to profitability was to replace the airline's existing high-cost structure with something more efficient. Rather than go through the difficult process of an internal overhaul, Milton opted to create an entirely different company, with new employees and a fresh vision. On September 22, 2002, Zip Air commenced service with a fleet of six planes coated in various shades of fluorescent paint. Offering competitive low fares, convenient schedules, and electronic ticketing and check-in, Zip at that time had 15 flights daily between four destinations in Western Canada, and hoped to grow to a fleet of 20 aircraft within two years. "The status quo is not an option for Air Canada," says Zip CEO Steve Smith. "In the short-haul world, we need to reduce our costs because the revenue pile is coming down."

Despite having to accept union jurisdiction over Zip employees, Zip was able to reduce labour costs substantially. Overall pilot costs at the new carrier were about 30 percent lower than at Air Canada. Zip also saved up to 40 percent on overall costs paid to flight attendants and airport workers. Convincing the unions to accept such a big pay cut was no small achievement for Milton, but the victory is not permanent. If Zip is profitable, labour leaders will demand payback, and costs will rise accordingly. Meanwhile, the existing pilot contract allows Zip to operate a maximum of 20 aircraft. Once the carrier reaches that ceiling, Air

Canada's senior management will likely start pushing for an increase so it can continue to cannibalize the mainline operation and move all domestic traffic over to Zip. That in turn could create an awkward relationship between Zip employees and their counterparts at Air Canada. In short, the success of Zip could ultimately be its downfall. "It's up to management and the unions not to kill the baby we've created," says Smith. "We're going to be 100 percent focused on keeping our costs in line."

Another problem with Zip's low cost/low price strategy is the danger of getting caught in a price war. In January 2003, both Zip and WestJet slashed fares on routes where they compete head-to-head in Western Canada, and many observers called it a costly battle for market share. Zip kicked off the fare wars when it began selling heavily discounted tickets for February travel on six routes. "This is the first time we've really gone to the market to say that we're a low-fare carrier and we will be aggressive in the pricing world," Smith says. Fares started as low as $39.99 one-way between Calgary and Victoria and $79.99 between Winnipeg and Abbotsford, before surcharges. WestJet responded by lowering the bar—offering Web fares from $37.50 and $77.50, which Zip subsequently matched. Following these price announcements, Avi Dalfen, an analyst at Research Capital Corp., published a research note stating that both airlines would lose money at those fare levels, even if they managed to fill the planes. "Given the intensifying fare competition in WestJet's core market, we are cutting our target share price to $16 from $19 and reiterating our 'hold' recommendation," said Dalfen. On the Toronto stock market, Air Canada shares fell eight cents to $4.39 and WestJet shares fell 84 cents to $15.06 as a result of the price cuts.

The discounting came just days after a Quebec court struck down a key provision of the Competition Act that gave the competition commissioner the power to unilaterally issue a cease-and-desist order against a dominant airline such as Air Canada engaging in anti-competitive behaviour. "For consumers, this is fabulous," says Rick Erickson, an independent industry analyst. "But the deals are short term—they can't continue to offer prices like this." Another analyst, Ben Cherniavsky of Raymond James Ltd., was just as pessimistic, suggesting that the pricing pressure would have a negative effect on yields, and adding, "In our view, this is the hallmark of a fare war because it represents targeted discounting in response to a competitive threat, as opposed to blanket price cuts across the system."

Sources: McArthur, K. (2003, January 22). WestJet, Zip slash fares in the West. *The Globe and Mail*, p. B2; Nogier, T. (2003, January 23). Carrier wars taking off. *Calgary Sun*, p. 50. Verburg, P. (2002). Emergency exit. *Canadian Business, 74*(19), 16–17.

PRICING STRATEGIES FOR NEW PRODUCTS

At the core of pricing is the consumer's perception of price in relation to quality and value for money. This perception can be influenced by the way in which a company charges for its services. When a new product enters the market, it is vital to obtain market share and create the desired image for the product in the consumer's eyes. New products face unique problems. If the product is truly new—something never before available in the market-place—it will be extremely difficult for consumers to develop a sense of what price is appropriate. If there are no similar products with which to compare it, they may either undervalue the innovation or perhaps overvalue it. Detailed research on price sensitivity, clearly outlining the unique features of the new product and researching the best way to communicate this information to consumers, will be important. But as noted in Chapter 5, most innovations are not "new to the world," and product variations require an examination of where the product will sit in the marketplace in comparison with competitors (see pp. 156–160).

Three strategies commonly used for the introduction of new products are prestige pricing, market skimming, and penetration pricing.

prestige pricing

setting prices high to position a product at the upper or luxury end of the market

1. **Prestige pricing**. This method sets prices high to position a product at the upper or luxury end of the market. For example, tourism and hospitality operators that wish to be seen as top-end operators or establishments must enter the market with high prices to reflect this quality image. The product itself will need to deliver this quality level (in terms of décor, menu, locations, fittings, etc.). A coach company introducing a new luxury vehicle with airline-style seats, individual light and air-conditioning controls, panoramic windows, onboard catering, and amenities can price the transportation as a prestige product. If consumers value these attributes, they will pay the additional premium price.

market skimming

this policy of "skimming the cream" calls for setting high prices at the launch stage and progressively lowering them as the product becomes better established

2. **Market skimming**. This policy of "skimming the cream" calls for setting high prices at the launch stage and progressively lowering them as the product becomes better established and progresses through its life cycle. The policy takes advantage of the fact that most products are in high demand in the early stage of the life cycle, when they are novel or unique or when supplies are limited. Demand can be managed by setting very high prices initially to attract those prepared to meet them, and gradually reducing the price to meet different market segments' price elasticities. The particular value of this policy is that it provides a high inflow of funds to the company when the marketing costs are highest. If the product anticipates a very short life cycle—as in the case of major events such as the Olympic Games—and organizing and marketing costs must be recovered quickly, market skimming is a sensible policy to pursue.

penetration pricing

pricing at a lower level to get maximum sales and market share; used when an organization is trying to get maximum distribution for the product or service in the initial stages

3. **Penetration pricing**. This strategy is the opposite of market skimming, as prices are set at a very low initial level. If an organization is trying to achieve maximum distribution for the product in the initial stages, it will probably price at a lower level to obtain maximum sales and market share. This method is commonly used in the marketing of fast-moving consumer goods, when rapid distribution-stocking is essential to the success of the product. If the market is price sensitive (such as in the fast-food sector), penetration pricing is an efficient way to gain a quick foothold. The intention is to set low prices only until this market share has been established and then to gradually raise prices to market levels.

SNAPSHOT

SPACE TOURISM PRICED OUT OF THIS WORLD

The fantasy of taking a vacation in outer space came true for an American millionaire on April 28, 2001, when Dennis Tito blasted off aboard a Russian rocket to become the world's first space tourist. Tito didn't have the amenities imagined by science fiction fabulists, such as orbital hotels and fast-food restaurants where space ships stop during interstellar journeys. But his trip, starting from the same launch pad that made Soviet cosmonaut Yuri Gagarin the first man in space, could mark a new era of paid space flight.

The founder of an investment firm, Tito reportedly paid up to US$20 million for the week-long trip. But some entrepreneurial

companies envision the time when space tourism could be more affordable and widespread.

SNAPSHOT *continued*

One of those companies is Space Adventures, a privately owned firm with headquarters in Arlington, Virginia. Space Adventures is planning to take its first wave of tourists into space by the end of 2005. The company currently pegs the price tag for the suborbital flights (travelling at a minimum of 62 miles in altitude), for individuals above the age of 18 who are in reasonable health, at US$98 000. The company has developed a payment plan for customers to pay for their trip over a four-year period. The payment consists of a $6000 downpayment, three annual payments of $12 000, and a final payment of $56 000 to be made 180 days before the flight. Despite the high price tag, hundreds of people who are hoping to be on the first suborbital space tour have already paid in full, according to Tereza Predescu from Space Adventures.

The company has developed a four-day itinerary for potential tourists, which includes accommodation and meals at a "spaceport." The three-day training session before the flight includes health screenings, flight-safety training, centrifuge training (to accustom space tourists to zero gravity), and simulated training on a reusable launch-vehicle simulator. On the fourth day customers will take off and fly for 30 to 90 minutes, and have the once-in-a-lifetime opportunity to view the limits of Earth and the universe from space. Once back on earth, Space Adventures is planning to make the space experience more tangible for its customers by providing them with customized videos from the flight.

There are some who caution against over-enthusiasm about space tourism. "I think tourist projects are a bit too early for space," said cosmonaut Sergei Avdeyev, who holds the record for total time in space: 747 days over three missions. "With ordinary tourism, you go buy a tour and fly off. You get certain conditions: if you don't like your room, you can change it; if you don't get enough fruit at the hotel, you can go out and buy more," he said. "All of these things that surround tourism are not envisaged here."

However, the demand for space travel is real. In 2002, a study polled affluent Americans about their level of interest in public space travel and their willingness to pay for specific space travel options. The bottom line: wealthy citizens around the world could and would pay to take that trip into space. For an orbital flight, people are willing to pay up to US$5 million, although orbital space travel is a fairly elastic market; demand increased significantly when the price dropped to US$1 million.

Sources: Orbital space travel & destinations with suborbital space travel. (2003). Retrieved August 15, 2003, from http://www.futron.com/spaceandtelecom/brochures/spacetourism/overview.htm; T. Predescu, director of communications for Space Adventures, personal communication, June 2, 2003; Space Adventures Web site: http://www.spaceadventures.com; Space tourist embarks on dream orbit. (2001, April 27). *Calgary Herald*, p. A3.

OTHER PRICING TECHNIQUES

Promotional Pricing

Promotional pricing is used by companies when they temporarily sell products below their normal list price (or rack rate). Usually this is done for a short period of time, often to introduce new or revamped products. Promotional pricing is used in the restaurant sector in these situations. The assumption is made that consumers will buy other items at normal price levels along with the promotionally priced items. Promotional pricing is often used in conjunction with product-bundle pricing (see below).

The time-share industry is often associated with controversial promotional pricing offers. In the spring of 2003, many Canadians received a letter and a certificate from Ramada Plaza Resorts. The letter informed consumers that they had been chosen to take part in a marketing study and promotion. In return they were offered five nights on a cruise to the Bahamas. All they had to do was phone a 1-800 number to book the vacation. But this wasn't a free offer: consumers were just offered a discount. Included in the letter was a cheque for $1600, but that didn't cover the whole cost of the trip. Callers would be asked for a credit card number to reserve their spot, and then they would have to pay US$700 to get the deal.

What Ramada doesn't say in the letter is that the marketing study is really a time-share presentation that each customer has to attend at the resort. And once the trip is booked, there are hidden charges and extra fees for upgrading hotels or changing itineraries. In fact, in the U.S., Ramada Plaza Resorts was sued for misleading consumers in 2000 and was ordered to refund millions of dollars. They are still banned from offering their promotion in more than a dozen states.[5]

Product-Bundle Pricing

product-bundle pricing

grouping together a company's products to promote them as a package

When a company groups several of its products together to promote them as a package, it is using **product-bundle pricing**. An example would be a hotel offering a weekend special that includes a room, dinner in a restaurant, valet parking, room-service breakfast, and late checkout for a set price. In some cases the package will include products that customers might not normally buy (such as the valet parking); this is often done to improve usage during slow periods. In 2003, Marriott and Renaissance Hotels bundled Web services and long distance charges for guests in 180 properties. Travellers could purchase high-speed Internet access and unlimited local and long-distance phone calls within the United States for US$9.95 per day.

In other areas of hospitality, product bundling is a normal policy, as is seen in the fast-food sector, or in restaurants where people may not be familiar with the food. Package tours are also a popular type of product bundling (see *Marketing in Action* for an example). Wholesalers package airfare, ground transport, accommodation, sightseeing tours, and admission to attractions, and because of their bulk purchases they can negotiate significant discounts. These companies can then offer packages to customers that work out to be considerably cheaper than buying the individual components separately. Bundling therefore offers cost advantages to the company as well as convenience to the consumer.

MARKETING IN ACTION

PRODUCT-BUNDLE PRICING IN ADVENTURE TOURISM

Brewster's Mountain Lodges & Adventures is a family-owned and -operated group of businesses that has been providing travellers with accommodations and adventures for over 100 years. The Brewsters offer a variety of other travel and excursion options that include ski packages, romance packages, golf packages, overnight pack-train packages, corporate and conference events, wedding facilities, sleigh rides, carriage rides, trail rides, back-country lodging, Western barbecues, rafting, and fishing trips.

On May 30, 2002, the Brewster family introduced their new "all-inclusive" Adventure Package (see Table 6.1), which takes guests to the various Brewster destinations in Kananaskis, Banff, and Lake Louise. The concept, new to these areas, provided guests with one-stop adventure-shopping convenience, including all pre-selected meal arrangements, thus making trip planning quicker and easier. The Adventure Package starts at Brewster's Kananaskis Guest Ranch. Adventure seekers stay at the ranch for two nights and engage with the beautiful scenery of the Alberta Foothills and the Canadian Rocky Mountains, participating in rafting, golf, and horseback riding.

Table 6.1

An All-Inclusive "Adventure Package," Summer 2003

PACKAGE INCLUDES:

Two nights at Brewster's Kananaskis Guest Ranch
Two nights at Brewster's Mountain Lodge
Two two-hour guided trail rides along the shores of the Bow River
Half-day guided river rafting on the Kananaskis River
Half-day guided trail ride to Lake Agnes or Plain of Six Glaciers
Half-day guided fishing excursion on Lake Minnewanka
Buffet breakfast at Brewster's Kananaskis Guest Ranch
Buffet breakfast at Brewster's Mountain Lodge
Hearty daily boxed lunches (choices available)
Two evening dinners at Brewster's Kananaskis Guest Ranch
Two fine dining evening meals in Banff during stay at Brewster's Mountain Lodge

PACKAGE COSTS:

$789.00 (US$543.00) per person, based on double occupancy
$549.00 (US$378.00) per person for additional persons ages 13 and over
$489.00 (US$337.00) per person for additional persons ages 8 to 12

MARKETING IN ACTION *continued*

The adventure continues in Banff, where participants experience a guided fishing excursion and a comfortable two-night stay in Brewster's Mountain Lodge, a Western-inspired hotel in downtown Banff offering superb rooms with handcrafted log furniture and Western décor, where guests can enjoy some local fine dining at nearby restaurants. In Lake Louise, considered one of the most scenic places in the world, adventurers saddle up at Brewster's Lake Louise Stables for another half day of horseback riding, which includes lunch.

Brewster's principal, Janet Brewster-Stanton, says, "We are excited about this package because it is one of the first of its kind in this area. All meals, lodging, and activities are included. Rather than making 8 to 10 contacts during the vacation planning process, this package encompasses it all! All-inclusive adventures in the Canadian Rockies."

Sources: Gamblin, A. (2002). *Brewster Rocky Mountain Adventures delivers new "all-inclusive" adventure packages*. Retrieved June 3, 2002, from http://www.kananaskisguestranch.com/adventurepackages.htm.

Price Spread and Price Points

price spread

a range of products and prices that will suit the budget of all target markets

Organizations in tourism and hospitality try to offer a **price spread**—a range of products that will suit the budget of all target markets. A holiday park, for example, may offer campsites with tents, standard cabins, en suite cabins, and family units, each different from the other in terms of size, location, types of fittings and furnishings. Table 6.2 on page 188 shows the range of prices offered by Banff Mount Norquay, the resort profiled in the opening vignette in this chapter. The range of prices that an organization can set is virtually unlimited. However, research in the restaurant sector has suggested that if the price spread is too wide, consumers will tend to order from among the lower-priced items.[6]

price points

the number of "stops" along the way between the lowest-priced item and the highest-priced item

Price points are the number of "stops" along the way between the lowest-priced item and the highest-priced item. Price points vary among industry sectors and types of business. In a restaurant, it is possible to create a menu with a wide range of dishes and to allot a different price to each dish. Restaurants will generally pick several price points and group dishes around those prices. There may be several dishes priced at $10–$13, then several priced around $19–$20, then others at $23–$28. The idea here is to simplify costing and menu planning, and to create points of comparison for the consumer.

One company that has tried to simplify price points is Air Canada. In May 2003, the company implemented a new, simplified Internet booking system that gave customers a choice of five different fares. They ranged from the most flexible fare, which included luxury airport service, to one-time, non-refundable bargains. This system replaced the previous, convoluted system of 25 fare categories that, when combined, could yield over 200 different ticket combinations. On Air Canada's Web site, consumers could now gain access to complete information about the availability, terms, and conditions of fares—information that was previously not always made public. In the first week of the new fare structure, consumer bookings increased by 25 percent.

Table 6.2

Banff Mount Norquay Lift Ticket Prices, 2002–2003*

REGULAR TICKETS (NOT UPGRADEABLE)				
Categories	**Adult 18+**	**Youth/Student**	**Child 6–12**	**Senior 55+**
Full-day	49.00	38.00	16.00	38.00
Afternoon	37.00	32.00	14.00	32.00
Night skiing	24.00	22.00	12.00	22.00
Last hour	14.00	14.00	10.00	14.00
ADVANTAGE (UPGRADEABLE TO REGULAR TICKETS—A.M. PURCHASES UPGRADE TO FULL DAY ONLY)				
Categories	**Adult 18+**	**Youth/Student**	**Child 6–12**	**Senior 55+**
Sundance carpet lift	12.00	12.00	12.00	12.00
Cascade/ Snowboard park	33.00	26.00	12.00	26.00
HOURLY (NOT UPGRADEABLE—VALID FROM TIME OF PURCHASE OR UNTIL CLOSING)				
Categories	**Adult 18+**	**Youth/Student**	**Child 6–12**	**Senior 55+**
2 hours	26.00	24.00	10.00	24.00
2.5 hours	28.00	26.00	11.00	26.00
3 hours	30.00	28.00	12.00	28.00
3.5 hours	33.50	30.00	13.00	30.00
4 hours	37.00	32.00	14.00	32.00
4.5 hours	40.00	34.00	15.00	34.00
5 hours	43.00	36.00	16.00	36.00
MULTI-DAY (MUST BE USED ON CONSECUTIVE DAYS)				
Categories	**Adult 18+**	**Youth/Student**	**Child 6–12**	**Senior 55+**
2 days	82.00	70.00	31.00	70.00
3 days	121.00	100.00	96.00	100.00
4 days	153.00	126.00	61.00	126.00
5 days	179.00	198.00	76.00	148.00

*All prices are in Canadian dollars.

Source: Banff Mount Norquay Web site (2002). Retrived Juanuary 15, 2002, from http://www/banffnorquay.com.

Discriminatory Pricing

discriminatory pricing

selling a product at two or more prices, despite the fact that the product costs are the same

Organizations often alter prices to suit different customers, products, locations, and times. This **discriminatory pricing** allows the organization to sell a product or service at two or more prices, despite the fact that the product costs are the same. For example, many restaurants charge higher prices in the evening than they do at lunchtime, even if the food is identical, because of demand differences. Ski resorts may charge more for a weekend ski pass than during the week if the majority of their customers drive up on a Saturday or Sunday.

These are examples of "time-based" discriminatory pricing, but a market may also be segmented to encourage increased participation from special groups, such as senior citizens or students. In this case, the groups would be offered special concessions, as seen in Banff Mount Norquay's cheaper prices for children, students, and seniors (see Table 6.2). The market must be capable of being segmented if discriminatory pricing is going to be an effective strategy. Segments will have highly distinct sensitivities, and being able to price differently to the various segments is key to success in maximizing profits.[7] Care should also be taken to ensure that the strategy is legal and that it does not lead to customer resentment.

Discounting

volume discounting

offering special prices to attract customers who agree to major purchases

From time to time, most businesses will need to consider discounting their standard prices. Many tourism organizations engage in **volume discounting**—offering special rates to attract customers who agree to major purchases. Hotels and airlines for example, offer special prices (or upgrades) to corporate clients to encourage volume business, and loyalty programs frequently offer discounts to ensure that travellers use a particular brand. The discount will often reflect the level of overall demand. Airlines and hotels traditionally discount during slow periods and low seasons. In 2003, hit by the quadruple whammy of post–September 11 terrorism fears, an ailing economy, the war in Iraq, and the outbreak of severe acute respiratory syndrome (SARS), hotels in Canada were usually willing to offer a better price than the quoted rack rate. A *Financial Post* journalist phoned several hotels in Toronto to ask for discounts or upgrades, and with the exception of just one property, all were willing to cut prices—sometimes offering rooms for less than half price.[8]

A discounted price is really a wise move only if it increases demand, brings new users, or increases consumption by regular users. Organizations that discount key products but don't lower costs to offset the discount are taking an economic risk unless the discount is only for a very short period or is designed to overcome a very specific problem. There is also the risk that discounting may not lead to increased demand. The main beneficiaries of discounts are often "inelastic" regular users who would buy the product regardless of the price. Discounting fever swept the fast-food industry in 2003 as chains struggled to win back customers and boost stagnant sales. But experts said that the discounting did more harm than good by cutting into profit margins and restraining sales growth, and many failures were predicted.[9]

Some have suggested that discounting has also caused structural changes in the packaged-holiday industry by undermining the profitability of some smaller companies to the point that it is no longer viable for them to stay in the industry. In the United Kingdom, for example, the largest three tour operators, Thomson, Airtours, and Thomas Cook, control about 70 percent of the market because of their success at packaging. Sheldon, discussing the relationship between pricing and industry structure, noted a division in the tourism industry between the few large firms and the many small ones, and pointed to the relatively short lives of many small companies.[10] However, several large tour operators have also failed, and many mergers or acquisitions have been recorded in the industry.

Yield Management

Yield is the profit that is made on the sales of goods and services; it is calculated based on the number of customers, how much they spend, and the number of products they buy. **Yield management** is the practice of developing strategies to maximize opportunities for the sale of an organization's perishable products, such as airline seats, hotel rooms, and tour seats, and therefore improving its long-term viability. More simply, it has been defined as "lowering the price … according to expected demand, and relying heavily on computers and modelling techniques."[11] It was initiated by the airline industry in the 1980s as a way to increase revenue from existing routes and aircraft. Computer technology made it possible for airlines to predict the number of seats that would be sold on a given flight—called the load factor. By analyzing costs, and also determining the price sensitivity of various types of airfares, airlines discovered that by offering seats at a variety of special fares they could boost load and revenues. It was mentioned earlier that Air Canada at one time had 25 fare categories that, when combined, could yield over 200 different ticket combinations.

Many have argued in favour of yield-management techniques, using price to balance the market conditions of supply and demand. Duadel and Vialle, for example, distinguished between "'spoilage," the underutilization of resources, and "spill," selling too cheaply early, with the result that later, higher-yielding demand has to be denied.[12] The practice of yield management is now common in other sectors of tourism, from hotels to ski resorts. Different rates are offered for certain groups of customers, and restrictions are placed on the use of these rates by other groups. The Fairmont Palliser in Calgary, for example, has seen tremendous improvements in revenue per available room since its implementation of a new yield management program in 1997. The company's strategy is to charge a maximum price until demand at that level falls and then to lower the price until all available capacity has sold. This example shows that yield management systems, if used properly, can provide considerable extra revenue. A good system will benefit both the business and the consumer.

Even theatres are using yield management techniques to maximize revenue. Table 6.3 shows the wide variety of ticket prices offered by Ontario's Stratford Festival in 2003. There are over 40 possible combinations of regular ticket prices, over 30 different types of discount tickets, and also special concessions for students, seniors, and families. It is interesting to note that the price list (included in Stratford's 2003 Visitor's Guide) highlights the fact that prices are significantly lower when converted to U.S. dollars. Many Canadian tourism organizations are realizing that American tourists do not automatically make these currency conversions and instead assume that the Canadian dollar is worth the same as the American dollar.

Table 6.3

Ticket Prices for the Stratford Festival, 2003

REGULAR TICKET PRICES							
Categories	Price Code	A+ Seats	A Seats	B Seats	C Seats	D 'Rush' Seats	Avon Box Seats
Regular	R	76.15–87.57	69.65–80.10	65.15–74.92	49.48–56.90	39.40	65.15–80.10
Musical	M	85.65–98.50	79.65–91.60	74.65–85.85	61.15–70.32	51.15	74.65–91.60
Summer Regular	W	82.15–94.47	75.65–87.00	71.15–81.82	51.48–59.20	41.40	71.15–87.00
Summer Musical	WM	91.65–105.40	85.65–98.50	80.65–92.75	64.15–73.77	54.15	80.65–98.50
Studio Theatre	SD		50.00–57.50				
Studio Sunday Evening	SE		28.15–32.37				
Celebrated Writers	CW	23.65	23.65	23.65	23.65	23.65	23.65
DISCOUNT TICKETS							
Categories	Price Code	A+ Seats	A Seats	B Seats	C Seats	D 'Rush' Seats	Avon Box Seats
Preview	P	55.39–63.70	50.71–58.32	46.21–53.14	35.24–40.53	31.92	46.21–58.32
Musical Preview	MP	67.25–77.34	62.57–71.96	56.49–64.96	46.36–53.31	38.86	56.49–71.96
June Special	J	61.32–70.52	56.12–64.54	52.52–60.40	39.98–45.98	31.92	52.52–64.54
50% Off	T	42.78–9.20	39.20–45.09	33.58–38.62	25.74–29.60	20.70	33.58–45.09
Fall Roads	F	65.03–74.78	59.50–68.43	55.68–64.03	42.36–48.71	33.79	55.68–68.43

TABLE 6.3 *continued*

STUDENT, SENIOR, AND FAMILY SAVINGS

Categories	Price Code	A+ Seats	A Seats	B Seats	C Seats	*D 'Rush' Seats	Avon Box Seats
Senior Regular	SR						
Senior		35.65	35.65	35.65	33.65	33.65	46.21–58.32
Student		23.65	23.65	23.65	22.65	22.65	46.21–58.32
Non-Senior/ Non-Student		55.39–63.70	50.71–58.32	46.21–53.14	35.24–40.53	31.92	46.21–58.32
Senior Musical	SM						
Senior		39.65	39.65	39.65	37.65	37.65	56.49–71.96
Student		23.65	23.65	23.65	22.65	22.65	46.21–58.32
Non-Senior/ Non-Student		67.25–77.34	62.57–71.96	56.49–4.96	46.36–53.31	38.86	56.49–71.96
Student Regular	S						
Senior		35.65	35.65	35.65	33.65	33.65	46.21–58.32
Student		23.65	23.65	23.65	22.65	22.65	46.21–58.32
Non-Senior/ Non-Student		55.39–63.70	50.71–58.32	46.21–53.14	35.24–40.53	31.92	46.21–58.32
Student Musical	SM						
Senior		39.65	39.65	38.65	37.65	37.65	56.49–71.96
Student		23.65	23.65	23.65	22.65	22.65	46.21–58.32
Non-Senior/ Non-Student		67.25–77.34	62.57–71.96	56.49–64.96	46.36–51.31	38.86	56.49–71.96

Categories	Price Code	A+ Seats	A Seats	B Seats	C Seats	*D 'Rush' Seats	Avon Box Seats
Family Experience 18 and under (up to two with each full-price ticket purchased)							
Regular		32.00–36.80	32.00–36.80	32.00–36.80	32.00–36.80	32.00	32.00–36.80
Musical		34.00–39.10	34.00–39.10	34.00–39.10	34.00–39.10	34.00	34.00–39.10
Student Full-Time			28.15*	28.15*	28.15		

STUDENT, SENIOR, AND FAMILY SAVINGS *continued*

Note: Rush tickets (maximum four per patron) are available only for "D" seating at the Festival and Avon theatres. They may be purchased in person at the Festival Theatre Box Office beginning at 9 a.m. on the day of the performance only. Telephone orders may be taken after 9:30 a.m., or earlier at the manager's discretion, depending on in-person demand. All prices and handling charges include the federal Goods and Service Tax. Each ticket price includes $2 toward Stratford Festival renewal projects. All prices are in Canadian dollars and are thus significantly lower when converted to U.S. funds. At current exchange rate ($1 U.S. = $1.50 Cdn at the time of printing), U.S. patrons enjoy savings of over 30% on the Canadian prices as listed.
*Individual Student pricing is available in the "A seating" section of the Studio Theatre and the "B seating" section of the Tom Patterson Theatre.

Source: Stratford Festival. (2003). *Visitor's guide,* 72.

Kimes has suggested that consumers seem to accept yield management in the airline industry, where they receive specific benefits if they accept certain restraints.[13] However, she raised the question of how customers react to it in other sectors, suggesting that a customer who pays more for a similar service and cannot perceive the difference in the service may view the situation as unfair. Kimes developed her argument on the basis of a **reference price**, derived from market prices and the customer's previous experience. At a normal (or reference) price, a high standard of service and amenities will please the client, but these same standards will only satisfy clients who are paying premium prices. Customers enjoying normal or superior standards on a holiday for which they paid low prices will be pleased or delighted. In contrast, customers receiving normal levels of service in return for high prices will feel at best exploited and at worst angry. This could result in complaints and negative word of mouth, undermining the credibility of the company concerned.

Employing yield management, both hotels and airlines use overbooking to cover no-shows and late cancellations. Because overbooking is a risky practice, companies using yield management must be prepared to offer inducements, such as free travel vouchers, in case overbooking occurs. In fact, some suggest that overbooking be avoided wherever possible because of the additional costs of "walking" guests to another hotel, potential ill will, and even possible legal liability. Hiemstra says that when hotels have significant problems with no-shows, they should develop overbooking strategies because it is costly to have rooms remain unused when they could be rented with better planning.[14] The first requirement in developing such a policy is to have good historical records of the

reference price

a price derived from market prices and the customer's previous experience occurrence of no-shows from which to calculate their probability. These records need to be carefully analyzed to determine seasonality, day of the week, or other patterns with which the practice may be associated. Costs associated with overbooking a room must also be determined and compared with the opportunity costs of not renting a room. Reciprocal arrangements with nearby hotels in the same quality segment can minimize the direct costs, but the cost of ill will is more difficult to estimate.

STRATEGIC AND TACTICAL PRICING

strategic pricing

setting prices early, in accordance with the long-term view of corporate strategy, product positioning, and value for money in the marketplace

tactical pricing

making short-term pricing decisions in response to changes in the marketing environment

Organizations in the tourism and hospitality industries operate pricing policies at the strategic and tactical levels. In **strategic pricing**, prices are determined early on in the planning of the marketing strategy, as the nature of the business means that prices have to be set a long way in advance so that brochures and guides can be published. These pricing decisions are based on the long-term view of corporate strategy, product positioning, and value for money in the marketplace.

While strategic pricing is concerned with the overall plans for the implementation of pricing policy, **tactical pricing** relates to day-to-day techniques in pricing, which can be rapidly altered to suit changing conditions in the marketplace. Thus, a strategy of discriminatory pricing that involves the setting of different prices for different market groups (e.g., business travellers and leisure travellers) may be introduced, but the actual prices to be charged and the ways in which these fares will be adjusted will require tactical decisions. The fact that organizations cannot stock services means that if the planned supply exceeds demand in the marketplace for whatever reason, the organization must sell excess capacity. This often means resorting to tactical strategies, in the form of promotional pricing or discounting, for example. Hotels have become skilled at using last-minute tactical pricing methods to fill unoccupied rooms. Customers can often negotiate a substantial reduction on the rack rate if they phone the hotel during the evening on which they want a room.

A good example of tactical pricing in the Canadian restaurant sector occurred in the spring of 2003, when the outbreak of bovine spongiform encephalopathy (BSE) or "mad-cow disease" in Canada discouraged consumers from eating beef. In response, many restaurants selling predominantly meat reduced their prices in order to tempt consumers back to their establishments. For example, Montana's Cookhouse ran a promotion giving customers $5 off purchases of $20 or more and $10 off purchases of $30 or more.

One of the strategic decisions that must be taken is whether to price differently to different geographic areas. Should the price set be common to all customers, or should it vary to reflect different market demand in various countries? It may be more costly to sell a package tour to the Japanese than to Americans, because of higher costs in Japan, or it may be necessary in one country to boost agents' commission levels to secure their support. Other strategic decisions must be designed to respond to the marketing initiatives of competitors. A tour operator may wait for its major competitor to launch its brochure before setting prices, or it may rely on its strong brand and set high prices to psychologically distance its own products and those of competitors. The opening vignette in Chapter 2 featured Four Seasons Hotels and Resorts, whose revenue per available room in the highly competitive U.S. market is more than 30 percent higher than that of its closest chain competitor, Ritz-

Carlton. This success has been derived from focusing exclusively on serving high-end travellers and charging them prices much higher than the competitors'. If a rival tries to match Four Season's high prices, then the group simply pushes up its prices even higher.

Other popular strategies include **all-in pricing** or **all-inclusive pricing**. This type of pricing was used originally in holiday camps in the United Kingdom, where customers were provided access to every entertainment facility in the camp for a single price. The strategy proved highly successful, and Club Med built on this model for its chain of holiday resorts around the world. Club Med now advertises "total all-inclusive" holidays, so that consumers pay for no extras whatsoever (see Figure 6.5). Today, Canadians are very familiar with booking all-inclusive holidays in resorts like the Caribbean and Mexico. Theme parks also normally adopt the all-inclusive strategy by charging just one fee for the use of all their attractions.

**all-in pricing
(all-inclusive pricing)**

charging consumers a single price for the various products or services on offer

Figure 6.5   Club Med Print Advertisement, 2003

A contrasting strategy involves charging a low basic entrance fee and recouping profits through *add-ons*, which require that customers pay for each individual attraction. Organizers at the Calgary Stampede have used this strategy for the fun fair set in the middle of the Stampede grounds. Guests pay a small entrance fee but then have to pay for all of the rides. This is similar to **off-set pricing** or **bait pricing**, in which an operator such as an attraction will set a very low entry charge, possibly even a "loss leader" at below cost, in order to attract visitors who then find themselves facing extra charges for every event. Hotels in Las Vegas provide an example of bait pricing. Prices are extremely reasonable for rooms and food and drink because profits are reaped through gambling on the premises.

**off-set pricing
(bait pricing)**

charging a low basic price and charging for extra services

TOURISM AND HOSPITALITY CHARACTERISTICS THAT AFFECT PRICING POLICY

Although some of the following points have already been referred to in this chapter, a separate discussion of the particular features of the tourism and hospitality industry that affect pricing is warranted here.

1. High Level of Segmentation in the Industry

The tourism industry is highly segmented, with varying elasticities of demand in the segments. These demand segments may be associated with different income levels, age groupings, seasonality, and types of pleasure or business. Groups are also not homogeneous in their demands. Some may be business travellers with expense accounts and others may be pleasure travellers spending their own funds.

2. Variability of Demand

Different product offerings also face much variability in the level of demand within customer segments associated with different days of the week, holidays, different seasons of the year, and normal fluctuations in local personal or business situations. For hotels, this variability causes difficulty in forecasting normal room demands for an individual property, and requires that each day of the year be projected and priced differently.

3. Perishable Nature of the Product

The tourism product is perishable, i.e., it cannot be stored and sold at a later date. In addition, suppliers may not wish the surplus to be sold through the same channel as the standard product, as this may affect future demand and pricing. This is why outlets exist that allow the supplier to remain anonymous. For example, the Internet provides an outlet for tour operators and airlines to offload surplus holidays or flights at reduced margins without changing their main brochures.

4. High Fixed Costs

High fixed costs in major tourism sectors exacerbate the perishable nature of the business of selling holidays, seats, or hotel rooms. This means that an organization saves little by not filling to capacity. In the hospitality sector, for example, variable costs associated with the rooms department account for only one-fourth of total room department income, while fixed costs associated primarily with paying for the building and overhead expenses account for a large share of the remaining revenue. This feature gives strong incentive to rent rooms at relatively low rates rather than leaving them vacant.

5. Cost Fluctuations

For many operators in the tourism industry, there is a high probability of unpredictable but major short-term fluctuations in cost elements such as oil prices and currency exchange rates. A tour operator running packages to various European and South American destinations may, according to exchange rates and the general climate of tourism in each country, have to vary its prices.

6. Vulnerability to Demand Changes

As the terrorist attacks in the United States in 2001, and in Bali in 2002, highlighted, the industry is vulnerable to demand changes resulting from unforeseen economic and political events. The Iraq war and the fear of attacks on American cities meant that Canadian consumers' demand for holidays in the United States fell in 2002. In fact, recent travel warnings about grave dangers at destinations have advised travellers to avoid or take extreme care in 121 countries.[15] Such warnings were bound to have an impact on pricing strategies for these destinations and for the other 128 destinations that were considered safe by the Canadian government.

7. High Level of Customers' Psychological Involvement

Customers display a particularly high level of psychological involvement in choosing vacation products, in which price may be a symbol of status as well as value.[16] They are therefore likely to invest considerable care in their choice. In the packaged holiday market, where the tour operators or travel agents emphasize prices rather than destination attributes in their promotions, the customers' attention is likely to be focused on comparing prices rather than on what each destination offers, potentially resulting in a reduced commitment to the resort visited. Under these conditions, there is more likely to be a mismatch between the tourists' holiday expectations and their destination experiences, resulting in dissatisfaction and complaint.

8. Seasonal Demand

One of the most common ways of setting holiday price differentials is the seasonal banding that is typical of tour operators' brochures—and familiar to all who purchase inclusive holidays—in the form of price and departure date matrices. Seasonality of demand leads to differing price expectations. Commercial business demand for some hotels often declines in high summer. This leads to domestic consumers anticipating lower rates and higher availability in mid-week. Conversely, many tour operators and airlines are able to increase prices in high summer when demand is at its peak. An interesting pricing strategy was set by the Eden Roc Resort & Spa in Miami in the 1990s. The resort charged guests the same amount in dollars as the day's highest temperature. The idea was to give guest no cause for complaint even in the event of a cold snap!

9. Tactical Price Cutting and Price Wars

If supply exceeds demand, there is near certainty of price cutting by major competitors. This leads to the high possibility of price wars being provoked in sectors such as transport, accommodation, tour operating, and travel agencies, in which short-term profitability may disappear. Cooper et al. have discussed the resulting dynamics of price-based marketing practices. They describe how, in attempting to increase market share by cutting its prices, a company provokes a hostile re-pricing reaction from its competitors because this is an attempt to take the competition's market share. The overall results may be an increase in the market size, as more customers are attracted by the lower prices, but overall revenue might not be increased. The long-term result is that the market remains unstable because of smaller margins.[17]

10. Low Prices

Price competition in many sectors has led to an industry characterized by low prices. Low prices have not only stimulated demand for holidays currently on offer, but have also altered the timing of demand—for example, by extending the holiday season—and have changed the demographic profile of holidaymakers to include all age groups and most socioeconomic groups of society. Low prices have therefore contributed to the commodification of holiday products noted and criticized by many analysts of the industry.[18, 19] However, a lower price provides an increased access to the product, bringing the product to a new group of potential purchasers that have different behavioural characteristics. One example of this is the way that cruising holidays are now promoted to a broader market on the basis of reduced prices.

11. Fixed Capacity

Even though demand may be highly variable and unpredictable, in many sectors of the industry supply available in the short run tends to be relatively fixed. For a hotel, for example, it takes a long time to expand a building or to build a new one. Adding part-time or seasonal labour may be useful in better serving guests during periods of peak occupancy, but it can add little to available room inventory. As a result, pricing policies are largely restricted to allocating existing supplies among competing demands. This restriction adds importance to effective no-show policies.

12. The Customer's Total Purchases

Some sectors of the industry have to consider the customer's total purchases when considering prices and profits. Hotels should not consider room rates and restaurant prices separately. Selling a room cheaply to a guest who will use the restaurant and bars extensively may be more profitable than selling it to someone who pays full rate for the room but purchases nothing else. For example, mixed-offering destinations such as Whistler, B.C., do not have to concern themselves too much with visitors not skiing, as they can earn huge profits from selling other on-snow activities, as well as earn revenue from the restaurants and retail units owned by Intrawest, the resort's parent company.

13. Increased Use of the Internet

Canadians looking for travel packages are keen users of the Internet. In 2003, 77 percent of travellers browsed the Internet for information and more than two in three package travellers used the Internet to help plan summer trips.[20] At a recent Mountain Travel Symposium in Whistler, Dr. Peter Yesawich, president of Yesawich, Pepperdine, and Brown said there are new priorities for travel consumers that will increasingly affect the way travel retailers do business. He said that many travel consumers are "empowering" themselves by learning the routines of Internet research and transacting for airfares. They are also increasingly aware of their ability to exercise more control over their purchases. Eighty-two percent of hotel customers attempt to negotiate lower prices on their rooms. Brand loyalties are fragile, and 77 percent of the same group said they would switch to another similarly branded property if the price was right. "Fifty-eight expect a complimentary breakfast," Yesawich said. He added that the terrorist attacks of September 11,

2001, dramatically altered traveller priorities, a fact that was immediately demonstrated by the need for families to connect. As this receded, consumers said they would travel, but only with price incentives. These deals came, but many were distributed "underground," by the Internet. Such deals have helped some consumers to become more self-reliant, and the most adventurous are building their own holidays, Yesawich said, adding that they are being encouraged to make online purchases with Internet-only discount rates.[21]

14. Late Booking

Price reductions for late booking are a widespread holiday industry response to its unsold capacity, and are typically promoted by travel agents and tour operators shortly before departure. However, operators are increasingly using Web site pricing options to accommodate late bookers. It wasn't long ago that most businesses made only rack rates available through the Web. Today, pricing is more complex, and many travel Web sites now have a whole menu of pricing options online. It is now typical to see last-minute discounts; Web-only offers; discounted pricing for groups; incentive rates for travel agents, tour operators, and reservation agents; and a variety of packages at different price points, including such add-ons as meals, activities, and transportation.[22] Care must be taken with late booking. If a lot of spare capacity is available on short notice, then the consumer may learn to expect inexpensive late deals. If too many people wait to book their holidays at the last minute, it can often lead to panic reductions in prices by operators and can alter price expectations of holidays.

CHAPTER SUMMARY

The key factors determining pricing decisions are marketing objectives, costs, other mix variables, channel member expectations, buyer perceptions, competition, and legal and regulatory restrictions. The analysis of buyers' reactions to price change uses the concept of "elasticity of demand." If demand increases in line with price cuts, the product is said to be elastic. But if demand remains relatively unaltered by price changes, then the product is said to be inelastic.

Generally, companies use pricing as part of their positioning of a product, employing one of three strategic approaches: premium pricing, value-for-money pricing, and undercut pricing. Basic approaches to pricing fall into three main categories: cost-based methods; demand-based methods; and competition-oriented pricing. Three strategies commonly used for the introduction of new products are prestige pricing, market skimming, and penetration pricing. Other pricing techniques include promotional pricing, product-bundle pricing, price spread and price points, discriminatory pricing, discounting, and yield management.

Particular features of the tourism and hospitality industry that affect pricing include the high level of segmentation of industry; variability of demand; the perishable nature of the product; high fixed costs; cost fluctuations; vulnerability to demand changes; the high level of customers' psychological involvement; seasonal demand; tactical price cutting and price wars; low prices; fixed capacity; the customer's total purchases; increased use of the Internet; and late booking.

KEY TERMS

all-in-pricing (all-inclusive pricing), p. 195	market skimming, p. 183	promotional pricing, p. 179
break-even analysis, p. 178	monopoly, p. 178	psychological pricing, p. 179
buyer-based pricing (sensitivity pricing), p. 179	negotiating, p.180	reference price, p. 193
competition-oriented pricing (going-rate pricing), p. 180	off-set pricing (bait pricing), p.195	strategic pricing, p. 194
	penetration pricing, p. 183	tactical pricing, p. 194
	premium pricing, p. 177	target rate of return, p. 171
cost-based pricing, p. 178	prestige pricing, p. 182	undercut pricing, p. 177
cost-plus pricing, p. 179	price lining, p. 179	value-for-money pricing, p. 177
discriminatory pricing, p. 189	price–quality trade-off, p. 171	variable costs, p. 178
elasticity of demand, p. 175	price points, p. 187	volume discounting, p. 189
fixed costs, p. 178	price spread, p. 187	willingness to pay (WTP) assessment, p. 176
market share, p. 171	product-bundle pricing, p. 185	yield, p. 190
	profit maximization, p. 171	yield management, p. 190

DISCUSSION QUESTIONS AND EXERCISES

1. What are the benefits and costs of a tourism operator providing discounts?
2. When would a new restaurant introduce a new product with premium pricing? When might it use undercut pricing?
3. What pricing strategy is Space Adventure using for space tourists? How could the company find out about price sensitivity for its proposed new package?
4. Collect advertisements for hotels in your area and find examples of product-bundle pricing. Explain how they work. Try to calculate the savings that the bundle offers.
5. Explain the differences between prestige pricing, market skimming, and penetration pricing, using examples from a sector of tourism and hospitality apart from hotels.
6. What type of pricing strategy is Banff Mount Norquay following in the opening vignette? Can you see any disadvantages to this strategy?

CASE STUDY

WILLINGNESS TO PAY FOR NATIONAL PARKS IN CANADA

Conflicts between environmentalists and ski resort developers can be found around the world, and there is no better example than in Banff National Park in Alberta, Canada. The dilemma of balancing the protection of national park values while making provision for their enjoyment is longstanding, and has become progressively more acute with the continued increase in recreation and tourist demand. It has been

argued that an opportunity may exist for resorts to gain a competitive advantage by positioning themselves as environmentally responsible, but little is known about skiers' environmental knowledge and awareness, or about their willingness to pay for "greener" tourism products. A proposed cap on the number of skiers permitted to visit Banff National Park and the huge increase in tourist numbers predicted by the World Tourism Organization make a rise in prices inevitable. It is therefore critical that tourism providers understand how much skiers are willing to pay to preserve the environment in the National Park.

The hypothesis that tourists will pay more for environmentally friendly tourism products lacks empirical verification. Are skiers really worried about the environmental impacts of skiing, and, if so, how much are they willing to pay for a deeper environmental commitment from ski destinations, whether enforced or not? These questions formed the main objectives of a research project by the University of Calgary, designed to clarify exactly how much skiers are willing to pay for a more environmentally friendly skiing product.

Most studies of "willingness to pay" (WTP) rely on one of two analytical methods: travel cost and the contingent valuation method (CVM). In practice, however, the travel-cost approach is employed more often to value and defend nature-based tourism as a land use rather than to guide pricing. While the travel-cost method is grounded in observed market behaviour, CVM poses hypothetical, "what if" questions about how individuals would respond to specified prices for tourism products—in this case, how much they are willing to pay for specific improvements in the environment where they are skiing. Individuals are asked about their "contingent valuation" ("If 'this' happens, what would you be willing to pay?").

CVM first came into use in the early 1960s, and there are now over 2000 papers and studies demonstrating use of this method, including several applications to the tourism industry. Over the years, more and more scholars have entered the debate as to the efficacy of CVM, in real and potential terms, as a means for valuing public goods. Although the reliability of CVM is subject to controversy, guidelines of good practice are available, and it is generally agreed that a well-designed and thoroughly piloted contingent valuation questionnaire can produce accurate value estimations.

For the research study at Banff National Park, a research instrument in the form of a survey was developed, based on the willingness-to-pay literature and on in-depth interviews with officials from Parks Canada, ski resort operators, and environmental groups. The survey was designed to discover whether or not skiers would pay more for environmentally friendly skiing products, and, if so, how much. A model recommended for contingent valuation surveys was adopted. According to this model, respondents are presented with a questionnaire consisting of three parts:

1. Questions about the respondents' characteristics and their preferences relevant to the goods being valued.
2. A detailed description of the tourism product being valued (in this case an environmentally friendly ski destination) and the hypothetical circumstance under which it is made available to the respondent.
3. Closed-ended questions that elicit the respondent's level of willingness to pay for the product being valued.

The quota-sampling method was used in the study to ensure that a representative sample was collected from three nationalities, to allow for cross-cultural comparisons. A target group of 300 skiers, divided evenly between visitors from Canada, the United States, and the United Kingdom was set. These three nationalities form the largest segments of visitors to Banff in the skiing season. Skiers were approached on buses as they travelled to the different ski areas in the national park, and also at the base lodges as they rested. Critics of CVM tend to prefer in-person interviews rather than mail and telephone surveys, as they facilitate respondent understanding.

Results

Respondents were asked about their likelihood of choosing a "green" ski destination over another, and whether or not they would pay more for ski resorts that instigated sound environmental policies. The results are shown in Table 6.4 on page 202. Skiers indicated that they would be more likely to visit a resort that instigated all of the policies except for one. Skiers (especially those from the United Kingdom and the United States) would not be pleased if night skiing were prohibited to avoid disrupting wildlife movement. The only individual

Table 6.4

Likelihood of Visiting and Paying More for "Greener" Ski Resorts

SKI RESORT'S POTENTIAL ENVIRONMENTALLY FRIENDLY CHANGES AND POLICIES	MORE LIKELY TO VISIT (%)		MORE LIKELY TO PAY MORE (%)	
	YES	NO	YES	NO
Ensure sensitivity to impacts to wildlife populations and habitats resulting from development from ski area construction and operation.	74.3	25.7	35.6	64.4
Adopt sustainability principles for water management.	64.2	35.8	31.6	68.4
Instigate environmental education programs.	62.6	37.4	29.1	70.9
Monitor the number of skiers to minimize negative environmental impacts.	62.5	37.5	34.7	65.3
Create traffic-free environment and efficient public transportation system.	80.6	19.4	53.2	46.8
Build and maintain environmentally friendly hotels.	75.6	24.4	37.6	62.4
Encourage and provide recycling facilities.	77.9	22.1	29.9	70.1
Base development on sound ecological knowledge rather than just economic considerations.	74.8	25.2	35.5	64.5
Restrict or eliminate certain forms of combustion to reduce air pollution.	75.3	24.7	37.6	62.4
Communicate to the public the resort's role as a responsible environmental steward.	70.5	29.5	30.2	69.8
Position and market the resort as the first true "green" ski resort.	62.5	37.5	34.8	65.2
Restrict access to some ski areas to protect wildlife, shrubs, and trees.	66.0	34.0	32.4	67.6
Provide incentives to tourists arriving by public transport (e.g., cheaper lift tickets).	79.9	20.1	42.9	57.1
Prohibit night skiing to avoid disrupting wildlife movement.	45.3	54.7	21.1	78.9

Table 6.5

Willingness to Pay (WTP) for Environmentally Friendly Skiing

	INCREASED AMOUNT THAT SKIERS WERE WILLING TO PAY*			
	All Skiers Surveyed ($)	Canadian Skiers ($)	British Skiers ($)	American Skiers ($)
Mean WTP	16.41	10.39	18.61	20.17
Standard deviation	20.31	15.27	22.19	21.57
Median	10.00	5.00	12.00	15.00
Number of observations	332	111	105	116

*All monetary amounts are in Canadian dollars.

policy that the majority of skiers said they would pay for was a traffic-free resort that had an efficient public transport system; and this was only 53 percent of the sample.

The mean WTP, the standard error, and the median WTP were calculated for each population. These are shown in Table 6.5. Mean WTP is the traditional measure used in cost–benefit analysis, while median WTP, which corresponds to the flat amount that would receive majority approval, is a standard public-choice criterion. According to the results, skiers on average are willing to pay CDN$16 more per day to visit an environmentally friendly ski resort. However, univariate analysis of variance between the three countries indicated a significant difference across cultures. American skiers will pay $20.17 and British skiers $18.61, both of which are significantly higher amounts than the $10.39 that Canadians are prepared to pay. Taken as a whole, 65 percent of skiers would be prepared to pay more: 59 percent of Canadian and British skiers, and 67 percent of Americans, would pay more for an environmentally responsible ski destination. The mean WTP amount for the 217 skiers who would pay more was $25 per day.

Results of a stepwise multiple regression analysis of the WTP amounts on relevant predictor variables indicated a strong correlation between WTP and the cost of the holiday. WTP amounts were also likely to rise with income, confirming previous WTP studies that found that people with higher incomes tend to exhibit higher WTP for the environment than those with lower levels. The third significant correlation was with the environmental consciousness level of skiers. As their perceived level of environmental consciousness went up, so did their WTP. Previous studies have shown that consumers who exhibit high levels of environmental awareness and consciousness make more green purchasing decisions than those exhibiting low levels.

Source: Hudson, S., & Ritchie, J. R. B. (2001.) Cross-cultural tourist behaviour: An analysis of tourist attitudes towards the environment. *Journal of Travel and Tourism Marketing, 10* (2/3), 1–22.

QUESTIONS

1. What do the results of this study tell us about willingness to pay for skiing in Banff National Park?
2. Why do you think that respondents' willingness to pay seems to increase as they work through the questionnaire?
3. Does a price increase at Banff National Park appear to be viable?

WEB SITES

www.banffnorquay.com
Banff Mount Norquay Resort

www.brewsteradventures.com
Brewster's Mountain Lodges and Adventures

www.canadiancabins.com
Canadian Mountain Cabins

www.one4yacht.com
One4 Yacht Fractions

www.spaceadventures.com
Space Adventures

www.stratfordfestival.ca
Stratford Festival (Canada)

ENDNOTES

1. Dickman, S. (1999). *Tourism & hospitality marketing*. Oxford: Oxford University Press.
2. Catrett, J., & Lynn, M. (1999). Managing status in the hotel industry: How Four Seasons came to the fore. *Cornell Hotel and Restaurant Administration Quarterly*, February 26.
3. Frabotta, D. (2000). Super 8: 2,000 in 2000: CEO Weller praises company's franchisees for their spirit, passion. *Hotel and Motel Management*, 215(8), 3.
4. Foss, K. (2002, January 31). Duck-hunting doctor in U.S. offers free hernia surgery. *The Globe and Mail*, p. A8.
5. Tighe, T. (2003, May 1). Holiday pitch too good to be true. *The Calgary Herald, Your City*, p. N11.
6. Carmin, J., & Norkus, G. (1990). Pricing strategies for menus: Magic or myth? *Cornell Hotel and Restaurant Administration Quarterly, 31*(3), 50.
7. Hiemstra, S. J. (1998). Economic pricing strategies for hotels. In T. Baum & R. Mudambi (Eds.). *Economic and management methods for tourism and hospitality research* (pp. 215–232). New York: Wiley.
8. Menzies, D. (2003, April 5). There's plenty of room in the inn. *Financial Post*, p. IN4.
9. Heinzl, J. (2003, February 3). Fast-food discounting hard to swallow. *The Globe and Mail*, pp. B1, B4.
10. Sheldon, P. (1986). The tour operating industry: An analysis. *Annals of Tourism Research, 13*(3), 349–356.
11. Lundberg, D. E., Krishnamoorthy, M., & Stavenga, M. H. (1995). *Tourism economics*. New York: Wiley, 106.
12. Duadel, S., & Vialle, G. (1994). Yield management: Applications to air transport and other service industries. Paris: Institut du Transport Aerien.
13. Kimes, S. E. (1994). Perceived fairness of yield management. *Cornell Hotel and Restaurant Administration Quarterly, 43*(1), 21–31.
14. Hiemstra, S. J. (1998) Economic pricing strategies for hotels. In T. Baum & R. Mudambi (Eds.). *Economic and management methods for tourism and hospitality research* (pp. 215–232). New York: Wiley.

15. Dickens, J. (2002, October 30). Travellers warned of high-risk zones. *The Courier-Mail*, p. 6.

16. Laws, E. (1998). Package holiday pricing: Cause of the IT industry's success, or cause for concern? In T. Baum & R. Mudambi (Eds.), *Economic and management methods for tourism and hospitality research* (pp. 197–214). New York: Wiley.

17. Cooper, C., Fletcher, J., Gilbert, D., & Wanhill, S. (Eds.). (1993). *Tourism: Principles and practice.* London: Pitman.

18. Krippendorf, J. (1987). *The holiday makers.* London: Heinemann.

19. Urry, J. (1990). *The tourist gaze.* London: Sage.

20. Canadians logging on to destination Web sites. (2000). Retrieved September 26, 2000, from http://tourismtogether.com/tourismweb/news.

21. Davis, T. (2002). Ski operators meet in Whistler to review "extraordinary" 2001. Retrieved April 19, 2002, from http://www.canadatourism.com/en/ctc/ctx/ctx-news/search/newsbydateform.cfm.

22. Hudson, S., & Lang, N. (2002). A destination case study of marketing tourism online: Banff, Canada. *Journal of Vacation Marketing, 8*(2), 155–165.

Distribution

CANADIAN MOUNTAIN HOLIDAYS

Canadian Mountain Holidays (CMH), a helicopter tourism pioneer, was founded in 1965 and operates in 12 mountain areas of southeastern British Columbia. The Banff-based company has annual revenues of about $55 million and claims an 80 percent repeat-booking figure in the winter. CMH has the leasehold rights from the B.C. government to 15 765 km² of remote territory in the Purcell, Cariboo, Selkirk, and Monashee mountain ranges. Boasting several times the number of heliski visits that its next competitor has, CMH has 21 helicopters and eight remote lodges—many accessible in winter only by helicopter. Lodges have been designed specifically to meet the needs of helitourists. Each lodge has a dining room and a fully stocked lounge, and each is equipped with a sauna and a Jacuzzi. There is even a resident qualified massage practitioner who can rejuvenate skiers'

tired muscles. The company divides its business into three strands: heliskiing, helihiking, and mountaineering.

Since its inception over 35 years ago, CMH has hosted more than 125 500 skier weeks. Each winter CMH sells 7000 holidays and actually has a waiting list of 3000. About 50 percent of customers are from the United States and 40 percent are from Europe. A seven-day package costs about $6000 and includes 100 000 vertical feet of skiing, and accommodation and food for seven nights. CMH does not advertise its heliskiing holidays, relying instead on word of mouth. This strategy has been successful for the company largely because its product appeals to a certain type of person.

CMH invented helihiking (an abbreviation for helicopter-assisted hiking) in 1978, and from June to September it runs excursions that depart from five mountain lodges. All-inclusive packages range from family adventures and photography workshops to alpine ecology. Stays can be at one or a combination of five lodges, and three-night helihiking packages cost approximately $2000. Helicopters transport guests to remote wilderness areas around B.C., where participants can decide from day to day whether they want to be mountaineers scaling steep ridges or to stroll leisurely along the glaciers and flower-filled meadows. The mountaineering program was created to satisfy the needs of helihiking guests who wanted more skills-development, more challenge, and more accomplishments. With a helicopter, guests can access four different peaks in four days, whereas normally this would take four weeks.

According to the company's chief marketing officer, Marty von Neudegg, CMH is just a group of mountain guides taking people into the mountains to have fun, and the company philosophy reflects this attitude. The company's greatest marketing vehicle is "encouraged word of mouth" and CMH does very little advertising. Von Neudegg says that there are three marketing areas for the company: sales, advertising, and service. However, 90 percent of the marketing budget is spent on service, in order to encourage customer loyalty. CMH produces colourful brochures for each of its three activity strands (winter brochures being produced in six languages), expensive videos are made for all three activities in up to six languages, and a Web site exists for each activity.

CMH also hosts marketing events called "An Evening with CMH" throughout North America, Europe, Japan, and Australia. These are invitation-only evenings at which CMH staff and guides entertain and provide information to past guests and their friends. These events are very successful, generating conversion rates in excess of 75 percent of all participants.

When CMH began marketing in Europe during the late 1960s and early 1970s, Europeans had no knowledge of Canadian heliskiing opportunities. Rather than following the normal route of mass-media advertising, CMH chose to place no advertisements at all. Instead, the company found one person in each nation to be the CMH agent, and this person had to know the product and its market intimately. These agents sold heliskiing to one person at a time. This took place many years before the term "one-to-one" marketing had been coined. Although the distribution system has become more sophisticated over the years, these 12 agents still work in Europe and bring in 40 percent of the business. For the U.S. and Canadian markets CMH employs its own travel agency, based in Banff.

CMH is also part of the "Adventure Collection," a group of nine adventure companies that have joined together to form an alliance based on the principle that each company is deeply committed to the environment and culture through which it takes its guests. The alliance prints a collective brochure that is sent to guests of all nine companies, and the companies jointly promote each other's trips. They also combine itineraries to create new trips in order to give travellers more choices.

Source: Hudson, S. (Ed.). (2003). *Sport and adventure tourism*. Binghamton, NY: Haworth.

Objectives

On completion of this chapter, readers should understand

- the two main types of distribution channels used in tourism and hospitality;
- the key intermediaries involved in the tourism and hospitality distribution system;
- the main forms of channel conflict in tourism and hospitality;

- the two main types of channel organization in tourism and hospitality;
- the two major forms of vertically integrated marketing system—alliances and franchises; and
- how a company designs its distribution system and how and it ensures the effective execution of the distribution strategy.

Chapter Overview

The opening vignette provides an example of a company choosing an unusual but successful method of distributing its product. This chapter examines the various ways in which tourism and hospitality products are distributed. It begins by looking at the nature and types of distribution channels and the different functions of a distribution system. The key intermediaries involved in the tourism distribution system are then discussed, including travel agents, tour operators, convention and meeting planners, and travel specialists; the increasing use of the Internet as a part of the distribution channel is also analyzed. The next section of the chapter is concerned with channel conflict and organization; it explores the two main forms of channel conflict—horizontal conflict and vertical conflict—and the two main types of channel organization—the conventional marketing system and the vertical marketing system. Two major forms of vertically integrated marketing system are alliances and franchises. Both have advantages and disadvantages, which are considered in detail and illustrated with several examples from the Canadian tourism industry. Finally, attention is given to how a company designs its distribution system and how it ensures the effective execution of the distribution strategy.

THE DISTRIBUTION SYSTEM

distribution system

the "place" aspect of a company's marketing mix; its purpose is to provide an adequate framework for making a company's product or service available to the consumer

An organization's **distribution system** is centred on the "place" aspect of a company's marketing mix. Its purpose is to provide an adequate framework for making a company's product or service available to the consumer; in the tourism industry, distribution systems are often used to move the customer to the product. The true rationale behind a company's distribution system can be traced back to its specific needs and wants. Figure 7.1 shows that each distinct distribution participant has a unique set of needs and wants. The motivation for developing an effective distribution network, therefore, is to help the different members meet their individual needs. By choosing to combine the activities of the various members, participants in the distribution system can work together to identify opportunities to fulfill each other's needs.

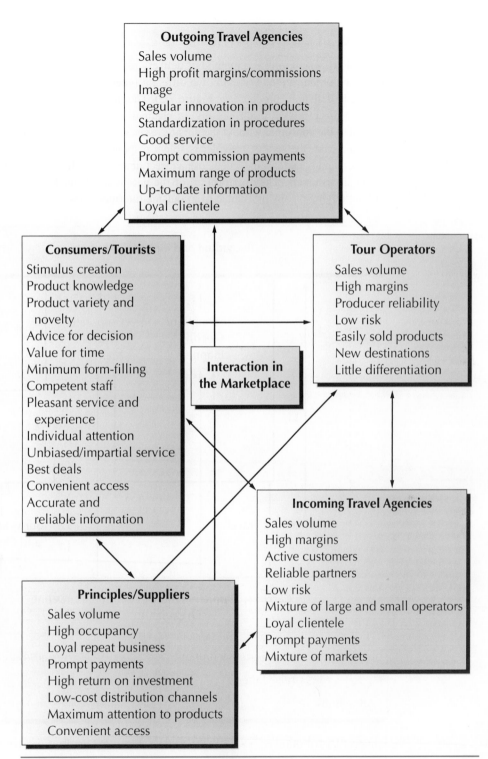

Figure 7.1 Needs and Wants of Tourism Distribution Channel Members

Source: Buhalis, D., & Laws, E. (2001). *Tourism distribution channels: Practices, issues and transformations.* New York: Continuum.

The Nature and Types of Distribution Channels

distribution channel

a direct or indirect delivery arrangement used by a supplier, carrier, or destination marketing organization

direct distribution channel

a channel through which a company delivers its product to the consumer without the outside assistance of any independent intermediaries

A **distribution channel** is a method of delivery used by a supplier, carrier, or destination marketing organization. There are two different types of distribution channels that a firm can use to deliver its product (see Figure 7.2). The first and most simple form of distribution is a **direct distribution channel**, a channel through which a company delivers its product to the consumer without the outside assistance of any independent intermediaries. In such a case, the service provider is solely responsible for the delivery of its product. Most bed and breakfasts in Canada use a direct distribution channel to market products to potential customers. They perform all of the necessary channel functions on their own, without relying on any assistance from outside intermediaries.

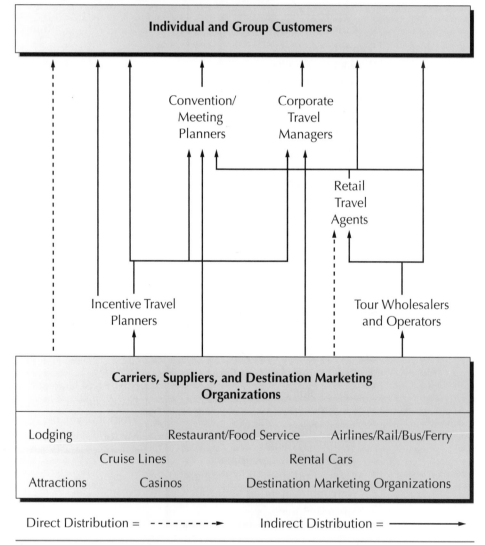

Figure 7.2   Types of Distribution Channels

Source: Morrison, A. M. (2002). *Hospitality and travel marketing* (3rd ed.). Albany, NY: Delmar Thomson Learning, 340.

indirect distribution channel

a channel through which a company distributes its product with the assistance of independent intermediaries

The second type of distribution channel used to deliver a product is an **indirect channel**. In this case, the service provider makes use of independent intermediaries to help facilitate the distribution if its product. Outside intermediaries such as travel agents, tour operators, and other tourism specialists assist the supplying company by helping to attract consumers to the product or destination. The opening vignette explains how, in its early stages, Canadian Mountain Holidays used an indirect distribution system to market its holidays in Europe, using specialist agents.

Functions of the Distribution System

In order for a company's distribution system to operate effectively, members must perform several key functions. One member can carry out these functions alone, or they can be executed by a number of different channel participants. The functions are listed below, and tasks should be assigned to those members that are best equipped to carry out particular functions.

1. *Acquiring information.* The purpose of this task is to gain access to relevant, complete, accurate, and timely information, thus enabling the company to assess its marketing environment. Information can be acquired through both primary and secondary research, using both qualitative and quantitative techniques (see Chapter 4).
2. *Promotion.* The purpose of promotion is to communicate the benefits of the destination's product to the consumer. This can be achieved through a variety of means, including the use of brochures, videos, magazine advertisements, and Web sites (see Chapters 8, 9, and 10).
3. *Contact.* Making contact with potential customers is critical to a company's success. It is important that the company establishes contact with its target market in order to be able to effectively communicate the benefits of its product.
4. *Negotiation.* The negotiation of high-quality arrangements and contracts is key to any business relationship. In the case of a tourism distribution system, it is important for the member to negotiate agreements with regard to price, operating procedures, and other issues that may arise among the system's participants.
5. *Physical distribution.* Obviously, a distribution system cannot be effective if there are no means to actually deliver the service to the consumer. The service provider is responsible for ensuring the successful distribution of its product at this stage.
6. *Financing.* An important task for every member of the distribution channel is to acquire the necessary resources to pursue its activities. Without funds in place, it may be impossible for the company to distribute its product.

MARKETING INTERMEDIARIES

marketing intermediaries

channels of distribution that include travel agents, tour operators, travel specialists, and the Internet

Marketing intermediaries are channels of distribution that include travel agents, tour operators, travel specialists, and the Internet. Their purpose is to help the service provider complete the six different functions listed above. Through the use of channel intermediaries, a company is able to expand the strength of its distribution network and to reach a much larger portion of its target market. As a result, the combined marketing efforts of the entire distribution network will lead to an increase in the number of customers using the service, thus boosting overall revenues.

Travel Agents

travel agents

marketing intermediaries that offer the tourism customer a variety of services, including everything from transportation plans and tour packages to insurance services and accommodation

Travel agents offer the tourism customer a variety of services, including everything from transportation plans and tour packages to insurance services and accommodation. They are the most widely used marketing intermediaries in the tourism industry. There are approximately 3560 full-service International Air Transport Association (IATA) travel agencies in Canada, down from a high of 4100 in the late 1990s.[1] Despite the drop, Canada has the highest number of agencies per capita of any country, the result of a small population being spread over a huge land mass. Some of the major travel agency chains include Marlin Travel, Uniglobe, Algonquin, Maritime Travel, Thomas Cook, and American Express. An agency will earn a commission for each sale, the amount depending on the type of product sold.

Travel agencies perform four distinct functions that pertain to a company's distribution system.

1. *Distribution and sales network.* Travel agents are a key player in the distribution and sale of a company's product under an indirect distribution system. Travel agents essentially act as tour brokers that bring the buyers and sellers of travel products together. The agents have access to an extensive network of suppliers and customers and are able to help facilitate interaction between the two by identifying the particular needs of each group.

2. *Reservations and ticketing.* Making reservations and issuing tickets are two of the more traditional roles of travel agents. Through the use of a global distribution system (GDS) such as Galileo, Abacus, or Sabre, travel agents can place reservations in numerous locations throughout the world. However, with the arrival of ticketless travel systems in the 1990s, the role of travel agents in issuing tickets (particularly airline tickets) is slowly diminishing.

3. *Information provision and travel counselling.* Travel agents have a wealth of information at their disposal. They possess an extensive knowledge of tourism destinations and are well equipped to offer advice to the inexperienced traveller. Whether a customer is looking for a quick flight across the country or planning a major expedition around the world, travel agents can provide valuable assistance in planning a trip.

4. *Design of individual itineraries.* The person-to-person nature of the travel agent business allows the travel agent to gain an in-depth understanding of customers' travel needs. By identifying what a customer's specific needs are, the agent can put together a personalized itinerary that best suits those needs. Travel agents can arrange trip components including transportation, accommodation, insurance, activities, and tours, all with the intent of satisfying the traveller's particular needs and expectations.

Despite the benefits that travel agents can provide to a company's distribution system, the emergence of new and cheaper distribution tools such as the Internet has placed the future role of travel agents in doubt. For this reason, a large number of travel agencies are seeking new positioning strategies to maintain their foothold in the tourism market. With airline carriers' elimination of base commissions for travel agents in 2002 (an event that prompted the Canadian Standard Travel Agency Registry [CSTAR] to file a class action suit against Air Canada, American Airlines, Delta Airlines, Continental Airlines, Northwest Airlines, United Airlines, and the International Air Transport Association [IATA] on behalf of 3700 accredited travel agencies in Canada), many agents are charging service fees to customers. Agents used to earn up to 10 percent on all airline tickets sold, and according to the Association of Canadian Travel Agents (ACTA), travel agencies processed approximately 70 to 75 percent of all airline tickets purchased by Canadian travellers in 2002.[2] Approximately one-third of agency business came from the sale of scheduled airline tickets. Apart from charging fees to customers, agencies are now looking at other ways to make up for the loss of airline commissions, including selling more package tours and cruises and focusing on selling their expertise.

The role of Global Distribution Systems (GDS) in the hospitality sector, and in the job of the travel agent, is significant. Hotel bookings through these systems were down in 2001, but the Hotel Electronic Distribution Network Association (HEDNA) points out that 2001 was still the second strongest year ever for hotel bookings through the systems. In its eighth annual "Survey of Global Distribution System Hotel Reservations," HEDNA found that 46 753 000 reservations for hotels were delivered by GDS in 2001. This figure represented a decrease of 4.2 percent when compared to 2000. However, it was above the levels of 1999. Hotel bookings made through Amadeus, Galileo, Sabre, Sahara, and Worldspan in 2000 totalled 48 787 000, while in 1999 those systems accounted for 43 781 000 bookings. The HEDNA survey also indicates that, based on an average daily rate of US$125.36 and an average length of stay of 2.2 days, 2001 GDS hotel bookings produced over 103 million room nights and US$12.9 billion in revenue for hotels around the world.[3]

However, despite the success of GDS, the future of travel agents is not rosy. Since a 1994 peak of 24 000 agencies, one of every three agencies has disappeared. Agents sold $83.5 billion worth of air transportation in 2000, but this dropped 16 percent, to $69.9 billion, one year later. Very tangible factors contributed to this decline: shrinking airline commissions; migration of travel purchases to the Internet; airlines' practice of encouraging travellers to bypass agents, including the advent and proliferation of Web-only fares; and sharp reductions in travel spending as a result of the economic recession and the post-September 11, 2001, environment. However, despite the decline in their number, travel agencies will continue to provide a valuable service to consumers. The availability of travel information has exploded, yet that explosion has created complexity and confusion. Thus, while traditional agents have lost market share to online purchasing, expert advice from travel advisors is likely to remain a vital service in the tourism marketplace. *The Profile* on Millenium Sun Travel below reinforces this theory.

PROFILE

JEANNIE HENKE, MILLENIUM SUN TRAVEL

I began my home-based travel agency approximately nine years ago. I was in the unique position of working for an airline, and I was bridging relationships with retail travel agencies in the community. For the next two to three years, I worked as a sales rep making referrals to A-list travel agencies and making a small commission. At that time, most suppliers (wholesalers and tour operators) did not recognize agents working on their own through their home. I also retained my employment with the airline; working on a casual basis and on maternity leave, I was able to earn an income and maintain industry experience. As my children entered school age, I was able to devote more time to building up my home-based business and to expanding my marketing from referrals received only from family and friends to corporate connections. I prefer to work only on a referral basis.

These days I work directly with most tour operators, car agencies, and hotels for full commission, whereas if I worked through a retail agency I would be splitting an agreed commission. I specialize in group travel, and my target markets are therefore the corporate or leisure traveller. However, I do not turn individual bookings away, unless I feel that taking them on is not feasible. My most likely client is the corporate group traveller taking his or her clients on incentive trips. I also arrange executive corporate retreats and other groups such as sports or school groups. I have two to three key corporate accounts that I service, and I allow their personnel to have after-hours access to my services for booking travel-related work. As a small-business and sole-proprietor owner, I provide my clients with the extra customer service that a lot of them feel is missing on the retail end. As one client has expressed, "I book on the Internet or with a chain, but I need a little 'TLC.'" I also provide any of my clients who make personal referrals to me a small referral fee as an incentive to do their personal bookings.

Throughout the year, I attend product launches or trade shows put on by tour operators, tourist boards, or consulates. These provide me with current information regarding particular destinations that I then market to my clients. Because of the weak Canadian dollar and post–September 11 environment, I've had to switch gears by focusing on marketing Canada and sun destinations such as Mexico. My competitors are retail agencies, the Internet, and in some cases the tour operators themselves. I do not charge the service fee that most retail agencies are now charging, a fee which many of my clients complain about after receiving what they consider to be unsatisfactory service from a retail agency. I don't have the quotas that some "chains" have to meet, and I do offer discounts, a practice that is in some cases against retail policies. The Internet also has its problems, such as clients not being able to change flights, speak to an actual human being when a problem arises with their tickets, etc. My clients have come to trust my travel skills and knowledge, and this in turn allows them free valuable time to carry on with more important aspects of their business. Since "bigger" is not always better, I am not acquiring any more accounts and am servicing only the accounts that I do have, in order to provide them with the quality of service that they have become accustomed to. Since I work only on a referral basis, when I manage to secure a key account this causes a chain reaction whereby the client refers me to several of their colleagues in their professional field. These referred clients are happy to use my services, since they assume that I must be good in order for their colleague to use my services exclusively. Due to referrals, over the past four to five years I have increased my business revenue up to approximately $400 000. This increase in profits allows me flexible time to volunteer in my children's school and also to acquire all the tax deductions available to a home-based business.

Based on recent changes in the tourism industry, I have started working with local charter outfits that provide short-haul flights

PROFILE *continued*

from Calgary to Edmonton for corporate group travel. With the increase in airport security requirements, airport fees, change fees, delays, and the requirement of arriving at the airport two hours early for a flight of less than one hour, I am using charters that hold 10 to 22 passengers. Corporate clients enjoy the convenience of showing up at the airport 15 minutes before departure, and they don't have to pay the huge change fees that the scheduled airlines are regulated to collect.

My success as a travel agent is due to the experience and connections that I have been able to cultivate over the years. Even though airlines have imposed caps on agent commissions, people still consider it a necessity to travel. The income availability in Calgary, the large number of corporate head offices, and the fact that Calgarians value their leisure time generate a large market for travel and tourism. I work outside of the traditional work force, but I am not alone: over the past few years, the number of travel agents working from home has increased significantly.

Source: J. Henke, owner and agent, Millenium Sun Travel, personal communication, June 2, 2003.

Tour Operators

tour operators

organizations that offer packaged vacation tours to the general public

Tour operators are organizations that offer packaged vacation tours to the general public. These packages can include everything from transportation, accommodation, and activities to entertainment, meals, and drinks. Tour operators typically focus their marketing efforts on the leisure market, which represents the dominant buying group of travel packages. Some of the larger tour operators include Conquest Tours; Signature Vacations, owned by U.K.-based First Choice; Sunquest/Alba and their parent company, MyTravel; Air Canada Vacations; Air Transat Holidays; and World of Vacations. There were 83 Canadian tour operators commissionable to travel agents in 1998, including a number of smaller specialty operators in the areas of eco/adventure travel. Like the travel agency industry, tour operators and wholesalers are concentrated in Ontario, Quebec, and British Columbia.

Tour operators have the ability to bring in large volumes of customers. They receive discounted rates from the various service providers in exchange for providing a large number of guaranteed visitors. Tour operators make their profits by providing low-margin travel packages to a large number of consumers. Typically, organizations that offer travel packages must sell between 75 and 85 percent of the packages available in order to break even. The majority of tour operators distribute their travel packages through travel agencies. Each travel agency represents an average of four tour operators, and has traditionally been an important player in the distribution of tour operator products.

With the rising use of the Internet as a distribution mechanism, a large number of tour operators are choosing to restrict their offerings to only a select number of specialized travel packages. Companies such as G.A.P Adventures in Toronto, Canadian Mountain Experiences in Banff, and Atlantic Tours Gray Line in Halifax are tour operators specializing in offering unique tour packages to different markets. G.A.P Adventures has chosen to target young, adventurous individuals interested in purchasing travel packages to the developing world, while Canadian Mountain Experiences focuses on offering a variety of ski packages throughout the Canadian Rockies. Atlantic Tours, on the other hand, specializes in escorted sightseeing tours throughout the Canadian Atlantic provinces (see opening vignette in Chapter 10). By reducing the scope of their operations, these companies have managed to differentiate themselves as specialized tour operators in each of their respective areas, and have thus been able to focus their efforts on appealing to particular niche markets.

Convention/Meeting Planners and Corporate Travel Managers

Convention and meeting planners plan and coordinate their organizations' external meeting events. These planners work for associations, corporations, large nonprofit organizations, government agencies, and educational institutions. Some combine the task of convention planning with that of corporate travel management, whereas other organizations split up the tasks. The convention and business markets are lucrative ones in Canada. In 2000, Americans made 2.36 million business trips of one or more nights to Canada, which is an increase of 0.4 percent over 1999. They spent $1.78 billion, an increase of 3.8 percent over the previous year. Also in 2000, overseas visitors made 782 700 business trips of one or more nights to Canada. To build on this, the CTC has created the Meetings, Conventions & Incentive Travel Program (MC&IT) to target meeting and incentive travel decision makers with an integrated approach that has two main strategies: relationship building and advertising. Existing relationships are strengthened and new ones developed through direct mail, business development, familiarization tours and site inspections, trade shows, and special events.

An example of such a program was created in 2003, when the Province of Ontario, the CTC, and the Hudson's Bay Company (HBC) were partners in a marketing initiative that focused on the meetings and convention business in the United States. The campaign, whose slogan was "Ontario, Canada … Great meetings come naturally," urged professional American planners to book meetings and conventions at Ontario destinations. As an incentive, planners received gifts for their delegates: coupons worth $20 at HBC.

The private sector is also involved in the marketing of conventions and exhibitions. The Canadian Management & Incentive Group (CMG), for example, assists in all event, meeting, travel incentive, and group needs. CMG is the Canadian partner of Global Event Partners, which is composed of more than 55 affiliated partners—20 within the United States and 35 in other countries. According to officials, CMG is the "one-stop shop" for all travel programs, domestic or international. The company can assist in everything from sightseeing tours and ground transportation to entertainment, event coordination, and team-building exercises. Spousal and children's programs are also available. On the incentive side, CMG can arrange for travel packages, reward evenings and dinners, spa weekends, gift certificates, and merchandise rewards. For special events, the company arranges pre- and post-convention packages, city tours, dinners, concerts, theatre packages, fashion shows, and art and museum tours. Additional services available for special events range from security and catering to photography and design and staging.

Travel Specialists

travel specialists

intermediaries that specialize in performing one or more functions of a company's distribution system

Travel specialists are intermediaries that specialize in performing one or more functions of a company's distribution system. Hotel representatives, for example, specialize in providing contact with a hotel's customers in order to identify their specific accommodation needs. Advertising agencies can also act as specialists, performing the promotional aspect of a company's distribution system. By using travel specialists in its distribution system,

tour brokers

companies that sell
motorcoach tours,
which are attractive to
a variety of markets

motivational houses

companies that provide
incentive travel, offered
to employees or distrib-
utors as a reward for
their efforts

junket representatives

companies that serve
the casino industry as
intermediaries for pre-
mium players

a company can designate particular functions to the intermediaries that are best equipped to perform them. Focusing on one specific operation within the distribution channel allows the travel specialist to effectively perform the function at hand in the best possible way.

Other examples of specialist intermediaries are tour brokers, motivational houses, and junket representatives. **Tour brokers** sell motorcoach tours, which are attractive to a variety of markets. Such tours are important to hotels en route as well as to the attractions that the tours visit. **Motivational houses** provide incentive travel, offered to employees or distributors as a reward for their efforts. Incentive trips usually involve staying in high-class accommodation in resort areas, but not necessarily in warm destinations: winter sports incentives are becoming increasingly popular in North America. Finally, **junket representatives** serve the casino industry as intermediaries for premium players. Junket reps maintain lists of gamblers who like to visit certain gaming areas such as Las Vegas, Reno, or Atlantic City, and they work for one or two casinos rather than the whole industry. Junket reps are paid a commission on the amount the casino earns from the players or, in some cases, on a per-player basis.

The Internet

Canadians are turning in increasing numbers to the Internet to help them plan and book their travel. Some stakeholders in the travel industry, such as airlines, car rental companies, and international hotel chains, have been quick to grasp the potential of marketing and selling their services online. They have recognized an opportunity to bypass intermediaries and to sell their basic products and services directly to the customer. Hotel bookings in Canada, for example, are expected to increase from 9 percent of total bookings to 20 percent by 2005. Companies such as Delta Hotels have developed Web-based booking tools for both leisure and group sales. Increasingly, package holiday tour operators are including direct sales via the Internet in their sales strategy, thus bypassing the travel agent. These travel companies are adopting both organic (internal) and acquisitive growth strategies. Many traditional companies have developed their own Web sites and interactive divisions (see *Snapshot* on Air Canada's Destina.ca, pp. 220–221), while others are acquiring Internet companies.

However, some critics have suggested that the tourism industry has traditionally been relatively slow on the uptake of new information technologies, particularly in the travel agency sector.[4] Many researchers have focused on the impact of the Internet on travel agents and on the role of electronic intermediaries in the travel business.[5] Since the Internet encourages direct and immediate contact between suppliers and customers, together with a decrease in transaction and commission costs, there is a strong case for the elimination of intermediaries entirely. However, the last decade has witnessed the emergence of electronic brokers, an electronic version of the traditional model, whose role is that of aggregating and disseminating travel information to customers. Examples are Travelocity and Expedia, which offer information and reservations for flights, hotels, and car rental.

In contrast to the commercial sector, destination marketing organizations (DMOs) have been slow to adopt information technology (IT) in their operations. Most DMOs did not start considering electronic distribution until public awareness of the Internet increased in the mid-1990s, and a key issue that DMOs have had about Web development has been whether to field enquiries themselves or pass them on through links to member Web sites. Only a few DMOs have designed and developed their Internet sites to enable customers to move quickly and easily from travel planning to reservations. An increasing amount of research is focused on the challenges faced by DMOs in keeping pace with the evolution of new technologies. The largest study to date was conducted by the World Tourism Organization (WTO), which evaluated the Web sites of 25 DMOs and found great variations in sophistication and quality.[6]

In Canada, a 2002 survey showed that 8 out of 10 Canadians who are connected to the Internet use it as a source of travel information and planning, 4 in 10 saying it has had a significant influence on how they make travel decisions.[7] The survey found that only 14 percent of Web users think they can get a better deal from a travel agency than online, and just 18 percent said they prefer printed travel catalogues to online information. Forty percent of those surveyed visited Air Canada's Web site, making it the most visited of all Canadian travel Web sites. After Air Canada, travel-related Web sites most visited by respondents included Travelocity.ca, Yahoo.ca/travel, Expedia.ca, Parks Canada, Sympatico.ca/travel, WestJet, and VIA Rail. VIA Rail was one of the early adopters of Internet technology, and in 1998 made 23 500 bookings online.

Figure 7.3 shows a model of online distribution applicable to many destinations, and illustrates the various ways customers can reach individual Web sites. In the diagram, the browser window is depicted below the customer because it can have an impact on the ultimate message delivery, usability, and pathway to the operator Web sites. The most common means of navigating through the online maze from customers to operator is typically for the customers to select the search engine or index service of their preference. For example, if they are looking for a hotel in the Banff area, they will type in, or funnel down through search categories to, something like "Banff Canada" or "Banff Canada Hotels." Alternatively, they may go through an index structure by geography (North America, Canada, Alberta, Banff), by service type, or through a topical index that includes entries such as "Travel," "Accommodations," and "Hotels." The other route they may take is to click on a link from a search engine to a destination travel guide or an electronic broker. These possible pathways are shown in the diagram in Figure 7.3.

The diagram also indicates that some customers may book travel through a corporately managed Web site. These are sites operated by national companies, such as Howard Johnson, Sheraton, Marriott, Best Western, and Fairmont, that distribute hotel room reservations for the area via their corporate reservation systems. Customers may also book directly, through the various destination travel guides. An important part of the diagram in Figure 7.3 is the cross-link marketing, whereby complementary services supply each other with links to each other's Web sites. In this case, the user stumbles perhaps on a transportation Web site, explores the links to a hotel and to an attraction, and ends up purchasing a hotel reservation and a sightseeing trip via the online systems on those other Web sites.

Obviously, individual operators would prefer to reach the customer directly, but the majority, especially the smaller operators, have to rely on electronic intermediaries to direct customers their way, in much the same way as they used to rely on travel agents. And while the Internet may be one of the most effective marketing channels for tourism companies, its costs are rising sharply. It is important, therefore, that operators keep track of the impact of Web sites on the bottom line. Michael Porter, a marketing strategy specialist, has recently suggested that the Internet is not necessarily a blessing and that it

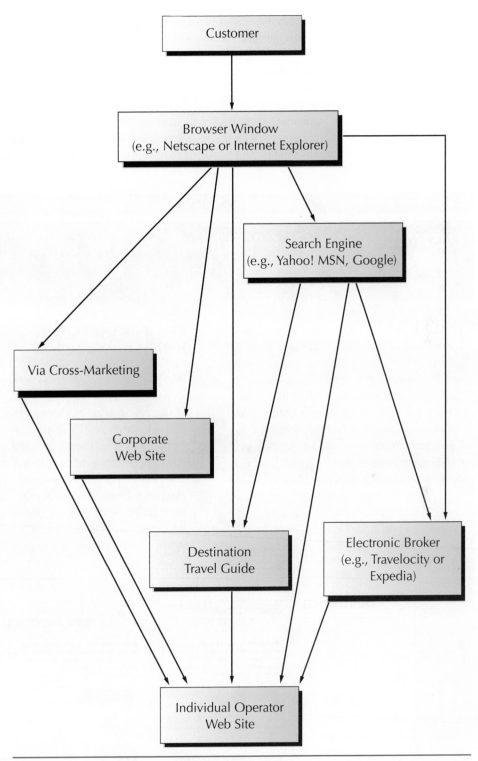

Figure 7.3 Intermediaries Involved in the Online Distribution of Destination Tourism Products and Services

tends to alter industry structures in ways that dampen overall profitability.[8] He predicts that many of the companies that succeed will be the ones that use the Internet as a complement to traditional ways of competing. Porter has also suggested that average profitability is under pressure in most industries that are influenced by the Internet, a comment backed up by Alford, who estimates that 80 percent of online travel businesses currently trading will not exist in two to three years' time.[9] Porter says that to gain competitive advantage in such a climate, individual companies will have to set themselves apart from the pack: "As buyers' initial curiosity with the Web wanes and subsidies end, companies offering products and services online will be forced to demonstrate that they provide real benefits."

SNAPSHOT

DESTINA.CA TARGETS GROWING ONLINE TRAVEL MARKET

In March 2002, Air Canada launched its own online travel venture—Destina.ca—to compete with U.S.-based giants such as Expedia.ca and Travelocity.ca. It positioned itself clearly as the "uniquely Canadian" online travel site. "When you look at the growth of the online travel market and the fact that there was no Canadian offering in it, we felt that it was a great opportunity to build a profitable business," says Lise Fournel, president and CEO of Destina.ca. Fournel's subtle criticism—which conveniently ignores the existence of Expedia.ca and Travelocity.ca—may well be the first of many shots fired as the big online travel players square off to battle for a share of Canada's exploding online travel market. This market is expected to grow from the $600 million reported in 2000 to $4.5 billion in 2005.

Clearly Destina.ca isn't going to be shy about going after its share of that lucrative market—both on the leisure and on the business travel side. In fact, it has long-term strategic and operational deals in place with both Air Canada and Aeroplan. The Aeroplan deal sees Destina.ca becoming the frequent flyer program's exclusive online partner, an arrangement that will allow its users to earn Aeroplan miles from every purchase they

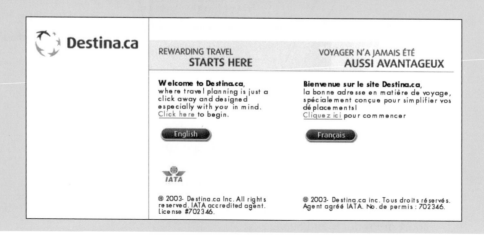

make at the site. In conjunction with Air Canada, Destina.ca had special fares available in Canada, to the United States and other international desinations, to mark its launch. It also featured special promotions on hotel accommodation from Renaissance, Delta, and Hyatt, and on cars from Budget.

Along with adding product, Destina.ca is also investing money and resources in customer service. Fournel explains that the company already has between 30 and 35 "customer care" agents in place to deal with any issues about which site users have questions or concerns. Interestingly enough, Destina.ca has indicated that for its first three weeks of operation it will not be applying a service fee for online bookings, as an incentive for customers to visit and use the site. Fournel says that after that Destina.ca will apply fees to products on which it doesn't receive a commission. She adds that most travel services sold on the site won't be subject to fees and that Destina.ca will continue to monitor the situation to determine any additional response. However, the bottom

line for Destina.ca is that it plans to move quickly to the merchant model approach because, as Fournel comments, "We believe that's where most of the revenue is."

Fournel admits that travel agents may be unhappy with the new online travel venture, but she makes it abundantly clear that Destina.ca is not the competition. "Travel agents have to understand that we're not competing with them. We are competing with the online U.S. travel sites. This is our competition," Fournel told *Canadian Travel Press* after Destina.ca's launch in Toronto. She added, "There is still a place for travel agents to offer one-on-one type services to their customers and bring added value to the equation." Fournel also suggested that while agents aren't really the customer base that Destina.ca is seeking, they might well be able to use the site to offer product to their customers.

Source: Mowat, B. (2002). Destina targets growing online travel market. Retrieved April 30, 2002, from http://www.canadatourism.com/en/ctc/ctx/ctx-news/search/newsbydateform.cfm.

CHANNEL CONFLICT AND ORGANIZATION

Channel Conflict

channel conflict

conflict that occurs when one member of a distribution channel perceives another to be engaged in behaviour that prevents or hinders the first member from achieving its goals

horizontal conflict

conflict between organizations at the same level of the distribution channel

In order for companies within a distribution channel to be successful, it is necessary that they work together in cooperation. When every member in the value chain works together, it allows the channel to combine its resources to perform in a more efficient and effective manner. The success of the entire channel will in turn benefit all of the individual members of that channel. Unfortunately, many companies in the tourism and hospitality industry tend to focus on their own, individual performance rather than on that of the entire chain. Thus a cooperative marketing system is often difficult to achieve, and a common occurrence is **channel conflict**, in which one member perceives another to be engaged in behaviour that prevents or hinders the first member from achieving its goals.

There are two main forms of channel conflict: horizontal conflict and vertical conflict. **Horizontal conflict** takes place between organizations at the same level of the distribution channel. An example is a conflict over territory between two Tim Hortons franchises. Due to the rapid growth of this company, it is common for two separate franchises to compete for the

vertical conflict

conflict between organizations at different levels of the same distribution channel

directional selling

a vertically integrated travel agent's sale, or attempted sale, of the foreign package holidays of its linked tour operator in preference to the holidays of other operators

same market segment of customers. **Vertical conflict** occurs between organizations at different levels of the same channel, and it is more common. An example is the argument between travel agents and airlines over the latter's cutting of base commissions for the former (see pp. 212–213). In the United Kingdom in the late 1990s, independent travel agents complained to the government about the practice of **directional selling**, which is a vertically integrated travel agent's sale, or attempted sale, of the foreign package holidays of its linked tour operator in preference to the holidays of other operators. The practice was facilitated by the lack of transparency of ownership links. It caused considerable conflict both between the large tour operators and between travel agents and tour operators.[10]

Conflicts may be caused by simple misunderstandings. For franchisees, for example, understanding the decisions made by the franchiser can sometimes be difficult. Dennis Murray, a Thrifty car rental franchisee says, "It can be exceptionally challenging when a decision made by the franchiser seems undesirable to a franchisee's particular location, but it is better for the entire system in the end." Cooperating to achieve overall channel goals sometimes means giving up individual company goals. Although channel members are dependent on each other, they often act alone in their own short-run best interests. They frequently disagree about the roles each should play or who should do what for which rewards. Such disagreements over goals and roles generate channel conflict.

Channel Organization

There are two main types of channel organization: the conventional marketing system and the vertical marketing system.

conventional marketing system

a distribution system that consists of a loose collection of independent organizations, each of which tries to maximize its own success

1. **The conventional marketing system.** The conventional marketing system was the traditional system that organizations adopted because the conventional hierarchical structure was consistent with the structure within individual organizations. This distribution system consists of a loose collection of independent organizations, each of which tries to maximize its own success (see Figure 7.4). For example, many small hotels pay a commission to travel agents, but no formal contract is signed between the hotel and the agent. The hotel simply communicates its policy and can, if it wishes, make rooms unavailable to travel agents on a temporary basis. Although this system has worked in the past, trends of globalization and technological advancement have forced many tourism organizations to reorganize their distribution channel into a vertical marketing system in order to remain competitive.

vertical marketing system

a system in which all members of the distribution channel work together as a unified whole

2. **The vertical marketing system.** In this situation, all members of the distribution channel work together as a unified whole (see Figure 7.5). They become vertically integrated so that they can all work together to achieve a common goal. Usually, one member dominates the system and leads the entire channel toward its shared goal by reducing conflict within the system. This leader may be appointed either formally or informally. Formal leadership can be obtained through ownership control over the other members (e.g., Air Canada's ownership of Destina.ca) or by forming contractual agreements with the other members in the channel (e.g., Destina.ca's deal with Budget for specially priced car rentals). Informal control is usually given to the channel member with the most brand ownership or financial strength, or is simply designated on the basis of the role that the leader plays within the system.

Figure 7.4 The Conventional Marketing System

Figure 7.5 The Vertically Integrated Marketing System

The vertical marketing system has five main advantages over the conventional marketing system. It

1. *allows economies of scale.* The entire chain is able to produce goods or services less expensively than competitors due to economies of scale (i.e., declines in unit costs of production as the volume of production increases), thus giving all channel members a competitive advantage.
2. *makes managing conflict easier.* With just one member dominating the channel, this leader has the authority to punish those channel members that are creating conflict, as well as to implement solutions to resolve such situations.
3. *eliminates duplication.* The vertical integration of the distribution channel allows all duplicated duties to be eliminated. This increases the efficiency of the chain.
4. *levers bargaining power.* The vertical integration of the channel gives the system and its members more power to bargain than when channel members work individually.
5. *creates shared goals.* The system allows for all the members of the channel to benefit from an achieved goal, rather than only one specific member benefitting.

There are two main forms of the vertical marketing system: alliances and franchises. Both carry with them advantages and disadvantages; which form an organization chooses depends on which one best matches that company's specific goals.

Alliances

alliance

partnership formed when two or more organizations combine resources through a contractual agreement that allows them to overcome each other's weaknesses by benefitting from each another's strengths

An **alliance** is a partnership formed when two or more organizations combine resources through a contractual agreement that allows them to overcome each other's weaknesses by benefitting from each another's strengths. In this form of distribution channel, each organization shares everything from information to resources to strategies, but the key advantage to alliances is increased distribution. Those organizations joined through the alliance will enjoy access to new markets through new and diversified sales locations. For example, Tourism Vancouver joined together with VISA to create an alliance that would benefit both parties. The three-year marketing partnership was developed to promote both domestic and international travel to Vancouver, which in turn would increase the use of VISA cards. This alliance benefits not only Tourism Vancouver and VISA but also the customer, who receives valuable package offerings. In another recent alliance, Summerfield Suites by Wyndham and Avis Rent a Car teamed up to offer clients who were booking 60 consecutive nights at any Summerfield Suites property 25 000 frequent flyer miles with a Wyndham airline partner and 10 percent off Avis's mini-lease rates for 60-day car rentals. Known as Extended Stay Rewards, the program was targeted at business travellers on a long assignment or families relocating to a new city. Extended Stay Rewards was available through 2002.

Marketing in Action on the opposite page provides an in-depth analysis of three alliances in the Canadian tourism industry.

THREE TOURISM ALLIANCES IN CANADA

1. Bearfoot Canada

On November 5, 2002, Jim Watson, then president and CEO of the Canadian Tourism Commission (CTC) announced the launch of the Okanagan Shuswap Bioregion Product Club, branded as "Bearfoot Canada." This major initiative saw the development of a permanent nature-based travel strategy for the Okanagan and Shuswap regions in the southern interior of British Columbia. The new product club was a partnership that brought together 30 adventure and eco-tourism businesses and linked them with environmental organizations, tourism associations, economic development agencies, the private sector, and local government.

The idea was that this alliance of partners would act as a catalyst and clearinghouse for adventure travel/ecotourism development and travel packaging within the Okanagan and Shuswap regions. Its aim being the protection of natural habitat areas while still encouraging people to make minimal-impact visits to the sites, Bearfoot Canada developed new travel opportunities within a number of Bearfoot Routes that were of importance to communities and to the natural habitat of the region. The club also published a series of Bearfoot Guides that helped tour guides and travellers interpret habitat and culture accurately.

The CTC contributed $86 500 to the partnership over three years, while the Adventure Okanagan Co-operative, along with community business and corporate partners, contributed $159 450 for a total of $245 950, which saw the development of new tourism products and the consolidation of this tourism segment. Watson indicated that further to the World Ecotourism Summit hosted by the CTC and Tourisme Québec in May 2002, this latest effort complemented the CTC's mission to address some of the challenges tourism faced in Canada. He said, "Tourism is strengthened by 'untouched' natural surroundings and 'genuine' communities, but success in tourism can also negatively impact these resources. The right kinds of tourism, properly managed, can create prosperity for communities and profits for businesses while protecting and even enhancing the environment and the community."

2. Conquest Alliance with Skyservice

When Conquest Vacations unveiled its new air services deal with Skyservice early in 2002, it really marked the first phase of the operator's launch of a new strategy designed to take advantage of the business opportunities that it believed clearly existed in the Canadian leisure travel marketplace. The agreement with Skyservice allowed Conquest to operate close to 75 weekly flights to 10 Canadian cities, also including the option to expand its service to additional destinations as the market dictates. More importantly, though, it set the stage for the operator to launch a full-blown land program that will mesh neatly with its air operations. Conquest was the first off the blocks with a strategy that will see the major mass-market operators aggressively pursuing domestic Canadian business in a way that they have perhaps never done before. "We go where the trends are," observed Conquest president Robbie Goldberg during the unveiling of the Skyservice deal, "and this summer, Canadians will be travelling in Canada." Goldberg pointed out further that the domestic market accounted for about 30 percent of Conquest's business, but the miserable state of the Canadian dollar and a clear indication by consumers that they wanted to stay close to home in 2002 suggested that that percentage would rise in later years.

With 30 years in the business under his belt, Goldberg is well known for not missing opportunities when they present themselves and for being able to shrewdly manage his company out of some rather dicey situations. Calling the fall of 2001 the "autumn of the double elevens"—a reference to both the events of September 11 and the collapse of Canada 3000 on November 11—Conquest's president said that his company has had to "change the way we do business and take stock of what we were doing." "We've changed some of our strategy and I believe that there's an opportunity to expand our Canadian business," Goldberg added. And while he's not convinced that Canadians are ready yet to fully embrace the idea of taking one-week package holidays in their own country as they do to southern destinations, Goldberg does believe there's an opportunity to "do some partnerships with people who are providing travel services, just like we're doing with Skyservice." In fact, Conquest is already talking to hoteliers, car rental companies, and even small tour and ground operators to put the pieces of its Canada program together. As Goldberg sees it, the formula is simple: if it wants to expand its business, it needs to bring new destinations on board; and its program with Skyservice allows it to do just that.

3. Golf Industry Targets the United States

The Canadian golf industry and tourism marketing partners spent an additional $1 million in 2002 to expand their marketing activities in the United States. The joint-marketing campaign was developed and launched by the Canadian Golf Tourism Alliance in partnership with the Canadian Tourism Commission as part of new marketing activities developed to stimulate American travel recovery in light of the slowdown after September 11, 2001. The campaign was added to the Alliance's $1.2 million "Golf. It's In Our Nature" marketing program, launched in September 2001 to encourage more American travellers to plan a golf vacation in Canada. Program partners included the Canadian Tourism Commission, the Ontario Tourism Marketing Partnership, and the golf tourism sector. "The increased partnership and marketing opportunities with the Canadian Tourism Commission will help the Canadian golf tourism industry increase our presence in the highly competitive U.S. market," says Murray Blair, president of the Canadian Golf Tourism Alliance. "It will help us keep pace with many other golf destinations in the U.S. and around the world that have expanded their advertising this year in response to the slowdown in overall leisure travel."

Under the expanded program, the Canadian Golf Tourism Alliance, ClubLink Corporation, and Niagara Tourism launched "Ontario Golf Trails," a major new golf tourism product involving courses in Toronto, Niagara, and Muskoka. As well, the Alliance significantly expanded its consumer marketing campaigns in the U.S. Northwest and Northeast markets. The launch of "Ontario Golf Trails," a collection of two- to five-day golf trail packages that included Toronto, Niagara, and Muskoka courses, was developed by ClubLink, the Niagara Parks Commission, and partners including the Canadian Golf Tourism Alliance, the Canadian Tourism Commission, and the Ontario Tourism Marketing Partnership. It was supported by a $645 000 multimedia marketing campaign in the New York, Ohio, Michigan, and Pennsylvania markets between April and August 2002. "This is the first true golf trail product introduction in Canada," said

Charles Lorimer, vice-president of sales and marketing for ClubLink, Canada's largest golf course operator. "It's designed to capitalize on an emerging trend among U.S. golf travellers looking to play several courses on a short get-away visit to Southern Ontario."

Canadian golf courses have been gaining respect south of the border for their quality and great value. In 2001, U.S. golfers spent in excess of US$320 million on golf travel in Canada. Revenues from the Canadian golf industry total more than $4.2 billion. Other highlights of the Canadian Golf Tourism Alliance's "Golf. It's in Our Nature" 2002 marketing campaign included an updated Web site—www.canadagolf.com—and a new Canada Golf toll-free visitor info line, both of which make it easier than ever to plan and book a Canadian golf vacation. Travellers can reserve tee-times online and shop for special package deals available only over the Internet.

Sources: Desaulniers, G. (2002). Tourism development goes Bearfoot. Retrieved November 7, 2002, from http://www.canadatourism.com/en/ctc/ctx/ctx-news/search/newsbydateform.cfm; Mowat, B. (2002). Conquest alliance with Skyservice. Retrieved February 25, 2002, from http://www.canadatourism.com/en/ctc/ctx/ctx-news/search/newsbydateform.cfm; Golf industry shoots for U.S. market. (2002). *Tourism, 6*(4), 11.

Franchises

franchises

businesses that are established when a franchiser grants a franchisee the right to engage in offering, selling, or distributing its goods or services under its marketing format

Franchises are businesses that are established when a franchiser grants a franchisee the right to engage in offering, selling, or distributing its goods or services under its marketing format. Franchising has become increasingly popular in Canada. For example, Tim Hortons, the food franchise, had revenues of nearly $600 million in 2001. Due to its increased coverage within Canada, the company is increasing its distribution by developing franchises internationally; it has already established over 150 stores throughout the United States. In the hotel sector, Days Inn continues to expand within Canada. Days Inn is the world's largest franchised hotel chain in terms of units, with over 1900 properties and more than 164 000 rooms. There are more than 80 independently owned and operated Days Inn locations in Canada, and the Realstar Group, master franchiser in Canada, plans to increase the number of Days Inn locations to 120 in the next four years.

Normally the franchisee will pay a fee to purchase a full-service franchise, as well as paying an annual percentage of sales. For example, in the car rental business, Thrifty franchisees pay a monthly fee of 5 percent of their gross revenue from rental and parking activities, which helps pay for headquarters support and for select programs for franchises. There is also an advertising fee, but many services are provided to franchisees for free.

Franchisees often run more than one franchise. For example, George Carisch is a multi-unit franchisee who owns 59 Arby's outlets in Canada. He, like many people in the world of franchising, claims that the relationship between franchiser and franchisee is one of the most important and challenging aspects of the business. Some of the advantages and disadvantages to both franchiser and franchisee are outlined below.

Franchiser Benefits

1. The main benefit to the franchiser is the increased distribution coverage, as franchises usually service markets nationally or globally. This global coverage is becoming increasingly important in the face of globalization.

2. Increased revenue through obtaining a percentage of the franchisees' sales
3. Expansion of the brand, allowing access to new market segments
4. Increased bargaining power with suppliers
5. The creation of economies of scale in areas such as purchasing and advertising

Franchiser Costs

1. Increased expenditure due to the need to monitor all franchisees' activities
2. Limitation of the franchising organization's ability to expand other methods of distribution (like alliances) due to territorial conflict
3. Increased number of decision makers within the system leading to a higher likelihood of conflict
4. Limitation of options for changing current operations because changes must occur throughout the entire franchise

Franchisee Benefits

1. Brand name recognition reduces risk by ensuring consumer awareness of the company. Thrifty Canada franchisees, for example, benefit from worldwide brand recognition and widespread advertising, as well as frequency-based programs linked with internationally and nationally recognized airlines, hotels, and other organizations.
2. Methods of operation are already decided, reducing the amount of time and money to start the company. This includes everything from the franchise layout and equipment to the entire marketing plan.
3. Costs are reduced, due to economies of scale gained from aspects like advertising and purchasing. One of the major benefits for Thrifty franchisees, for example, is help with buying cars, as car manufacturers will provide incentives for purchases when a company is part of a bigger system.
4. Free consulting on business issues
5. Assistance with financing

Franchisee Costs

1. The new organization must continually pay fees and royalties for the benefits that it will be receiving, such as the use of brand name and advertising.
2. Decision making is limited because of the amount of planning already done by the franchiser.
3. If one company in the organization performs badly, every company in the franchise is affected.

Overall, although there are costs to franchising, choosing this method of distribution has benefits to both franchiser and franchisee. This is why the number of franchises in Canada has seen such rapid growth. A successful restaurant franchise, White Spot, is profiled in the Case Study in this chapter, and the *Snapshot* on the opposite page underlines how much hotel franchises actually cost.

HOW MUCH DOES A HOTEL FRANCHISE ACTUALLY COST?

Most investors in hotels today require some type of chain affiliation before they will consider becoming involved in a hotel project. They believe that the benefits of having an established brand image, a central reservations system, coordinated marketing, and a frequent traveller program are worth the cost of associating with a hotel chain. Hotel companies that have an established brand give independent lodging owners the right to use their brand logo, reservations system, and other programs by either granting a franchise or actually taking over the property's management through a management contract. Globally, franchising has become the most popular method of obtaining brand identity because the hotel owner does not have to relinquish operational control.

The total cost of a hotel affiliation ranges from 2.3 percent of rooms revenue for Best Western to 11.3 percent for a Marriott hotel (see Table 7.1 on page 230). Most hotel brands cost between 8 percent and 10 percent of rooms revenue, the median being 8.3 percent. Other organizations achieving low percentages include Master Host Inns at 4.4 percent, Guesthouse Inns at 5.3 percent, and Key West Inns at 5.4 percent.

Hotel franchise affiliations usually entail several types of fees. They start with an initial fee typically based on a dollar amount per room. Ongoing fees usually include a royalty fee for the use of the trade name and service marks, an advertising or marketing contribution fee, reservation expenses, and frequent traveller program costs. Other fees often include computer software, training programs, global distribution systems, and equipment

rentals. The total of all these fees and expenses are used in calculating the percentage of rooms revenue to be paid to the franchiser. Table 7.2 on page 232 indicates the costs a franchisee might incur over a 10-year period, based on a mid-rate, 200-room chain hotel.

As the table shows, the cost of using a hotel chain affiliation can be significant. The total 10-year cost for a Best Western hotel, for example, would be more than $1 million, although the chain does have the lowest percentage of rooms revenue (2.3 percent). HVS International recommends that owners carefully evaluate the price/value relationship of all the potential hotel brands before signing a long-term franchise agreement. Unlike most franchise agreements that require 5-, 10-, or even 20-year commitments, Best Western memberships are renewed annually, with no long-term lock-in and no management fees, making this company very attractive to potential franchisees.

Best Western is more a membership association than a franchise, and is based on a simple idea and plan—uniting independent hoteliers to promote their properties and increase profitability. In addition to having the use of an internationally recognized brand name, members benefit from worldwide reservations and marketing services, the mass buying and bargaining power of thousands of hoteliers, and the experience and services of a professional headquarters staff. Costs of all major services and programs are included in the annual fees and dues. Some specialized services and programs are available at nominal charges, on a cost-recovery basis.

SNAPSHOT *continued*

Table 7.1

Cost of a Hotel Franchise over a 10-Year Period, as Percentage of Rooms Revenue

FIRST-CLASS CHAIN	% OF TOTAL ROOMS REVENUE, 2000	MIDRATE CHAIN	% OF TOTAL ROOMS REVENUE, 2000	ECONOMY CHAIN	% OF TOTAL ROOMS REVENUE, 2000
AmeriSuites	9.10	Best Western	2.30	AmeriHost Inn	9.70
Courtyard	9.50	Candlewood	8.10	AmericInn	7.80
Crowne Plaza	9.60	Clarion Hotel	7.50	Baymont	9.60
Doubletree	9.00	Club Hotel by Doubletree	9.60	Best Inns/ Suites of America	7.70
Doubletree Club	9.00	Comfort Inn/Hotel	10.50	Days Inn	10.30
Doubletree Guest Suites	9.00	Comfort Inn & Suites	10.50	Downtowner Inns	5.70
Embassy Suites	8.90	Comfort Suites	10.50	EconoLodge	8.40
Howthorn Suites	7.70	Country Inn & Suites	9.20	Guesthouse Inns	5.30
Hilton	10.10	Fairfield Inn	9.40	Homegate Suites	10.30
Hilton Garden Inn	10.00	Four Points	8.80	Howard Johnson	10.10
Homewood Suites	8.90	Hampton Inn/Suites	9.50	Key West Inn	5.40
Marriott	11.30	Holiday Inn	9.60	Key West Inn & Suites	5.40
Omni	6.80	Holiday Inn Select	9.60	Knights Inn	8.60
Park Plaza	8.90	Holiday Inn Sunspree	10.10	Mainstay Suites	9.60
Radisson	8.20	Holiday Inn Express	10.10	Microtel	8.30

TABLE 7.1 *continued*

FIRST-CLASS CHAIN	% OF TOTAL ROOMS REVENUE, 2000	MIDRATE CHAIN	% OF TOTAL ROOMS REVENUE, 2000	ECONOMY CHAIN	% OF TOTAL ROOMS REVENUE, 2000
Renaissance	8.70	Howard Johnson/Hotel	9.60	Motel 6	8.90
Residence Inn	8.10	Master Host Inns/Resort	4.40	Passport Inn/Suites	5.70
Sheraton	8.80	Park Inn	8.00	Ramada Ltd.	9.80
Staybridge Suites	9.20	Quality Hotel		Red Carpet Inn/Suites	6.30
Summerfield Suites	9.00	Quality Inn	9.30	Red Roof Inns	10.40
Westin	9.30	Quality Inn & Suites	9.30	Rodeway Inn	7.00
Wyndham	9.80	Quality Resort	9.30	Scottish Inns/Suites/Lodge	5.70
		Quality Suites	8.80	Shoney's Inn	8.80
		Ramada	9.40	Shoney's Inn & Suites	8.80
		Sleep Inn	9.30	Studio 6	7.60
		Sleep Inn & Suites	9.30	Sundowner Inns	7.10
		SpringHill Suites	10.20	Super 8	8.40
		TownePlace Suites	10.10	Travelodge	10.10
		Wellesley Inn	8.30	Villager Lodge	8.20
		Wellesley Inn & Suites	8.30		

SNAPSHOT *continued*

Table 7.2

HVS International Hotel Franchise Cost Analysis Guide

BASED ON MID-RATE 200-ROOM CHAIN HOTEL	TOTAL INITIAL COSTS ($)	TOTAL ROYALTY COSTS ($)	TOTAL RESERVATION COSTS ($)	TOTAL MARKETING COSTS ($)	TOTAL FREQUENT TRAVELLER COSTS ($)	TOTAL MISCELLANEOUS COSTS ($)	TOTAL 10-YEAR COSTS ($)	% OF TOTAL ROOMS REVENUE, 2000
Best Western	64 750	53 200	277 400	516 480	100 480	114 000	1 126 310	2.3
Comfort Inn	60 000	2 574 399	858 113	1 029 736	196 140	445 073	5 163 401	10.5
Hampton Inn	90 000	1 961 401	—	1 961 401	196 140	431 540	4 640 482	9.5
Holiday Inn	100 000	2 451 752	767 258	612 938	198 140	581 297	4 711 385	9.6
Ramada	71 000	1 961 401	1 103 288	1 103 288	—	370 475	4 609 453	9.4

Note: All monetary amounts are in US dollars.

Source: Rushmore, S. (2001, June). "What do hotel franchises actually cost? *Hotels, 35*(6); *Membership makes the difference*. (2002). Best Western membership document, Phoenix Arizona, 1–10.

DESIGNING THE DISTRIBUTION SYSTEM

Tourism organizations must decide how to make their services available to their selected target market by choosing their distribution mix strategy. This can be a complex decision. They must select a mix that will provide them with the maximum amount of exposure to potential travellers as well as ensure that the strategy chosen aligns with the company or destination image. In addition, the strategy should maximize control over sales and reservations and should work within the organization's budget.

An organization can consider three broad distribution strategy choices:

intensive distribution

strategy in which an organization maximizes the exposure of its travel services by distributing through all available outlets or intermediaries

exclusive distribution

strategy in which an organization deliberately restricts the number of channels that it uses to distribute its product or service to its customers; an effective method for marketing prestige products

selective distribution

strategy between intensive and exclusive distribution, in which a company uses more than one but less than all of the possible distribution channels

1. **Intensive distribution.** In this case the organization maximizes the exposure of its travel services by distributing through all available outlets or intermediaries. This strategy is most useful for an organization that is trying to obtain high market coverage. An example of a Canadian tourism organization that uses this strategy is Air Canada.

2. **Exclusive distribution.** Here the organization deliberately restricts the number of channels that it uses to distribute its product or service to its customers. Because only a limited number of intermediaries are given the right to distribute the product, the result is often a strengthening of the company's image and an increase in the status of those who purchase the product. This strategy is an effective method for prestige tourism products and is used by companies like Canadian Mountain Holidays, profiled in the opening vignette.

3. **Selective distribution.** In this strategy between intensive and exclusive distribution, a company uses more than one but less than all of the possible distribution channels. The Rocky Mountaineer (see Case Study in Chapter 9) employs selective distribution, using sales representation in 18 countries to sell over a half-million tours each year.

Before an organization begins to design its distribution strategy, it is important that it consider the following five factors:

1. *Market coverage.* The amount of market coverage should be considered in coordination with the organization's goals and objectives, as this factor will directly impact the particular distribution mix that is best for the company.

2. *Costs.* Only the most cost-effective distribution methods should be implemented, and they should make effective use of the organization's budget.

3. *Positioning and image.* The distribution strategy chosen should be consistent with the position and image that the company wants to achieve and maintain.

4. *Motivation of intermediaries.* Intermediaries should be provided with appropriate incentives in order to motivate them to sell the product or service to consumers. The Quebec City Convention Bureau, for example, hosts about 700 tour operators and 400 meeting planners on custom itineraries each year. Thse trips provide an excellent promotional forum for giving intermediaries a first-hand appreciation of the facilities and services being offered.

5. *Characteristics of the tourism organization.* Each organization has unique characteristics and needs that are specific to its operations. These needs must be considered when designing the distribution strategy. For example, if an organization operates in a manner that requires it to communicate directly with the consumer in order to be successful, then it must develop its distribution strategy to meet those needs.

The opening vignette showed how an exclusive distribution strategy worked well for Canadian Mountain Holidays. Another example of a company playing "hard to get" comes from a ramshackle Victorian farmhouse two hours northwest of Toronto. Here, a back-road Ontario purveyor of suckling pig and home-grown squab has been ranked as one of the top 10 restaurants in the world. Eigensinn Farm, the rustic eatery of famed chef Michael Stadtlander, earned ninth place on a list of the 50 best dining establishments on the planet, according to a recent restaurant guide.[11] The restaurant, inconveniently located hours from the city, seats no more than 16 people per evening. It serves six-course dinners that include game and livestock raised on its own acreage, seasoned with herbs grown in its own garden. According to recent marketing theory, customers crave exclusivity,[12] and Eigensinn Farm certainly provides evidence that playing "hard to get" can sometimes be effective!

Cruise lines, too, have a carefully planned distribution strategy. These companies have traditionally used exclusive distribution, but are gradually moving toward selective distribution. Roughly 90 percent of cruises are sold through traditional travel agencies, and in today's economy suppliers are reluctant to jeopardize these firmly established, reliable relationships, despite the agency commissions involved. However, online cruise sales reached approximately $900 million in 2003, up 61 percent from 2002.[13] Even though only 10 percent of cruises are predicted to be sold online by 2005, the Internet is now an important part of the equation, as many consumers will make their travel decisions online, even if they ultimately purchase offline. Cruise lines work with online travel agencies to sell discount and last-minute inventory, but they use their own Web sites for marketing purposes rather for than direct sales. Many companies don't even feature consumer booking engines on their sites. In the United States, 54 percent of online cruise sales in 2002 were generated from online travel agencies, Travelocity.com grabbing one-third of this business.

DISTRIBUTION CHANNEL MANAGEMENT

channel management

a process that includes selecting and motivating individual channel members and evaluating their performance over time

Once the tourism organization has decided on its distribution mix strategy, it must implement and manage the chosen distribution channel. **Channel management** includes selecting and motivating individual channel members and evaluating their performance over time.

Selecting Channel Members

Tourism organizations must share information and work closely with the members of their distribution system. It is critical, therefore, that an organization selects the best suited channel members in order to ensure an effective distribution system. When selecting channel members, the service provider should determine the characteristics that distinguish the most valuable marketing intermediaries from the others. Evaluation criteria may include such aspects as a channel member's number of years in business, the services and products it already carries, its past growth and financial history, its level of cooperativeness, and its reputation and image.

Motivating Channel Members

After an organization has selected its distribution channel members, it must continually motivate these members to perform their best. Three incentives are commonly used to motivate a company's intermediaries. The first one is financial, and includes commissions and bonuses. The second incentive often used in the tourism industry is the provision of educational trips for intermediary staff, during which they can experience the supplier's product for themselves. Such "familiarization trips" are common in the travel agency sector. Another incentive, again quite common in travel agencies, is to provide intermediaries with reduced-price holidays. This type of incentive gives intermediaries greater knowledge of the product and enthusiasm for selling it to consumers.

Evaluating Channel Members

Tourism organizations must constantly monitor each channel member's performance in order to ensure the success of the channel as a whole. Performance can be measured through the generation of sales, customer delivery time, and/or the success of combined promotional efforts among intermediaries. Channel members who perform well should be recognized and rewarded, and assistance should be provided to those who are struggling to meet the company's goals and objectives. The organization should also "re-qualify" its channel members periodically and replace the weaker members that harm the overall effectiveness of the distribution system. One reason that Best Western likes to renew contracts annually is so that it can maintain control over the distribution channel. The company has also implemented a "quality assurance process," whereby a quality inspection team will use the same criteria to review every one of the member hotels around the world. Finally, the Best Western Web site gives customers the opportunity to provide online feedback regarding service quality.

CHAPTER SUMMARY

A company's distribution system is essential to delivering its product to the consumer. There are two different distribution channels that the service provider or principal can pursue: direct or indirect channels. In a direct channel, a company delivers its product to the consumer without the outside assistance of any independent intermediaries. In an indirect channel, the supplier makes use of several marketing intermediaries in order to help distribute its product. These intermediaries are independent associations that are not under the company's control, including such organizations as travel agents, tour operators, convention and meeting planners, travel specialists, and the Internet sites.

The conventional marketing system consists of a loose collection of organizations, each of which tries to maximize the benefits of the channel for its own best interests. However, under a vertical marketing system, organizations work together to achieve group objectives established by the channel as a whole, resulting in benefits for each independent party.

There are two main forms of vertical marketing systems: alliances and franchises. Alliances are partnerships formed when two or more organizations combine resources through a contractual agreement that allows them to overcome each other's weaknesses by benefitting from one another's strengths. Franchises are formed when a franchiser grants a franchisee the right to engage in offering, selling, or distributing the franchiser's goods or services under its marketing format.

When designing its distribution system, a company can choose among three different types of strategy: intensive distribution, in which an organization maximizes the exposure of its travel services by distributing through all available outlets or intermediaries; exclusive distribution, in which an organization deliberately restricts the number of channels that it uses to distribute its product or service to its customers; and selective distribution, in which a company uses more than one but less than all of the possible distribution channels. But before an organization begins to design its distribution strategy, it is important that it consider the following five factors: market coverage, costs, positioning and image, motivation of intermediaries, and the characteristics of the tourism organization itself. In order for the company to ensure the effective execution of its distribution strategy, it must select individual channel members, motivate these members, and monitor their performance over time.

KEY TERMS

alliance, p. 224
channel conflict, p. 221
channel management, p. 234
conventional marketing system, p. 222
direct distribution channel, p. 210
directional selling, p. 222
distribution channel, p. 210
distribution system, p. 208

exclusive distribution, p. 223
franchises, p. 227
horizontal conflict, p. 221
indirect distribution channel, p. 211
intensive distribution, p. 233
junket representatives, p. 217
marketing intermediaries, p. 211

motivational houses, p. 217
selective distribution, p. 233
tour brokers, p. 217
tour operators, p. 215
travel agents, p. 212
travel specialists, p. 216
vertical conflict, p. 222
vertical marketing system, p. 222

DISCUSSION QUESTIONS AND EXERCISES

1. How does the tourism and hospitality industry's distribution system differ from that of other industries?

2. Explain the difference between the structure of a conventional marketing system and that of a vertical marketing system. Can you think of two companies in the Canadian tourism industry that use these two different strategies?

3. Choose a company within the Canadian tourism industry and explain how it uses its distribution strategy to attract customers to its product. Do you think that the company is using the most effective distribution channel available to it? What do you recommend that the company do to improve its distribution system?

4. Considering two different franchise organizations in Canada, compare the different distribution strategies used by each franchise. Which franchise do you think is more effective in distributing its product or service to consumers?

5. What are the two different types of channel conflict that can arise in a distribution system? Give one example for each type from the tourism industry in Canada. How can these conflicts be resolved?

6. How would you evaluate the performance of a channel member as the manager of a large hotel franchise?

CASE STUDY

WHITE SPOT RESTAURANTS: A FRANCHISING SUCCESS STORY

In 1914, a 12-year old boy named Nat Bailey left his home in Minnesota to make a living on his own. He crossed the Canadian border into British Columbia and settled in Vancouver, where for many years he sold peanuts, hot dogs, and hamburgers at sporting events. Recognizing that there was money to be made in the food service industry, he scraped enough cash together to buy a Model T Ford that he converted into a small restaurant on wheels. The success of Bailey's venture led to his establishment of the White Spot Barbeque, on Granville Street, where Bailey managed to woo the appetites and patronage of Western diners by employing a simple, three-pronged recipe for success that endures to this day: quality, service, and consistency. The intervening years of expansion eventually led to the development of today's White Spot Restaurants, a collection of family casual-dining spots that includes 58 full-service operations and 28 quick-service outlets. The family of corporately owned and franchised operations generated $120 million in system-wide sales in the year 2000. From the modest Granville Street cabin that functioned with three employees, the company's staff has grown to 3500—a work force that in 2001 served 13 million White Spot customers.

In 1993, a full 65 years after the launch of the first White Spot restaurant, the company opened its first franchise location in Vernon, B.C. Today, Canada's two most westerly provinces are home to 38 franchised, full-service restaurants and 23 Triple-O franchises, the company's branch of quick-service operations. The remainder of White Spot's eateries are company-owned and -operated. White Spot management has a clear vision when it comes to the selection of new recruits. Company president Warren Erhart says potential franchises are not required to have a food-service background, but a previous track record in the business field is a definite asset. Some of the core values sought by the franchiser mirror the principles held by the

founder: integrity, innovation, a high energy level, communication skills, and a strong sense of community involvement.

Paul Gilley, one of White Spot's earliest recruits, represents a model example of what the company seeks in its franchisees. In 1994, he signed up for his first full-service franchise in Langley, B.C., and over the next five years purchased four additional operations, primarily in the Greater Vancouver Area. Gilley seemed ideally suited to join the White Spot family. He had spent a number of years in the retail sector, holding the position of head of Blockbuster Video for B.C., doing a stint in heavy equipment sales, and spending a few years as a Vancouver-based franchisee for AAMCO Transmissions. When Gilley learned that franchise opportunities with White Spot were available, the man who had grown up with the restaurant legend opted to invest. "White Spot was a highly respected name in the West and I had been a customer all my life," he says.

Gilley advises potential franchisees that being a people person is important, as is the willingness to work hard in a vibrant and challenging environment. "The expectations of White Spot customers are high, and you have to constantly work to maintain the level of quality and service the restaurant

Table 7.3

Franchise Costs for White Spot Restaurants

NATURE OF INVESTMENT	HIGH ($)	LOW ($)	TO WHOM PAID
Initial franchise fee	75 000	75 000	Franchiser
Construction of leaseholds improvements	420 000	250 000	Contractor
Acquisition and installation of fixtures and equipment	280 000	240 000	Suppliers and installation contractors
Initial inventory/supplies	20 000	15 000	Franchiser and suppliers
Start-up costs (advertising, etc.)	50 000	30 000	Franchiser and suppliers
TOTAL	**845 000**	**610 000**	

Source: Carter, D. (2002). Success marks the Spot. *Franchise Canada, 2*(5), 26–31. Retrieved May 30, 2002, from http://www.whitespot.ca.

has become known for," he says. Although Gilley says that the process of growing a White Spot business requires long hours (restaurants operate from 6:30 a.m. to 11 p.m.) and a resolute focus, the opportunity for financial reward is unquestionable. While Gilley admits that several variables exist, his experience shows that it is entirely possible to discharge the capital investment required to purchase a full-service franchise in five years or less.

Depending on size and location, the cost to purchase a full-service White Spot franchise ranges from $610 000 to $845 000 (see Table 7.3). An approved franchisee's investment portfolio incorporates a base franchise fee of $75 000, plus the costs of restaurant construction or renovation of existing retail space, fixtures and equipment, initial inventory and supplies, and start-up costs such as advertising. Erhart says that approved franchisees, who participate in a three-month training program, are not just buying a restaurant in which they can become independent and successful entrepreneurs; they are buying into a respected legend in the foodservice field. "The financial rewards possible are

borne out by the number of existing franchisees who have been able to purchase a second or third restaurant," he says.

Company management is a reliable source of ongoing support for both new and seasoned White Spot franchises. Operating under the umbrella of the company's Vancouver-based head office, a staff of business consultants is available to provide franchisees with advice and assistance on everything from operational procedures to marketing, human relations, and financial matters. "Our business consultants are accessible to franchisees 24 hours a day, seven days a week," says Erhart. An important element in the franchisee/franchiser relationship is a two-way line of communication. "New franchisees bring fresh blood to the company, and their ideas for the advancement of White Spot restaurants are welcomed," says Erhart. Franchisees are invited to sit on various committees that examine all aspects of the business, from corporate direction to menu development.

As for the future, White Spot aims to continue to be a leader, not a follower, in the foodservice field; it is a front-runner in the full-service restaurant sector. The company president asserts that staying at the top of the heap will involve keeping pace with the ever-changing demands of the dining public. While renowned tried-and-true favourites will not be abandoned, White Spot will continue to add menu items according to customer trends. In addition to the chain's evolving menu, White Spot continually invests in the brand through the renovation of existing restaurants. Over the last decade, the company has upgraded many of its operations to include full bars. "As we renovate our restaurants, it is important for us to maintain the comfort levels our guests have come to love, at the same time incorporating a social element with the addition of our bar/lounge areas," says company marketing director Chiyoko Kakino. White Spot is also planning to expand into Central and Eastern Canada, a beckoning market previously untapped by the Western Canadian food chain. The current planning strategy ultimately calls for several franchised outlets, primarily in high-population centres such as Toronto.

Source: Carter, D. (2002). Success marks the Spot. *Franchise Canada, 2*(5), 26–31.

QUESTIONS

1. Do you think White Spot should be considering expanding into Central and Eastern Canada? What specific franchising problems may arise from a planned expansion?
2. The benefits and costs of franchising were discussed in this chapter. What specific benefits and costs apply to both franchiser and franchisee in the White Spot case?
3. Why do you think that White Spot chooses to own and operate some of its restaurants itself? Why not put them all out to franchise?
4. What skills do you think would be required to operate a White Spot franchise? Check out the White Spot Web site for material to support you answer.

WEB SITES

www.adventurecollection.com
The Adventure Collection

www.aircanada.ca
Air Canada

www.acta.ca
Association of Canadian Travel Agents

www.bestwestern.com
Best Western hotels

www.canadagolf.com
Canadian Golf Tourism Alliance

www.cmhski.com
Canadian Mountain Holidays

www.cstar.ca
Canadian Standard Travel Agency Registry

www.conquestvacations.com
Conquest Vacations

www.destina.ca
Destina.ca (Air Canada's online travel agency)

www.expedia.ca
Expedia.ca (online travel agency)

www.hoteldiscounts.com
hoteldiscount!com (online hotel agency)

www.hedna.org
Hotel Electronic Distribution Network Association

www.iata.org
International Air Transport Association

www.skyserviceairlines.com
Skyservice

www.thrifty.ca
Thrifty Car Rental

www.timhortons.com
Tim Hortons

www.travelocity.ca
Travelocity.ca (online travel agency)

www.whitespot.ca
White Spot Restaurants

ENDNOTES

1. Agencies closing up shop expected to accelerate. (2002). *Travel Week, 30*(14), 1.
2. Pashby, C. (2002, March 28). Travel agents band together to fight cuts. *Canmore Leader*, p. A19.
3. Canadian Tourism Commission. (2002). GDS hotel bookings down but not out. Retrieved March 1, 2002, from http://www.canadatourism.com/en/ctc/ctx/ctx-news/search/newsbydateform.cfm.
4. Christian, R. (2001). Developing an online access strategy: Issues facing small to medium-sized tourism and hospitality enterprises. *Journal of Vacation Marketing, 7*(2), 170–178.
5. Reinders, J., & Baker, M. (1998). The future for direct retailing of travel and tourism products: The influence of information technology. *Progress in Tourism and Hospitality Research, 4*, 1–15.
6. World Trade Organization Business Council. (1999). *Marketing tourism destinations online. Strategies for the information age.* Madrid: World Trade Organization.
7. Buhasz, L. (2002, March 30). Travellers rely on the Web. *The Globe and Mail*, p. T3.
8. Porter, M. E. (2001). Strategy and the Internet. *Harvard Business Review, 79*(3), 63–78.
9. Alford, P. (2000). E-business models in the travel industry. *Travel & Tourism Analyst, 3*, 67–86.
10. Hudson, S., Snaith, T., Miller, G.A., & Hudson, P. (2001). Distribution channels in the travel industry: Using mystery shoppers to understand the influence of travel agency recommendations. *Journal of Travel Research, 40*(2), 148–154.
11. Abraham, C. (2002, November 3). Tiny Ontario restaurant makes world 10-best list. *The Globe and Mail*, pp. A1–A2.
12. Brown, S. (2001). Torment your customers: They'll love it. *Harvard Business Review, 79*(9), 83–88.
13. Travel down 5% but U.S. online sales up 37% in 2002. (2003). *Travelweek, 31*(14), 10–11.

Marketing Communications:
The Role of Advertising and
Sales Promotions

DAYS INNS RECEIVES ADVERTISING AWARD

In 2002, Days Inn Canada was honoured by the Canadian Franchise Association with a Gold Frankie in the Television category for its television advertisement "The Affair." Aimed at addressing brand image, "The Affair," written by Pirate Radio & Television and produced and directed by Apple Box Productions—both of Toronto—opens with a grainy video surveillance tape in which we see a man entering a Days Inn. We hear a voice-over, in which the man's wife tells two private investigators, "I started getting suspicious about a month ago. Every Thursday night, he'd say he was working late." Next we see the private investigators burst into the hotel room, only to see the boxer-short-clad husband, who has been lying on the bed with remote control and *TV Guide* in hand, jump up in fright. "I - I - I just love the room," he says, followed by a quick montage of room shots. The advertisement ends with the narrator's voice-over, which says, "If lovin' us is wrong, we don't want to be right."

"We are very honoured to receive this award from the Canadian Franchise Association," says Melissa Evans, Days Inn Canada's vice-president of marketing. "The Days Inn product has changed dramatically over the past few years with the addition of a number of new construction properties as well as a tremendous amount of renovations at our existing properties. This commercial positions Days Inn in a new light that reflects these changes." Frankie Awards honour creative achievement by businesses in the franchise sector and are presented annually by the Canadian Franchise Association. The Association represents over 350 companies in the franchising business in Canada. This is the second time "The Affair" has been honoured. In February 2002, Days Inn Canada was presented with a 2001 Finalist Certificate award in the New York Festivals Television & Cinema Advertising Awards Competition, in the Travel/Tourism category.

Source: Winters, B. (2002). They loved it, they really loved it—CFA honours Days Inn with a "Frankie." Retrieved May 6, 2002, from http://www.canadatourism.com/en/ctc/ctx/ctxnews/search/newsbydateform.cfm.

Objectives

On completion of this chapter, readers should understand

- the role of promotion within marketing;
- the various marketing promotion tools used in tourism and hospitality;
- the communication process;
- the importance of integrated marketing communications (IMC);

- the stages involved in an integrated marketing communications campaign plan;
- the role of advertising in the promotional mix;
- sales promotion objectives and techniques used in tourism and hospitality; and
- types of joint promotions.

Chapter Overview

Effective communication with target customers is carried out by a variety of methods, referred to as "marketing communications." The opening vignette offers an example of the successful implementation of the promotional technique known as "advertising." The next three chapters look at the various promotional techniques used by tourism and hospitality providers. Chapter 8 begins with an introduction of the role and types of promotional tools used in tourism and hospitality. A section follows that focuses on the communication process. The chapter then discusses the rise of integrated marketing communications (IMC) as a result of the recognition that advertising can no longer be crafted and executed in isolation from other promotional mix elements. Consideration is then given to the communication techniques of advertising and sales promotion. Chapters 9 and 10 analyze the remaining communication tools, including public relations, personal selling, word of mouth, direct marketing, and Internet marketing.

THE ROLE OF PROMOTION IN MARKETING

In many people's perception, marketing is promotion, for promotion is the highly visible, public face of marketing. However, promotion is only one element of the marketing mix, its role being to convince potential customers of the benefits of purchasing or using the products and services of a particular organization. Organizations use marketing communications—promotional tools used to communicate effectively with customers— for many reasons other than simply launching new products. They may, for example, be trying to encourage potential customers to try their product at the same time as encouraging their existing customers to purchase or use the same product again. Together with marketing, marketing communications dramatically increased in importance in the 1980s and 1990s, to the extent that effective, sustained communication with customers is now seen as critical to the success of any organization, whether in the private, public, or not-for-profit sector, from international airlines to tourism destinations and attractions.

MARKETING PROMOTION TOOLS

Promotions decisions will be determined by the overall marketing plan, as illustrated in Figure 8.1. Chapter 2 explains how marketing objectives are derived from the strategic tools of targeting and positioning (see pp. 50–55). The marketing mix is then used to achieve these objectives, and promotions are just one part of this marketing mix.

Figure 8.1 The Role of Promotions in the Marketing Strategy

promotional mix

a company's total marketing communications program

The blend of promotional elements outlined in Table 8.1 on page 246 is known as the **promotional mix**, and promotional management involves coordinating all the elements, setting objectives and budgets, designing programs, evaluating performance, and taking corrective action. Promotion can be a short-term activity, but considered at a strategic level it is a mid- and long-term investment aimed at building up a consistent and credible corporate or destination identity. Promotion, when used effectively, builds and creates an identity for the product or the organization. Brochures, advertisements, in-store merchandising, sales promotions, and so on, create the identity of the company in the mind of the consumer, and all aspects of the promotional effort should therefore project the same image to the consumer.

This chapter discusses the first two tools listed in Table 8.1—advertising and sales promotion—and Chapters 9 and 10 discuss the remaining five promotional tools.

It is worth clarifying that promotion management deals explicitly with the promotional mix. In contrast, **marketing communications** is an all-encompassing term (and activity) that includes communication via any and all of the marketing mix elements. How a product is packaged, priced, and distributed all communicate an image to a customer just as much as how the product is promoted.

marketing communications

an all-encompassing term (and activity) that includes communication via any and all of the marketing mix elements.

Table 8.1

The Promotional Mix Used in Tourism and Hospitality

PROMOTIONAL TOOL	TOURISM AND HOSPITALITY APPLICATION
Advertising	Television, newspapers, magazines, billboards, Internet, brochures, guidebooks
Sales promotion	Short-term incentives to induce purchase. Aimed at salespeople, distributors such as travel agents, and consumers. Can be joint promotions. Include merchandising and familiarization trips.
Public relations	All non-paid media exposure appearing as editorial coverage. Includes sponsorship of events and causes.
Personal selling	Meetings and workshops for intermediaries; telephone contact and travel agents for consumers
Word of mouth	Promotion by previous consumers to their social and professional contacts. Often perceived by consumers to be the most credible form of promotion.
Direct marketing	Direct mail, telemarketing, and travel exhibitions
Internet marketing	Direct e-mail marketing, Internet advertising, customer service, and selling and market research

THE COMMUNICATION PROCESS

The marketing literature reflects a long-standing interest in explaining the principles of the communication process that takes place between the sender and receiver of a message. The most commonly adopted generalized model comprises four components: sender, message, medium, and receiver. The communication process is outlined in Figure 8.2. The diagram presents a scenario in which the message is prepared in a symbolic form by the sender (a cruise line for example) for the prospective audience, perhaps as a visual representation. This process is referred to as "encoding." The message is then transmitted by way of a suitable medium such as a television advertising campaign. The receiver sees the message and decodes it; "decoding" is the method by which the message is filtered or internalized. The major concern of the sender at this stage is that the message is not distorted in the process by what is termed "noise." For example, a television advertisement showing a cruise ship at the same time as a news item referring to a sinking ship would fail to convey a convincing message. Likewise, the message might be distorted by clutter, which means the audience may see an excessive number of commercial messages that just get in the way of the advertiser's intended message.

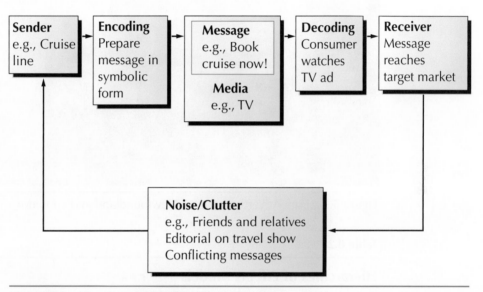

Figure 8.2 The Communication Process

How Communication Works

There are a number of models that show how communication works, particularly in advertising. The models developed invariably assume that customers follow a number of predetermined stages, commencing with awareness and progressing to purchase. The most commonly cited model is that first proposed by Strong,[1] called the **AIDA model** (attention, interest, desire, and action). The idea of this model is that communication should first attract the receiver's attention, then engage the receiver's interest, then create in the receiver a desire for the product or service, and then inspire action in the receiver. For example, in the print advertisement for Newfoundland and Labrador in Figure 8.3 on page 248, the tail of a humpback whale with a giant iceberg in the background grabs the reader's attention; this visual image works with the print copy to gain the reader's interest and to provoke the desire in him or her to travel to that part of Canada. The Web site and 1-800 number are included in the ad to inspire action. Though undoubtedly over-simplistic, the AIDA model is a memorable and useful checklist of the aims of advertising, and it provides a framework for other, more complex theories. All of the models of communication that have been developed are known as "hierarchies of effects models," as they assume a progression from one stage to the next (see Table 8.2 on page 248).

AIDA model

a memorable and useful checklist of the aims of advertising, standing for **a**ttention, **i**nterest, **d**esire, and **a**ction

Figure 8.3 Print Advertisement for Newfoundland and Labrador

Table 8.2

Hierarchies of Effects Models

TYPE OF EFFECT	STRONG (1925)	LAVIDGE & STEINER (1961)	ROGERS (1962)	BROADBENT & JACOBS (1984)	COLLEY (1961)	WELLS ET AL. (2003)
Cognitive	Attention	Awareness → Knowledge	Awareness	Problem Recognition → Information Search	Awareness → Comprehension	Perception → Learning
Affective	Interest → Desire	Liking → Preference → Conviction	Interest → Evaluation	Attitude → Intention	Conviction	Persuasion
Behavioural	Action	Purchase	Trial	Behaviour → Adoption	Action	Behaviour

All the hierarchies of effects models have as their basis the assumption that an effective advertisement makes the receiver think about the product, feel positively toward it, and do something to purchase it. Lavidge and Steiner label these the cognitive, affective, and conative stages of the response.[2] The cognitive stage involves the rational, conscious part of the brain; the affective stage involves the emotions; and the conative stage, a resulting change in behaviour. The authors distinguish between simple awareness and real knowledge of the product, and grade the affective response from mere liking, through preference, to conviction. Rogers argues that the effect of advertising is to interest the consumer enough to evaluate the merits of the product and then to give it a trial before adopting it.[3] Broadbent and Jacobs go further in saying that it is often the trial and not the advertisement that convinces the customer to change an attitude toward a product.[4] Colley presents the DAGMAR model (**d**efining **a**dvertising **g**oals for **m**easured **a**dvertising **r**esults), which begins with awareness, moves to comprehension, then to conviction, and ends with action.[5]

Finally, Wells et al. suggest that there is a set of categories of typical effects that advertisers hope to achieve.[6] The first category is perception, which means the advertiser hopes the ad will be noticed and remembered. Then there are two categories of effects that are focused either on learning, which means the audience will understand the message and make the correct associations, or on persuasion, which means the advertiser hopes to create or change attitudes or touch emotions. The last major category of effects is behaviour: getting the audience to try or buy the product or perform some other action. These factors of message effectiveness are further illustrated in Table 8.3.

DAGMAR model

a hierarchies of effects model that stands for defining advertising goals for measured advertising results

Table 8.3

Message Effectiveness Factors

KEY MESSAGE EFFECTS	SURROGATE MEASURES	COMMUNICATION TOOLS
Perception	Exposure	Advertising; Public relations
	Attention	Advertising; Sales promotion
	Interest	Advertising; Sales promotion; Public relations
	Memory: recognition/recall	Advertising; Sales promotion; Public relations
Learning	Understanding	Public relations; Personal selling; Direct marketing; Advertising
	Image and association; brand links	Advertising; Public relations; Point-of-purchase ads
Persuasion	Attitudes: form or change Preference/intention	Public relations; Personal selling; Sales promotion
	Emotions and involvement	Advertising; Public relations; Personal selling
	Conviction: belief, commitment	Personal selling; Direct marketing

TABLE 8.3 *continued*

KEY MESSAGE EFFECTS	SURROGATE MEASURES	COMMUNICATION TOOLS
Behaviour	Trial	Sales promotion; Personal selling; Direct marketing
	Purchase	Sales promotion; Personal selling; Direct marketing
	Repeat purchase; Use more	Sales promotion; Personal selling; Direct marketing

Source: Wells, W., Burnett, B., & Moriarty, S. (2003). *Advertising principles and practice.* Englewood Cliffs, NJ: Prentice Hall, 9.

In the table, the key categories of message effects are listed down the left-hand side. The second column, "surrogate measures," refers to the effects that advertisers seek to achieve and that they later use to evaluate how effective the advertisement was in achieving its objectives. The third column lists the communication tools that may be most appropriate for achieving the objective. The table illustrates that advertising is just one part of the communication mix, and that there are situations in which other communication tools may be more effective. For example, sales promotions are more effective in getting people to respond with a purchase or other types of actions.

THE GROWTH OF INTEGRATED MARKETING COMMUNICATIONS (IMC) IN TOURISM

integrated marketing communications (IMC)

the unification of all marketing communications tools, as well as corporate and brand messages, so they send a consistent, persuasive message to target audiences

Perhaps one of the most important advances in marketing in recent decades has been the rise of **integrated marketing communications (IMC)**—the unification of all marketing communications tools, as well as corporate and brand messages, so they send a consistent, persuasive message to target audiences. This approach recognizes that advertising can no longer be crafted and executed in isolation from other promotional mix elements. As tourism markets and the media have grown more complex and fragmented, consumers find themselves in an ever more confusing marketing environment. Tourism marketers must address this situation by conveying a consistent, unified message in all their promotional activities. IMC programs coordinate all communication messages and sources of an organization. An IMC campaign includes traditional marketing communication tools, such as advertising or sales promotion, but recognizes that other areas of the marketing mix are also used in communications. Planning and managing these elements so they work together helps to build a consistent brand or company image.

An Integrated Marketing Communications (IMC) Campaign

An integrated marketing communications campaign is composed of a complex set of interlocking, coordinated activities strategically designed to meet a set of objectives and to solve some critical problem within a specified time period, usually a year or less. The campaign is designed around a creative theme that extends across time and includes various advertising vehicles or marketing communication activities. Table 8.4 outlines an IMC campaign plan, the components of which are discussed in more detail below.

Marketing in Action in this chapter provides an example of an IMC campaign—Travel Alberta's "Alberta Made to Order" campaign—that used a variety of communication tools to send one consistent message to consumers and trade. Another example is Tourism Vancouver's winter 2002 communications program, which featured an "indulgence" theme to coincide with the time of year when people seek rest and relaxation to recoup from the hectic holiday season. The Indulgence Package included a two-night stay at one of Vancouver's top hotels, complimentary parking, breakfast for two, and one other amenity, ranging from spa passes or champagne to handmade chocolates or dinner vouchers. The Tourism Vancouver winter packages and specials were available via the organization's Web site (www.tourismvancouver.com) and were marketed through a mix of radio promotions and events. The program was also supported with print insertions in the *Seattle Times*, which profiled the destination within a larger British Columbia focus. The Web site featured special sections providing information and listings on arts, culture,

Table 8.4

An IMC Campaign Plan

STEPS IN THE CAMPAIGN	DETAILS
1. Situation analysis	Product and company research Consumer and stakeholder research Industry and market analysis Competitive analysis
2. SWOT (strengths, weaknesses, opportunities, and threats) analysis	Internal strengths and weaknesses External opportunities and threats Problem identification
3. Campaign strategy	Objectives Targeting Positioning
4. Message strategy	Message development research The creative theme Tactics and executions
5. Media plan	Media mix Scheduling and timing
6. Other marketing communications activities	Sales promotion Direct marketing Public relations
7. Appropriation and budget	Based on the cost of reaching the target market
8. Campaign evaluation	Measure the effectiveness of stated objectives

and retail options for the visitor during the winter season. All Indulgence Packages, plus room-only product, could be booked online throughout the three-month campaign. Getaways could also be booked by calling a 1-800 number provided in the ad.

1. Situation Analysis

situation analysis

a business review that summarizes all the relevant information available about the product, the company, the competitive environment, the industry, and the consumers

The first section of most campaign plans is a situation analysis, which is a business review that summarizes all the relevant information available about the product, the company, the competitive environment, the industry, and the consumers. This information is obtained using primary and secondary research techniques (see Chapter 4).

2. SWOT Analysis

SWOT analysis

a technique that provides scope for an organization to list all its strengths, weaknesses, opportunities, and threats

The section of the plan that follows a situation analysis builds on this analysis by evaluating the significance of the research. Some plans include a section called "Problems and Opportunities"; others call it a SWOT analysis, meaning an analysis of the strengths, weaknesses, opportunities, and threats the company or brand faces (see Chapter 2). In the case of Travel Alberta, research had illuminated the problem of a general lack of awareness of travel opportunities in Alberta among consumers. This had to be addressed in the communication campaign.

3. Campaign Strategy

After the situation analysis and the SWOT analysis, most advertising and IMC campaign plans focus on the key strategic decisions and programs that direct the campaign. The strategy section identifies the objectives that will solve the key problems identified at the end of the SWOT analysis. It also specifies the target stakeholder audiences and how the strategy will handle competitive advantage and the product's position. Objectives guide the development of the campaign's strategy. These objectives are established based on an understanding of the hierarchy of effects and the various ways in which communication can affect an audience. At the end of the campaign, the company can compare its results against these objectives to measure the campaign's success. Chapter 2 highlights the factors necessary for effective and actionable objectives (see p. 50), and these also apply to communications objectives. For example, it is important that objectives are measurable, either directly or indirectly. The objectives for the Travel Alberta campaign, for example, were to encourage Albertans to visit all six regions of the province, to alter current travel preferences, and to increase the amount of travel within Alberta (see *Marketing in Action*).

In many cases, the final response required from an IMC campaign is purchase. But purchase is the result of a long process of consumer decision making. The marketing communicator needs to know where the target audience stands in relation to the product and to what state it needs to be moved. The audience may be in any of a large variety of buyer readiness states such as awareness, knowledge, liking, preference, conviction, or purchase. For example, Travel Alberta discovered in consumers a general lack of awareness of travel opportunities within Alberta, so the organization made an attempt to change this situation through advertising. It used television and editorial coverage to generate more knowledge and positive feelings toward travel opportunities in Alberta. The campaign was successful in changing preferences, as research after the campaign discovered that the percentage of survey respondents that had Alberta as a "top of the mind" travel destination had increased by more than 20 percent. Finally, Albertans were obviously convinced enough to take action, as domestic tourism in Alberta increased considerably in the year following the campaign (see *Marketing in Action*).

4. Message Strategy

The message strategy (and the choice of what type of creative approach to use for the various stakeholder audiences) flows from an understanding of the key communication problems and objectives. The message, or creative strategy, outlines the impression the campaign intends to convey to the target audience. Variations on the creative approach are tested through **concept testing**, in which a simple statement of the idea (usually a sketch with a key phrase) is tried out on people who are representative of the target audience to get their reactions to the product. The message strategy in a campaign includes this creative concept and its variations, known as executions, which carry the concept across different media, situations, stakeholder audiences, and times of year. Often an "umbrella" theme is used, as in Travel Alberta's "Alberta Made to Order" program. A strong umbrella theme not only holds the various ads in a campaign together but also creates synergy, meaning that the impact of the whole campaign is greater than the sum of the individual parts.

concept testing

testing new product concepts with a group of target consumers to find out if the concept has strong consumer appeal

5. Media Plan

In the Travel Alberta campaign, the media plan included using TV, radio, brochures, newspapers, and other promotional vehicles to stimulate people to spend more time travelling in Alberta. All these media outlets are referred to as the **media mix**—created by media planners by selecting the best combination of traditional media vehicles (print, broadcast, etc.); nontraditional media (electronic media, unexpected places like the floors of stores); and marketing communication tools such as public relations, direct marketing, and sales promotion to reach the targeted stakeholder audiences. If a product has an awareness problem, widespread mass media would probably increase the general level of awareness. If the problem is lack of trial, sales promotion may be the most important tool. If the product appeals to a very small market, then the Internet may be the best means of reaching that target audience. Media planners allocate media dollars to accomplish reach and frequency objectives. In a high-reach campaign, money is allocated to get the message to as many people as possible. In a high-frequency campaign, the money is allocated to fewer media, thus reaching fewer people, but message repetition increases.

media mix

a combination of traditional media vehicles (print, broadcast, etc.); nontraditional media (electronic media, unexpected places like the floors of stores); and marketing communication tools such as public relations, direct marketing, and sales promotion, used to reach the target audiences

6. Other Marketing Communications Activities

The concept of a communication mix in an IMC plan includes more than just traditional advertising media. In most cases, advertising campaigns are supported by other forms of marketing communications, such as sales promotion and public relations. An organization has to decide which IMC tool can best reach a mass audience (advertising), involve an audience (events), or build credibility and believability (public relations). This decision is made through a process called **zero-based planning**, in which the decision about which marketing communications tools to use is based on an analysis of the year's situation analysis, SWOTs, and communication objectives, rather than just tweaking last year's budget with decisions based on what was done in the past.

zero-based planning

the practice of analyzing the strengths and weaknesses of the various marketing communications tools and then matching them to the problem identified in the situation analysis

7. The Appropriation and Budget

After developing the campaign plan, managers create a budget that estimates the costs of the various recommended campaign steps. If this budget exceeds the amount of funds available—the appropriation—either costs have to be shaved or the appropriation has to increase. Once the appropriation is set, the money can be allocated among the various communications activities. The budget size for communications has a tremendous range.

For example, Tourisme Montréal's 2002 advertising campaign cost $8 million (see *Snapshot,* pp. 262–263). At the other end of the scale, the Green Tourism Association in Toronto had only $3000 to spend on their promotional campaign (see Case Study).

Marketing experts remind campaign planners to base their budgets on the cost of reaching the target market rather than on the cost of certain kinds of marketing communication activities. Once the potential customer targets are identified, then it should be possible to quantify the value of the brand's customers and prospects, so that targets can be selected and prioritized based on what they are currently and potentially worth to the company.[7] This makes setting **return-on-investment goals** possible—that is, calculating the expected profit returns based on the costs of reaching a customer or group of customers. This calculation is also called break-even analysis or payout planning.

8. Campaign Evaluation

The last stage in the development of a campaign plan consists of preparing a proposal stating how the campaign will be evaluated. This is an important step as it determines whether or not the campaign effort was effective, and the key part of an evaluation is measuring a company or brand's effectiveness against its stated objectives. However, clients of agencies should consider many things, including the extent to which the message reached the right people; the ads actually said what was intended; the ads achieved what was expected; consumer perceptions were changed; product sales increased; the media mix was effective; lessons could be learned from the campaign; and the campaign could be improved in the future.

There are many evaluative research techniques available to marketers to measure effectiveness. Memory tests are often used, and are based on the assumption that a communication leaves a mental residue with the person who has been exposed to it. Memory tests fall into two major groups: recall tests and recognition tests. In a traditional **recall test**, a commercial is run on television network and the next evening interviewers ask viewers if they remember seeing the commercial. This type of test, in which the specific brand is mentioned, is called aided recall. Alternatively, the interviewers may ask consumers what particular ads they remembered from the previous day, and this is known as unaided recall. If the commercial fails to establish a tight connection between the brand name and the selling message, the commercial will not receive a high recall score. Another method of measuring memory, called a **recognition test**, involves showing the advertisement to people and asking them whether they remember having seen it before.

The **persuasion test** is another evaluative research technique used to measure effectiveness after execution of a campaign. In this technique, consumers are first asked how likely they are to buy a particular brand. Next, they are exposed to an advertisement for the brand. After exposure, researchers again ask them what they intend to purchase. The researcher analyzes the results to determine whether intention to buy has increased as a result of exposure to the advertisement. Persuasion tests are expensive and have problems associated with audience composition, the environment, and brand familiarity. However, persuasion is a key objective for many advertisers, so even a rough estimate of an advertisement's persuasive power is useful.

return-on-investment goals

working out the expected profit returns based on the costs of reaching a customer or group of customers; also called break-even analysis or payout planning

recall test

a test that evaluates the memorability of an advertisement by contacting members of the audience and asking what they remember about the advertisement

recognition test

a test that evaluates the memorability of an advertisement by contacting members of the audience, showing them the ad, and then asking whether they remember having seen it before

persuasion test

a test that evaluates the effectiveness of an advertisement by measuring whether the ad affects consumer's intentions to buy a brand

PUSH AND PULL PROMOTIONAL STRATEGIES

push strategy

a promotion strategy that calls for using the sales force and trade promotion to push the product through channels; the producer promotes the product to wholesalers, the wholesalers promote to retailers, and the retailers to consumers

pull strategy

a promotion strategy that calls for spending a large amount on advertising and consumer promotion to build up consumer demand; if successful, consumers will ask their retailers for the product, the retailers will ask the wholesalers, and the wholesalers will ask the producers

One final factor to consider in the promotional strategy will be the position of the organization in the distribution channel. For example, does a retailer (i.e., the travel agent or the venue) carry out its own promotion for the travel product, or does the producer (i.e., the tour operator or destination organization) have to promote the product in order to bring the public into the travel agent to buy it? This is known as the choice between push and pull promotional strategies. A **push strategy** calls for using the sales force and trade promotion to push the product through channels; the producer promotes the product to wholesalers, the wholesalers promote to retailers, and the retailers to consumers. In contrast, a **pull strategy** calls for spending a large amount on advertising and consumer promotion to build up consumer demand; if successful, consumers will ask their retailers for the product, the retailers will ask the wholesalers, and the wholesalers will ask the producers. The two strategies are contrasted in Figure 8.4.

The choice of strategy will depend on the degree of influence each member of the distribution channel has on the consumer's decision process and on the relative power of the producer's and the retailer's brand names. In most cases, a combination of the two strategies will be used, with each player in the channel marketing itself to the others and providing support for joint promotions. In the Travel Alberta case (see *Marketing in Action*), a pull strategy was used to entice consumers to travel within Alberta through advertising and promotion, whereas a push strategy was used to promote the product through the channel using a detailed brochure produced for the industry, which encouraged individual tourism organizations to consider packaging or product partnership programs (see Figure 8.5 on page 256).

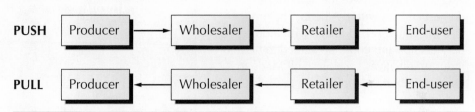

Figure 8.4   Push and Pull Promotional Strategies

MARKETING IN ACTION

TRAVEL ALBERTA'S "ALBERTA MADE TO ORDER" CAMPAIGN

The Case Study in Chapter 4 shows that the domestic tourist market in Alberta is definitely not homogeneous but does have certain common characteristics. Albertans have an overall preference for recreating in mountains, forests, and parks; they want to explore and do new things; and they are attracted to the idea of tourism packages. Travel Alberta's "Alberta Made to Order" campaign, launched as a response to these findings, is an excellent example of a research-based marketing program that provides useful guidelines for other

MARKETING IN ACTION *continued*

destinations and managers of tourism organizations wishing to exploit the potential of domestic tourism.

The research study showed Travel Alberta that Alberta's tourism marketing needed to offer a brand image that acknowledged the joint consumer desires for mountains, forests, and parks on the one hand, and for exploring and doing new things on the other. The "Alberta Made to Order" umbrella marketing program was designed to accomplish this task. Initial research showed that consumers link the phrase "made to order" to the concept of customization and suitability—to the delivery of an ideal vacation built to satisfy their needs. The brand image was designed for use by both Travel Alberta and Alberta's tourism industry. The goal of the program was to encourage Albertans to visit all six regions of the province, to alter current travel preferences, and to increase the amount of domestic travel within Alberta. The program also integrated brand image with industry partnerships and could be altered to tie into industry initiatives such as "Golf Made to Order," "Alberta's North Made to Order," and "Edmonton Made to Order."

A detailed brochure produced for the industry encouraged individual tourism organizations to consider packaging/product partnership programs. Working with a variety of partners (over 80 projects with cooperative funding were launched), Parcom Travel (Travel Alberta's in-province marketing agent) created and developed strong awareness of travel programs; it used television, radio, newspaper, and other promotional vehicles to stimulate people to spend more time travelling in Alberta, primarily through the concept of short getaway breaks. Throughout all vehicles of communication, information was carefully shaped to speak directly to the five different consumer tourism cluster segments identified in the research. Articles and components were timed to gen-

erate consumer interest in particular areas of the province (while ensuring a strong representation of all six regions and product clusters). The communication vehicles also provided Alberta's tourism industry with ongoing opportunities to buy into and provide their "call to action" through advertising participation aimed at spurring industry sales (see Figure 8.5).

The consumer survey established that television, followed by newspapers and glossy publications, was the preferred media for tourism promotions. Two 30-second commercials were therefore developed to create high awareness of the new branding. Launched in May 2000, the "Alberta Made to Order" television commercials were seen by more than 90 percent of adults 54 years and under about 20 times by

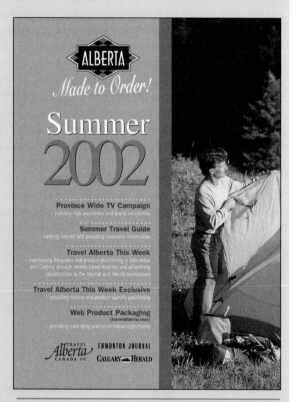

Figure 8.5 Front Page of Travel Alberta Flyer Sent Out to the Tourism Industry in 2002

MARKETING IN ACTION *continued*

the end of June. Taking the 2000 program beyond the awareness created by the commercials, Travel Alberta's promoted its Web site (www.travelalberta.com) and 1-800 number in all media materials. The program also included Travel Alberta's 72-page summer magazine and weekly one- to two-page travel features in the *Edmonton Journal* and *Calgary Herald* as well as in selected weeklies and rural tabloids. The editorial style was personal, in a response to the research that indicated that word of mouth was the most reliable form of communication for Albertans. A special-event motor home also delivered tourism product information at events and locations around the province all summer (see Figure 8.6). In addition, Travel Alberta worked with a media sponsor to record videos of Albertans at various events or destinations

that they visited throughout the province. Albertans who spotted themselves as "stars" on television could call in and win prizes.

From independent surveys conducted at the conclusion of the 2000 campaign and compared to similar surveys done in 1997 and 1998, Travel Alberta discovered that the percentage of survey respondents that had Alberta as a "top of the mind" travel destination had increased by more than 20 percent. The percentage of survey respondents aware of slogans, themes, or catchy phrases promoting travel in Alberta had increased by more than 13 percent.

Source: Hudson, S., & Ritchie, J. R. B. (2002). Understanding the domestic market using cluster analysis: A case study of the marketing efforts of Travel Alberta. *Journal of Vacation Marketing, 8*(3), 263–276.

Figure 8.6   Travel Alberta Motor Home Used to Promote the "Alberta Made to Order" Campaign

TOURISM ADVERTISING

Advertising has emerged as a key marketing tool in the tourism and hospitality industries. These industries require potential customers to base buying decisions upon mental images of product offerings, since they are not able to physically sample alternatives. As a result, advertising is a critical variable in the tourism marketing mix, and it covers a wide range of activities and agencies. Its role reflects that of promotion in general, which is to influence the attitudes and behaviour of audiences in three main ways: confirming and reinforcing, creating new patterns of behaviours, or changing attitudes and behaviour. Thus tourism and hospitality companies use images to portray their products in brochures, posters, and media advertising. Destinations do the same, attempting to construct an image of a destination that will force it into the potential tourist's list of options, leading ultimately to a purchase decision. Whatever the tourism or hospitality product, its identity is the public face of how it is marketed, and the importance of advertising in tourism marketing should therefore not be underestimated.

Defining Advertising

advertising

any paid form of non-personal presentation and promotion of ideas, goods, or services by an identified sponsor, using mass media to persuade or influence an audience

Advertising can be defined as paid non-personal presentation and promotion of ideas, goods, or services by an identified sponsor, using mass media to persuade or influence an audience. This standard definition of advertising has six elements. First, advertising is a paid form of communication, although some forms of advertising, such as public service announcements, use donated space and time. Second, not only is the space paid for, but the sponsor is identified. Third, most advertising tries to persuade or influence the consumer to do something, although in some cases the point of the message is simply to make consumers aware of the product or company. Fourth, the message is conveyed through many different kinds of mass media, and fifth, advertising reaches an audience of potential consumers. Finally, because advertising is a form of mass communication, it is also non-personal.

PROFILE

TIM HORTONS PROVING THAT ADVERTISING DOESN'T HAVE TO BE FLASHY OR CONTROVERSIAL TO SELL

So there you are, confined by the cold, clammy stone walls of Glasgow, away from the warmth and civilization of Canada. What are you going to do to bring a touch of home to these bleak environs? In early 2003, Tim Hortons ran an advertising campaign based in Scotland. Here, a group of poor Canadian students at the University of Glasgow forced to survive on haggis and bannock appeal to Tim Hortons for help and receive a care package of coffee to keep their spirits up. The campaign was based on a true human insight: it is nice to have the comforts of home when you can't be at home. The Tim Hortons product fits nicely into this insight.

The campaign was well received by critics. "It celebrates the incredible fact that a doughnut chain named after a hockey player has become a Canadian cultural icon. Tim Hortons has truly reached icon status as a Canadian brand, a positioning most clients would kill for," says Michael Clancy, director of strategic and creative planning for Brandworks International. "The casting is especially good: real, earnest, Canadian, believable. And the mini-travelogue of Scotland is superb. The footage is beautiful and the sound of skirling pipes completes the effect."

Barry Campbell, senior creative director for Allard-Johnson Communications is just as complimentary. "The staff of the agency must have thoroughly enjoyed working on this piece of business because of the partnership they enjoy with Tim Hortons," he says. "The agency clearly understands their customer and the business they are in. If it didn't, the agency could never have produced a spot that relies so heavily on credibility. We encounter testimonials every day but most of them roll by into obscurity even if we do believe their claims. This one entertains and informs after repeated viewings."

Enterprise Creative Selling, the Toronto-based agency behind the ads for Tim Hortons, may be one of the most influential advertising agencies in Canada, at least judging by the millions of Canadians who dutifully line up to purchase whatever product it features in its ads—whether it is coffee cake, bagels, or iced cappuccino. Although its commercials almost never win advertising industry awards, it has helped build Tim Hortons into a Canadian icon, proving that advertising doesn't have to be flashy or controversial to work. "We'd love to win an award or two," says Alison Simpson, general manager of the 43-staff agency, "but it is not our driving force. We define great creative [advertising] by the results it delivers."

Tim Hortons seems to be convinced. The doughnut chain has stuck with Enterprise for more than 11 years, an unusually long time in an industry in which clients and agencies are forever playing musical chairs. "Enterprise's advertising is not the only reason why we are where we are, but it has certainly helped us," said Bill Moir, executive vice-president of marketing for Tim Hortons. One of the biggest challenges for Enterprise has been trying to keep up with Tim Hortons' growth. The chain's sales have climbed steadily and are now well over $2 billion. This has put pressure on Enterprise to produce more ads to sustain Tim Hortons' double-digit growth. In 1996, Enterprise created just eight television commercials for the chain. In 2002, it produced a total of 22. That doesn't include separate French-language ads that started in 2001. Before that, Quebec advertising was adapted from spots running in English Canada.

The ads, like the products they promote, don't try to be overly sophisticated. That would alienate Tim Hortons' core customer. But the commercials are not afraid to be goofy or contrived. Sentimental music and sweeping shots of Scottish countryside with an emotional story of a Canadian who misses Canada—all of this works to sell an average cup of coffee. The ads are also simple, don't take themselves too seriously and, above all, focus on the product. Says Ken Wong, professor of marketing at Queen's University, "Their advertising in general is not brilliant, but it is disciplined. Essentially the agency is saying 'We don't care if we win creative awards. All we care about is what works for the client.'"

Sources: Heinzl, J. (2002, March 15). Enterprise finds that hokey sells. *The Globe and Mail*, p. B7; Tim Hortons in Scotland mood piece stands up after repeated viewings. (2003, February 10). *Financial Post*, p. 12.

Developing an Advertising Program

advertising objective

a specific communication task to be accomplished with a specific target audience during a specific period of time

The process of developing an advertising program includes six important stages. These are illustrated in Figure 8.7 on page 260 and discussed below.

1. Setting the Objectives

In planning and managing advertising, a key factor is the setting of objectives. An **advertising objective** can be defined as a specific communication task to be accomplished with

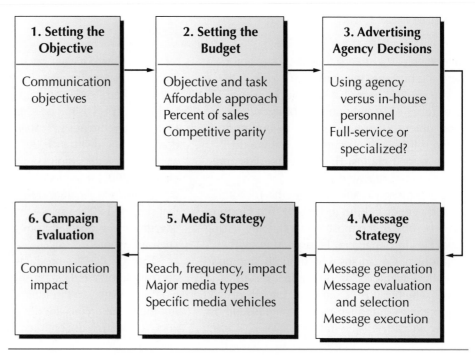

Figure 8.7   The Process of Developing an Advertising Program

a specific target audience during a specific period of time. In general terms, advertising has four major tasks: informing, persuading, reminding, and selling. However, advertising in tourism and hospitality can have many uses. These might include creating awareness; informing about new products; expanding the market to new buyers; announcing a modification to a service; announcing a price change; making a special offer; selling directly; educating consumers; reminding consumers; challenging competition; reversing negative sales trends; pleasing intermediaries; recruiting staff; attracting investors; announcing trading results; influencing a destination image; creating a corporate image; soliciting customer information; improving employee morale; and contributing to cooperative/partnership advertising ventures.

The Canadian Tourism Commission was quick to respond in the aftermath of the tragic events of September 11, 2001, by promptly providing useful and timely information to the industry and by launching successful marketing campaigns in Canada and the United States to promote tourism to and within Canada. The objective of the "Go Explore Stay Near" print ad below was to encourage the travel trade to promote travel in Canada (see Figure 8.8).

2. Setting the Budget

Ideally, the advertising budget should be calculated on the basis of the objectives set in the first stage of the process. The media plan must reach sufficient numbers in the target market to produce the size of response that will achieve the sales target. Several methods can be used to set the advertising budget. The **objective and task** method involves developing the promotion budget by (1) defining specific objectives, (2) determining the tasks that must be performed to achieve these objectives, and (3) estimating the costs of performing these

objective and task method

developing the promotion budget by (1) defining specific objectives, (2) determining the tasks that must be performed to achieve these objectives, and (3) estimating the costs of performing these tasks

Figure 8.8 "Go Explore Stay Near" Print Ad from the Canadian Tourism Commission

affordable method

setting the promotion budget at what management thinks the company can afford

percentage of sales method

setting the promotion budget at a certain percentage of current or forecasted sales or as a percentage of sales price

competitive parity method

setting the promotion budget to match competitors' outlay

tasks. Using this method requires considerable experience of response rates and media costs, as well as confidence in the accuracy of predictions. Cautious managers prefer to base the advertising budget on what they know from previous experience they can afford to spend. This is often referred to as the affordable method. The percentage of sales method involves setting the promotion budget at a certain percentage of current or forecasted sales or as a percentage of sales price. In tourism and hospitality, the percentage of gross sales generally set aside for marketing is somewhere between 4 and 12 percent, advertising being allocated about a quarter of this amount. The actual percentage will vary according to the product's position on the product life cycle (see Chapter 5). For example, new products will require more advertising to launch them into the market.

Another way of setting the budget is the competitive parity method, which sets the promotion budget at the level needed to achieve parity or "equal share-of-voice" with competitors. It may seem unwise to spend significantly less than competitors if you are aiming for a similar share of the same market. In the hotel business the advertising expenditures for the average hotel is 1 percent of sales, but for limited-service hotels, advertising expenditure is higher, representing 2 percent of sales.

All these methods have their weaknesses when used individually. The objective and task method could produce a higher cost figure than the company can afford. The percentage of sales method can lead to the budget being cut because of declining sales. And basing the budget on the competition's assumes that competitors have the same objectives, the same level of financial resources, and an understanding of their target market preferences. None of the methods takes into account the fact that different creative ideas can produce very different consumer responses, and in practice, companies often use a combination of methods—plus the lessons of previous years—in calculating the budget. The exact figure will depend on how adventurous an approach the corporate culture or the individual manager is prepared to take.

3. Advertising Agency Decisions

Since advertising is usually considered the most important tool in the marketing communications mix, companies must decide carefully whether they are going to do the work themselves or hire an outside agency. Only very small businesses, such as guesthouses or local visitor attractions, are likely to undertake their own advertising without professional help. At the very least, advertising agencies can help with the purchase of advertising space at discounted rates. Most advertising agencies enjoy working on tourism and hospitality accounts as intrinsically interesting products, and may welcome the account as a stimulating break from their usual subject matter.

The best advertising agencies create value for their clients, as seen in the Tim Hortons example (see *Profile*). An agency can clearly interpret what the customer wants and then communicate information about the client's product so meaningfully, so uniquely, and so consistently that customers reward that product with their loyalty. An agency can add perceived value to the product of its client by giving the product a personality, by communicating in a manner that shapes basic understanding of the product, by creating an image or memorable picture of the product, and by setting the product apart from its competitors.

SNAPSHOT

TOURISME MONTRÉAL LAUNCHES HUGE ADVERTISING CAMPAIGN

In 2002, in an attempt to revitalize the Montreal tourist industry, which was badly hurt by the terrorist attacks on September 11, 2001, and the economic slowdown of 2001, Tourisme Montréal launched the biggest advertising campaign ever mounted by a Canadian city. With the help of other parties (see opposite), the organization was able to spend $8 million to jump-start the tourist industry, which generates nearly 60 000 jobs and over $1.7 billion in spending in the region. The campaign was announced by Charles Lapointe, president and chief executive officer of Tourisme Montréal, in the presence of elected officials and representatives of the tourist industry. "The advertising campaign of unprecedented scale that Tourisme Montréal is about to launch on North American markets will intensify the promotion of Montréal, which has been losing speed compared to the competition for some time," said Lapointe. "By relying on a strong brand image that promotes 'Montréal as a European-style city in North America that offers a unique experience because of how passionately we celebrate life,' we hope to propel Montréal to the ranks of the most prized destinations in North America."

"Along with traditional promotion channels, our new campaign will use avant-garde tools at the forefront of technology, giving us the benefit of the Internet as a formidable and indispensable instrument for travel marketing," Lapointe continued. During the weeks following the announcement, attractive brochures promoting Montreal as a destination and offering appealing packages were inserted in nearly 25 U.S. and Canadian publications (see Figure 8.9). No fewer than 17 million copies were distributed in this way in prestigious newspapers and magazines such as the *New York Times, Los Angeles Times, Boston Globe, Chicago Tribune, Gourmet, National Geographic Magazine, GQ, New Yorker, Condé Nast Traveler, Travel & Leisure, Food & Wine, Globe and Mail, Ottawa Citizen*, and others. In addition to the inserts, one-third-page ads ran four times in more than 15 North American publications, reaching 30 million readers.

The Montreal communications agency Marketel was chosen to conduct this campaign. For the first time in Canada, companies outside the travel industry agreed to invest in an advertising campaign of such scale. Along with its traditional public and private sector partners, Tourisme Montréal was able to convince companies like Panasonic, Audio Products International, Temper Pedic, Neff Kitchens, Time Pieces, Fairmont, Walker Zanger, and others to join the effort to jump-start the Montreal tourist industry, a true economic engine in the region. This addition to the constant and sustained contribution from

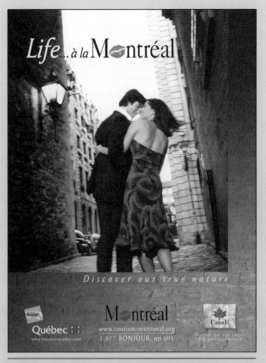

Figure 8.9   Front Cover of Brochure Promoting Montreal, Inserted in Nearly 25 U.S. and Canadian Publications

the Canadian Tourism Commission, Tourisme Québec, Canada Economic Development, the Eastern Townships and Laurentians Associations of Tourism and Recreation, the Tremblant Resort Association, Air Canada, VIA Rail, Casino de Montréal, the Hotel Association of Greater Montréal (AHGM), Gogo Worldwide Vacations, Yankee Holidays, Montréal Vacations, Collette Vacations, Hospitalité Canada, as well as hotels and tourist attractions enabled Tourisme Montréal to appreciably increase the budget, and therefore the impact, of its campaign.

Source: Bellerose, P. (2002). Tourisme Montréal launches huge advertising campaign. Retrieved April 17, 2002, from http://www.canadatourism.com/en/ctc/ctx/ctx-news/search/newsbydateform.cfm.

Hiring an advertising agency has three main benefits. The agency provides objective advice, experienced staffing, and tailored management of all advertising activities and personnel. Agencies are also partly paid from media discounts and often cost the company very little. Since a client can drop its agency at any time, most agencies work hard to do a good job. But despite the advantages that independent agencies offer their clients, there are instances where companies have an in-house agency or an advertising department. Many retailers, for example, have in-house agencies, as they tend to operate with small profit margins and find they can save money by doing their own advertising. Also, retailers must develop and place their ads under extremely tight deadlines, so they prefer to have control over their advertising.

There are two main types of advertising agency: the full-service agency and the specialized agency. In advertising, a **full-service agency** is one that provides the four major staff functions: account management, creative services, media planning and buying, and account planning (which is also known as research). A full-service advertising agency will also have its own accounting department, a traffic department to handle internal tracking on completion of projects, a department for broadcast and print production, and a human resources department. However, tourism and hospitality organizations often use the services of a **specialized agency**. This type of agency will specialize in certain functions (e.g., writing copy, producing art, media buying), audiences (e.g., minority, youth), or industries (e.g., health care, computers, leisure). For example, Toronto-based Boom Communications is an advertising agency forged specifically to help advertisers reach baby boomers. In addition, there are specialized agencies in all marketing communication areas, such as direct marketing, sales promotion, public relations, events and sports marketing, and packaging and point-of-sale. In 2003, the Canadian Tourism Commission chose Palmer Jarvis DDB to support its worldwide marketing programs. In 2002, the agency was ranked as Canada's number one agency in *Marketing Magazine*'s "Scouting Report," based on client feedback and a review of its business and creative portfolio.

Ad agencies have traditionally been paid through commissions and some fees. Under this system, the agency receives about 15 percent of the media costs as a rebate. But both advertisers and agencies have become increasingly unhappy with the commission system. Larger advertisers complain that they pay more for the same services received by smaller ones simply because they place more advertising. Advertisers also believe that the commission system drives agencies away from low-cost media or non-commissionable media and short advertising campaigns. Agencies are unhappy because they perform extra services for an account without receiving additional revenue. As a result, the trend is now toward paying either a straight fee or a combination of commission and fee. Some large advertisers are even tying agency compensation to the performance of the advertising campaigns. Other trends in the business include increasing consolidation, which is creating huge agency-holding companies, and increasing diversification as agencies have sought growth by moving into related marketing services. These new mega-group agencies offer a complete list of integrated marketing and promotion services under one roof, including advertising, sales promotion, public relations, direct marketing, and marketing research.

full-service agency

an advertising agency that provides the four major staff functions: account management, creative services, media planning and buying, and account planning

specialized agency

an advertising agency that specializes in certain functions (e.g., writing copy, producing art, media buying), audiences (e.g., minority, youth), or industries (e.g., health care, computers, leisure)

4. Message Strategy

The message strategy is the fourth stage in the process of developing an advertising program. Studies have shown that creative advertising messages can be more important than the number of dollars spent on the message. Creative strategy plays an increasingly important role in advertising success. Developing a creative strategy requires three message steps: generation, evaluation and selection, and execution.

Providers of tourism and hospitality products face an inherent barrier to effective communication with their customers: the intangibility of the product. A hotel or airline flight is experienced only at or after the time of purchase. This characteristic of services in general poses genuine challenges for message *generation*. Advertisers need to make tangible an intangible product, using emotion and experience. British Airways have always been creative in achieving this goal in its advertising. A few years ago this company produced an ad for its business class lounge that associated the lounge with a green oasis in the middle of the desert. A more recent campaign, using TV and print to promte the comfort of business class, shows a man sleeping overnight on a bed in the middle of Times Square, New York (see Figure 8.10).

Creative people have different ways of developing advertising messages. Many start by talking to customers, dealers, experts, and competitors. Others imagine consumers using the product and in this way determine the benefits that consumers seek. Although advertisers may create many possible messages, only a few will be used in the campaign, and the second step in developing a creative strategy—*evaluation and selection*—will determine the final message to be used. According to Kotler et al., the advertiser must evaluate possible ads on the basis of three characteristics.[8] First, messages should be meaningful and should point out benefits that make the product more desirable or interesting to consumers. Second, messages should be distinctive. They should tell the consumer how the product is

Figure 8.10 British Airways Creative Print Advertisement

better than competing brands. Finally, messages must be believable. This goal is difficult to achieve, as many consumers doubt the truth of advertising.

In the third step of developing a creative strategy, *execution*, the creative staff must find a style, tone, words, and format for executing the message. Any message can be presented in a variety of execution styles. The following styles are commonly used in tourism and hospitality:

1. *Slice of life.* This style shows people using the product in a normal setting. Although the Tim Hortons Scotland campaign did not fit into this category, most of the companies' ads are true to the experience of visiting a Tim Hortons and normally show consumers enjoying the products at breakfast or lunchtime.

2. *Fantasy.* This style creates a wonder world around the product or its use. The human psyche is receptive to fantasy, and companies like Disney have capitalized on this type of advertising that is effective in an industry that appeals to one's desire to escape.

3. *Mood or image.* This style of builds a mood or image around the product or service, such as beauty, love, or serenity. Destination marketers often attempt to create an emotional relationship between the destination and potential visitors—as in the Yukon advertisement in Figure 8.11. In this type of advertising, branding activities concentrate on communicating the essence or the spirit of a destination via a few key attributes and associations.

4. *Lifestyle.* This style shows how a product fits with a lifestyle. For example, an airline advertising its business class featured a businessman sitting in an upholstered chair in the living room, having a drink, and enjoying the paper. The other side of the ad featured the same person in the same relaxed position with a drink and a paper in one of the airline's business-class seats.

5. *Musical.* This style shows one or more people or cartoon characters singing a song about a product. Almost 30 years ago, Coca-Cola wanted to "teach the world to sing in perfect harmony," and the pattern was set for an important ingredient in successful advertising: the use of music. Airlines have used music to good effect. Delta Airlines used music effectively in its "We Love to Fly" campaign, as did British Airways in its "World Images" campaign. The association various destinations have with music is often used in advertising campaigns. For instance, the haunting strains of Irish music are the background sounds in an ad for Ireland.

6. *Testimonial evidence.* In this style, celebrities we admire, created characters (McDonald's Ronald McDonald, for example), experts we respect, or people "just like us" whose advice we might seek out speak on behalf of the product to build credibility. The Tim Hortons Scotland campaign (see *Profile*) relied heavily on credibility for its effectiveness.

7. *Technical expertise.* In this style of advertisement, the company shows its expertise with the product. Hotels, for example, may use this style in advertising directed toward meeting and convention planners, to show that they have the technical qualities to support the meeting planner. Holiday Inn has used this execution style (see Figure 8.12 on page 268), and airlines also often make use of expertise to reassure the consumer about the technical qualities of their pilots and mechanics.

Figure 8.11   Print Advertisement for the Yukon

5. Media Strategy

The media plan section in an advertising plan includes media objectives (reach and frequency), media strategies (targeting, continuity, and timing), media selection (the specific vehicles), geographic strategies, schedules, and the media budget. The range of advertising media available to today's advertiser is increasingly bewildering and is becoming ever more fragmented. While these changes offer the prospect of greater targeting, they also make the job of the media planner more difficult. Table 8.5 on page 269 provides a reference guide to the range of the main advertising media and lists their major advantages and disadvantages.

Given cost constraints, media planners usually select the media that will expose the product to the largest target audience for the lowest possible cost. The process of measuring this ratio is called efficiency—or **cost per thousand (CPM)**. To calculate the CPM, two figures are needed: the costs of the unit (e.g., time on TV or space in a magazine) and

cost per thousand (CPM)

the process of selecting the media that will expose the product to the largest target audience for the lowest possible cost ("M" is the Roman numeral for 1000)

Figure 8.12 Holiday Inn Uses Technical Expertise to Differentiate Its Hotels

the estimated target audience. The cost of the unit is divided by the target audience's gross impressions to determine the advertising dollars needed to expose the product to 1000 members of the target.

$$CPM = \frac{\text{cost of message unit}}{\text{gross impressions}} \times 1000$$

For example, the show *Pilot Guides* has 92 000 target viewers, and the cost of a 30-second announcement during the show is $850.

$$CPM = \frac{\$850}{92\,000} \times 1000 = \$9.24$$

There are many components to the media mix, and how an organization blends them depends on a number of factors, particularly the nature of the product or service and the target audience. For example, tour operators and major destinations rely heavily on television advertising, but niche players such as special interest operators tend to focus their advertising in specialist publications. Decisions also have to be made about reach and frequency. Nova Scotia, for example, relies heavily on the response it gets from television advertising during the annual East Coast Music Awards. Viewers all over Canada with a predisposed interest in Atlantic Canada tune in to the program, and Nova Scotia tourism

Table 8.5

The Advantages and Disadvantages of the Major Advertising Media

MEDIA TYPE	ADVANTAGES	DISADVANTAGES
Print Media		
Local press	High market coverage Short lead time Easily laid out Frequency/immediacy Relatively inexpensive Allows for repetition of ads Creates local image	Audience reads selectively Short life span Low attention Media clutter Poor reproduction quality
National press	Large circulation Many creative options for layout Appeals to all income levels Relatively cheap for national coverage Frequency allows repetition Allows audience/geographical selectivity	Audience reads selectively Short life span Poor reproduction Low attention Clutter
Consumer magazines	Large circulation High pass on readership High-quality reproduction and colour Relatively long life and read in leisurely fashion Well-segmented audience High information content Allows sales promotion inserts	Expensive Distant copy dates Clutter
Specialist trade journals	Well-segmented audience Short lead times Potential for high information content ads	Clutter Competitors' ads may be featured
Circulars	Low production and distribution costs Blanket coverage in target areas	Poor image Distribution abuse Short attention span
Inserts in free press and magazines	Relatively cheap Good for direct response ads	Short life span May be seen as having a poor image
Posters	Cheap Target specific areas/groups Longevity (especially on public transport—buses, etc.)	Short exposure time Poor image Clutter Audience segmentation difficult

TABLE 8.5 *continued*

MEDIA TYPE	ADVANTAGES	DISADVANTAGES
Broadcast Media		
Television	Opportunity for high creativity and impact (sound, visual, etc.) Good for image Appeals to all income levels Relatively cheap for national coverage Frequency allows repetition Allows audience/geographical selectivity High attention gaining	Relatively high production and airtime costs Short life span Clutter Fleeting attention
Commercial radio	Large localized audience Gains local recognition Flexible deadlines Well-segmented audience Allows repeat messages	Production can be expensive Allows audio message only Clutter Short life span Fleeting message Low attention; audience distraction high
Cinema	Possibility to segment audience or mass market Allows frequent exposure Potential for high creative impact of colour and visuals—large screen and sound	Relatively high production and air time costs Competitors' ads may be featured Fleeting message Difficult to establish audience profile
Out of Home		
Billboards	High impact Low cost and large readership Longevity Ability to create awareness	Brief exposure Limited message—unsuitable for complex ads Needs large-scale distribution Creativity needed for impact
Transit	Can be targeted to specific audiences with high frequency Allows for creativity Can provide detailed information at a low cost	Brief exposure Image factors
Other Media		
Direct mail	Allows tracking Prepared mailing lists Allows audience/geographical selectivity High information content	Relatively high production costs of creating and maintaining databases Potential for poor image

TABLE 8.5 *continued*

MEDIA TYPE	ADVANTAGES	DISADVANTAGES
Other Media continued		
Exhibitions/ trade fairs and shows	Large target audience Reach large numbers of customers simultaneously Good for attracting new, maintaining existing customers	Costs of set-up and staffing can be expensive Clutter
Sponsorship and events	Possibility to reach attractive segments or mass market Allows company to build credibility and benefit from reflected success Potential for unusual, attention-grabbing activity Builds company recognition	Relatively costly Transience of celebrity and lack of control over others' actions Time-consuming to build relationships and links with partners Difficult to evaluate impact
Point-of-sale displays, in-store merchandising	Relatively inexpensive Reinforces ad message Incentive for trade location to stock product	Reaches customers already likely to purchase
Ambient media		
	Good coverage Good segmentation potential Many creative options	Creativity a constant challenge Targeting can be difficult Impact wears off quickly
Internet		
	Global impact Immediacy Many creative options for design Possibility of direct response and audience profiling	Short life span Creativity and Web design costs Low attention Targeting can be difficult

staff answer about 20 000 calls from across the country during the program. More than a third of those callers end up visiting the province, and officials claim that the advertising is worth about $8 million in economic activity.[9]

While tourism and hospitality advertising makes use of all of the main media, the key vehicles are print and electronic media advertisements and brochures. In fact, the most popular medium used by tourism advertisers is undoubtedly the travel brochure. For many organizations, the design, production, and distribution of their annual tourism brochure is the single most important and most expensive item in the marketing budget. The position of the brochure as a major travel medium is being threatened by new technology, such as CD-ROMs, videos, and the Internet. However, the brochure is changing in response to such challenges. In Ontario, for example, a new snowmobile trail guide is used to promote Northern Ontario as a four-season destination. The Snowmobile Passport Trail Planner, highlighting the snowmobile trails of Northern Ontario, has been embraced as an excellent reference tool for travellers to the region. The publication, a quick reference to the nearly 40 000 kilometres of groomed trails in the North, was released in early January 2003 by the Northern Tourism Marketing Company (NTMC), all 50 000 copies of the book being earmarked for distribution.

Other destinations are presenting their brochures as magazines (such as the *Alberta Motor Association*) that include guest articles and short stories. A new magazine from the CTC, called *Pure Canada*, covers a variety of topics from "Canada's Best New Chefs" to "Bicycling in Nova Scotia." Award-winning journalists and photographers are responsible for the editorial coverage, with the objective of making the magazine an exciting read and visually stimulating. An added element of the magazine is an innovative marketing partnership with Fodor's Travel Publications that has led to the inclusion of a 62-page "Fodor's Micro Guide to Canada" in every issue. This helpful feature includes destination overviews, maps, travel tips, and "must-see locations" in Canada.

ambient advertising

advertising that uses new, unexpected ways of getting messages across

One of the fastest growing sectors of media is ambient advertising. This approach includes place-based advertising and uses new, unexpected ways of getting messages across. Examples of ambient advertising include ads on the back of grocery receipts, on gas pumps, in elevators, on ATM screens, on shop floors, on washroom walls, on toilet paper, on pizza boxes, on welcome mats, on tickets, and on airline boarding cards. Performance advertising—in which actors stage live performances to promote products—has also begun in Canada. Molson and Proctor & Gamble are just two of the companies capitalizing on the spontaneity and human quality this type of advertising brings. In 1999, Virgin Atlantic made innovative use of ambient media in the tourism sector when it painted the traditionally green and white Hong Kong harbour's Star Ferry bright red with its own logo. A further use of ambient advertising is the use of airfields as a context in which to view ads cut into crop fields. An example of such an attempt to capture the interest of the business traveller occurred at Munich airport, where arriving passengers saw a giant ad for Swissair growing in the fields below. A 250-metre-long aircraft, grown in green barley against a background of brown straw, depicted the red and white Swissair logo—the colours created by using pigments.

6. Campaign Evaluation

Managers of advertising programs should regularly evaluate the communication and sales objectives of advertising. The key purposes of evaluation were highlighted earlier in the chapter, in the discussion of the stages of an IMC campaign, as were the evaluative research techniques available to marketers (see p. 254). These purposes and techniques are no different for an advertising campaign, and will therefore not be repeated here. The campaign evaluation stage is often the most difficult in the advertising cycle, largely because while it is relatively easy to establish certain advertising measures (such as consumers' awareness of a brand before and after the campaign), it is much harder to establish shifts in consumer attitudes or brand perception. Despite such uncertainties, the evaluation stage is significant not only because it establishes what a campaign has achieved but also because it will provide guidance as to how future campaigns could be improved and developed.

Effective Advertising

The advertising environment has changed dramatically in recent years, and in this climate of constant change the "rules" of advertising are also changing. During the 1950s and 1960s, successful advertising was felt to result when advertising agencies followed certain rules that were grounded in the experience of that time. Table 8.6 lists the eight old, as well as the eight new, rules of the advertising game.

However, at the time of writing, the advertising industry is facing serious challenges, which may bring even the new rules into question. Poorly performing economies, combined with new technology that may threaten the way advertising operates, have created a need to rethink advertising as a strategic alternative. Advertising will survive and grow only if it focuses on being effective. All advertisers are expecting specific results, based on their stated objectives. It is no longer acceptable to tell a client "Our ads work. We just don't know how, when, and with what results."

Effective ads work on two levels. First, they should satisfy consumers' objectives by engaging them and delivering a relevant message. Second, the ads must achieve the advertiser's

Table 8.6

Rules of the Advertising Game

THE EIGHT OLD RULES OF ADVERTISING	THE EIGHT NEW RULES OF ADVERTISING
1. You must have a unique selling proposition (USP).	Emotional selling propositions are paramount.
2. You must offer rational benefit.	Irrational appeals are legitimate and predominate.
3. Humour doesn't sell.	Humour can and does work for many brand personalities.
4. You must have a memorable slogan.	Slogans are good but only if they are memorable.
5. You must have a logo in the ad.	You don't always need to feature your logo.
6. You must show the product in the ad.	You don't always need to feature your product.
7. Every ad in a campaign must look the same.	Ads in a campaign should be linked but don't need to be identical.
8. Creative adds don't sell.	Creative ads do sell.

Source: Aitchison, J. (1999). Cutting edge advertising. How to create the world's best print for brands in the 21st century. Singapore: Prentice Hall.

objectives. The advertiser's objectives differ from consumers'. Ultimately, advertisers want consumers to buy and keep buying the advertised goods and services. To move consumers to action, they must gain their attention. They must hold consumers' interest long enough to convince them to change their purchasing behaviour, try a product, and stick with a product. The Tim Hortons advertising campaign discussed in this chapter (see *Profile*) strives to keep consumers' interest. The ads grab attention and are likely to satisfy the viewer's curiosity and need for entertainment. Additionally, because the campaign is so likeable, it will reinforce the good feelings or satisfaction of consumers who already buy from Tim Hortons.

The basic guideline in producing good advertising must be to use whichever combinations of slogans, logos, or tag lines work best in terms of the creative execution and brand strategy. Advertising for hotels is a case in point. Much of this advertising is not creative. It frequently features the hotel itself, its reception desk, and some of its facilities. And yet, for a consumer, this type of advertising is unlikely to create a point of differentiation for a hotel or a hotel chain. Occasionally hotel advertising will attempt to break ground, and the opening vignette indicates how Days Inn managed to win an advertising award for an unusual, creative television ad.

SALES PROMOTIONS

sales promotion

a technique used by a company to increase the value of its product by offering an extra incentive to purchase the product

Whenever a marketer increases the value of its product by offering an extra incentive to purchase the product, it is creating a **sales promotion**. In most cases, the objective of a sales promotion is to encourage action, although it can also help to build brand identity and awareness. Like advertising, sales promotion is a type of marketing communication. Although advertising is designed to build long-term brand awareness, sales promotions are primarily focused on creating immediate action. Simply put, sales promotions offer an extra incentive for consumers, sales reps, and trade members to act. Although this extra incentive usually takes the form of a price reduction, it may also be additional amounts of the product, cash, prizes and gifts, premiums, special events, and so on. It may also be a fun brand experience, as in Radisson Hotels & Resorts' "Go *Spy Kids 2* Family Package" promotion (see *Snapshot,* p. 278–279). Furthermore, a sales promotion usually has specified limits, such as an expiration date or a limited quantity of the merchandise.

The use of sales promotion is growing rapidly for many reasons: it offers the manager short-term bottom-line results; it is accountable; it is less expensive than advertising; it speaks to the current needs of the consumer to receive more value from products; and it responds to marketplace changes. Sales promotions can also be extremely flexible. They can be used at any stage in a product's life cycle and can be very useful in supporting other promotional activities.

Tactical promotional techniques designed to stimulate customers to buy have three main targets: individual consumers, distribution channels, and the sales force. Table 8.7 highlights the sales promotion objectives for each target market, along with typical techniques used to achieve these objectives in the tourism and hospitality industry. As the table shows, many tools can be used to accomplish sales promotion objectives. Some of the main tools used are discussed below, including samples, coupons, gift certificates, premiums and point-of-purchase displays (often referred to as merchandising), patronage rewards, contests, sweepstakes, and games.

Table 8.7

Sales Promotion Objectives and Techniques Used in Tourism and Hospitality

	OBJECTIVES	TECHNIQUES
Customer	Sell excess capacity—especially as the delivery date approaches Shift the timing of product purchases/peaks and troughs Attract and reward regular/loyal customers Promote trial of products (new users) Generate higher consumption per capita Increase market share Defeat/pre-empt competitors' promotions	Price cuts/sale offers including Internet Discount vouchers/coupons Disguised price cuts Extra product Additional services Gifts Competitions Passport schemes for regular customers Prize draws Point-of-purchase displays and merchandising materials Contests, sweepstakes, and games
Distribution Channels	Secure dealer support and recommendations Achieve brochure display and maintain stocks Support for merchandising initiatives Improve dealer awareness of products Build room value Increase room rate	Extra commission and overrides Prize draws Competitions Parties/receptions Trade and travel show exhibits Educational seminars Recognition programs Flexible booking policies
Sales Force	Improve volume of sales through incentives Improve display in distribution outlets Achieve sales "blitz" targets among main corporate accounts Reward special efforts	Bonuses and other money incentives Gift incentives Travel incentives Prize draws Visual aids

Samples

sampling

giving away free samples of a product to encourage sales, or arranging in some way for people to try all or part of a service

Sampling involves giving away free samples of a product to encourage sales, or arranging in some way for people to try all or part of a service. As many tourism and hospitality services are intangible, sampling is not always a straightforward process. However, restaurants and bars often give customer free samples of menu items or beverages. Sampling for the travel trade often comes in the form of familiarization trips. A familiarization trip (commonly referred to as a "fam trip") is a popular method used to expose a product to intermediaries in the channel of distribution. For example, a hotel might have a group of travel agents visit the facility to familiarize them with the features and benefits. If travel agents are impressed with a facility during a fam trip, they will convey their enthusiasm to customers, and bookings will increase. The trips are free or reduced in price and can be given to intermediaries by suppliers, carriers, or destination marketing groups.

Coupons

Coupons are vouchers or certificates that entitle customers or intermediaries to a reduced price on a good or service. Coupons are used extensively in the tourism and hospitality industries, especially among restaurants, hotels, rental car companies, tourist attractions, and cruise lines. Besides stimulating sales of a mature product, coupons are also effective in promoting early trial of a new product. But many marketing professionals feel that too much promotional use of coupons creates a commodity out of a differentiated product. Overuse has also led to coupon wars and other forms of price discounting, all the while detracting from the intrinsic value of a company's product or service. Figure 8.13 shows an example of coupon use: in this ad, an Alberta theme park offers two coupons for the summer for 2003. Calaway Park, positioned just outside Calgary, gains over 85 percent of its attendance through some form of promotions.

Gift Certificates

Gift certificates are vouchers or checks that are either selectively given away by the sponsor or sold to customers, who in turn give them to others as gifts. In February 2003, Signature Vacations, in a joint promotion with a variety of Canadian retailers, launched an

Figure 8.13 Coupons for Calaway Park, Alberta

online contest dubbed "Where's Juan?" in which travel agents could win gift certificates from the retailers participating in the promotion. The contest stated that Juan had gone on vacation for the month of February, and the only clues to his whereabouts were the post-cards he kept sending. The contest, which ran to February 28, could be entered from Signature's Web site for travel agents (just4you.signaturevacations.com). There were three winners each week: the person who found Juan first; a random winner from all agents who correctly identified the resort where he was hiding out; and a random winner from those who had also made a booking for that resort during the previous week. Prizes were from Chapters, Famous Players, Shoppers Drug Mart, and Canadian Tire. The contest was open to agents from across Canada except, for legal reasons, those from Quebec.

Premiums

premiums

goods offered either for free or at low cost as an incentive to buy a product

Premiums are goods offered either for free or at low cost as an incentive to buy a product. There are several varieties of premiums, including self-liquidators (sold at a price to recover the sponsor's cost) and free premiums (distributed by mail, in or on packages). Most marketing professionals agree that, to be effective, premiums must be of an appropriate quality and durability, be appealing, and have high perceived value to certain customer groups.

Such promotions can be expensive and—far from creating loyalty—they encourage consumers to switch brands constantly. In 2003, Canadian breweries realized that the perceived advantages of in-case promotions are largely illusory. Between 2000 and 2003, they had became hooked on in-case promotions, offering T-shirts, mini–Stanley Cups, NASCAR caps, coasters, bottle openers, and countless other trinkets. However, early in 2003, the industry realized it had to tame the monster it had created. While a desirable item can produce double-digit sales gains, demand tumbles when a giveaway ends and drinkers move on to seek the next prize. Worse, because of their high cost and fleeting effectiveness, in-case programs rarely pay for themselves. A single promotion can cost millions of dollars, including a sizable amount for television commercials that air in heavy rotation to create demand for the latest token. Both Molson and Labatt decided to move away from in-case promotions at the same time and to reallocate marketing dollars to new product launches and other activities.

Point-of-Purchase Displays

point-of-purchase merchandising

a technique used to promote a product at locations where it is being sold

Point-of-purchase merchandising is a technique used to promote a product at locations where it is being sold. The value of point-of-purchase merchandising has long been recognized in retailing and is making rapid inroads in restaurants, hotels, car rental companies, and travel agencies. In the food and beverage industry, menus and wine and drink lists are the key tools. In fact, many restaurants, such as Catch, in Calgary (see *Marketing in Action* in Chapter 5), put their menus on the Web for customers to view. Most wineries now offer free tastings in order to entice customers to purchase. In the travel agency business, brochures, posters, and window and stand-up displays are fairly common forms of sales promotion. Hotels also use a wide variety of merchandising techniques, including in-room guest directories, room-service menus, elevator and lobby displays, and brochure racks.

Patronage Rewards

Patronage rewards are cash or other prizes given to customers for their regular use of a company's products or services. The intent of such rewards is to encourage loyalty and to

contests

sales promotions in which entrants can win prizes based on some required skill that they are asked to demonstrate

sweepstakes

sales promotions that require entrants to submit their names and addresses; winners are chosen on the basis of chance, not skill

games

sales promotions similar to sweepstakes but involving the use of game pieces, such as scratch-and-win cards

create a positive change in the behaviour of the consumer. Examples are the frequent flyer plans that award points for miles travelled, such as Air Canada's Aeroplan reward plan. Many hotel chains also have frequent stay programs, and some restaurants have frequent diner programs. These will be discussed in more detail in Chapter 11.

Contests, Sweepstakes, and Games

In 2002, spending on games, contests, and sweepstakes by U.S.-based marketers rose 9 percent to US$1.8 billion.[10] **Contests** are sales promotions in which entrants win prizes based on some required skill that they are asked to demonstrate. The Signature Vacations online contest mentioned above required travel agents to demonstrate their destination product knowledge in order to win prizes. **Sweepstakes** are sales promotions that require entrants to submit their names and addresses. Winners are chosen on the basis of chance, not skill. **Games** are similar to sweepstakes, but they involve using game pieces, such as scratch-and-win cards. The *Snapshot* below highlights how Radisson Hotels & Resorts used a variety of sales promotions tools, including sweepstakes and games, to promote summer use of its hotels. The use of contests, games, and sweepstakes has been shown to increase advertising readership. These promotional tools can be useful in communicating key benefits and unique selling points, and can be targeted at both consumers and members of the trade.

SNAPSHOT

RADISSON HOTELS & RESORTS' SPY KIDS 2 *PROMOTION*

In the summer of 2002, Radisson Hotels & Resorts announced an exclusive Radisson Go *Spy Kids 2* Family Package that offered a fun-filled, value-packed summer travel deal in conjunction with the premiere of the blockbuster family movie *Spy Kids 2: The Island of Lost Dreams*. The Radisson Go *Spy Kids 2* Family Package included a low room-rate, free breakfast for four, an upgrade to the best available room at check-in, and a collectible *Spy Kids 2* Go Pack.

Radisson partnered with Dimension Films to develop the family leisure package. The promotion was available from May 23 through September 29, on an exclusive, limited basis, at Radisson Hotels & Resorts locations throughout Canada, the United States, and the Caribbean. "The *Spy Kids* movies add a lot of

fun and surprise to our family Go Package," said Brian Stage, executive vice-president of marketing and sales for Radisson Hotels & Resorts. "Consumers are reporting that they have less and less leisure time—in fact 58 percent of Americans say they don't have as much as they would like," said Kathy Sheehan, senior account director at RoperASW, a leading consumer research company. "People are seeking 'high peace' in our 'high pace' world. The fact that one of the top leisure activities cited was simply spending time with the family and relaxing means that this is good timing for the introduction of a promotion like the Radisson Go *Spy Kids 2* Family Package," Sheehan added.

The movie *Spy Kids 2: The Island of Lost Dreams* featured a family of super spies who

SNAPSHOT *continued*

worked together to save each other and help protect the family. The *Spy Kids 2* Go Pack, modelled after the movie, was loaded with games, a Kodak camera, snacks, and more, and was designed for guests to use during their stay and take home with them. "The *Spy Kids 2* Go Pack was created to add adventure, fun, and value for the entire family," said Diana Reichert, senior marketing manager for Radisson Hotels & Resorts Canada.

The Radisson Go *Spy Kids 2* Ultimate Adventure Sweepstakes at the company's Web site (www.radisson.com) also invited guests to enter a draw that offered a chance to win prizes. The first prize was a seven-day, six-night stay for a family of four at the Radisson Aruba Resort. Radisson also worked with leading companies including Kodak, the Nabisco Biscuit Division of Kraft Foods, and other top companies on this promotion.

Source: Murdoch, J. (2002). Rescue your family vacations with Radisson. Retrieved May 30, 2002, from http://www.canadatourism.com/en/ctc/ctx/ctx-news/search/newsbydateform.cfm.

JOINT PROMOTIONS

joint promotion

a promotion in which two or more organizations that have similar target markets combine their resources to their mutual advantage

Both the Radisson Hotels and Signature Vacations promotions involved partnership with other companies and are therefore examples of joint promotions. In a **joint promotion**, two or more organizations that have similar target markets combine their resources to their mutual advantage. This collaboration can reduce the cost of the incentives offered, and it may be a one-off joint promotion or a long-term campaign such as a trade association campaign using an "umbrella" brand name. Perhaps the best way to describe such promotions is by focusing on some further examples.

A well-publicized joint promotion occurred during the Winter Olympics of 2002, when Budget Rent A Car of Canada and Roots Canada teamed up to benefit Olympic athletes through their "Drive To Win" promotion. From February 1 to April 30, 2002, customers at participating Canadian Budget locations could scratch a game card to win prizes from Roots and Budget and to have an opportunity to win the grand prize of a brand new 2002 Jeep Liberty. Budget made a $5 donation from each eligible Budget rental during that time period to a charity directly benefitting Canadian Olympians. This "scratch and win" style contest featured instant-win prizes of Roots merchandise, Roots gift certificates, and discounts on Roots products and Budget rentals. The grand prize of a new 2002 Jeep Liberty was provided by DaimlerChrysler Canada and was drawn in May from ballots received at Roots and participating Budget locations.

In the summer of the same year, Campbell Soup Company cross-promoted Canada's summer attractions at over 2000 grocery stores. Part of the promotion included a householder mailing of over 15 million retail flyers announcing the in-store promotion. Attractions were invited to participate at no cost other than the redemption value of coupons offered in the campaign. The campaign was aimed at regional and local markets and was intended to bolster attendance and sales at many of Canada's tourism services and attractions.

At the same time, Travel Alberta and the Alberta Cattle Commission joined forces to promote travel to Alberta along with Alberta beef. Alberta beef was on the menu at Travel

Alberta tourism promotions across North America. The partnership was piloted at a trade show and marketing blitz in Seattle, which received positive reviews. The promotion included celebrity chef John Berry, who prepared an Alberta beef prime rib dinner for firefighters at a Seattle fire hall.

If soup and beef can attract visitors to Canada, then so can a Porsche. In 2003, a $3 million promotion deal among Porsche, the Canadian Tourism Commission, and Travel Alberta was initiated by the CTC's German office and was designed to steer affluent travellers to Alberta and other Canadian destinations. In addition to the promotional and direct marketing opportunities tied to an IMAX film called *Top Speed*, the CTC received 10 pages of promotional space in Porsche's custom magazine, *Christophorus*. These pages include a combination of advertising and editorial copy promoting travel to Canada. *Top Speed* was shot partly in the Kananaskis region, just outside Banff National Park in Alberta, and included shots of Porsches zooming down mountain highways and around winding forest roads. Travel Alberta's partnership with the CTC and Porsche was featured on the front page of *Marketing Magazine*.

Finally, an example of a joint promotion being carried out by an association using an umbrella brand name comes from Vancouver. In 2000, 15 of the city's best-known summer festivals and celebrations entertained visitors and locals for 247 days. The combined audience of 2 million included more than 160 000 out-of-town visitors. In 2001, local organizers decided to create a giant "Vancouver, City of Summer Festivals" umbrella that would jointly promote these 15 events. "Working under the City of Summer Festivals umbrella, we are going to build on the awareness, publicity and independent marketing we carry out on behalf of our individual events," said Stephen Drance of Festival Vancouver. "We'll continue as independent productions, but all of us can help each other by pooling our promotional, marketing, and publicity opportunities. For instance, cross-promoting all 15 events through each of our brochures adds to the overall marketing efforts and gives everyone even more exposure. The same is true when it comes to linking our Web pages, or being side-by-side on the event pages of Tourism Vancouver and Tourism B.C. publications as City of Summer Festival events."[11]

CHAPTER SUMMARY

In marketing communications, the blend of promotional elements is known as the promotional mix; this includes advertising, sales promotions, public relations, personal selling, word of mouth, direct marketing, and Internet marketing. The communication process takes place between the sender and receiver of a message, and there are four components in the process: sender, message, medium, and receiver. Models developed to show how advertising works include the AIDA model (**a**ttention, **i**nterest, **d**esire, and **a**ction) and the DAGMAR model (**d**efining **a**dvertising **g**oals for **m**easured **a**dvertising **r**esults). These and others are known as the hierarchies of effects models.

Perhaps one of the most important advances in marketing in recent decades has been the rise of integrated marketing communications (IMC)—the recognition that advertising can no longer be crafted and executed in isolation from other promotional mix elements. The IMC campaign plan summarizes the marketplace situation, the underlying campaign strategy, the main creative strategies and tactics, media and other marketing communication areas of sales promotion, direct marketing, and public relations. It concludes with a section on how to evaluate the campaign's effectiveness.

Advertising can be defined as any paid form of non-personal presentation and promotion of ideas, goods, or services by an identified sponsor, using mass media to persuade or influence an audience. There are six important stages in developing an advertising program: setting the objectives; setting the budget; advertising agency decisions; message strategy; media strategy; and campaign evaluation.

The use of sales promotions is increasing rapidly for many reasons: it offers the manager short-term bottom-line results; it is accountable; it is less expensive than advertising; it speaks to the current needs of the consumer to receive more value from products; and it responds to marketplace changes. Many tools can be used to accomplish sales promotion objectives; these include samples, coupons, gift certificates, premiums and point-of-purchase displays, patronage rewards, contests, sweepstakes, and games. In joint promotions, two organizations that have similar target markets combine their resources to their mutual advantage. This collaboration can reduce the cost of the incentives offered, and it may be a one-off joint promotion or a long-term campaign such as a trade association campaign using an "umbrella" brand name.

KEY TERMS

advertising, p. 258
advertising objective, p. 259
affordable method, p. 261
AIDA model, p. 247
ambient advertising, p. 272
competitive parity method, p. 261
concept testing, p. 253
contests, p. 278
cost per thousand (CPM), p. 267
coupons, p. 276
DAGMAR model, p. 249
full-service agency, p. 264
games, p. 278

gift certificates, p. 276
integrated marketing communications (IMC), p. 250
joint promotions, p. 279
marketing communications, p. 246
media mix, p. 253
objective and task method, p. 260
percentage of sales method, p. 261
persuasion test, p. 254
point-of-purchase merchandising, p. 277
premiums, p. 277

promotional mix, p. 245
pull strategy, p. 255
push strategy, p. 255
recall test, p. 254
recognition test, p. 254
return-on-investment goals, p. 254
sales promotion, p. 274
sampling, p. 275
situation analysis, p. 252
specialized agency, p. 264
sweepstakes, p. 278
SWOT analysis, p. 252
zero-based planning, p. 253

DISCUSSION QUESTIONS AND EXERCISES

1. Find an example of an advertisement from a tourism or hospitality organization. What execution style is it using? How effective is the ad, and what changes would you make to improve its effectiveness?

2. What are the main factors that determine an airline's choice of advertising media? If possible, obtain details or examples of advertising from specific airlines to support your answer.

3. Why is it that the "old rules" of advertising in Table 8.6 might not be so applicable today? Do the "new rules," proposed in 1999, still apply today?

4. Which do you think is an effective advertisement: one that creates an emotional bond with consumers or one that is designed to inform consumers about the product's unique benefit? Or do you have another definition and explanation?

5. How can sales promotions be used to support other elements of the marketing communications mix? Give examples to support your answer.

6. Do you think sales promotions create loyalty or encourage switching to competitors' products? Use examples from your own experience.

CASE STUDY

PROMOTING URBAN ECOTOURISM IN TORONTO

Urban green tourism is a relatively new and emerging concept that was pioneered by a group of interested individuals and organizations who came together in 1993 to explore the potential and marketability of ecotourism in Toronto by establishing the Green Tourism Association (GTA) of Toronto. While the word "green" usually relates to parks, organic products, and recycling, for the GTA the term was far more inclusive. In this case, "green" adapts the World Tourism Organization's definition of sustainability and thus refers to environmental responsibility, local economic vitality, cultural sensitivity, and experiential richness.[12] Specifically, the GTA was incorporated as a nonprofit organization in 1996, its mission being to "develop and cultivate a green tourism industry within the Toronto region, an industry that is ecologically sound, fosters appreciation of and respect for diverse cultural and natural heritage, and strengthens local economies and communities." This goal translates into a three-part mandate to

1. promote and market urban green tourism to tourists and residents;
2. support urban green tourism businesses; and
3. work to green the tourism industry.

The GTA promoted urban green tourism through its green map, green guidebook, and Web site to educate travellers and industry about greener practices. These three promotional means are discussed below.

1. The Green Map

In 1999, the green map was launched by the GTA. It was the twenty-second map in the international Green Map System™, the first map to provide a unified source of information that links tourism to the environment. Linking with the Green Map System™ allowed the association to become part of an international network of green maps and to use established icons for the Toronto map. The Green Map System™ is a globally connected, locally adaptable framework for community sustainability. Billed as the "*Other* Map" of Toronto, it colourfully highlights "green" activities and sites, including businesses, green spaces, ecotours, galleries and heritage sites, organic and natural food stores, and sustainable transportation options, among others. A tourist map generally highlights areas of interest for visitors, such as attractions, landmarks, museums, etc., thus providing an easy reference for touring. Toronto's green map highlights such areas but additionally provides environmental awareness. Old shorelines, hidden creeks, and watersheds are shown in relation to the city's attractions; these can easily be seen as the map is laid over an aerial photograph of the city. Short paragraphs on the map also add a green perspective, addressing topics such as natural history, environmental visits, green spaces and parklands, special gardens, and tips on how to be a green tourist. In total, 375 businesses, attractions and resources are featured on the map, which is produced on recycled paper with vegetable ink.

Although the GTA had only $3000 to spend on promotion of the map, a broad market was reached, including multiple levels of industry, government, tourists, and residents. Some of the marketing and distribution statistics are as follows:

- total direct and indirect media reach: over 4 million people;
- public relations costs: over $50 000;
- 29 media promotions (print, radio, and television);
- 33 000 of the 60 000 maps produced were distributed within the first two weeks;
- 8 percent of inquiries at visitor information sites throughout the summer asked for green information or a copy of the map.

The $3000 spent on promotion resulted in considerable media interest, and GTA received a large amount of free coverage in articles, editorial coverage,

and TV interviews. This expression of media and public interest was a clear demonstration that the topic struck a chord. Indeed, requests for copies of the map came from all over the world—as far away as Australia and Turkey. The multiple requests for additional information, the wide-ranging exposure, and the increased funding options led to the expansion of the organization and to many new or expanded projects, including the development of a green tourist guidebook and the GTA Web site and resource centre.

2. The Green Guidebook

In 2000, the GTA was ready to launch a guide to complement the *Other* Map. In addition to an expanded list of environmentally friendly behaviour and experiences, including outdoor, wildlife, cultural, and local neighbourhood options, it also provided information on large "mainstream" operators such as some of the best-known and largest hotel properties and attractions. In addition, brief historical accounts of the various Toronto neighbourhoods and main arteries; access to information; favourite things to see and do that are "off the beaten track"; lesser-known places to eat; and small, "alternative" types of businesses such as cooperatives and fairly traded produce outlets were described or listed. Again, the media were very interested in the concept, which resulted in extensive exposure:

- international media reach within the first year: over 16 million;
- public relations value of over $150 000;
- more than 75 media promotions (print, radio, and television).

3. The Web site: www.greentourism.ca

Urban green tourism encompasses more than just tourism. That is why the GTA decided to use the Web to link the many areas that support sustainable development, healthy living, and responsible tourism. Through the online resource centre, it is possible to research ecotourism tours, responsible/sustainable tourism offerings, sustainable transportation options, green accommodation initiatives, tips on greening businesses and the environment, and a library of publications and case studies. The multitude of links provides resources both locally and globally, connecting the surfer to critical issues, codes of ethics, tips, facts, and discussion items that contribute to urban green tourism. The Web site provides increased exposure to GTA members through reciprocal links.

Organizational sustainability is determined by financial support received from public and private sources. Although the GTA initiatives were enthusiastically received by the media, residents, and visitors to Toronto, the association continued to struggle to stay afloat financially. Continued over-reliance on public sector grants to pursue its work caused the organization to do little multi-year planning. Most businesses identify success as improving profit margins while lowering overall costs, and it is usually awareness of bottom line initiatives that convinces businesses to take the next step in becoming more environmentally sensitive. While there is increasing evidence that addressing environmental issues can achieve significant cost reductions for corporations, the most spectacular savings are realized by large organizations.

Whether large or small, businesses want to see a return on any investment. Marketing initiatives have to focus on creating exposure and on reaching the various identified markets and segments. Businesses will want to hear how a product or campaign will ultimately bring more customers through their doors. Although the association has tried to quantify its impact on demand since its inception, it is very difficult to obtain either baseline information or to regularly monitor attitudes and behaviour of residents and tourists to determine changes in motivations. But most businesses require tangible proof that visitors coming to Toronto are indeed looking for "greener" experiences and that joining the association or advertising through its various publications would translate into additional revenues for companies.

This lack of industry buy-in, at least in monetary terms, has resulted in a very limited marketing budget, and therefore in a lack of media tracking, advertising expenditures, and print runs. This in turn reduces the appeal for businesses to take out a GTA membership. At the same time, interest in the urban green tourism concept and the GTA's work has generated a number of invitations nationally and internationally, including to the International Year of Ecotourism Preparatory Conference in Brazil. In 2002, the association received a total of 1241 information requests, an increase of 121 percent over 2001.

Sources: *Green Map System.* (2000). Retrieved November 15, 2002, from http://www.ecotourism.org; Green Tourism Association Web site: http://www.greentourism.ca.

QUESTIONS

1. Critically analyze the three methods of promotion currently used by the GTA.
2. What more can be done to entice businesses to take out a GTA membership?
3. How can the GTA capitalize on the worldwide interest in its concept?
4. Should the GTA pursue paid membership (smaller numbers) or use an expanded network of "green" supporters to gain greater acceptance in the marketplace?
5. Should the association's publications list only association members, or also non-members that are seen as important tourism resources (e.g., major attractions, hotels, etc.)?

WEB SITES

www.daysinn.com
Days Inn

www.greentourism.ca
Green Tourism Association of Toronto

www.radisson.com
Radisson Hotels & Resorts

www.timhortons.com
Tim Hortons

www.tourism-montreal.org
Tourisme Montréal

www.tourismvancouver.com
Tourism Vancouver

www.travelalberta.com
Travel Alberta

ENDNOTES

1. Strong, E. K. (1925). *The psychology of selling.* New York: McGraw-Hill.
2. Lavidge, R. C., & Steiner, G. A. (1961). A model for predictive measurement of advertising effectiveness. *Journal of Marketing*, October, 59–62.
3. Rogers, E. M. (1962). *The diffusion of innovations.* New York: Free Press.
4. Broadbent, S., & Jacobs, B. (1985). *Spending advertising money.* London: Business Books.
5. Colley, R. H. (1961). *Defining advertising goals for measuring advertising results.* New York: Association of National Advertisers.
6. Wells, W., Burnett, B., & Moriarty, S. (2003). *Advertising principles and practice.* Englewood Cliffs, NJ: Prentice Hall.
7. Hayman, D., & Schultz, D. (1999, April 26). How much should you spend on advertising? *Advertising Age*, 32.
8. Kotler, P., Bowen, J., & Makens, J. (2003). *Marketing for hospitality and tourism.* Upper Saddle River, NJ: Prentice Hall.
9. Foot, R. (2002, January 18). Saint John hosts CBC awards show but denied ads. *National Post*, p. A7.
10. Heinzl, J. (2003, May 24). Firms' marketing departments are big winners in contest mania. *The Globe and Mail,* pp. B1, B4.
11. Judas, W. (2002). "Vancouver, a City of Summer Festivals." *Tourism, 6*(3), 8.
12. Blackstone Corporation. (1996). *Developing an urban ecotourism strategy for Metropolitan Toronto.* Toronto: Green Tourism Association.

Marketing Communications:
Public Relations, Personal Selling, and Word of Mouth

INNISKILLIN WINES

Wine tourism is hot. After a deep sleep of almost 50 years, the Canadian wine industry has experienced a dramatic rebirth over the last two decades, and Canadian wineries are capitalizing on the growth of wine tourism. The wineries in the Niagara region, for example, attract over 300 000 visitors annually, and a push to develop regional cuisine is gaining momentum. There are 14 wineries in the vicinity of the town of Niagara-on-the-Lake. They are all successful vintners, and they all offer tours and tastings of their wines. The challenge for these wineries is to combine a business focused on a consumer product with a successful tourist destination. Moreover, it is difficult for one winery to ensure that it stands out as unique in a cluster of competitors.

One winery attempting to differentiate itself is Inniskillin Wines. Founded in 1975 by Donald Ziraldo and Karl Kaiser, the company produces and bottles wines from select wine grapes grown in the Niagara Peninsula. Inniskillin's wine tour was developed in

1992 with the building of its new Barrel Aging Cellar, in recognition of growing visitation to the winery and in keeping with Ziraldo's leadership in the Canadian wine industry. Inniskillin's tour takes visitors through 20 viewing stations. Commentary, illustrations, and photographs are set up at the stations, all of which have specifically designed windows that offer views into the winery facilities.

Inniskillin Wines uses public relations to maintain a consistent and positive public image and also to stay at the forefront of the minds of both those who purchase their product and those who visit the area around Niagara-on-the-Lake and who may visit their winery. The public image that Inniskillin wants to portray can be summed up by the statement that appears at the bottom of every company press release: "Inniskillin is Canada's premier estate winery, producing truly distinctive estate wines that rank among the world's finest."

Inniskillin ensures that any event of note related to the winery or the company's wines is communicated to the public through press releases. The following selected list of Inniskillin press releases provides an idea of the wide range of events that warrant a press release. An actual press release is shown later on in this chapter (see pp. 294–295).

January 17, 2001	Celebrity Icewine Picking
February 21, 2001	Inniskillin and Keg Restaurants create Perfect Wine and Food Pairing at Niagara Culinary Institute
February 28, 2001	Inniskillin Wines Named Official Wine Supplier of the Toronto 2008 Olympic Bid
May 8, 2001	Food Network Canada and Inniskillin Wines Kick It Up a Notch with Food Network Canada's *Emeril Live!* in Toronto This June
June 25, 2001	Inniskillin Wins "Best Canadian Winery" and "Best Icewine" Trophies at the International Wine and Spirits Competition
July 13, 2001	Inniskillin Okanagan Wines and Earl's Restaurants Team Up to Provide a Unique Canadian Dining Experience

Inniskillin wants the public to know about its current state of production, so the company publicizes its harvest, particularly the icewine picking. The company also forms partnerships with other companies, such as The Keg and Earl's Restaurants to make its wines more accessible to the public. The winery associates its products with celebrities when appropriate, such as with the event with Chef Emeril Lagasse and Food Network Canada, and its Celebrity Icewine Picking, which in the past has featured Blue Rodeo's Jim Cuddy, CBC's Ron McLean, and actor/singer Michael Burgess.

Perhaps the most important idea that is communicated through Inniskillin's press releases is the recognition and renown that its wines receive at competitions around the world. Although Inniskillin enters many of its wines into competitions, its icewine is by far its signature product. The making of icewine requires a great deal of attention and skill and, not surprisingly, requires advantageous climatic conditions. In 1991, Inniskillin's 1989 icewine won Le Grand Prix d'Honneur at Vinexpo in Bordeaux, France, the fair's highest award and, according to Inniskillin's Web site, "the greatest of international accolade for Canadian icewine."

The Inniskillin winery at Niagara-on-the-Lake hosts events year-round at the Brae Burn Estate. In 2003, 13 events were scheduled between February and December. Events range from tastings and sessions on wine and food pairings to events that are part of tours and galas in partnership with the other wineries in the Niagara region. Events are open to the public, and many have no cost but require reservations. Inniskillin clearly desires to make understanding wine and winemaking a year-round experience for its consumers.

Source: Getz, D. (2000). *Explore wine tourism.* New York: Cognizant Communication Corporation; Inniskillin Wines Web site: http://www.inniskillin.com.

Objectives

On completion of this chapter, readers should understand

- the roles and functions of public relations;

- public relations techniques;

- the roles and objectives of personal selling;

- the sales process and the staffing of sales personnel; and

- the importance of word of mouth in the promotional mix.

Chapter Overview

The opening vignette highlights how a winery in Niagara uses public relations (PR) as a key part of its communications program. This chapter begins by focusing on public relations, examining the roles and functions of public relations and the main public relations techniques used in tourism and hospitality. Personal selling is the focus of the next section of the chapter, which discusses the roles and objectives of personal selling, the sales process, and the roles of a sales manager. The chapter then concludes with a section on word-of-mouth communication—an important but often misunderstood form of promotion in tourism.

PUBLIC RELATIONS

Definition of Public Relations

public relations (PR)

the activities that a tourism or hospitality organization uses to maintain or improve its relationship with other organizations or individuals

publicity

attention received through news media coverage

Public relations (PR) includes all the activities that a tourism or hospitality organization uses to maintain or improve its relationship with other organizations or individuals. Although public relations has a distinguished tradition, people often mistake it for **publicity**, which refers to attention received through news media coverage. Public relations is broader in scope than publicity, its goal being for an organization to achieve positive relationships with various audiences (publics) in order to effectively manage the organization's image and reputation. Its publics may be external (customers, the news media, the investment community, the general public, government bodies) and internal (shareholders, employees). Figure 9.1 shows the different publics who may have an influence over the organization. Managing the relationships and communications with each and every public is essential to effective public relations.

Roles and Functions of Public Relations

The three most important roles of public relations and publicity in tourism and hospitality are maintaining a positive public presence, handling negative publicity, and enhancing the effectiveness of other promotional mix elements.[1] In this third role, public relations paves the way for advertising, sales promotions, and personal selling by making customers more receptive to the persuasive messages of these elements. Ultimately, the difference between advertising and public relations is that public relations takes a longer, broader view of the importance of image and reputation as a corporate competitive asset and addresses more target audiences. PR, then, is concerned with the image of the whole company and, as

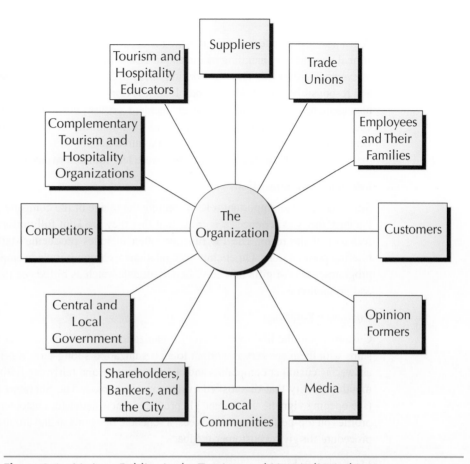

Figure 9.1 Various Publics in the Tourism and Hospitality Industry

such, is sometimes regarded as separate from the marketing function, which is allocated to such divisions as "corporate affairs." The functions of the PR department include the following:

Establishing Corporate Identity

The objectives of establishing a corporate identity are similar to those of branding: to create an image of consistency, reliability, and professionalism that is easily recognized by the public. Everything that the organization owns or produces must project the same image: for example, Inniskillin Wines' placement of the same image statement at the bottom of every company press release (see opening vignette).

Government Relations

The organization's business may be affected by changes in the law or in government policy, and a company may wish to ensure that politicians are aware of the impact their decisions will have. For example, the ski areas of Western Canada positioned in the national parks have been lobbying the government for many years to allow them to develop and upgrade in order to compete with ski areas outside of the parks. Lobbying can be done by individual companies, professional bodies, or specially formed groups.

Crisis Management

When a serious incident occurs, it is the PR department's job to take the pressure off operational managers by handling media enquiries and ensuring that the organization's version of events is presented. The organization needs to be seen to be acting swiftly, efficiently, and responsibly to deal with the problem. It is important that an organization has a crisis management plan in place before an incident occurs. For example, in 2003, with the United States on "Code Orange" alert and the possibility of war looming, the nonprofit United States Tour Operators Association assured people on tours and vacation packages that they would be well cared for if they were left stranded overseas.

Internal Communications

Since staff play an important role in creating the image of the company and the quality of the customer's experience, it is important that they are kept fully informed and made to feel part of the team. The PR function often includes producing staff newsletters and briefing presentations. Other employee relations techniques include employee recognition programs, cards or gifts that mark important dates such as birthdays, incentive programs, and promotions.

Customer Relations

Customers are the lifeblood of every organization, and techniques that improve relationships with them are very important to an organization's long-term survival. For example, answering customer complaints and claims promptly and fairly can limit the bad word-of-mouth publicity that dissatisfied customers can spread. The Sheraton Suites in Calgary (see opening vignette in Chapter 11) produces a newsletter for customers, which includes profiles on top-performing employees, a schedule of events in and around Calgary, and the procedure for giving customer feedback.

Marketing Publicity

Marketing publicity is part of the wider PR function and is therefore part of the promotional mix. Its objective is to secure editorial space to achieve marketing goals. Editorial space in a newspaper, or indeed in a television show, can be extremely effective (see *Snapshot*, p. 301–302).

PROFILE

PUBLIC RELATIONS AT AIR CANADA

In a fiercely competitive airline industry, Air Canada uses an ongoing marketing campaign to communicate to customers its mission of offering value-added customer services, technical excellence, and passenger safety.

However, the traditional channels used to communicate to the customer, such as television and print advertising, have become subject to an increasing amount of clutter that reduces their effect on the target market. Air

PROFILE *continued*

Canada has consequently placed an increasing emphasis on newer and more creative ways of reaching its audience, and public relations is now an integral part of its marketing mix.

Air Canada uses public relations in a number of forms to promote its airlines, including sponsorship programs, supporting charities and awards, running contests, and providing ongoing news releases. Its management of public relations helps to generate awareness about the company and creates a favourable image for the brand. It also helps to generate sales and control promotion costs.

The company is involved in sponsorship programs for a variety of organizations, each of which provides exposure to a different target market. Every year, the airline sponsors high-profile sporting events: examples were the 2002 PGA Air Canada Golf Championship (see Figure 9.2 on page 292) and the 2002 Air Canada Grand Prix in Montreal. Such events draw huge crowds and attract a great deal of media attention. The company also sponsors a number of sporting teams, including all six Canadian NHL hockey teams and the Toronto Raptors of the NBA. Air Canada's sponsorship also plays a major role in the arts and culture community; the company is involved with a vast range of organizations, from the Vancouver Film Festival to the Orchestre Symphonique de Montréal.

Air Canada also sponsors many charities. "Dreams Take Flight" is one of the initiatives that the company is proud to support. This organization helps children who are socially disadvantaged or have physical or mental disabilities. Offering financial support to this and other charities helps to create the image of Air Canada as being a company who cares about people and invests in the community. The company also sponsors many awards. For example, Air Canada is a major sponsor of the Aboriginal Awards and the National Press Club World Freedom Press Awards.

Generating positive views about a company and its products can be a very successful means of marketing because customers often perceive information that they receive from the news as more credible than that found in traditional advertisements and promotions. However, there is some talent required in creating interesting news stories that the media will choose to cover. Air Canada has been successful in continuously generating a large number of press releases about the company that appear in local newspapers, magazines, and on television. Charities, sponsorships, and other forms of community involvement are the kinds of events that create a positive image for Air Canada in the news. The PR department at Air Canada is also keen to publicize information about new in-flight product offerings and company awards and achievements. Favourable news releases about the company appear on the corporate Web site, with links to the original sources.

Air Canada also uses *enRoute,* the company's in-flight magazine, as an important marketing communications tool. The magazine serves a broader public relations role as well: *enRoute* is a sponsor of the CBC Literary Awards, and the in-flight entertainment programming is used to promote Canadian film and music. Air Canada also has the distinction of being the largest promoter of Canadian wines on an international scale.

As for the future, the public relations department at Air Canada is looking forward to focusing on proactive media relations and PR initiatives. Unfortunately, in recent years the airline has moved from crisis to crisis, and therefore much of the PR effort has been directed into crisis management issues. The airline is increasingly making use of its Web site to provide public information over and above promoting products and selling tickets. For example, the public were directed to the

PROFILE *continued*

By attending the Air Canada Championship, you can help contribute
to over 30 charities in Canada. Now that's something worth applauding.

Northview Golf and Country Club – Vancouver, B.C., August 26 – September 1

AIR CANADA *Championship* | AIR CANADA

Figure 9.2 Print Advertisement Promoting the Air Canada Golf Championship

Web site for all developments on the impact of the events of September 11, 2001, on operations, and the same was done during the Iraqi war early in 2003. Then, when the company filed for protection under the Companies' Creditors Arrangement Act (CCAA) in April 2003, the PR department worked extremely hard to persuade all stakeholders that business was operating as usual. For example, all e-mail subscribers to Destina.ca (Air Canada's online tour operator) received a personal e-mail informing them about the "restructuring" of Air Canada.

Source: P. Leblanc, senior director of communications, Air Canada, personal communication, March 21, 2003.

Public Relations Techniques

A variety of PR techniques are available to tourism and hospitality organizations. Nine of the key techniques are highlighted in Figure 9.3 and discussed below.

Figure 9.3 Selected Public Relations Techniques Available to Tourism and Hospitality Organizations

1. Press Releases and Press Conferences

press release (news release)

a short article about an organization or an event that is written in an attempt to attract media attention, which will then hopefully lead to media coverage

A **press release** or **news release** is a short article about an organization or an event that is written in an attempt to attract media attention, which will then hopefully lead to media coverage. Preparing press releases is probably the most popular and widespread public relations activity. To be effective, the release must be as carefully targeted as an advertising media schedule. It should be sent to the right publications and be written in a style that those publications would use. The headline should give a clear idea of the subject. The release should then open with a paragraph that summarizes the main points of the news story by stating who did what, when, why, and where. The style should be that of a news report, and the story must be genuinely interesting to the publication's readers. Ideally, it should tell them something new that is happening and should contain a strong human angle. Other useful contents of a press release include a photograph and quotations, and it is essential to provide a contact name and telephone number in case journalists require further information. An example of a press release sent out by Inniskillin Wines (see opening vignette) appears in Figure 9.4 on page 294.

January 16, 2002
Niagara-on-the-Lake, Canada

Celebrity Icewine Picking 2002

Inniskillin is waiting patiently for the ideal night temperatures to start Icewine picking while also trying to coordinate with the weather for the pre-selected date for the daytime Celebrity Icewine Picking.

Mother Nature is again this year presenting a challenge!!!

We are aiming for a 12:30 p.m. start on Friday, January 18th for the Celebrity Icewine Picking, which also allows guests to attend the Xerox Images of Winter Icewine Gala that same evening in Niagara Falls, which is put on by the Niagara Grape and Wine Festival.

This year **Inniskillin President, Donald Ziraldo** welcomes celebrities from the field of music and sports. Well known **Blue Rodeo** musician **Jim Cuddy** and *Hockey Night in Canada's* sportscaster **Ron MacLean** will join Ziraldo and media guests to participate in Canada's other winter ice "sport"—Icewine Picking. Both Cuddy and MacLean have become Canadian wine enthusiasts and are anxious to tackle the winter harvest!

Jim Cuddy is lead singer and one of the principal song writers for rock band **Blue Rodeo**. Together since the mid-80s, Blue Rodeo has released 12 albums, including their Greatest Hits album Vol. 1 in the fall of 2001. With countless awards and honours, Blue Rodeo is one of the longest lasting, most successful bands in Canadian music history. A truly great talent whose love of wine recently led him to write the foreword for *Vines Buyer's Guide to Canadian Wine.*

Ron MacLean is best known to hockey fans as the energetic host of *Hockey Night in Canada* and co-host of the Coaches' Corner with the colourful Don Cherry. MacLean has covered the Olympics for CBC at the Sydney Summer Olympics and will be heading shortly to Salt Lake City for the 2002 Winter Olympics.

Celebrity pickers from previous years will also join the guests:
Actor/Singer Michael Burgess, Actor Jonathan Welsh, and Loblaws' Executive Chef Christine Chamberlain.

Accompanying this group will be various photographers, journalists, and film crews from as far away as the U.K. and California.

After the chilly vineyard task the group will move into the Loft of the old restored barn for an Icewine tasting followed by lunch.

Donald Ziraldo will present a structured tasting profiling:
- the Inniskillin Riedel Vinum Extreme Icewine Glass;
- 99 Chenin Blanc, 99 Oak-Aged Vidal, 99 Cabernet Franc, 95 Vidal; and
- the aging potential of Icewine through tasting the 95 Vidal Icewine from the underground Library.

Contact:
Debi Pratt
Director of Public Relations, Inniskillin Wines
Tel: 905-468-2187 #310
Toll free: 1-888-466-4754
dpratt@inniskillin.com

Inniskillin is Canada's premier estate winery,
producing truly distinctive estate wines
that rank among the world's finest.

Figure 9.4 Sample Press Release

Source: Inniskillin Web site: http://www.inniskillin.com/news/pressReleases.

Just as press releases can be effective media-attention grabbers, so can special press conferences. A press conference is a meeting at which a prepared presentation is made to invited media people. An example of such a conference took place at the beginning of 2002 when, on January 22 and 23, Newfoundland's Ministry of Tourism partnered with the Canadian Tourism Commission in London, U.K., as well as with Air Canada, Vision, and Buena Vista Productions to launch the movie *The Shipping News* at a gala event in London. The movie is based on E. Annie Proulx's Pulitzer Prize–winning novel of the same title and is set in Newfoundland. The screenings at this London conference presented the film to U.K. tour operators and media. The thinking behind this special press conference was that the movie would generate increased U.K. tourist interest in Newfoundland, as it brings the province and its history to a wider audience.

feature stories

articles of human interest that entertain, inform, or educate readers, viewers, or listeners

2. Feature Stories

Feature stories or features are articles of human interest that entertain, inform, or educate readers, viewers, or listeners. They are longer and have less immediate news value than news releases. However, such features can be extremely effective, and organizations in the tourism and hospitality sectors often encourage journalists to write stories about their products. For example, in 2000, Rocky Mountaineer Railtours (RMR) worked with Monica Campbell Hoppe, of the Canadian Tourism Commission in Los Angeles, to bring Bob Shue, travel editor of the *Denver Post*, to Calgary to ride the Rocky Mountaineer (see Case Study). He rode in early spring and his articles about his experience were published on June 11, 2000. Shue dedicated most of the travel section of the *Denver Post* to Western Canada. RMR experienced a 73 percent increase in bookings in the first six weeks following the articles' publication, and over the course of the year saw an 88 percent overall increase from the previous year. In 2001, the numbers remained high and a year-to-year comparison of guests coming from Colorado between 1999 and 2001 showed a 63 percent increase.[2]

The generation of media coverage for a destination is often an important part of the marketing plan. Tourism Calgary, for example, estimated that familiarization tours and information requests from media in 2001 and 2002 generated media articles with a value of more than US$1.04 million. The G8 summit in Kananaskis in 2002 provided an excellent opportunity to generate media coverage of the area. Tourism Calgary staff worked closely with organizers and industry partners prior to, during, and following the summit to ensure that the event received maximum exposure. The G8 summit attracted 1943 representatives of media from 36 countries and 333 media outlets, and brought an additional $193.1 million to Calgary and area businesses.

3. Travel Exhibitions and Roadshows

Many hospitality and travel organizations exhibit at travel trade shows, exhibitions, or conventions. Generally, these occasions bring all parts of the industry (suppliers, carriers, intermediaries, and destination marketing organizations) together. Exhibiting at a trade show is similar to putting together a small promotional mix. Some exhibitors send out direct mail pieces (advertising) to intermediaries, inviting them to visit their booths. The booth displays (merchandising) portray the available services and may be tied in with recent advertising campaigns. Representatives working the booth hand out brochures and business cards and try to develop sales leads (personal selling—see pp. 303–314). They may also give away free samples or vouchers (sales promotions). When the trade show is over, exhibitors often follow up with personalized mailings (direct mail) or telephone calls (telemarketing).

One of the largest trade shows in Canada is "Rendez-vous Canada" (RVC), an annual showcase that puts Canada's export-ready tourism products in front of qualified international buyers. The trade show held in Halifax, Nova Scotia, in 2002 proved to be very successful, attracting more than 1700 participants. More than 22 000 appointments between international buyers and sellers of Canadian tourism products were scheduled in advance and, for the first time, delegates were able to schedule additional appointments onsite at RVC. In addition to holding business meetings, delegates were able to enjoy the sights, sounds, and hospitality of Atlantic Canada during a series of networking functions that offered the possibility of creating new partnerships.

Some trade shows are held in major cities across the country, taking the form of roadshows that move from one city to the next. Each year, for example, the Canadian Tourism Commission (CTC) Roadshow visits various cities in Canada to present new partnering opportunities, market trends, and program updates developed by the commission and available to the industry. The CTC promotes the Canadian tourism industry by positioning Canada as a premier, four-season, world-class destination and works closely with the industry to achieve this. Partnering is an integral part of the CTC's strategy and is the essence of the Roadshow objectives.

Another important annual event is Canada Media Marketplace, the cornerstone of the CTC's media relations program in the United States. The event, which alternates between New York and Los Angeles, attracted 158 print and broadcast journalists in 2002 and resulted in millions of dollars worth of editorial coverage for Canada during the ensuing months. These stories generate a significant financial yield for to the industry. Charels McDiarmid of the Wickaninnish Inn in Tofino, B.C., says, "We booked between $60 000 and $80 000 worth of bookings in the first couple of weeks after a story on the inn appeared in the *L.A. Times* last year, and it is still generating business for us."[3]

4. Hosting and Sponsoring Events

event sponsorship

the financial support of an event (e.g., a car race, a theatre perform-ance, or a marathon road race) by a sponsor in return for advertising privileges associated with the event

Event sponsorship is the financial support of an event (e.g., a car race, a theatre per-formance, or a marathon road race) by a sponsor in return for advertising privileges asso-ciated with the event. Sponsorships are usually offered by the organizer of the event on a tiered basis, which means that a lead sponsor pays a maximum amount and receives max-imum privileges, whereas other sponsors pay less and receive fewer privileges. Some of Canada's leading advertisers are involved in event marketing and sponsorships. Among the leaders are Labatt and Molson, the Royal Bank of Canada, Imperial Tobacco, Coca-Cola, Pepsi-Cola, and VISA. Investment in sponsorships is mainly divided among three areas: sports, entertainment, and cultural events. Sporting events attract the lion's share of sponsorship revenue.

Events are occurrences staged to communicate messages to target audiences. Public relations departments arrange press conference, grand openings, public tours, and other events to create opportunities to communicate with specific audiences. Tourism and hos-pitality companies can draw attention to themselves by arranging or sponsoring special events, such as the Trout Forest Music Festival in Northwestern Ontario (see Case Study in Chapter 12). The sponsorship of events is also an effective way of gaining publicity, as it allows the sponsor to invite and host suppliers, journalists, distributors, and customers, as well as bring repeated attention to the company's name and products.

The last few decades have seen an increase in destinations' hosting of sporting events. These events bring valuable attention to the host destinations. For example, Calgary's hosting of the Winter Olympic Games in 1988 had a dramatic impact on levels of aware-ness and knowledge of the city of Calgary.[4] More recently, the Olympic Winter Games in 2002 put Utah on the map in the minds of winter sports enthusiasts, many of whom had never visited Utah before. For example, Ogden, host to the Olympic curling venue and the Olympic downhill race at nearby Snowbasin Resort, reported that ski-group bookings for the 2002–2003 season were up 300 percent from the 2001–2002 season. Ogden Convention and Visitors Bureau credited the increase to Olympic exposure.

5. The Sponsorship of Causes

cause-related marketing

a technique whereby companies contribute to the well-being of society and associate themselves with a posi-tive cause that will reflect well on their corporate image

The sponsorship of causes is part of the wider activity of **cause-related marketing**, a technique whereby companies contribute to the well-being of society and associate them-selves with a positive cause that will reflect well on their corporate image. Cause-related marketing is a rapidly expanding public relations trend in North America, particularly during this period of increasing public cynicism toward big business.[5] A company may run a promotion with a charitable organization and donate a portion of its business profits to the cause (for an example, see *Profile* on Air Canada). Alternatively, the company may decide to build a long-term relationship with a cause. Brands can benefit from strategic alignments with causes or with not-for-profit organizations. The emotional attributes associated with cause-linked brands differentiate them from their rivals (this is called "cause branding"). However, a weakness of cause-related marketing is that it is often short-term, opportunistic, and is seen by more and more people as self-serving and exploitative.[6]

An example of real social responsibility comes from the restaurant chain White Spot (see Case Study in Chapter 7). Founder Nat Bailey's belief that a business that receives from the community should also give back to it remains a steadfast component of the company's corporate philosophy. A deep sense of community involvement is one of the core values the company seeks in potential franchisees. The White Spot family supports a variety of community-based sports teams and, off the playing field, the restaurant chain has a long history of helping institutions such as Vancouver's Children's Hospital, the Variety Club, United Way, Junior Achievement, and the White Spot Junior Pie Band, an award-winning musical group the company has sponsored for nearly four decades. Promoting driver safety has also been a high priority. Since the 1980s White Spot Restaurants has distributed tens of thousands of "If You Drink, Don't Drive" stickers.

The *Snapshot* below provides another example of cause-related marketing in the tourism and hospitality industry. CHIP Hospitality supports two major causes–assisting Aboriginal students and fighting homelessness– through two initiatives, called "CHIP Hospitality—Future Tourism Leaders" and "Friends in Need."

SNAPSHOT

CHIP HOSPITALITY AND CAUSE-RELATED MARKETING

CHIP Hospitality of Vancouver, one of Canada's leading hotel management companies, helps Aboriginal students further their studies in tourism through a scholarship program that supports the Foundation for the Advancement of Aboriginal Youth (FAAY). "CHIP Hospitality is proud to join with FAAY to offer Aboriginal youth expanded career opportunities through the support of education," says CHIP Hospitality's president, Minaz Abji. "We hope this will be an important step towards helping these young people develop the knowledge and skills to become successful participants in Canada's growing tourism industry."

CHIP Hospitality has made a three-year commitment to FAAY, and its funds will provide six scholarships of $2000 each year for post-secondary students. The "CHIP Hospitality—Future Tourism Leaders" scholarships will be available to Canadian Aboriginal students enrolled in studies focusing on the hospitality industry at any accredited post-secondary educational institution in Canada. "I am very pleased to welcome CHIP Hospitality to the FAAY family," says Jocelyne Soulodre, president and CEO of the Canadian Council for Aboriginal Business (CCAB). "These scholarships will be distributed across the country and will help Aboriginal students prepare themselves for rewarding careers in the Canadian tourism industry." CCAB is Canada's leading organization dedicated to promoting the full participation of Aboriginal people in the Canadian economy. Established in 1994, FAAY is Canada's oldest general

SNAPSHOT *continued*

interest scholarship and bursary program for Aboriginal youth. The foundation has awarded almost $750 000 to approximately 600 Aboriginal students in all areas of study. CHIP Hospitality joins 10 other leading Canadian and U.S. companies in supporting FAAY's scholarship program.

In 2003, CHIP Hospitality's hotels across Canada donated more than $117 000 to help fight homelessness in their communities as a result of the success of the hotel management company's "Friends in Need" holiday season initiative. "Homelessness affects every city in Canada and we have made it a corporate mission to fight it at the grassroots level by building local partnerships in every community in which we operate," says Abji. "Friends in Need" is a national initiative of CHIP Hospitality, a subsidiary of CHIP REIT (Canadian Hotels Income Properties Real Estate Investment Trust). Thirty-five CHIP Hospitality–managed hotels in 29 cities across Canada offered special holiday season rates of up to 75 percent off, with $10–12 per room sold going to local charities to fight homelessness. CHIP Hospitality hotels booked over 10 800 room nights from the promotion in 2003, and the proceeds went to support projects at 31 local charities from St. John's to Vancouver and in Seattle. The "Friends in Need" promotion is part of CHIP Hospitality's "Hotels with Heart" initiatives, in

which the company takes a leadership role in issues critical to the vitality of its communities and associates.

Since launching the "Friends in Need" initiative nationally in 2000, CHIP Hospitality has raised a total of $298 000 for local shelters, soup kitchens, and youth support groups thanks to the strong support of the community and travellers. "Our community and visitors really rallied behind the program," says John Kearns, general manager of Marriott Residence Inn, Vancouver, one of CHIP Hospitality's hotels. "Having begun the "Friends in Need" program in Fredericton, I am very happy to see it go nationwide," says Pat Carlson, director of the Fredericton Homeless Shelter. "This program has meant that we have been able to plan better in our budget process and that means reducing some of the stress associated with keeping our doors open. These kinds of partnerships are pivotal to building a stronger community and they demonstrate that big business does have a heart."

Sources: Eisenhauer, B. (2002). CHIP Hospitality provides funds for Aboriginal students. Retrieved April 25, 2002, from http://www.canadatourism.com/en/ctc/ctx/ctx-news/search/newsbydateform.cfm; Eisenhauer, B. (2003). CHIP Hotel raises over $117 000 to fight homelessness. Retrieved January 21, 2003, from http://www.canadatourism.com/en/ctc/ctx/ctx-news/search/newsbydateform.cfm.

publications

annual reports, brochures, and company newsletters and magazines that can draw attention to a company and its products, and can help build the company's image and convey important news to target markets

6. Publications

Companies rely extensively on communication materials to reach and influence their target markets. **Publications** such as annual reports, brochures, and company newsletters and magazines can draw attention to a company and its products, and can help build the company's image and convey important news to target markets. Audio-visual materials, such as films, videocassettes, and DVDs are coming into increasing use as promotion tools. Many destination marketing organizations, such as Tourism Vancouver, use videos to promote their destinations, and large companies such as Disney send promotional videos directly to consumers as well as to members of the travel trade. Smaller companies, such as Canadian Mountain Holidays (CMH) (see opening vignette in Chapter 7), will produce videos (CMH, for example, makes videos for heliskiing, helihiking, and mountaineering in up to six languages) and then show them to specific audiences such as intermediaries or targeted audiences.

7. Winning or Sponsoring Awards

In many industries, such as the car industry, it has become common practice for companies to promote their achievements. Automotive awards presented in magazines such as *Motor Trends* have long been known to carry clout with potential car buyers. The winning of awards has become increasingly important in tourism and hospitality sectors as well. For individual operators, the winning of an award is a campaign opportunity, a fact recognized by award-winning organizations such as Virgin Atlantic and Whistler Resorts. These organizations will use the third-party endorsements in their advertising to build credibility and attract customers.

Most of the awards in tourism and hospitality promote best performance and are often an indication of quality. They can therefore provide excellent publicity for winners. An example of a successful awards scheme is the Alberta Tourism Awards (ALTO), which began in 2001. Contestants can enter one or more of eight different categories such as Marketing Excellence or Friends of Tourism, and independent judges review all submissions before deciding on the winner. Each award is sponsored to the tune of $3500 by various organizations that in turn benefit from the publicity that the awards generate. For example, the Sustainable Tourism award is sponsored by EPCOR Utilities Inc. All ALTO finalists are recognized at an annual gala ceremony held in conjunction with the Travel Alberta Tourism Industry Conference.

8. Celebrity Visits

Encouraging celebrities to use tourism and hospitality products can result in considerable media coverage, and can therefore help to promote that particular product. For example, Richard Branson built Virgin Atlantic Airways with the help of a strong public relations campaign that included inviting as many rock stars as possible to fly on his airline. Destinations, too, can benefit from celebrity visits. The ski resorts at Whistler, B.C., have a reputation for attracting high-profile film and music stars, like Arnold Schwarzenegger, Kevin Costner, and British singer Seal, as well as business magnates like Microsoft's Bill Gates. Many consider the 1998 visit to Whistler by Prince Charles and his sons, Princes William and Harry, as the biggest thing to have happened on the Whistler celebrity scene.

Celebrities can also be used to represent destinations for PR purposes. In October 2002, singer Anne Murray was appointed honorary Canadian Tourism Ambassador by Jim Watson, president and chief executive officer of the Canadian Tourism Commission (CTC). "Anne Murray is truly a Canadian treasure," says Watson. "The grace and style with which she represents her music and her country have had a direct impact on people visiting Canada to learn more about Anne and her home." "We are thrilled that Anne is our newest honorary Tourism Ambassador," adds Watson. "Through the Anne Murray Centre in Springhill, Nova Scotia, she has helped promote awareness of the music of Nova Scotia and Canada, while positively impacting tourism in the area." The Anne Murray Centre provides visitors with a first-hand view of the incomparable mix of awards, photographs, memorabilia, and audio-visual highlights of Anne Murray's life and career in a series of award-winning, three-dimensional displays.

9. Product Placement

product placement

the insertion of brand logos or branded merchandise into movies and television shows

Product placement is the insertion of brand logos or branded merchandise into movies and television shows, and it is another tactic for generating publicity. Since television viewers have a tendency—and now the technology—to zip through or avoid commercials, product placement has become increasingly popular with many companies. In fact, product placement is now so blatant that the brand is integrated right into the script of the movie. The movie *Castaway*, staring Tom Hanks, was little more than an extended commercial for FedEx courier company. In addition to featuring countless FedEx packages and logos, the film even managed to accommodate a brief history of the courier's corporate rise. *Survivor*, the popular reality TV show, has featured brands such as Reebok, Mountain Dew, Budweiser, and Doritos, and seemingly every movie starring Tom Cruise is loaded with product placements—even those that are set 50 years into the future!

Tourism and hospitality companies have been quick to take advantage of this growing trend to generate publicity through product placement. British Airways was one of the first companies to be endorsed by James Bond in his movies, and Virgin paid a large amount for a promotional tie-in with the 1999 film *Austin Powers: The Spy Who Shagged Me*. The movie contained a huge plug for "Virgin Shaglantic," and star and writer Mike Myers promoted the film in the United States by appearing on posters for Virgin Atlantic with the headline "There's only one virgin on this poster, baby." Hotels have also got in on the act. The Plaza Hotel was heavily featured in *Home Alone II: Lost in New York*. In the same movie, the family spent considerable time discussing an Avis car rental.

Destinations, too, have begun to see product placement as an opportunity to gain exposure (see *Snapshot* below). Many are keen to persuade producers to make films, television series, or commercials in their country or province. For example, as was mentioned earlier, Newfoundland's Ministry of Tourism partnered with the Canadian Tourism Commission in London, U.K., to launch the movie *The Shipping News*, as the movie is set in Newfoundland. In recent years, tourism officials have persuaded many U.S. film producers to take advantage of favourable exchange rates by filming in Canada. For example, numerous films—including *The Edge*, *Mystery Alaska*, and *Snow Dogs*—have used Canmore and Kananaskis Country in Alberta as a backdrop.

SNAPSHOT

JAPANESE NEWS PROGRAM BROADCASTS FROM CANADA

In 2002, as part of the Canadian Tourism Commission's Asia Pacific marketing program, the Canadian Tourism Commission, VIA Rail, and major tourism industry partners arranged for Japan's largest network television station and sole public broadcaster to bring its national morning news program to Canada for the first time. The popular Japanese morning show, *Ohayou Nippon* (*Good Morning Japan*), with 23 million viewers, was broadcast live from coast to coast from July 7 to 18, 2002. The NHK network show is Japan's top-rated morning news and talk show and was broadcast live from Gastown in Vancouver, B.C., on July 8 before continuing to Kelowna, B.C., on July 9. In total, *Canada—The Transcontinental Fantastic Journey* was broadcast from 10 cities in 7 provinces to showcase Canada.

The NHK crew, including Japanese news anchors and celebrity reporters, travelled aboard VIA Rail and made stops across the country to explore Canada's culture, history, and lifestyle, as well as to showcase some of the country's best tourist attractions. Along the way, they visited the Okanagan wineries, Toronto's Kensington Market, and Montreal's world-renowned Just for Laughs Comedy Festival. The 12-day journey by rail wrapped up at Green Gables House, in Cavendish, P.E.I., to celebrate the 50th anniversary of the publication of L. M. Montgomery's "Anne of Green Gables" books in Japan. NHK aired four minutes of live network daily programming over a two-week period and broadcast a 25-minute daily travelogue titled *Canada—The Transcontinental Fantastic Journey* on high-definition television in the morning, repeating it on satellite television in the afternoon. The Canadian programming was expected to reach over 20 million Japanese viewers daily.

"With close to half a million inbound visitors per year, Japanese travellers are an important audience for our tourism industry," says Jim Watson, former president and CEO of the Canadian Tourism Commission. "This unique partnership with NHK and VIA Rail is a tremendous opportunity for us to bring a wide range of Canadian experiences direct into the homes of millions of Japanese television viewers, from Vancouver's "Hollywood North," and First Nations music and culture in Saskatoon to a passion for gardening in Mont-Joli, Quebec. We are confident that Japanese viewers will enjoy this glimpse of the many faces and attractions of Canada and decide to bring their families here for a closer look," continues Watson.

"The transcontinental railway is such a huge part of Canada's history and identity. There is no better way to experience the sights and sounds of our great country," says Steve Del Bosco, vice-president of marketing for VIA Rail. "We're privileged to be a part of this project and to help provide a truly Canadian experience which promotes Canada's unique flavour and culture to NHK's millions of viewers around the world." The crew's full itinerary included stops in Vancouver, Kelowna, Jasper, Edmonton, Saskatoon, Toronto, Montreal, Quebec City, Mont-Joli, and Cavendish. In addition to the CTC and VIA Rail, organizations supporting this project included Tourism B.C., Travel Alberta, Tourism Saskatchewan, Ontario Tourism, Tourism Québec, and Tourism P.E.I.

Source: Wallace, F. *Canada says "Good Morning" to 20 million Japanese viewers a day*. Retrieved July 5, 2002, from http://www.canadatourism.com/en/ctc/ctx/ctx-news/search/newsbydateform.cfm.

PERSONAL SELLING

personal selling

a personalized form of communication in which a seller presents the features and benefits of a product to a buyer for the purpose of making a sale

Personal selling is a personalized form of communication in which a seller presents the features and benefits of a product to a buyer for the purpose of making a sale. The high degree of personalization that personal selling involves usually comes at a much greater cost per contact than mass communication techniques. Marketers must decide whether this added expense can be justified, or whether marketing objectives can be achieved by communicating with potential customers in groups.

Some tourism and hospitality organizations favour personal selling far more than others, as for them the potential benefits outweigh the extra costs. Companies such as MyTravel, parent company to brands including Sunquest, AlbaTours, The Holiday Network, and Tours Maison, place a great emphasis on personal selling. And in this age of evolving technology and ubiquitous electronic communication, one element hasn't changed in the meetings and convention business: the industry is still driven by personal relationships. As Tony Pollard, president of the Ottawa-based Hotel Association of Canada likes to say, "You can't shake hands with a fax and you can't shake hands with an e-mail." Ralph Strachan, chair, president, and CEO of Tourism Toronto adds, "Getting in the door, getting the attention of your client and making an impression is the name of the game."

Roles of Personal Selling

While the salesperson's job is to make a sale, his or her role goes well beyond this task. Personal selling plays a number of important roles in the tourism and hospitality industry, six of which are discussed below.

1. Gathering Marketing Intelligence

The salesperson must be alert to trends in the industry and to what the competitor is doing. Competitive knowledge is important when the salesperson faces questions involving product comparisons, and information on competitor's promotions can be very useful for the marketing department. Data collected by the salesperson is often reported electronically to the company's head office, where managers can retrieve the information and use it appropriately at a later date. At the Banff Rocky Mountain Resort in Banff, Alberta, director of sales Shelley Grollmuss says, "One way we gather market intelligence is by doing site inspections of our competitors' hotels. We keep a file on each competing hotel with their promotional literature and rates. Local chambers, CVBs, provincial tourism organizations, the CTC, and the Conference Board of Canada are also great resources for market intelligence and trends."[7]

2. Locating and Maintaining Customers

Salespeople who locate new customers play a key role in a company's growth. Salespeople can identify qualified buyers (those most likely to purchase travel services), key decision makers (those who have the final say in travel decisions), and the steps involved in making travel decisions. This important information can be gathered effectively through inquiries by salespeople and from sales calls to an organization.

3. Promoting to the Travel Trade

Many organizations find personal selling to be the most effective communication tool in promoting to key travel decision makers and influencers in the travel trade, such as corporate travel managers, convention or meeting planners, tour operators, and retail travel agents. The purchasing power of these groups is impressive, and there are relatively few of them, which justifies the added expense of personal selling. Shelley Grollmuss says, "We promote to the travel trade in two markets. We use the Canadian Meetings & Incentive Travel Show (CMITS) for the meetings and convention market and Rendez-vous for the tour and travel market."

4. Generating Sales at Point of Purchase

Personal selling can significantly increase the likelihood of purchase and the amount spent by customers at the point of purchase. Reservations staff at hotels and car rental desks have a great opportunity to up-sell (sell upgraded accommodations or cars), and staff in restaurants and travel agencies can have a major influence on the purchase decision of the customer. Increased sales are a result of the proper training of service and reservations staff in personal selling techniques.

5. Using Relationship Marketing

Sales representatives provide various services to customers: consulting on their problems, rendering technical assistance, arranging finance, and expediting delivery. These representatives are very important for building relationships with customers and maintaining their loyalty. Careful attention to individual needs and requirements is a powerful form of marketing for tourism and hospitality organizations. Key customers really appreciate the personal attention they receive from professional sales representatives and reservations staff. This appreciation normally results in increased sales and repeat use, and the focus is on creating and keeping long-term customers. This is just one part of a process that has become known as "customer relationship management" (CRM).

6. Providing Detailed and Up-to-Date Information to the Travel Trade

Personal selling allows an organization to pass on detailed information to the travel trade and provides an opportunity to deal immediately with a prospect's concerns and questions. This is especially important for an organization that relies on travel trade intermediaries for part or all of its business. Tour operators, for example, should have regular contact with travel agents in order to update them on changes in the marketing environment. In 2003, MyTravel merged its sales personnel into a single team to represent all of its brands. The move to consolidate and centralize inside sales meant that one representative of MyTravel replaced the three or more that a travel agency might have been accustomed to dealing with. Company reps were able to more readily explain the differences between the brands to help agents make the most out of the expansive product line.

Objectives of Personal Selling

Although sales objectives are custom-designed for specific situations, there are general objectives that are commonly employed throughout the tourism and hospitality industry.

1. Sales Volume

Occupancy, passenger seats or miles, and total covers (restaurant seats) are common measures of sales volume within the industry. Catch restaurant in Calgary, for example, employs two salespeople who are paid on the basis of the volume of covers that they generate for the establishment. An emphasis on volume alone, however, leads to price discounting, the attraction of undesirable market segments, cost cutting, and employee dissatisfaction. Some sectors, such as exclusive resorts, unique adventure holidays, and upper-end cruises, restrict prospecting to highly selective segments, believing that price and profits will take care of themselves. Others may establish sales volume objectives by product lines to ensure a desired gross profit. This system is the basis for yield management (see Chapter 6).

2. Cross-Selling, Up-Selling, and Second-Chance Selling

cross-selling

offering a customer the opportunity to purchase allied products that go beyond the obvious core products

up-selling

upgrading price and profit margins by selling higher-priced products

second-chance selling

trying to sell additional services to a customer who has already booked services

Cross-selling occurs when a seller offers a buyer the opportunity to purchase allied products that go beyond the obvious core products. Cross-selling is now integral to virtually every segment of the travel industry, travel insurance being one of the most profitable cross-sells in the industry. Good opportunities exist for tourism companies, such as hotels and resorts, to upgrade price and profit margins by selling higher-priced products such as suites through **up-selling**. At the Ripley Ridge Retreat in Calgary (see *Snapshot* in Chapter 10, pp. 331–332), cross-selling and up-selling are tools used frequently in the sale of wedding packages. "We can turn a $300 wedding into a $3000 wedding just while the prospect is walking round the property," said Cara Ripley, marketing director. "We will try and satisfy needs as best we can, and we attempt to sell as many services as we can, from accommodation for the rehearsals to champagne breakfasts and brunches."

A related concept is **second-chance selling**, in which a salesperson may contact a client who has already booked an event such as a three-day meeting. The salesperson may try to sell additional services such as airport limousine pick-up, or try to upgrade rooms or food and beverage services.

3. Market Share

Some sectors of the tourism industry are more concerned with market share than others. Airlines, cruise lines, major fast-food chains, and rental car companies, for example, are often more focused on market share than restaurants, hotels, and resorts are. As a consequence, salespeople are sometimes required to measure market share or market penetration and are held accountable for a predetermined level of either or both. At the Banff Rocky Mountain Resort hotel, sales director Shelley Grollmuss looks at the hotel's market share relative to other hotels in the Banff/Canmore corridor. "We actually gather market share information from a variety of hotels, compile that data and send it back to the hotels that participate in our report. This information is also forwarded to our head office. The report tracks occupancies and revenues for each month," she says.

4. Product-Specific Objectives

Occasionally, a sales force will be charged with the specific responsibility of improving sales volume for specific product lines. This objective may be associated with up-selling and second-chance selling, but may also be part of the regular sales duties of the sales force. Such objectives might be to sell more hotel suites, holiday packages to Mexico, honeymoon packages, or more premium car rentals. A common approach used to encourage the sale of specific products is to set objectives for them and to reward performance with bonuses or other incentives.

The Sales Process

The sales process consists of the following seven steps (see Figure 9.5).

1. Prospecting and Qualifying

prospecting

the process of searching for new accounts

Prospecting is the process of searching for new accounts. It has been said that there are three truisms about prospecting: most salespeople don't like to prospect; most salespeople do not know how to prospect; and most companies are inept at teaching or training salespeople to prospect. There are two key elements to successful prospecting. The first is to determine positioning strategy, i.e., to whom you should prospect. The second is implementing a process to find and ultimately contact those prospects on a one-to-one basis. Jones, speaking about the hospitality sector in particular, suggests that there are five key steps in this one-to-one prospecting (see Figure 9.6).[8] The first step in the prospecting process is to create an ideal customer profile based on current best customers, and the next step is to decide what segments represent good prospects. The third step involves brainstorming to determine all of the possible sources of leads available to find new customers

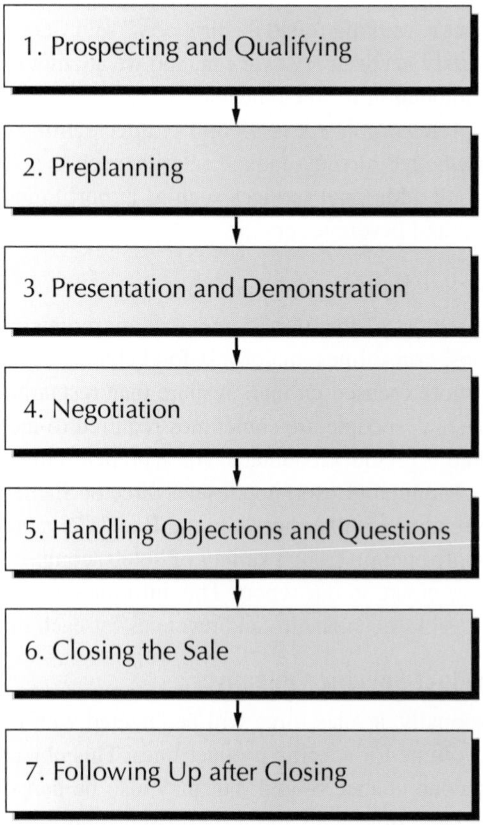

1. Prospecting and Qualifying

↓

2. Preplanning

↓

3. Presentation and Demonstration

↓

4. Negotiation

↓

5. Handling Objections and Questions

↓

6. Closing the Sale

↓

7. Following Up after Closing

Figure 9.5   The Sales Process

that fit the ideal customer profile, and in the fourth step, the salesperson determines which of the lists will be best for prospecting. The fifth and final step is deciding on how to make the initial contact.

Shelley Grollmuss says, "We do our prospecting from a variety of directories and our head office also does telemarketing across Canada."[9] Smaller operations such as Ripley Ridge Retreat in Calgary (see *Snapshot* in Chapter 10, pp. 331–332) tend to wait until customers contact them through word of mouth or through their Web site. For example, a bride- and bridegroom-to-be may key in "Calgary weddings" on the Internet, find the Ripley Ridge Web site, and then call the company's 1-800 number.

Step 1: Ideal Customer Profile
Identify top customers
Create profile of ideal customer
What makes this customer good business?

Step 2: Prospecting Segment Choice
Target customers
Focus on market segments/subsegments that
   match Ideal Customer Profile
What segments represent good prospects?

Step 3: Sources of Leads
"Brainstorm" from sources
   Lists
   Files
   Referrals
What are the possible sources of leads?

Step 4: Target Sources
Decide on best sources to target
Link sources to the Ideal Customer Profile
Will the source of leads provide the profile information?

Step 5: Initial Contact
Determine the key players in the decision making
Assess customer needs
Who should be the initial contact?
What are his/her customer needs?
How should he/she be contacted?

Figure 9.6 One-to-One Prospecting Steps Outline

Source: Jones, D. L. (2001). Prospecting in a down economy. *HSMM Marketing Review*, Fall/Winter, 46–49.

2. Preplanning

A successful sales call, made either by telephone or in the field, requires careful preplanning and preparation. Shelley Grollmuss admits that "sometimes the preplanning is not as in-depth as it should be due to time constraints." There are two elements to preplanning a sales call: the pre-approach and the approach. In the pre-approach stage, a salesperson needs to learn as much as possible about the prospect in order to be able to establish a rapport during the sales call and to have the foundation on which to build the sales presentation itself. The approach then follows and involves all the activities that lead to the sales presentation. These include arranging the appointments with prospects, establishing rapport and confidence at the start of a sales call, and checking preliminary details prior to the sales presentation. Sales representatives have three principal objectives in their approaches: to build rapport with the prospect, to capture a person's full attention, and to generate interest in the product.

3. Presentation and Demonstration

The salesperson now tells the product "story" to the buyer, often following the AIDA formula of gaining attention, holding interest, arousing desire, and inspiring action. Companies have developed three different styles of sales presentation. The oldest is the canned approach, which uses memorized sales talk that covers the main points. The formulated approach identifies early the buyer's needs and buying styles and then uses an approach formulated for this type of buyer. It is not canned but follows a general plan. The need/satisfaction approach starts with a search for the customer's real needs by encouraging the customer to do most of the talking. This approach calls for good listening and problem-solving skills. Shelley Grollmuss uses a formulated approach to win business: "I will meet with a client, ask them a variety of questions about their company and meeting needs, then I will show them my picture book and tell them about how our property can accommodate them."

According to experts, there are certain words that make listeners take notice. Apparently, the 15 most persuasive sales words are: discover, money, guaranteed, love, proven, safe, own, best, good, easy, health, new, results, save, and free.[10] It has been suggested that a salesperson needs to introduce a "wow" factor: an intangible element that causes an emotional response in potential buyers, making them take a second look, draw in breath, and say, "Wow, I have to buy that!"[11] There are two ways to create the wow factor. The first is by introducing a product that is unique. More often than not, this is impossible, so the second way is to add the factor to the sales personality by generating enthusiasm, and delivering what is promised.

4. Negotiation

Much of selling to the travel trade involves negotiation skills. For meeting planners and hotel groups, for example, the two parties need to reach agreement on the price and other terms of the sale. The hotel salesperson will be seeking to win the order without making deep concessions that will hurt profitability. Although price is the most frequently negotiated issue, other factors may be taken into account, and numerous bargaining tools exist. Sales force members should be taught to negotiate using services or bundled services as the primary negotiating tool rather than price. For the hotel salesperson, negotiations should begin with rack rates, and price concessions should be given only when absolutely essential. Other negotiating tools, such as upgrades, airport pick-up, champagne in rooms, etc., should be employed. A hotel might package these amenities into bundles of services and brand them with names such as the Prestige Package, in order to entice buyers into making a booking.

At the Banff Rocky Mountain Resort, Shelley Grollmuss often provides complimentary upgrades or additional services that are of minimal cost to the hotel. "However, we try to make our proposal look as enticing as possible from the start. These days you are rarely given the opportunity to negotiate on the room rate—it has to be attractive and competitive from the start. Meeting rooms rates and additional hotel service are often negotiated once they have decided on their location." At the Ripley Ridge Retreat in Calgary, prices for corporate retreats are usually competitive enough to win the business, but Cara Ripley will discount a maximum of 10 percent if a corporate customer requests it. "We find that most people don't ask because our prices are low enough already, but to be successful you have to understand how to negotiate in order to close a sale."

5. Handling Objections and Questions

When most sales presentations are completed, prospects ask questions and raise one or more objections. Objections come in all forms, even through body language. Resistance can be psychological (e.g., preference for an established hotel) or logical (e.g., price). There are several effective ways to handle objections. One is to restate the objection and to prove diplomatically that it is not as important as it seems. Another is the "agree and neutralize" tactic or the "yes, but" approach. In this approach, sales representatives initially agree that a problem exists, but go on to show that the problem is not relevant or accurate. No matter which approach is used, objection must be met head-to-head.

6. Closing the Sale

Closing means getting a sales prospect to agree with the objectives of the sales call, which normally implies making a definite purchase or reservation. Closing the sale can be the most important stage of the sales process, but many salespeople are not comfortable about asking for the order or do not recognize the opportune moment to wrap things up. A sales call without a close is unsuccessful, and every salesperson must ask for the business or at least some commitment to continue the dialogue. Knowing when and how to close are the keys to success. As with objections, this again requires careful attention to the prospect's words and body language. Closing techniques include actually asking for the order, offering to help the secretary write up the order, asking whether the buyer wants A or B, asking how the buyer would like to pay, or by indicating what the buyer will lose if the order is not placed immediately.

At the Ripley Ridge Retreat, it is the job of Shawn Ripley to close the sale for a wedding after showing a prospective bride and/or groom around the property. Asking for the business happens when the tour of the property finishes inside the reception room (which contains a cash machine), where Shawn will ask the customer if he or she would like to check availability, block a certain date off, and then leave a $100 deposit. According to the retreat's owners, 100 percent of prospective customers will book on the spot.

7. Following Up after Closing

A salesperson's work is not finished until all the required steps and arrangements are made to deliver the promised services. In some cases, such as the organization of major association conventions or the planning of incentive travel trips, this "delivery" work is extensive. However, the follow-up is essential if the salesperson wants to ensure customer satisfaction and repeat business. "Follow up or foul-up" is the slogan of many successful salespeople. It is often advisable to give buyers some kind of reassurance that they have made the right decision. This reduces the buyers' level of **cognitive dissonance**—a state of mind that many customers experience after making a purchase, in which they are unsure whether they have made a good or bad decision. An important part of post-sale activity also involves immediate follow-up after prospects or their clients have actually used the services. Many travel agents use this effectively by telephoning clients soon after their trips to find out what they liked and did not like. Shelley Grollmuss says, "We always have the salesperson that booked a piece of business follow up with the client directly after their function to ensure that everything went as anticipated."

cognitive dissonance

a state of mind that customers experience after making a purchase, in which they are unsure whether they have made a good or bad decision

Sales Management

sales management

the management of the sales force and personal selling efforts to achieve desired sales objectives

Sales management is the management of the sales force and personal selling efforts to achieve desired sales objectives. A sales manager has five key roles to play: recruiting salespeople, training them, motivating and rewarding them, sales planning, and sales performance evaluation.

1. Recruiting Salespeople

A sales manager's first job is to hire competent people to fill available positions. In tourism and hospitality, it is uncommon for field sales representatives to be hired without sales experience. The more established practice is for entry-level people to be order takers, who are eventually promoted to sales representative positions. Hiring salespeople from competitors and related outside organizations is also common. Research has shown that no one set of physical characteristics, mental abilities, and personality traits predicts sales success in every situation. Salespeople's success depends more on the actual tasks assigned to them and the environment in which they operate. Most customers say they want salespeople to be honest, reliable, knowledgeable, and helpful. Companies should look for these traits when selecting candidates. Another approach is to look for traits common to the most successful salespeople in the company. A study of super-achievers found that super-sales performers exhibited the following traits: they were risk-taking, had a powerful sense of mission, had a problem-solving bent, cared about the customer, and engaged in careful planning.[12]

2. Training Salespeople

Sales training programs are very important to the continuation of success in personal selling. For example, every year, the Canadian Institute of Travel Counsellors (CITC) holds two Executive Certified Travel Manager retreats. Participants in the retreats spend much of the program analyzing a travel agency case study. They deal with a range of issues and review the current obstacles and opportunities before the agency to determine what marketing and sales efforts should be employed, as well as what requirements agency staff have. At the close of the program, an individual strategic plan is drawn up for the case study agency that may then be used as a model to implement strategies for course participants' agencies.

Many employers recognize the benefits of professional certification and give preference to certified individuals when hiring. The Canadian Tourism Human Resource Council (CTHRC) recently launched the second edition of the *Sales Manager National Occupational Standards* (English and French) to the Canadian tourism industry. The standards describe the skills, knowledge, and professionalism necessary in a sales manager in the accommodations sector. However, they are also applicable to other tourism sectors.

Standards are the building blocks for achieving professional certification in the occupation, and are often used in training programs. To ensure that its 27 certificate occupations remain current and relevant, the CTHRC brings industry representatives together for standards updates and revisions on a three- to five-year cycle, or as deemed necessary by industry. Other national occupational standards currently in development are for catering managers, banquet managers, banquet servers, and room service attendants.

Sales training that ultimately benefits the Canadian tourism industry may not necessarily take place in Canada. In 2003, responding to the needs of major tour operators in the United Kingdom for sales training on Canada's urban tourism products, eight of Canada's "big cities" organized an exclusive one-week sales and training mission, with impressive results.[13] Representatives of destination marketing organizations (DMOs) from Victoria, Vancouver, Calgary, Edmonton, Ottawa, Montreal, Quebec City, and Halifax conducted training sessions in two teams for approximately 250 sales and reservations staff at the offices of 13 U.K. tour companies. The teams promoted the Canadian provincial capitals and gateway cities as exciting, four-season, cosmopolitan destinations, featuring new experiences and activities, within easy access to natural attractions. The $40 000 initiative was very successful. Feedback from the U.K. tour operators and their staff to the urban product–specific training was positive. The city DMO representatives reported that there was excellent dialogue with the Canada product managers at each tour company regarding ways to position Canada's cities. The Canada Cities Consortium is already looking ahead to the expansion of the program and to leveraged funding opportunities.

3. Motivating and Rewarding Salespeople

The majority of salespeople require encouragement and special incentives to work at their best level. This is especially true of field selling, as the nature of the job makes it open to frequent frustration: sales reps usually work alone, their hours are irregular, and they are often away from home. Even without these factors, most people operate below capacity in the absence of special incentives, such as financial gain or social recognition. Sales managers therefore need to understand motivation theories and to provide financial and nonmonetary incentives to keep sales-force motivation at its peak.

Financial incentives include salary and commissions, as well as fringe benefits such as paid vacations, insurance programs, and medical programs. Often bonuses are given when predetermined volumes of sales and profits, or sales quotas, are achieved. In the tourism industry, free travel is a very important fringe benefit, especially for travel agency and airline staff. Non-monetary compensation and motivators are reward/recognition programs and job advancement opportunities. Sales promotions can also be used to motivate a sales force (see p. 274). However, they tend to work best in achieving short-term objectives and are not advisable over the long-term.

4. Sales Planning

The heart of sales planning is the sales plan, usually prepared annually and containing a detailed description of personal selling objectives, sales activities, and the sales budget. These selling objectives are frequently set as forecasts of unit or sales volumes or some other financial target derived from expected sales levels. This sales forecast is very useful to others outside the sales department and is a key planning tool for the entire organization. Expected sales levels influence the allocation of personnel and financial resources in many other departments. But the selling objectives may also be nonfinancial, such as the number of sales calls, new sales prospects converted to customers, or the number of inquiries answered successfully.

The sales department budgets are another part of the sales plan. Typically these will include the sales forecast, the selling expense budget, the sales administration budget, and the advertising and promotion budget. Given the relatively high cost of personal selling, this budget plays a key role in planning and controlling the sales effort. Finally, the sales plan will include the assignment of sales territories and quotas. **Sales quotas** are performance targets set periodically for individual sales representatives, branch offices, or regions. They help sales managers motivate, supervise, control, and evaluate sales personnel. The sales manager is likely to use a combination of past territory performance and market indices to allocate quotas for each territory.

sales quotas

performance targets set periodically for individual sales representatives, branch offices, or regions

5. Evaluating Sales Performance

The final function of sales management is the measurement and evaluation of sales performance. "Sales analysis" is the term used most frequently for the evaluation of performance. This analysis can be done by considering total sales volume or by looking at sales by territory or customer groups. One of the most important methods of evaluation is to judge actual results against sales forecasts and budgets.

MARKETING IN ACTION

SELLING BEDS AT THE WESTIN EDMONTON

"It really is a buyer's market," says Mark Nisbett, director of sales and marketing at The Westin Edmonton, a 20-storey hotel situated near the North Saskatchewan River in the heart of downtown Edmonton. Nisbett is reflecting on the market conditions in 2003, a year when the hotel industry in Alberta had already been hit by an ailing economy, the war in Iraq, and the outbreak of severe acute respiratory syndrome (SARS).

The Westin is part of Starwood Hotels & Resorts, and the four-star hotel has 413 guest rooms and suites, as well as 22 000 square feet of meeting and banquet space. Selling to groups is the main focus of the sales team at The Westin, and Nisbett identifies two types of clients: those who know what they want and just call to book a meeting or a banquet; and those whom the sales team have to work a lot harder to close because they may be looking at other properties or even other destinations.

MARKETING IN ACTION *continued*

However, Nisbett admits that being part of the Starwood group gives The Westin national sales coverage. "We have a lot of leads generated through Starwood that we can then follow up."

But competition for group business is fierce. For example, a medical association from San Francisco recently expressed an interest in hosting its conference at The Westin Edmonton, but the association was also looking at Vancouver, Toronto, and Calgary. "It is up to our sales team to go out and win that business, perhaps coordinating with other hotels in Edmonton. We will have to find out exactly what the needs and wants are for that association, and then put a bid package together with other hotels in the city. What happens then is that the meeting planners will make a couple of site visits to a hotel in each destination and weed out the properties that they are not interested in," says Nisbett.

These site visits are an important part of the sales process. Nisbett likes The Westin to be the Edmonton property that hosts the buyers, because he then has a great opportunity to wow them when they are on site. "When a buyer visits the hotel we do everything possible to impress. For example, we may put pictures up of the prospective buyers everywhere back-of-house prior to the visit, so that all members of staff can give the buyer personal attention." Preparation for the site inspection is very important. By finding out beforehand everything they can about the company, exactly who they are and exactly what their needs are, the Westin sales team can then tailor the site inspection to those needs. "It shows the client that we are interested in their business if we have taken the time to find out what they are all about," says Nisbett.

However, not all selling takes place at the hotel. Sales managers travel three to four times a year to major Canadian cities for sales purposes, and occasionally to cities outside of Canada. "We prefer to bring buyers to our hotel so that they can experience the product, but sometimes it is necessary to travel to close a sale," says Nisbett. "For example, we have a contract outstanding at the moment with the Canadian Diabetes Association, who are a little hesitant to book with us despite a satisfactory site visit, so we will send someone to Toronto to close the sale. If we think we can influence a decision by making a personal sales call, then we will spend the money to do that."

Sales planning is a key part of Nisbett's job. "What we do is forecast the entire year, based on existing bookings and historical data, and then plot a grid for our sales managers. We then work out a minimum target for each period, and the sales managers will be armed with this knowledge when they meet with a buyer." If a buyer or meeting planner is not prepared to pay this target room rate, then the sales personnel may negotiate by offering services such as free parking. Each sales manager has a room-night target and a revenue target. For example, in 2003, the corporate sales manager had a target of 8800 room nights at an average rate of $123 per night. "He or she can reach the target by booking more rooms at a lower rate or fewer rooms at a higher rate—as long as the revenue target is reached," says Nisbett. Food and beverage sales are also becoming very important, and sales managers are encouraged to get buyers to commit to a certain amount of food and beverage sales, even if the event is three years away.

Most of the training for The Westin sales team is Web-based; it is live and interactive and contains about six different modules covering topics such as negotiating, handling objections, and making presentations. Salespeople can take them on their own, and each module takes about two and a half hours. Nisbett can see how well they have performed on each module, so if he sees one salesperson has not done well with presentations, he can

MARKETING IN ACTION *continued*

offer extra training. Turnover is high among salespeople in the hotel industry, so the Starwood philosophy is to "pay for performance" to try to keep high-quality salespeople. Sales managers earn a base salary of about $38 000 to $44 000, but that can increase with a lucrative incentive scheme. The highest commission a sales manager has earned while Nisbett has been at The Westin was $34 000, but the norm is in the $15 000–$20 000 range.

However, sales managers can also win incentive trips to luxury resorts by meeting predetermined targets. Nisbett says more often than not, the first thing they say when they return is that "there is no way I am not going on that trip again next year." This then encour-

ages them to meet targets the following year. Other incentives used by Nisbett include team-building exercises outside the hotel (such as a game of golf), reward points, and extra holidays. Nisbett also offers small cash incentives for good performance on the Starwood Mystery Shopping program. In this program, telephone calls are made by third-party researchers to various Starwood Hotels as well as to key competitors, and sales managers are scored on factors such as greeting, qualification of needs, presentation, handling of objections, attempts to close, and professionalism.

Source: M. Nisbett, director of sales and marketing, The Westin Edmonton hotel, personal communication, July 15, 2003.

WORD OF MOUTH

word of mouth

communication about products and services between people who are perceived to be independent of the company that is producing or providing the product

Word of mouth is communication about products and services between people who are perceived to be independent of the company that is producing or providing the product.[14] It is a communication tool that works particularly well for the tourism and hospitality industry, and is worthy of special attention. Recommendations or advice from friends, relatives, peers, and influential persons are without doubt one of the most powerful communications media. Word of mouth can be controlled only to a degree, but it must be a priority nevertheless for tourism businesses, and it is indeed used in a variety of sectors of tourism. For example, Inniskillin Wines (see opening vignette) has recognized that even non-buyers are primary sources of communications about the winery and the wines tasted, and can have a potentially tremendous impact on future visits and remote sales. The Vancouver Convention & Exhibition Centre also values the power of word of mouth. Its "Be a Host" program assists local people to help sell Vancouver as a destination in their respective industries, and has helped to establish credibility and profile for the centre.

Word-of-mouth communications can be conversations or just one-way testimonials. They can be live or canned. They can be conveyed in person, by telephone, by e-mail, via a listserv group, or by any other means of communication. They can be one-to-one, one-to-many (broadcast), or group discussions. The essential element is that they are from or among people who are perceived to have little commercial vested interest in persuading someone else to use the product and therefore no particular incentive to distort the truth in favour of the product. In contrast, advertising is the communication of a message that is chosen, designed, and worded by the seller of the product, in a medium that is owned or rented. A sales message is a "company line" delivered by a representative of the company. On the other hand, word of mouth is originated by a third party and transmitted spontaneously in a way that is independent of the producer or seller, and can therefore have a high level of credibility.

According to Silverman, word of mouth is far and away the dominant communication force in the marketplace. Yet it is also the most neglected.[15] Silverman suggests that this is so because most people think that they can't do much about word of mouth. Most marketers believe, implicitly or explicitly, that word of mouth is out of their control. They believe that advertising and other marketing media can influence it, to be sure, but not directly. However, Silverman believes that word of mouth can be strongly influenced and even harnessed, and in that sense, controlled.

Word of mouth is a communication tool that works well for the tourism and hospitality industry. In his recent book, *The Anatomy of Buzz*, Emanuel Rosen takes a substantive look at creating word-of-mouth excitement about a product.[16] Rosen suggests that the best starting points are "hubs," also known as influencers and opinion leaders. Some hubs are obvious, such as regional and national media outlets. For instance, if a local talk-show host discusses a restaurant on Monday, it will probably be full on Tuesday. Oprah Winfrey's "book club" is an example of this phenomenon. Other hubs are less obvious. They include fashion leaders in junior high schools (social leaders who made skinny scooters popular), gurus on college campuses (technical leaders who spread the word via the Internet), and people on the boards of local charities (community leaders who attend many social functions). The best hubs also span networks, in addition to influencing people in their own network. The leapfrogging of word of mouth from one network to another accelerates the rate of beneficial buzz.

Often generated within the hive of the Internet, "buzz" has become essential to a product's success in today's fast-paced business environment. As Rosen (a former marketing executive for Niles Software) explains, in pre-Internet days a new product would appear in stores, consumers would buy it or not, and the company would then take however long it wished to evaluate the launch. Today, however, consumers immediately voice their views—on message boards, review sites, company sites, complaint sites, via e-mail, or on their own Web sites—and so have a strong and immediate influence on whether a launch succeeds.

Rosen points out that hubs are where you find them. Sometimes they come to you. People who attend specialized conferences often are hubs for their organizations. Other times, you have to seek them out. People who are looked up to by others as experts and who talk to a lot of people are good prospects. People who are known by friends and colleagues as being interested in cuisine and fine wine are considered experts whose opinions are sought when a new restaurant opens. Certain tourist segments can be more influential than others. For example, gay tourists, who attend events like the Gay Games, are a minority of consumers, but they tend to be "hyperconsumers" who not only consume more but also influence the purchases of their gay and straight friends and colleagues, thus providing vital word-of-mouth endorsements for destinations, products, brands, and companies.[17] Word of mouth is also considered to be the main force of influence in the backpacker market.[18]

Destinations use word of mouth as part of their communications strategy. In 2003, Tourism PEI and the Tourism Industry Association of Prince Edward Island (TIAPWI) invited all Islanders to call or e-mail friends and/or relatives in other Canadian provinces to "Come Home to the Island" to rediscover the magic and beauty of the Island and renew old friendships. In the form of a contest, Islanders were asked to personally invite their friends and family in the rest of Canada to enter to win a trip to Prince Edward Island. Islanders could either phone their family and/or friends or send them an innovative e-card from the contest's Web site. To enter the contest, friends or family could visit the Web site or respond to the e-card and request a Visitor Guide package, or they could call a toll-free number and quote the contest code word "home." Minister of Tourism Jeffrey Lantz noted, "This initiative allows for every Islander to get involved in making tourism a success on PEI. It is a proactive way of encouraging people to travel to Prince Edward Island."[19]

Silverman suggests that word of mouth is powerful for 10 key reasons.[20]

1. *It has independent credibility.* A decision maker is more likely to get the whole, undistorted truth from an independent third party than from someone who has a vested interest in promoting the company's point of view. It is this unique credibility that gives word of mouth much of its power. So if you are thinking about backpacking around Australia, you are more likely to take advice from friends who have been there than from a travel agent.

2. *It delivers experience.* Lack of positive experience with a product or service is usually the single greatest factor holding it back from greater and faster acceptance. Again, hearing about other backpackers' experiences will act as the accelerator or the brake on your booking your backpacking holiday.

3. *It is more relevant and complete.* Word of mouth is "live," not canned like most company communication. When your friend tells you about a country she thinks you would like, she is telling you because she thinks that you—not some anonymous stranger—would like it. She wouldn't tell you about it if she thought you weren't interested in going.

4. *It is the most honest medium.* Because it is custom-tailored, and because people participating in it are independent of the company, it is the most honest medium. And customers know it. Advertising and salespeople can be biased and not fully truthful. The inherent honesty of word of mouth further adds to its credibility.

5. *It is customer-driven.* Closely related to the two reasons given above, word of mouth is the most customer-driven of all communications channels. Customers determine whom they will talk to, what they will ask, and whether they will continue to listen or politely change the subject.

6. *It feeds on itself.* Word of mouth tends to breed and is self-generating. If 10 people have 10 experiences each while backpacking around Australia, that's one hundred direct experiences. If they each tell 10 people about their own experiences, that's an additional 1000 (indirect) experiences, which can be just as powerful as the direct experiences. It doesn't take long for everyone to hear about the wonders of Australia, often several times each, which provides additional confirmation (e.g., "everybody's talking about it").

7. *It has expert power.* The "hubs" referred to earlier have one overriding attribute that gives them their influence: trust. People trust them to filter, distill, and objectively evaluate the overwhelming amount of information, make sense of it, and present it in a recommendation that is most likely to be right. Tiers of experts and influencers tend to initiate word of mouth, sustain it, give it even more credibility, and supply the initial "bang" that can start the chain reaction of word of mouth.

8. *Influencers like to influence.* One of the reasons that the initial stages of word of mouth are sustained and can spread so rapidly is that influencers like to influence. That's one of the reasons that they are influencers. If they didn't enjoy the process, they would keep their mouths shut and their keyboards still.

9. *It saves time and money.* Another attribute of word of mouth is that it can be extremely efficient. If you want to visit a destination that you don't know too much

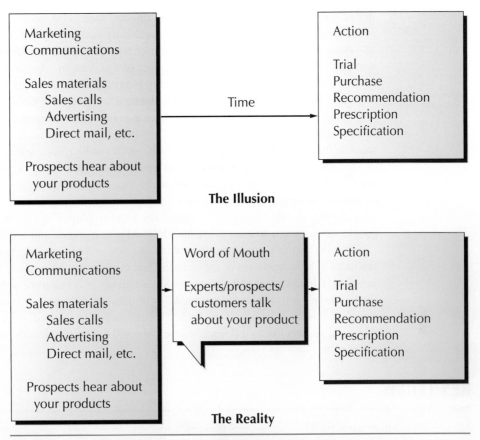

Figure 9.7   What Causes Sales? Illusion versus Reality

Source: Silverman, G. (2001, September). The power of word of mouth. *Direct Marketing, 64*(5), 47–63.

about, the best way is often to find a few people who have either been there or collected information about the place, and learn from them what they have found out.

10. *It is an illusory force.* Word of mouth is an invisible, illusory force (sometimes even called "underground" communication, or "the grapevine," as well as "the buzz"). A company can gain competitive advantage by making competitors think that increased sales are due to active promotional efforts, so the illusion is that the advertising, or the sales message, or the mailing caused the effects. In fact, many products or services succeed despite the marketing supporting them, for reasons different from the positioning of the product or the most emphasized benefits. Figure 9.7 explains this illusory force.

CHAPTER SUMMARY

Public relations includes all the activities that a tourism or hospitality organization uses to maintain or improve its relationship with other organizations or individuals. The functions of the PR department include establishing corporate identity, government relations, crisis management, internal communications, customer relations, and marketing publicity. The main techniques used in public relations are press releases and press conferences, feature stories, travel exhibitions and roadshows, hosting and sponsoring events, sponsoring causes, publications, winning or sponsoring awards, celebrity visits, and product placement.

Personal selling is a personalized form of communication that involves a seller presenting the features and benefits of a product or a service to a buyer for the purpose of making a sale. In the tourism and hospitality industry, personal selling plays a number of important roles: gathering marketing intelligence, locating and maintaining customers, promoting to the travel trade, generating sales at point of purchase, relationship marketing, and providing detailed and up-to-date information to the travel trade. Objectives of personal selling include achieving sales volume, up-selling and second-chance selling, market share or market penetration, and product-specific objectives. The sales process consists of seven steps: prospecting and qualifying, preplanning, presentation and demonstration, negotiation, handling objections and questions, closing the sale, and following up after closing. A sales manager has three key roles to play. The first is to recruit salespeople, the second is to train them, and the third is to motivate and reward them.

Word of mouth is communication about products and services between people who are perceived to be independent of the company that is providing the product, in a medium perceived to be independent of the company. Silverman suggests that word of mouth is powerful for 10 reasons: it has independent credibility, it delivers experience, it is more relevant and complete, it is the most honest medium, it is customer-driven, it feeds on itself, it has expert power, influencers like to influence, it saves time and money, and it is an illusory force.

KEY TERMS

cause-related marketing, p.297	press release (news release), p. 293	public relations (PR), p. 288
cognitive dissonance, p. 310		sales management, p. 310
cross-selling, p. 305	product placement, p. 301	sales quotas, p. 312
event sponsorship, p. 297	prospecting, p. 306	second-chance selling, p. 305
feature stories, p. 295	publications, p. 299	up-selling, p. 305
personal selling, p. 303	publicity, p. 288	word of mouth, p. 314

DISCUSSION QUESTIONS AND EXERCISES

1. How important are public relations and publicity to tourism and hospitality organizations? Give examples to support your answer.
2. With reference to the *Profile* on Air Canada, do you think the company is proactive or reactive in terms of public relations?
3. You have just won a tourism award and would like to publicize your achievements. Write a press release for the local newspaper in an attempt to get them to run a story relating to your win.
4. Which do you think is the most important step in the sales process? Explain your answer.
5. Think of some recent examples when someone has attempted to up-sell or cross-sell a product to you. Explain why they succeeded or failed. What are the disadvantages of these selling techniques?
6. Why is it, do you think, that word of mouth is the most neglected promotional tool in the marketplace?

CASE STUDY

THE ROCKY MOUNTAINEER

The train
will carry you,
the scenery will move you.

CANADIAN ROCKIES BY RAIL

This year, experience the natural beauty of the Canadian Rockies.
For a free brochure, see your travel agent or call 1-800-665-RAIL (7245).

ROCKY MOUNTAINEER RAILTOURS®
www.rockymountaineer.com

Figure 9.8 Rocky Mountaineer Print Advertisement

Imagine a trip, by train, through the heart of the spectacular Canadian Rockies, specifically scheduled so that the breathtaking mountain scenery can be enjoyed entirely by daylight. Some of the most beautiful places in Canada are seen from the country's oldest form of mass transportation—passenger rail. This could be an ideal tourism product, one that would be easy to promote and easy to sell. Nevertheless, in the spring of 1990, the newly privatized Rocky Mountaineer passenger train service and its parent company, Mountain Vistas Railtour Services, (later the Great Canadian Railtour Company) were facing many challenges, not the least of which was marketing this wonderful product on a minuscule budget.

Passenger rail was a staple of Canadian transportation from the time the railways were first constructed in the late 19th century. However, by the late 20th century, the two major Canadian railways—Canadian National and Canadian Pacific—had withdrawn from passenger service, leaving that sector dominated by VIA Rail, a Crown corporation. The Rocky Mountaineer passenger service was created in 1988 and travelled between Vancouver and Calgary, making an overnight stop in Kamloops, B.C. The trip was designed so that guests could enjoy the fabulous views of the Rocky Mountains by daylight. In the fall of 1989, the Canadian government decided to privatize the Rocky Mountaineer, and by April of 1990, Mountain Vistas Railtour Services bought and immediately began operating the Rocky Mountaineer. In that first season, the company made one return trip per week between Vancouver and Jasper and Calgary, at a cost of $350 for a one-way fare.

The new company was headed by Peter Armstrong, who had previously turned Vancouver's Gray Line tour-bus business into a profitable operation. He assembled a team for the Rocky Mountaineer that brought together experts in both tourism and railways. The marketing of the Rocky Mountaineer would be crucial, so Armstrong recruited the help of skilled marketers. Rick Antonson, formerly of the Edmonton Convention & Tourism Association, became the vice-president of sales and marketing. Murray Atherton, who had worked for Armstrong at Gray Line and had his own hospitality consulting firm, was brought in to reach the overseas tour companies, particularly those in the United Kingdom. Finally, Mike Leone, who had handled media relations in the United States for Expo 86, was entrusted with the company's public relations.

The company's first trip was for the Pacific Asia Travel Association (PATA), a booking committed to by VIA Rail. Despite the haste with which Mountain

Vistas had to prepare for this trip, it was a great success. The company benefited from this initial trip in a number of ways. First, Tourism Canada (CTC's precursor) had filmed portions of the trip for their own promotions and Mountain Vistas was able to get a couple of hundred copies of this video into circulation. Second, the PATA trip provided the company with first-hand knowledge provided by overseas tour operators on the best ways to sell travel products in their home markets. Finally, the then minister of external affairs for the federal government, Joe Clark, remarked during the trip that it was "the most spectacular train trip in the world." The company registered that quotation as a trademark and uses it in promotional materials.

A huge obstacle for the fledgling company was the reports in the media on the "demise" of passenger rail in Canada. This was particularly troublesome in the United States, where a PBS special and the evening news reported the end of passenger rail between Vancouver and Toronto. With such a limited marketing budget, it would be difficult to bring all the pertinent media on board for familiarization tours to promote the Rocky Mountaineer. Mike Leone's skill at public relations brought the Rocky Mountaineer press coverage and feature write-ups in the United States, all in an effort to overcome the public mindset that rail travel had disappeared.

The most important marketing task for that first year was to obtain the bookings to fill the trains. Given the financial constraints, very few dollars were available for marketing and the company had to make every one count. There were few tour operator contacts passed on by VIA, leaving only the very shell of an operator network. Murray Atherton was getting up at 2:00 a.m. to contact tour companies in the United Kingdom, trying to "paint the dream, paint the picture" for the tour operators. This personal selling was crucial, as the new company was building its tour contacts from scratch.

Marketing the second season was complicated by the fact that the company was well into the first season before it could confirm the schedule for the second year. It was also trying to develop offerings and contracts that would suit the needs of diverse markets, including Europe and Southeast Asia. As well, the company had had no capacity at the time to arrange travel packages beyond its two-day service, and had referred that business to other tour companies.

During a trip to London with Tourism Canada in September, a Mountain Vistas representative discovered that a Canadian tour operator had just cancelled a luxury train trip across Canada that had been arranged with Thomas Cook, and the cancelled trip was featured in a publication that had already gone to print. The company scrambled to have a Rocky Mountaineer brochure sent overnight to Thomas Cook for insertion into the publication. Its ability to capitalize on this opportunity led to a $10 000 deal and an eight-page feature in the Thomas Cook travel magazine.

For all their challenges, the people behind the Rocky Mountaineer knew they had a winning product to sell, and the company has gone from strength to strength. In 2003, it celebrated its fourteenth season as North America's largest privately owned passenger rail service. It has sales representation in 18 countries and welcomes guests from the United States, United Kingdom, Australia, Germany, Mexico, and many other countries. It has transported over a half million guests and has over 150 departures each year. The company now offers over 40 different vacation packages that allow guests to "explore the breathtaking scenery of British Columbia and Alberta by land, sea, and rail."

These days, the company has a strong communications program that includes print media campaigns, direct media campaigns, and other communication efforts that attract travel media from all over the world. Figure 9.8 is an example of a print ad used by the company in 2003. The popularity of the Rocky Mountaineer is evidenced by its continued growth as well as its international recognition. The Rocky Mountaineer has been named one of the "20 Best Rail Experiences in the World" three times by *The International Railway Traveler* magazine and was voted "Best Attraction" by the North American Association of Travel Writers in 1998. The future looks very bright indeed for "The Most Spectacular Train Trip in the World"®.

Source: Grescoe, P. (2000). Trip of a lifetime: The making of the Rocky Mountaineer. Vancouver: Hurricane.

QUESTIONS

1. Which tourism and hospitality promotional tools are best suited to a product like the Rocky Mountaineer?
2. Why were public relations so important for the Rocky Mountaineer in its early days?
3. What other promotional tools were developed as a result of the Rocky Mountaineer's focus on personal selling?
4. What media mix should the company be using today? Compare and contrast with the mix used in 1990.

WEB SITES

www.aircanada.com
Air Canada

www.atlantictours.com
Atlantic Tours

www.canadatourism.com
Canadian Tourism Commission

www.greenfieldhospitality.com
Greenfield Hospitality (a management consulting firm specializing in hospitality, travel, and tourism)

www.rockymountaineer.com
Rocky Mountaineer

ENDNOTES

1. Morrison, A. M. (2002). *Hospitality and travel marketing* (3rd ed.). Albany, NY: Delmar Thomson Learning.
2. Media fams work. (2002). *Tourism, 6*(3), 13.
3. Media marketplace—Our best foot forward. (2002). *Tourism, 6*(5), 5.
4. Ritchie, J. R. B., & Smith, B. H. (1991). The impact of a mega-event on host region awareness: A longitudinal study. *Journal of Travel Research, 30*(1), 3–10.
5. Earle, R. (2000). *The art of cause marketing*. New York: McGraw-Hill.
6. Smith, G., & Stodghill, R. (1994, March 21). Are good causes good marketing? *Business Week*, 64.
7. S. Grollmuss, director of sales, Banff Rocky Mountain Resort, personal communication, July 3, 2003.
8. Jones, D. L. (2001). Prospecting in a down economy. *HSMM Marketing Review*, Fall/Winter, 46–49.
9. S. Grollmuss, director of sales, Banff Rocky Mountain Resort, personal communication, July 3, 2003.
10. Brooks, B. (2002, June). Prospecting: How to stay in the mind of your prospect and win. *Home Business,* 40, 42.
11. Farber, B. (2001). That's a shocker. *HSMM Marketing Review*, Fall/Winter, 85–86.
12. Garfield, C. (1986). *Peak performers: The new heroes of American business*. New York: Avon.
13. Daniels, M. (2003). Canada's cities' mission a first. Retrieved March 31, 2003, from http://www.canadatourism.com/en/ctc/ctx/ctx-news/search/newsbydateform.cfm.
14. Silverman, G. (2001, September). The power of word of mouth. *Direct Marketing, 64*(5), 47–63.
15. Ibid.
16. Rosen, E. (2000). *The anatomy of buzz: How to create word of mouth marketing*. New York: Doubleday Currency.
17. Pritchard, A., Morgan, N. J., Sedgley, D., & Jenkins, A. (1998). Reaching out to the gay tourist. *Tourism Management, 19*(3), 273–282.
18. Australian Tourist Commission. (2003). *Australia a popular destination for backpackers*. Retrieved September 26, 2003, from http://www.australia.com.
19. MacDougall, S. (2003). "Come Home to the Island" contest launched. Retrieved June 25, 2003, from http://www.canadatourism.com/en/ctc/ctx/ctx-news/search/newsbydateform.cfm.
20. Silverman, G. (2001, September). The power of word of mouth. *Direct Marketing, 64*(5), 47–63.

Marketing Communications: *Direct Marketing and Internet Marketing*

DENNIS CAMPBELL'S POSTCARD CAMPAIGN

At eighteen, Dennis Campbell believed he could build a successful tourism business based on Nova Scotia's Scottish history and heritage. To do this he registered a company in 1987 called Halifax City Guide Services and tagged it "the company with the kilts." By 1995, the company—

now called Atlantic Ambassatours Limited—was grossing $3.5 million and had become the number one tour operator in Atlantic Canada after merging with Atlantic Tours. These days, the Atlantic Tours product is the main revenue generator, selling the four Atlantic Provinces as a motorcoach destination to customers all over the world. To do this, Campbell, who is president of the company, sends one hundred thousand brochures to travel agents in Canada and the United States, and has a marketing budget of $400 000.

However, in building his business in the early days, Campbell's best idea was the least expensive one. Called the "postcard campaign" by Campbell, it was simple, creative, and possessed the boldness that only someone with nothing to lose would dare. Campbell was trying to attract the attention of his "dream client list." A dream client was a Holland America, a Carnival Cruise Line, a Cunard Cruise Line, a Tauck Tours— "someone who has the potential to give us a couple hundred thousand dollars worth of business" said Campbell. These companies were at the conventions, but Campbell was aware that "they were practically a fortress.

They don't want to talk to you because they get bombarded—our dream client is everyone's dream client." He realized that mailing or phoning was not going to work, so he decided to start sending them postcards until he had their attention. "I sent one every month, and I wrote out for each month what the message would be."

He started with the cruise lines. He obtained the list of these lines and started writing postcards. Using Paul Stouffer at Holland America, for example, his first postcard read "Dear Paul, We are a short excursion company that provides kilted guides, bagpipers, and all kinds of neat things. The next month's read "Dear Paul, Hope you got our postcard last month. We would like you to consider using us." Third month's read "Dear Paul, We're not going to stop sending you postcards until we have your business." The next postcard read "Dear Paul. Don't mean to sound pushy like the last postcard, but we really want your business."

After bombarding Holland America's Seattle offices with postcards, Campbell finally encountered his target—Paul Stouffer, the head of shore excursions for the cruise lines—at a Miami trade show. When he found him, he approached him and said, "Paul Stouffer? Dennis Campbell. Would you like a postcard?" Apparently, he laughed and said, "Dennis Campbell! Dennis, listen, I'll make you a deal. Stop sending me those damn postcards and I'll give you our business." The same thing happened with Cunard Cruise Lines. When Campbell called Cunard Cruise Lines and said, "It's Dennis Campbell, I'm going to be down in New York, can I meet with you?" The response of the woman on the phone was, "Dennis Campbell, I'd like anything more than a postcard! I'd love to meet with you!"

The postcard mailing worked with Carnival, Cunard, Holland America, Clipper, and Silver Seas. In the summer cruise seasons of 1994–1995, the unique campaign, which used about 200 nine-cent postcards and stamps, brought in $600 000 in sales from some of the world's biggest cruise lines. A key part of the campaign was Campbell's insistence that each card be handwritten so as not to lose its effect. He even asked his mother to write them as she had much nicer handwriting than her son!

The Atlantic Ambassatours Limited now owns the group of companies: Atlantic Tours Limited, Nova Tours, Absolute Charters, Seymour Splash Tours, Gray Line of Nova Scotia, and Gray Line of New Brunswick. In 2003, the company had 30 year-round staff and just over 100 seasonal staff, with revenues in excess of $6.5 million. The company still uses postcard campaigns today as one of its most effective ways to get incremental business.

Source: Lynch, A. (1996). Ambassatours: Heritage drag pays off. In A. Lynch (Ed.). *Sweat equity: Atlantic Canada's new entrepreneurs* (pp. 181–194). Halifax: Nimbus.

Objectives

On completion of this chapter, readers should understand

- the difference between direct marketing and direct response advertising;

- the key direct response advertising tools;

- the role of the Internet as part of a communications strategy; and

- the ways in which the Internet is being used by the tourism and hospitality industry.

Chapter Overview

The opening vignette highlights a particularly innovative direct mail campaign that worked for one Canadian tour operator. This chapter looks at two important and growing areas of tourism and hospitality marketing: direct marketing and Internet marketing. The key advantages of direct marketing are discussed in the first section of this chapter, as are the major direct marketing tools. The remainder of the chapter discusses the Internet, which the tourism and hospitality industry is using to perform six key marketing functions: direct e-mail marketing, advertising, distribution and sales, providing information, customer service and relationship marketing, and marketing research.

DIRECT MARKETING AND DIRECT RESPONSE ADVERTISING

direct marketing

a marketing system, fully controlled by the marketer, that develops products, promotes them directly to the final consumer through a variety of media options, accepts direct orders from customers, and distributes products directly to the consumer

Direct marketing is a marketing system, fully controlled by the marketer, that develops products, promotes them directly to the final consumer through a variety of media options, accepts direct orders from customers, and distributes products directly to the consumer. It is rapidly becoming a vital component of the integrated marketing communications mix, and a recent study suggests that by 2005, direct marketing will be worth $12.9 billion of revenues in Canada, up 38 percent from the $9.4 billion it was worth in 2000.[1] Overall sales as a result of this investment are expected to reach $81.7 billion, up from $51.2 billion in 2000. Direct marketing has increased in popularity as businesses have come to place more importance on customer satisfaction and repeat purchase. Direct marketing makes use of databases, which allow precision targeting and personalization, thus helping companies to build continuing and enriching relationships with customers. There are eight key advantages of direct marketing, which are listed in Table 10.1.

These advantages of direct marketing are fundamental in their implications for achieving more cost-effective marketing. They are especially useful to businesses that are too small to engage in large-scale advertising or to achieve cost-effective access through retail distribution channels. It is worth emphasizing that many of the benefits derive from the use of new information technology that was not available to earlier generations of marketing managers. Bearing in mind that most large tourism and hospitality businesses, such as hotels, car rental companies, and scheduled airlines, have a large proportion of frequent-repeat customers that are vital to their profitability, the advantages of direct marketing in this industry cannot be underestimated. It is no coincidence that hotel groups and airlines have been competing ever more strenuously in recent years to bind their loyal customers to them with a wide variety of membership or club schemes, frequent traveller rewards, and other "special relationship" arrangements for their key accounts.

Table 10.1

The Key Advantages of Direct Marketing

1. Precision targeting	Direct marketing is aimed at a specific individual. It provides opportunities to target not only general groups of potential buyers but specific buyers individually.
2. Personalization	Direct marketing provides an opportunity to personalize messages and build stronger links between the company and the consumer. It enables the sender to use names, and thus to target promotions to the individual.
3. Flexibility	Not only can the contents of each direct marketing message be changed to suit the specific requirements of each participant, but the message can also be delivered to specific geographic locations.
4. Privacy	Offers made by direct marketing methods are not readily visible to competitors. Direct marketing does not broadcast an organization's competitive strategy as widely as mass communication advertising.
5. Measurability	A major advantage of direct marketing is the ability it gives a company to measure the effectiveness of various response fulfillment packages sent out to prospects, in terms of converting inquiries into sales, costs per booking, response by market segments, and so on.
6. Low cost	Direct marketing has the advantage of generally lower costs per transaction than other forms of communication.
7. Detailed knowledge of consumers	Direct marketing methods allow the gathering of valuable consumer information—not only names and addresses, but also lifestyle information and purchasing behaviour.
8. Fast or immediate response	Because of the format of direct marketing, offers can be made quickly—and can be quickly accepted. This has become more applicable recently with the advent of the Internet.

direct response advertising

advertising through any medium, designed to generate a response by any means that is measurable (e.g., mail, television, telephone, fax, or Internet)

Direct response advertising is one segment of the direct-marketing industry, and it plays a major role in influencing consumer purchase patterns. It can be defined as advertising through any medium, designed to generate a response by any means that is measurable (e.g., mail, television, telephone, fax, or Internet). If traditional mass media are used, the message will include a toll-free telephone number, mailing address, or Web site address where more information can be obtained. The major forms of direct response advertising are direct mail, telemarketing, the Internet, and direct response television (DRTV) (see Figure 10.1 on page 326). In 2001, direct mail advertising amounted to $1.2 billion in Canada, or 14 percent of net advertising revenues. In comparison to the United States, Canada is an undeveloped market for direct response communications. Currently, a Canadian spends only about one-third the amount that an American does making purchases through direct response communication vehicles. Such a low figure supports the premise that there is tremendous potential for direct response initiatives in Canada.

Figure 10.1 presents some of the communication strategies of the four main forms of direct response advertising, discussed below.

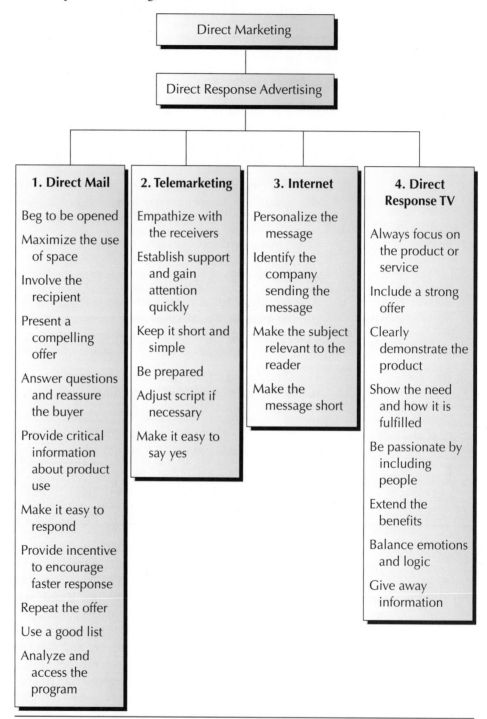

Figure 10.1 Strategic Considerations for Major Forms of Direct Response Advertising

1. Direct Mail

direct mail

a type of direct response advertising in which an offer is sent to a prospective customer by mail

Direct mail, in which an offer is sent to a prospective customer by mail, is by far the most common form of direct response advertising. The use of mail is widespread due to its ability to personalize the message (the name can be included in the mailing), its ability to convey lengthy messages (printed sales messages can be sent with reply cards or contracts that can be returned by prospects), and its ability to provide a high degree of geographic coverage economically (the mailing can be distributed to designated postal codes anywhere in Canada). There are numerous options available to companies wishing to use direct mail—examples include sales letters, leaflets and flyers, folders, brochures, DVDs, and CD-ROMs. An example of an innovative direct mail piece is that developed by the Vancouver Convention and Exhibition Centre (VCEC) in 2002. Business planners were sent a pop-up cardboard model of a laptop computer containing a CD-ROM that would give respondents an orientation to the VCEC and a direct link to its Web site.

solo direct mail

a direct mail piece sent out by one company and delivered by the company itself

cooperative direct mail

a direct mail offer delivered as part of a package that includes offers from other companies

Essentially, an organization has the option of using **solo direct mail**—delivering a mail piece by itself and absorbing the costs associated with such a mailing (as in the postcard campaign highlighted in the opening vignette), or **cooperative direct mail**—delivering an offer as part of a package that includes offers from other companies. Tourism Calgary uses cooperative direct mail to attract more meetings and convention business to the city. An aggressive group-marketing effort involving Tourism Calgary, the TELUS Convention Centre, and the Calgary Stampede's Roundup Centre, aimed at Canadian and U.S. business travel markets, was launched in 2001 and continues today. Using direct mail as a key component of the campaign, about 250 prescreened U.S. meeting planners

Figure 10.2 Vancouver Convention and Exhibition Centre Direct Mail Piece

received a hand-crafted cedar box containing information on the destination as well as a Western blanket. The 2001 mail campaign won an award from the New York Festivals and a second from the Direct Marketing Association.

The three basic steps involved in direct mail marketing are obtaining a proper prospect list, conceiving and producing the mail piece, and distributing the final version. However, the first step is the backbone of the entire campaign. Both the accuracy and definition of the list can have a significant bearing on the success or failure of a campaign. Companies recognize that it costs six to seven times as much to acquire a new customer as it does to keep an existing one, so they compile databases to keep track of existing customers and form relationships with them through the mail and electronic means.

Lists are secured from internal and external sources. There is no better prospect than a current customer, so a company's internal database must be monitored and updated routinely. In direct mail terms, an internal customer list is referred to as a "house list." As an alternative, companies can take steps to form lists of potential customers. Such customers are referred to as "prospects." A list broker can assist in finding these prospects—those that perhaps mirror the demographic and psychographic profile of existing customers. The use that many hotels and airlines make, for example, of American Express or other credit card company membership databases illustrates the value of third-party address lists. Such lists can usually be accessed at a cost per 1000 names. A company can also purchase a response list, which is a list of proven mail-order buyers, or a circulation list, which is a magazine subscription list.

2. Telemarketing

telemarketing

using the telephone to reach customers or prospective customers

call centre

a central operation from which a company operates its inbound and outbound telemarketing programs

A form of direct marketing that combines aspects of advertising, marketing research, and personal sales, **telemarketing** uses the telephone to reach customers or prospective customers. Telemarketing developed massively through the 1990s through the combination of technology-led development of consumer databases, telephone communications, and creation of call centres. A **call centre** is a central operation from which a company operates its inbound and outbound telemarketing programs. There are now more than 6000 such centres in Canada, and the industry was worth $15 billion in 2000.[2] Inbound telemarketing refers to the reception of calls by the order desk, customer inquiry, and direct response calls often generated through the use of toll-free numbers. Outbound telemarketing, on the other hand, refers to calls that a company makes to customers to develop new accounts, generate sales leads, and even close a sale.

Telemarketing is becoming increasingly popular in tourism and hospitality industries. For example, in its first year of operation, Greenfield Hospitality Services Inc., a business-to-business telemarketing team of five agents, completed 25 projects and made over 150 000 outbound phone calls for clients in the Canadian hospitality and tourism industry. Greenfield's clients include notables such as Resorts Atlantic, Rogers Media (*Meetings and Incentive Travel* magazine and *Marketing Magazine*), Kostuch Publications (*Hotelier* magazine, *Foodservice and Hospitality* magazine), Tourism Whistler, the Renaissance Hotel at Skydome, the Ottawa Marriott, the Toronto Marriott Bloor-Yorkville, and Meetings Prince Edward Island. Looking ahead, the Teleservices Division will continue to serve the needs of hospitality and tourism organizations, and will diversify operations with programs aimed at the publishing industry, government, and the association markets. The company also plans to venture into the U.S. marketplace.

The primary advantage of telemarketing is that it can complete a sale for less cost than is needed to complete a sale using such techniques as face-to-face sales calls or mass advertising. However, for this method to be effective, proper training and preparation of telemarketing representatives needs to be as comprehensive as it is for personal selling. Planning the message is as important as the medium itself. A drawback to telemarketing is the fact that consumers react negatively to it. The majority of Canadians consider telemarketing calls unwelcome and intrusive, and they are ranked as one of the least desirable sales techniques. Furthermore, half of the population thinks there are too many calls, and the same numbers of people react to them by hanging up.[3] Despite this behaviour, organizations believe that the advantages of telemarketing, such as call reach and frequency and cost efficiency, outweigh the disadvantages.

3. Internet

The role of the Internet in direct response advertising is discussed in the next section of this chapter. Needless to say, direct e-mail marketing, often eliciting direct e-mail response, is one of the most promising applications in online advertising.

4. Direct Response Television

Direct response television is one of the fastest growing segments of the direct response industry. Advertisers are attracted to this medium because it allows them to track response rates. Today, savvy advertisers like American Express do very little advertising without a built-in response mechanism that allows them to judge results. There are essentially three forms of direct response television: 60-second (or longer) commercials that typically appear on cable channels, infomercials, and direct–home shopping channels. In all cases, the use of toll-free telephone numbers and credit cards make the purchase more convenient for the viewer.

infomercial

a commercial, usually 30 minutes long, that presents in great detail the benefits of a product or service on the television

Cable television lends itself to direct response because the medium is more tightly targeted to particular interests. The Shopping Channel (TSC), for example, has annual sales of $150 million, reaching millions of households. Direct response television also makes good use of the infomercial format. An **infomercial** is a commercial, usually 30 minutes long, that presents in great detail the benefits of a product or service. Criticized in the past for being exclusively "get-rich-quick" concepts, infomercials are now being created that are highly informative and well produced, although tourism and hospitality organizations have been slow to adopt this form of direct response advertising.

Digital television is likely to have a huge impact on the sale of tourism products and services, even though interactive television sets with computer capabilities are still a novelty. In much the same way as the Internet, digital television heralds a revolution in the marketing of tourism products and services, enabling advertising to be combined with purchase transactions. Add the fact that television viewers see holidays and travel as a top home-shopping preference and digital television would seem to offer tremendous opportunities. Digital television offers consumers travel services via digital travel agents or online tour operators, allowing them to make an immediate booking for the destination or tour featured on the television screen. This is an exceptionally effective sales tool.

Many travel agents believe that digital television will be a greater threat to business than the Internet, precisely because it is an incredibly interactive medium facilitated by a very familiar tool—the television remote control. As yet, few large tour operators have developed Web sites that enable a customer to book online, as few customers seem to want to book this way, seeing it to be too time-consuming and insecure. Travel agents consider digital television to be more of a threat because the television is a focus of family activity, and using the television remote control does not require any computing knowledge and therefore lacks the barriers to adoption presented by the Internet.

INTERNET MARKETING

While traditional advertisers have been looking for ways to use the Internet, direct marketers saw the potential of e-marketing immediately. The Internet provides the same components found in direct mail and telemarketing, but it has greater sampling opportunities. Online music stores have thousands of music clips for shoppers to listen to before making a purchase, and some retailers, such as Eddie Bauer, allow online visitors to "try on" clothes. Companies also send e-mail messages offering special prices on items based on customers' past purchasing patterns. The Internet is also providing companies with new ways to gather information about consumers. One of the more ambitious companies—the giant bookseller Amazon.com—encourages consumers to create their own network of contacts that its marketers can then use to promote products. Amazon.com owns PlanetAll, a Web-based address book, calendar, and reminder service. A subscriber enters a friend's information and then Amazon can not only remind these subscribers about upcoming birthdays, but can also suggest books that those friends and relatives have indicated that they would like to receive as gifts.

The majority of Canadian businesses (60 percent) now have a Web presence, but most of them are not using the Internet to its full marketing potential, according to a study by the Canadian Marketing Association (CMA).[4] The study found that the use of online marketing effort has been relegated to a relatively small number of marketing tools and tactics. The most common e-marketing tactic being employed is outbound e-mail, which is used by 46 percent of all respondents, followed closely by banner ads (38 percent) and online collaborative tools such as mortgage calculators (34 percent). The study also found that the majority of Canadian companies gather and store consumer information, but few analyze this data when determining future strategies. In fact, only about half of those companies surveyed by the CMA claim to be putting customer information they gather from the Web to any use whatsoever. Canadian companies are just beginning to use customer relationship management. Two-thirds are aggregating customer data, but nearly three-quarters are only building their databases and not yet putting customer knowledge to use. Forty percent of the respondents to the CMA survey are dissatisfied with their ability to effectively measure online marketing and Web site performance. Current online metrics focus on operational measures, with little use of key measurement testing in the areas of customer validation, online merchandising measurement, and other business metrics.

In spite of the failure of some very high-profile companies over the past decade or so, the Internet is thriving and even transforming the tourism industry. The impact of e-marketing can be felt across all sectors in the industry, from large hotel chains to small outfitters. The advantage of this business model is that it is based on a sound foundation—consumer demand. Customers are looking to the Internet to research, plan, and even book their trips at rates that are increasing every year. The *Snapshot* on pages 331–332 shows how a small family business in Calgary has capitalized on the power of the Internet to develop a successful tourism business.

SNAPSHOT

RIPLEY RIDGE RETREAT

"Without the Internet, Ripley Ridge Retreat would not exist," says Cara Ripley, director of marketing for Ripley Ridge Retreat, a family-owned business run by Shawn and Cara Ripley in cooperation with Shawn's parents, Bill and Shirley Ripley. The retreat is located on seven and a half acres of beautiful aspen forest nestled in the Paskapoo Slopes on Calgary's western edge, adjacent to Canada Olympic Park. Operations began as a one-room bed and breakfast (B&B) in the summer of 1997. Between 1998 and 2001, the accommodation choice grew to include another B&B suite, two cabins, and a guesthouse. A meeting facility was added in the fall of 2001, and a spa in January 2003. The names Ripley Ridge Retreat and Nature's Essence Spa became registered trade names in 2002. Food, lodging, and spa business licences were granted in January 2003.

Ripley Ridge Retreat appeals to people who appreciate nature, enjoy unique accommodation styles with personalized service, like to learn about the heritage of the area, and have an interest in health and well-being. Three distinct market segments exist: couples between the ages of 27 and 44 travelling without their children for a quick getaway, generally from Alberta; well-travelled older couples between the ages of 45 and 65—generally high-income professionals; and small groups of women getting together for a brief vacation from their families. Guest surveys reveal that all three market segments use the Internet and word of mouth as their primary sources of information when researching accommodation choices. "When we ask people how they heard of us, they all say the Internet, but none of them know exactly how!" says Cara Ripley.

Advertising for the retreat is primarily conducted online through various listings on Web sites servicing the target markets, such as BedandBreakfast.com and DiscoverCalgary.com. Print advertising is limited due to a small advertising budget and minimal return on investment. "We have had a few brochures in the past, but they don't seem to bring us any business," commented Cara. "Brochure costs are very high, as are distribution costs. The only place we can really distribute them is through Tourism Calgary and Travel Alberta, and we have found that they just haven't resulted in bookings. In fact, the one year we distributed brochures throughout Travel Alberta information centres (50 in each), we found that they were not given out, and then they were thrown out at the end of the season. (Travel Alberta now recycles or sends back unused brochures.) Also brochures at airports don't work because people flying into Calgary have already booked their accommodation for the first night or two."

Other promotional activities include direct mailouts to target markets such as women's organizations, yoga studios, and past clients. Flat sheets have also been developed for the staff lounges at Air Canada and WestJet. Publicity is generated through prize giveaways for target market associations and for high-profile charities including the Canadian Cancer Association, Canadian Diabetes Association, and Planned Parenthood.

SNAPSHOT *continued*

A public relations campaign was also launched in the summer of 2003 to include disc jockeys from Alberta radio stations, travel writers, and television personalities.

However, the Internet remains the company's most powerful promotional tool, and all of the company's promotional activities drive people to its Web site. "Our primary marketing strategy is Internet based and the return on investment exceeds traditional marketing efforts 1000:1, at least," says Cara. "We were able to grow our business from a one bedroom B&B with $4000 per year revenue to a retreat with three private cabins, two B&B suites, corporate meeting space with high speed Internet, spa facilities, and over 4000 ft of interpretive nature trails with $150 000 annual revenue—in just four years. Revenue projections for 2003 are $250 000. Over 95 percent of our current business comes from people who have visited our Web site."

The company has a very aggressive Internet strategy, driving qualified traffic to the Web site by using keyword strategies, portals, affiliates, link exchanges, and offline media. Ripley Ridge Retreat is located on strategic Web sites such as Bed & Breakfast Inns Online (www.bbonline.com), BBCanada (www.bbcanada.com), and on other sites that list good-quality B&Bs and small inns. "We have a keyword strategy that we use. If you look us up using various keywords such as 'Calgary accommodations,' we are usually first, second, or third. People are always wondering how we get our name up there, but we don't tell them!" says Cara.

How does the company convert surfers into buyers? By using an "entertaining, informative, compelling, secure, and easy-to-use site," says Shawn Ripley. According to him, visuals are very important: "For accommoda-

tions, you have to enable the surfer to experience as much of the product as is possible. Beyond that, you have to make it easy for people to book." The Web site itself is divided into two main parts. One is designed completely in Flash (a high-graphics program) and is aimed at high-speed users and those who require a lot of sensory stimuli in the decision-making process. "It also shows a high level of investment and hopefully imparts an image of a serious business on the other end of the site," says Shawn. The other portion is designed just in HTML (hypertext markup language) and allows users with a slower connection and those who are more information-driven to find information and make decisions quickly. "Both sections of the site use a lot of visuals that attempt to show how unique our product is. However, visitors do comment that the site undersells the real thing—an encouraging reaction showing that we still have a lot of room for improvement [of the Web site]."

The site itself is user-friendly, and a toll-free number is provided for people who wish to speak to someone at the retreat. Reservations can be made online via a secure server. Shawn says it is rare to have a visitor come to the retreat who doesn't make a comment like "Your Web site is simply fantastic. It's really why I'm here."

"I feel that although we have a very comprehensive Internet strategy at the moment, we've only just touched on the true potential of this venue for tourism products," says Shawn. "Take care of the fundamentals and then your imagination is really the only limitation."

Source: C. Ripley and S. Ripley, owners, Ripley Ridge Retreat, personal communication, July 8, 2003.

THE USE OF THE INTERNET IN TOURISM AND HOSPITALITY

The Internet is being used by the tourism and hospitality industry to perform six key functions: direct e-mail marketing, advertising, providing information, distribution and sales, customer service and relationship marketing, and marketing research.

1. Direct E-mail Marketing

direct e-mail marketing

marketing in which a user chooses to receive messages from a particular advertiser via the Internet

spam

e-mail advertisements sent to lists of recipients who have not agreed to receive them

One of the most promising applications in online advertising is **direct e-mail marketing**, in which a user chooses to receive messages from a particular advertiser. This form of advertising is relatively inexpensive, has high response rates and is easy to measure, and is targeted at people who want information about certain goods and services. Unlike banner advertising in its various forms, sending sales messages by e-mail seems quite acceptable to Internet users, since they agree to accept the message. The success of an e-mail campaign—like that of a direct mail campaign—depends on the quality of the list, which can be created in-house or be rented from a list broker. Typically, these lists include opt-in names and addresses. "Opt-in" means that the people on the list have agreed to receive direct e-mail. E-mail advertisements sent to lists that are not opt-in are called **spam**. Spam refers to the inappropriate use of a mailing list or other networked communications facility as a broadcast medium. It is unsolicited "junk" e-mail. One of the problems with e-mail is the low cost of sending messages, which results in users receiving an increasing number of unwanted messages. The consequence is that more and more e-mail goes unopened, and gaining permission to send someone an e-mail is becoming more important.

Establishing first contact is the toughest goal of any e-mail marketer. The most obvious place to find prospects is at other Web sites, newsgroups, and mailing lists. This method of marketing still works, but many mailing lists and newsgroups have settled into their own set of experts. It is harder to penetrate market share this way. E-mail marketing is still in its infancy online, and many of the so-called lists are not tested or even targeted. The best means of survival is still endorsed mailing to a group of interested customers, which is why it is important to allow people to remove themselves from lists.

The goal is to have customers make first contact, and then have the marketer follow up. This can be done by giving customers something of real value, such as a good special report or newsletter, to encourage them to make contact. For example, in 2003, Hilton Canada, the Canadian Tourism Commission, and Air Canada joined together with Fourth Wall Media to run a "Why Canada?" campaign directed at meeting planners in the United States. The campaign involved sending four interactive e-mails to the U.S. planners, and the pilot campaign received twice the amount of responses anticipated. Along with offering tips as to "Why Canada," "What to Do," "Where to Go," "How to Get There," and "Where to Stay," the campaign also rewarded planners who participated with the chance to win a Hilton weekend getaway to Quebec City and The Ice Hotel or an executive leather briefcase. The campaign received an extremely positive response: of the 3600 e-mail recipients, 1400 entered the contest. The quartet of partners is therefore planning to develop more e-mail marketing initiatives.

2. Advertising

These days, the Internet is an important part of the media mix, and Internet advertising is seen by some as the convergence of traditional advertising and direct response marketing (see Figure 10.3). Online advertising holds four distinct advantages:

1. *Targetability.* Online advertisers can focus on users from specific companies, geographical locations, and nations, as well as categorize them by time of day, computer platform, and browser. They can target using databases, a tool that serves as the backbone of direct marketing. They can even target based on a person's personal preferences and actual behaviour.
2. *Tracking.* Marketers can track how users interact with their brands and learn what is of interest to their current and prospective customers. Advertisers can also measure the response to an ad (by noting the number of times an ad is clicked on, the number of purchases or leads an ad generated, etc.). This is difficult to do with traditional television, print, and outdoor advertising.
3. *Deliverability and flexibility.* Online, an ad is deliverable 24 hours a day, 7 days a week, 365 days of the year. Furthermore, an ad campaign can be launched, updated, or cancelled immediately. This is a big difference from print or television advertising.
4. *Interactivity.* An advertiser's goal is to engage the prospect with a brand or a product. This can be done more effectively online, where consumers can interact with the product, test the product, and, if they choose, buy the product.

banner ad

an advertisement placed as a narrow band across the top of a Web page; the most common form of advertising on the Internet

Online marketers can advertise via e-mail (as discussed earlier) and by sponsoring discussion lists and e-mail newsletters. But the most common form of advertising on the Internet is the **banner ad**—an advertisement placed as a narrow band across the top of a Web page. In terms of appearance and design, banner ads are often compared to outdoor posters. The content of the ad is minimal. Its purpose is to stir interest, so that the viewer clicks the ad for more information. Once the banner ad is clicked, the viewer sees the advertisement in its entirety, usually via a link to the advertiser's home page. The design characteristics of the banner ad are critical, since the goal is to encourage clicking. The Web site the ad links to must be interesting, or the surfer will quickly return to the previous page. The Web editors at TourismTogether.com, Travel Alberta's industry intranet site, offer readers ten tips for developing an effective Web site. These are shown in Table 10.2.

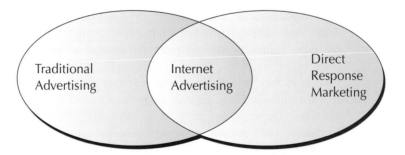

Figure 10.3   The Internet as the Convergence of Traditional Advertising and Direct Response Marketing

Source: Zeff, R., & Aronson, B. (1999). *Advertising on the Internet* (2nd ed.). New York: Wiley, 13.

Table 10.2

Ten Tips for a Better Web Site

1. Navigation	Keep it simple (KIS), and make sure it's consistent from page to page. No matter where you place your menu bar—either at the top or down the side—always include a small text menu at the bottom of every page.
2. Privacy policy	With all of the concern over privacy on the Web, if you collect any type of information from your visitors (even if it's just an e-mail address), you need to include a privacy policy. There are many online templates that will help you to create one easily. Once made, post a link to it on every page of your site.
3. Contact information	Post your contact information at the bottom of every page of your site, along with your e-mail address. Don't make the viewer fill out a whole form when he or she just wants to send a simple comment. Include your e-mail address, hotlinked and ready to go.
4. Logos and graphics	Please keep your graphics down to a reasonable size. No one wants to wait two minutes while your huge, beautiful logo loads onto the screen.
5. Fonts	Stick to standards. Remember, if you stray from using the standard fonts that everyone has installed on their computers (such as Arial, Verdana, and Times New Roman), the viewer won't see your fonts as intended.
6. Make it sticky	Include interactive features if possible, such as live news feeds. Use chat rooms, discussion boards, etc. You want to create a sense of community—a place to which people will want to return.
7. Newsletter	If you're going to have a Web site, you need to offer an e-mail newsletter, even if it's strictly going to be about sale items, specials, or site updates. You need to start collecting a list of your visitors' e-mail addresses so you can keep in touch with them.
8. Browsers	Make sure you take a peek at your site in both Netscape and Internet Explorer. Recent statistics show that Internet Explorer has about 80 percent of the market share, but you'll still want to make sure that the other 20 percent can view your site without any problems.
9. Screen resolution	This is a highly debatable subject. The norm these days seems to be 800 x 600, although there are still a small number of people limping along in 640 x 480.
10. Index page	On the very first page of your site (the homepage), the first paragraph should answer the "5 W's," basically telling visitors who you are and what you're offering. Surfers are a very impatient group. Stop them before they click away.

Source: 10 tips for a better Web site. (2003). Retrieved April 2, 2003, from http://main.tourismtogether.com/inforesources.

Published research into the effectiveness of tourism Web sites is still very limited. According to marketing experts, the success factors for marketing tourism on the Web include the following: attracting users, engaging users' interest and participation, retaining users and ensuring that they return, learning about user preferences, and relating back to users to provide customized interactions.[5,6] Learning about user preferences would appear to be the most important element of this model, as it will affect the remaining elements, and yet very few studies have attempted to understand the behaviour of tourists online. Although statistical measures can be obtained through log files, it is difficult to ascertain the meaning behind the results (e.g., whether clicking on a link was an accident or an intended behaviour). Surveying visitors might be a better way to understand consumer preferences and to establish the effectiveness of a site.

Research that has looked at content of Web pages suggests that it is crucial that content is accurate, attractive, and easily searchable.[7] Interactivity is also an imperative, as the very behaviour of consumers changes when they log onto the Internet. They not only search for information but also expect interaction and entertainment.[8] A positive experience on the Web site increases the time spent at the site and therefore increases the dollar amount spent.[9] Offering virtual tours is one way of providing interactivity. Tourism Vancouver, for example, provides customers with online virtual tours of Greater Vancouver's leading attractions and tourism products, at www.tourismvancouver.com (see Figure 10.4). Through new interactive maps available on the Web site and syndicated through other sites such as Canada.com and MyBC.com, potential visitors to Vancouver can take virtual tours of an extensive selection of places, including Capilano Suspension Bridge, Stanley Park, and Vancouver International Airport.

It is also important for tourism operators and destinations to consider the language of their online visitors. The Prince Edward Island tourism Web site (www.peiplay.com) now has more than 20 pages available in Japanese, allowing potential visitors from halfway around the world a chance to search for activities, transportation, or general information in their own language and at any time of day (the latter of which helps to reduce the barriers presented by time zones) (see Figure 10.5). The link is accessible from the Web site's homepage, where Japanese script directs visitors to a Japanese-language home page, and then to pages that outline "Things to Do" and "Places to Stay" and offers a "Vacation Planner." The text on the "Getting Here" page has been specially adapted to the needs of residents of Japan and will eventually include references to partner tour companies. Special attention is paid to the pages related to L. M. Montgomery and Anne of Green Gables, a favourite theme among many young Japanese women.

3. Providing Information

As mentioned in Chapter 7, a significant proportion of Canadians use the Internet as a source of travel information and planning. However, a key challenge for the Canadian tourism industry is to convert surfers into buyers. U.S travellers are more active users of the Internet for planning, booking, and purchasing both travel and non-travel items. Canadians, on the other hand, use the Internet predominantly for research and planning purposes.

The Web is being used not just to provide information to individual consumers. In 2003, The Canadian Tourism Commission (CTC) launched GoMedia Canada (www.gomediacanada.com), a comprehensive, national travel portal for Canadian-based media. This unique Canadian travel resource is designed for media who need to access information

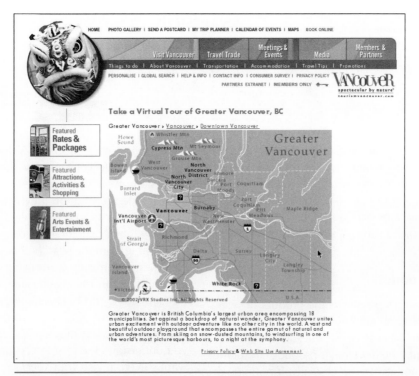

Figure 10.4   Tourism Vancouver Virtual Tour Web Page

Figure 10.5   Prince Edward Island Tourism's Japanese Homepage

HOW TO CONVERT WEB SITE HITS INTO SALES

One of the common questions asked by Web site owners is, "I'm getting plenty of hits but no sales—what is going on?" Kevin Sinclair, author of two free e-books, *Success Secrets* and *How to Choose a Home Based Business* offers some tips on how to address this issue.

Your Product

The first area to review is the product or service that you are offering. Does a market exist for it? To answer this question you need to find out whether similar products are being sold on the Internet successfully. If not, you may need to rethink your Internet strategy. If others are selling a similar product successfully, then this would tend to confirm that there is a market for your product. Next, look at the strategy and pricing being adopted by your competitors. How do you compare? Why should your visitors buy from you rather than from one of your competitors? Answering these questions will provide you with valuable information you can use to improve your situation and generate more sales. Also, take a critical look at your product quality. Does it live up to the claims you are making on your Web pages? If not, improve your product so that it does, or modify your Web site to be more truthful about it.

Provide Solutions

Your visitors are looking for a solution to a problem. Do you know what problems your visitors are looking for solutions to? Does your Web site show how your product will solve your visitors' problem? You will need to put yourself into your visitors' shoes to better understand what they are seeking, so that you can provide the solution they need. One way to better understand your visitors is to monitor how they are getting to your site. If they are coming from the search engines, knowing what search terms they are using can provide some clues. This means you may need to invest in some sort of statistical package for tracking. You may find some surprises when you review the statistics about your site. Once you understand the problem your visitors want solved, revise your Web site to show that your product will provide the solution they need.

Site Design

Your site needs to look like it is a commercial Web site rather than an amateur one. The design needs to be consistent from page to page, and the site needs to be easy to navigate. Contact details including physical address, phone numbers, and e-mail address need to be shown. Graphics need to be minimized to ensure that your homepage downloads quickly. Also, ensure that your Web host provides a fast connection to the Internet. Most people will not wait for a page that takes a long time to download. They will just move on to your competitor. Also, make it easy to order. A large number of people abandon a Web site in the middle of the ordering process. A common reason for this is that the ordering process is too time-consuming and complicated. Make yours simple and quick and you will lose fewer sales.

Testimonials and Guarantees

Testimonials and guarantees can have a huge impact on your level of sales. On the Web, a key priority is to build credibility. The common methods used are having a privacy statement, publishing a newsletter, publishing testimonials from satisfied customers, and providing a strong guarantee. Take every opportunity to gather comments from your customers about how your product has helped them. A way of getting comments is a customer feedback survey. This can be used for the purpose of gaining testimonials as well as seeking ways to improve your product or develop additional products your customers may need. A strong guarantee will provide your visitor with greater confidence to purchase your product. Try to make your guarantee simple and without too many conditions. Always honour your guarantee without question or delay.

Source: Sinclair, K. (2003). How to convert hits into sales. Retrieved April 2, 2002, from http://main. tourismtogether.com/inforesources.

about Canada as a tourism destination. Journalists can now leverage essential resources to assist them with the research, writing, editing, and filing of assignments. Designed as a time-saving tool, GoMedia Canada provides the latest CTC media releases, links to the tourism industry, information on media tours, market research, and a comprehensive travel wire complete with still photography and video footage. Some of the most evocative travel stories, produced by some of Canada's best travel writers, are also available to Canadian media on a rights-free basis. The site allows journalists to store information and bookmark references for future use. And once their story is filed, they can ship the designed page, transcript, or photo electronically in universally accepted formats such as PDF or HTML.

4. Distribution and Sales

Chapter 7 provided an in-depth analysis of the distribution of travel products online, but to reiterate the importance of the Internet, here are some key statistics. Online travel spending by Canadians is expected to reach $11 billion by 2006, a huge increase from the $1.5 billion spent in 2001.[10] Internet use overall grew by 45 percent between 1999 and 2002, and Canadians looking for travel packages are keen users of the Internet. In 2003, 77 percent of travellers browsed the Internet for information, up 10 percent from 2002, and more than two in three package travellers used the Internet to help plan summer trips.[11] In the business travel world, too, online transactions more than tripled in 2002, and it is estimated that between 20 and 30 percent of all corporate travel bookings were made over the Internet in 2003.

In North America, Travelocity.com continues to be the most popular place to purchase travel online by a two-to-one margin over any other travel site. The product depth of the Canadian version, Travelocity.ca, includes 700 airlines, more than 55 000 hotels, more than 50 rental car companies, direct booking of VIA Rail, and thousands of vacation packages and cruises. Online consolidators such as the Hotel Reservations Network (HRN) have also emerged as key distributors of the travel product. HRN's Web sites include hoteldiscount!com, TravelNow.com, and condosaver.com, plus more than 20 000 affiliate sites. It is projected that over half of all Canadian adults will use the Internet to book their travel by 2004. Destina.ca, Air Canada's online travel agency, attracted over one million visitors in its first two months of operation.

Many companies are forming online partnerships in order to distribute their travel products. For example, World Wide Trails (WWT), a new Northern Alberta–based company, has put together its Adventure Travel Affiliate Program for Canadian travel agents interested in making inroads into the adventure market. Describing itself as an "adventure library," the marketing firm has partnered with more than 50 adventure tour operators to offer more than 300 itineraries at www.worldwidetrails.com. Included in the program is an adventure travel online booking engine as well as incentives such as familiarization trips, monthly draws, and bonuses to top-selling agents and agencies on a regional, provincial, and national basis. Agents can also call for personalized service. There is no cost to join, though WWT splits commission on all tours booked.

Another example of a Canadian online partnership is an initiative between the Railway Association of Canada (RAC) and the Canadian Tourism Commission (CTC). Between them, these organizations have gathered a number of train-related tourist excursions and attractions under one umbrella, called Canada by Rail. The group has created a comprehensive, user-friendly, one-stop Web site resource for all rail-related leisure opportunities in every region in Canada (www.canadabyrail.ca). The site was officially launched in December 2002, and the response has been very positive. Already, the resource offers information and links, by province and area of interest, to museums, rail excursions, historical societies, bed and breakfasts, restaurants, hotels, and RAC members offering tourist services. The photographs in the photo gallery have proven very popular and can be downloaded.

Hotels in particular are increasingly turning to the Internet to increase sales. According to a recent survey of hotels, by Arthur Andersen, respondents expect the percentage of total bookings made online to triple over the next three years, to 15.4 percent.[12] Part of this expectation is due to the fact that online agencies have been building up their hotel business as a way to diversify from low-margin air sales. Non-hotel sites are also expanding into hotel reservations. Southwest, for example, launched a hotel reservations service in 2001 using the Galileo global distribution system. Expedia is also having tremendous success online. In March 2001, it announced that it had sold more than one million room nights in less than three months. In comparison, it took Expedia three years to sell its first million room nights. Through its Travelscape division, which operates on the merchant model, Expedia contracts for special room blocks to resell to consumers at a margin, thus guaranteeing revenue for the hotel. Hotels can sign on to become an "Expedia Special Rate Hotel" through Travelscape, to help fill unsold inventory. Travelscape helps hotels maximize revenue during peak, shoulder, and off-peak travel periods; it also offers hotels an Extranet tool that allows them to manage inventory and rates online.

Delta Hotels and Resorts was the first hotel chain in Canada to offer one-stop shopping with Expedia. In 2003, Expedia Canada announced a strategic deal with Delta Hotels to provide vacation packages to any of Delta Hotels' 37 properties across Canada. In addition, more than 450 airlines and all major car rental companies are available on www.deltahotels.com for booking. As well, Delta hotel properties are available for sale across all Expedia sites, including Expedia.ca, Expedia.com, and others. Expedia Canada is also providing telephone and e-mail–based customer support for the online flight and car rental bookings of Delta Hotels' online guests.

Travelocity, as the top online agency, gives hotels access to more than 25 million customers. In March 2001, the online agency expanded its hotel offerings through its relationship with hotel consolidator Hotel Reservations Network (HRN). In addition to Travelocity's current inventory of more than 50 000 hotel properties, this alliance gives members real-time access to the discounted independent vacation rental inventory provided through HRN's condosaver.com, giving the participating properties a new avenue of broad distribution. Hotel Reservations Network is one of the hottest hotel booking sites on the Internet, although it has roots as a call centre business. In fact, it claims to be the Internet's top provider of discount hotel accommodations and supplier of room availability during sold-out periods. HRN booked $305 million on the Internet in 2000.

PROFILE

QUÉBEC RESORTS AND COUNTRY INNS CREATES A POWERFUL E-MARKETING TOOL

Québec Resorts and Country Inns is a rapidly expanding network bringing together some of the hotel and restaurant industry's biggest names from Québec's 12 distinct tourism regions. In 2001, with the goal of better reaching its customers, travellers, travel organizers, and other associations, the network launched a new innovative Web site (www.hotelleriechampetre.com; see Figure 10.6). As a gateway to approximately 20 inns and hotels in Quebec, the Québec Resorts site offers its online clientele several individual and group packages for each of Quebec's four seasons, along with current online deals.

Each page of information is updated regularly. Visitors to the site can arrange business meetings or conferences online, find information using an interactive approach, secure online bookings, find seasonal specials, or purchase gift certificates for relatives, friends, or valued employees. Visitors may also subscribe to an electronic tourism newsletter, access recipes by great chefs, view a road map to better locate the inn or hotel, and peruse media summaries of the services

offered by the members of the Québec Resorts network.

Thanks to the intranet portion of the Québec Resorts Web site, building customer

Figure 10.6 Québec Resorts and Country Inns Web Site Homepage

PROFILE *continued*

profiles; customizing offers; and continually updating packages, promotions, online deals, electronic newsletters, recipes, contests, news, road maps, media summaries, and image databases is very easy. The immediacy and relevance of the information found on the site make for a powerful marketing management tool and research tool for anyone wishing to arrange a vacation or a business meeting at one of the 24 inns and hotels belonging to the network.

By using the site's Extranet service, each of the 24 network members can manage and update packages, promotions, online deals, recipes, and news, both quickly and independently, without the need for outside help of any kind. The information contained on the Web site is constantly updated, making the site the most relevant tool for every visitor interested in any of the hotels and inns in the Québec Resorts network.

At the end of 2002, new sections were added to the site to enable visitors to instantly access information related to theme getaways. Sections now exist for very specific needs, such as "Planning your wedding," "Meetings and conferences," and "Spa-relaxation." Québec Resorts and Country Inns hopes that these new features will keep visitors on their Web site longer and ultimately increase the number of online buyers, which currently stands at 1 to 2 percent.

Sources: Ran, G. (2001). Québec Resorts/Hôtellerie Champêtre Network creates a powerful e-marketing tool. Retrieved April 19, 2003, from http://www.canadatourism.com/en/ctc/ctx/ctx-news/search/newsbydateform.cfm; Québec Resorts and Country Inns introduces its new website!(2002). Retrieved December 23, 2002, from http://www.hotelleriechampetre.com.

5. Customer Service and Relationship Marketing

The Internet is moving marketers much closer to one-to-one marketing. The Web not only offers merchants the ability to communicate instantly with each customer, but it also allows the customer to talk back, and that makes it possible for companies to customize offers and services. *Marketing in Action* in this chapter shows how New Brunswick hotels use Internet marketing to tailor communications to the advantage of both marketer and customer. Tourism Québec is also taking advantage of the precision targeting that Internet marketing allows. In April 2003, the organization launched a new gay-focused Web site called "Visiting Gay-Friendly Quebec: Fun-Loving and Free-Living." Designed to appeal to international gay and lesbian travellers, the site focuses on Montreal in particular—as one of the strongest "out" gay communities in North America—and on Quebec's gay culture in general. Along with information on gay clubs and restaurants, the site has up-to-date information about events such as Divers/Cité, Montreal's gay-pride festival, and Black & Blue Festival, one of the largest gay circuit parties in the world.

The Internet also allows organizations to provide 7-day, 24-hour service response. For example, it is now relatively easy for customers to check on the status of their bookings or their frequent flyer/visitor programs at any time of the day on the Internet.

permission marketing

marketing in which consumers volunteer to be marketed to on the Internet in return for some kind of reward

Many consumers too are looking to build relationships on the Web. Godin introduced the concept of **permission marketing**, in which consumers volunteer to be marketed to on the Internet in return for some kind of reward. This type of marketing uses the interactivity offered by the Web to engage customers in a dialogue and, as a consequence, in a long-term interactive relationship.[13] Permission marketing is based on the premise that the attention of the consumer is a scarce commodity that needs to be managed carefully. Its emphasis is on building relationships with consumers instead of interrupting their lives with mass marketing messages. Understanding the degree to which a potential consumer is receptive to this kind of marketing is crucial, as was mentioned in the section in this chapter on direct e-mail marketing (see p. 333).

6. Marketing Research

The Internet has introduced some exciting new ways of conducting surveys. The two main alternatives are using either e-mail or the Web to deliver and receive questionnaires. Many hospitality and travel organizations have placed HTML questionnaires on their Web sites to collect information from people visiting their sites. For example, Panorama Village— the four-season resort owned by Intrawest—runs regular surveys to collect data from past and prospective customers.

Researchers are still experimenting with online surveys, and there are no conclusive guidelines about the strengths and weaknesses of online research. However, the relative speed and flexibility of online surveys are seen to be two major advantages. Additionally, there is the potential of reaching a large and growing audience of people on the Internet. Internet software is available to take the written survey and convert it into e-mail or Web-compatible formats, e-mail or administer online surveys, and then automatically collect responses, enter them into a database, and calculate descriptive statistics. By using this software on a busy Web site, it is possible to collect hundreds of responses in a short time period. However, Tierney has suggested that it may be increasingly difficult to get potential Web surfers to become survey respondents.[14] Since the respondent must click on the link to find an online survey, an incentive is often necessary to get the user to do so. But the use of incentives with Internet surveys has been shown to cause at least three methodological concerns: response bias, multiple entry, and unwanted entries.

MARKETING IN ACTION

NEW BRUNSWICK HOTELS OFFER NEW ONLINE TRAVEL SERVICE

Tourism is big business in New Brunswick, which is also one of Canada's most wired provinces. In 2002, the province's travel industry reported a record $985 million in revenues from 1.5 million visitors, the majority of whom arrived during the summer months. There are currently 1571 tourist operators and 11 704 available rooms in hotels, motels, bed and breakfasts, cottages, and country inns in New Brunswick. However, despite its launch of a Web site in 1998, technology had passed the province by. "We only updated it when we had the time," says Bill Thompson, deputy minister with New Brunswick's Tourism and Parks, "and that wasn't acceptable. We wanted something that could be kept up to date. If we're going to be in the modern world of the online travel agent, as a province we have to meet their standards."

So in March of 2003, 1500 tourism businesses in New Brunswick got a new electronic marketing tool when the province

MARKETING IN ACTION *continued*

introduced MyTravelHost, a Web site designed to help them increase bookings and compete online with large chain hotels, resorts, and travel operators (see Figure 10.7). The Web portal, developed by T4G Ltd., a Toronto technology-consulting firm, is an electronic service the company says will allow operators to deliver timely and relevant information to travellers. The estimated cost was $450 000, and the objective is to sell every room in the province every night during the tourism season.

MyTravelHost, which T4G calls a "tourism customer care and management platform," is accessible to consumers online or at information kiosks throughout New Brunswick, and to call centre employees who staff a tourism hotline run by the New Brunswick's Tourism and Parks Department. Every hotelier—large and small—is able to enter and modify the information about their property and offer services such as online reservations. "One of the strengths is that it can be updated instantly," says Dave

 Your biggest tourism challenge just got easier.

My Travel Host is a full customer care solution for tourism organizations that helps enable regional authorities to work with local operators and offer a consistent brand through the various channels that travelers buy from. My Travel Host addresses a number of weaknesses that are endemic in the information management and service delivery capabilities of tourism authorities around the world. These weaknesses include incomplete coverage of the product offering, uncoordinated campaign execution, poor brand control, inadequate customer service capability, lack of product or customer analysis, high maintenance costs, and high costs of print publication and distribution. Through the innovative application of technology, My Travel Host helps tourism authorities reduce the overall cost of operations by providing for the managed use and re-use of information, and increased revenue through a consistent multi-channel approach.

Multi-Channel Interface: My Travel Host supports interfaces for the call centre, the web, and for kiosks so that information is available anywhere, anytime and through any channel. Whether customers are accessing information on the web, visiting an information centre, or calling in to a central phone number, they have access to the same set of consistent information.

Operators: Self-Service Operators are able to enter and modify data on their existing properties, decreasing the amount of effort required by the Tourism Authorities to keep content current.

Reservations: Whether it is through the web, a customer care representative, or from a kiosk, we are able to connect customers to reservations systems to effect bookings for large and small tourism operators.

Campaign Management: My Travel Host's campaign management system enhances inventory realization by maximizing bookings throughout the year and distributing the volume of tourists over longer periods.

Product Repository: All product information (accommodations, tickets, sports etc.) is stored in a single repository. This allows for consistent communication of a single brand.

Customer Repository: All customer information is stored in a single repository. Whether dealing with the customer online, through an operator, or in person, this repository allows for a consistent and highly productive interaction.

Trip Planner: My Travel Host supports the ability to dynamically assemble trip plans and modify them while on a particular trip. This is either a self-service or an operator assisted function. Trip planning information can be accessed before, during, or after the visit.

Analytics Information: All aspects of the interaction with the customer are stored for future use and analysis. This information includes the number of visitors per channel, total number of visitors, visitors that have booked accommodation, and many other important business metrics.

My Travel Host
A T4G SOLUTION
we'll get you there

"We needed a partner with the most up-to-date technology who could enable us to meet a variety of technical requirements. T4G was just that partner."

NB Tourism and Parks Minister,
L. Joan MacAlpine

Accommodations are available on-line, all the time. My Travel Host levels the playing field for large and small operators, enabling them to compete on a global scale through each and every selling channel.

Maximum traveler convenience and lower cost of operations for operators are ensured through a robust interface with upstream and downstream systems and booking engines.

Collateral bookings and trip planner functionality ensure maximum industry participation from the region.

Personalization is raised to a new level as the call centre is equipped to assign a personal agent or concierge to each traveler for the duration of their stay.

Real-time communication for the traveler, combined with the ability to access travel plans and trip information anytime improves sell-through for operators and increases customer satisfaction.

Figure 10.7
MyTravelHost Web Site Homepage

MARKETING IN ACTION *continued*

Hyndman, T4G's director of hospitality services. "For example, if at any point we learn that a particular traveller is a keen golfer, we can begin to tailor communications to that individual—they will see special golf information and offers."

Geoff Flood, president of T4G, says that tourism authorities are in the business of marketing their destination, helping tourism operators sell their product, and ensuring that visitors have the best possible experience before, during, and after their visit. "The problem in the past was that the big guns got all of the exposure and the little guy didn't get any," he says. "This new system will allow the operators to improve the quality, integrity, and delivery of all their information."

Fred Fettah, general manager of the Lord Beaverbrook Hotel in Fredericton, says that the direct information and easy access is important to the hotel's customers. "We are privately owned and not part of a chain, so effectively utilizing electronic channels is critical," he says. "We need this type of site because clients want as much convenience at their fingertips as possible. People today want one-stop shopping. They want to look at the hotel, the rates, and what's going on in the city. This is an excellent tool, and the more the province invests in the future, the better it is for us."

Source: Barker, P. (2003, March 17). Hotels have no reservations about online travel service. *National Post*, p. BE2.

CHAPTER SUMMARY

Direct response marketing is rapidly becoming a vital component of the integrated marketing communications mix in the tourism industry. There are eight key advantages of direct marketing: precision targeting, personalization, flexibility, privacy, measurability, low cost, detailed knowledge of consumers, and fast or immediate response. Direct response advertising is one segment of the direct-marketing industry, and it plays a major role in influencing consumer purchase patterns. It can be defined as advertising through any medium, designed to generate a response by any means that is measurable (e.g., mail, television, telephone, fax, or Internet). Most large tourism and hospitality businesses, such as hotels, car rental companies, and scheduled airlines, have a large proportion of frequent-repeat customers who are vital to their profitability, so the advantages of direct marketing in this industry cannot be underestimated.

In spite of the failure of some very high-profile companies over the past decade or so, the Internet is transforming the tourism industry. The impact of e-marketing can be felt across all sectors in the industry, from large hotel chains to small outfitters. The advantage of this business model is that it is based on a sound foundation—consumer demand. Customers are looking to the Internet to research, plan, and even book their trips at rates that are increasing every year. The Internet is being used by the tourism and hospitality industry to perform six key functions: direct e-mail marketing, providing information, advertising, distribution and sales, customer service and relationship marketing, and marketing research.

KEY TERMS

banner ad, p. 334	direct marketing, p. 324	permission marketing, p. 342
call centre, p. 328	direct response advertising,	solo direct mail, p. 327
cooperative direct mail, p. 327	p. 325	spam, p. 333
direct e-mail marketing, p. 333	infomercial, p. 329	telemarketing, p. 328
direct mail, p. 327		

DISCUSSION QUESTIONS AND EXERCISES

1. Which direct response advertising technique do you think would be most effective for a growing ski resort attempting to attract new skiers?

2. The chapter talks mainly about the advantages of direct marketing. But what, in your opinion, are the disadvantages of the various tools mentioned?

3. Explain how direct marketing and Internet marketing are related.

4. What are the main advantages and disadvantages of Internet marketing?

5. The Internet is being used by the tourism and hospitality industry in six key areas. In which area do you foresee the greatest future potential?

6. Take a look at an existing Web site for a particular tourism or hospitality organization. Referring to Sinclair's tips, make a list of the strengths and weaknesses of the Web site.

CASE STUDY

HOW DO BED AND BREAKFASTS IN CANADA MARKET THEMSELVES ON THE INTERNET?

Small, family-owned businesses like bed and breakfasts (B&B's) have tended to grasp the potential of the Internet quicker than most larger companies, and generally the smaller the business, the larger the portion of available marketing dollars it invests in the Internet.[15] But what do these B&B's spend that money on, and how do they specifically use the Internet as a marketing tool? In 2002, an online survey was used to answer these questions. A review of the previous research on entrepreneur-led family businesses shows a scarcity of empirical work. Some suggest that because the entry barriers are low, small family businesses can set up an Internet presence, which helps level the playing field between small and large (non–family-owned) firms. Other research shows that small, family-owned businesses use the Internet because of its cost-effectiveness and because they wish to reach consumers beyond their borders. The overall objectives of the online survey were to confirm the above hypotheses, but also to

1. understand the importance of the Internet as a marketing tool for family-owned accommodations;

2. study the relationships between Internet use and (a) owner characteristics, (b) growth, and (c) internationalization;

3. develop theories identifying factors that facilitate and inhibit the adoption and implementation of Internet technology in family-owned businesses; and

4. investigate the effectiveness of family-owned business Web sites in converting surfers into buyers.

Initially, in-depth interviews with B&B owners were conducted in Alberta and British Columbia. Questions were asked pertaining to the use of the Internet, e-mail, Web sites, reservation systems, etc. Owners were asked for what purpose they used the Internet (i.e., to market rooms, increase exposure, project a professional image, etc.); what factors influenced or constrained their use of the Internet; how much they used e-mail as a marketing or communication tool or as a vehicle for taking reservations; what were the key advantages and disadvantages of using the Internet; what were success strategies for converting surfers to buyers; and how they advertised their Web sites.

Based on the analysis of these interviews, and on previous studies, an online survey was developed and hosted on a university Web site. An e-mail address list of 1048 B&B's was compiled from various guidebooks, online guides, and brochures. These establishments were contacted via e-mail and

directed to the Web site to complete the survey. An incentive was offered to encourage response: respondents were given the chance to win one of seven videos called *The Inside Story: How to Market a Bed & Breakfast on the Internet* (donated by the producer of the video, Locklin Productions). The survey was designed to move respondents easily through the questionnaire, and a pilot study indicated that the average completion time was approximately 10 minutes. In addition to their use of the Internet as a marketing tool, respondents were questioned about such factors as the number of beds in their property, the average price of rooms, years of operation, and the age and education of owners, to allow cross-tabulations and regression analysis. The survey was "live" for two months, and in total 353 usable responses were collected, giving a response rate of 33.7 percent.

The first question asked respondents how their customers heard about them (see Table 10.3). A large proportion (88 percent) of owners said that customers found them via the Internet "often" or "always." Word of mouth and accommodation

Table 10.3

Communication Methods That Attract Bed and Breakfast (B&B) Customers

HOW CUSTOMERS FOUND B&B'S	NEVER (%)	SOMETIMES (%)	OFTEN (%)	ALWAYS (%)
Word of mouth	2	36	57	5
Tourist office/Chamber of Commerce	12	56	30	2
Brochures	9	60	30	1
Internet	3	9	67	21
Accommodation guidebooks	7	46	42	5
Other guidebooks	27	56	15	2
Magazines and newspapers	56	38	6	0
Signs	43	45	11	1
Direct mail	85	13	1	1
In Canada, provincial or regional promotions	45	39	14	2

guidebooks were the second and third most powerful communication tools. Interestingly, direct mail was very unlikely to attract customers, as were magazines and newspapers.

Having established that the Internet was the key communication tool for B&B's, owners were asked questions pertaining to their Web sites. A quarter of respondents were in the first two years of running their sites, 35 percent were in the third or fourth years of operation, and the remaining 40 percent had been operating their sites for five years or more. For 36 percent of respondents, more than 60 percent of bookings were made online, and for the same number of owners, more than 60 percent of inquiries turned into reservations. There was a small positive correlation between the number of Web site opera-

tional years and the percentage of reservations made via the Internet, indicating that experience is likely to increase the number of bookings taken online. There was also a correlation between years in operation and Internet inquiries, indicating that inquiries are also more likely to increase the longer an owner has been operating a Web site.

Respondents were asked why they had a Web site. Table 10.4 lists the reasons in order of importance. There is clearly a trend toward using the Web as a marketing tool and as an avenue for delivering information, although 56 percent do use the Web to make online reservations. However, the Web is used less for relationship marketing or research purposes, as only 27 percent use it to obtain feedback from customers. Web sites tended to be updated when

Table 10.4

Reasons for a Bed and Breakfast (B&B) Having a Web Site

REASON FOR HAVING A WEB SITE	PERCENTAGE OF B&B OWNERS WHO AGREED (%)
To use as a marketing tool	92.3
To increase business exposure	83.0
To expand customer base outside Canada	81.5
To target more customers with less expense	81.0
To expand customer base within Canada	79.8
To answer questions about accommodation	78.4
To project a professional image	75.6
To impart knowledge quickly	71.3
To use e-mail as a marketing or communication tool	71.3
To improve customer service	63.9
To make reservations directly	56.3
To provide quotes to customers	54.5
To level the playing field between small and big business	39.2
To offer paperless documentation	38.6
To obtain feedback from customers	27.6

necessary, and exactly 50 percent of respondents said they measured the efficiency of their sites.

In terms of using online tools, very few used video or audio advertising, and only 16 percent offered information in other languages. The same low number used a secure server for making online credit card reservations. However, nearly half of respondents (46 percent) had links to businesses to help customers make travel plans, and 43 percent used the Web to give live e-mail assistance to customers. E-mail was not used very often to contact new or potential clients or suppliers. However, respondents did use e-mail for contacting existing clients and, more frequently, for answering online inquiries. Over 70 percent of owners reported using e-mail for taking reservations.

Owners were asked how customers found their Web sites. The most common method was through Web site search engines, 70 percent of customers often or always finding the B&B homepage in this way. A lesser percentage (about 40 percent) found the Web sites through guidebooks, online guidebooks, via word of mouth, or through Web site links. Occasionally, customers would find a Web site as a response to print media, or as a response to direct e-mail marketing, press releases, or broadcast media.

B&B owners were asked what they thought the advantages and disadvantages of using the Internet were. Table 10.5 lists these, in order of importance. Respondents clearly perceived more advantages than disadvantages.

Respondents were asked what they did to convert surfers into buyers. The most used methods were to answer queries within 24 hours (86 percent), provide as much information as possible (85 percent), keep the Web site up to date (71 percent) and make it easy for customers to reserve a room (63 percent). Nearly 60 percent of owners felt that employing professionals to design the Web site assisted in converting surfers into buyers. Once again, only 15 percent of owners used a secure server for secure online booking, and only 7 percent had a privacy policy, even though they identified security as being the major disadvantage of using the Internet.

Over 50 percent of businesses had been operating for six years or more, but still 24 percent of the sample was not yet profitable. Most owners (83 percent) had between one and five rooms, and the

Table 10.5

Advantages and Disadvantages of Using the Internet in Running a Bed and Breakfast (B&B)

ADVANTAGES	PERCENTAGE OF B&B OWNERS WHO AGREED (%)
Can reach a worldwide marketplace	89.8
Low cost	81.0
Ease of updating marketing information	79.0
Interactivity	65.3
Building customer relationships	51.4
Measurement of efficiency	45.7
Transmission of sound and video	44.6
Customer belief in security	6.3

TABLE 10.5 *continued*

DISADVANTAGES	PERCENTAGE OF B&B OWNERS WHO AGREED (%)
Not secure	44.0
Cannot screen customers	41.5
Poor technical knowledge	34.1
Customer privacy concerns	31.8
Too long to develop Web presence	25.0
Customers more likely to cancel	17.9
Cost	7.7

most popular price range was between $81 and $100 (47 percent). However, 41 percent had rooms in the $40–$80 range, 32 percent charged between $100 and $130, and some (19 percent) had rooms with a price tag of over $150. Half of the owners spent up to $1000 on marketing each year, 20 percent had an annual marketing budget of $1001 to $2000, and a further 30 percent spent more than $2000 on marketing each year. For over half of the respondents, 50 percent of this money was spent on Web site maintenance. Interestingly, there was a negative correlation between the number of rooms and the percentage of marketing dollars spent on the Web site, indicating that the smaller the estab-

lishment, the more they were likely to spend, in relative terms, on their Web sites.

Finally, there was a small positive but significant correlation between the number of years of Web site operation and both the percentage of international bookings and the number of reservations made via the Internet, indicating that more experienced operators were more adept at converting surfers into buyers, and that they were also using the Internet to reach consumers beyond their borders. As for owner characteristics, there was no correlation between the education level of owners and Internet use, but there was a significant relationship between the age of the owner and general Internet use.

QUESTIONS

1. In two paragraphs, summarize the results of the study.
2. Since many studies suggest that security and privacy are key concerns for consumers in terms of online transactions, why do you think the bed and breakfasts in the study did not have secure online servers?
3. It appears that the majority of owners do not use the Internet for direct e-mail or for relationship marketing. Why do you think this is?
4. Critically analyze an existing Web site for a bed and breakfast in Canada. What improvements would you make?

WEB SITES

www.bonjourquebec.com
Bonjour Québec (Tourism Quebec's new gay-focused Web site)

www.canadabyrail.ca
Canada by Rail

www.destina.ca
Destina.ca (Air Canada's online travel agency)

www.gomediacanada.com
GoMedia Canada (Canadian Tourism Commission's media Web site)

www.ksinclair.com
Kevin Sinclair's Web site (provides information on developing an effective Web site)

www.peiplay.com
Prince Edward Island visitors' guide

www.hotelleriechampetre.com
Québec Resorts and Country Inns

www.ripleyridge.com
Ripley Ridge Retreat

www.tourismtogether.com
TourismTogether.com (provides information on Internet marketing)

www.worldwidetrails.com
World Wide Trails (an alliance of adventure tour operators)

ENDNOTES

1. Direct response spending expected to go nuts. (2001, February 12). *Marketing*, 15.
2. Lazarus, E. (2001, February 12). The new call centre Mecca. *Marketing Direct*, 24.
3. Gooderham, M. (1997, May 7). Level of antipathy a wake-up call for telemarketers. *The Globe and Mail*, p. C11.
4. Internet use by Canadian businesses evolves. (2002). Retrieved April 2, 2002, from http://main.tourismtogether.com/inforesources.
5. Parsons, A. M., Zeisser., M., & Waitman, R. (1998). Organizing today for the digital marketing of tomorrow. *Journal of Interactive Marketing, 12*(1), 31–46.
6. Gretzel, U., Yuan, Y. L., & Fesenmaier, D. R. (2000). Preparing for the new economy: Advertising strategies and change in destination marketing organizations. *Journal of Travel Research, 39*(2), 146–156.
7. Beirne, E., & Curry, P. (1999). "The impact of the Internet on the information search process and tourism decision-making. In D. Buhalis & W. Schertler (Eds.). *Information and communication technologies in tourism* (pp. 88–97). Wien, Austria: Springer-Verlag.
8. Schwartz, E. I. (1998). *Webonomics: Nine essential principles for growing your business on the World Wide Web.* New York: Broadway.
9. Hoffman, D. L., & Novak, T. P. (1996). Marketing in hypermedia computer-mediated environments: Conceptual foundations. *Journal of Marketing, 60*(July), 50–68.
10. Barker, P. (2003, March 7). Hotels have no reservations about online travel service. *National Post,* p. BE2.
11. Canadians logging on to destination Web sites. (2000). Retrieved September 26, 2000, from http://tourismtogether.com/tourismweb/news/buzz/sep.
12. Anderson, K. (2001). 2001 occupancy rates down; hotels turn to the Web. Retrieved April 2, 2002, from http://main.tourismtogether.com/inforesources.
13. Godin, S. (1999). *Permission marketing.* New York: Simon & Schuster.
14. Tierney, P. (2000). Internet-based evaluation of tourism Web site effectiveness: Methodological issues and survey results. *Journal of Travel Research, 39*, 212–219.
15. Hudson, S., & Lang, N. (2002). A destination case study of marketing tourism online: Banff, Canada. *Journal of Vacation Marketing, 8*(2), 155–165.

Providing Service Quality through Internal Marketing

"IT'S OUR PLEASURE!"—SERVICE EXCELLENCE AT THE SHERATON SUITES CALGARY EAU CLAIRE

The Sheraton Suites Calgary Eau Claire has a reputation for service excellence. The hotel was awarded the Starwood Select Best in Brand in North America for both 2001 and 2002, with the highest guest satisfaction score among 240 Sheraton properties. The Starwood Select Best in Brand award recognizes exceptional levels of hospitality, service and attention to detail, as well as upscale facilities and variety of amenities. The Sheraton Suites was also the winner of the Alberta Tourism Award (ALTO) for Service Excellence in 2002. This particular award honours an organization in the tourism industry that demonstrates "a commitment to service excellence, delivering outstanding customer service to their visitors, employees, suppliers and other stakeholders."[1]

But exactly what does it take to win awards like this?

For Randy Zupanski, general manager of the hotel, there are two key reasons why the Sheraton Suites Calgary Eau Claire is so different from its competitors: customer loyalty and quality employees. First, a focus on customer loyalty is driven by the "It's Our Pleasure" program—a recognition and reward program for guests. On every fifth stay, a guest receives a gift, one that is meaningful to the guest, and the value of the gift increases the longer a customer remains loyal. For example, on the fifth stay a guest may receive a bottle of wine in his or her room, and by the twenty-fifth stay, a personalized bathrobe will be given as a loyalty gift. Meanwhile, the hotel collects valuable data on the personal preferences of customers and stores this data in a database. For example, if a guest likes extra towels and feather pillows, then these will be waiting in the room when the guest arrives, with a note saying "It's our pleasure to provide you with these items...."

Zupanski suggests that the majority of hotels put in the customer service effort after the guest arrives, whereas the Sheraton Eau Claire takes care of preferences before arrival. A guest relations officer is employed for the sole purpose of coordinating the "It's Our Pleasure" program, and a room is not ready for a guest until this officer has ensured all preferences are taken care of. "We probably employ an extra 14 shifts a week to control this program, but it brings attention to the guest that the room has been specifically prepared for him or her," says Zupanski. Another way that the hotel builds loyalty and develops customer relationships is by holding a weekly cocktail party at the hotel every Wednesday. Four or five managers are on hand to greet the guests, and since 65 percent of guests are from the corporate sector, it is a unique opportunity for business travellers to meet hotel managers and get to know them. These meetings are another opportunity for managers to gain more knowledge about guest preferences that they can then add to the database.

The second, and perhaps most important, reason that the Sheraton Eau Claire is an award winner is the quality of its employees. The hotel hires "nice people with great attitudes" and takes training very seriously. Three training programs include a full day spent on the "It's Our Pleasure" scheme, using role-playing to emphasize the meaning and importance of employee empowerment. Employees are trained in the art of service recovery and are taught the importance of customer contact. Energy is put into "key contact areas," so that before a guest reaches his or her room, there has been plenty of opportunity for personal contact from the valet, bellman, reception staff, or the general manager him- or herself. For Zupanski, pride is the key, and every effort is made to recognize the achievement of employees and to ensure that they are happy and proud of their jobs. Loss of employees to other hotels is extremely low, he says, and if employees do leave, it is to go into other industries, not to other hotels.

The results of these efforts are not just manifested in the winning of awards. The hotel has occupancy rates 15–20 percent higher than its nearest competitor, and room rates are $15–20 above those of competing hotels. Since opening, the Sheraton Suites Eau Claire has lead the market with an overall market share on revenue per available room (RevPAR) of 140 percent among its competitive set, which includes Hyatt, Fairmont, Westin, Delta, and the Marriott. Only time will tell whether or not arrogance and complacency will set in at the hotel as a result of winning so many awards. In the meantime, the Sheraton Suites Calgary Eau Claire provides an excellent example of the value of internal marketing.

Source: R. Zupanski, general manager, Sheraton Suites Calgary Eau Claire, personal communication, April 5, 2003.

Objectives

On completion of this chapter, readers should understand

- the internal marketing process;
- the link between service quality and customer satisfaction;

- the measurement tools and the behavioural consequences of service quality;
- the link between customer satisfaction and loyalty;
- relationship marketing strategies; and
- the importance of service recovery.

Chapter Overview

The opening vignette introduces the concept of internal marketing and provides a good example of a hotel that has differentiated itself by focusing on employees and customer loyalty. This chapter begins by defining internal marketing and examining the four key steps in the internal marketing process. The next section focuses on delivering service quality, and includes discussions of the "gaps model" of service quality, the measurement of service quality, and the behavioural consequences of service quality. The third main section of the chapter discusses loyalty and relationship marketing. Various customer retention strategies are introduced, as are the benefits of relationship marketing to both company and customer. The final part of the chapter analyzes service recovery and offers guidelines for tracking and handling complaints.

THE INTERNAL MARKETING PROCESS

internal marketing

marketing aimed internally, at a company's own employees

Internal marketing was introduced in Chapter 1 as an integral part of the services marketing triangle (see Figure 1.2), and can be defined as marketing aimed internally, at a company's own employees. Internal marketing takes place through the fulfilling of promises. Promises are easy to make, but unless providers are recruited, trained, equipped with tools and appropriate internal systems, and rewarded for good service, the promises may not be kept. Internal marketing was first proposed as a way to deliver consistently high service quality by Berry, Hensel, and Burke in 1976.[2] However, despite the rapidly growing literature on internal marketing, very few organizations actually apply the concept in practice. One of the main problems is that a single unified concept of what is meant by internal marketing does not exist. Lack of investment in internal marketing may also be the result of corporate distraction. Companies that are busy trying to boost revenues and cut costs may not see why they should spend money on employees, thus missing the point that these are the very people who ultimately deliver the brand promises the company makes. Or lack of such investment may reflect a conscious decision by executives who dismiss internal efforts as "feel-good pseudoscience," failing to understand that research consistently demonstrates that service quality problems (people problems more than product problems) are what push customers away and into the arms of competitors.[3]

Yet there are some encouraging signs. In the spring of 2002, Interbrand, a leading brand strategy and design firm, asked marketers what impact the events of 2001 had on their brand-building efforts in 2002. One area of significant change was that internal

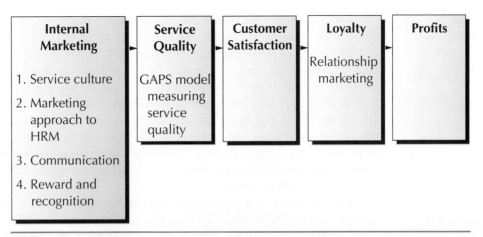

Figure 11.1 The Link between Internal Marketing and Profits

branding had become ranked third in importance, moving up from seventh. Current thinking suggests that brands are a reflection of the best parts of the organization's culture, values, and beliefs. The greatest ambassadors of the brand are the employees, and it is with them that branding should start and progress. A strong internal brand makes for a strong external one. Interbrand attributed the change of heart to recent economic and political events that have underscored the need for an organization's messages to reflect its values and culture.[4] Also, researchers and practitioners seem to be agreeing on the objectives and definition of internal marketing. There is growing awareness that an effective internal marketing program will have a positive effect on service quality, customer satisfaction and loyalty, and eventually profits. Figure 11.1 illustrates the link between internal marketing and profits.

The main objective of internal marketing is to enable employees to deliver satisfying products to guests. This takes place through a four-step process.

1. Establishment of a Service Culture

Organizational culture refers to the unwritten policies and guidelines, to what has been formally decreed, and to what actually takes place in a company. It is the pattern of shared values and beliefs that helps individuals understand organizational functioning and thus provides them with norms for behaviour in the business. In the past few decades, researchers have begun to analyze the linkage between culture and the marketing of services. Due to the unique characteristics of services (i.e., intangibility, inseparability of production and consumption, perishability, and heterogeneity), the nature of the culture of a service organization is particularly important and worthy of attention.

Marketing culture refers to the unwritten policies and guidelines that provide employees with behavioural norms, to the importance the organization as a whole places on the marketing function, and to the manner in which marketing activities are executed. Since service quality is one dimension of marketing culture, it follows that the kind of marketing culture an organization has would be particularly important for a service organization, as the simultaneous delivery and receipt of services brings the provider and customer physically and psychologically close. Research has shown a strong positive relationship between the kind of marketing culture a service organization has and its profitability and degree of marketing effectiveness.[5]

service culture

a culture that supports customer service through policies, procedures, reward systems, and actions

A **service culture** is a culture that supports customer service through policies, procedures, reward systems, and actions. An internal marketing program flows out of a service culture. A services marketing program is doomed to failure if its organizational culture does not support servicing the customer. Such a program requires a strong commitment from management. If management expects employees to have a positive attitude toward customers, management must have a positive attitude toward the customer and the employees. The change to a customer-oriented system may require changes in hiring, training, reward systems, and customer complaint resolution, as well as empowerment of employees. It requires that managers spend time talking to both customers and customer-contact employees. The *Snapshot* on pages 366–367 highlights how a service organization can measure its service culture.

A service culture will be developed over time through the actions of management. For example, the general manager of Sheraton Suites Calgary Eau Claire has fostered a service culture in his hotel by spending time greeting guests and inquiring about their welfare during morning checkout and afternoon check-in. He also spends time working alongside customer-contact employees while they serve customers. This action makes it clear to employees that management does not want to lose touch with operations and that management cares about both employees and customers.

In organizations that have weak service cultures, there are few or no common values and norms. Employees are often bound by policies and regulations, although these policies make no sense from a customer-service perspective. As a result, employees become insecure about making decisions outside of the rules and regulations, and they are therefore unable to satisfy customers. Turning potentially dissatisfied guests into satisfied guests is a major challenge for tourism and hospitality organizations, and empowering employees to go the extra mile in satisfying guests is recognized as one of the most powerful tools available to a service organization. **Empowerment** is the act of giving employees the authority to identify and solve guest problems or complaints on the spot, and to make improvements in the work processes when necessary. Often this will mean decentralizing decision making and flattening organization charts in order to give more power to the front-line employees who directly serve customers. It also means that managers must have greater levels of trust in their subordinates and must respect their judgment.

empowerment

the act of giving employees the authority to identify and solve guest problems or complaints on the spot, and to make improvements in the work processes when necessary

Empowerment is regarded as an essential aspect of internal marketing, and as essential for the operationalization of Gronroos's interactive marketing concept, a part of the services marketing triangle introduced in Chapter 1 (see p. 8). In order for interactive marketing to occur, front-line employees need to be empowered—that is, they require a degree of control over the service task performance in order to be responsive to customer needs and to be able to perform service recovery. However, the degree of empowerment is contingent on the complexity and variability of customer needs and the degree of task complexity. Also, empowerment does not suit all employees because of the extra responsibility that it inevitably entails.

2. Development of a Marketing Approach to Human Resource Management

A marketing approach to human resources management (HRM) involves the use of marketing techniques to attract and retain employees. This means using marketing research techniques to understand the employee market. Different employee segments look for different benefits, and it is important to understand what benefits will attract employees.

Advertising for staff can then be developed with prospective employees in mind, building a positive image of the company for present and future employees and customers. Marketing can help by working with the human resources (HR) department to identify the key elements in employee motivation, including the effect of incentives and the development of training and improvement programs. Marketing can help most of all with research, working with HR to determine, internally, what can be done to improve the delivery of "customer-facing" people and to help understand what motivates employees, channel partners, and customer-service representatives. If marketers are good at understanding customers, consumers, and end-users of products and services, they should be able to lend those talents to HR to help them understand internal marketing conducted by internal marketers.

Such a marketing approach to developing positions and benefits helps to attract and retain good employees. Companies should ensure that they recruit employees who are highly motivated, customer-oriented, and sales-minded because changing employee attitudes and behaviours is more difficult and costly once the employees have been recruited. Employees also need the right type and level of training to perform their jobs. This can help to reduce ambiguity surrounding their role and can help employees to meet the needs of customers more effectively.

More and more managers are trying to tap into the psyche of employees as the continuous turnover of staff takes its toll on the industry. Employee turnover in the hospitality industry is often 10 times what it is in other industries. Some managers are finding that giving increased responsibility is improving retention and performance. "We created a self-managing work team in our kitchen department, and not only has it improved profitability immensely, but that department has the lowest turnover in the hotel," says David Kaiser, general manager of Best Western Denham Inn & Suites, in Leduc, Alberta. "We educated all the staff on the financial side of the business, and they are rewarded for profitability. Everyone knows how each activity impacts the profitability. For instance, food costs are typically quite high, and in a traditional kitchen set-up, the chef is responsible. In our operation, everyone down to the dishwasher knows what the food costs and how waste, storage, and portions impact the bottom line."[6]

Keeping a job interesting may also mean transferring employees to other departments or even to another location. Businesses such as Fairmont Hotels & Resorts in Canada offer employee exchange programs to boost staff loyalty. Employees can spend a few months working at Banff, Lake Louise, or other desirable locations. It is not, however, just entry-level positions that are difficult to keep filled. Turnover among hospitality industry sales and marketing professional is at almost 25 percent. A National Restaurant Association poll of more than 400 foodservice managers also found that about one-quarter of the respondents intended to leave their positions in the near future, with at least half of those planning to depart the foodservice business entirely.[7]

According to Jon Katzenbach, author of *Why Pride Matters More Than Money*, feelings of pride can motivate people to excel far more effectively than money or position.[8] He says that institutions such as Southwest Airlines and Marriott International, which manage to sustain the emotional commitment of a large proportion of their employees over good times and bad, seldom rely on monetary incentives. Instead, they find ways to instil institution-building pride in what people do, in why and how they do it, and in those with whom they do it. Pride builders accomplish this by (a) setting aspirations that touch emotions, (b) pursuing a meaningful purpose, (c) cultivating personal relationships of respect, (d) becoming a person of high character, and (d) injecting humour along the way. For the Sheraton Suites Calgary Eau Claire (see opening vignette), instilling pride in employees is a key motivator. Katzenbach warns that those who want to develop pride-building capability are advised to avoid the most common pitfalls: overly relying on monetary incentives, assuming that pride only follows performance, creating laundry lists of things to do, managing by numbers, and assuming that top-down initiatives will penetrate the front line without significant help from a cadre of pride builders.

Continuous training can also help improve employee morale and reduce turnover of employees. The Canadian Tourism Human Resource Council (CTHRC) provides human resource development solutions for the tourism industry, and in 2002 it introduced the *Performance First HR Tool Kit*, a pragmatic guide to human resource management. The kit (which includes a manual and CD) provides the "ready made tools" needed to recruit, select, hire, train, coach, and manage employees effectively. Several customizable, user-friendly templates and forms are available in the kit, including application forms, interview evaluations, job-offer letters, training plans, and employee manuals suited to the position.

MARKETING IN ACTION

INTERNAL MARKETING AT FAIRMONT HOTELS & RESORTS

Fairmont Hotels & Resorts is a good example of a company that aims its marketing efforts toward its employees. Fairmont is the largest luxury hotel management company in North America and has achieved great success since it opened in 1914. The company now operates 77 hotels with about 30 000 rooms and employs 28 000 people. The company sees internal marketing as critical in achieving guest satisfaction, and consequently Fairmont is world-renowned for its excellent guest service.

Fairmont knows that it is important to segment the employee market as well as the guest market, and to develop a marketing mix to attract the best staff for its company. Attracting self-motivated, results-oriented staff for Fairmont is key to its employee marketing mix, which is why it has an extensive recruiting and hiring process to select the best employees to interact with its guests. Once hired, the employee participates in a mandatory two-day orientation offered by the Fairmont Learning Organization (FLO). New recruits learn Fairmont's service culture (policies, procedures, reward systems, and actions) and organizational culture (mission, vision, values, and history of the company). It is imperative that employees believe in their product and value it, as employee satisfaction and customer satisfaction are directly related. If one of these decreases, it could mean a warning that the company is not customer-focused. The company measures the success or failure of its internal marketing programs through employee turnover rate—currently running at about 20 percent, with industry averages five or six times higher. Staff loyalty

MARKETING IN ACTION *continued*

in turn encourages customer loyalty; repeat guests make up 60 percent of Fairmont's business.

Empowerment is about turning the traditional organizational structure upside down, with the customers and employees at the top of the structure and management at the bottom. Management and employees now work to serve the guest, versus serving the CEO or "boss." Focusing on the needs and wants of the customer and granting employees the power to achieve the ultimate guest service creates an atmosphere in which employees are not afraid to tell supervisors of a mistake in order to rectify it and satisfy the guest. At Fairmont a mistake is considered an "oops." The company-wide emphasis is on giving each employee—at both the corporate and the property levels—the tools, training, authority, and support they need in order to make informed decisions and take appropriate actions to deliver the highest level of service excellence to Fairmont guests. The goal is to empower employees to create customized experiences that make lifetime memories for guests—what Fairmont calls "wow" experiences. Service recovery is taken very seriously at Fairmont. Employees are trained to handle difficult or non-routine situations. However, training manuals can only prepare employees to handle normal, non-routine guest requests. It is internal marketing programs, such as the FLO, that provide employees with the right attitude, knowledge, communication skills, and authority to deal with any demands. Staff are trained to empathize with guests—to recognize how the guests feel, to reassure them that Fairmont does care and understands the problem, and to determine if further action needs to be taken or incentives given in order for the guests to return to Fairmont in the future.

Employee reward and recognition programs are an important part of the process of internal marketing. Once Fairmont has attracted and recruited the right employees, attention is focused on keeping employees satisfied and motivated to continue to impress the guest. Benefits and perks are important factors in compensating employees. Substantial discounts of up to 50 percent off food, beverages, and hotel rates are offered as employee incentives to encourage them to use these products/services, thus facilitating first-hand knowledge. Employees are part of the product, and encouraging them to be excited about Fairmont hotels and services will in turn make the customer more excited. Fairmont also has a number of recognition awards that are presented throughout the year. These benefits and awards market the company to the employees and install a positive attitude within the workplace. Internal communication at Fairmont is also taken seriously. A bi-monthly newsletter is distributed in each specific hotel, and a company-wide newsletter, *The Dialogue*, keeps staff up to date on new company procedures.

Fairmont Hotels & Resorts is a company that has used internal marketing to its advantage and that is setting the standard in guest service in the hotel industry. By successfully aiming internal marketing at its employees, Fairmont continues to achieve its mission of "earning the loyalty of [its] guests by exceeding their expectations and providing warm personal service."

Sources: Cohen, S. (2001). Concierges go the extra mile to make visitors' stays memorable. *The Business Journal,* Kansas City, *19*(50), 24; Liddle, A. J. (2002, January 28). Regional powerhouse chains. *Nations Restaurant News, 36*(4), 100–102; Mueller, S. (2000). "How do you set your hotel apart from others? *The Business Journal,* Kansas City, *17*(51), 44; The Fairmont Learning Organization. (2001, September). *MyFairmont Serviceplus Training Binder.*

3. Dissemination of Marketing Information to Employees

Managers need to pay significant attention to the communication of marketing (and other organizational) strategies and objectives to employees, so that they understand their own role and importance in the implementation of the strategies and in the achievement of the objectives. Research evidence suggests that the frequency, quality, and accuracy of downward communication moderates employee role ambiguity and hence increases job satisfaction. Managers need to find appropriate communication mechanisms for their particular organizations and for the task at hand. Supportive senior management is fundamental to the success of internal marketing, as it indicates to all employees the importance of internal marketing initiatives and thereby facilitates interfunctional coordination.[9] Such communication mechanisms may come in the form of company meetings, training sessions, newsletters, e-mails, annual reports, or videotapes.

Unfortunately, many companies exclude customer-contact employees from the communication cycle. The director of marketing may tell managers and supervisors about upcoming promotional campaigns, but some managers may feel that employees do not need to have this information. However, it is important that staff are informed about marketing promotions. They should hear about promotions and new products from management, not from external advertisements meant for customers. Changes in the service delivery process should also be communicated. In fact, all action steps in the marketing plan should include internal marketing. For example, when a company introduces a new mass media campaign, the implementation should include actions to inform employees about the campaign. Because service advertising and personal selling promise what people *do*, frequent and effective communication across functions—horizontal communication—is critical. If internal communication is poor, perceived service quality is at risk. If company advertising and other promises are developed without input from operations, contact personnel may not be able to deliver service that matches the image portrayed in marketing efforts.

4. Implementation of a Reward and Recognition System

For employees to perform effectively, it is important that they know how they are doing, so communication must be designed to give them feedback on their performance. In a recent Canadian survey, almost 90 percent of employees reported that "being made to feel like a valued employee is important in motivating them to achieve company goals."[10] The survey was conducted by Bob Macdonald, president of Maritz Canada Inc. Macdonald argues that in order to feed an employee's energy level and overall desire to perform, organizations need to clearly communicate performance objectives, as well as provide relevant training, feedback, and recognition in the form of non-cash rewards. However, the rewards should be tailored to the interests of the employees they are designed to motivate. Group excursions are popular with employees in the 18-to-29 age groups, while older employees prefer personal trips. More men than women, for some reason, appreciate getting "company-logo merchandise" as a reward. For some, the ideal reward is the gift of a personal chef for the evening, and for others time off with pay is the perfect reward.

Some companies recognize superior performance with reward points that can be redeemed for an array of gifts. At the high end, the rewards can range from airline tickets to big-screen televisions. Sometimes recognition alone is enough. Macdonald says that 73 percent of the surveyed employees reported that receiving "recognition as top performer" was important (the *Snapshot* below highlights the importance that Radisson Hotels & Resorts places on recognizing top performing employees). Furthermore, most employees want regular feedback. Macdonald found in his survey that only 15 percent of employees said that their companies offer that extra something for a job well done. He suggests that most employers do not offer non-monetary rewards because they are concerned about the cost or are not sure what their employees would value. Macdonald says that as the labour market tightens, retention of top performers will become an issue for employers. He adds that employees have made clear, in repeated surveys, that money is important—but it takes more than money to engage them in their jobs.

SNAPSHOT

RADISSON EMPLOYEES OF THE YEAR

Canadian Radisson Hotels & Resorts made their presence known at the 2002 Annual Business Conference for Carlson Hospitality Worldwide (Radisson's parent company) held in Las Vegas, Nevada, when they demonstrated the "Power of One" and received two of the global hotel company's top awards. Chris Hales, general manager of the Radisson Hotel Toronto-Markham, was named the brand's top general manager and awarded the 2001 Esprit Award. Jose Diaz, bellperson at the Radisson Hotel Winnipeg Downtown was selected from over 47 000 Radisson employees worldwide to be named Employee of the Year for 2001. Jay Witzel, president and chief operating officer of Radisson Hotels & Resorts, presented both awards.

The Esprit Award is given to the general manager who establishes a high level of employee and guest engagement; is recognized for excellence in guest services, RevPAR, and profit growth; and is an active participant within the brand—a general manager who is a leader, but who also serves. As part of this award, a Voyageur Scholarship has been established in Hales's name at Johnson and Wales University, a respected hospitality school. Hales, a 27-year veteran of the

industry, joined Radisson as general manager of the Markham hotel in 1997. He was selected from more than 430 Radisson general managers in 60 countries to receive this honour. "Chris embodies the vision of Radisson to create valuable relationships with the guests we serve," says Witzel. "It's a role that takes not only confidence and competence, but a strong commitment to our goal of creating great places in great places." "I was as honoured as I was surprised to receive this award, and it is one that I share with our entire team at the Radisson Hotel Toronto-Markham," says Hales. "It is their dedication, enthusiasm and 'Yes I Can' spirit that adds the 'shine and polish' to our hotel."

The Employee of the Year is given to the employee who embodies and consistently displays four key characteristics that add to the success of any hotel: an overwhelming "Yes I Can" attitude, an unwavering commitment to teamwork, a drive to contribute to the success of the hotel, and an outstanding desire to contribute to the community. "Our employees are at the heart of our business model, delivering the Radisson brand promise each day with professionalism and dedication," says Witzel. "In choosing this year's

Employee of the Year, one individual stood out among the nominees as someone who always goes above and beyond to help others." In nominating Jose Diaz, a member of the bellstand department at the Radisson Hotel Winnipeg Downtown, fellow staff members and guests alike gave him high praise: "He has an 'anything possible, you-name-it' guest service and satisfaction atti-tude." "He really is the very first person every guest should meet upon arrival." "His demeanour with guests reflects a genuine love of people."

Diaz joined the hotel in 1995 in the housekeeping department and transferred to the position of bellperson in 2000. He acknowledges that he has two important influ-ences in his life to which he can attribute his personal success: his team of fellow employees at the Radisson, and his mother, who Diaz claims "taught me that it is nice to be important, but it's more important to be nice." Recognition for his hard work and dedi-cation to guests is not new to Diaz. He was also given the Associate of the Year award by CHIP Hospitality, a subsidiary of Canadian Hotel Income Properties Real Estate Investment Trust (CHIP REIT). The Radisson Hotel Winnipeg Downtown is owned by CHIP REIT and managed by CHIP Hospitality. Diaz was selected from the employees at 37 hotels that are owned and/or managed by CHIP REIT. And last year he was chosen by the mayor's office as one of the Stars of the City of Winnipeg after being nominated by a number of hotel guests. "Jose leaves a positive impres-sion with every guest he interacts with. From the corporate executive to the leisure traveller, Jose treats everyone as a VIP," says David Chizda, general manager of Radisson Hotel Winnipeg Downtown. "We know that Jose is always there, providing 100 percent guest sat-isfaction with all of our guests and with his fellow associates alike."

Source: Murdoch, J. (2002). Radisson names Canadians as their top GM, top employee. Retrieved February 27, 2002, from http://www.canadatourism.com/en/ctc/ctx/ctx-news/search/newsbydateform.cfm.

DELIVERING SERVICE QUALITY

Service quality has been increasingly identified as a key factor in differentiating service products and building a competitive advantage in tourism. The process by which cus-tomers evaluate a purchase, thereby determining satisfaction and likelihood of repurchase, is important to all marketers, but especially to services marketers because, unlike their manufacturing counterparts, they have fewer objective measures of quality by which to judge their production. **Service quality** can be defined as customers' perceptions of the service component of a product, and these perceptions are said to be based on five dimen-sions: reliability, assurance, empathy, responsiveness, and tangibles.[11]

service quality

customers' perceptions of the service compo-nent of a product

customer satisfaction

the difference between the service that a customer expects and the perceived quality of what is actually delivered

Many researchers believe that an outgrowth of service quality is **customer satisfac-tion**, measured as the difference between the service that a customer expects and the per-ceived quality of what is actually delivered.[12] According to this view, satisfaction represents a global judgment rather than a transaction-specific measure. Satisfaction is also thought to have an affective element that is experiential and that is most appropriately assessed after consumption. Satisfying customers has always been a key component of the tourism industry, but never before has it been so critical. In these uncertain times, and with increased competition, knowing how to win and keep customers is the single-most important business skill that anyone can learn. Customer satisfaction and loyalty are the keys to long-term profitability, and keeping the customer happy is everybody's business. Becoming customer-centred and exceeding customer expectations are requirements for business success.

Well-publicized research shows that companies can increase profits from 25 to 85 percent by retaining just 5 percent more of their customers,[13] but the newest research indicates that merely "satisfying" customers is no longer enough to ensure loyalty.[14] There is little or no correlation between satisfied (versus highly satisfied) customers and customer retention. This means that it is not enough just to please customers. Each customer should become so pleased with all elements of their association with an organization that buying from someone else is unthinkable.

"Customer-centred" is an exact term that connotes much more than focusing on or understanding the customer. The true customer-centred company has the willingness and ability to bring the customer to the very centre of its organizational being.[15] Customers' needs and expectations are communicated throughout, and every employee evaluates every process, every task, and every decision by considering how it will add value for the customers. All employees must be convinced that the customer really does come first. The issue of understanding needs and expectations is an important part of the quest for customer satisfaction. The "gaps model" of service quality (see Figure 11.2 on page 364) provides a method of graphically illustrating these needs and expectations.[16]

The Gaps Model of Service Quality

This conceptual model enables a structured thought process for evaluating and "designing in" customer satisfaction. The model begins with expected service as viewed by the customer. Every customer has certain expectations about a service, which may come from word of mouth, personal needs, group needs, past experience, and/or external communications. When the service is delivered and the customers' expectations are exceeded, the customers perceive the quality as relatively high. When their expectations have not been met, they perceive the quality as relatively low. Thus, as stated above, customer satisfaction can be defined as the difference between what the customer expects and the perceived quality of what is actually delivered. Often there is a gap between expected service and the actual service as perceived by the customer, and in the model, this is gap 5. The magnitude of this gap is driven by four other possible gaps, each of which denotes failure in some aspect of service delivery. The five gaps are discussed below.

Gap 1: The Difference between the Customer's Expectations of Service and Management's Perception of Those Expectations

Many reasons exist for managers not being aware of what customers expect: they may not interact directly with customers, may be unwilling to ask about expectations, or may be unprepared to address them. The four key factors responsible for gap 1 are the service provider's inadequate marketing research orientation, lack of upward communication, insufficient relationship focus, and inadequate service recovery. The importance of both relationship marketing and service recovery are discussed later in this chapter. By building

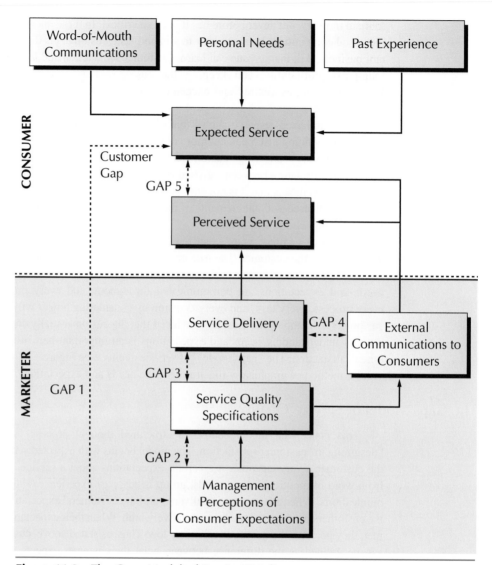

Figure 11.2 The Gaps Model of Service Quality

Source: Parasuraman, A., Zeithaml, V. A., and Berry, L. L. (1985). A conceptual model of service quality and its implications for future research. *Journal of Marketing, 49* (4), 40.

stronger relationships, understanding customer needs over time, and implementing recovery strategies when things go wrong, gap 1—the customer expectations gap—can be minimized.

Gap 2: The Difference between the Management's Perception of Customer Expectations and the Way That These Perceptions are Then Translated into Specifications or Processes

Gap 2 occurs when managers know what their customers want but are unable or unwilling to develop systems that will deliver it. Some of the reasons that have been given for gap 2 are poor service design, absence of customer-defined standards, and inappropriate physical evidence and servicescape. One of the most important ways to avoid gap 2 is to design services clearly, without oversimplification, incompleteness, subjectivity, or bias. To do this, tools are needed to ensure that new and existing services are developed and improved in as careful a manner as possible. (See, for example, the *Snapshot* on pp. 366–367, showing how Whistler Lodging Company introduced new technology in order to improve customer satisfaction and reduce gap 2). Service blueprinting is often used as an implementation tool to address the challenges of designing and specifying intangible service processes. Service organizations must also explore the importance of physical evidence, the variety of roles it plays, and strategies for effectively designing physical evidence and the servicescape to meet customer expectations (see Chapter 5 for a discussion of the servicescape).

Gap 3: The Difference between Management's Specifications of Service and the Actual Service That is Delivered to the Customer

Even when guidelines exist for performing services well and treating customers correctly, high-quality performance is not a certainty. Research on customer experience has identified many of the critical inhibitors to closing gap 3. These include employees who do not clearly understand the roles they are to play in the company, employees who see conflict between customers and company management, the wrong employees, inadequate technology, inappropriate compensation and recognition, and lack of empowerment and teamwork. To deliver better service performance, these human resource issues must be addressed across functions. A second cause of gap 3 is the challenge involved in delivering service through intermediaries such as travel agents or franchisees. It is a huge task for organizations to attain service excellence and consistency in the presence of intermediaries who represent them, interact with their customers, and yet are not under their direct control. Other variables in gap 3 include the customers—who may not understand their roles and responsibilities and may negatively affect each other—and the failure to match supply and demand. Because services are perishable and cannot be inventoried, service companies frequently face situations of over- or under-demand. Marketing strategies for managing supply and demand should be used to reduce gap 3.

Gap 4: The Difference between the Delivery of the Service and External Communications about the Service

Gap 4 is created when promises do not match performance. Broken promises can occur for many reasons: over-promising in advertising or personal selling, inadequate coordination between operations and marketing, and differences in policies and procedures across service outlets. There are also less obvious ways in which external communications influence customers' service quality assessments. Service companies frequently fail to capitalize on opportunities to educate customers in using services appropriately. They also frequently fail to manage customer expectations of what they will receive in service transactions and relationships. Therefore, in addition to improving service delivery, companies must also manage all communications to customers, so that inflated promises do not lead to overly high expectations. Many companies profiled in this book—such as Canadian Mountain Holidays and WestJet— make it a policy to "under-promise and over-deliver." Unfortunately, there are too many examples of companies that do just the opposite. Aeroplan, Air Canada's frequent flyer program, for example, promises free flights for loyal customers. However, the reality is that those free flights are very difficult to book, and there is also a booking fee. Only one attempt in five to book a flight using accumulated mileage is successful.[17] This difference between what is promised and what is delivered can cause customer frustration, perhaps driving the customer to the competition.

Gap 5: The Difference between Customer's Expectations and Perceptions

The central focus of the gaps model is gap 5, the customer gap: the difference between the service a customer expects and the service the customer perceives that he or she receives. Firms need to close this gap in order to satisfy customers and to build long-term relationships with them. To close this all-important customer gap, the four other gaps—the provider gaps—need to be closed.

SNAPSHOT

IMPROVED CALL CENTRE INCREASES SATISFACTION FOR WHISTLER CUSTOMERS

Speedy response is the lifeblood of all call centres. If callers are left too long on the line, they will hang up. If they do, the callers' business may be lost forever. That is why Whistler Lodging Company switched to a new Internet protocol (IP)–based telephone system at its head office in 2002. The company had been struggling along with a leased Centrex system since relocating to Vancouver from Whistler a year before. "We knew from the start the Centrex system would not give us what we wanted," says Drew Stotesbury, executive vice-president of O'Neill Hotels & Resorts Ltd. of Vancouver (parent company of Whistler Lodging). "We did it because we needed a band-aid solution until we could get what we wanted." What they wanted was an IP-based telephone system covering not just the 15-seat call centre, but also the entire head office. By 2005, the IP system, supplied by Delphi Solutions Corp. of Markham, Ontario, will be extended to include the 10 properties and 80 rental homes and condominium apartments that the company operates at Whistler.

The improvement in service to customers has been remarkable, Stotesbury says. During

the six months ending January 31, 2002, the abandoned call rate under the old Centrex system was a worrisome 13.8 percent. By

SNAPSHOT *continued*

March 2002, using Delphi's IP solution, the abandoned call rate plunged to just 3.4 percent. "The latest period also reflects about 10 percent more incoming calls," he adds. During the high season, the centre handles between 300 and 400 calls a day from customers making reservations, changing them, seeking information, or purchasing lift tickets. The annual average, however, is closer to 200 calls per day. The call centre staff are also impressed with the new system. By the time they take a call, they know exactly what to expect. Before the IP solution, when an agent answered a call, he or she did not know whether the person on the other end of the line had just called in or had been waiting for five minutes and getting increasingly aggravated. Nor was there any way of knowing what property the caller was interested in or what kind of service he or she wanted.

Today, however, the system uses simple keyboard prompts to separate callers into nine queues. Callers are asked to indicate which of four different Whistler Lodging companies they are calling and whether the call is to make new reservations, change or inquire about existing reservations, obtain general or specific information, or purchase lift tickets. By the time the agent gets the call, he or she knows which property is involved and what service is required. The agent can answer the call with a cheery "Welcome to Mountain Memories," for example. Supervisors can see how many calls they have waiting and which queue they are in. Priority is given to new reservations. The management features of the new system allow call-centre supervisors to instantly shift agents away from responding calls in the information queue to revenue-generating reservations if the number of phone calls warrants such a move.

One immediate benefit of the new system is that Whistler Lodging no longer pays $1200 per month to lease a phone system. The total cost for installing the new system in the call centre and head office was about $80 000, but that cost is quickly being recaptured through increased efficiencies—and fewer lost calls. Ultimately, the customer is being offered a better service, and this will lead to improved customer satisfaction and a positive effect on the bottom line.

Source: Belford, T. (2003, March 3). Whistler Hotels answer callers faster, smarter. *Financial Post*, p. BE5.

Measuring Service Quality

importance–performance analysis (IPA)

a procedure that shows both the relative importance of various attributes and the performance of the company, product, or destination under study in providing these attributes

The two main research instruments that have been developed over the years to analyze the concepts of quality and consumer satisfaction in the service industry are importance–performance analysis (IPA) and SERVQUAL. **Importance–performance analysis (IPA)** is a procedure that shows both the relative *importance* of various attributes and the *performance* of the company, product, or destination under study in providing these attributes. Its use has important marketing and management implications for decision makers, and one of the major benefits of using IPA is the identification of areas for service quality improvements. Results are displayed graphically on a two-dimensional grid, and through a simple visual analysis of this matrix, policy makers can identify areas where the resources and programs need to be concentrated. Introduced over 20 years ago,[18] IPA is well documented in the literature.

Figure 11.3 on page 368 shows the importance and performance mean scores of ski attributes from a study in Switzerland.[19] The action grid identifies where each of the

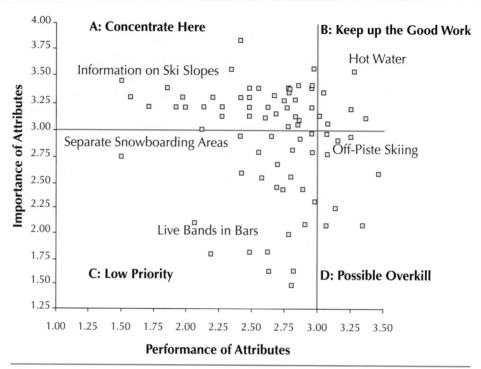

Figure 11.3 Importance–Performance Grid with Attribute Ratings for a Ski Destination

Source: Hudson, S., & Shephard, G. (1998). Measuring service quality at tourist destinations: An application of Importance–Performance Analysis to an Alpine ski resort. *Journal of Travel and Tourism Marketing, 7*(3), 69.

attributes falls in terms of the four quadrants, with examples pinpointed in each quadrant. In this variation, the largest number of attributes (42 percent) was plotted into the "Concentrate Here" area of the action grid. Respondents rated these attributes high in importance but low in performance. These attributes included the majority of services on the ski slopes, comfortable beds, value for money in bars and restaurants, and the prices in the ski shops.

SERVQUAL is an instrument developed by Parasuraman, Zeithaml, and Berry,[20] which is used to measure the difference between consumers' expectations and perceptions of service quality. Exploratory research conducted in 1985 showed that consumers judge service quality by using the same general criteria, regardless of the type of service. Parasuraman et al. capture these criteria using a scale composed of 22 items designed to load on five dimensions reflecting service quality. The dimensions are: assurance, empathy, reliability, responsiveness, and tangibles. Each item is used twice: first, to determine customers' expectations about companies in general, within the service category being investigated; second, to measure perceptions of performance of a particular company, within this same service category. These evaluations are collected using a seven-point Likert scale. According to the authors, the service quality is determined as the difference between customers' expectations and perceptions.

SERVQUAL

an instrument used to measure the difference between consumers' expectations and perceptions of service quality

Other researchers have suggested that the mere fact of asking respondents to mark their perceptions of performance already leads them to compare mentally their perceptions and their expectations. In other words, the estimation of perceptions might already include a "perception minus expectation" mental process. They suggest that performance on its own, or SERVPERF (which stands for "service performance"), is the measure that best explains total quality. Attempts have been made to compare the relative predictive validity of these alternative measures for evaluating quality. In all the studies, the various methods (IPA, SERVQUAL, SERVPERF) were compared to find that measures of performance alone have higher predictive validity than do measures that incorporate expectations or preferences. In other words, the service quality measurements of IPA, SERVQUAL, and SERPERF do not produce statistically different results. The studies also found that the inclusion of importance weights did not improve the predictive validity of the measures. One could therefore argue that with no statistical difference between the tests, any of them can be used to measure satisfaction. Such a finding would enable managers to employ the most straightforward test of satisfaction, so there would be justification in measuring performance only.

However, although the perceptions format offers the most predictive power—a finding that has consistently emerged in the literature—it offers little diagnostic potential and, indeed, may result in inappropriate priorities being established. From a managerial perspective, it would seem important to track trends of the extent to which expectations are met over time as well as trends in performance. The use of difference scores gives managers a better understanding of whether increasing expectations or diminishing performance might be responsible for declining service quality and customer satisfaction. An examination of minimum expectations may also be fruitful. Similarly, disregarding importance may mean losing useful insights. Without considering attribute importance, one has no indication of the relative importance that respondents attach to particular aspects of service performance. In addition, the fact that IPA is easily interpreted by managers could be of critical value for managers who do not use sophisticated software packages.

Service Quality Ratings

Measuring service quality has become an important consideration in many sectors of tourism and hospitality. For example, every year, inspectors all over Canada travel to hotels, motels, inns, lodges, resorts, and bed and breakfasts to rate them for the Canada Select Accommodation Rating Program. It is a voluntary program in which inspectors arrive at the facility unannounced and rate the public areas as well as 10 percent of the rooms. They have a set of hard-and-fast criteria that they use to determine the amenities and services that are available, and they also assess the general quality of the surroundings, such as the furniture, walls, and floors. Overall cleanliness and the state of repair are factors in the rating. Properties are grouped into six categories based on shared characteristics such as general locations, facilities, services, and market appeal (rating criteria are different within each category).

In 2003, the inspections cost $165, with additional charges for larger properties up to a maximum of $550. The inspectors usually sit down and discuss the inspection with the operator before they leave. Most people feel that the rating is fair, and more and more businesses are joining the program. Table 11.1 on page 370 gives the star rating descriptions. Canada Select ratings are available on printed materials and on the Internet, and the

Table 11.1

Canada Select Accommodation Rating Program: Star Rating Descriptions

★	**Modest** accommodations meeting the Canada Select standards of cleanliness, comfort, and safety
★★	**Moderate** accommodations with additional facilities and some amenities
★★★	**Above average** accommodations with a greater range of facilities, guest amenities, and services available
★★★★	**Exceptional** accommodations with an extensive range of facilities, guest amenities, and services.
★★★★★	**Luxurious** properties; among the very best in the country in terms of their outstanding facilities, guest services, and quality provided

Source: Canada Select. (2002). Retrieved February 15, 2002, from http://www.canadaselect.com.

benefits to the consumer include the ability to choose accommodation with confidence, knowing an independent authority has rated the property. In general, Canada Select's national rating standard provides reliable information to the travelling public on what to expect from a roofed accommodation. Canada Select is truly a national program: all 10 provinces and the Yukon participate in the program.

The Behavioural Consequences of Service Quality

During the 1980s, the primary emphasis of both academic and managerial effort focused on determining what service quality meant to customers and on developing strategies to meet customer expectations. Since then, many organizations have instituted measurement and management approaches to improve their service. The service quality agenda has now shifted and reconfigured to include other issues. The issue of highest priority today involves understanding the impact of service quality on profit and other financial outcomes of the organization. Executives of many companies in the 1980s were willing to trust their intuitive sense that better service would lead to improved financial success. They therefore committed resources to improving service prior to having documentation of the financial payoff. Some of these companies, such as Four Seasons and Ritz-Carlton, have been richly rewarded for their efforts. But executives in other companies have been reluctant to invest in service improvements without solid evidence of their financial soundness. However, research on the relationship between service quality and profits has begun to accumulate. Findings from these studies show that companies offering superior service achieve higher-than-normal market share growth;[21] that the mechanisms by which service quality influences profits include increased market share and premium prices;[22] and that businesses in the top quintile of relative service quality realize on average an 8 percent higher price than their competitors.[23]

Another fruitful area of research is that which examines the relationship between service quality and behavioural intentions. Zeithaml, Berry, and Parasuraman have developed a conceptual model that depicts the behavioural consequences of service quality as intervening variables between service quality and the financial gains or losses from retention or defection (see Figure 11.4). The left portion of the model is at the level of the individual customer and proposes that service quality and behavioural intentions are related and, therefore, that service quality is a determinant of whether a customer ultimately remains with or defects from a company.

By integrating research findings and anecdotal evidence, a list of specific indicators of customers' favourable behavioural intentions can be compiled. These include saying positive things about the company to others, recommending the company or service to others, paying a price premium to the company, and remaining loyal to the company. Loyalty may be manifested in a variety of ways—for example, by expressing a preference for a company over others, by continuing to purchase from it, or by increasing business with it in the future. Customers perceiving service performance to be inferior are likely to exhibit behaviours signalling that they are poised to leave the company or spend less money with the company. These behaviours include complaining, which is viewed by many researchers as a variety of negative responses that stem from dissatisfaction and predict or accompany defection.

After testing this model, the authors found strong empirical support for the intuitive notion that improving service quality can increase favourable behavioural intentions and decrease unfavourable intentions. The findings demonstrate the importance of strategies that can steer behavioural intentions in the right directions, including (1) striving to meet

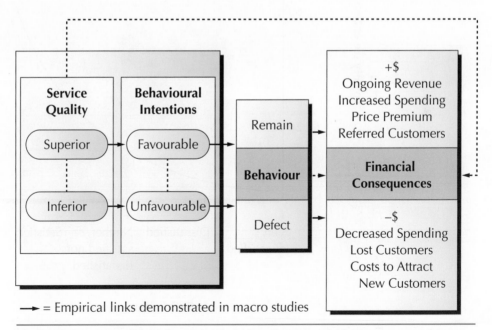

Figure 11.4 A Model of the Behavioural and Financial Consequences of Service Quality

Source: Zeithaml, V. A., Berry, L. L., & Parasuraman, A. (1996). The behavioral consequences of service quality. *Journal of Marketing, 60*, 31–46.

customers' "desired-service" levels (rather than merely performing at their "adequate-service" levels), (2) emphasizing the prevention of service problems, and (3) effectively resolving problems that do occur. However, multiple findings suggest that companies wanting to improve service, especially beyond the desired-service level, should do so in a cost-effective manner.

LOYALTY AND RELATIONSHIP MARKETING

The Link between Satisfaction and Loyalty

customer loyalty

a measure of how likely customers are to return to an organization, and of their willingness to build relationships with the organization

As Figure 11.1 shows (see p. 355), customer satisfaction is a requisite for loyalty. Customer satisfaction is a measure of how well a customer's expectations are met. **Customer loyalty**, on the other hand, is a measure of how likely customers are to return to an organization, and of their willingness to build relationships with the organization. Customer expectations must be met or exceeded to build loyalty. As Figure 11.5 indicates,

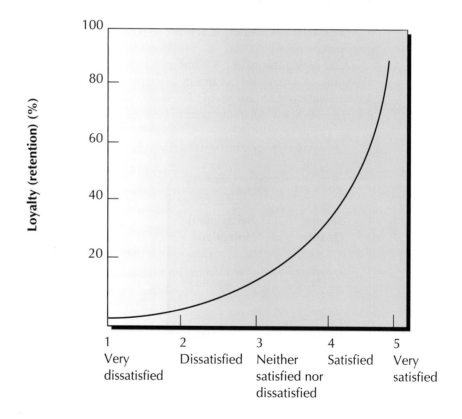

Satisfaction measure

Figure 11.5   Relationships between Customer Satisfaction and Loyalty in Competitive Industries

Source: Heskett, J. L., Sasser, W. E., Jr., & Schlesinger, L. A. (1997). The service profit chain: How leading companies link profit and growth to loyalty, satisfaction, and value. New York: Free Press, 83.

there is an important relationship between customer satisfaction and loyalty. The relationship is particularly strong when customers are very satisfied. Thus, businesses that simply aim to satisfy customers may not be doing enough to engender loyalty. They must instead aim to more than satisfy—or even delight—their customers.

However, it is important to understand that there are several reasons why satisfied customers may not become loyal customers in the tourism industry. First, many travellers prefer to visit different places and may not return to the same destination or hotel even if they are extremely satisfied. Second, some travellers are very price-sensitive and shop for the best deal they can get regardless of satisfaction measures. Finally, customers expect to be satisfied with their purchase, so satisfaction ratings are often inflated. This underscores the need to have extremely satisfied customers in order to encourage loyalty.

Loyal customers are therefore more valuable than satisfied customers. A satisfied customer who does not return and does not spread positive word of mouth has no value to the company. On the other hand, a loyal customer who returns and spreads positive word of mouth has a very high value, and it is therefore important that companies identify those patrons who are likely to become loyal customers.

Relationship Marketing

relationship marketing
marketing that attracts customers, retains them, and enhances their satisfaction

Once a company has identified potential loyal customers, the next stage is to create a relationship with these customers that will eventually lead to customer loyalty. This is called **relationship marketing**, a form of marketing that attracts customers, retains them, and enhances their satisfaction.[24] In the past, tourism and hospitality marketers have tended to put more emphasis on attracting new customers. More recently, the idea of nurturing the individual relationships with current and past customers has received greater attention. Most marketers now accept that it is less expensive to attract repeat customers than to create new ones, and this is the basic concept behind relationship marketing. The key outcome of all relationship marketing efforts is to make individual customers feel unique and to make them believe that the organization has singled them out for special attention.

Retention Strategies

According to Morrison, this individualization or customization can be achieved by doing the following:[25]

1. *Managing service encounters.* This means training staff to treat customers as individuals—by using their names or knowing their preferences and interests, for example.
2. *Providing customer incentives.* Customer incentives or inducements can be given to encourage repeat use of the business. Pages 375 and 376 highlight some loyalty programs in the hospitality sector in Canada.
3. *Providing special service options.* Similar to offering customer incentives, this involves giving special extras to repeat or club customers, such as the high-speed Internet offered by Fairmont to its guests enrolled in the Fairmont President's Club (FPC).
4. *Developing pricing strategies to encourage long-term use.* This involves offering special prices to repeat customers, such as annual memberships to theme parks or season ski passes.

5. *Maintaining a customer database.* Keeping and using an up-to-date database on individual customers is an important part of relationship marketing. Ritz-Carlton, for example, even keeps details on the pillow preferences of their guests.
6. *Communicating with customers through direct or specialized media.* Relationships can be enhanced by using non–mass media approaches to communicate directly with individual customers. Direct e-mail marketing has been particularly useful for organizations in recent years in helping to develop relationships with individual customers.

Zeithaml and Bitner build on this group of strategies by suggesting that there are four different levels of retention strategies that encourage relationship marketing: financial bonds, social bonds, customization bonds, and structural bonds.[26] These are illustrated in Figure 11.6.

At level 1, the customer is tied to the organization primarily through financial incentives—often in the form of lower prices for greater volume purchases or lower prices for customers who have been with the company for a long time (e.g., frequent flyer programs). In other cases, firms aim to retain customers by simply offering loyal customers the assurance of stable prices, or at least smaller price increases than those paid by new customers. Other types of retention strategies that depend primarily on financial rewards are focused on bundling and cross-selling of services. The Delta loyalty scheme profiled

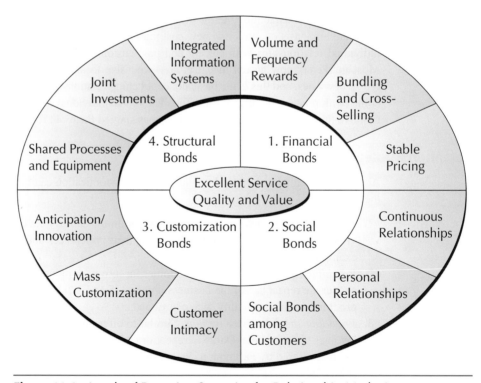

Figure 11.6 Levels of Retention Strategies for Relationship Marketing

Source: Zeithaml, V. A., & Bitner, M. J. (2000). *Services marketing: Integrating customer focus across the firm.* New York: McGraw-Hill, 153.

on page 275 is an example of a reward scheme linked to other services, which gives additional benefits to customers.

Level 2 strategies bind customers to the business through more than just financial incentives. Marketers using this retention strategy build long-term relationships through social and interpersonal, as well as financial, bonds. Services are customized to fit individual needs, and marketers find ways of staying in touch with their customers, thereby developing social bonds with them. Social, interpersonal bonds are common among professional service providers and their clients, as well as among personal care providers and clients. Sometimes relationships are formed with the organization due to the social relationships that develop among customers rather than between customers and the service provider. For example, people who vacation at the same place during the same weeks every year build bonds with others who vacation there at the same time.

Level 3 strategies involve more than social ties and financial incentives, and two commonly used terms fit within the customization bonds approach: mass customization and customer intimacy. Both of these strategies suggest that customer loyalty can be encouraged through intimate knowledge of individual customers and through the development of one-to-one solutions that fit the individual customer's needs. The Ritz-Carlton, for example, maintains a computerized guest history profile of thousands of individual repeat guests. When guests visit any Ritz-Carlton, members of staff already know about their likes and dislikes. Casinos also maintain sophisticated databases of guest preferences, as well as their wagering habits.

Level 4 strategies are the most difficult to imitate and involve structural as well as financial, social, and customization bonds between the customer and the firm. Often structural bonds are created by providing the client with customized services that are technology-based and that serve to make the customer more productive. An example would be a reservations system installed in a travel agency by a tour operator. The agent is therefore structurally bound to that operator in its operations.

Loyalty Schemes

An example of an innovative loyalty scheme comes from the Delta Lodge at Kananaskis, in Alberta. The guest loyalty program, "Scale Our Mountains," was launched in April 2002, and aimed to celebrate those guests who frequent the Delta Lodge with unique "extras" to enhance their stay. The experience began for those taking in their third excursion to the resort. Guests were welcomed to their room with added touches, including handmade goodies created by the Delta Lodge's Executive Chef, along with gifts for children. Guests' fourth, sixth, and ninth stays were also recognized, with privileges the likes of complimentary suite upgrades and additional nights' stays. Program members were also able to take more than memories home with them, as additional stays promised a handcrafted Aboriginal dreamcatcher or a Delta Lodge at Kananaskis signature fleece vest as a keepsake. Outdoor enthusiasts also reaped the rewards as the loyalty program offered its members the opportunity to indulge in outdoor adventure year-round. Based on their number of stays, members received complimentary lift tickets for the slopes at Nakiska or free access to a nearby golf course. Loyalty members are also able to amass even more benefits from the program by simply recommending the Delta Lodge to family, friends, and business colleagues. Two or more referrals resulting in bookings afford members discounts for future stays.

Fairmont Hotels & Resorts also have a popular guest loyalty program: Fairmont President's Club (FPC). Guests enrolled in FPC generally enjoy a range of amenities and services that include room-upgrade certificates and complimentary health club access. In spring 2002, Fairmont Hotels & Resorts offered complimentary high-speed Internet access to gold- and platinum-tier members of FPC. In addition, Fairmont Gold, the newly branded "club floor" offered complimentary high-speed Internet access. Other features added for gold and platinum FPC members at about the same time were 10 percent off treatments and complimentary facility access to Willow Stream—The Spas at Fairmont, the company's branded spa offering.

Benefits of Relationship Marketing

Both parties in the customer–company relationship can benefit from customer retention. It is not only in the best interest of the organization to build and maintain a loyal customer base; customers themselves also benefit from long-term associations. Table 11.2 summarizes the various benefits of relationship marketing for both the company and the customer. Assuming they have a choice, customers will remain loyal to a company when they receive greater value relative to what they expect from competing organizations. Value represents a trade-off for the consumer between what they give and what they get. Consumers are more likely to stay in a relationship when the "gets" (quality, satisfaction, specific benefits) exceed the "gives" (monetary and non-monetary costs). When companies can consistently deliver what the customer considers to be value, the customer clearly benefits and has an incentive to stay in the relationship.

The benefits to an organization of maintaining and developing a loyal customer base are numerous, but they are linked directly to the bottom line. Among service organizations, reducing customer defections by just 5 percent can boost profits by 25 to 85 percent.[27] Retained customers are much more profitable than new ones because they purchase more and they purchase more frequently, often at a price premium, while at the same time requiring lower operating costs. They also make referrals that cost the business nothing. And, of course, their acquisition cost is nothing, which is significant because it costs a company five to seven times more to prospect for new customers than it does to maintain the current ones.[28]

Table 11.2

Benefits of Relationship Marketing to the Company and the Customer

BENEFITS TO THE COMPANY	BENEFITS TO THE CUSTOMER
Increased purchases	Social benefits
Lower costs	Confidence and trust
Employee retention	Special treatment
Increased profits	Reduced risk
Less customer defection	Increased value
Free advertising through word of mouth	Customized services

lifetime value of a
customer

a calculation that con-
siders customers from
the point of view of
their potential lifetime
revenue and prof-
itability contributions
to a company

To understand the financial value of building long-term relationships with customers, companies sometimes calculate lifetime values. The lifetime value of a customer is a calculation that considers customers from the point of view of their potential lifetime revenue and profitability contributions to a company. This value is influenced by the length of an average lifetime, the average revenues generated in that time period, sales of additional products and services over time, and referrals generated by the customer. For example, Stew Leonard, the very successful Connecticut grocer, has calculated the lifetime value of each of his store patrons as US$50 000.[29]

Focusing on the "Right Customers"

The idea of targeting the "right customers" for relationship marketing has emerged in the literature and in practice over the last few decades. Reichheld, for example, stresses that companies aspiring to relationship marketing should make formal efforts to identify those customers who are most likely to remain loyal, and should develop their overall strategy around delivering superior value to these customers.[30] Targeting profitable customers for relationship marketing involves studying and analyzing loyalty- and defection-prone customers, searching for distinguishing patterns in why they stay or leave, what creates value for them, and who they are.

Innovative service companies today are beginning to recognize that not all customers are worth attracting and keeping. Many customers are too costly to do business with and have little potential to become profitable, even in the long term. To build and improve upon traditional segmentation, companies are now trying to identify segments that differ in current and/or future profitability to the organization. After identifying profitability bands, the company offers services and service levels in line with the identified segments. Virtually all companies are aware at some level that their customers differ in profitability—in particular that a minority of their customers account for the highest proportion of sales or profits. This has often been called the 80/20 rule: 20 percent of customers produce 80 percent of sales or profits. This 80/20 customer pyramid is shown in Figure 11.7.

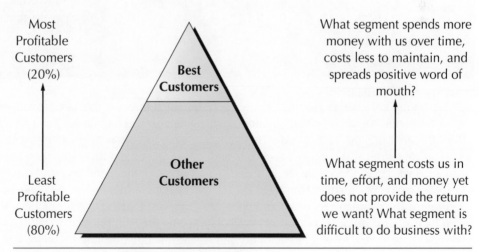

Figure 11.7   The 80/20 Customer Pyramid

Source: Zeithhaml, V. A., & Bitnen, M. J. (2000). *Services marketing: Integrating customer focus across the firm.* New York: McGraw-Hill, 470.

A few years ago, Thomas Cook Travel divided its customers into A's (those who bring in more than US$750 or more in annual revenues), B's (those who bring in US$250–$749), and C's (those who bring in less than US$250). The company found that 80 percent of its customers were C's. By focusing in on the more profitable customers (A's and B's), and by charging C's for their time-consuming demands (a $25 deposit was taken for researching any trip), the company increased its profits considerably. The growth of the company's A- and B-level clients also increased by 20 percent.[31]

However, a customer's unprofitability may not be the only reason a company chooses to refuse or terminate a relationship with him or her. For various reasons, the belief that "the customer is always right" does not always apply in service industries. It would not be beneficial to either the company or the customer for a company to establish a relationship with a customer whose needs the company cannot meet. Every server in the restaurant business has met the "customer from hell," a paying guest whose behaviour is beyond rude and who seems determined to ruin the evening for everyone concerned. These disruptive customers have even been segmented in some research articles, into classifications like "Egocentric Edgars," "Freeloading Fredas," and "Dictatorial Dicks."[32, 33] Such customers are often impossible to satisfy, and may place too much stress on employees and the organization.

Similarly, it would not be wise to forge relationships simultaneously with incompatible market segments. In many tourism businesses, customers experience the service together and can influence each other's perceptions about the value received. For example, a conference hotel may find that mixing executives in town for a serious training program with students in town for a sporting event may not be wise. If the student group is a key long-term customer, the hotel may choose to pass up the executive group in the interest of retaining the students' business.

PROFILE

MOUNTAIN RIVER OUTFITTERS

Operating in Canada's Northwest Territories, Mountain River Outfitters (MRO) is an adventure tour operator providing a complete logistical service to both hikers and canoeists who wish to explore the wild and beautiful region of Canada's Northwest Territories. The company is owned and operated by five local residents of Norman Wells, who all share a great love of the outdoors and the Sahtu Region. Their goal in being in business is to make the great unspoiled wilderness, which they say they are "fortunate enough to be able to call home," just a little more accessible to visitors from other places.

Mountain River Outfitters operates for only two months of the year and caters to a very specific and numerically stable niche. Over the last four years, the numbers of people visiting the Sahtu Region to take part in canoeing or hiking adventure vacations has not increased. However, between 1999 and 2002, the company has experienced phenomenal

PROFILE *continued*

growth (relatively speaking), with sales increasing from $6000 in 1999 to $42 000 in 2002. This growth has resulted from a complete rethinking of the business and from the development of a business strategy based primarily on providing excellent service quality and customer satisfaction.

MRO's core business prior to 2000 was the provision of a water taxi service. After paddling one of the white-water rivers that cascade down from the Mackenzie Mountains, canoe groups inevitably end up on the Mackenzie River, many miles from Norman Wells and often downstream of that community. Rather than paddle the Mackenzie River to Norman Wells, from where they would fly home, groups often preferred to be picked up by motor boat. Hikers attempting, or having completed, a hike on the CANOL Trail would use the water taxi to cross the Mackenzie River from Norman Wells to the trail head (a distance of four kilometres). Water taxi services were provided on a price-per-head basis, and competitive advantage was derived entirely from the low price (compared to the alternative of chartering an aircraft).

The quality of service was poor, primarily because the equipment used was inadequate, but also because there was little empathy toward the needs of the customer: customers were told when they could be picked up, the service being considered as a favour for which the customer should be thankful. Compounding the problems affecting service quality, it was usual for MRO to make huge promises and to lead customers to believe that the company could provide far more than was possible or practicable. For example, arrangements would be made to rent canoes to customers, even though MRO did not actually own any!

The journey, by water taxi on the river, was often unpleasant (because of bad weather) but was endured by customers who could not afford alternative means of travelling back to Norman Wells and who did not fully understand beforehand what they were letting themselves in for. The reputation of MRO in the small circle of people "in the know" was infamous. However, the company was recognized as a reliable operation that never failed to pick up people as arranged. MRO had realized that customers might have needs other than the water taxi and had provided some additional outfitting services on an ad hoc and inconsistent basis. The provision of these services was, however, very much a sideline and did not significantly add to business revenues.

In 2000, Mountain River Outfitters changed its approach to business by putting the needs of the customer first and by investing in new equipment. A complete outfitting service was developed, through which a group of canoeists or hikers would be looked after from the time they arrived in Norman Wells prior to their departure for the wilderness to the time they left Norman Wells to begin their journey home. This new approach represented a significant increase in the scope of services the company offered, and required a relationship to be built between the customer and the business. This relationship is initiated when a prospective customer first contacts the company (usually by e-mail after perusing the Web site). By establishing a dialogue with customers over the months before they arrive, MRO develops personalized offerings to fit their individual needs, allowing customer expectations to be appropriately managed. When customers eventually arrive in Norman Wells, they feel as if they know their outfitter, and they are met at the airport as friends. They also know exactly what they should and should not expect from their outfitter. During the time they spend in Norman Wells, they are

PROFILE *continued*

extended every courtesy—including the use of a company vehicle. This same courtesy is provided to customers after their return to Norman Wells, up to the point when they fly home.

An investment in new equipment (especially in a new boat) has improved the quality of the water taxi experience. The water taxi journeys are often several hours long, and a courtesy lunch and refreshments are now offered as standard. The customer is no longer told when they can be picked up—although it is sometimes necessary to tell a customer when he or she cannot be picked up (only one trip can be made each day, and clashes between customers inevitably occur during the planning stages). Investment in canoes and other outdoor equipment has increased the revenue potential of the business. Canoe rentals now represent 50 percent of revenues, and it is through rental revenue that the company can afford to provide many of the complimentary and more ephemeral services that cannot be directly priced. Customers are billed only for water taxi service and canoe rental (plus any extras they have requested prior to their arrival, such as supplies or food). All other aspects of the full service provided are provided without charge. This pricing strategy means that customers are not "nickeled and dimed" for every last thing, and it means that they always feel that they are getting far more than they are paying for. Customer expectations are therefore exceeded.

Relationship building and a new reputation for responsiveness and reliability have also been crucial in encouraging the repeat patronage of certain commercial canoe-guiding companies. These companies provide Mountain River Outfitters with a core source of revenue from year to year, without which investment in new equipment would have been impossible.

Source: N. Dale, manager, Mountain River Outfitters, personal communication, May 5, 2003.

SERVICE RECOVERY

service recovery

the process by which a company attempts to rectify a service delivery failure

Service delivery failure is likely to occur at some point in time for organizations in the service industry. Though it is unlikely that businesses can eliminate all service failures, they can learn to effectively respond to failures once they do occur. This response is often referred to as **service recovery**, defined as the process by which a company attempts to rectify a service delivery failure. An effective recovery will retain customer loyalty regardless of the type of failure. In one study, customer retention exceeded 70 percent for those customers who perceived effective recovery efforts.[34] Another study reported that customers who experienced a service failure told nine or ten individuals about their poor service experience, whereas satisfied customers told only four or five individuals about their satisfactory experience.[35] Therefore, an effective recovery process may lead to positive word of mouth, or at least diminish the negative word of mouth typically associated with poor recovery efforts. Figure 11.8 shows the various ways that a customer can respond following a service failure.

Such advantages of effective service recovery efforts display the importance of these efforts in satisfying current customers and reducing defections. The average business does not hear from 95 percent of dissatisfied customers, and every complaining customer

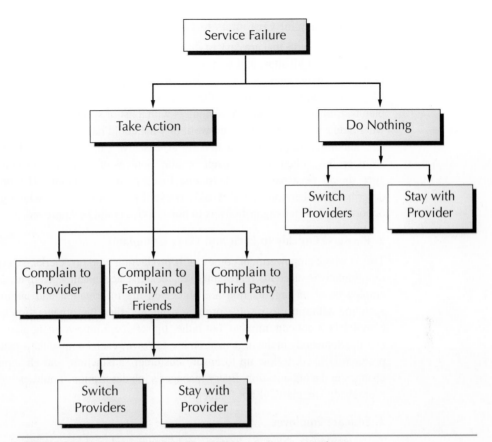

Figure 11.8 Customer Response Following Service Failure

Source: Zeithaml, V. A., & Bitner, M. J. (2000). *Services marketing: Integrating customer focus across the firm.* New York: McGraw-Hill, 168.

represents 26 dissatisfied but non-complaining customers. As was mentioned above, reducing customer defections can boost profits. In addition, retained customers are much more profitable than new ones because they purchase more and they purchase more frequently, while at the same time requiring lower operating costs. It is therefore critical that companies attempt to reduce customer defections, and Harari has suggested that to do this, companies must take a strategic look at customer complaints.

The events that actually wind up irritating and frustrating customers are the end points of a process that needs to be fixed immediately. Products that don't work, outdated features, incorrect invoices, poor phone etiquette, user-unfriendly software, slow turnaround time—these are symptoms of the problem. The real problem lies somewhere in the organization's systems, policies, culture, and habits that created the bad customer experience (faulty product, invoice, etc.). These are what need to be addressed. Until they are repaired, they are bleeding the company in terms of internal costs (rework, overtime, duplication of effort, etc.) and lost revenues. The point is not merely to make things right for the complaining customer, but to simultaneously tackle the underlying problem that created the negative experience in the first place. Harari offers eight guidelines for tracking and handling complaints.[36]

1. Make It Easy for Customers to Complain

Create survey cards that are easy to fill out and that have return postage. Include these with all products, at all sites, and with invoices or other correspondence. Position suggestion boxes in as many sites as possible. Establish electronic accessibility to central terminals. Make sure that home phone numbers are on all business cards. Proactively solicit complaints. Call customers and ex-customers with a list of specific questions. Carefully probe what didn't work, what didn't go well, or what could have been done better. Every manager should be responsible for making at least five calls per month. Hold regular small focus groups; solicit specific, even "minor," sources of hassle and irritation. Every manager should be a part of at least one focus group per month. The opening vignette describes the Sheraton Suites' weekly cocktail party at the hotel, which gives guests the opportunity to offer suggestions as to how service could be improved.

2. Respond Quickly to Each and Every Complaint

This is where empowerment comes in. If production workers, clerks, salespeople, service representatives, account representatives, dealers, accountants, engineers, and all other employees of an organization are not given the information and authority (including spending authority) to resolve problems quickly, then the organization's concern about complaints is not commitment, but rather lip service. Empowerment also implies responsibility. Somebody in the organization has to "own" each complainer—that is, see that the problem is fixed, follow up to ensure customer satisfaction, and champion appropriate changes in the organization. Every manager's job description should include being such a "somebody" regularly, if not frequently.

3. Educate Employees

Teach employees about the strategic and financial value of complaints, about the need for urgency in responding, and perhaps most important, teach them that everyone owns the problem—not just the "customer service" people. This can be done in orientation, in management-development sessions, in memos and briefings, and in meetings and speeches.

4. Approach Complaints as Operational Problems and Strategic Opportunities

Approaching complaints as opportunities means putting complaints in the category of research and information, not of personal attacks. It means replacing blame analysis with problem analysis. It means viewing complaints in the Renaissance tradition, in which the critic was an ally who helped the object of the criticism to better focus on reality.

5. Make Complaints and Complainers Visible

Post quantitative complaint data publicly (for employees and for customers). Post raw, unedited letters and phone call transcripts on bulletin boards. Reprint them in newsletters. Read and discuss them in meetings. Publicize responses to the complaints. Identify and applaud the employees who did the responding. Invite complainers to address people in the organization and to work with them on improvements. Pay them if necessary. Include a "customer panel" in every management retreat.

6. Adjust Quality Measures, Performance Reviews, and Compensation Accordingly

What gets measured and rewarded gets done. Quality measures should always incorporate pervasive customer complaints. Key questions for managers' performance evaluation and pay might include the following: How many complaints have you solicited? How many "firefighting" teams have you been on? How have you used the input of complainers to improve this organization? Rewarding managers for discovering and acting on complaints should be encouraged. Winners of the Nova Scotia Pineapple Awards for service excellence, for example, are often employees whose service recovery goes above and beyond what is expected to enrich a visitor's stay in Nova Scotia.

7. Reward Complainers

Complainers can help a business prosper, and their advice is often priceless. Visible displays of gratitude not only make good common sense but also send a signal to complainers and to the organization. Consider thank-you notes and phone calls, small cash rewards, plaques and certificates, gifts, "consultant of the month" awards, feature stories in company newsletters, and periodic celebrations with complainers as guests of honour.

8. Stop Calling Them "Complainers"!

Or "difficult customers" or "jerks." They are critics, allies, consultants, or guests of honour. Call them anything as long as it reflects their contribution to the success of the organization.

CHAPTER SUMMARY

Internal marketing can be defined as marketing aimed internally at a company's own employees. The main objective of internal marketing in the service industry is to enable employees to deliver satisfying products to guests; it is a process that involves four steps: the establishment of a service culture, the development of a marketing approach to human resource management, the dissemination of marketing information to employees, and the implementation of a reward and recognition system. A solid internal marketing program will lead to good service quality, defined as the customer's perception of the service component of a product. Such perceptions are said to be based on five dimensions: reliability, assurance, empathy, responsiveness, and tangibles.

An outgrowth of service quality is customer satisfaction. The issue of understanding needs and expectations is an important part of the quest to achieve customer satisfaction. The "gaps model" of service quality provides a method of graphically illustrating these needs and expectations, and this conceptual model enables a structured thought process for evaluating and "designing in" customer satisfaction. The two main research instruments that have been developed over the years to analyze the concepts of service quality and consumer satisfaction in the service industry are importance–performance analysis (IPA) and SERVQUAL.

Although many organizations now measure service quality and have instigated management approaches to improve their service, the service-quality agenda has now shifted and reconfigured to include other issues. The issue of highest priority today involves understanding the impact of service quality on profit and other financial outcomes of the organization. This has led in turn to a focus on customer loyalty and relationship marketing, which involves attracting customers, retaining them, and enhancing their satisfaction. It has been suggested that there are four different retention strategies that encourage relationship marketing: financial bonds, social bonds, customization bonds, and structural bonds.

Finally, service failure is apt to occur at some point in time for businesses in the service industry. Though it is unlikely that companies can eliminate all service failures, they can learn to effectively respond to failures once they do occur. This response is often referred to as service recovery, defined as the process by which a firm attempts to rectify a service delivery failure. Harari offers eight guidelines for tracking and handling complaints: make it easy for customers to complain; respond quickly to each and every complaint; educate employees; approach complaints as operational problems and strategic opportunities; make complaints and complainers visible; adjust quality measures, performance reviews, and compensation accordingly; reward complainers; and stop calling them complainers.

KEY TERMS

customer loyalty, p. 372
customer satisfaction, p. 362
empowerment, p. 356
internal marketing, p. 354

importance–performance
   analysis (IPA), p. 367
lifetime value of a customer,
   p. 377
relationship marketing, p. 373

service culture, p. 356
service recovery, p. 380
service quality, p. 362
SERVQUAL, p. 368

DISCUSSION QUESTIONS AND EXERCISES

1. Apart from those companies discussed in the chapter, name a tourism or hospitality organization that has an obvious service culture. What is the evidence of this culture?

2. If you were the manager of a hotel and wanted to apply the gaps model to improve service, which gap would you start with? Why? In what order would you proceed to close the other gaps?

3. Think about a service organization that retains you as a loyal customer. Why are you loyal to this provider? What would it take for you to switch?

4. With regard to the same organization, what are the benefits to the firm of keeping you as a customer? Calculate your "lifetime value" to the organization.

5. Why is it important for a tourism organization to have a strong service recovery strategy?

6. Think of a time when you received poor service from a tourism or hospitality company. Was any recovery effort made? What should or could have been done differently? What was your response (refer to Figure 11.8)?

CASE STUDY

WESTJET AIRLINES

WestJet Airlines is a company that has, so far, beaten the odds to become a favourite of both travel agents and consumers in Canada. It is, after all, the airline that boards passengers by sock colour or zodiac sign; concocts promotions that enable passengers with names like "Love" and "Heart" to fly free on Valentine's Day; and has seen gate agents break out flutes to entertain stranded passengers during an ice storm. And compared to rigid, often humourless Air Canada, WestJet earns raves from the travel trade. "They'll do almost anything for you," one Ontario agent gushed to *Canadian Travel Press*.

Bill Lamberton, vice-president of marketing and sales for WestJet, says the formula is simple: "We foster a caring culture." While company employees earn industry averages (not overblown union scales that help hamper other airlines), staffers also earned an average $11 500 bonus in 2000 and take part in profit sharing and share purchase plans. This evokes "pride and passion" in every employee in the company, says Lamberton. "When someone picks up the phone, they're a shareholder. The person at the gate is a shareholder." Another key ingredient of WestJet's success is its underlying philosophy to emulate and "Canadianize" the model of successful U.S. discount carrier, Southwest Airlines. Moreover, besides looking to fill a niche as a discount carrier and "price leader," WestJet has no overriding strategy to compete head to head with behemoth Air Canada, something that neither Canadian Airlines nor Canada 3000 could accomplish. "We had to be different," says Lamberton. To that end, WestJet does not seek to encourage Air Canada clientele to "change stripes." Instead, it focuses on Canadians who aren't flying at all. "Our goal is to stimulate travel, to get people out of buses and cars. Market stimulation, that's what WestJet is all about!" says Lamberton. To date, the airline has also generally chosen to fly routes that don't directly compete with Air Canada; for example, five of the six routes the carrier flies in Ontario are unduplicated. And primary hubs are Winnipeg and Hamilton, Ontario, again somewhat out of Air Canada's way, prompting Lamberton to comment, "We offer alternatives."

WestJet knows that its no-frills image is not everyone's cup of tea. The key is for agents and consumers to know what they're getting into. That means, for example, reminding passengers to eat before they board the plane. It also means following the philosophy, "under-promise, over-deliver." "We don't want to be all things to all people; but to some people we are the right option," says Lamberton. And after more than half a decade, that strategy has been wildly successful. The company's revenue has risen to $478.4 million in 2001, from $37.3 million in its inaugural year, 1996. And despite the events of September 11, 2001, profits that year were $37.2 million, compared to Air Canada's $1.5 billion loss. In 2002, WestJet served 21 cities in Canada, with plans to expand, primarily in Central and Atlantic Canada. In fact, by 2008, as few as 36 and as many as 58 WestJet planes are expected to be flying the Canadian skies, with all of the original fleet retired and replaced by then as well.

Clive Beddoe, president and CEO of WestJet, was one of Canada's Entrepreneurs of the Year in 2000 because of his willingness to take risks. He was already a wealthy and successful businessperson (in plastics), but was willing to risk everything to move into an industry in which the failure rate is extremely high. WestJet's entry into the marketplace in early 1996 was a watershed in the Canadian airline industry, as it was the first true low-cost, low-fare, short-haul scheduled carrier. What has enabled this airline to make money for its owners in each year of its existence while many others fight to simply survive? Some suggest it is the fact that WestJet operates an airline in a nontraditional manner and achieves nontraditional results.

WestJet has been praised by passengers for its service and light-hearted humour, which starts from the first booking call—if you're put on hold, you will hear a message full of corny jokes, as well as helpful information. In the airport, passengers may be boarded by the colour of their hair or shoes. On board, flight attendants spice up safety instructions with jokes, and the order in which passengers leave the plane is sometimes based on how quickly their row can relay a roll of toilet paper. At other times the pilot may sing, or attendants will offer prizes for the passenger with the most lipstick in her purse or the one with the biggest hole in his socks. Invariably, a WestJet passenger leaves the aircraft with a smile. As WestJet spokesperson Siobhan Vinish says, "We take our job seriously, but not ourselves."

But Beddoe—University of Calgary's Distinguished Business Leader for 2003—has also designed a shrewd corporate marketing and business plan, with the goal of winning customer loyalty in the hypercompetitive airline business. "The degree of enthusiasm for us is probably greater than I expected, but not much," says Beddoe. WestJet's approach is two-pronged. On one hand is a balanced pricing mechanism that aims to maximize revenue while keeping fares low. On the other is a sharp eye—in fact, 2400 sets of sharp eyes belonging to employees—watching costs. The airline has five different fare classes, or buckets, plus a seat-sale class to stimulate underperforming or new routes. Rather than fight for market share with larger carriers, WestJet's strategy is to use low process and unrestricted tickets to lure people who would otherwise have driven or stayed at home. Beddoe says the essential element in keeping costs low is the work force. "Traditionally in the industry, employees said 'OK, you made money, where's my cut?' The only thing I could think of was to align the interests of the employees and the company." One result is a generous profit sharing plan that enables employees to earn the equivalent of 30 percent of their annual salary.

But the airline industry is extremely vulnerable to changes in the environment. In 2001, as a result of September 11, air traffic fell off as much as 50 percent. International air carriers like Swissair, Sabena of Belgium, and Canada 3000 crumbled. Airlines across North America called for government bailouts and compensation packages as 100 000 people lost jobs in the industry. The domestic airline industry in Canada went through a consolidation process with only two players—WestJet and Air Canada—left standing. Despite the drop in passenger numbers and fares around the world after September 11, WestJet managed to continue growing by adding new destinations and airlines to its fleet, and was well positioned to fill the competitive void left by the grounding of Canada 3000. "We just continued to do what we'd set out to do from the beginning of the year. We had a plan for the year and we sustained it" said Beddoe. "We felt confident that travel would come back. We saw what happened after the Gulf War in the early 1990s. It was short-lived, but there was a catastrophic reaction within the industry when people stopped travelling."

Beddoe says it was WestJet's culture that brought the airline through tough times after September 11. "We were the first airline in North America to be fully operational, with every one of our scheduled flights flying," he said. "On the 12th of September we were given the rules by which we were going to operate and our people worked through the night to figure how we were going to apply those rules and how to disseminate those operating procedures and standards out to all of our bases. By four o'clock in the morning we were able to be up and operational and ready to go." The display of excellence in leadership, corporate performance, innovation, focus on customer relationships, and human resource practices was truly evident around this single catastrophic event. "It was probably the most extreme example of how well this culture of teamwork can work and how it can be applied to create extraordinary results," says Beddoe.

However, Beddoe is aware that additional terrorist attacks, the fear of such attacks, or increased hostilities could further impact the airline industry and WestJet, and could cause a decrease in travel and an increase in costs to airlines and airline travellers. In the aftermath of the terrorist attacks, the availability of insurance for airlines has decreased and the costs of such insurance have increased. In the event that the Canadian government does not renew its indemnity regarding war and terrorism insurance, it is possible that such insurance will not be available to the Canadian airline industry, including WestJet.

Industry watchers also argue that an economic downturn could hurt a carrier dependent on leisure travellers, and that WestJet's expansive growth will make it difficult for the company to keep its distinctive culture alive. But Beddoe says WestJet is prudent as well as ambitious. It has protected itself against rising fuel prices with hedging contracts, and he noted that British Columbia has been one of WestJet's fastest growing markets, even though the province has been in a recession. The carrier will also continue to rely on travel agents, who currently account for 38 percent of bookings, although its "distribution channel of choice will always be the Internet." To that end, the airline pays 9 percent commission to agents for Internet bookings, compared to 7 percent for bookings that come through computer reservations systems such as Sabre. Meanwhile, WestJet also sees its corporate clientele growing. Currently, 60 percent of passengers are considered VFR ("visiting friends or relatives"), 35 percent business, and only 5 percent as "true vacation" (not visiting friends or relatives).

Can WestJet's corporate culture be sustained? Beddoe argues that Southwest Airlines, on which WestJet has been based, has kept its culture alive 25 years even as its work force swelled to 30 000. Having said this, Beddoe realizes that protecting the culture is essential. "It's focus number one. Our risk, in my view, is internal, not external. And that's why we put so much emphasis on it." However, Beddoe is cautious about becoming too arrogant and conceited. "It's not me who made all this happen, it's 2400 people here that make it happen. The focus is on the teamwork and that no matter how good we are at what we're doing, we can always be better."

Sources: Baginski, M. (2002). WestJet celebrates sixth anniversary. Retrieved February 26, 2002, from http://www.canadatourism.com/en/ctc/ctx/ctx-news/search/newsbydateform.cfm; Fitzpatrick, P. (2001, October 16). Wacky WestJet's winning ways. *National Post*, p. C1; Quinn, P. (2001, September 12). Success stories. Flying in the face of adversity. *Financial Post*, p. E1; Welner, C., & Briggs, D. (2002). Reaching for the skies. *Alberta Venture, 6*(5), 26–27; WestJet annual information form, March 20, 2002.

QUESTIONS

1. The case study highlights several reasons for WestJet's success. In your opinion, which one is the most important?
2. Is the culture at WestJet as important to the success of the organization as its management team believes it to be?
3. How serious is the threat from conventional airlines that want to imitate the WestJet culture? What does it take to imitate organizational culture?
4. As WestJet continues to expand, will it be more difficult to sustain its culture?
5. How does WestJet's culture affect customer service?

WEB SITES

www.canadaselect.com
Canada Select (rated accommodations Web site)

www.cthrc.ca
Canadian Tourism Human Resource Council

www.deltalodgeatkananaskis.ca
The Delta Lodge at Kananaskis

www.fairmont.com
Fairmont Hotels & Resorts

www.go2bc.ca
Go2 (a resource for those interested in careers in tourism)

www.tians.org/pineapple
Nova Scotia Pineapple Awards

www.radisson.com
Radisson Hotels & Resorts

www.sheratonsuites.com
Sheraton Suites Calgary Eau Claire

www.canadaselect.travel.bc.ca
Travel BC (searchable database with accommodation listings)

www.westjet.com
WestJet Airlines

www.whistlerestays.com
Whistler Lodging Company

ENDNOTES

1. Travel Alberta. (2003). *ALTO tourism awards application form.* Edmonton: Author.
2. Berry, L. L., Hensel, J. S., & Burke, M.C. (1976). Improving retailer capability for effective consumerism response. *Journal of Retailing, 52*(3), 3–14.
3. Booker, E. (2003). Spend some serious time, money on internal marketing. *B to B, 88*(2), 8–10.
4. Ibid.
5. Webster, C. (1995). Marketing culture and marketing effectiveness in service firms, *The Journal of Services Marketing, 9*(2), 6–22.
6. Sutherland, S. (2002). Hospitality trends, *Alberta Venture, 6*(4), 49–53.
7. Ibid.
8. Katzenbach, J. (2003). *Why pride matters more than money.* New York: Crown Business.
9. Rafiq, M., & Ahmed, P. K. (2000). Advances in the internal marketing concept: Definition, synthesis and extension. *The Journal of Services Marketing, 14*(6), 449–462.
10. Galt, V. (2003, February 12). Can't pay more? Try some little extras. *The Globe and Mail*, p. C2.
11. Parasuraman, A., Zeithaml, V. A., & Berry, L. L. (1988). SERVQUAL: A multiple item scale for measuring consumer perceptions of service quality. *Journal of Retailing, 64*, 12–20.
12. Cronin, J., & Taylor, S. (1994). "SERVPERF versus SERVQUAL: Reconciling performance-based and perception-minus-expectations measurements of service quality." *Journal of Marketing, 58*(1), 125–131.
13. Reichheld, F. F., & Sasser, W. S., Jr. (1990). Zero defections: Quality comes to services. *Harvard Business Review, 68*, 105–111.
14. Heskett, J. L., Sasser, W. E., Jr., & Schlesinger, L. A. (1997). *The service profit chain: How leading companies link profit and growth to loyalty, satisfaction, and value.* New York: Free Press, 83.
15. Hauck, M. (2001). How to ensure the satisfaction of your meeting planner customers. *HSMAI Marketing Review,* Fall/Winter, 50–52.

16. Parasuraman, A., Zeithaml, V. A. and Berry, L. L. (1985). A conceptual model of service quality and its implications for future research. *Journal of Marketing, 49*(4), 41–50.

17. Cohen, A. (2002, January 8). "Mileage junkies feed their habit. *Financial Times,* p. 10.

18. Martilla, J. A., & James, J. C. (1977). Importance–Performance Analysis. *Journal of Marketing, 41*(1), 13–17.

19. Hudson, S., & Shephard, G. (1998). Measuring service quality at tourist destinations: An application of Importance–Performance Analysis to an Alpine ski resort. *Journal of Travel and Tourism Marketing, 7*(3), 61–77.

20. Parasuraman, A., Zeithaml, V. A. and Berry, L.L. (1985). A conceptual model of service quality and its implications for future research. *Journal of Marketing, 49*(4), 41–50.

21. Buzzell, D., & Gale B. T. (1987). *The PIMS principles.* New York: Free Press.

22. Phillips, L. D., Chang, D. R., & Buzzell, R. (1983). Product quality, cost position and business performance: A test of some key hypotheses. *Journal of Marketing, 47*(Spring), 26–43.

23. Gale, B. (1992). Monitoring customer satisfaction and market-perceived quality. *American Marketing Association Worth Repeating Series,* Number 922CSO I. Chicago: American Marketing Association.

24. Berry, L. L. (1983). Relationship marketing. In L. L. Berry, G.L. Shostack, & G. Upah (Eds.), *Emerging perspectives on services marketing* (pp. 25–28). Chicago: American Marketing Association.

25. Morrison, A. M. (2002). *Hospitality and travel marketing* (3rd ed.). Albany, NY: Delmar Thomson Learning.

26. Zeithaml, V. A., & Bitner, M. J. (2000). *Services marketing: Integrating customer focus across the firm.* New York: McGraw-Hill.

27. Reichheld, F. F., and Sasser, W. S., Jr. (1990). Zero defections: Quality comes to services. *Harvard Business Review, 68,* 105–111.

28. Zeithaml, V. A., & Bitner, M. J. (2000). *Services marketing: Integrating customer focus across the firm.* New York: McGraw-Hill.

29. Zeithaml, V. A., & Bitner, M. J. (2000). *Services marketing: Integrating customer focus across the firm.* New York: McGraw-Hill, 145.

30. Reichheld, F. F., & Sasser, W. S., Jr. (1990). Zero defections: Quality comes to services. *Harvard Business Review, 68,* 105–111.

31. Rasmusson, E. (1999). Wanted: Profitable customers. *Sales and Marketing Management, 151*(5), 28–34.

32. Withiam, G. (1998). Customers from hell. *Cornell Hotel and Restaurant Administration Quarterly, 39*(5), 11.

33. Zemke, R., & Anderson, K. (1990). Customers from hell. *Training, 27*(2), 25–33.

34. Kelley, S. W., Hoffman, K. D., & Davis, M. A. (1993). A typology of retail failures and recoveries. *Journal of Retailing, 69*(4), 429–452.

35. Collier, D. A. (1995). Modeling the relationships between process quality errors and overall service process performance. *Journal of Service Industry Management, 64*(4), 4–19.

36. Harari, O. (1997). Thank heavens for complainers. *Management Review, 86*(3), 25–29.

Destination Marketing

MARKETING FIRST NATIONS TOURISM IN THE YUKON

According to many tourism experts, First Nations communities in Canada are sitting on a gold mine of tourism potential. Studies have revealed a potential of up to 18 million international visitors over the next five years. The United Kingdom alone is home to 13.5 million potential long-haul pleasure travellers, and of those, 4.1 million have expressed high levels of interest in Aboriginal tourism. Germany has 9 million potential tourists interested in Aboriginal culture, France has 1.5 million, the Netherlands has 1.7 million, and Italy has 4.9 million. In Canada, 700 000 Canadians had an Aboriginal tourism experience in 1999.

But marketing and promoting First Nations tourism is not always the responsibility of traditional destination marketing organizations (DMOs). For example, in the Yukon it is the Yukon First Nations Tourism Association (YFNTA) that is dedicated to promoting and maintaining the cultural integrity of native tourism in that region. The YFNTA was incorporated in 1994 and has First Nations tourism-business owners populating its board of directors. The association has the following guiding principles:

- *Marketing and Promotion.* To market and promote the growth of First Nations tourism in a manner that maintains the cultural integrity of each Yukon First Nation.
- *Networking and Communication.* To develop positive working relationships between the Yukon First Nations Tourism Association and communities, industry, and government.
- *Product and Entrepreneurial Development.* To assist in the development of Yukon First Nations tourism products that promote cultural awareness and maintain cultural integrity.
- *Human Resource Development.* To provide First Nations tourism training and education in a manner consistent with cultural requirements and national standards.
- *Lobbying and Advocacy.* To represent the interests of the Yukon First Nations Tourism Association openly, honestly, and with integrity.

The positioning of the YFNTA articulates the First Nations people, history, and culture as central to an understanding of the Yukon. The organization's mission statement makes this very clear: "The Yukon First Nations Tourism Association is dedicated to promoting and maintaining the cultural integrity of native tourism." By bringing together tourism businesses and attractions that are run by the First Nations, the YFTNA strives to bring the visitor to an understanding of not only the landscape of the Yukon but also of the people who have lived there for thousands years as well as those who are more recent arrivals.

The YFTNA *Visitor Guide* and Web site do more than list tourist attractions, accommodations, and shopping. They have been carefully crafted to provide a wealth of information that goes beyond directions and maps. In fact, the bulk of the *Visitor Guide* is used to provide information under such headings as "our history," "the land gives us life," "our cultural heritage," and "Yukon First Nations arts." The facts in these sections are fascinating and cover topics ranging from ancient trade routes and

traditional remedies to modern land claims and cultural gatherings. Everything is written so that it is easily understood by non-natives, and unfamiliar terms are explained for the visitor. Interspersed with the information in the *Visitor Guide* are explanations of etiquette and cultural differences, and how best to respect the traditions of the First Nations.

There are several maps provided in the guide, one of which is a typical tourist guide map that shows major roads, towns and cities, and tourist attractions. However, the other maps provide a division of the Yukon by culture groups and by nations. Each of the First Nations is located and described for visitors, so they can have at least a moderate understanding of the people that are their hosts. The attractions and business listings at the back of the guide focus on the attractions that have First Nations content and on First Nations businesses.

Visitors are encouraged to seek out cultural tourism experiences that are often paired with popular wilderness/adventure experiences. There are also many events hosted by Yukon First Nations that are open to visitors. Through the YFNTA, visitors are invited to learn more about the cultures of the First Nations and to participate in appropriate ways. That said, both the *Visitor Guide* and the Web site remind visitors that many in the Yukon still practise a traditional lifestyle, and their privacy, seasonal campsites, and burial grounds are to be respected.

The YFNTA provides businesses that are part of the association with a way to differentiate themselves from other tourism businesses in the Yukon. The association has strongly positioned itself to convey to the visitor that an understanding of the First Nations peoples is vital to an understanding and appreciation of the Yukon.

Sources: Aboriginal tourism in Canada. (2003, February 5). *Winnipeg Free Press*, p. B2; Yukon First Nations Tourism Association. (2001). *Yukon First Nations Tourism Association Welcome Visitor Guide 2001/02*, Whitehorse, Yukon; Yukon First Nations Tourism Association Web site: http://www.yfnta.org.

Objectives

On completion of this chapter, readers should understand

- the principles of destination marketing;
- the role of destination marketing organizations (DMOs);
- the growing importance of responsible marketing;

- the two strategies to consider in the marketing of destinations;
- the principles of destination branding;
- the marketing of events and conferences; and
- the marketing of sport and adventure tourism.

Chapter Overview

The opening vignette provides an example of an emerging destination basing its positioning on its cultural tourism and its wilderness and adventure experiences. In the Yukon, tourism is now the territory's top private sector employer. More than 280 000 visitors each year spend upward of $160 million, creating an estimated 2000 jobs. As tourism expands around the globe, it brings new opportunities for destination marketing, such as the high levels of interest in Aboriginal tourism. But at the same time, this globalization leads to a dilution of established destination identities and to increased competition among emergent tourism destinations. This chapter looks at both the opportunities and challenges inherent in marketing destinations. It begins by discussing the principles of destination marketing and defining, characterizing, and classifying destinations. A summary of the objectives and benefits of destination marketing is followed by a more in-depth look at the role of destination marketing organizations (DMOs). A short section on identifying target markets is followed by a section on tourism development, which focuses on the growing importance of responsible marketing. There are two strategies to consider in the marketing of destinations—promotion versus facilitation—and these are discussed in turn. The next section presents a review of the theories of destination branding. Finally, the chapter looks at the marketing of two particularly important sectors for destinations: events and conferences, and sport and adventure tourism.

THE PRINCIPLES OF DESTINATION MARKETING

destinations

places that have some form of actual or perceived boundary, such as the physical boundary of an island, political boundaries, or even market-created boundaries

To understand the principles of destination marketing it is important to comprehend what is meant in the tourism industry by the term "destination." Destinations are places that have some form of actual or perceived boundary, such as the physical boundary of an island, political boundaries, or even market-created boundaries. The tourism destination can comprise a wide range of elements that combine to attract visitors to stay for a holiday or day visit, but there are four core elements that make up the destination product: prime attractors, built environment, supporting supply services, and socio-cultural dimensions (such as atmosphere or ambience) (see Table 12.1).

It would be misleading to define the destination as a composite product, for this implies that it can be marketed as a packaged bundle of benefits in the same way that a fast-moving consumer good can. As the prime attractors and cultural attributes of the host

Table 12.1

Characteristics of a Destination

CHARACTERISTICS	DESCRIPTION	EXAMPLES
Prime attractors	The main attractors that appeal to visitors and that differentiate one destination from another	Rocky Mountains and national parks in Canada; pyramids in Egypt; Niagara Falls in the United States and Canada
Built environment	The physical layout of a destination, including waterfronts, promenades, historic quarters, and commercial zones. Major elements of infrastructure such as road and rail networks, plus open spaces and commercial facilities	London Docklands in the United Kingdom; Venetian canals in Italy; West Edmonton Mall in Canada (see *Profile*)
Supporting supply services	Essential facilitating services such as accommodation, communications, transport, refreshment and catering, entertainment, and amenities	Essential at most destinations
Sociocultural dimensions	Cultural attributes: bridges between past and present, the mood or atmosphere—ranging from sleepy to vibrant. The degree of friendliness and cohesion between the host community and visitors	The friendliness of Canadians; chaotic transport in China; the music in Ireland; the laid-back attitude of Fijians

Source: Adapted from Lumsdon, L. (1997). *Tourism Marketing*. Oxford: Thomson Business Press.

community are a major appeal to the visitor, the offering is far more complicated than that of a composite product. Since many of these elements are inherited from previous generations, the marketer has little control over such external factors. Furthermore, the mix of public and private sector provision makes traditional approaches to branding and marketing planning difficult to apply. The other main difference between a destination and other types of product is that the visitor becomes part of the overall appeal and forms an integral part of the contemporary destination.

Classifications of Destinations

Kotler, Bowen, and Makens distinguish between macro-destinations such as the United States and micro-destinations such as the states, regions, and cities within the United States.[1] However, there are many different types of destinations, including those listed in Table 12.2 on page 394.

Table 12.2

Classifications of Destinations

DESTINATION TYPE	DESCRIPTION
Major international destinations	Destinations on "must-see" lists. Examples are places such as Paris, New York, London, and Vancouver, which have mass appeal to large numbers of international travellers.
Classic destinations	Destinations where the natural, cultural, or historical appeal encourages long-stay holidays. Examples are Saint-Tropez or Lourdes in France, or Banff National Park in Canada.
Human-made destination resorts	Destinations where visitors view the resort as the destination itself and rarely venture outside the perimeters. Examples are the all-inclusive resorts in the Caribbean or Mexico, or the Hilton Hawaiian Village in Honolulu.
Natural landscape or wildlife tourism destinations	Destinations that have high natural appeal and are habitats of rare species of flora, fauna, or wildlife. Examples are the Galapagos Islands in Ecuador, the Serengeti wildlife reserve in East Africa, and the Queen Charlotte Islands in B.C.
Alternative destinations	More contemporary destinations such as cruises, theme parks, massive shopping centres like West Edmonton Mall, and time-share properties.
Business tourism destinations	Destinations where retailing and entertainment sectors encourage longer stays by business executives and partners. This is often accompanied by a thriving hospitality sector and a desire to heighten the destination's image through events marketing. An example in Canada is Toronto.
Stopover destinations	Destinations that are situated between generating areas and holiday destinations. Often characterized by having a wide-ranging budget accommodation sector and a strong mix of restaurants and cafés. Calgary is often identified as a stopover destination.
Short break destinations	Destinations that have national appeal—and often international appeal if suitable attractions exist. Niagara Falls is a classic example.
Day trip destinations	Destinations that attract primarily regional, day-visitor demand; the most common of all destinations. They range from seaside ports to major retailing centres in all parts of the world. The Laurentians is a popular day trip destination for people in Montreal.

There is an increasing grey area in the distinction between attractions and destinations. Some human-made attractions such as Disney World in Florida, while technically attractions, appear to have more in common with destinations than with most other attractions. In terms of the area they cover and their visitor numbers, as well as the fact that they have on-site accommodation, for example, they appear to be more like destinations. However, the fact that they are usually single-ownership rather than multiple-ownership operations confirms that they are not like other destinations, as does the fact that they usually have a single core product or theme, unlike most destinations. But attractions like West Edmonton Mall in Alberta (see *Profile*) are often seen as shopping destinations as well as being labelled as major attractions.

PROFILE

WEST EDMONTON MALL: ATTRACTION OR SHOPPING DESTINATION?

The race is on for the title of "world's largest mall." A planned 48-hectare addition to the Mall of America in Bloomington, Minnesota, could make West Edmonton Mall (WEM) in Alberta the world's "second" largest shopping mall. But for the time being, WEM is still touted as the world's largest entertainment and shopping centre, and it remains Alberta's number one attraction, drawing 21 million visitors a year. The more than 800 stores and services and 110 eating establishments within its 49 hectares make WEM a shopper's paradise. But "hanging out at the mall" takes on a whole new meaning at WEM, where the 3700-square-metre Galaxyland (the world's largest indoor amusement park) offers 25 rides, including Mindbender, the world's largest indoor triple-loop roller coaster, and Space Shot, one of the world's tallest indoor tower rides.

The enormous World Waterpark at WEM contains the world's largest indoor wave pool and the world's tallest indoor bungee jump. The full-size skating rink inside the mall is the second home of the Edmonton Oilers hockey team and offers public skating and rentals throughout the week. Other attractions include the Sea Life Caverns and Dolphin Lagoon, the Ice Palace, Professor WEM's Adventure Golf, Go Karts, and the Palace Casino.

When first planned and built in September 1981, at a cost of $1.2 billion, the mall was intended to be a retail shopping mall for the residents of Edmonton. But the developers were quick to see the potential for more than shopping. Gary Hanson, general manager of

PROFILE *continued*

WEM, says, "When the developers added phase two of the project, they had already established that the mall needed components other than just shopping. That's when they introduced the entertainment component."

WEM is in many ways a one-stop destination. Two hotels—the attached 355-room Fantasyland Hotel and the nearby West Edmonton Mall Inn—provide visitors with everything they need on site. The Fantasyland Hotel is an attraction unique to WEM. The hotel offers guests the opportunity to choose from 11 different exotic themed rooms. Tour operators have recognized that WEM is a destination of choice for many people and have partnered with the mall to provide vacation getaway packages to customers that include return airfare, accommodation at one of the mall's two hotels, and value-added incentives such as coupon books. Many of these visitors come from the United States. Shopping is a primary trip motivator for American tourists, and the Travel Industry Association of America (TIA) has claimed that the average spending per person per trip is US$333. The TIA also says that travellers who shop want to visit different, rather than familiar, stores, 73 percent wanting to shop in stores that they do not have in their own city.

"Despite the fact that shopping has been identified as the number one activity of travellers, we know that people are not going to come here only for shopping," says Hanson. "We know that visitors want to do other things. For example, the German market wants to experience wilderness and stay in five-star hotels. So we partner with all the activity providers associated with the Edmonton region—fishing, golf, skiing, and so on. They use us to market their products, and we use them to market our product."

After 20 years, the vision keeps growing. In the next 10 to 15 years, the mall's owners plan to expand to become a "lifestyle" centre, where shopping, entertainment, living, and work space all come together. A $145 million expansion plan includes the addition of 500 residential apartments, office space, more retail area, an 8000-seat multi-use facility, and a third hotel.

Sources: Olsen, D. (2003, April 12). Battle of the mega malls. *National Post*, p. PT6; West Edmonton Mall: An Anchor for Alberta. (2002, December 6). *Tourism*, p. 6; Wilson, V. (2002). *Southern Ontario introduces shopping getaway packages.* Retrieved September 16, 2002, from http://www.canadatourism.com/en/ctc/ctx/ctx-news/search/newsbydateform.cfm.

OBJECTIVES AND BENEFITS OF DESTINATION MARKETING

A fair proportion of destination marketing tends to be carried out by public sector bodies, and hence it tends to be quite complicated. These public bodies are often involved in destination marketing for a wide range of reasons other than just attracting tourists. These objectives might include

1. improving the image of an area in the hope that this will encourage industrialists to relocate their factories and offices to the area;
2. providing jobs for local residents;
3. increasing the range of facilities that are available for the local community;

4. giving local residents more pride in their local area, which can happen when people see that tourists want to visit their region;
5. providing a rationale and funding for improvements to the local environment; and
6. trying to make the destination politically more acceptable.

However, public sector bodies can earn income from tourism in a number of ways, so economic benefits are just as important. Revenue may come in the form of sales taxes or hotel room taxes, and from admissions to publicly owned attractions. A large tourism benefit comes from the multiplier effect, as tourist expenditures are recycled through the local economy. Governments use economic impact models to estimate overall employment gains in goods and services consumption resulting from tourism multipliers. Tourism is often used to shift the burden of taxes to nonresidents. Taxation of tourists has in fact become very popular, and it includes taxes on airline tickets, hotel taxes, and other user fees. Many in the tourism industry have suggested that these taxes should go back into promoting tourism and developing the infrastructure to support tourism.

THE ROLE OF DESTINATION MARKETING ORGANIZATIONS (DMOS)

destination marketing organizations (DMOs)

government agencies, convention and visitors bureaus, travel associations, and other bodies that market travel to their respective destination areas.

The role of national tourist boards in proactively marketing and advertising destinations that they represent has changed substantially in the last few decades.[2] A major development of the 1980s and 1990s was the appearance of private–public sector **destination marketing organizations (DMOs)** or National Tourist Organizations (NTOs), complementing and sometimes replacing the advertising and marketing activities of conventional, fully state-funded tourism offices. DMOs are government agencies, convention and visitors bureaus, travel associations, and other bodies that market travel to their respective destination areas. This trend is being reinforced by the very rapid expansion of the World Wide Web and the Internet as media that give the tourism industry the ability to market, promote, advertise, sell, provide information, and accept reservations. The appearance of regional tourist boards with an agenda to promote and advertise only their own attractions in foreign markets is another trend that is likely to develop. Meanwhile, the world's leading names in travel have moved pronouncedly to the use of advertising and promotions that create brand awareness.

The growth in tourism has lured many government agencies and other groups into marketing their destinations to pleasure and business travellers. Nearly every state, province, and territory now has a separate body that is responsible for marketing. Nationally, organizations such as the Australian Tourist Commission, the British Tourist Authority, and the Canadian Tourism Commission are investing millions of dollars in tourism marketing and development. At a state or province level, marketing agencies spend millions of dollars promoting tourism. Their marketing programs target both individual travellers and travel trade intermediaries. Often they enter into cooperative marketing with suppliers, carriers, intermediaries, and other destination marketing organizations. *Marketing in Action* in Chapter 8 highlights the ways in which cooperation and industry partnerships helped Travel Alberta to stimulate domestic tourism. Many agencies also provide seed money to other DMOs for their individual marketing programs.

convention and visitor bureaus (CVBs)

regional or city-level organizations responsible for marketing a specific destination

At a regional or city level, **convention and visitor bureaus (CVBs)** have been created to be responsible for destination marketing. In the United States, nearly every community with a resident population of more than 50 000 now has a CVB. Approximately 500 of the larger bureaus belong to the **International Association of Convention & Visitors Bureaus (IACVB)**, which provides educational resources and networking opportunities to its members and distributes information on the CVB industry to the public. The individual bureaus divide their attention between the travel trade—particularly convention/meeting planners and tour operators—and individual travellers. Their goal is to bring more conventions, meetings, and leisure travellers to their communities. These bureaus represent a broad group of suppliers in their destination areas and are often funded through local accommodation and restaurant taxes.

TOURISM DEVELOPMENT

Understanding the Impacts of Tourism

International Association of Convention & Visitors Bureaus (IACVB)

an organization that provides educational resources and networking opportunities to its members and distributes information on the CVB industry to the public

The tourism marketer is likely to be involved in the process of developing a destination, in terms of either building new resorts or rejuvenating old ones (see *Snapshot,* pp. 418–420). Part of the process involves estimating future demand, as in a feasibility study, but increasing emphasis is being placed upon evaluating the likely impacts—such as direct or indirect economic impact—of any development. Techniques have also been developed to monitor other impacts, such as the environmental and social impacts of tourism. Common analytical frameworks include an environmental audit, environmental impact analysis, carrying capacity, and community assessment techniques. It is beyond the scope of this book to cover these techniques in detail, but the tourism marketer needs to have knowledge of the most current models and techniques applied to the evaluation of environmental and social impact. Many definitions of tourism marketing state that consumer satisfaction can only take place within the framework of environmental and societal responsibility. The destinations that fail to grasp this fact will find it increasingly difficult to remain competitive.

The Destination Life Cycle

tourism area life cycle (TALC)

the stages a destination goes through, from exploration to involvement to development to consolidation to stagnation to rejuvenation or decline (also known as the "tourism destination life cycle")

It has been argued that the nature of the marketing strategy adopted by a destination is often dictated by the tourism destination life cycle, also known as the **tourism area life cycle (TALC)**.[3] Like the product life cycle (see Chapter 5, p. 144), the tourism area (or destination) life cycle follows a pattern as outlined in Figure 12.1, moving from exploration to involvement to development to consolidation to stagnation to rejuvenation or decline. The assumption is that at each stage the tourism marketer will plan the marketing effort to fit the next predicted phase of development, or possibly in the later stages, to suit the resort's ultimate decline. One Canadian destination that has moved rapidly through the life cycle in the last few decades is Newfoundland and Labrador. In 1996, Newfoundland and Labrador's tourism industry was little more than a footnote on the province's economic statement. Today, it is a powerhouse of the economy. With more than a 40 percent increase in nonresident visitation since 1996, more and more hoteliers, restaurateurs, and tour companies are entering the industry. One could therefore argue that Newfoundland and Labrador is in the consolidation stage of the TALC.

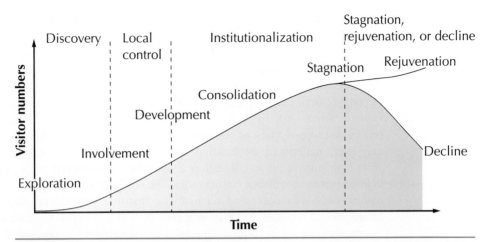

Figure 12.1 The Tourist Area Life Cycle

Source: Butler, R. W. (1980), adapted by Cooper, C., Fletcher, J., Gilbert, D, & Wanhill, S. (1993). *Tourism: Principles and practice.* London: Pitman, 90.

The life cycle also suggests that the destination will appeal to different markets as it matures. This fits with Plog's consumer typology framework, introduced in Chapter 3 (see pp. 81–82), which suggests that the adventurous, outgoing (allocentric) visitor seeks unfamiliar and unspoiled destinations.[4] Those who are more passive and like the familiar (psychocentrics) prefer mature destinations. Midcentrics (a mixture of the two extremes) head for resorts that are more developed, or are becoming mature.

Although the destination life cycle is useful, it does have its problems, just like the product life cycle. The assumption that destinations will inevitably progress from one stage to another may not always apply, and it is difficult to determine when a destination has reached a particular stage in the life cycle. Also, defining and analyzing destinations as a whole might be misleading. Certain parts of cities or destinations might suffer from stagnation while other parts flourish. Related to this point is the possibility that different life cycle patterns might exist in the same destination for different tourist segments. Despite these problems, the destination life cycle is a useful concept for destination marketers to be aware of. In a review of the subject, Cooper suggests that the destination life cycle can be used in three ways: (1) as an applied model of destination evolution; (2) as a guide for marketing and planning; and (3) as a forecasting tool.[5] In practice, the second and third points both involve marketing, since forecasting is integral to effective marketing planning.

Responsible Marketing of Destinations

The theory of sustainable tourism emphasizes the critical importance of environmental stewardship. Similarly, a common thread running through all of the existing literature on competitiveness suggests that, to be competitive, a destination must be sustainable from an environmental perspective. However, destinations are generally still inexperienced in handling environmental issues creatively. A substantial fraction of environmental spending relates to the regulatory struggle itself and not to improving the environment, particularly in the tourism sector. But corporate managers in certain industry sectors have begun to consider environmental management as a critical component for sustaining competitive advantage, and in the tourism industry it is time for managers to start recognizing environmental improvement as an economic and competitive opportunity, rather than an annoying cost or inevitable threat.

responsible marketing

the balancing of environmental initiatives and environmental communication in order to achieve sustainable competitive advantage

Yet, if environmental improvement is to provide a competitive opportunity the company must consider **responsible marketing**, which is the balancing of environmental initiatives and environmental communication in order to achieve sustainable competitive advantage. Unfortunately, there has been no consistent approach to environmental marketing practices in tourism. Some destinations neglect their environmental obligations, perhaps because of a lack of guidelines and examples of best practice, or perhaps because they don't understand the benefits. Others exploit environmental communication for short-term gains or fail to tell visitors about their environmental initiatives. Many studies indicate that environmental considerations are now a significant element of travellers' destination-choosing process, and much of what first-time visitors learn about a destination's environmental qualities that may influence their choice depends on the effectiveness of information and the motivation stimulated by commercial brochures or Web sites.

Figure 12.2 provides a model of responsible marketing that managers in the tourism industry can use to improve their environmental marketing practices. The model is based on previous literature in marketing and in strategic and environmental management, and it adopts the view that a destination can be plotted on a two-by-two matrix to identify its position regarding responsible marketing. The vertical axis represents environmental action and the horizontal axis represents communication of these activities. Destinations can take up one of four theoretical positions within the model. They can be classified as *inactive* when they tend not to see the benefits of allocating any resources toward environmental activities and when they have a low level of commitment to both environmental improvement and communication of environmental activities. Those that see the benefits of environmental action (perhaps for regulatory purposes) but fail to communicate these efforts are *reactive*. Destinations that exploit consumer interests in environmentally friendly products without considering resource characteristics, environmental ethics, or a long-term perspective are seen as *exploitive*. The position in the model most likely to remain sustainable (and competitive) is that in which environmental action and environmental communication of this action is high, and these destinations are labelled as *proactive*. In the proactive position, the destination and its associated products/services are developed sensitively, with regard to their long-term future, and consumers are aware (both before purchase and during the visit) of the concern for the resources involved.

Chapter 1 describes the conflict between ski areas in Banff National Park and environmentalists (see *Snapshot,* pp. 25–26). In the past, the ski areas there have taken up an inactive or reactive position. However, in North America, there is evidence of both a new management style and a new commitment to have skiing coexist with the environment. The Aspen Skiing Company, for example, was the first to appoint an environmental affairs director, and its green campaign has won numerous awards. Aspen communicates its initiatives via the ski industry's first environmental Web site and an intra-company environmental newsletter. However, Aspen is an exception, and an opportunity exists for Banff ski areas to take a proactive approach to environmental stewardship.[6]

It is important to recognize that a destination's position in the model may only be temporary, as it may be in transit between one place in the model and the next. Further, there are likely to be a variety of contingency factors that will affect a destination's position. Previous research suggests that these influences include the level of environmental pressures from stakeholders, managerial interpretations of environmental issues, the level of environmental regulations, and the size and the financial position of the company.

Environmental Communication

	Low	High
Low	**Inactive** No support or involvement from top management Environmental management not necessary No environmental reporting No employee environmental training or involvement	**Exploitive** Some involvement of top management Environmental issues dealt with only when necessary External reporting but no internal reporting Little employee training or involvement
High	**Reactive** Some involvement of top management Environmental management is a worthwhile function Internal reporting but no external reporting Some employee environmental training or involvement	**Proactive** Top management involved in environmental issues Environmental management is a priority item Regular internal and external reporting including an environmental plan or report Employee environmental training or involvement encouraged

Environmentally Responsible Action (row label spanning Low and High)

Figure 12.2   A Model of Responsible Marketing

MARKETING IN ACTION

TOURISM DEVELOPMENT: THE QUÉBEC CITY AND AREA TOURISM AND CONVENTION BUREAU

The Québec City and Area Tourism and Convention Bureau is taking a zoned approach to tourism development, according to its latest marketing plan. The approach follows Quebec City's elevation to mega-city status following the recent government-mandated municipal mergers. The plan states that the development priorities were determined not only on the basis of their feasibility but also on the possibility of having them ready

MARKETING IN ACTION *continued*

for market within a five-year time span. The ambitious plan, once completed, would have the effect of turning what is primarily a city destination into a multifaceted destination offering a wide range of tourism products and placing a much greater emphasis on outdoor activities. In the Jacques-Cartier region, examples of project possibilities include the development of the Duchesnay Forestry Camp as a base for ecotourism, and a heightening of the tourism impact made by area focal points such as Parc de Jacques-Cartier, Stoneham, Villages des Sports, and Lac Beauport.

In Portneuf, the plan calls for the building of major tourist facilities at the mouth of the Jacques-Cartier River, around the Cap Santé fish ladder, and the site of Fort Jacques-Cartier. At the same time, the bureau wants to spur tourism in the Portneuf Wildlife Reserve and build the zone as an active resort area offering ecotourism, adventure pursuits, golf, cycling, snowmobiling, and day fishing. For the city itself, outside Old Quebec the plan suggests developing the zoo and aquarium for tourism, completing the regional cycling network, and improving access to the historic neighbourhoods of Beauport and Charlesbourg.

In Old Quebec, the bureau's aim is to secure ongoing financing for nationally and internationally known events such as the winter Carnaval and the summer Festival d'été. It urges the development of at least one low-season event and a solution to the problem of tour-bus traffic in the Old Town. The recommendations for the Côte-de-Beaupré region

include making Mont-Sainte-Anne a world-class, four-season resort and integrating the products offered by the Cap-Tourmente Wildlife Reserve. The plan for Île d'Orléans calls for the creation of a safe cycling network and the building of a seigniorial system interpretation centre at Mauvide-Genest Manor. At the same time, the zone should highlight the history of the founding families and build on the fame of Felix Leclerc.

In its marketing outline, the bureau states firmly that Quebec must become a unique winter city destination that is decorated, illuminated, and lively, while also offering a total winter experience by reinforcing the links between the city, the mountains, and nature. For the summer, the aim is to work at integrating travel tour, urban destination, and active resort products. The plan for the future is to make the Quebec City area a unique, world-class destination, and a true city resort, with the addition of a unique offer in every zone. Other priorities include attracting a diverse client base and a growing individual clientele, having a common approach to business travel marketing, and developing a four-season market and product vision. At the same time, the bureau wants financing for tourism development, improved air access for international visitors, and a true culture of tourism with a first-rate welcome.

Source: Canadian Travel Press. (2002). Greater Quebec is in the zone, Retrieved May 7, 2002, from http://www.canadatourism.com/en/ctc/ctx/ctx-news/search/newsbydateform.cfm.

IDENTIFYING TARGET MARKETS

Chapter 2 discusses in detail the importance of segmentation and targeting (see pp. 42–44 and pp. 51–52), and a lengthy discussion on this subject is therefore unnecessary here. However, it is worth underlining the importance of destinations understanding what motivates tourists, how they make their decisions, and how they evaluate and perceive destinations. Having gained such understanding, destinations must then segment the market—whether it is into subcategories such as business travellers, conference and convention delegates, incentive travellers, and tourists, or into classifications such as the typologies proposed by Plog (see Chapter 3, pp. 81–82).[7] There are also growing tourism markets that destinations need to court. Chapter 2 describes the four growing segments of the baby-boomer market, the gay market, the senior market, and the family market (see pp. 51–52). But there are also others, such as those travellers interested in sport tourism and those looking for environmentally friendly tourism.

An unusual tourism market that has emerged in Ontario is the market for visiting maple syrup operators. Maple syrup producers in Ontario welcome visitors every spring to taste pure maple syrup and other maple products. Destination Ontario, developer of the largest Internet network of tourism-related businesses in the eastern half of Ontario, promotes a collection of 42 maple syrup operators and 7 maple syrup festivals in eastern Ontario. Using the planning features of the Web site (www.realontario.ca), visitors can plan a trip, add sugar bushes to their personal travel itinerary, and get step-by-step driving directions directly to a syrup producer's door.

A destination can identify its natural target market in two ways. The first is to collect detailed information about its current visitors in order to determine which visitors should be targeted. The second approach is to audit the destination's attractions and select segments that might logically have an interest in these attractions. Marketers should not, however, make the assumption that current visitors reflect all of the potentially interested groups. After a destination identifies its natural target markets, tourism planners should conduct research to determine where these tourists are found. If many segments are identified, the relative potential profit from each should be evaluated. The potential profit of a target tourist segment is the difference between the amount the tourist segment is likely to spend and the cost of attracting and serving this segment. Ultimately, potential tourist segments should be ranked and selected in order of their profitability.

Whatever tourist segments a destination seeks, it needs to be very specific in its targeting. A ski area attracts skiers, yet even with such givens, potential visitors must be segmented by additional characteristics. For example, Lake Louise in Banff National Park appeals to image-conscious, upper-income, and professional skiers, whereas Norquay, just an hour away, attracts a more price-conscious family market. Marketing organizations need to be aware of these subtle differences. Likewise, destinations need to closely monitor the relative popularity of their various attractions by determining the number and type of tourists attracted to each. Information should be collected continuously on the changing needs and wants of existing markets, emerging markets, and potential target markets. The research conducted by Tourism Whistler, for example, has contributed considerably to the unprecedented growth and rising stature of Whistler as a world-class year-round destination. By identifying and targeting potential target markets such as British and South American skiers, Whistler has become the country's most acclaimed recreational destination. Tourism Whistler regularly conducts customer surveys to gauge satisfaction levels, to identify areas that need improvement, and to formulate strategies.

PROMOTION VERSUS FACILITATION

promotion strategy

reaching prospective visitors via expenditure on a promotional mix intended to achieve destination awareness and influence prospective customers' attitudes and purchasing behaviour; a traditional approach to destination marketing

Middleton and Clarke have suggested that there are two possible strategies to consider in the marketing of destinations.[8] The first, the **promotion strategy**, is concerned with reaching prospective visitors via expenditure on a promotional mix intended to achieve destination awareness and influence prospective customers' attitudes and purchasing behaviour; the other, the facilitation strategy, is concerned with exercising a facilitating influence over the tourism industry (see Figure 12.3). Figure 12.3 shows that at the budget-decision stage, DMOs have the choice of apportioning funds between the two routes shown: direct control of the promotional mix (on the left) and marketing facilitation (in the middle of the diagram). Facilitation forms the important bridge between DMO and the component sectors of the industry, while the promotion strategy reflects the more traditional approach to destination marketing.

Promotion Strategy

The promotional campaigns of most DMOs fall into three main categories: strategic campaigns, aimed, for example, at attracting visitors in the shoulder season; traditional image-building campaigns, which aim simply to build and maintain awareness of the destination; and "damage control" campaigns typified by Montreal's advertising campaign that followed the terrorist attacks of September 11, 2001 (see *Snapshot* in Chapter 8, pp. 261–263). Media investment in attracting tourists has grown rapidly in recent years, and most destination marketing organizations are involved in a range of promotional activities. These include the following six types.

1. Brochures

Brochures are produced for both promotional and informational purposes, although both functions may be served by a single brochure. As well as a general brochure covering the whole destination, a range of other brochures may also be offered. These may cover smaller geographical entities within the overall destination region. Alternatively, they may be targeted at specific market segments such as sport tourists or business travellers.

2. Advertisements

Due to the challenge of limited budgets referred to earlier in the chapter, most destinations' ads are placed in print media rather than on the more expensive, but more effective, medium of television. Most resort advertising is seasonal and takes place when it is thought potential visitors will be making their holiday decisions. The majority of ads seek to encourage potential consumers to request a copy of the destination's brochure, although more recently ads have been created to drive the audience to a destination Web site or to combat tourism crises. For example, in June 2003, the Tourism Authority of Thailand offered a US$100 000 SARS-free guarantee in all its print ads, saying that "Any tourist who enters and stays in Thailand legally between May 20 and Nov 19, 2003, and contracts SARS within the kingdom is eligible to receive $100 000 if death results within 90 days of the entrance date. Up to US$10 000 for hospitalisation." Presumably, the authority undertook a risk assessment, but this is a good example of the use of monetary incentives to combat tourism crises.

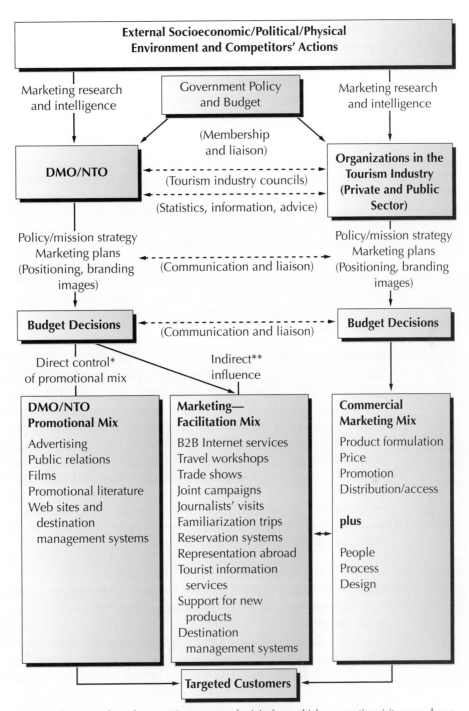

External Socioeconomic/Political/Physical Environment and Competitors' Actions

Marketing research and intelligence

Government Policy and Budget

Marketing research and intelligence

(Membership and liaison)

DMO/NTO

(Tourism industry councils)

Organizations in the Tourism Industry (Private and Public Sector)

(Statistics, information, advice)

Policy/mission strategy
Marketing plans
(Positioning, branding images)

(Communication and liaison)

Policy/mission strategy
Marketing plans
(Positioning, branding images)

Budget Decisions

(Communication and liaison)

Budget Decisions

Direct control*
of promotional mix

Indirect**
influence

DMO/NTO Promotional Mix

Advertising
Public relations
Films
Promotional literature
Web sites and
    destination
    management systems

Marketing— Facilitation Mix

B2B Internet services
Travel workshops
Trade shows
Joint campaigns
Journalists' visits
Familiarization trips
Reservation systems
Representation abroad
Tourist information
    services
Support for new
    products
Destination
    management systems

Commercial Marketing Mix

Product formulation
Price
Promotion
Distribution/access

plus

People
Process
Design

Targeted Customers

* Expenditure mainly in the countries or areas of origin from which prospective visitors are drawn
** Expenditure in the countries or areas of origin and at the destination

Figure 12.3   The Destination Marketing Process for DMOs/NTOs

Source: Middleton, V. T. C., & Clarke, J. (2001). *Marketing in travel and tourism.* Oxford: Butterworth-Heinemann, 338.

3. The Press and Public Relations

The press and public relations play a significant role in the marketing of destinations, and Chapter 9 provides many examples of destinations using familiarization trips, celebrity visits, press releases, product placement, and television broadcasts to attract attention and improve their image with the general public. For agencies that have limited budgets, this low-cost form of promotion is particularly attractive.

4. Personal Selling

Relatively little personal selling is carried out by destination marketing agencies. However, some destinations find personal selling to be the most effective communication tool in promoting to key travel decision makers and influencers in the travel trade, such as corporate travel managers, convention or meeting planners, tour operators, and retail travel agents. The purchasing power of these groups is impressive, and there are relatively few of them, which justifies the added expense of personal selling. Chapter 9 gives a recent example of a sales training exercise conducted by eight of Canada's "big cities" that organized an exclusive one-week sales and training mission in the United Kingdom. The personal-selling teams promoted the capitals and gateway cities as exciting, four-season, cosmopolitan destinations, featuring new experiences and activities, within easy access to natural attractions (see p. 311).

5. Sales Promotions

Due to the lack of control over the destination product and pricing, sales promotions are used relatively little in destination marketing. However, "added value" promotional offers may be made available, featuring elements of the destination product over which the destination marketing agency does have control. An interesting promotion involving residents, and called "Invite the World," was launched in 2003 by Tourism Vancouver. The promotion was modelled after a similar campaign launched in 1985 for Expo 86. "Invite the World" was a marketing campaign that encouraged Vancouverites and British Columbians to become ambassadors and to invite friends from all over the globe to experience the city and province. Each resident who did so was automatically entered into a weekly draw to win a tourism package consisting of weekend getaways, dinners, tickets to major events and attractions, and other prizes.

6. Trade Fairs and Exhibitions

Many DMOs exhibit at travel trade shows, fairs, exhibitions, or conventions. Generally these occasions bring all parts of the industry together. Examples are provided in Chapter 9, but a recent example comes from Newfoundland and Labrador, which hosted the 2003 Travel & Leisure Show. Many Canadian DMOs exhibited at the show, including Travel Alberta, Tourism Calgary, Tourisme Québec, Tourisme Saguenay, Tourisme Montréal, and, of course, Tourism Newfoundland and Labrador. The large the number of DMOs participating in the show reflected the increasing interest in domestic tourism in light of the turbulent external environment at the time.

Facilitation Strategy

Considering the fact that DMO budgets for marketing purposes are equivalent to an average of 0.5 percent or less of tourism expenditure, as well as the fact that most DMOs

facilitation strategy

creates marketing
bridges between a des-
tination marketing
organization and indi-
vidual operators in the
tourism industry; exer-
cises a facilitative influence over the industry

cannot influence more than around 10 percent of all prospective visitors, the question of how effective many DMO marketing campaigns are in practice is a valid one. An alternative strategy, relevant to all DMOs, is one of marketing facilitation. The **facilitation strategy** creates marketing bridges between a DMO and individual operators in the tourism industry, and between "umbrella" campaigns and industry marketing expenditure. The opening vignette in Chapter 4, for example, shows how marketers in Superior North market and promote all communities and businesses/operators in the region under a single, four-season destination umbrella. Figure 12.3 presents some of the most common facilitation strategies used by DMOs around the world.

One of these strategies is the participation in joint marketing schemes. Many destinations have formed partnerships with travel, recreational, and communication businesses on joint promotional efforts. They advertise in national magazines and travel publications and do vertical marketing with business travel promotions to link to the business-leisure segment of the travelling public; and they target intermediaries such as travel agents. For example, when Australians prepare for adventure, they head to Paddy Pallin, a chain of retail stores selling gear and clothing for the outdoor adventure enthusiast. Prompted by the Canadian Tourism Commission, the retailer recently embarked on a campaign to increase sales, using trips to Canada's Yukon as the main draw. The campaign was built around a "Win a Trip to the Yukon" contest that required entrants to have made a minimum $50 purchase at any Paddy Pallin store. In-store contest promotions included window displays, staff badges, and point-of-purchase materials. The chain expected a high return on the effort, and so invested in a national advertising campaign to drive traffic to the stores. For the Yukon, the contest promoted adventure travel to a target market, capturing names and addresses for subsequent fulfillment mailings. It worked: there were a total of 5000 entries into the competition, and 1200 requested further information on the Yukon and Canada.

Another effective way to attract potential travellers is to offer them convenient packages that not only include the basic necessities but also contain visits to the icon attractions in the destination. Packaging destinations either for the general mass tourism market or for niche specialist markets can significantly increase a destination's appeal. Inbound operators are usually responsible for packaging the destinations, putting together the combination of stopovers, attractions, accommodations, and tours; deciding the best transportation to use along the way; and allocating the amount of time to be spent at each destination. While some might argue that it is impossible to see Canada in two or three weeks, inbound operators, working with suppliers in both countries, package short tours that do have mass appeal. These operators, working with the Canadian Tourism Commission and provincial tourism offices, as well as with regional tourism groups and individual suppliers, create tours and promotional materials that will help to win business in the highly competitive international marketplace.

Packages put together by destinations are often used to attract visitors in the off-peak season, when accommodation providers are desperate to increase their occupancy rates and will offer low prices. The package is then built around the hotel. They can also be used in cities to stimulate demand on weekends, when businesspeople have left and the hotel is quiet. Packages can also be used to promote a certain image of a destination that the agency wishes to develop, such as arts and cultural breaks in industrial cities, for example. Such themed weekend breaks have become very popular in recent years.

DESTINATION BRANDING

destination branding

creating a superior proposition that is distinctive from competitors' and imparts meaning above and beyond the functional aspects of the destination

The subject of **destination branding** has received increased attention over the last few decades. In an increasingly competitive global marketplace, the need for destinations to create a unique identity—to differentiate themselves from competitors—has become more critical than ever. As suggested in Chapter 5, a brand in the modern marketing sense offers the consumer relevant added value, a superior proposition that is distinctive from competitors', and imparts meaning above and beyond the functional aspects. Today, most resorts claim to have luxury accommodation, superb attractions, friendly people, and a unique culture and heritage. However, these factors are no longer differentiators, and successful destination branding lies in its potential to reduce substitutability.

Challenges of Destination Branding

But destination branding has its challenges. Morgan and Pritchard, in a recent book on destination branding, suggest that there are five key challenges faced by destination marketers.[9]

1. Limited Budgets

The first challenge facing destination marketers is their extremely limited budgets by comparison with those of marketers of many consumer goods and services. While one corporate giant such as Sony would spend in excess of US$300 million on advertising annually, the World Tourism Organization (WTO) estimates that the world's governments are spending approximately US$350 million each year on destination advertising—accounting for about half of the promotional budgets of national tourism organizations. Combine this problem with evidence that tourism promotion does not persuade uncommitted vacationers (but rather acts to confirm the intentions of those already predisposed to visit), and destination marketers have genuine cause for concern. As a result, they have to outsmart rather than outspend the competition—and that means creating innovative, attention-grabbing advertising on a budget and maximizing the amount spent on media. In Canada, destination marketing budgets are generally quite low. For example, in 2003, the marketing budgets for Nova Scotia and Saskatchewan were about $13 million each, while Prince Edward Island and Tourism Victoria had just $7 million each to spend on marketing.

2. Politics

Public sector destination marketers are hampered by a variety of political pressures and have to reconcile a range of local and regional interests and promote an identity acceptable to a range of constituencies. Destination brand building is frequently undermined by the short-term mindset of the tourism organization's political masters. Effective advertising can also be confounded by bureaucratic red tape. For example, political considerations within a province can often dictate the range of photographs that are included in a campaign.

3. External Environment

It has become evident at the beginning of the 21st century that destinations are particularly vulnerable to external forces such as international politics, economics, terrorism, and environmental disasters. September 11, 2001, an ailing economy, the war in Iraq, and the outbreak of severe acute respiratory syndrome (SARS) were just some of the crises that have derailed destination promotional planning in Canada in the past few years. The *Profile* in Chapter 1 describes how the Canadian Tourism Commission (CTC) and its partners came together to try to mitigate the impact of these crises and put in place several initiatives to help restore consumer confidence and stimulate travel.

4. Destination Product

As was mentioned at the beginning of this chapter, the tourism destination comprises a number of elements that combine to attract visitors to stay for a holiday or day visit. These elements include accommodation and catering establishments; tourist attractions; arts, entertainment, and cultural venues; and the natural environment. Destination marketers have relatively little control over these different aspects of their product, and a diverse range of agencies and companies are partners in the task of crafting brand identities. While packaged goods normally have an obvious core—so that their advertisements can anchor themselves to product performance and attributes—with destinations the situation is much less clear.

5. Creating Differentiation

The final challenge of destination branding is that of creating differentiation in spite of the pressures on destination marketing. Countries often promote their history, their culture, and their beautiful scenery in their marketing, but most destinations have these attributes, and it is critical to build a brand on something that uniquely connects a destination to the consumer now or has the potential to do so in the future. For example, Moose Jaw, Saskatchewan, has seen tourism grow between 12 and 17 percent over the last decade, mainly because of the Temple Gardens Mineral Spa. The waters that lie 1350 metres beneath Moose Jaw have revitalized what had been a sleepy tourist destination, and the number of guests from the United States continues to grow, as do the number of visiting groups, including travelling sports teams.

Brand Building

Morgan and Pritchard suggest that there are five stages in the process of building a destination brand.[10]

1. Market Investigation, Analysis, and Strategic Recommendations

The first stage is to establish the core values of the destination and its brand. This stage should consider how contemporary or relevant the brand is to today's tourism consumer and how it compares with key competitors. In 2002, Tourism Vancouver Island's new marketing brand, "Vancouver Island, Victoria and the Gulf Islands," replaced the former "The Islands" brand, implemented 22 years ago when Tourism Vancouver Island's marketing was focused on neighbouring regions where consumers knew that the brand referred to Vancouver Island and the Gulf Islands. As market reach grew, Tourism Vancouver Island decided to evaluate the effectiveness of the brand. "We've been considering a brand change for some time," explains Tourism Vancouver Island executive director and CEO, Dave Petryk. "We initiated a survey in B.C. and Seattle/King County, and results clearly showed that potential visitors didn't recognize 'The Islands' as Vancouver Island and the Gulf Islands. In fact, research showed that people often thought our advertisements referred to the Hawaiian Islands, or the San Juans, or even to the Caribbean."

2. Brand Identity Development

Once this market investigation is complete, the next stage is to develop the brand identity. Of importance here is the brand benefit pyramid (see Figure 12.4). Critical to the success of any destination brand is the extent to which the destination's brand personality interacts with the target market. A brand's personality has both a head and a heart: its "head" is its logical features, while its "heart" is its emotional benefits and associations. Brand propositions and communications can be based around either. Brand benefit pyramids sum up consumer's relationships with a brand and are frequently established during the consumer research process, in which consumers are usually asked to describe what features a destination offers and what the place means to them. Using their answers, it should then be relatively easy to understand what particular benefit pyramids consumers associate with the destination in question.

3. Brand Launch and Introduction

The third stage in brand building is to communicate the vision and launch the brand. This may be done through a single announcement or as a part of huge international advertising campaign. An example of the former took place in the spring of 2002, when the Bedwell

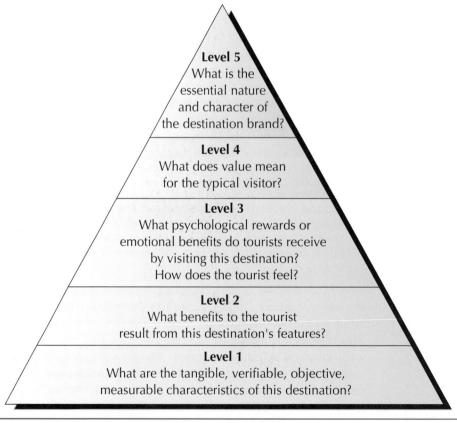

Figure 12.4   The Destination Brand Benefit Pyramid

Source: Morgan, N., & Pritchard, A. (2002). Contextualizing destination branding. In N. Morgan, A. Pritchard, & R. Pride (Eds.), *Destination branding* (pp. 11–41). Oxford: Butterworth-Heinemann, 31.

Harbour Resort and Marina, long a familiar and favourite port-of-call for leisure boaters and international travellers to the Gulf Islands of British Columbia, decided to rename themselves "Poets Cove at Bedwell Harbour." In announcing the re-branding exercise, Lorne Prokopy, partner and consulting architect to the Poets Cove project said, "In honour of the great classic poets, including Tennyson, Wordsworth and Browning, the resort will capture the old-world romance and charm that can only be found in the serene misty mornings and sun-filled afternoons of South Pender Island."[11]

4. Brand Implementation

The implementation stage involves translating the brand personality and proposition into deliverable messages. A logotype or brand signature and a design style guide, which ensures consistency of message and approach, should also reinforce the brand values. The *Snapshot* below shows how many Canadian provincial capitals have branded themselves with slogans. The vision should be expressed in the brand's core values that are consistently reinforced through the product and in all marketing communications. Every execution in all media contributes to maintaining brand presence.

5. Monitoring, Evaluation, and Review

The final stage is to evaluate the brand's performance in the marketplace. Continuous monitoring and evaluation of the communications is the key here, as are open-mindedness and a willingness to embrace change on the part of the brand managers. Any change must be managed with the overall consistency of the brand. The secret is to continually evolve and enrich the original brand personality, building on the initial strengths to increase their appeal and broaden the market.

SNAPSHOT

POSITIONING THE CAPITALS OF CANADA

Marketers of Canada's capitals are working harder than ever to broaden their appeal by packaging innovative new themes and historical, cultural, and geographic attractions to sell their cities as exciting four-season travel destinations. Many have branded themselves with slogans designed to impress and attract. Here is how they are positioning themselves:

Charlottetown: *Birthplace of Canada*
Edmonton: *Canada's Festival City*

Fredericton: *New Brunswick's Riverfront Capital*
Halifax: *One of Canada's Great Cultural Capitals*
Iqaluit: *Canada's Newest and Most Northern Capital City*
Ottawa: *Canada's Capital*
Quebec City: *The New Capital*
Regina: *The Queen City*
St. John's: *The City of Legends*
Toronto: *Diversity Our Strength*
Victoria: *City of Gardens*
Whitehorse: *Our People Our Strength*
Winnipeg: *Embrace the Spirit*

SNAPSHOT *continued*

Yellowknife: *Diamond Capital of North America*

Many of the cities have capitalized on their cultural assets. For example, the marketing of Halifax as an entertainment and cultural centre began in 1998 when the city hosted the highly successful inaugural version of the East Coast Music Awards. Since then Halifax's stature as an entertainment and cultural capital has expanded considerably, fuelled in part by the growth of a vibrant East Coast music scene. Winnipeg invites visitors to "Embrace the Spirit" of the city by experiencing unique historical and cultural attractions such as the Circle of Life Thunderbird House—a focal point for Aboriginal art, dance, music, and theatre among Winnipeg's Aboriginal population, the largest of any city in Canada. Prince Edward Island's capital, Charlottetown, has built on the city's image as the birthplace of Canada to promote its unique historical and cultural assets. And St. John's is using its popular "City of Legends" theme to market its rich mix of history and Newfoundland culture.

Other capitals have used rivers, oceans, or ports to differentiate themselves. Fredericton, capital of New Brunswick, is a good example. Three hundred years of development at Fredericton is tied to the majestic Saint John River, which runs through the heart of the capital. When Fredericton re-branded itself in 2002, it chose "Atlantic Canada's Riverfront Capital" as a theme to build on this unique setting and create a more active and experiential interpretation of the city for visitors. Canada's northern capitals are successfully packaging their culture, climate, and geography to build a unique brand of adventure tourism. They are increasingly popular destinations for European visitors looking for "hard" adventure—canoeing, camping, hiking, and wildlife spotting—in the wide open spaces of the Yukon. Yellowknife, the "Diamond Capital," is synonymous with exploration and adventure, from the tales of the early bush pilots to current mining initiatives. And Iqaluit, Canada's smallest capital, on the shores of Koojeesee Inlet at the head of Frobisher Bay, is a centre of Inuit culture and a starting point for adventure on Baffin Island or other areas of Nunavut.

Finally, some capitals are basing their positioning on festivals and special events. World-class festivals, such as the Toronto's Caribana, the Edmonton Fringe Festival, and the Halifax Busker Festival, are slowly becoming known throughout the world as high-quality attractions. Edmonton has successfully billed itself as "Canada's Festival City" for many years, thanks to a stable of 15 annual festivals and events.

Source: Higgins, G. (2003). Sharing the capital experience. *Tourism, 7*(3), 10–12.

MARKETING EVENTS AND CONFERENCES

For business and leisure travellers, events and conferences often play a key role in bringing people to destinations. These can vary from conventions and exhibitions for the business market to huge sporting events like the Olympics or the soccer World Cup, which attract millions of sport tourists. From the destination's perspective, event tourism is the development and marketing of events to obtain economic and community benefits. To the consumer, it is travel for the purpose of participating in or viewing an event. A study by the Toronto Convention and Visitors Association estimated that the SARS benefit concert in 2003 featuring the Rolling Stones would deliver a one-time economic boost of more than $52 million to the city, notably in the hotel and associated hospitality industries. However, another objective of the event was to restore Toronto's SARS-tarnished image, but although Canadian news media lavished attention on the concert, global coverage was spotty. The long-term impact of the concert on Toronto's image remains to be seen.

One example of a Canadian destination that has successfully attracted events and conferences over the last decade is Saint John, New Brunswick. In 2002, Saint John hosted a record number of 330 events, attracting 63 000 delegates to the city, compared to 207 events in 1999 that brought in about 29 000 people. These conventions, meetings, trade shows, sporting events, concerts, festivals, and reunions were worth an estimated $47 million in direct expenditures to Saint John in 2002. Much of the credit for this success is due to Venue Saint John, a strategic private/public sector alliance of 15 organizations whose goal is to attract and host events in Saint John. Noted for its creative approach, increased productivity, cost savings, and improvement of the economy of the city, Venue Saint John was named the Grand Prize winner in the Industry category of the 2002 Tourism Innovation Competition. Table 12.3 provides a list of events that Venue Saint John assisted with in 2002 and shows that the organization's impact is wide-ranging.

Events are often introduced to cope with seasonality and to boost tourism receipts during normally quiet times of year. For example, eight years ago, Whistler, B.C., held its first World Ski and Snowboard Festival in April in order to increase occupancy rates at the

Table 12.3

Events Hosted by Venue Saint John in 2002

DATE	EVENT
January–February 2002	East Coast Music Awards: attracted over 2300 delegates from across Canada
July 2002	Canadian National Square Dance Convention: attracted 5000 participants from around the world
May–June 2002	Canadian National Fencing Championships: attracted 1500 participants Canadian Medical Association Annual General Meeting: attracted 600 delegates
August 2002	Marathon by the Sea: has grown from 200 to 1200 participants and has gained international recognition in a few short years
June 2002	Dietitians of Canada Conference: attracted 500 delegates
September 2002	Shriners Convention: attracted 1500 delegates Scottish Rite of Freemasons of Canada Annual General Meeting: attracted 1000 delegates

Source: Retrieved July 5, 2003 from http://www.venuesaintjohn.com.

end of the winter season. Now in its eighth year, the event is North America's largest snow-sport and music event, attracting thousands of enthusiasts from all over the world. Hotel rooms are fully booked during the event, which spans two weekends in order to maximize occupancy rates. In addition to ski and snowboard competitions, film events, parades, and a lively club scene at night, more than 30 acts are booked for the Outdoor Concert Series. The concerts usually attract audiences of up to 10 000 revellers. According to an independent research study commissioned by the festival organizers, the 2003 festival resulted in a $26 million impact on the resort. The staging of major events in Whistler is not a new experience, and although the destination lost the World Cup skiing competition to Lake Louise, it was successful in its bid to be the host city for the 2010 Olympic Winter Games. The estimated cost of the joint Vancouver/Whistler Olympic bid was about $20 million, but hosting the games is expected to generate $1.3 billion in revenue from ticket sales, sponsorships, and television rights.

In Canada, several organizations are involved in the marketing of events and festivals. For example, Festivals and Events PEI, a federation of more than 80 festivals, events, and suppliers, promotes events on Prince Edward Island. Festivals get little exposure outside of their own home province or territory. And despite the millions of visitors who attend Canadian festivals across the country every year and the substantial revenues they generate for the tourism industry, marketing of the festival sector has been relatively taken for granted. World-class festivals such as the Montreal Jazz Festival and the Edmonton Fringe Festival remain relatively unknown outside of their own home provinces. Smaller community events and celebrations also have much to offer and would interest visitors touring through a particular province or region.

The convention and exhibition market, another lucrative market for destinations, has experienced unparalleled growth during the past 20 years. High-quality convention and exhibition centres can be found in virtually every city around the world, and Canada is no exception (see Chapter 7, p. 216 for a more detailed discussion of the convention market).

MARKETING SPORT AND ADVENTURE TOURISM

Sport Tourism

sport tourism

travel away from a person's primary residence to participate in a sporting activity for recreation or competition; travel to observe sport at the grass roots or elite level; and travel to visit a sport attraction

The Canadian Tourism Commission has identified sport tourism as the fastest-growing tourism sector, and many destinations are seeking to capitalize on this growth. Although sport tourism is a relatively new concept in contemporary vernacular, its scope of activity is far from a recent phenomenon. The notion of people travelling to participate and watch sport dates back to the ancient Olympic Games, and the practice of stimulating tourism through sport has existed for over a century. Within the last few decades, however, destinations have begun to recognize the significant potential of sport tourism, and they are now aggressively pursuing this market niche. Broadly defined, **sport tourism** includes travel away from a person's primary residence to participate in a sporting activity for recreation or competition; travel to observe sport at the grass roots or elite level; and travel to visit a sport attraction such as a sports hall of fame or a water park.[12]

Five major areas of sport tourism have been identified: attractions, resorts, cruises, tours, and events,[13] each of which is discussed below.

Sport Tourism Attractions

Sport tourism attractions are destinations that provide the tourist with things to see and do related to sport. Attractions could be natural (parks, mountains, wildlife) or human-made (museums, stadiums, stores). This core area of sport tourism also includes visits to (a) state-of-the-art sports facilities and/or unique sports facilities that generally house sports events, such as stadiums, arenas, and domes; (b) sport museums and halls/walls of fame dedicated to the sport heritage and to honouring sport heroes and leaders; (c) sport theme parks, including water slides, summer ski jumps, and bungee jumping; (d) hiking trails developed for exploring nature; and (e) sport retail stores.

An example of a popular hall of fame in Canada is the Hockey Hall of Fame, founded in 1943 to establish a memorial to those who developed Canada's great winter sport—ice hockey. On June 18, 1993, the Hockey Hall of Fame opened the doors of its current home in BCE Place, Toronto. The new $35 million facility comprises 5300 square metres, including 930 square metres in the magnificently restored Bank of Montreal building located at the corner of Yonge and Front Streets, the balance housed in the shopping/food court concourse level at BCE Place. The new Hockey Hall of Fame quickly established a reputation as a world-class sports and entertainment facility and one of Toronto's prime tourist attractions, bringing in over 500 000 visitors in its first year.

Sport Tourism Resorts

Sport tourism resorts are well-planned and integrated resort complexes that have sport or health as their primary focus and marketing strategy. In many situations, these vacation centres have high-standard facilities and services available to the sport tourist. The sport tourism resort category includes amenity and destination spas, golf and tennis resorts, water and snow sport resorts, as well as nature retreats offering outdoor adventure and exploration. Generally speaking, these resorts have state-of-the-art sport equipment and facilities and offer visitors various levels of activity opportunities and educational programs led by instructors who have a great deal of expertise and personal visibility. These resorts do vary in their focus, however, ranging from those that have high-level international standards and specialize in specific and highly developed skills to campground services specializing in recreational sporting activities. An extension of the sport resort category is sport camps. An example of such a sporting complex is Canada Olympic Park (COP) in Calgary. Since its construction in 1986, the COP has hosted thousands of sports enthusiasts from all over the world at sport camps for both amateur and professional sports participants.

Sport Tourism Cruises

The sport tourism cruise category incorporates all boat-related trips that use sports or sporting activities as their principal market strategy. Many ships built today resemble hotels and resorts and have unique sport installations. They also use guest sport celebrities as a marketing tool. To further satisfy the sport tourist, cruise ships often arrange special transportation to provide guests with opportunities to participate in activities such as snorkelling and water skiing in unique and varied water environments. Other planned activities include provision of on-board sport competitions and/or modified games (e.g., a golf driving range on deck) and special presentations or clinics from invited sport celebrities. "Cruise-and-drive" programs allow tourists to board their own vehicles to facilitate transportation to desired sport destinations. Private yachts may also be chartered, which may be sailed directly to the sport destination of the sailor's choice. The use of watercraft for sporting activities (e.g., recreational and competitive sailing or jet skiing) is also an important dimension to this category.

Sport Tourism Tours

Sport tourism tours bring visitors to their favourite sport events, facilities, or destinations around the world. These tours may be self-guided or organized, depending upon access, location, and nature of the activity. For example, many ski tour packages provide air, accommodation, local transportation, and ski-lift tickets with no special guide or amenities. At a more organized level, some companies specialize in travel packages that fly fans to a sports event—such as a hocky game—in another city, put them up in a hotel for a couple of nights, provide tickets to the game, arrange for a cocktail party and pre-game briefing with media as well as a post-game reception with players and coaches, and then return them safely home. This type of tour is especially appealing to sport aficionados who want to follow their team on the road or take in a major event such as the Super Bowl or Indianapolis 500, and for those whose dream is to walk the fairways of Augusta National during the Masters golf tournament. The major Canadian company in this market is Roadtrips, which boasts that it can take fans to just about any sport event in the world, from Formula 1 car racing to the Masters golf tournament to World Cup soccer. While sport devotees are the most passionate customers, corporations form the biggest part of the sport tourism tour business, since companies often reward their best employees with trips to the biggest sporting events in the world.

Sport Tourism Events

Finally, the sport tourism event category includes sport activities that attract a sizable number of visiting participants and/or spectators. The type of visitor depends on the sport event: some are obviously more spectator-driven than others (e.g., the Olympic Games versus the National Amateur Shuffleboard Championship). Furthermore, these sport tourism events have the potential to attract nonresident media and technical personnel such as coaches and other sports officials. High-profile sport events such as the Super Bowl, Olympic Games, or World Cup are often referred to in the literature as "tourism hallmark events" or "mega events."[14] Of the five categories of sport tourism, the sport event category has the most significant economic impact on host destinations. It is increasingly common for organizers to calculate the amount of new dollars or hotel room nights that are generated by an event. Events designed to attract large numbers of spectators can bring thousands, or even millions, of dollars into a local economy. However, smaller participatory events, such as tournaments or marathons, can also bring benefits, particularly to smaller cities or less populated regions (see *Snapshot,* pp. 418–420). Since participatory events often make use of existing infrastructure and volunteer labour, they can be relatively inexpensive to host, thereby yielding high benefit-to-cost ratios. Further, participatory sport events have been shown to be an effective way to attract new visitors and to generate return visits.

Recent data suggests that sport tourism is a high-impact and growing segment of the Canadian tourism industry. The CTC's research division estimates that sport travel in Canada is valued at approximately $1.3 billion annually or 4 percent of the tourism market.[15] Currently, about 200 000 sport events occur annually in this country, and nearly

Figure 12.5 Saskatchewan: Capitalizing on Golf Tourism

40 percent of travellers participate in, or are spectators at, a sport event every year. Many destinations are investing in this profitable sector of tourism. For example, in September 2002, the government of Ontario announced that it was investing $15 million over four years in snowmobiling to strengthen recreation and Northern Ontario tourism. Tourism plays a key role in the economy of many rural and northern communities, and snowmobiling contributes $1 billion annually to the Ontario economy. In the same province, Brantford is branded as the "Tournament Capital of Ontario" (TCO) and hosts a growing number of regional, provincial, national, and international sporting events each year that attract thousands of participants, coaches, and spectators. London, in Southwestern Ontario, also considers sport to be one of the most significant contributors to the city's promotion and growth. Finally, Saskatchewan is publicizing its 250 golf courses in order to attract the growing number of golf tourists (see Figure 12.5).

The mission of the Canadian Sport Tourism Alliance (CSTA) is to increase the capacity and competitiveness of communities across Canada in hosting sporting events. Its objectives are to provide the sport tourism industry with a credible image and profile; to facilitate networking, educational, and communication opportunities between sport and tourism partners; to facilitate access to national tools and best practices; to ensure the delivery of high quality services in the sport tourism industry; to build investment in sport tourism from the public and private sectors; and to set targets for expansion of the industry and to monitor their achievement. All cities and sport-friendly businesses and organizations are invited to join the CSTA. Benefits include a reduced registration at all CSTA conferences, updates on sport tourism trends, and ongoing electronic and print communication.

SNAPSHOT

DESTINATION MARATHONS

A growing segment of the sport tourism market is that formed by destination marathoners. Destination marathoners are runners who combine the physical and spiritual rush of completing a 42-kilometre (26.2-mile) road race with the pleasures of a vacation. Every one of the 50 United States now caters to these travellers who follow their passion—whether it is to Alaska's Midnight Sun Marathon, New York City's beloved five-borough block party, or races at Disney World, at Mount Rushmore, and in Nashville (where country-music bands play at each mile along the race course). London, Berlin, Athens, and Paris play host to a few of Europe's top races, and even the Great Wall of China has its own marathon, held each May. A directory of international marathon races on the MarathonGuide.com Web site listed 81 races just in May and June of 2003. Table 12.4 provides a sample of some of the marathons from around the world.

Table 12.4

Marathon Calendar from around the World

MONTH	MARATHON
January	Walt Disney World Marathon, Orlando, Florida; Las Vegas Marathon
February	Tahiti Nui Sunrise Marathon, Moorea
March	Napa Valley Marathon, California; Rome Marathon; Thailand Temple Run, Bangkok
April	Country Music Marathon, Nashville, Tennessee; Paris International Marathon; London Marathon
May	Great Wall Marathon, Tianjen Province, Republic of China
June	Mayor's Midnight Sun Marathon, Anchorage, Alaska; Safaricom Marathon, Lewa Wildlife Conservancy, Kenya; Edinburgh Marathon
July	Nova Scotia Marathon, Barrington
August	Quebec City Marathon; Marathon by the Sea, Saint John, New Brunswick
September	Maui Marathon, Hawaii; Berlin Marathon
October	Melbourne Marathon
November	New York City Marathon; Athens Marathon
December	Honolulu Marathon, Hawaii

SNAPSHOT *continued*

The marathon is one of the most storied races of all time. Originally conceived as a race for the 1896 Olympics in Athens, the marathon immediately captured the imagination and hearts of the running public. Transported to Boston in 1897 by American spectators, the history of the marathon in the New World is almost as long as the history of the marathon itself. But once the exclusive domain of Olympic athletes and hard-core fitness fiends, today's marathon is geared toward people who compete not to win, but to finish. New races are springing up across Canada and the United States, and even successful, long-established marathons are diversifying into new options such as shorter runs, concerts by big-name musical acts, elaborate fitness expos, and hotel discounts. Even though Mbarak Hussein of Kenya won the 2002 Honolulu Marathon in 2 hours and 12 minutes, the course stayed open for another 8 hours to see over 26 000 racers pass the finishing post. To cater to these marathon travellers, Honolulu puts on a luau with guest musicians such as Brian Wilson and Van Morrison, and on race day holds a 10-kilometre walk for runners' families and friends.

Destination marathons have also become popular in Canada. A growing number of Canadians—especially those in the baby-boomer bracket—are planning their holidays around marathon events. Popular marathons include Woody's RV World Marathon, in Red Deer, Alberta; Casino Niagara Marathon, in Niagara Falls, Ontario; and the Royal Victoria Marathon, in Victoria, B.C. One that has received recent accolades is Marathon by the Sea, in Saint John, New Brunswick (see Figure 12.6). The event has been attracting runners and their families since 1995, and it has become the largest participative sport event in the province's history, with runners and walkers of all ages and physical ability completing a 8-mile race, a half marathon, or a full 42-kilometre marathon.

Marathon by the Sea's purposes are to test people's limits, to encourage them to take part in an event that motivates a healthy lifestyle, and to create pride in the community. The event has attracted a growing number of entrants from across Canada and the United States. About 270 people attended the first year, and up to 988 participants took part in 2002. The event also involves over

Figure 12.6 Print Advertisement Used to Promote Marathon by the Sea

SNAPSHOT *continued*

300 volunteers and has grown to become a three-day event with a festival-like atmosphere. Total revenue brought into the city for this weekend-long event is estimated at $273 400.

The 2000 Ultimate Guide to Marathons rated Marathon by the Sea the 7th Top Summer Destination in North America, and the following year race director Lori Weir won the Venue Saint John Sport Planner of the Year Award, an award that recognizes sport event leaders who bring recognition and business to Saint John and the Venue Saint John partnership. The same year, Marathon by the Sea caught the eye of *Runners World* magazine, the most widely read running magazine in the world, and Saint John was a featured destination in a subsequent issue.

Sources: Cummings, S. (2002). Sport Planner of the Year Award, Saint John. Retrieved May 9, 2002, from http://www.canadatourism.com/en/ctc/ctx/ctx-news/search/newsbydateform.cfm; MarathonGuide.com Web site: http://www.marathonguide.com; Mate, S. (2002, September 4). The marathon tourist. *The Globe and Mail*, p. R10; Winik, M. (2003). Going the distance. *Travel + Leisure, 33*(4), 124–128.

Adventure Tourism

Adventure tourism brings together travel, sport, and outdoor recreation, and, like sport tourism, is one of the fastest-growing segments of the tourism industry. The Adventure Travel Society classifies adventure tourism according to activity,[16] distinguishing between "hard" and "soft" adventure tourism activities. Mountaineering is classified as a hard adventure activity, along with activities like white-water rafting, scuba diving, and mountain biking. Soft adventure activities include camping, hiking, biking, animal watching, horseback riding, canoeing, and water skiing. The soft outdoor adventure market is huge in Canada (see Table 2.1 in Chapter 2 for a detailed analysis of this sector).

As the adventure tourism bug has spread to the masses, adventure companies are attracting a growing number of people who are not necessarily passionate about one particular activity, and there is a strong trend in the industry toward multi-activity soft adventure tourism packages in nature-based environments. In fact, what is sold as the ultimate multisport adventure is the "Survivor" tour. The incredible success of the TV series of the same name has encouraged companies to launch Survivor-themed trips that offer participants multiple challenges.

Adventure tourism companies tread a careful line between selling adventure as an idea and delivering adventure as an experience. In this respect, adventure is socially constructed and has been subjected to a process of commodification. Three key factors have facilitated this commodification: a deferring of control to experts; a proliferation of promotional media; and the application of technology in adventurous settings.[17] These factors have combined to create a cushioning zone between the normal home (often urban) location of everyday life and the extraordinary experience of an adventure holiday.

To explain the rise of this commodification, consider Spirit of the West Adventures, a Vancouver Island outfitter that takes small groups of guests on camping and kayaking trips to see the killer whales in B.C.'s Johnstone Strait. The company provides a wilderness camping experience without the inconvenience of having to "rough it." Each couple is housed in a four-person tent kept high and dry on cedar platforms. Guides and cooks prepare snacks and meals such as barbequed sockeye salmon and prawn shish kebab, followed by wine and chocolate-dipped fruit. "We sometimes jokingly call it 'float-and-boat,' an eating trip with some kayaking thrown in between meals," says Sprit of the West owner John Waibel. "What out guests want is a chance to have an outdoor adventure without the risk of being uncomfortable."

Waibel's customers are among a growing number of aging North Americans that many in the outdoor recreation business are referring to as "bobos": bourgeois bohemians. They are looking for an escape to nature from their stressed-out urban lives, but the catch is that they want the experience without the hassle of hauling a lot of gear into the backcountry, sleeping on lumpy ground, and hunting for kindling to cook smoky, second-rate meals. Alberta-based Pure West Lifestyles & Adventures is another company catering to these "bobos." It offers camping adventures along the foothills of the Rocky Mountains "without the hassles of packing in tents and equipment." In fact, participants don't even have to walk much. The company's Web site promises access by all-terrain vehicles "so you and your family can enjoy the remote wilderness without the exhausting long hikes on foot usually required to get to such secluded and pristine backcountry locations."

These adventure tourists are also referred to as GRAMPIES, that is, people who are "growing, retired, and moneyed, in good physical and emotional health."[18] It is estimated that by 2040 in excess of half the population in the developed world will be over the age of 50. This means more people in good health with a more informed global perspective—more GRAMPIES—and thus more adventure tourists.

CHAPTER SUMMARY

To understand the principles of destination marketing, it is important to comprehend what is meant by the term "tourism destination." Destinations are places that have some form of actual or perceived boundary, such as the physical boundary of an island, political boundaries, or even market-created boundaries. There are many different types of destinations, including major international destinations, classic destinations, human-made destination resorts, natural landscape or wildlife tourism destinations, alternative destinations, business tourism destinations, stopover destinations, short break destinations, and day trip destinations.

There are two strategies to consider in the marketing of destinations: promotion and facilitation. The first is concerned with reaching prospective visitors via expenditure on a promotional mix intended to achieve destination awareness and influence prospective customers' attitudes and purchasing behaviour; the other is concerned with exercising a facilitating influence over the tourism industry. Facilitation forms the important bridge between destination marketing organizations (DMOs) and the component sectors of the industry, while the promotion strategy reflects the more traditional approach to destination marketing.

The subject of destination branding has received increased attention over the last few decades. Destination brand builders face five key challenges: limited budgets, politics, the external environment, the destination product, and creating differentiation.

The destination brand-building process comprises five stages: market investigation; analysis and strategic recommendations; brand identity development; brand launch and introduction; brand implementation; and monitoring, evaluation, and review.

For business and leisure travellers, events and conferences often play a key role in bringing people to destinations. From the destination's perspective, event tourism is the development and marketing of events to obtain economic and community benefits. To the consumer, it is travel for the purpose of participating in or viewing an event. Events are often introduced to cope with seasonality and to boost tourism receipts during normally quiet times of year.

The Canadian Tourism Commission has identified sport tourism as the fastest-growing tourism sector, and many destinations are seeking to capitalize on this growth. Five major areas of sport tourism have been identified: attractions, resorts, cruises, tours, and events.

Adventure tourism brings together travel, sport, and outdoor recreation, and, like sport tourism, is one of the fastest-growing segments of the tourism industry.

KEY TERMS

convention and visitor bureaus (CVBs), p. 398
destination branding, p. 408
destination marketing organizations (DMOs), p. 397
destinations, p. 392
facilitation strategy, p. 407
International Association of Convention & Visitors Bureaus (IACVB), p. 398
promotion strategy, p. 404
responsible marketing, p. 400
sport tourism, p. 414
tourism area life cycle (TALC), p. 398

DISCUSSION QUESTIONS AND EXERCISES

1. Considering the characteristics and classifications of destinations, do you think the West Edmonton Mall is an attraction or a destination?
2. Research the marketing activities of a local destination marketing organization. Is it following a promotion or facilitation marketing strategy?
3. It is suggested in this chapter that a major change in the role, the structure, and the skills of DMOs is required. Why do you think this is?

4. Apply the model for responsible marketing to a destination you are familiar with. What position does the destination take, and how could it become more sustainable?
5. Apply the Destination Brand Benefit Pyramid (Figure 12.4) to a local destination. What does the exercise tell you about the destination's brand?
6. Find an example of a destination that is attempting to attract sport tourists. Which of the five areas of sport tourism discussed in the chapter is the destination focusing on?

CASE STUDY

THE TROUT FOREST MUSIC FESTIVAL

"Catch the Trout" is the invitation. The logo is a trout in a fedora playing the banjo. If that's not enough to catch a person's attention, the Trout Forest Music Festival (TFMF) certainly is. In August of 1996, 106

guests gathered in Pakwash Park in Northwestern Ontario for the first TFMF, also known as "Troutfest" and "Music in the Woods." The festival was moved in its second year to Waterfront Park in the town of Ear Falls, Ontario. By 2001, attendance at the festival was so high as to almost double the population of Ear Falls during the festival—quite a feat, as the town's population is 1316 people. Only 1500 adult tickets to the festival are available, and guests come primarily from the local region, Northwestern Ontario, and Southern Manitoba.

TFMF relies heavily on grants and donations that come from a wide range of sources, including the Canadian Heritage Ministry, the Canada Council for the Arts, the Ontario Trillium Foundation, the Ontario Arts Council, the SOCAN Foundation, CKDR AM 800 Radio, VIA Rail, Weyerhaeuser Company, Human Resources Development Canada, and the Township of Ear Falls, as well as from at least 88 other large and small organizations. The Trout Forest Music Festival has six stated objectives, which are critical, as the support of the Canadian Heritage Ministry is contingent upon the fulfillment of these objectives. They are as follows:

1. To provide a quality music experience for festival goers of every age, in an intimate outdoor setting.
2. To promote the development of regional artists by providing an appropriate venue to showcase their talents and provide opportunities to interact with and learn more from more experienced musicians.
3. To showcase new types of music experiences to promote a wider appreciation of music by the regional audience.
4. To promote local First Nations music and artists.
5. To unite people of various ages and walks of life from across the region as volunteers sharing a common love of music and sharing in a common task.

The overall purpose of the festival is clearly stated by its organizers: "The Trout Forest Music Festival organization is a grassroots, nonprofit collective of folk music enthusiasts who are committed to providing quality live entertainment to their audiences." The artists are drawn from the pool of talented musicians across Canada. The TFMF has assembled a team of directors, crew, and volunteers

that continue to make the festival a success. The theme varies each year: in 2001, the festival had a bi-coastal theme, with many performers from the East Coast; in 2002 the theme was "Latin Music in the Woods"; and the theme in 2003 was an "East Coast Kitchen Party."

The festival has three stages that featured 25 performers from across Canada in 2002. Live music is also performed in the beer garden area that becomes the Jam Pit in the evenings. Consistent with their goals of encouraging interaction between performers and guests, festival organizers have designated an area around the bonfire in the evening, after the stages close, for performers and guests to gather with their instruments and join in the music and share the experience. In addition, the festival features creative arts that are for sale, a family area, and camping that is reserved for out-of-town guests. The festival takes place in Waterfront Park in the township of Ear Falls and has the full support of the town.

The TFMF has close connections with some other well-known folk festivals across Canada. In its second year, when it was experiencing many difficulties in planning, the director of the Winnipeg Folk Festival at the time offered assistance and expertise on behalf of the Winnipeg Folk Festival, which is the largest folk festival in the country. TFMF is also a member of the Ontario Council of Folk Festivals. In 2001, Lloyd Romaniuk, the executive director of the TFMF, was a guest of the Stan Rogers Folk Festival in Canso, Nova Scotia, with the assistance of the Canada Council for the Arts. Canso is a similar-sized community that supports and benefits from a similar-sized festival. Both festivals want to support local and Canadian culture and provide a new level of economic benefits to their communities. It is these connections with the folk music community that allow TFMF to find the performers for Troutfest. Romaniuk attended both the East Coast Music Awards and the Atlantic Scene Festival in 2003 to find and book the best talent for the festival in August.

The festival is not confined only to Ontario. In April of 2003, for the first time, TFMF took its spirit on the road to put on a benefit concert in Winnipeg, called the Trout Forest Mini-Festival. Thirty percent of attendees at the TFMF are residents of Manitoba, so this was part of an outreach program to increase attendance at the Troutfest in Ear Falls. The TFMF continues to grow and intends to solidify its calling by hiring some full-time staff to complement the vast numbers of volunteers. The festival has begun strategic operational planning and uncovered a need to increase audience support. The outreach program is a part of this forward-thinking planning. The TFMF's commitment to folk music in Canada includes supporting other festivals and making efforts toward building a "network of festivals that can assist each other." It also brings together communities across Northern Ontario for a common purpose, and the board of directors now includes members from Kenora, Red Lake, and Winnipeg, to complement those from the local community.

Sources: Amory, R. (2001, August 25). Catch the trout in the forest. *Saturday Miner and News*, Kenora; Canadian Heritage continues to support Troutfest. (2003). Retrieved March 16, 2003, from http://www.troutfest.com; Trout Forest Music Festival. (2003). Retrieved March 16, 2003, from http://www.troutfest.com.

QUESTIONS

1. Using only the stated objectives of the TFMF, describe the demographic profile of their main target markets.
2. Given these target markets, what has the TFMF changed to accommodate these groups?
3. What additional features has the TFMF added to connect the guests with the music?
4. Why are connections with other folk festivals in similar-sized communities beneficial to the TFMF?
5. Find some information on a festival in your area. How does it compare to the TFMF?

WEB SITES

www.fredericton.ca
City of Fredericton

www.city.iqaluit.nu.ca
City of Iqaluit

www.canadascapital.gc.ca
City of Ottawa

www.stjohns.ca
City of St. John's

www.city.whitehorse.yk.ca
City of Whitehorse

www.city.yellowknife.nt.ca
City of Yellowknife

www.realontario.ca
Destination Ontario

www.tourism.ede.org
Edmonton Tourism

www.festivalspei.com
Festivals and Events PEI

www.marathonbythesea.com
Marathon by the Sea

www.marathonguide.com
MarathonGuide.com (guide to marathons around the world)

www.purewest.com
Pure West Lifestyles & Adventures

www.quebecregion.com
Quebec City and Area Tourism

www.roadtrips.com
Roadtrips (sport tourism operator)

www.kayak-adventures.com
Spirit of the West Adventures

www.torontotourism.com
Toronto Tourism

www.visitcharlottetown.com
Tourism Charlottetown

www.halifaxinfo.com
Tourism Halifax

www.tourismregina.com
Tourism Regina

www.tourismvictoria.com
Tourism Victoria

www.tourism.winnipeg.mb.ca
Tourism Winnipeg

www.troutfest.com
Trout Forest Music Festival

www.islands.bc.ca
Vancouver Islands Tourism

www.venuesaintjohn.com
Venue Saint John

www.yfnta.org
Yukon First Nations Tourism Association

ENDNOTES

1. Kotler, P., Bowen, J., & Makens, J. (2003). *Marketing for hospitality and tourism.* Upper Saddle River, NJ: Prentice Hall.
2. Gauldie, R. (2000). Advertising and promotion in the travel industry. *Travel & Tourist Analyst, 4,* 71–84.
3. Butler, R. W. (1980). The concept of a tourist area life cycle of evolution: Implications for management of resources. *Canadian Geographer, 24*(1), 5.
4. Plog, S. C. (1974). Why destination areas rise and fall in popularity. *Cornell Hotel and Restaurant Quarterly, 14*(4), 55–58.
5. Cooper, C. (1994). The destination image: An update. In A. V. Seaton (Ed.), *Tourism: The state of the art.* Chichester: Wiley.
6. Hudson, S. (2002). Environmental management in the Rockies: The dilemma of balancing National Park values while making provision for their enjoyment. *Journal of Case Research, 22*(2), 1–14.
7. Plog, S. C. (1974). Why destination areas rise and fall in popularity. *Cornell Hotel and Restaurant Quarterly, 14*(4), 55–58.
8. Middleton, V. T. C., & Clarke, J. (2001). *Marketing in travel and tourism.* Oxford: Butterworth-Heinemann.
9. Morgan, N., & Pritchard, A. (2002). Contextualizing destination branding. In N. Morgan, A. Pritchard, & R. Pride, (Eds.), *Destination branding* (pp. 11–41). Oxford: Butterworth-Heinemann.
10. Ibid.
11. Zwueste, B. (2002). Bedwell Harbour Resort applies poetic license. Retrieved April 26, 2002, from http://www.canadatourism.com/en/ctc/ctx/ctxnews/search/newsbydateform.cfm.
12. Gibson, H., Attle, S., & Yiannakis, A. (1998). Segmenting the active sport tourist market: A life span perspective. *Journal of Vacation Marketing, 4*(1), 52–64.
13. Delpy Neirotti, L. (2003). An introduction to sport and adventure tourism. In S. Hudson (Ed.), *Sport and adventure tourism* (pp. 1–25). Binghamton, NY: Haworth.
14. Getz, D. (1991). *Festivals, special events and tourism.* New York: Van Nostrand.
15. Sport tourism impact. (2002). *Tourism, 6*(6), 6.
16. *Adventure travel society.* (2000). Retrieved August 12, 2000, from http://www.adventuretravel.com.
17. Beedie, P., & Hudson, S. (2003). The commodification of mountaineering through tourism. *Annals of Tourism Research, 30*(3), 625–643.
18. Christiansen, D. (1990). Adventure tourism. In J. Miles & S. Priest (Eds.), *Adventure education* (pp. 433–441). Pennsylvania: Venture.

Glossary

advertising: Any paid form of non-personal presentation and promotion of ideas, goods, or services by an identified sponsor, using mass media to persuade or influence an audience.

advertising objective: A specific communication task to be accomplished with a specific target audience during a specific period of time.

affordable method: Setting the promotion budget at what management thinks the company can afford.

AIDA model: A memorable and useful checklist of the aims of advertising, standing for **a**ttention, **i**nterest, **d**esire, and **a**ction.

alliance: Partnership formed when two or more organizations combine resources through a contractual agreement that allows them to overcome each other's weaknesses by benefitting from each another's strengths.

all-in pricing (all-inclusive pricing): Charging consumers a single price for the various products or services on offer.

allocentrics: Travellers who prefer exotic destinations, unstructured vacations rather than packaged tours, and more involvement with local cultures.

ambient advertising: Advertising that uses new, unexpected ways of getting messages across.

attitudes: Ingrained feelings about various factors of an experience.

augmented product: The add-ons that are extrinsic to the product itself but may influence the decision to purchase.

banner ad: An advertisement placed as a narrow band across the top of a Web page; the most common form of advertising on the Internet.

beliefs: The thoughts that people have about most aspects of their life.

benchmarking: A management technique that allows companies to compare how well they are performing relative to their competitors.

benefits: The rewards the product gives the consumer.

Boston Consulting Group (BCG) model: A technique designed to show the performance of an individual product in relation to its major competitors and the rate of growth in its market.

brandicide: The process of taking a well-known brand and extending it into a new area that will "kill" the brand.

branding: A method of establishing a distinctive identity for a product based on competitive differentiation from other products.

break-even analysis: A pricing technique that considers fixed and variable costs, customer volumes, and profit margins.

budget competitors: Companies that compete for the same consumer dollars.

buyer-based pricing (sensitivity pricing): Allows for high prices when the demand is high and for lower prices when the demand is low, regardless of the cost of the product.

call centre: A central operation from which a company operates its inbound and outbound telemarketing programs.

cash cow: A product that generates a high volume of income in relation to the cost of maintaining its market share.

cause-related marketing: A technique whereby companies contribute to the well-being of society and associate themselves with a positive cause that will reflect well on their corporate image.

channel conflict: Conflict that occurs when one member of a distribution channel perceives another to be engaged in behaviour that prevents or hinders the first member from achieving its goals.

channel management: A process that includes selecting and motivating individual channel members and evaluating their performance over time.

cognitive dissonance: A state of mind that customers experience after making a purchase, in which they are unsure whether they have made a good or bad decision.

competition-oriented pricing (going-rate pricing): Technique in which an organization fixes the prices of products in relation to competitors' prices.

competitive parity method: Setting the promotion budget to match competitors' outlay.

competitor analysis: A review of competitors that allows the organization to identify and highlight the market trends and the level of loyalty of consumers.

competitor intelligence: Keeping track of competition by having a clear understanding of who the competition is and knowing how the company is doing in comparison to the competitors.

concept testing: Testing new product concepts with a group of target consumers to find out if the concept has strong consumer appeal.

consumer attitudes: A consumer's enduring favourable or unfavourable cognitive evaluations, emotional feelings, and action tendencies toward some object or idea.

consumer behaviour analysis: The study of why people buy the products they do and how they make decisions.

consumer research: One type of applied research that focuses on the consumer.

contests: Sales promotions in which entrants can win prizes based on some required skill that they are asked to demonstrate.

convention and visitor bureaus (CVBs): Regional or city-level organizations responsible for marketing a specific destination.

conventional marketing system: A distribution system that consists of a loose collection of independent organizations, each of which tries to maximize its own success.

cooperative direct mail: A direct mail offer delivered as part of a package that includes offers from other companies.

core product: The basic need function served by the generic product.

cost-based pricing: Adding a certain dollar amount or percentage to the actual or estimated costs of a service to arrive at a final price.

cost per thousand (CPM): The process of selecting the media that will expose the product to the largest target audience for the lowest possible cost ("M" is the Roman numeral for 1000).

cost-plus pricing: Adding a standard mark-up to the cost of the product to reach the price charged.

coupons: Vouchers or certificates that entitle customers or intermediaries to a reduced price on a good or service.

cross-selling: Offering a customer the opportunity to purchase allied products that go beyond the obvious core products.

cultural environment: Institutions and other forces that affect society's basic values, perceptions, preferences, and behaviours.

culture: The norms, beliefs, and rituals that are unique to each person.

customer loyalty: A measure of how likely customers are to return to an organization, and of their willingness to build relationships with the organization.

customer satisfaction: The difference between the service that a customer expects and the perceived quality of what is actually delivered.

DAGMAR model: A hierarchies of effects model that stands for **d**efining **a**dvertising **g**oals for **m**easured **a**dvertising **r**esults.

demographics: Statistics that describe the observable characteristics of individuals.

destination branding: Creating a superior proposition that is distinctive from competitors' and imparts meaning above and beyond the functional aspects of the destination.

destination marketing organizations (DMOs): Government agencies, convention and visitors bureaus, travel associations, and other bodies that market travel to their respective destination areas.

destinations: Places that have some form of actual or perceived boundary, such as the physical boundary of an island, political boundaries, or even market-created boundaries.

differentiation: A strategy that consists of an innovative technological breakthrough, which can take competitors a long time to imitate. A competitive advantage can be gained by a product that is newer, better, and/or faster.

direct competitors: Companies that offer similar goods and services to the same consumer at a similar price.

direct distribution channel: A channel through which a company delivers its product to the consumer without the outside assistance of any independent intermediaries.

direct e-mail marketing: Marketing in which a user chooses to receive messages from a particular advertiser via the Internet.

directional selling: A vertically integrated travel agent's sale, or attempted sale, of the foreign package holidays of its linked tour operator in preference to the holidays of other operators.

direct mail: A type of direct response advertising in which an offer is sent to a prospective customer by mail.

direct marketing: A marketing system, fully controlled by the marketer, that develops products, promotes them directly to the final consumer through a variety of media options, accepts direct orders from customers, and distributes products directly to the consumer.

direct response advertising: Advertising through any medium, designed to generate a response by any means that is measurable (e.g., mail, television, telephone, fax, or Internet).

discriminatory pricing: Selling a product at two or more prices, despite the fact that the product costs are the same.

distribution channel: A direct or indirect delivery arrangement used by a supplier, carrier, or destination marketing organization.

distribution system: The "place" aspect of a company's marketing mix; its purpose is to provide an adequate framework for making a company's product or service available to the consumer.

diversification: Seeking opportunities outside the present business.

dog: A product that provides neither cash flow nor long-term opportunities and does not hold great promise for improved performance.

economic forces: Those forces that affect consumer purchasing power and spending patterns.

elasticity of demand: The sensitivity of customer demand to changes in the prices of services.

empowerment: The act of giving employees the authority to identify and solve guest problems or complaints on the spot, and to make improvements in the work processes when necessary.

event sponsorship: The financial support of an event (e.g., a car race, a theatre performance, or a marathon road race) by a sponsor in return for advertising privileges associated with the event.

exclusive distribution: Strategy in which an organization deliberately restricts the number of channels that it uses to distribute its product or service to its customers; an effective method for marketing prestige products.

executive summary: A few pages, usually positioned at the beginning of the marketing plan, that sum up the plan's main sections.

experience: Occurs when a company intentionally uses services as the stage, and goods as props, to engage individual customers in a way that creates a memorable event.

facilitation strategy: Creates marketing bridges between a destination marketing organization and individual operators in the tourism industry; exercises a facilitative influence over the industry.

factual survey: The respondent is asked to state certain facts, such as age or number of children.

family life cycle: The stages through which families might pass as they mature.

features: The objective attributes of a tourism product.

feature stories: Articles of human interest that entertain, inform, or educate readers, viewers, or listeners.

fixed costs: Costs that do not vary with the amount of the service provided.

focus: A strategy that concentrates on designing a good or service to meet the needs of one segment of the market better than the competition does.

focus group: Type of research in which the researcher acts as a facilitator to obtain views representative of a wider population; usually comprises 8 to 10 people.

forecasting: A market-research–based but future-oriented process that relies on expectations, vision, judgment, and projections for factors such as sales volume and revenue trends, consumer profiles, product profiles, price trends, and trends in the external environment.

franchises: Businesses that are established when a franchiser grants a franchisee the right to engage in offering, selling, or distributing its goods or services under its marketing format.

full-service agency: An advertising agency that provides the four major staff functions: account management, creative services, media planning and buying, and account planning.

games: Sales promotions similar to sweepstakes but involving the use of game pieces, such as scratch-and-win cards.

general competitors: Companies that provide the same service.

gift certificates: Vouchers or checks that are either selectively given away by the sponsor or sold to customers, who in turn give them to others as gifts.

goals: The primary aims of the organization.

horizontal conflict: Conflict between organizations at the same level of the distribution channel.

importance–performance analysis (IPA): A procedure that shows both the relative importance of various attributes and the performance of the company, product, or destination under study in providing these attributes.

in-depth interview: A qualitative research technique in which an interviewer will meet an interviewee for about 45 minutes to one hour.

indirect distribution channel: A channel through which a company distributes its product with the assistance of independent intermediaries.

infomercial: A commercial, usually 30 minutes long, that presents in great detail the benefits of a product or service on the television.

integrated marketing communications (IMC): The unification of all marketing communications tools, as well as corporate and brand messages, so they send a consistent, persuasive message to target audiences.

intensive distribution: Strategy in which an organization maximizes the exposure of its travel services by distributing through all available outlets or intermediaries.

internal marketing: Marketing aimed internally, at a company's own employees.

International Association of Convention & Visitors Bureaus (IACVB): An organization that provides educational resources and networking opportunities to its members and distributes information on the CVB industry to the public.

interpretive survey: The respondent acts as an interpreter as well as a reporter.

joint promotion: A promotion in which two or more organizations that have similar target markets combine their resources to their mutual advantage.

junket representatives: Companies that serve the casino industry as intermediaries for premium players.

learning: The way in which visitors receive and interpret a variety of stimuli.

learning and enrichment travel: Refers to vacations that provide opportunities for authentic, hands-on, or interactive learning experiences.

life cycle model: Suggests that travel patterns and destinations vary as people move through their life cycle.

lifestyle analysis: Examines at the way people allocate time, energy, and money.

lifetime value of a customer: A calculation that considers customers from the point of view of their potential lifetime revenue and profitability contributions to a company.

low-cost leadership: The simplest and most effective strategy for dealing with competition, but one requiring large resources and strong management to sustain. It may be short-lived, as it is easy for competitors to match a low price in an attempt to drive off the challenge.

macroenvironment: The larger societal forces that affect the microenvironment: competitive, demographic, economic, environmental and natural, technological, political, cultural and social, and legal forces.

market development: Identifying and developing new markets for current products.

market penetration: Modifying an existing product for the current market.

market share: The percentage relationship of an organization's sales to total industry sales.

market skimming: This policy of "skimming the cream" calls for setting high prices at the launch stage and progressively lowering them as the product becomes better established.

marketing: The process of planning and executing the conception, pricing, promotion, and distribution of ideas, goods, and services to create exchanges that satisfy individual (customer) and organizational objectives.

marketing communications: An all-encompassing term (and activity) that includes communication via any and all of the marketing mix elements.

marketing information system (MIS): The way in which an organization gathers, uses, and disseminates its research in the marketing context.

marketing intermediaries: Channels of distribution that include travel agents, tour operators, travel specialists, and the Internet.

marketing plan: A written, short-term plan that details how an organization will use its marketing mix to achieve its marketing objectives.

marketing research: The systematic and objective search for and analysis of information relevant to the identification and solution of any problem in the field of marketing.

Maslow's hierarchy of needs: Maslow's theory that human needs are arranged in a hierarchy, from the most pressing to the least pressing; these needs in order of importance are physiological needs, safety needs, social needs, esteem needs, and self-actualization needs.

media mix: A combination of traditional media vehicles (print, broadcast, etc.); nontraditional media (electronic media, unexpected places like the floors of stores); and marketing communication tools such as public relations, direct marketing, and sales promotion, used to reach the target audiences.

microenvironment: Forces close to the organization that can affect its ability to serve its customers: the organization itself, marketing channel firms, customer markets, and a broad range of stakeholders or publics.

mission statement: A brief simple phrase or sentence that summarizes the organization's direction and communicates its ethos to internal and external audiences. It also answers the question, "What business are we in?"

monopoly: A supply situation in which there is only one seller.

motivational houses: Companies that provide incentive travel, offered to employees or distributors as a reward for their efforts.

motivations: Inner drives that people have that cause them to take action to satisfy their needs.

needs: The gaps between what customers have and what they would like to have, seen as the force that arouses motivated behaviour.

negotiating: A technique used to establish prices when at least two parties are involved and they have a conflict of interest with respect to one or more issues about the product.

niche marketing: The tailoring of products to meet the needs and wants of narrowly defined geographic, demographic, or psychographic segments.

objective and task method: Developing the promotion budget by (1) defining specific objectives, (2) determining the tasks that must be performed to achieve these objectives, and (3) estimating the costs of performing these tasks.

objectives: The specific aims that managers accomplish to attain organizational goals.

off-set pricing (bait pricing): Charging a low basic price and charging for extra services.

opinion survey: The respondent is asked to express an opinion or make an evaluation or appraisal.

packaging: The process of combining two or more related and complementary offerings into a single-price offering.

penetration pricing: Pricing at a lower level to get maximum sales and market share; used when an organization is trying to get maximum distribution for the product or service in the initial stages.

percentage of sales method: Setting the promotion budget at a certain percentage of current or forecasted sales or as a percentage of sales price.

perception: An overall mind-picture of the world, shaped by information that people filter and then retrieve.

perceptual mapping: Technique used to identify the relationship between the level of perceived importance of certain aspects of a product on the part of the tourist and the actual performance on the part of the supplier.

permission marketing: Marketing in which consumers volunteer to be marketed to on the Internet in return for some kind of reward.

personal selling: A personalized form of communication in which a seller presents the features and benefits of a product to a buyer for the purpose of making a sale.

persuasion test: A test that evaluates the effectiveness of an advertisement by measuring whether the ad affects consumer's intentions to buy a brand.

point-of-purchase merchandising: A technique used to promote a product at locations where it is being sold.

portfolio analysis: An approach to evaluating a very diverse group of goods and services, based on long-term planning and economic forecasts.

positioning: Establishing an image for a product or service in relation to others in the marketplace.

positioning statement: A phrase that reflects the image an organization wants to create.

premium pricing: Setting prices above market price, to reflect either the image of quality or the unique status of the product.

premiums: Goods offered either for free or at low cost as an incentive to buy a product.

press release (news release): A short article about an organization or an event that is written in an attempt to attract media attention, which will then hopefully lead to media coverage.

prestige pricing: Setting prices high to position a product at the upper or luxury end of the market.

price lining: Pre-establishing price lines (levels) that the company feels confident will attract customers.

price points: The number of "stops" along the way between the lowest-priced item and the highest-priced item.

price–quality trade-off: Acceptance of the higher cost of a better quality of product.

price spread: A range of products and prices that will suit the budget of all target markets.

primary data: Information collected for the specific purpose at hand.

product-bundle pricing: Grouping together a company's products to promote them as a package.

product category competitors: Companies that produce the same product or class of products.

product development: Developing a genuinely new product to be sold to existing customers.

product differentiation: A technique that enables organizations to seek to gain competitive advantage by offering a product that has features not available in the offerings of competitors.

product life cycle (PLC) analysis: A way of plotting products or services to identify what stage they are at in their life cycle; a valuable way of reviewing a product's past and current position and making predictions about its future.

product mix: The portfolio of products that an organization offers to one market or several.

product placement: The insertion of brand logos or branded merchandise into movies and television shows.

profit maximization: Corporate objective that causes managers in organizations to make decisions in such a way as to maximize profits.

projection techniques: Called "what if?" techniques, as they involve measures to get subjects to respond to hypothetical, or projected, situations.

promotional mix: A company's total marketing communications program.

promotional pricing: A temporary reduction in price.

promotion strategy: Reaching prospective visitors via expenditure on a promotional mix intended to achieve destination awareness and influence prospective customers' attitudes and purchasing behaviour; a traditional approach to destination marketing.

prospecting: The process of searching for new accounts.

psychocentrics: Travellers who prefer familiar destinations, packaged tours, and "touristy" areas.

psychographic analysis: Attempts to measure people's activities, interests, and opinions.

psychological pricing: Using slightly lower prices to give consumers the perception of added value.

publications: Annual reports, brochures, and company newsletters and magazines that can draw attention to a company and its products, and can help build the company's image and convey important news to target markets.

publicity: Attention received through news media coverage.

public relations (PR): The activities that a tourism or hospitality organization uses to maintain or improve its relationship with other organizations or individuals.

pull strategy: A promotion strategy that calls for spending a large amount on advertising and consumer promotion to build up consumer demand; if successful, consumers will ask their retailers for the product, the retailers will ask the wholesalers, and the wholesalers will ask the producers.

push strategy: A promotion strategy that calls for using the sales force and trade promotion to push the product through channels; the producer promotes the product to wholesalers, the wholesalers promote to retailers, and the retailers to consumers.

qualitative research: Research methods and techniques that use and give rise to qualitative (subjective) information.

quantitative research: Research to which numerical (empirical) estimates can be attached.

question marks: Fairly speculative products that have high-risk potential. They may be profitable, but because they hold a small market share, they may be vulnerable to competition.

recall test: A test that evaluates the memorability of an advertisement by contacting members of the audience and asking what they remember about the advertisement.

recognition test: A test that evaluates the memorability of an advertisement by contacting members of the audience, showing them the ad, and then asking whether they remember having seen it before.

reference groups: Groups that have a direct (face-to-face) or indirect influence on a person's attitude or behaviour.

reference price: A price derived from market prices and the customer's previous experience.

relationship marketing: Marketing that attracts customers, retains them, and enhances their satisfaction.

repertory grid technique: Structured research technique that requires respondents to select from a group of three items.

responsible marketing: The balancing of environmental initiatives and environmental communication in order to achieve sustainable competitive advantage.

return-on-investment goals: Working out the expected profit returns based on the costs of reaching a customer or group of customers; also called break-even analysis or payout planning.

sales management: The management of the sales force and personal selling efforts to achieve desired sales objectives.

sales promotion: A technique used by a company to increase the value of its product by offering an extra incentive to purchase the product.

sales quotas: Performance targets set periodically for individual sales representatives, branch offices, or regions.

sampling: Giving away free samples of a product to encourage sales, or arranging in some way for people to try all or part of a service.

secondary data: Information that already exists somewhere, having been collected for another purpose.

second-chance selling: Trying to sell additional services to a customer who has already booked services.

segmentation analysis: The practice of dividing total markets up into groups on the basis of similar characteristics.

selective distribution: Strategy between intensive and exclusive distribution, in which a company uses more than one but less than all of the possible distribution channels.

service culture: A culture that supports customer service through policies, procedures, reward systems, and actions.

service quality: Customers' perceptions of the service component of a product.

service recovery: The process by which a company attempts to rectify a service delivery failure.

servicescape: The environment in which the service is delivered and in which the firm and customer interact, and any tangible components that facilitate performance or communication of the service.

services marketing mix: The original four P's of the marketing mix—product, place, promotion, and price—plus the people, the physical evidence, and the process.

services marketing triangle: A model that illustrates the three interlinking groups that work together to develop, promote, and deliver services: the company, the customer, and the provider.

SERVQUAL: An instrument used to measure the difference between consumers' expectations and perceptions of service quality.

situation analysis: A business review that summarizes all the relevant information available about the product, the company, the competitive environment, the industry, and the consumers.

"smart" rule: Rule used in the development of the mission statement in order to ensure that the statement is **s**pecific, **m**easurable, **a**ttainable, **r**elevant, and **t**rackable.

social class: The position one occupies within society, determined by such factors as income, wealth, education, occupation, family prestige, value of home, and neighbourhood.

solo direct mail: A direct mail piece sent out by one company and delivered by the company itself.

spam: E-mail advertisements sent to lists of recipients who have not agreed to receive them.

specialized agency: An advertising agency that specializes in certain functions (e.g., writing copy, producing art, media buying), audiences (e.g., minority, youth), or industries (e.g., health care, computers, leisure).

sport tourism: Travel away from a person's primary residence to participate in a sporting activity for recreation or competition; travel to observe sport at the grass roots or elite level; and travel to visit a sport attraction.

stars: Products that have a dominant share of a fast-growing market.

strategic marketing plan: A written plan for an organization covering a period of three or more years into the future.

strategic pricing: Setting prices early, in accordance with the long-term view of corporate strategy, product positioning, and value for money in the marketplace.

sweepstakes: Sales promotions that require entrants to submit their names and addresses; winners are chosen on the basis of chance, not skill.

SWOT analysis: A technique that provides scope for an organization to list all its strengths, weaknesses, opportunities, and threats.

tactical pricing: Making short-term pricing decisions in response to changes in the marketing environment.

tangible product: The specific features and benefits residing in the product itself—styling, quality, brand name, design, etc.

target market: A clearly defined group of customers whose needs the company plans to satisfy.

target rate of return: Corporate objective that aims to achieve a particular return on the assets employed in an organization.

telemarketing: Using the telephone to reach customers or prospective customers.

tour brokers: Companies that sell motorcoach tours, which are attractive to a variety of markets.

tourism and hospitality products: A group of selected components or elements brought together in a "bundle" to satisfy needs and wants.

tourism area life cycle (TALC): The stages a destination goes through, from exploration to involvement to development to consolidation to stagnation to rejuvenation or decline (also known as the "tourism destination life cycle").

tourism market: A market that reflects the demands of consumers for a very wide range of travel and hospitality products.

tour operators: Organizations that offer packaged vacation tours to the general public.

travel agents: Marketing intermediaries that offer the tourism customer a variety of services, including everything from transportation plans and tour packages to insurance services and accommodation.

travel specialists: Intermediaries that specialize in performing one or more functions of a company's distribution system.

undercut pricing: Setting prices lower than the competition and using the price as a trigger to purchase immediately.

unique selling proposition (USP): A feature of a product that is so unique that it distinguishes the product from all other products.

up-selling: Upgrading price and profit margins by selling higher-priced products.

VALS™: A typology framework that divides the population into eight lifestyle groups, defined according to factors such as self-image, aspirations, values, and products used.

value-for-money pricing: Charging medium prices and emphasizing that the product represents excellent value for money at this price.

variable costs: Costs that increase as more of a service is provided.

vertical conflict: Conflict between organizations at different levels of the same distribution channel.

vertical marketing system: A system in which all members of the distribution channel work together as a unified whole.

virtual focus groups: Online "chat" sessions, in which one to dozens of pre-recruited respondents type in responses to a guided online discussion.

volume discounting: Offering special prices to attract customers who agree to major purchases.

willingness to pay (WTP) assessment: Asking potential customers what they would be willing to pay for the product.

word of mouth: Communication about products and services between people who are perceived to be independent of the company that is producing or providing the product.

yield: The profit that is made on the sales of goods and services; calculated based on the number of customers, how much they spend, and the number of products they buy.

yield management: The practice of developing strategies to maximize opportunities for the sale of an organization's perishable products, such as airline seats, hotel rooms, and tour seats, and therefore improving its long-term viability.

zero-based planning: The practice of analyzing the strengths and weaknesses of the various marketing communications tools and then matching them to the problem identified in the situation analysis.

Index

TEXT ACKNOWLEDGMENTS

p. 5: Reprinted from *Marketing in Travel and Tourism*, Middleton, V.T.C. & Clarke, J. (2001), with permission from Elsevier. **p. 8:** From *Services Marketing: Integrating Customer Focus Across the Firm*, Zeithaml, V.A. & Bitner, M.J., 2000, p. 16, used by permission of the McGraw-Hill Companies. **p. 28:** Used by permission of Pier 21. **p. 30:** Used by permission of *National Post*. **p. 41:** Canadian Tourism Commission. **p. 42:** Reprinted with the permission of The Free Press, a Division of Simon & Schuster Adult Publishing Group, from COMPETITIVE STRATEGY: Techniques for Analyzing Industries and Competitors by Michael E. Porter. Copyright © 1980, 1998 by The Free Press. All rights reserved. **p. 52:** Reprinted with permission from *Foodservice and Hospitality* magazine, 2002. **p. 80:** SRI Consulting Business Intelligence. **p. 82:** Used by permission of Cornell Hotel and Restaurant Quarterly. **p. 91:** Reprinted with permission from *Foodservice and Hospitality* magazine, 2003. **p. 140:** Reprinted from *The Development and Management of Visitor Attractions*, Swarbrooke, J. (1995), with permission from Elsevier. **p. 209:** Reprinted by permission of Thomson Learning UK. **p. 210:** From *Hospitality and Travel Marketing, 3rd Edition* by Morrison, © 2002. Reprinted with permission of Delmar Learning, a division of Thomson Learning: www.thomsonrights.com. Fax 800 730-2215. **p. 219:** From Hudson, S., & Lang, N. "A Destination Case Study of Marketing Tourism Online: Banff, Canada," *Journal of Vacation Marketing*, 2002. Reprinted by permission of Henry Stewart Publications. **p. 237:** Used by permission of Franchise Canada. **p. 249:** From *Advertising Principles & Practice*, 6/e by Wells/Burnett/Moriarty, © 2003. Reprinted by permission of Pearson Education, Inc., Upper Saddle River, NJ. **p. 307:** Reprinted by permission of Hospitality Sales and Marketing Association International (HSMAI). **p. 317:** Reprinted by permission of George Silverman, President, Market Navigation, Inc. **p. 322:** Reprinted by permission of Nimbus Publishing. **p. 334:** Reprinted by permission of the Zeff Group. **p. 364:** Reprinted by permission of the American Marketing Association. **p. 366:** Reprinted by permission of the author. **p. 371:** Reprinted by permission of the American Marketing Association. **p. 374:** From *Services Marketing: Integrating Customer Focus Across the Firm*, Zeithaml, V.A. & Bitner, M.J., 2000, p. 153, used by permission of the McGraw-Hill Companies. **p. 405:** Reprinted from *Marketing in Travel and Tourism*, Middleton, V.T.C. & Clarke, J. (2001), with permission from Elsevier. **p. 410:** Reprinted from *Destination Branding*, Morgan, N., Pritchard, A., & Pride, R., (2002), with permission from Elsevier.

PHOTO ACKNOWLEDGMENTS

Photos used in *Marketing in Action* box titles are © Paul A. Souders/Corbis/Magma. Photos used in *Profile* box titles are © Charles O'Rear/Corbis/Magma. Photos used in *Snapshot* box titles are © Ariel Skelley/Corbis/Magma.

p. 2: Courtesy of G.A.P Adventures. **p. 28:** Courtesy of Pier 21. **p. 34:** Courtesy of Four Seasons Hotels. **p. 57:** Courtesy of Superior North Community Futures Development Corporation. **p. 68:** Photodisc. **p. 87:** Dick Hemingway. **p. 100:** Courtesy of Superior North Community Futures Development Corporation. **pp. 119 and 120:** Courtesy of Travel Alberta. **p. 136:** Ice Hotel Quebec-Canada © Xavier Dachez. **p. 147:** Courtesy of Catch Restaurant. **pp. 153 and154:** Courtesy of The Manitoba Museum. **p. 164:** Courtesy of Weekendtrips.com. **p. 168:** Courtesy of Banff Mount Norquay. **p. 183:** Space Adventures. **p. 195:** Courtesy of Club Med. **p. 206:** Courtesy of Canadian Mountain Holidays. **p. 220:** Courtesy of Destina.ca. **p. 237:** Al Harvey. **p. 242:** Sabine Traweger. **p. 248:** Courtesy of Newfoundland and Labrador Tourism. **pp. 256 and 257:** Courtesy of Travel Alberta. **p. 261:** Courtesy of the Canadian Tourism Commission. **p. 263:** Courtesy of Tourisme Montréal. **p. 265:** Courtesy of British Airways. **p. 267:** Courtesy of Tourism Yukon. **p. 268:** Courtesy of Holiday Inn on King, Toronto. **p. 276:** Courtesy of Calaway Park. **p. 286:** Courtesy of Inniskillin Wines. **p. 292:** Courtesy of Air Canada. **p. 319:** Courtesy of Rocky Mountaineer Railtours. **p. 322:** Courtesy of Atlantic Tours. **p. 327:** Courtesy of Vancouver Convention and Exhibition Centre. **p. 337 (top):** Courtesy of Vancouver Tourism; **(bottom):** Courtesy of Prince Edward Island Tourism. **p. 341:** Courtesy of Quebec Resorts and Country Inns. **p. 344:** Courtesy of MyTravelHost.net. **p. 352:** Courtesy of The Sheraton Suites Calgary Eau Claire. **p. 366:** Courtesy of Tourism Whistler. **p. 390:** Courtesy of Yukon First Nations Tourism Association. **p. 395:** Courtesy of West Edmonton Mall. **p. 417:** Courtesy of Tourism Saskatchewan. **p. 419:** Courtesy of Marathon by the Sea.